CHAMBERS

Global Practice Guides

Trade Marks

Contributing Editor

Dale Cendali

Kirkland & Ellis LLP

2018

AF864930

Chambers Global Practice Guides

For more than 20 years, Chambers Global Guides have ranked lawyers and law firms across the world. Chambers now offer clients a new series of Global Practice Guides, which contain practical guidance on doing legal business in key jurisdictions. We use our knowledge of the world's best lawyers to select leading law firms in each jurisdiction to write the 'Law & Practice' sections. In addition, the 'Trends & Developments' sections analyse trends and developments in local legal markets.

Disclaimer: The information in this guide is provided for general reference only, not as specific legal advice. Views expressed by the authors are not necessarily the views of the law firms in which they practise. For specific legal advice, a lawyer should be consulted.

Series Editor

Claire Oxborrow
Editor, Global Practice Guides. Graduated with a First in Modern History from the University of St Andrews in 2005. During postgraduate studies at the LSE she worked as a visiting lecturer at the University of Roehampton. After completing the GDL and the LPC she spent time as a volunteer at the Brunel Museum.

Publisher **Chambers & Partners**
Series Editor **Claire Oxborrow**
Business Development Director **Brad Sirott**
Editorial Contributions **Liz Wilson**

Orders to **Chambers & Partners**
Published by **Chambers & Partners**
(a division of Orbach & Chambers Ltd)

No.3 Waterhouse Square
138 Holborn, London
EC1N 2SW
Tel +44 20 7606 8844 **Fax** +44 20 7831 5662
Web www.chambersandpartners.com

Copyright © 2018
Chambers and Partners
ISBN 978-0-85514-738-9

Printed and bound in Great Britain by Bell and Bain Ltd, Glasgow

CONTENTS

INTRODUCTION

Contributing Editor

Dale Cendali
Kirkland & Ellis LLP

Kirkland & Ellis LLP Intellectual Property Law Practice is one of the oldest such practices in a full-service firm in the country, having been an integral part of Kirkland since 1925. Located in the Firm's Chicago, London, Los Angeles, New York, Palo Alto, San Francisco and Washington, D.C. offices, Kirkland has approximately 230 intellectual property lawyers who are experienced in a variety of technical disciplines and registered to practice before the US Patent and Trademark Office. More than 70% of the lawyers are engineers and scientists trained with degrees and professional backgrounds in technical areas.

Contributing Editor

Dale Cendali is a nationally recognised leader in the field of intellectual property litigation, having successfully litigated and tried numerous high-profile cases, and having argued before the US Supreme Court. Her practice encompasses copyright, trade mark, false advertising, patent, internet, and trade-secrets law, as well as defamation, the right of publicity, privacy, complex contract disputes and similar areas, including electronic discovery. Dale heads Kirkland's Copyright, Trademark, Internet and Advertising practice group.

Trade Marks: Trends and Developments

The value of trade marks has never been higher. As evidenced by the explosion of logos, such as the now ubiquitous logo for the streetwear fashion brand Supreme (appearing as a white font in a red square), on plain white t-shirts or sneakers in the market, the consuming public has a pronounced affinity for brands. See https://www.forbes.com/sites/andriacheng/2018/02/07/flaunting-logos-is-coming-back-into-fashion/#76b34f028723 This rise in what some call "logo culture," is partly attributable to social media, which is particularly well-suited for optimising labels and brands. This value has encouraged the extension of existing brands into new categories and industries, resulting in increased trade-mark filings worldwide, see http://www.wipo.int/export/sites/www/ipstats/en/docs/infographic_madrid_2017.pdf (showing 5% increase in trade-mark applications filed under the Madrid Protocol) and more trade-mark litigation. See http://www.compumark.com/press-releases/three-quarters-brands-experienced-trademark-infringement-past-year/

Both legacy and new brands are expanding beyond the traditional boundaries of single-industry business (eg, "just" luxury apparel) into industries such as restaurants, hotels, or other hospitality-based businesses. Furthermore, brands have increasingly taken part in collaborations with other brands in both adjacent (eg, Supreme and Louis Vuitton) and distinct (eg, streetwear brand KITH and Coca-Cola) markets. As these brands enter new territories, leveraging their substantial goodwill, it has become more challenging for trade-mark law practitioners who must carefully examine marketplace proximity and assess whether consumers would in fact be confused or, alternatively, have experienced a rise in sophistication such that they can discern between third-party uses of similar marks. Together, this has altered the way that consumers view brands and trade marks, paving the way for a new globalised perspective on branding.

Growth in United States Patent and Trademark Office Filings

In Fiscal Year 2017, (1 October 2016 through 30 September 2017), more than 425,000 new trade-mark applications were filed with the United States Patent and Trademark Office. This was an increase of more than 10% from the previous year and the US register of trade marks now contains more records than ever before. As noted above, this likely reflects the desire for brands to extend their reach into new goods and services. It may also reflect an increased interest by businesses and individuals to provide additional notice to their competitors that they are using the applied-for term as a source-identifier and wish to protect that term as a trade mark.

United States Supreme Court Allows Registration of 'Disparaging' Trade Marks

In *Matal v. Tam*, a case involving the band The Slants, the US Supreme Court declared that a portion of the US Federal trade-mark statute, the Lanham Act, which banned "offensive" trade-mark registrations, was unconstitutional because the law violated the First Amendment. The United States Patent and Trademark Office had previously opposed registering the name of the band because it found that the name "The Slants" was disparaging to people of Asian descent. The Supreme Court's decision also meant that the Washington Redskins, which have been involved in a 20-year legal battle based on a claim that the mark was "offensive," can keep its registrations intact.

Social Media Fuels New Trade-Mark Applications

The social media giants, eg, Facebook, Instagram, Snapchat, and Twitter, have expanded the scope of their trade-mark portfolios. In addition to registering the names of the platforms, the companies have also applied for, or already registered, marks such as the Instagram photograph "filters," Sierra and Hudson and Facebook's "thumbs-up" button. Businesses have also upped their enforcement of marks on social media, while companies have been quick to capitalise on United States Patent and Trademark Office's decision that a 'hashtag' is registerable. See https://tmep.uspto.gov/RDMS/TMEP/current#/current/ch1200_d1ff5e_1b5ad_3bc.html

Kirkland & Ellis LLP
601 Lexington Avenue
New York, NY 10022
United States

Tel: +1 212-446-4846
Fax: +1 212-446-4900
Email: dale.cendali@kirkland.com
Web: www.kirkland.com

KIRKLAND & ELLIS

BRAZIL

LAW AND PRACTICE: p.11

Contributed by Licks Attorneys

The 'Law & Practice' sections provide easily accessible information on navigating the legal system when conducting business in the jurisdiction. Leading lawyers explain local law and practice at key transactional stages and for crucial aspects of doing business.

Law and Practice

Contributed by Licks Attorneys

CONTENTS

Licks Attorneys handles large and strategic litigation and counselling on intellectual property in Brazil. The firm's trade mark group supports clients throughout the entire trade-mark life cycle, providing clear advice for trade-mark protection and enforcement, through to surveillance services, monitoring clients' trade marks in the web environment and aiming to act quickly against any infringement. In addition to negotiating, drafting and registering agreements involving trade marks, Licks' transactional group has been working to develop training programmes to establish standards for intellectual property and innovation deployment and protection, adopting preventive anti-counterfeiting measures.

Authors

Eduardo Hallak is a partner at the firm. His extensive practice includes: trade mark, trade dress and publicity rights matters, patents, copyright, and licensing and technology transfer; he also handles cases related to food and drug law, industrial designs, the internet, e-commerce & software, and anti-counterfeiting. Eduardo is a member of the Brazilian Intellectual Property Association, the American Intellectual Property Law Association, the Pharmaceutical Trade Marks Group and the International Trademark Association. He has published and lectured extensively on legal issues pertaining to intellectual property. He is individually recognised in the Trademark Practice in Brazil, World Trademark Review 2018.

Ana Montenegro is head of the firm's trade marks department. She specialises in trade marks, industrial designs, copyright, licensing, regulatory, data protection, food and drug law. Ana is a member of the Mediator's Panel of the World Intellectual Property Organization for the INPI-BR Mediation Chamber (2013), and of the American Chamber of Commerce – Intellectual Property Committee. She is individually recognised in the Trademark Practice in Brazil, World Trademark Review 2018.

1. Types of Trade Marks & Registration

1.1 Types of Trade Marks

According to Article 122 of the Brazilian IP statute, any visually perceptible distinctive signs, when not prohibited under law, are susceptible to registration as trade marks. In this connection, the Brazilian legal system allows the registration of different types of signs:

- nominative, figurative, composite and three-dimensional trade marks: used to identify products or services in the market;
- certification trade marks: used to attest to the conformity of products or services with certain technical standards or specifications, particularly regarding its quality, nature, material, and employed methodology; and
- collective trade marks: used to identify products or services provided by members of a certain entity.

Famous and well-known trade marks are protected according to the Paris Convention and Trade-Related Intellectual Property Rights (TRIPS) Agreement rules, but specific provisions in the Brazilian IP statute also grant different degrees of protection for trade marks, based on their level of recognition in the market:

- famous trade marks: registered in Brazil, will be guaranteed special protection in all branches of activity; and
- well-known trade marks will enjoy special protection in a determinate field of activity, regardless of whether they are locally registered.

The trade dress cannot be registered in Brazil, but its protection has been recognised by Brazilian courts based on unfair competition provisions.

1.2 Trade-Mark Rights

According to Article 129 of the Brazilian IP statute, trademark rights are acquired by means of a valid registration issued by the Brazilian PTO (INPI), which assures its titleholder exclusive rights to use the sign in the national territory.

As a rule, Brazil adopts the first-to-file system, which means that the first person/entity to file a trade mark before the INPI, if the application meets all legal formalities, is entitled to its registration. However, Article 129, §1° of the Brazilian IP statute establishes an exception to that, granting preferential registration rights to any person who, in good faith, at the date of priority or of the application, was using an identical or similar trade mark for at least six months in the country, to identify or certify identical, similar or akin products or services.

1.3 Standards for Registering
As a rule, the INPI rejects the registration of trade marks that are not inherently distinctive or are not provided with distinctiveness by comparison to other registered trade marks.

Despite that, secondary meaning has been widely accepted by Brazilian courts, consolidating case law that recognises the possibility of a sign acquiring distinctive character through its extensive use in the market, and the applicability of Article 6 quinquies of the Paris Convention.

1.4 Trade-Mark Register
The INPI is the Brazilian trade-mark register, and has an online database available for public consultation through an electronic system. In order to access INPI's database and electronic system, users are required to create a personal account using basic data (such as legal nature, name, address, ID number, e-mail and contact phone).

Furthermore, to assure publicity to its acts, the INPI publishes an electronic Official Gazette on a weekly basis reporting any developments that have occurred in connection with trade-mark applications/registrations (namely office actions, abeyance, allowance or rejection decisions etc). The Official Gazette is made available to the public, in electronic format, every Tuesday.

1.5 Types of Registers
In Brazil there are no different types of registers (eg principal and supplemental).

1.6 Searching for Prior Trade Marks
It is highly advisable that before applying to register a trade mark in Brazil that an interested party obtains professional assistance to conduct availability searches in the INPI's online database, confirming whether the sign is already being used by any third parties to cover identical/similar products or services; and is free for registration relating to the desired products or services. These searches will only encompass filed/registered trade marks.

Comprehensive availability searches include information obtained through the INPI's online database, private databases connected to the INPI's system, state commercial registries and domain name registration database (Registro.br). For specific cases or upon a client's request, the prior searches may also include general use searches on the web, aiming to investigate the scenario of possibly unregistered marks.

1.7 Registration Requirements
To be eligible for trade-mark registration in Brazil, a sign must fulfil the following basic requirements:

- relative novelty or "availability";
- veracity, which forbids signs that induce a false indication regarding the origin, source, nature, quality or usefulness of the products or services; and
- distinctiveness; as well as not falling into the prohibitions set forth in Article 124 of the Brazilian IP statute.

In addition to the basic filing requirements, the applicant must provide:

- personal data, such as name, address, corporate type, e-mail and contact phone;
- confirmation of the products or services to be claimed;
- confirmation of the trade mark type and, if applicable, a sample of the trade mark in high resolution;
- priority number and date, if applicable;
- declaration confirming to be engaged in activities compatible with the products or services covered by the application;
- colour claim, if applicable;
- Power of Attorney; and
- proof of payment of the INPI's official fees for the requested service.

The Power of Attorney and the priority document may be presented to the INPI after the filing date, upon payment of additional official fees. The applicant has 60 days to submit the Power of Attorney; and four months to submit the priority document and its simple Portuguese translation.

1.8 Registering a Trade Mark
According to Article 128 of the Brazilian IP statute a trade mark can be registered by any natural or legal persons under public or private law (such as corporations, partnerships, joint ventures, unions and associations, among others). Under private law, natural or legal persons may only apply for registration of a trade mark related to the field of activity they are lawfully engaged in, either directly or through controlled companies.

The registration of collective trade marks may be applied for by a legal person who represents the collectivity, which may engage in an activity other than that pursued by its members. Registration of certification trade marks may only be applied for by a person who has no direct commercial or industrial interest in the product or service being certified.

1.9 Registering Signs
The Brazilian IP statute provides for the protection of visually perceptive signs, such as words, figures, designs, combinations of words and designs, combinations of colours

(when arranged in an unusual and distinctive manner) and three-dimensional shapes.

Other distinctive signs – that cannot be graphically represented – are not subject to registration before the INPI, namely single colours, scents, sounds, tastes, touch, motion, positions and trade dress (jointly referred to as non-traditional trade marks).

It is worth mentioning that many applicants are seeking strategies to overcome INPI's restrictive understanding, adjusting the presentation/nature of their non-traditional trade marks to obtain registration including requests for protection of:

- "word marks" that describe the graphic representation of sounds;
- "figurative marks" that depict sequential images of a movement evolution;
- "figurative marks" that stress an isolated colour depicting a position in the products' design/packaging; or
- "figurative marks" stressing colour schemes and layout of products/services partially to cover a trade dress.

1.10 Other Rights to Signs

The Brazilian legal system recognises the rights to company names, trade names and domain names.

The by-laws or articles of association (incorporation documents) that establish a company must include its name (company name). The company name becomes effective upon registration of such incorporation documents with a State Commercial Registry and is protected by the Civil Code and the Paris Convention.

A trade name is not mandatory information in incorporation documents, but protection arises from its use in commerce.

The rights related to domain names arise from their registration with the Brazilian registrar, so-called Registro.br (https://registro.br/). The procedure is done online and requires prior availability checking. If the desired domain name is not being used by any third parties, the registrant may secure it upon payment of the official fee of approximately USD10 per year.

Domain names can be registered by individuals or legal entities. Foreign legal entities are required to be represented by a Brazilian attorney or proxy holder and to execute an agreement committing to initiate commercial activities in Brazil within 12 months from registration or to assign the domain name to a Brazilian subsidiary within the same period. Domain names also have protection akin to a trade name.

1.11 Registration Procedure

The Brazilian legal system does not allow multi-class applications.

The registration procedure of a trade mark in Brazil includes the following formalities:

- submitting an electronic form with information on an applicant including; attorney of record, trade mark; products or services claimed and its international classification; Vienna classification related to any figurative elements of the trade mark, if applicable; and declarations of veracity and compatibility of activities;
- Power of Attorney; and
- proof of payment of the INPI's official fees.

After the trade-mark application is filed, the INPI issues an electronic official receipt and assigns a serial number to the new application. After that, the INPI conducts a formal analysis over the adequacy/sufficiency of the information provided. If the filing information is insufficient, but contains basic data on the applicant, trade mark and international class, the INPI will raise an office action to be complied with by the applicant within five days counted from its publication in the Official Gazette.

If the applicant does not comply with the office action, the application is declared non-existent. If the office action is complied with and the application meets the filing requirements, it will be published for opposition purposes in the Official Gazette within approximately 15 to 20 days, triggering a 60-day term for any third parties to file an opposition. No time extensions are allowed.

If an opposition is filed, the INPI will publish notice of such opposition in the Official Gazette, triggering a new 60-day term for the applicant to submit a formal reply. No time extensions are allowed.

If no oppositions are filed, the application will move forward to wait in a "line" for an analysis on the merits by the INPI (following chronological filing order). In any event, the INPI shall proceed with the application analysis after all opposition deadlines have lapsed.

Trouble-free trade-mark applications (without opposition proceedings or rejection decisions) take approximately two years to be analysed and decided by the INPI. Any such analysis' timeframe will be significantly impacted if any third parties file an opposition.

If the INPI publishes an allowance decision, the applicant has 60 days to pay the final fees related to first decennium protection and the issuance of digital registration certificate. Such a deadline may be extended for 30 days, upon payment of additional official fees. After confirmation of the payment the INPI will publish the registration grant notice in the Official Gazette, triggering the ten-year validity term of the trade mark. The digital registration certificate will be made available for download by the applicant within approximately three to four months after the publication of the registration grant notice.

If the INPI publishes a rejection decision, either based on absolute or relative grounds, the applicant will have 60 days to file an appeal. The timeframe of analysis of cases subject to appeal is approximately four to five years.

The appeal is decided by the INPI's president, with a focus on the opinion issued by the Trademark Board of Appeals of the INPI (in charge of analysing appeal arguments). The president's decision is binding to the applicant and terminates proceedings in the administrative sphere.

If the appeal arguments are accepted the INPI will publish the allowance notice and the applicant has 60 days to pay the registration fees, extendable for an additional 30 days.

If the appeal arguments are rejected, the application will be definitively shelved by the INPI. The applicant still has the possibility of seeking a review before federal courts within five years though, as any act by the INPI can be judicially reviewed, as per the Brazilian constitutional system.

1.12 Use in Commerce

The Brazilian legal system does not require the use of a trade mark in commerce as a precedent condition for its registration. It is also not necessary to demonstrate use of the trade mark as of the filing date.

Once a trade-mark registration is granted by the INPI and published in the Official Gazette, it shall remain valid for a period of ten years, which can be successively renewed for an additional ten-year term.

The title-holder must apply for renewal of the registration during the last year of its term of validity, by paying the relevant official fee of approximately USD330. The renewal period may be extended for six months after the registration's validity term expires (so-called extraordinary term), upon payment of increased fees of approximately USD500.

1.13 Registration of Series Marks

The Brazilian legal system does not allow for the registration of series marks, eg a number of trade marks within the same characteristics in a single application.

1.14 Length of Registration Process

Trouble-free trade-mark applications (without opposition proceedings or rejection decisions) take approximately two years to be analysed and decided by the INPI. If a trade-mark application faces an opposition filed by third parties or a rejection decision by the INPI, the average timeline of analysis and issuance of a final merit decision may significantly increase, to four up to five years.

Brazilian applicants are not required to have legal representation to initiate registration procedures before the INPI. However, according to Article 217 of the Brazilian IP statute, foreign applicants must permanently maintain a duly qualified attorney resident in the country, with powers to represent him or her administratively and judicially, including for receiving summons.

The INPI's official fee for filing a single-word mark application in one class is approximately USD130. If an applicant is an individual, local small company, research institution, NGO or government entity, the INPI shall grant a special discount of almost 60%, and such fees decrease to approximately USD50. The costs related to attorney fees vary from firm to firm.

1.15 Grounds for Refusal

Based on Article 124 of the Brazilian IP statute, the following circumstances are considered absolute grounds for refusal of a trade-mark application:

- crests, armorial bearings, medals, flags, emblems, official public distinctions and monuments, be they national, foreign or international, as well as any respective designations, figures or imitations;
- an isolated letter, digit or date, except when sufficiently distinctive;
- expressions, figures, drawings or any other sign contrary to morals and good customs or which offend a person's honour or image or are an affront to the liberty of conscience, beliefs, religious cults or to ideas and sentiments worthy of respect and veneration;
- designations or acronyms of a public entity or establishment, when registration is not requested by that public entity or establishment;
- signs of a generic, necessary, common, usual or simply descriptive character, when related to the product or service to be distinguished, or those commonly used to designate a characteristic of the product or service with respect to its nature, nationality, weight, value, quality and moment of production or of giving a service, except when presented in a sufficiently distinctive manner;
- signs or expressions used only as a means of advertising;
- colours and their names, except when arranged or combined in an unusual and distinctive manner;
- signs that suggest a false indication with respect to origin, source, nature, quality or utility of the product or service to which the mark is directed;

- reproductions or imitations of official seals, normally adopted for the guarantee of a standard of any type or nature;
- reproductions or imitations of titles, bonds, coins and bank notes of the Union, the States, the Federal District, the Territories, the Municipalities or of any country;
- technical terms used in the industry, science or art that is related to the product or service to be distinguished; and
- necessary, common or usual shapes of a product or of its packaging, or, furthermore, shapes that cannot be disassociated from a technical effect.

1.16 Process for Overcoming Objections

If the INPI's objection refers to formal aspects, an applicant may file a brief in compliance with it, submitting further information or documents as required by the INPI. If the applicant fails to comply in a satisfactory manner, the application may be declared non-existent by the INPI.

If the INPI's objection refers to grounds for refusal, the applicant may file an appeal within 60 days counted from the date of the publication of such a decision. If no appeal is filed, the application will be definitively dismissed by the INPI.

The general basis to overcome absolute ground objections include:

- sustaining that a trade mark deemed "descriptive" by the INPI is indeed merely evocative;
- attesting that signs deemed as "slogans" by the INPI are actually used to identify a product or service in the market;
- evidencing that a sign deemed "deceptive" by the INPI is not confusing for consumers; and
- claiming to have acquired distinctiveness through extensive use in the market for trade marks refused by the INPI due to "lack of distinctiveness".

As a rule, the INPI rejects the registration of trade marks that are not inherently distinctive and does not accept secondary meaning allegations. However, Brazilian case law recognises the possibility of a sign acquiring distinctive character through its extensive use in the market.

The general basis to overcome relative ground objections includes:

- evidencing the non-existence of the likelihood of confusion with senior trade marks; products or services covered thereof;
- submitting a co-existence agreement to demonstrate a lack of conflict, bearing in mind that the INPI is not obliged to accept it; and
- applying for limitations or restrictions in the specification of products or services covered by the trade mark, among others.

1.17 Consideration of Prior Rights

The INPI shall consider the existence of prior rights in its examination of a trade-mark application. For instance, they could be senior trade-mark rights, prior company/trade-name rights, image and patronymic rights and prior use.

Concerning the latter, according to Article 129, §1° of the Brazilian IP statute, any person who in good faith at the date of priority or of the application was using an identical or similar mark for at least six months in the country, to distinguish or certify a product or service that is identical, similar or akin, will have preferential rights to registration.

The INPI's long-standing position established that the existence of prior rights must be argued in an opposition proceeding; eg before a trade-mark registration is granted in favour of a third party.

However, the Brazilian Superior Court of Justice (STJ) recently adopted a more flexible interpretation, which allows a former user, in good faith, to argue their prior rights within the statutory term of five years counted from registration date.

1.18 Third-Party Rights

Article 158 of the Brazilian IP statute allows aggrieved third parties to participate during the registration procedure of a trade mark by filing opposition proceedings within 60 days counted from the first publication of the trade-mark application in the INPI's Official Gazette.

If an opposition is filed, the INPI will publish notice of such opposition in the Official Gazette, triggering a new 60-day term for an applicant to submit a formal reply. No time extensions are allowed for these specific deadlines.

As a rule, the INPI does not accept the late submission of third-party observations (eg briefs with the nature of opposition filed after the lapse of the 60-day legal term). In any event, the petition rights are guaranteed under the Brazilian Federal Constitution and, in the case of interest, third parties can submit briefs offering aids for the examination of a trade mark by the INPI.

The INPI, in turn, is not obliged to analyse these third-party briefs or consider their arguments to ground its merit decision about a trade mark's registrability.

1.19 Revoke, Change, Amend or Correct an Application

As a rule, a trade mark cannot be changed after an application is filed. However, based on the INPI's Guidelines for Trademark Examination, some specific circumstances allow modifications of a sign originally filed, such as:

- In cases of obvious mistakes made by an applicant such as: when typing the word elements of the trade mark; regarding the colour claim applied to figurative elements of the trade mark; in the presentation of composite, figurative or three-dimensional trade marks; and causing discrepancy between the trade mark's image and the declaration of its nominative elements. These correction requests must be filed before the allowance or rejection of the application, through a specific request and upon payment of the official fee of approximately USD20. The applicant must present documents that prove the mistake and the intention to file the correct sign. Furthermore, if a trade-mark application is filed in association with the symbol of registered trade marks ® and TM, the INPI will raise an office action enabling its deletion by the applicant.
- In cases where the INPI fails to insert in its electronic database any relevant information about the trade mark, colour claim, graphical representation of composite, figurative or three-dimensional trade marks; or the use of capital lettering. These correction requests must be filed before the allowance or rejection of the application, through a specific form request, no official fees apply.
- In the event that an applicant is required to present a defence against oppositions or administrative nullity actions, or the INPI issues a rejecting decision: the applicant will be allowed to delete the term or element considered conflicting or unregistrable, as long as such modification does not significantly alter the main characteristics of the sign and do not require its re-publication for opposition purposes in the INPI's Official Gazette.
- In a case where an applicant wishes to delete or restrict the specification of products or services covered by its trade mark, or such adequate coverage to the claimed international class. Such a request may be submitted by the applicant at any time during the prosecution or validity term of a trade mark, through a specific brief and upon payment of official fees.

Finally, it is important to clarify that an applicant may, at any time, at its sole discretion: apply for the withdrawal of a trade-mark application or renounce a trade-mark registration, without incurring any official fees; and submit a specific brief, requesting the change of its name, headquarters or address, upon the payment of official fees.

1.20 Assigning an Application or Granting a Licence

Articles 134 and 139 of the Brazilian IP statute allow both the assignment and license of trade marks during the application process.

It should be noted, however, that an applicant will not be allowed to remit royalties abroad due to assignment or licence of trade-mark applications, this is allowed only after the respective registrations are granted by the INPI.

1.21 Remedies Against the Trade Mark Office

Article 212 of the Brazilian IP statute establishes that an applicant may file an appeal against any decisions provided for in this law, including the refusal to register a trade mark, within a period of 60 days counted from its publication in the Official Gazette.

The appeal suspends the legal effectiveness of the first instance decision, until a final decision is rendered by the INPI's president, with a focus on the opinion issued by the Trademark Board of Appeals of the INPI (in charge of analysing appeal arguments). The president's decision is binding to the applicant and terminates proceedings in the administrative sphere.

Notwithstanding the above, both decisions issued by the INPI (first instance and the INPI's president decision) may be reviewed before federal courts, as per the Brazilian constitutional system. The applicant is not obliged to file an administrative appeal to overcome a decision issued by the first level prior to filing a lawsuit, and may choose to take discussions directly to courts.

1.22 Use of a Trade Mark

The Brazilian legal system does not require that an applicant use its trade mark in commerce before registration.

1.23 Dividing a Trade Mark

The Brazilian IP statute does not allow an applicant to divide a trade mark application filed before the INPI.

1.24 Length of Term of Protection

Trade-mark registrations are valid for a period of ten years, counted from the publication of their registration notice in the INPI's Official Gazette, and may be renewed for successive and equal periods of ten years.

A title-holder must apply for renewal of the registration during the last year of its term of validity, by paying the relevant official fee of approximately USD330. The renewal period may be extended for six months after the registration's validity term expires (so-called extraordinary term), upon payment of increased fees of approximately USD500.

1.25 Requirements for an Exhaustion

The Brazilian legal system adopts the principle of national exhaustion of trade-mark rights, which means that once the trade mark-owner (or its licensees/authorised parties) introduces the product into the Brazilian market, they can no longer prevent their free circulation, as per Article 132 of the Brazilian IP statute.

1.26 Participation in the Madrid System

Brazil is not a member of the Madrid System yet.

However, on 21 June 2017 the Brazilian President forwarded Message #201 for the analysis of the national Congress, which is related to the Madrid Protocol; and on 24 October 2017 the INPI's President submitted to the national Congress a work-plan in line with the INPI's structure to enable Brazil's entry in the Madrid Protocol.

This scenario shows that INPI is politically motivated to join the Madrid System; and has been working to reduce its backlog to meet the 18-month maximum period for trade-mark examination.

1.27 Consequences for Providing Incorrect Information

The consequences for providing incorrect information in connection with a trade-mark application or other filings may vary according to the type of wrongful information provided: in most cases, an applicant is required to pay fees and request a correction to assure accuracy of its future rights. In other cases, the INPI may dismiss some benefit granted to the applicant (eg discounted official fees) or the applicant may lose its rights (eg incorrect priority claim/documents) or the trade-mark application may even be dismissed (eg in the hypothesis of official fees not regularly paid or of non-compliance to formal office actions).

1.28 Updating or Refreshing a Design Mark

Please see **1.19 Revoke, Change, Amend or Correct an Application** for more.

1.29 Denotation

In Brazil, the symbol ® is used to indicate that a trade mark is registered before the INPI. If any person uses the referred symbol ® in connection with a trade-mark application (still pending analysis by the INPI), it may be considered as an act of unfair competition, as per terms of Article 195 of the Brazilian IP statute: "A crime of unfair competition is committed by who: I - publishes, by any means, a false affirmation, in detriment to a competitor, with a view to obtaining advantage; (…)".

2. Assignment and Licensing

2.1 Assignment Requirements or Restrictions

The Brazilian IP statute allows either an applicant or title-holder to apply for the assignment of a trade mark, who is then required to submit to the INPI a written agreement, executed by empowered officers of each party and two witnesses.

Article 165 of the Brazilian IP statute sets forth that the assignment must include all registrations for identical/similar trade marks covering related products or services, under penalty of ex officio cancellation of the non-assigned trade marks.

The assignment agreement may encompass both trade-mark applications and registrations.

2.2 Procedure for Assigning a Trade Mark

Parties must negotiate a trade-mark assignment agreement, which must contain:

- an assignor and assignee's complete data;
- powers of representation to the signatories of the assignment agreement and their respective signatures;
- indication of the number of trade-mark applications or registrations subject to the assignment; and
- the date and place where the agreement was executed.

To be valid in Brazil, this document must be legalised or apostilled (as per The Hague Apostille Convention), submitted in a bilingual format or together with its simple Portuguese translation.

The assignment document must be submitted to INPI together with:

- a specific form requesting the assignment of the trade marks (and a list indicating all assigned trade-mark applications and registrations);
- Power of Attorney;
- any other documents needed to attest that the assignment agreement signatories are duly empowered; and
- proof of payment of the INPI's official fees.

The INPI will review if the request meets all legal formalities and, upon acceptance, will publish the notice of assignment in the Official Gazette.

2.3 Registering or Recording the Assignment

The trade-mark assignment agreement must be recorded as a condition for the effective change of ownership before the INPI and any third parties. The transfer of ownership is formalised upon publication in the INPI's Official Gazette.

During the gap between the assignment taking place and the recordal publication by the INPI, the assigned trade mark(s) may be subject to incumbrances related to its former owner. For instance, if the former owner/assignor has a tax debt, the Brazilian IRS may obtain a court order to seize the trade mark(s) – impairing the effectiveness of the assignment agreement.

2.4 Trade Marks and Security

Article 5 of the Brazilian IP statute sets forth that industrial property rights are deemed as chattels, for any legal purposes. Thus, a trade-mark registration can either be given as a security, be subject to rights in rem, be assigned by way of security, or be levied in execution. The effectiveness of such guarantees depends on the registration of the relevant encumbrances before the INPI and its publication in the Official Gazette.

The property of the chattel is only vested by registration. In this sense, trade-mark applications may be offered by its owner as a security, but there is a risk of refusal by the creditor.

2.5 Licensing Requirements or Restrictions

The Brazilian IP statute allows either an applicant or title-holder to apply for the licensing of a trade mark, on an exclusive or non-exclusive basis. To do so, the contracting parties are required to submit to the INPI a written licence agreement, executed by empowered officers of each party and two witnesses.

The licence agreement may encompass both trade-mark applications or registrations. However, any royalty payments due to the licensing of trade-mark applications cannot be remitted abroad until the issuance of registrations by the INPI.

The price shall be agreed between the parties with the basis on a percentage of the net sales of products or services provided under the licensed trade marks. Any payments made between related companies (subsidiary) are limited to 1%, as per applicable tax and fiscal regulations.

2.6 Procedure for Licensing a Trade Mark

Parties must negotiate a trade-mark licence agreement, which must contain:

- a licensor and licensee's complete data;
- powers of representation to the signatories of a licence agreement and their respective signatures;
- indication of the number of trade-mark applications or registrations subject to the licence;
- the validity term of the licence;
- price and other commercial conditions; and
- the date and place where the agreement was executed.

To be valid in Brazil, a licence agreement must be legalised or apostilled (as per The Hague Apostille Convention), submitted in a bilingual format or together with its simple Portuguese translation.

The licence document must be submitted to INPI together with a specific form; Power of Attorney; and proof of payment of INPI's official fees. The INPI will conduct a formal review of the agreement and, upon acceptance, will publish the recordal in its Official Gazette and issue the recordal certificate. Such certificate is required by the Brazilian Central Bank for enabling royalties' remittance to foreign countries.

2.7 Registering or Recording the Licence

A licence agreement needs to be recorded with the INPI in order to produce certain effects like:

- the effectiveness before any third parties, besides granting legitimacy to the local licensee to represent the licensor before Brazilian courts (if such possibility is specifically provided in the agreement);
- enabling royalties' remittance to foreign countries; and
- enabling fiscal deductibility for the Brazilian licensee paying royalties.

To validate trade-mark proof of use the licence agreement does not have to be recorded with the INPI.

During the gap between the licence taking place and the recordal publication by the INPI, the licence will only be automatically effective between the parties.

2.8 Reasons to Deny Granting a Perpetual Licence

The term of a licence may not exceed the term of validity of the trade marks that will be licensed. The licence agreement can be renewed for successive periods, through the submission of a written additive, if the licensed registrations have been duly renewed by the licensor/title-holder.

3. Opposition Procedure

3.1 Legal Grounds and Timeframes

The legal grounds for an opposition procedure are the absolute or relative prohibitions set forth in Article 124 of the Brazilian IP Statute; bad faith; and other special rights afforded to trade marks under the Brazilian IP statute, such as:

- oppositions grounded on famous trade marks (an exception to the Specialty Principle) to prevent the registration of identical or similar trade marks in all fields of activity (Article 125 of the Brazilian IP statute;
- oppositions grounded on well-known trade marks (an exception to the Territoriality Principle) to prevent the registration of identical or similar signs that imitate or reproduce, wholly or in part, a trade mark of which an applicant could not reasonably fail to know in view of his or her activity, in a specific market segment (Article 124, XXIII; Article 126 of the Brazilian IP statute and Article 6 bis of the Paris Convention); and
- oppositions grounded on prior fair use: according to Article 129, §1° of the Brazilian IP statute, an opposition procedure may be initiated against a senior trade mark if the opponent party can evidence that it was using an identical or similar trade mark for at least six months in the country, to identify or certify identical, similar or akin products or services.

The INPI takes approximately three to four years to render decisions on the merits on opposed trade mark cases.

3.2 Filing an Opposition

Any individuals or companies that own senior rights over a trade mark, that could be damaged by the registration of an identical or similar trade mark to cover identical, similar or related products or services may oppose a trade-mark application.

The opponent party does not need representation, but it is highly advisable that the procedure is handled by a specialised attorney. The INPI charges approximately USD110 for official fees.

3.3 Opposition Procedure

Article 158 of the Brazilian IP statute allows any third parties, aggrieved by a trade-mark application to file an opposition procedure within 60 days counted from the first publication of the trade-mark application in the INPI's Official Gazette.

If an opposition is filed, the INPI will publish notice of such opposition in the Official Gazette within approximately two months, triggering a new 60-day term for an applicant to submit a formal reply. The submission of a reply by the applicant is not mandatory, and its absence will not cause the dismissal of the application.

The INPI takes approximately three to four years to render merit decisions on opposed trade mark cases.

3.4 Legal Remedies

Article 212 of the Brazilian IP statute establishes that an applicant may file an appeal against any decisions provided for in this law, including the refusal to register a trade mark, within a period of 60 days counted from its publication in the Official Gazette.

If the INPI rejects a trade-mark application, the applicant may file an appeal within 60 days counted from the publication of such a decision under penalty of dismissal. Once the appeal is filed it will be published in the Official Gazette within three months, triggering a new 60-day term for the opponent to present a possible reply.

The case will be decided by the INPI's president, with a focus on the opinion issued by the Trademark Board of Appeals of the INPI (in charge of analysing appeal arguments).

If the INPI grants the trade-mark registration, the aggrieved party can still file an administrative nullity action within 180 days counted from the publication of the registration notice in the Official Gazette.

Furthermore, decisions by the INPI may be reviewed before federal courts by filing the relevant lawsuit within a five-year statutory limitation.

4. Initiating a Lawsuit

4.1 Actions to Pursue Infringement

According to the Brazilian legal system a trade mark-owner (and, in some cases, a licensee) has standing to pursue civil or criminal actions to stop or prevent trade mark infringement, jointly or separately.

Infringement lawsuits must be filed before state courts, against any third parties that, wholly or partially, imitate or reproduce its registered trade mark to designate identical, similar or related products or services, leading to confusion before consumers; or imports, exports, sells, offers or exhibits for sale, hides or maintains in stock a product bearing that trade mark. Such an action is grounded on Article 129 of the Brazilian IP statute, that assures an owner exclusive rights to use the trade mark in the national territory.

Criminal actions must be initiated upon submission of a formal complaint before the police, who will then investigate the leads or evidences submitted to confirm whether a crime against a registered trade mark has been committed (and by whom). Such an action is grounded on Articles 189 and 190 of the Brazilian IP statute.

Different actions, in the civil sphere, are available for the protection of unregistered trade marks. The grounds for such actions are unfair competition provisions, that prohibit the use of fraudulent means to divert, for his or her own or a third party's benefit, another's clientele; and an applicant's right to care for the material integrity or reputation of its trade-mark application, which legitimises the remittance of cease-and-desist letters (C&D letters) or the filing of preventive lawsuits.

4.2 Initiating Infringement Proceedings

According to the Brazilian legal system, a trade mark-owner must file a trade-mark infringement proceeding before a state court, either on the site where an infringement occurred, or where an alleged infringer has its main place of business.

4.3 Effect of Decisions on Infringement Actions

The INPI is not a party in infringement lawsuits filed before state courts. Even though the INPI's decisions are not binding in any judicial cases, as judges are free to construe their own convictions, judges tend to decide trade-mark infringement cases with deference to administrative decisions issued by the INPI, as it is the competent authority to rule on trade-mark registrability.

4.4 Declaratory Judgment Proceedings

An alleged infringer may, at any time, file a non-infringement declaratory lawsuit as a strategic defence to a possible infringement lawsuit filed by a title-holder. Since a lawsuit intends to obtain a judicial declaration that a certain trade mark does not infringe trade-mark rights of a senior title-holder, a non-infringement declaratory lawsuit is generally filed before an infringement lawsuit and usually after the alleged infringer suffers objections in the administrative sphere and/or receives a C&D letter from a senior title-holder.

4.5 Jurisdiction of Courts

At first instance judges have jurisdiction to rule in trade-mark matters as infringement cases are dealt with by state courts, while validity or nullity cases are dealt with by federal courts, as per the Brazilian bifurcated system.

At second instance, the State Court of Appeals has jurisdiction over trade-mark infringement cases, while the Federal Court of Appeals has jurisdiction over trade-mark validity and nullity actions. Any appeals filed against State or Federal Courts of Appeals' rulings are filed before the STJ or the Supreme Court of the Justice (STF), when a case involves a violation of any provision of the Brazilian Federal Constitution.

4.6 Prerequisites to Filing a Lawsuit

Under Brazilian legislation there is no mandatory prerequisites to file a lawsuit.

Despite that, as matter of strategy and cost-effectiveness, it is advisable to send C&D letters to an infringer prior to initiating legal action, in an attempt to settle a dispute amicably and possibly build a case for future litigation (in case the infringer replies to the C&D letter and exposes its defence arguments).

4.7 Representation for Parties

According to the Brazilian legal system the parties in trade-mark litigation matters need to be represented by a lawyer.

4.8 Interim or Preliminary Injunctions

According to the Brazilian legal system both interim and preliminary injunctions are available and may be granted by a judge, without the prior hearing of the other party (ex parte injunctions), when a plaintiff successfully demonstrates urgency (which means, that if not promptly decided this situation will cause irreparable damages) and the likely success of the complaint.

Judges must analyse the hardship caused by a decision to grant an injunction against the hardship caused by not granting it. For specific cases, upon a judges' discretion, the plaintiff may be required to post a bond.

Ex parte preliminary injunction requests are usually decided within 24-96 hours of the filing of a complaint. The scope of the injunction may vary from immediately enjoining the defendant from using the trade mark under penalty of a daily fine to the immediate search and seizure of all infringing products.

4.9 Protection for Potential Defendant

To protect itself, a potential defendant may file a non-infringement declaratory lawsuit (please refer to **4.4 Declaratory Judgment Proceedings**); or counter attack by filing a separate invalidity lawsuit before federal courts (due to the mandatory presence of the INPI as a defendant), seeking to declare the nullity of a plaintiff's trade mark.

Bonds may be offered by a defendant in substitution for a preliminary injunction, but it is up to a judge to avail whether to substitute it or not.

4.10 Obtaining Information and Evidence

The Brazilian legal system does not provide for discovery (or discovery-alike) proceedings. Aiming to produce evidence, a plaintiff may submit to the courts a request to seize relevant documents or materials (even counterfeit products) in the possession of the infringer with the judge then deciding on the relevance of that request.

4.11 Initial Pleading Standards

The initial pleading standards to initiate a lawsuit consists of:

- asserting all pleadings of infringement: senior trade-mark rights, unfair competition, client deviation or loss of market share, dilution of the trade mark attractive power, among others;
- attesting to the entitlement of prior trade-mark rights;
- gathering documents and materials to be used as evidence of the infringement,

It is important to gather a robust set of evidence, including expert opinions and visual aids, including market surveys upon filing a lawsuit; although it is possible to submit further evidence (documents and materials) afterwards.

Unlike patent lawsuits, trade mark cases do not always require expert examination. It depends on the level of complexity of a case and the market at hand.

The Brazilian IP statute sets special provisions for trade-mark proceedings that differ from non-IP proceedings, such as the INPI must be included as a mandatory defendant in any validity and nullity lawsuits filed before federal courts; and during the proceedings, if preliminary injunctive relief is granted, a judge may suspend the effects of the trade-mark registration and of its use.

Pleadings may be supplemented by additional evidence during the evidentiary phase of the lawsuit (eg before a decision is rendered). As a general rule, claims set in the complaint, however, cannot be altered after the defendant is summoned.

4.12 Representative or Collective Actions

Although not prohibited under Brazilian law, it is not common to file representative or collective actions related to trade-mark proceedings.

According to the Brazilian legal system, collective actions are regulated by Law 7,347 of 1985, which sets forth that only patrimonial and moral damages can be caused to:

- the environment;
- consumers;
- assets and rights of artistic, aesthetic, historical, tourist and landscape value;
- collective and diffuse rights or interests;
- infraction to the economic order;
- urbanistic order;
- the honour and dignity of racial, ethnic or religious groups; or
- to the public and social wealth.

If a trade-mark registration is deemed to cause damages to a group of consumers, to assets and rights of artistic, aesthetic, historical, tourist and landscape value or infringes the economic order of the honour and dignity of racial, ethnic or religious groups, a civil action could be filed by Public Prosecutors or by any public association with the purpose of safeguarding collective interests.

4.13 Restrictions on Trade Mark-Owners

Brazilian Procedural Law establishes that, in the case of a completely groundless lawsuit of trade mark infringement (any type of action, actually), a judge may hold a plaintiff in bad faith and set a fine to be paid at the end of proceedings. This is extraordinarily rare, as access to courts is a fundamental right set in the Brazilian Constitution.

A trade mark-owner may also be subject to administrative proceedings before the Brazilian antitrust authority – CADE – under sham litigation claims. If CADE finds that the conduct harms fair competition, the trade mark-owner may be condemned to pay a fine, which could be fixed in 0.1 up to 20% of a company's net revenue. CADE's current case law offers varied standards for establishing conduct that is considered sham litigation.

5. Infringement

5.1 Action for Infringement

The necessary parties to a trade-mark infringement action are a title-holder (namely, the owner of the trade mark registration) and an alleged infringer.

It is possible for the trade-mark licensee to initiate an infringement lawsuit in lieu of the title-holder or as a joint plaintiff, if specifically provided for in the licence agreement and such agreement is duly recorded by the INPI.

The owner or licensee of a trade-mark application may start a lawsuit based on the use of its trade mark and unfair competition provisions.

5.2 Signs and Infringement

The following factors must be considered when determining trade mark infringement:

- the degree of distinctiveness of the trade marks, if the senior mark is not composed by distinctive element(s) it shall face the burden of co-existing with other trade marks composed by the same element(s);
- if observed successively, the trade marks bear similarities that may cause the risk of confusion or undue association for the public;
- if both trade marks cover identical, similar or related products or services, and are also susceptible to causing confusion or undue association regarding the product itself and its origin.

There are also market circumstances that may be further considered when determining trade mark infringement, such as if there is direct competition in a market segment, if the products target the same kind of consumers, and if they are sold through the same market channels, if the relevant products or services are indeed interchangeable, among others.

5.3 Use of a Sign by Defendant

It is necessary to establish that a defendant has used a sign as a trade mark with commercial intent.

5.4 Defences Against Infringement

An alleged infringer may sustain the following defence arguments:

- sufficient distinctiveness between trade marks;
- non-related products or services, targeted to different consumer markets;
- prior use in good faith;
- forfeiture of the senior trade mark due to non-use in a market;

- bad faith, in case a plaintiff has no exclusive rights to the trade mark or any of its composing elements (eg such as a registration granted by the INPI with a disclaimer); and
- a prior-registered company name, trade name or domain name.

It is also possible to cite exceptions provided in Article 132 of the Brazilian IP statute to:

- prevent tradesmen or distributors from using distinctive signs that belong to them, together with the mark of the product for its promotion and commercialisation;
- prevent the manufacture of accessories;
- prevent the free circulation of products placed on the internal market by him or herself or by another with his or her consent, without prejudice to the provisions of §§ 3 and 4 of Article 68; and
- prevent the mention of the mark in speeches, scientific or literary works or in any other type of publication, provided that it is without any commercial connotation and without prejudice to its distinctive character.

To some extent, fair use based on fundamental rights and a consumers' right to information may be alleged as well, such as in comparative publicity.

5.5 Role of Experts and/or Surveys

As a rule, judges are free to construe their own convictions; however; in more complex trade mark matters, it is not unusual for parties to submit opinions or surveys drafted by experts. If a judge deems it necessary to have an impartial technical opinion, it will appoint a court's expert.

Judges are not bound to decide based on the one-sided or court-appointed expert opinions, but depending on the arguments brought and the reputation of the selected experts, a judge may feel inclined to accept their views.

5.6 Administrative or Criminal Offence

According to the Brazilian IP statute, a crime against a trade mark is committed by someone who:

- reproduces a registered mark wholly or in part, without the authorisation of a title-holder, or imitates it in a manner that may induce confusion;
- alters the registered mark of a third party already applied to a product placed on the market;
- imports, exports, sells, offers or exhibits for sale, hides or maintains in stock a trade mark that reproduces a registered mark wholly or in part, or imitates it in a manner that may induce confusion:
- deals with products branded with an illicitly, wholly or partially reproduced or imitated mark of a third party; or
- deals with a product from his or her industry or commerce, held in a vessel, container or package carrying a legitimate mark of a third party.

The applicable penalty is of detention for three months to one year, or payment of a fine.

According to the Brazilian legal system the trade mark-owner (and in some cases the licensee) has standing to pursue criminal actions to stop or prevent trade-mark infringement. Criminal actions must be initiated upon submission of a formal complaint before the police, who will then investigate the leads or evidences submitted to confirm whether a crime against a registered trade mark has been committed (and by whom).

Such an action is grounded on Articles 189 and 190 of the Brazilian IP statute.

5.7 Custom Seizures

Customs' Seizure of Counterfeits

According to Section 605 of Decree Law No 6,759 of 2009 the seizure of counterfeits is usually limited to copyright and trade mark-infringing products. It is also possible to apply for inspection requests to patented products based on the provisions of the TRIPS agreement (Article 41(1) and others), which includes the protection of patents.

A title-holder would have to: formalise legal representation before the National Directory to Fight Counterfeiting (NDFC) by attaching a list of trade marks together with other relevant information about the distinctive features of the original branded products (photos, images, hidden labels, bar codes, watermarks, explanatory texts, presentations and others); and file Inspection Requests before the Central Co-ordination of Customs Affairs (COANA), aiming to list its intellectual property rights and triggering surveillance of any illegal imports.

If any suspicious or counterfeit products are seized, customs notifies the title-holder or its legal representatives about the preliminary seizure. The title-holder has ten days to submit a technical report to customs regarding the origin of said products (clarifying whether it is a legal shipment or not). An additional ten-day term is then initiated, enabling the owner of the seized products to reply.

If customs conclude they are dealing with counterfeit products, the title-holder is required to assert a penal claim to obtain the definitive apprehension or destruction of the merchandise based on Article 606 of the Decree 6,759 and Article 200 (followings) of the Brazilian IP statute. The title-holder bears all the costs and expenses incurred for the adoption of these measures.

Parallel Imports
The STJ's case law prohibits parallel imports (import of original products) without a trade mark-owner's consent.

6. Revocation/Cancellation

6.1 Remedies and Reasons
The Brazilian legal system provides for in and out of court remedies. Out-of-court remedies are taken before the INPI, through a nullity administrative proceeding that may be filed by a party with a legitimate interest within 180 days counted from the date of publication of the trade-mark registration.

In court remedies must be filed before federal courts, since it must involve the necessary joinder of the INPI. Any decisions issued by the trial level judge are subject to review by the Federal Court of Appeals.

As a rule, any trade-mark registration granted in violation of the Brazilian IP statute (absolute or relative grounds set forth in Article 124) might be subject to revocation/cancellation proceedings. Furthermore, Article 143 of the Brazilian IP statute sets forth that if a title-holder does not initiate the use of its trade mark after five years counted from its registration date, or interrupts its use for more than five consecutive years, the trade mark may be vulnerable to a forfeiture request filed by a third party with a legitimate interest and, therefore, be declared extinct.

6.2 Trade Mark Office and Civil Courts
Revocation/cancellation actions can be brought before the INPI or federal courts. Please refer to **6.1 Remedies and Reasons**.

6.3 Statutory Limitation or Time Period
The administrative nullity procedure must be initiated within 180 days counted from the date of publication of the trade-mark registration. As a general rule, a trade mark nullity lawsuit has a five-year statute of limitation from the date of issuance. There are exceptions to overcome the statute of limitation, such as bad faith (eg Article 6 bis of the Paris Convention) and when there are absolute grounds to annul the trade-mark registration.

6.4 Initiation of Revocation/Cancellation Proceeding
Out-of-court revocation/cancellation proceedings may be initiated by third parties with a legitimate interest or ex officio by the INPI. In court revocation/cancellation proceedings, namely the trade mark nullity lawsuit, may be filed before federal courts by any third party with a legitimate interest or the INPI.

According to the Guidelines for Trademark Examination issued by the INPI, the following conditions satisfy the requirement of a legitimate interest to initiate revocation/cancellation proceedings:

- own a senior identical or similar trade-mark application or registration to identify identical or similar products or services;
- personality rights;
- copyrights; and
- other rights that characterise that the third party develops activities in the same market segment or related to the products and services covered by the trade mark.

6.5 Partial Revocation/Cancellation
It is possible to apply for the partial revocation/cancellation of trade-mark registration in cases where only part of the products or services covered thereof have overlap with senior trade marks, have been granted in violation of the Brazilian IP statute provision or have not been used by a title-holder.

Courts or the INPI may also decide on a partial revocation/cancellation by imposing a disclaimer to the registration, establishing that part of it is not entitled to protection.

6.6 Possibilities of Amendment
As a rule, after revocation/cancellation proceedings are initiated with the INPI it cannot be amended, but a claimant, at its sole discretion, may withdraw prior to the issuance of a decision. However, the withdrawal request is not binding to the INPI, which may proceed ex officio.

It is also possible for a title-holder to amend its trade-mark registration subject to revocation/cancellation proceedings at any time, to restrict its specification of products or services.

As a general rule, the Brazilian Civil Procedure Code provides that claims in a lawsuit can be amended before a defendant is summoned.

6.7 Revocation/Cancellation and Infringement
Given that Brazil has a bifurcated system, lawsuits involving revocation/cancellation and infringement usually have different timeframes.

The timing for decisions by state courts (eg infringement cases) may vary according to the location, but usually ranges around five to ten months for a first-instance ruling. The timing for a decision by appellate state courts usually ranges around six to eight months.

The timing for a decision by federal courts (eg revocation/cancellation cases) may be impacted by the complexity of the set of evidences produced by parties, and the statutory double terms for the INPI to present briefs in a case. Trial level decisions usually take approximately two years to be rendered, and if the case goes to the Federal Court of Appeal it may take two to four years for a final decision.

Revocation/cancellation and infringement cases are not heard together. When a revocation/cancellation case is filed before an infringement lawsuit, it is possible to have the latter stayed until a final decision is rendered in the revocation/nullity case.

7. Trial & Settlement

7.1 Special Procedural Providions

Please refer to **4.10 Obtaining Information and Evidence**.

7.2 Determination of Cases

In Brazil, only cases dealing with crimes against life are determined by a jury. Therefore, trade-mark lawsuits will always be decided by judges, while on an appellate level cases will be decided by a panel of appellate judges. Judges within a local court are randomly assigned to cases, but forum shopping strategies are available.

7.3 Possibilities of Settlement

According to the Brazilian legal system a defendant has the following possibilities to settle a case: a conciliatory hearing, to be held after the admissibility examination of the initial complaint, unless both parties decline; and at any time, during the lawsuit. After parties reach a settlement, the judge will render a decision confirming the settlement terms. Any settlements that involve non-negotiable rights (eg trade-mark validity or term, among others) will be rejected by the courts.

7.4 Other Court Proceedings

According to the Brazilian legal system revocation/cancellation actions may influence the proceedings of an infringement lawsuit by suspending it, if they are filed before or concomitantly to the infringement lawsuit; or by giving cause to its dismissal or rejection of the claims if there is a prior and definitive decision on the merits cancelling a trade-mark registration.

The parties may request suspension and a judge can determine it ex officio.

8. Remedies

8.1 Existing Remedies

The main remedies available to a trade mark-owner under the Brazilian legal system are: damages; recovery of court fees and expert fees (if applicable); preliminary and final injunctive relief; search and seizure or destruction of counterfeit products; and freezing bank accounts in the event that an infringer fails to comply with a court order determining the payment of damages.

In Brazil, there is no provision for enhanced damages related to the wilful infringement of trade marks nor for punitive or treble damages.

The professional fees established between a client and attorney for representation cannot be recovered in a lawsuit.

With regard to a judge's discretion to order remedies, they are bound to the provisions set out in Brazilian regulations and to the extent of a plaintiff's claims.

8.2 Rights and Remedies

A prevailing defendant is entitled to receive reimbursement of certain costs, such as court fees (including expert fees, if applicable) and declaration for non-infringement, which results in ensuring the right to continue using a trade mark.

8.3 Different Types of Remedies

Defence remedies are the same despite different types of trade marks.

9. Appeal

9.1 Special Provisions

There are no special provisions for trade marks concerning the appellate procedure in lawsuits before the courts. The regular Civil Procedure Code rules apply.

9.2 Factual or Legal Review

Appeals imply a full review of the facts of a case. If a lawsuit reaches the Superior Courts, then the review is restricted to the specific violation to federal laws or constitutional provisions.

9.3 Length of Appeal from Trial Court

The timing for a decision by appellate state courts ruling in trade-mark infringement cases usually ranges around six to eight months.

The timing for a decision by the Federal Court of Appeal ruling in trade mark nullity actions usually ranges around two to four years.

10. Other Trade Mark Issues

10.1 Recognition of Dilution

The Brazilian jurisdiction recognises trade-mark dilution as a ground to oppose a trade-mark registration or to prevent the use of a trade mark in a lawsuit.

10.2 Protection of Famous Marks

The Brazilian IP statute has clear provisions related to well-known trade marks. Article 126 sets forth that trade marks that are well-known in their field of activity in terms of Article 6 bis (1) of the Paris Convention will enjoy special protection, independently of whether they have been previously filed or registered in Brazil. In this sense, the INPI may reject ex officio an application to register a trade mark that, wholly or partially, reproduces or imitates a well-known trade mark to designate identical, similar or related products or services.

It should be noted, however, that if an applicant initiates an opposition procedure based on a well-known trade mark, he or she is required to proceed with the filing of its trade mark before the INPI within 60 days counted from the opposition filing date, under penalty of dismissal (Article 158, §2° of the Brazilian IP statute).

Provided that there are no standards to define "well-known" trade marks or criteria to its assessment, the INPI considers if the trade mark under examination acquired a certain degree of recognition in the national territory in association to a specific market segment. An applicant has the burden of proof that its trade mark is entitled to such special protection, and must submit supporting evidence such as: dated advertising materials; the amount of investment made in advertisements; market surveys to demonstrate public acknowledgment and preference; and market-share data, among others.

10.3 Special Rules Regarding Geographic Indicators

In Brazil, geographic indicators (GIs) may be protected under two modalities:

- source indications: which covers the geographical name of a country, city, region or locality of its territory, which has become known as a centre of extraction, production or manufacture of a certain product or for providing a determined service; and
- appellation of origin: which is considered to be the geographical name of a country, city, region or locality of its territory, designating a product or service with qualities or characteristics exclusively or essentially related to the geographical environment, including natural and human factors.

Important facts to note include: geographical indications are not subject to a specific validity term, eg the protection for a registered geographical indication will remain valid unless the registration is cancelled; the use of geographical indicators is restricted to the producers and providers of services established in the locality; and certain quality requirements must be met for appellations of origin.

Throughout Rule #25 of 2013 the INPI established the conditions for registration of geographical indications in Brazil. The application for registration of a geographical indication must be made by a legitimate party, refer to only one geographic name, and contain the description and characteristics of the product or service to be related to the geographic area, besides an official document defining the limits of the geographic area. During the examination, the BPTO may issue office actions in order to enable the recognition of the geographical indicator.

Based on the EU-MERCOSUR Free Trade Agreement, the INPI recently issued Rule #79 of 2017 establishing new and simplified administrative proceedings to be adopted by the INPI for the recognition of GI registrations coming from the EU, according to the list provided by the EU's diplomatic representation and published by the INPI on 7 November 2017.

Such publication triggers a 30-day term for any third parties to present explanatory briefs challenging the recognition of the EU GIs in Brazil. If there is a challenge, the EU's diplomatic representation will be notified, and an applicant will have a new 30-day term to present a reply. After that, the INPI will analyse the case and issue a technical opinion ruling in favour or against the local recognition of the GI. The technical opinion ruling is final and binding to the GI applicant and the EU's diplomatic representation.

Finally, to prevent misuse and/or confusion, the Brazilian IP statute also sets forth that any: "Geographic indications, imitations thereof likely to cause confusion or signs that might falsely suggest a geographic indication" are not registrable as trade marks.

10.4 Special Rules Relating to Surnames

Article 124, XV of the Brazilian IP statute defines that "personal names or signatures thereof, family or patronymic names and images of third parties, except with the consent of the owner, his heirs or his successors" are not registrable as marks.

The INPI's Guidelines for Trademark Examination defines that although no-one can be prevented from using their own surname, when such use has a commercial intent this should be balanced between the interests of the consumer and trade-mark principles. Therefore, the manual reinforces the first-to-file principle in what relates to trade-mark registration, and infers that a use conflicting with a senior registered trade mark that causes the risk of confusion might not be allowed.

11. Costs

11.1 Costs Before Filing a Lawsuit

The Brazilian legal system does not provide for any procedures that would generate mandatory costs prior to the filing of a lawsuit. In order to file a lawsuit, a plaintiff would only have to pay court fees.

Additional costs may arise from possible remittance of a C&D letter, and obtaining legalisation/apostille of foreign documents.

11.2 Costs Regarding an Infringement Action

The typical costs for bringing an infringement action to conclusion in the first instance involve court fees, that for trade-mark infringement lawsuits are usually fixed at a 2% rate on the lawsuit value; and expert fees, in case expert examination is requested by parties and allowed by the judge.

The expert will propose the amount of his or her fee to act in a case, and the parties are summoned to agree or contest such amount. If the party(ies) contests, the judge will fix the expert's fee in a reasonable way. If the party(ies) agree with the expert's fee, they will be summoned to pay.

If one party requests an expert's exam, it is responsible for paying for it. If both parties request it, they split payment; and if the judge ordered an expert's exam the plaintiff is responsible for the payment.

11.3 Costs of Litigation

A plaintiff anticipates court fees, expert fees (if applicable), and the counterparty reimburses such costs if the lawsuit is decided in favour of the plaintiff. Each party will be responsible for paying professional fees for legal representation to its selected attorneys.

12. Alternative Dispute Resolution

12.1 Common Way of Settlement

There are no specific provisions related to alternative dispute resolution (ADR) inside the Brazilian IP statute. However, many trade-mark infringement cases end up in a settlement after the beginning of court procedures, especially in cases where a preliminary injunctive relief was granted and later confirmed by the Court of Appeals. It is important to note that ADRs are not available for invalidity issues, which can only be decided through an action filed before federal courts, with the INPI as a mandatory defendant.

The Brazilian Civil Procedure Code actively promotes conciliation during procedures. The conciliation or mediation hearing is held at the beginning of the trial phase of a case provided that the complaint filed with the court fulfils all the essential requirements and a prompt dismissal of the case due to the impossibility of the request is not applicable (Article 334). The timeframe for a defendant's answer only starts to run "from the hearing of conciliation or mediation, or the last session of conciliation, when any party fails to attend or, while attending, no compromise is reached" (Article 335, item I).

Although not necessarily common in trade-mark infringement cases, arbitration is also available in Brazil and governed by the Arbitration Law #9,307 of 1996. Article 1º of this Law limits the scope of issues that can be submitted to arbitration: "Persons capable of entering into contracts may settle through arbitration disputes related to freely transferable patrimonial rights".

Therefore, if the parties can agree to arbitration instead of resorting to the courts this could possibly lead to a faster final decision; but if a trade mark-owner needs, for example, injunctive relief for the immediate cessation of use of a confusingly similar mark, arbitration might not be the best option.

Although issues of trade-mark invalidity are not available for ADRs, the INPI had partnered with the World Intellectual Property Organisation (WIPO) in 2014 in order to draft mediation rules that would apply to proceedings before the INPI, mainly for trade-mark disputes between national companies. Nevertheless, it seems that the use of this centre was basically non-existent, since the INPI would not be bound to adopt the mediation results.

13. Trade Marks and Other Intellectual Property

13.1 Protection by Copyright

If provided with a minimum degree of originality, a logo, three-dimensional trade mark or an industrial design may be considered as "works of art" and entitled to such protection under Article 7, VIII of the Brazilian Copyright Law #9.610 of 1998).

Therefore, the owner of a logo, three-dimensional trade mark or industrial design not registered before the INPI, may successfully obtain a court order to determine the search and seizure or destruction of products bearing the works of art; and the payment of damages due to unauthorised use, reproduction, publication and other illicit actions involving the works of art under copyright law provisions. In that context, it is important to clarify that copyright does not need to be registered in order to be enforceable.

It should be noted that not all remedies available to title-holders of trade marks or industrial designs registered with the INPI are equally available under copyright law. For example, there are no criminal penalties for third parties in good faith – not the infringer – who commercially exploit the product bearing the works of art.

Three-dimensional trade marks cannot be protected as patents. It is worth mentioning that under Brazilian law, patents do not cover industrial designs: they are separate forms of industrial property rights. Therefore, unregistered three-dimensional trade marks could be protected as an industrial design (design patent), if the ornamental shape has absolute novelty and is further submitted for registration with the INPI.

As for trade dress, there is no specific protection under trademark rights or copyrights. The trade dress cannot be registered with the INPI and its enforcement is based on unfair competition provisions under the Brazilian IP statute.

Licks Attorneys
Rua da Assembleia, 10, suite 4108
Rio de Janeiro RJ, Brazil, 20.011-901

Tel: +55 21 3550-3700
Fax: +55 21 3550-3777
Email: info@lickslegal.com
Web: www.lickslegal.com

CANADA

LAW AND PRACTICE: p.33

Contributed by Blaney McMurtry LLP

The 'Law & Practice' sections provide easily accessible information on navigating the legal system when conducting business in the jurisdiction. Leading lawyers explain local law and practice at key transactional stages and for crucial aspects of doing business.

Law and Practice

Contributed by Blaney McMurtry LLP

CONTENTS

Blaney McMurtry LLP Intellectual Property Practice Group provides a full range of services and works with other members of the firm. We work with our clients to equip them with the knowledge required to determine proactively and strategically how to identify, perfect and manage their intellectual property assets which may include patents, trade-marks, copyright, industrial designs or trade secrets. Lawyers also assist with the development and implementation of strategies for the exploitation and enforcement of these rights, specifically: preliminary registrability; opinions for proposed trade-marks and trade names; monitoring and mark-watching services, by mark, applicant or product/service; preparation, filing and prosecution of trade-mark applications in Canada, the US and internationally; trade-mark management and renewal.

Authors

Ian S. Epstein is a partner specialising in insurance litigation and coverage, commercial litigation, intellectual property and immigration. Ian's expertise in intellectual property advocacy before the Canadian courts extends to brand and reputation management, patents, product liability, malicious prosecution, and actions against public authorities. He has extensive experience in risk management and insurance coverage matters. His commercial litigation practice includes property, entertainment contracts and claims.

Bruno P. Soucy is a partner specialising in intellectual property, copyright & trade-marks, corporate and commercial and information technology. After developing his practice in business law – including in the areas of M&A, secured lending, competition, advertising, corporate finance, commercial, corporate, entertainment, intellectual property, technology, e-commerce and privacy – Bruno began to specialise in the fields of intellectual property, advertising and technology law. He also developed expertise in various regulated industries, such as information technology, manufacturing (food and consumer goods), manufacturing (medical devices), consumer retail, financial services, professional services (engineering, accounting and management consulting), telecommunications and life sciences.

Andrea Rush is a partner specialising in trade marks, copyright, branding and technology. She is certified as a specialist in trade-mark law and a registered trademark agent, former Chair of the Law Society Specialist Certification Board, Law Society IP Year in Review and ALAI Toronto. She has recognised expertise before the Trademarks Opposition and Copyright Boards, Federal and Supreme Court of Canada. Andrea is a recent recipient of the Long-Term Achievement Award from the Law Society of Ontario; and a former recipient of the Charles Seton award from the Copyright Society of the USA, and Duff Rinfret Scholarship (Justice, Canada). Andrea has taught at Osgoode Hall Law School (LLM, e-commerce) and OCAD University (IP), Trustee CSUSA, INTA Panel of Neutrals, WIPO Mediation Centre, and served on a NAFTA business services SAGIT (sectoral advisory group on international trade).

1. Types of Trade Marks & Registration

1.1 Types of Trade Marks

The Trade-marks Act (RSC 1985, c T-13) (the "Act") and the Trade-marks Regulations (SOR/96-195) (the "Regulations") provide for registrability and enforceability of registered and unregistered marks within Canada, and are supplemented by common law and additional federal and provincial laws.

Trade marks can comprise:

- words, sounds, designs (including colour as a feature) or a combination of these used to distinguish the goods or services of one person or organisation from those of others;
- certification marks (known in some jurisdictions as "collective marks"), which can be licensed to individuals or business entities for the purpose of showing that certain goods or services meet a defined standard; and
- distinguishing guises/trade dress, which protect the shape of goods or their containers, or a way of wrapping or packaging goods.

The word "mark" is also used to refer to:

- a geographical indication;
- a mark protected by a federal act of incorporation;

- a mark protected by an act respecting the Royal Canadian Legion; and
- a prohibited mark.

Amendments to the Act projected to come into force in 2019 would augment eligibility for registration of a "sign" to include a word, personal name, design, letter, numeral, colour, figurative element, three-dimensional shape, hologram, moving image, mode of packaging goods, scent, taste and texture, positioning of a sign as well as a certification mark that is proposed to be used. Proposed Trade-marks Regulations have been published for public consultation, setting out rules of general application, affecting implementation of the Madrid Protocol and providing transitional provisions, repeal and coming into force of the amendments.

The Canada–European Union Comprehensive Economic and Trade Agreement (CETA) Implementation Act entered into force in Canada on 21 September 2017 to:

- protect EU geographical indications found in Annex 20-A of CETA;
- provide a mechanism to protect other geographical indications with respect to agricultural products and foods;
- provide for new grounds of opposition, a process for cancellation, exceptions for prior use for certain indications, for acquired rights and for certain terms considered to be generic; and
- transfer the protection of the Korean geographical indications listed in the Canada–Korea Economic Growth and Prosperity Act into the Act.

Marking requirements for goods such as precious metals, textiles, food, drugs and plants, and for delivery of services such as banking, gaming, use of packaging and labelling, and selection of business names are to be found in other federal and provincial legislation that coexists with the Act. For example, clearance of pharmaceutical names should be undertaken with the Canadian Intellectual Property Office (CIPO) and Health Canada, as each department of the federal government applies independent criteria for approval. Reference to "banking" services in an application should indicate compliance with the federal Bank Act. Reference to "lotteries" suggests an activity that is regulated by each of the provinces.

1.2 Trade-Mark Rights

Most trade-mark rights arise through use independent of registration. Rights in an unregistered mark arise under common law from use of the mark in Canada. Such common law rights only extend to the geographic area in which the mark enjoys goodwill or reputation. The Québec Civil Code and Charte de la langue française should be consulted with respect to the use of trade marks in Québec. Because rights arise in the absence of registration, it is useful to search beyond the Trademarks Database maintained by CIPO and to do so in both official languages, as the average consumer is deemed to be bilingual.

Unregistered marks may be more limited in venue of enforceability. Unregistered rights arise in the venue of use under passing off, whereas trade mark registration extends protection across the country, unless expressly restricted (eg, by registration or consent). Use in social media has increased the potential for enforcement of marks used and made known through internet communication received in Canada.

Registration is (currently) required for certification marks and recording is required by a public authority for a mark to be noted as "advertised" (rather than registered) on the CIPO database.

Registration supplements the options available for enforcement, conferring rebuttable presumptions and access to the Federal Court. Registration is required to assert depreciation of goodwill associated with a mark. In addition, a regime for obtaining assistance from border protection authorities with respect to counterfeit goods is available to owners of registered trade marks. To enlist the assistance of the Canada Border Services Agency (CBSA) in detaining suspected shipments of counterfeit products, a request must be presented to the CBSA together with trade mark and copyright particulars.

1.3 Standards for Registering

Depending on the type of mark, objections may be encountered by an applicant for registration during examination and prior to allowance of a mark, if opposed.

Certification marks must be used prior to filing (such a requirement will change when the amendments to the Act come into effect). The applicant cannot use the mark itself and must disclose the standards on which certification is based.

A public authority can secure a mark without undergoing opposition proceedings (a mark is noted on the CIPO database as "advertised" rather than registered) and benefit from protection that does not expire, and that is not limited to one or more classes of goods or services.

An applicant for a "famous mark" can be faced, during prosecution, with objections by the examiner or oppositions alleging that the mark is not registrable or that the applicant is not the person entitled to registration of the mark. Fame per se does not negate the need to refute likelihood of confusion, in view of the consumer protection element of Canadian trade mark law.

To register a distinguishing guise as a trade mark, the applicant must present evidence demonstrating that the distinguishing guise has acquired distinctiveness and actually serves to distinguish the goods of the applicant from those of others. Probable purchasers would include resellers and the consumers.

During the examination phase, an applicant may receive notification from CIPO setting out the bases for an examiner's objections (technical, absolute and relative grounds) and deadlines within which to respond. Time extensions to respond may be available during examination.

Evidence, such as incorporation of a name or use as a surname, may be filed to support the argument that a mark has acquired distinctiveness to overcome objections on the grounds of descriptiveness. Approval for advertisement and allowance by the registrar are discretionary.

1.4 Trade-Mark Register
CIPO is an agency of Innovation, Science and Economic Development Canada, a federal government department, and maintains a register that is available to the public, online, without charge. Details relating to pending and abandoned applications, and relating to active and inactive trade-mark registrations are available on the CIPO Trademarks Database. Contents of files (eg, images of actual documentation filed and correspondence) are not yet available to the public online.

CIPO also publishes online weekly the Canadian Trademarks Journal, which provides notification of applications that are advertised for opposition within the mandatory due dates (see below) for those who seek to oppose a trade mark application. Practice notices published by the Trademarks Office also appear online and provide useful guidance on Trademarks Office practice.

1.5 Types of Registers
There is only one trade mark register.

1.6 Searching for Prior Trade Marks
Searching of the Canadian federal Trademark Database is undertaken by examiners in conjunction with their review of each application. Searching is generally recommended to identify proactively any potential barriers to use and registration, risks of an adverse administrative decision and liability for infringement. Currently the delay between application and a first examiner's report may be several months, while adoption and first use of the mark may be undertaken beforehand.

Although there is no supplemental trade-mark register, other public registers may be consulted when clearing registrability of a trade mark, including registries of drugs, business names and domain names, telephone directories and French and English dictionaries (to determine the meaning in both English and French as the average Canadian is deemed to be bilingual). Private search firms may be enlisted for preparation of search reports. The databases may provide useful clues for further investigation of third-party use and the potential for co-existence or, conversely, clash.

1.7 Registration Requirements
An application may be filed online with a government filing fee. The application must set out the following information:

- The legal name and address of the applicant.
- The trade mark: word mark or visual representation of a design (which may claim colour as a feature) or of a sound.
- The goods and services, which should be described in ordinary commercial terms, preferably according to the Nice classification system, the use of which is currently still optional, although encouraged by the registrar.
- The filing bases, currently differentiating between proposed use and actual use, providing the date when use has occurred in Canada in respect of each of the goods and services, although this delineation will not be required when the amendments are implemented.
- The identity of the user(s) and predecessors in title by name (currently), if any.
- Details of a foreign registration on which the Canadian application is based.
- Particulars of any foreign application on the basis of which convention priority is claimed. Currently, the country of origin of the applicant must serve as the basis for a convention priority claim. Once amended, reliance on an application filed anywhere within the Paris Union, within six months of filing plus a seven-day grace period may be referenced.
- A declaration of use in Canada of a mark that is proposed to be used in Canada must be filed after allowance is a current requirement. This requirement will be eliminated under the proposed revisions.

A foreign applicant should appoint a duly authorised representative for service of correspondence in Canada.

The language of the application should be English or French (consistently throughout).

1.8 Registering a Trade Mark
A person (as defined in the Act, including an individual or a legal entity such as a lawful trade union, trade association, joint venture or a professional association) may register in Canada, without the need to be a citizen, resident or otherwise domiciled in Canada. A mark functions to identify a single source. The proposed amendments clarify that the reference to "person" includes two or more persons who, by

agreement, do not have the right to use the trade mark in Canada except on behalf of both or all of them.

1.9 Registering Signs

Amendments to the Act projected to come into force in 2019 would augment eligibility for registration of a "sign" to include a word, personal name, design, letter, numeral, colour, figurative element, three-dimensional shape, hologram, moving image, mode of packaging goods, scent, taste and texture, positioning of a sign as well as proposed certification marks.

Currently, registration is available for trade marks made up of:

- words, sounds, designs (including colour as a feature) or a combination of these used to distinguish the goods or services of one person or organisation from those of others;
- marks that can be licensed to many people or companies for the purpose of showing that certain goods or services meet a defined standard; and
- distinguishing guise/trade dress, which protects the shape of goods or their containers, or a way of wrapping or packaging goods.

1.10 Other Rights to Signs

The federal and provincial laws of Canada provide protection for source-identifiers in addition to trade marks, including:

- legal names and business names, which may be searched by reference to a federal business name register and a provincial register in each province;
- domain names, under the.CA registry by those who satisfy the local presence requirements; and
- products listed on the Health Canada Drug Products database.

Such rights generally arise through registration with one or more government authorities.

1.11 Registration Procedure

An application for registration may be filed by delivery to any of the regional offices of CIPO, or online, along with the prescribed fee. The application sets out, inter alia, the identity of the applicant, the mark and the basis (or bases) on which registration is sought. The first phase of scrutiny is by the examiner. Once the examiner completes examination and related searches, and is satisfied that the mark is registrable and that the applicant is entitled to registration of the mark, the application is approved for advertisement in the Trademarks Journal for opposition. If opposition proceedings are commenced but are withdrawn or are otherwise not successful, the application is allowed. A declaration of use is required for applications that were filed based on proposed use. Following allowance of the application, a registration fee must be paid before a registration will issue.

An applicant pays the same government filing fee regardless of the number of classes, but this will change when the amendments to the Act come into force. The registrar is sending requests for classification under the Nice system and a fee for each class will be imposed once the amendments are implemented.

Currently, payment of a registration fee and a declaration of use for proposed use applications are required. Both of these requirements will be eliminated once the amendments to the Act come into force. No evidence of use or samples of use need to be filed at the time of filing, nor on payment of the registration fee or renewal fee to secure registration of a mark.

Practice notices on the CIPO website set out the availability of extensions through the various stages of examination to registration.

1.12 Use in Commerce

An applicant is not required to file specimens of use at the time of filing, allowance of a trade-mark application or renewal of a trade-mark registration. As of now, use of the mark must commence before a registration will issue. During examination, specimens of use may be filed, to support a claim of acquired distinctiveness. During opposition, specimens of use may be necessary (see discussion below re opposition). After allowance, a declaration of use is required for an application based on proposed use. Following implementation of the amendments, such a requirement will cease to apply.

The tests for use in Canada on goods, services and for export, respectively, differ. The relationship between the owner of a mark and the user should be considered at the time of filing, controlled during the life of a mark. Advertising of services demonstrates use provided that the services are actually delivered within Canada.

1.13 Registration of Series Marks

Each application covers one mark only. Separate applications would be required for each variation of a particular mark.

Currently, the registrar may register marks that resemble each other and are owned by the same person as "associated marks", which cannot be assigned separately. Verification of associated marks is necessary during due diligence proceedings, as the inability to transfer a mark apart from the associated marks may negatively impact on valuation and impede timeliness if not feasibility of closing. Once the amendments to the Act come into effect, the registrar will abandon the practice of recording marks as "associated marks" on the Trademarks Register.

1.14 Length of Registration Process
In the absence of any office action or opposition, the time interval from application to registration is roughly 12 to 18 months, depending on delays arising during examination and the number of extensions that are requested by an applicant. Opposition proceedings progress along a schedule that may significantly add to the timeline, even if based on weak grounds.

Use of a trade-mark agent for searching, preparation and prosecution of an application and representation during opposition proceedings is recommended but not required.

In the absence of opposition proceedings, CIPO fees are often less than CAD750. Agent fees vary.

1.15 Grounds for Refusal
The examiner may refuse to approve an application based on absolute and relative grounds. The absolute grounds pertain to registration of a word that is:

- primarily merely the name or surname of an individual who is living or has died within the preceding 30 years;
- the trade mark is, whether depicted, written or sounded, either clearly descriptive or deceptively misdescriptive of the character or quality of the goods or services in association with which it is used or proposed to be used, or of the conditions of or the persons employed in their production or of their place of origin;
- the name in any language of the goods or services with which it is used or proposed to be used; and
- consists of a protected geographical indication, or consists of plant varieties under the Plant Breeders' Rights Act.

1.16 Process for Overcoming Objections
An official letter from the examiner will provide reasons for any objections raised, as well as at least one opportunity to respond. The nature of a response will depend on the type of objection.

When an objection is raised pertaining to descriptiveness or to a surname, an applicant may request reconsideration citing past decisions of the registrar or the courts. The Registrar and the Federal Court each maintain a list of authorities that are frequently relied on in trade mark proceedings before the examiner, the Opposition Board and in judicial proceedings.

During examination, rather than attempting to refute the examiner's objections by way of written argument, the applicant may file evidence that, through use, the applied-for mark has become known to the public so as to merit registration. For example, a surname objection can be overcome when through recognition it becomes a brand. An applicant may attempt to overcome an examiner's descriptiveness or name objection by filing to show that the applied-for mark has acquired distinctiveness or is not without distinctive character. Evidence of use may describe sale and advertising in Canada, and attach invoices, promotional materials and market research, including surveys, magazines, newspapers and web presence.

When likelihood of confusion is the basis for an examiner's objection, the applicant may assert that coexistence is feasible without likelihood of confusion. The examiner may be requested to take notice of the state of the federal trade mark register and dictionary definitions. State of the register evidence unsupported by evidence of use may not be accorded much weight by the Registrar.

Consents are not binding on the Registrar. However, the registrar will usually accept consent from a public authority that is recorded as the owner of the official mark if the citation is to a mark advertised under the Act. When requesting consent from a public authority, it is helpful to specify the limitations on intended use.

1.17 Consideration of Prior Rights
Registrability of an applied-for mark may be impeded by the existence of a previously filed application or a pre-existing registration likely to give rise to confusion. Examiners look at the filing date to ascertain priority. As a result, a prior filed application or registration will serve as a block to impede further examination of a subsequently filed application. Determinations of priority at the Trademarks Opposition Board and the Federal Court/provincial courts take into account length of use.

Confusion is assessed by reference to the average consumer having a vague or imperfect recollection of another mark. An open-ended list of factors is set out in the Act. The weight of each factor depends on the circumstances of the case.

A new procedure will permit a third party to correspond with CIPO during examination, to bring to the attention of the examiner considerations that may impact on whether or not an applied-for mark will be approved.

1.18 Third-Party Rights
Within two months after advertisement of an application for registration, a statement of opposition can be filed by any person(s), provided the opponent(s) assert at least one of the grounds of opposition set out in the Act, namely:

- the application does not conform to the requirements of the Act regarding the content of the application (eg, failure to describe the goods and services in ordinary commercial terms, or to state accurately the particulars of use, non-use or making known); failure to set out the standards of a certification mark, or to be satisfied of entitlement to registration;

- the trade mark is not registrable; eg, because the mark is primarily merely a name, clearly descriptive or misdescriptive of the goods or services or conditions of production or origin in English or French, the name in any language of the goods and services, a mark or denomination that is prohibited, a geographical indication, or a mark that is prohibited by the Olympic and Paralympic Marks Act;
- the applicant is not the person entitled to registration of the trade mark because of previous use or making known as a mark or a trade name in Canada by another person, or a previous filing or previous registration by another person; and
- the trade mark does not distinguish the goods or services in association with which it is used by its owner from the goods or services of others, nor is it adapted to distinguish them.

The material dates for each of the grounds of opposition differ and are set out in the Act. Decisions of the Trademarks Opposition Board can be appealed to the Federal Court.

Interlocutory motions may be filed to strike out all or part of a statement of opposition. Decisions arising therefrom may also be appealed to the Federal Court.

1.19 Revoke, Change, Amend or Correct an Application

Depending on timing, certain types of amendments are permissible following filing. Some changes to an application can only be made before advertisement. Some changes can be made any time (eg, to limit the statement of goods or services), while other changes cannot be made at any time. At no time can an application be amended to change:

- the identity of the applicant, except after recognition of a transfer by the registrar;
- the trade mark, except in respects that do not alter its distinctive character or affect its identity;
- the date of first use or making known in Canada of the trade mark to an earlier date, except where the evidence proves that the change is justified by the facts;
- the application from one not alleging use or making known of the trade mark in Canada before the filing of the application to one alleging such use or making known; or
- the statement of wares or services so as to be broader than the statement of wares or services contained in the application at the time the application was filed.

Errors in prosecution that cannot be corrected include:

- incorrect identification of the trade mark;
- failure to include goods or services in an application;
- missed due dates relating to claiming of convention priority, filing a statement of opposition or other steps within that proceeding;
- failure to renew after the expiry of a grace period; and
- failure to respond to a statement of opposition by filing a counterstatement.

An application may be amended to limit the goods or services claimed in the application at any stage of the application process and following registration, but not to extend the list. Settlement discussions may be premised on the willingness of a party to do so voluntarily.

Minor clerical errors may be corrected with the registrar's approval. Timing plays a role in determining whether a clerical error can be corrected. Errors in asserting priority can be corrected within the six-month priority filing period of the Paris Convention. Missing a due date to oppose, or the misfiling of a request for an extension to file a statement of opposition may result in loss of opportunity to oppose. Allowance without inclusion in an advertisement of a basis of entitlement may require re-advertisement.

1.20 Assigning an Application or Granting a Licence

Trade marks are transferable, whether registered or unregistered. It is useful to record the assignment during the application process and if an assignment occurs during the course of opposition or challenge, it is helpful also to amend the statement of opposition to reflect the change of ownership.

1.21 Remedies Against the Trade Mark Office

An appeal against a decision of the registrar lies with the Federal Court, within the timelines set out in the Act. The appeal is made by filing an originating notice of motion, by counterclaim in an action for infringement of a trade mark or by statement of claim in an action claiming additional relief under the Act.

1.22 Use of a Trade Mark

Currently, use is required prior to registration. The use must have occurred in Canada or in a foreign country if entitlement to registration in Canada is referenced in the Canadian application as based on a corresponding foreign registration. "Use" in relation to a trade mark is defined in a different manner depending on whether the subject matter is goods, services, or for export purposes.

An application may be filed based on proposed use in Canada — no use at time of filing. The applicant will need to demonstrate use by filing a declaration after allowance of the application and before a registration will issue. Extensions can be obtained pending use of the mark, which may be delayed for reasons such as the need to secure regulatory approval before a product launch. The requirement to file a declaration of use will be eliminated once the amendments to the Act come into force.

When an application claiming a date of first use is undergoing examination, the Trademarks Office does not receive or review specimens. However, an applicant may choose to file specimens of use for review by the examiner when responding to an official letter that objects where the applied-for mark is clearly descriptive/misdescriptive of the subject mark or is primarily merely a name or surname. During opposition proceedings, specimens of use will normally be filed to show how the mark was used in regard to the goods and/or services referenced in the application. Specimens are also filed in response to a notice of cancellation under the Actto counter the allegation of non-use. In all cases, it is necessary to show use of the mark as registered.

1.23 Dividing a Trade Mark

The proposed amendments will introduce the ability (not currently available) to file divisional applications, through which an applicant can retain the initial filing date for those portions of an application that are divided out. Currently, it is possible to delete from a declaration of use those goods or services recited in an application for the narrowed list. Those deleted claims can be captured by a new filing, albeit receiving a later filing date than would be the case by dividing an application. This question often arises after a mark has been allowed and it is necessary for an applicant to file a declaration of use (required for the time being in regard to applications based on proposed use).

1.24 Length of Term of Protection

The amendments propose to shorten the current term of protection — which is presently 15 years — to ten years. A grace period of six months from the date shown on notification from the Trademarks Office is available. An application for renewal of a trade mark should be accompanied by the required filing fee. Evidence of use is not required. The renewal application is straightforward and may be submitted online by the registered owner or an agent.

1.25 Requirements for an Exhaustion

The Supreme Court of Canada noted that "grey goods" were legitimately sourced from the trade mark-owner who had placed goods bearing the trade mark on to the Canadian market. The grey goods and the goods sold by authorised distributors were not different. The doctrine of exhaustion of trade-mark rights applied. In the absence of a disclaimer that lets consumers know of any differences, such as the absence of warranty services, remedies may be available for passing off, misleading advertising and other tortious conduct. Moreover, Canada-specific regulatory requirements such as labelling laws that apply to consumer products may be used to prevent import of grey goods into Canada.

Contractual restrictions regarding distribution of grey goods may be enforceable in some Canadian provinces and territories. The Ontario Court of Appeal has upheld a settlement in which the parties had agreed to refrain from grey marketing of confectionery goods. The settlement was held not to constitute an improper restraint of trade.

1.26 Participation in the Madrid System

Participation in the Madrid System is a core feature of the recent amendments to the Act that are expected to be implemented during the winter of 2019. On the registration of a trade mark in the international register on the basis of an application that contains a request under the protocol for the extension to Canada of the protection of a trade mark resulting from its international registration, an application will be deemed to have been filed under the Act by the holder of the international registration of the trade mark and in respect of the same goods or services that are listed in that request. Reference to the CIPO website is recommended regarding pertinent requirements of the Draft Regulation that remains subject to public consultation at the time of writing. Part 2 is entitled Implementation of the Madrid Protocol.

1.27 Consequences for Providing Incorrect Information

As indicated above, certain errors can be corrected. Others will negate registrability and enforceability. An applicant declares good faith (bona fide intention to use) when initiating the process. Affidavits filed in the course of examination, opposition and enforcement proceedings are sworn documents tendered by way of proof of truth. Unsworn evidence is inadmissible as hearsay evidence.

1.28 Updating or Refreshing a Design Mark

Variations that are insubstantial may be covered under an existing registration and support use of the mark as registered. Each case stands alone based on its facts. Accordingly, as a precaution, variations should be left to a fresh application, to avoid uncertainty over whether a variation is substantive and, hence, not covered by an existing registration. For this purpose, a style guide setting out restrictions on permitted variations is often recommended. Examples of variation between registration and actual use may include colours, font, punctuation, placement and size of components. Because logos and sound marks may also enjoy protection under the Copyright Act, care should be taken to avoid variation without permission from the author and/or copyright-owner, so as to avoid infringement of copyright and violation of moral rights that may not be held by the trade mark-owner.

1.29 Denotation

Symbols are optional. The designation of TM and its French equivalent, MC, are helpful, although not required. The designation of ® and its French equivalent, MD, are reserved for registered trade marks.

2. Assignment and Licensing

2.1 Assignment Requirements or Restrictions
The Act provides for assignment of trade marks. Currently, a written document evidencing the assignment should be filed to give public notice of the details of transfer. An assignment of a registered or unregistered mark that splits ownership of a mark by goods, services or territory may, depending on the facts of use, impact detrimentally on the distinctiveness of the mark.

2.2 Procedure for Assigning a Trade Mark
Because a trade mark is an intangible property right, a written document detailing the transfer of ownership should be executed. Optionally, the details of an assignment of trade-mark applications and registrations are registered at CIPO by filing a copy of the document. A letter to CIPO should name the entity shown on the trade mark register as the assignor, the proposed assignee and explain any discrepancies between the named assignor and the owner of the mark shown on CIPO's Trademarks Database.

2.3 Registering or Recording the Assignment
Registration provides public notice of a conveyance. A purchaser in good faith without notice should be entitled to rely on the information contained on the public register. As a practical matter, failure to record an assignment can have adverse consequences in commercial transactions that purport to transfer a portfolio of marks. Rectifying the chain of title on the record after the fact can pose challenges impacting on the ability to file new trade-mark applications in the name of the assignee, to record transfers that occur after the gap, to enforce the subject trade marks in the name of the new owner and support use of a mark during opposition and cancellation proceedings.

2.4 Trade Marks and Security
Security in personal property (real and intangible) is the subject of provincial legislation. The Actcreates a federal register that is a deposit system for documents that include security agreements and discharges of security interests. However, the deposit system maintained pursuant to the Act does not set up a priority system between lenders.

2.5 Licensing Requirements or Restrictions
The Act provides that if an entity is licensed by or with the authority of the owner of a trade mark to use the trade mark and the owner has, under the licence, direct or indirect control of the character or quality of the goods or services then the use, advertisement or display as or in a trade mark, trade name or otherwise by that entity is to the benefit of the owner of the mark in that country. The Act does not expressly require that the trade mark be registered, nor the subject of an application, nor that the licence be in writing.

The Act, which acknowledges that marks can be licensed, does not impose any limitations on the nature of the relationship between licensor and licensee. The Act does not require that licences be registered in the Trademarks Database maintained by CIPO.

2.6 Procedure for Licensing a Trade Mark
A licence is a contract. The basic requirements for formation of a contract may be informed by civil or common law, the underpinnings of which are consent and consideration. Good faith is an element of all contracts.

In the case of trade-mark licensing, the agreement should identify the mark subject to the licence as well as the scope (activities and territory) of permitted use, coupled with the consequences of non-authorised use and other grounds for termination. The agreement should ALSO explain how quality control is to be exercised by the owner and the consequence of non-compliance with the standards that are implemented by the owner.

2.7 Registering or Recording the Licence
While a licence need not be registered, it is useful to provide notice of the existence of a licence. Marking on goods and associating the mark with services provided under licence advantageously identify source and quality, thereby supporting distinctiveness of a mark.

2.8 Reasons to Deny Granting a Perpetual Licence
A registered trade mark is a creature of statute, the duration of which is finite (currently 15 years, to be shortened to ten) and requires renewal. Perpetuity exceeds expiry of the statutory period. Renewal is optional. Non-use leaves a registration vulnerable to cancellation. At common law, rights in a trade mark are created through use. Accordingly, a mark loses its raison d'être when it ceases to distinguish the source of goods or services. An owner should control the character and quality of the goods and services offered in association with a mark. Revocability of a licence for non-compliance with the standards set by the owner facilitates enforcement.

3. Opposition Procedure

3.1 Legal Grounds and Timeframes
Following examination for technical compliance, relative grounds and inherent registrability, the examiner may approve an application for advertisement in the Canadian Trademarks Journal. The date of advertisement begins a timeline for opposition due dates.

Bases of opposition pertain to:

- non-compliance with the Act or other legislation;

- opponent's prior filing, registration, making known, or use, in Canada of a confusing mark;
- inherent non-registrability such as clear descriptiveness or misdescriptiveness, name; and
- non-distinctiveness, ie, inability to distinguish the wares and services associated with the applied-for mark from those of others.

The grounds of opposition are set out in the Act, namely:

- the application does not conform to the requirements of the Act in regard to the content of the application (eg, failure to describe the goods and services in ordinary commercial terms, or to state accurately the particulars of use, non-use or making known), failure to set out the standards of a certification mark, or to be satisfied of entitlement to registration;
- the trade mark is not registrable; eg, because the mark is primarily merely a name, clearly descriptive or misdescriptive of the goods or services or conditions of production or origin in English or French, the name in any language of the goods and services, a mark or denomination that is prohibited, a geographical indication, or a mark that is prohibited by the Olympic and Paralympic Marks Act;
- the applicant is not the person entitled to registration of the trade mark because of previous use or making known as a mark or a trade name in Canada by another person, or a previous filing or previous registration by another person; and
- the trade mark does not distinguish the goods or services in association with which it is used by its owner from the goods or services of others, nor is it adapted to distinguish them.

The material dates for each of the grounds of opposition differ and are set out in the Act.

Interlocutory motions may be filed to strike out all or part of a statement of opposition. An opposition is an administrative proceeding and is therefore subject to rules of natural justice.

The proposed amendments will add to these grounds of opposition absence of use and absence of proposed use in Canada at the same time as eliminating use as a requirement for filing. It remains to be seen whether certain 45-class applications currently on file at CIPO based on proposed use will proceed to registration simply on payment of the CAD200 registration fee once the amendments are implemented, or will be delayed by opposition proceedings alleging lack of bona fide intention.

3.2 Filing an Opposition

Any person may file a statement of opposition, as set out in the Act. The government fee to initiate an opposition is CAD750 and the government fee to obtain any permitted extension is CAD125. Legal fees will vary by agent.

3.3 Opposition Procedure

The opponent begins by filing a request for an extension of time to file the statement of opposition, or by filing the actual statement of opposition. This document is filed by the opponent with CIPO for initial review. The statement of opposition sets out the grounds of opposition.

CIPO forwards the Statement of Opposition to the applicant's registered agent, or to the applicant if none has been appointed. In response, the applicant must file a counterstatement of opposition. This is a short document that denies the grounds. An extension of time to file the counterstatement can be obtained. The application is deemed abandoned if no counterstatement is filed within the required timeframe.

The next step is the filing of evidence that should show the issues raised in the statement of opposition, or a statement that no evidence will be filed. Evidence is filed in sequence, by way of affidavits that must be sworn and each of the exhibits commissioned. The opponent may reply to the applicant's evidence.

Upon request, the registrar will issue an order for the affiants to attend for cross-examination, non-compliance with which could result in the affidavit evidence being inadmissible. When cross-examinations are complete, transcripts are filed with the registrar.

The last step is argument; written followed by oral arguments in response. The registrar will first set a date for filing of the written arguments by each party. After receipt of both parties' written arguments, the registrar will exchange them simultaneously. Upon request, the registrar will set a date for oral hearing, which can be conducted in person or remotely (by phone).

Deadlines are strictly observed in opposition proceedings. A small number of exceptions are available. One extension, a "cooling-off period" of nine months, is available to each party, on consent of the other, for the purpose of settlement discussions.

3.4 Legal Remedies

An appeal from a final decision of the registrar to the Federal Court of Canada is available within two months from the date on which notice of the decision was communicated by the Registrar. After expiry of the foregoing two-month period, leave of the Court is required. Further appellate review may be available from the trial division to the Court of Appeal and, with leave, to the Supreme Court of Canada. The rules of each court set out the requirements for leave and the timelines for filing the documentation.

4. Initiating a Lawsuit

4.1 Actions to Pursue Infringement
Different approaches may be pursued by an aggrieved owner of a trade mark, registered or unregistered, to prevent and recover damages for unauthorised use that would lead to confusion or mistake of various types of marks and indications covered by the Act.

The Act prohibits use and adoption of (i) a mark so nearly resembling another mark that has by ordinary and bona fide commercial usage become recognised as designating the kind, quality, quantity, destination, value, place of origin or date of production of any goods or services, and (ii) a designation under the Plant Breeders' Rights Act that would be likely to be mistaken.

Prohibitions apply with respect to use in connection with a business, as a trade mark or otherwise of indications that identify agricultural products or food, wines and spirits that are listed with the minister and published on the CIPO website. A statement of objection may be filed to object to an indication.

The owner of a registered trade mark can assert infringement and depreciation of goodwill. Unregistered trade marks are also enforceable under the Act for passing off and on the bases of various common law torts. A trade-mark registration serves as a basis for proceeding in the federal courts as well as the courts of the various provinces.

4.2 Initiating Infringement Proceedings
Recovery in respect of unregistered marks is ordered by the courts of the provinces and available in the Federal Court if asserted in conjunction with infringement of a federal law. A registration affords the potential for assistance from border authorities in accordance with the Combating Counterfeit Products Act that came into force on 2 January 2015. Infringement proceedings can be initiated within the Federal Court of Canada or the superior court of any province.

While the civil courts of each province are also appropriate venues for trade mark proceedings — particularly enforcement of unregistered rights, tortious conduct associated with marks and breach of licence agreements — only the Federal Court can direct the Registrar to amend the CIPO Trademarks Database in consequence of submissions that may be made during infringement proceedings. Variation or cancellation of a registration may be helpful to a defendant in infringement proceedings. Moreover, decisions of the Federal Court are binding in each of the provinces. The foregoing may bear on choice of court.

The Opposition Board has jurisdiction over registration only, ie, not over use of a mark.

4.3 Effect of Decisions on Infringement Actions
Decisions of the Trademarks Office do not bind the courts, nor do they bind examiners or the Opposition Board. The Registrar's decisions are generally fact-specific and decided on a case-by-case basis, often by reference to the common list of authorities — decisions of the Federal Court trial and appellate divisions.

4.4 Declaratory Judgment Proceedings
Declaratory relief is available to each party. For example, a plaintiff may seek to confirm that its mark is valid and infringed by the defendant's use of a confusingly similar mark. A defendant may seek an order that the plaintiff's mark is invalid and should be struck from the Trademarks Register or that the defendant's use would not give rise to confusion.

4.5 Jurisdiction of Courts
The federal and provincial courts have trial and appellate divisions. The Supreme Court of Canada may grant leave to hear appeals from civil and criminal appellate courts that raise issues of national importance or public interest.

The standard of review of a decision of the Registrar, in an appeal under the Act, depends on whether new evidence has been filed that would have affected the Registrar's findings of fact or exercise of discretion. Where new evidence is filed that meets this threshold, the court must consider de novo the issue to which that additional evidence relates.

4.6 Prerequisites to Filing a Lawsuit
It is not necessary to send a formal demand letter before initiating a lawsuit, although it is frequently done unless there is a reason not to give notice. For example, there may be a concern — particularly in the case of counterfeit goods — that a defendant may destroy or alter key evidence if notified.

4.7 Representation for Parties
Representation by a lawyer is not required before the Opposition Board, nor before the courts, although it is preferable given the technical nature of the procedure and substance. In Ontario, the small claims courts offer unrepresented litigants simplified recovery, albeit with a cap of CAD25,000.

4.8 Interim or Preliminary Injunctions
Interim and interlocutory injunctions are useful remedies for trade mark-owners, but infrequently granted due to the high standard of proof required to establish irreparable harm (harm not otherwise compensable in damages).

An applicant for an interlocutory injunction must establish (i) a serious issue to be tried, (ii) that irreparable harm would be suffered if the injunction is not granted and (iii) the balance of convenience favours the requesting party. A factor to consider is the lapse of time before court action is initiated. It is critical to move quickly if harm is to be characterised as irreparable and not compensable in damages. An interim interlocutory injunction is reviewable after a short time set out in the order. A foreign plaintiff may be required to post a bond/security for costs. Permanent injunctions do not require proof of irreparable harm.

4.9 Protection for Potential Defendant

At any time, a potential or actual defendant can request the registrar to cancel any and all of the plaintiff's registrations that are not in use under the Act and oppose any and all of the plaintiff's marks that are within the opposition period (two months post advertisement in the Trademarks Journal). The defendant can also challenge the validity of the plaintiff's registrations as a separate court proceeding or, if the claim is before the Federal Court, within a counterclaim. To succeed in a challenge of this nature, a party must show that the trade mark was not registrable under the Act because of any one of the absolute grounds of registration, or that the mark is no longer distinctive of the registrant's goods or services.

A defendant may also refute the allegations of confusion and seek a declaration that it is not infringing the plaintiff's marks.

A foreign plaintiff may be required to post a bond for security for costs and damages that the defendant could suffer due to the litigation.

A defendant may make a formal offer to settle the case. In both the Federal Court and the provincial superior courts, formal offers (in contrast to revocable, confidential offers to settle that are exchanged between counsel on a confidential, without prejudice basis) may have a significant impact on the amount of costs ultimately awarded by the court.

4.10 Obtaining Information and Evidence

Evidence may be obtained by way of extraordinary remedies prior to commencement of a proceeding. Civil search warrants in the context of Anton Piller Orders and Mareva injunctions offer the opportunity to obtain information and evidence if there is a reasonable fear of destruction. Cross-examinations on affidavits take place in the context of an application, while discovery, offering a more extensive examination, takes place in the context of an action. A third party may be ordered to provide information that would be useful to the court, by way of subpoena.

4.11 Initial Pleading Standards

The level of detail must be sufficient to enable the responding party to plead in response, failing which the pleading may be struck in whole or in part. Pleadings may be amended and supplemented, by leave of the court or upon consent.

In trade-mark proceedings, appeals are of right from a decision of the Registrar to the Trial Division of the Federal Court and from the Federal Court Trial Division to the Federal Court of Appeal. Fresh evidence not before the Registrar may be filed on appeal to the Trial Division. An appellant may succeed on appeal if the Court determines that the decision of the Registrar was not reasonable having regard to the evidence before it or that the newly filed evidence is material and would have led the Registrar to a different result.

4.12 Representative or Collective Actions

Class actions for copyright infringement are under way in Canada. In contrast, for reasons related to preservation of distinctiveness, since a mark is owned by a single legal entity, rather than multiple individuals, certification of a class of aggrieved trade mark-owners is not common practice. However, multiple users of descriptive words may have a common interest in preventing appropriation of a word in common language to benefit a trade-mark registrant. The common use by competitors within an industry has proved useful in successfully counterclaiming for invalidity of a registered mark.

4.13 Restrictions on Trade Mark-Owners

The interface between IP (reasonable limitations) and competition legislation continues to be considered for all property rights. The proposed amendments to the Act would enable a court to direct cancellation of a registration that would be likely to limit unreasonably the development of any art or industry. A trade mark-owner should not imply to third parties (eg, retailers) that a defendant is infringing its mark before any such decision has been reached by a court. Forwarding to a retailer a copy of a demand letter addressed to a manufacturer that implies infringing conduct before a court has rendered a decision could support a claim for tortious interference with economic relations.

5. Infringement

5.1 Action for Infringement

Infringement is a term generally used with reference to registered trade marks. The Act enables a third-party licensee to require the owner to initiate infringement proceedings. If the owner refuses or neglects to do so within two months after being so called on, the licensee may institute proceedings for infringement in the licensee's own name as if the licensee were the owner, making the owner a defendant. This statutory right may be waived by agreement.

An owner of an unregistered mark that has been used or made known in Canada can proceed by way of a claim on the basis of passing off.

Third parties may be authorised to file an action for infringement or enforce unregistered trade-mark rights. For example, an agreement between an owner of an IP granting security in that portfolio may provide that the lender is authorised to take all actions useful or necessary to preserve the security, which would include monitoring unauthorised use and initiating actions for infringement and passing off, with co-operation of the trade mark-owner.

5.2 Signs and Infringement

Likelihood of confusion is central to the consumer protection orientation of the Act. All of the surrounding circumstances are open to consideration, by reference to the open list of factors recited in the Act. The factors are:

- inherent distinctiveness of the respective trade marks or trade names and the extent to which they have become known;
- length of time the trade marks or trade names have been in use;
- the nature of the goods, services or business;
- the nature of the trade; and
- the degree of resemblance between the trade marks or trade names in appearance or sound, or in the ideas suggested by them.

Confusion is to be determined based on the somewhat rushed, casual consumers' first impression, even where expensive goods are involved. Confusion is an element of depreciation of goodwill. The registered mark need not be identical to the unauthorised use. Disclaimers will not shield an unauthorised user from liability for disparaging imitation of a trade mark that is likely to cause confusion as to the source of the services. Depreciation of goodwill can also occur in regard to use of similar characters, containers and labels.

5.3 Use of a Sign by Defendant

"Use" (or misuse) by a defendant of a trade mark, to distinguish source, is required in regard to any infringement claim. This is not necessarily the case in terms of a claim based on depreciation of the plaintiff's goodwill in a trade mark. Remedies may be available under the Act where there is use or misuse of a trade name, domain name, or key word likely to cause confusion even in the absence of use or misuse by a defendant as a trade mark.

5.4 Defences Against Infringement

If a defendant's use of a mark is confusing and disparaging, the Act provides relief from depreciation of goodwill. Contrary to the Copyright Act, the Act does not provide defences of parody and fair use. Each law entails a separate assessment of wrongdoing.

Delay may preclude the ability to demonstrate urgency in securing an injunction. Co-existence may weaken or erode the distinctiveness of the mark sought to be enforced. Limitation periods may prevent recovery of damages; however, timing can run from the date the plaintiff had knowledge of the unlawful conduct.

A defendant's strategy may be to challenge the plaintiff's registered rights, asserting invalidity due to an absolute ground of entitlement to registration or other, such as non-use. If the plaintiff began the proceeding in the Federal Court, the challenge can be linked to a counterclaim that seeks an order to amend the Trademarks Register and expunge the plaintiff's registration.

5.5 Role of Experts and/or Surveys

Practitioners may consult with experts to gauge perception of the "ordinary person in a hurry" with a "vague recollection" of words, graphics and sounds. Experts may be helpful to practitioners and their clients when selecting and enforcing a mark.

Expert evidence is admissible if it meets the following criteria:

- relevance;
- necessity in assisting the trier of fact;
- absence of any exclusionary rules; and
- tendered by a duly qualified expert.

Canadian courts have been guarded in relying on surveys and expert opinion evidence, because non-technical subject-matter is within the ability of judges to assess, based on the judge's personal experience or knowledge. Survey evidence can still be useful, such as to assist courts in assessing the passing off of trade dress.

5.6 Administrative or Criminal Offence

Remedies for contempt of a civil court order may be ordered against directors and officers of corporations. A warrant of committal may be ordered by the Federal Court for arrest and imprisonment to secure compliance with court orders, including non-compliance with an injunction and failure to make the payment of costs and fines awarded by a court for infringement, passing off and contempt.

The Combating Counterfeit Products Act introduced criminal offence provisions in the Act relating to the import and sale of counterfeit products.

Design and sound marks are also protected under the Copyright Act, which contains criminal penalties for infringement: summary conviction and indictment. Forgery of a trade mark is an offence under the Criminal Code.

5.7 Custom Seizures
Since January 2015, the CBSA has been guided by procedures and protocols for processing suspected counterfeit and/or pirated goods with regard to IP, based on the following Canadian federal legislation: the Copyright Act, the Customs Act, the Customs Tariff, the Trademarks Act, and the Criminal Code.

Parallel imports — grey goods, which legitimately originate with the owner of a trade mark — are outside the scope of the border enforcement regime.

6. Revocation/Cancellation

6.1 Remedies and Reasons
Revocation/cancellation may arise on a voluntary basis (by request of the registered owner), by decision of the Registrar (under summary cancellation proceedings under the Act or failure to renew) or by order of the Federal Court (on the bases of non-registrability and non-distinctiveness).

6.2 Trade Mark Office and Civil Courts
Requests for cancellation of a registration for non-use, in whole or in part, may be initiated in the Trademarks Office under the Act by any person at any time after three years from the date of registration (or earlier where there are extraordinary circumstances) and are often initiated naming a law firm as a requesting party. There is a simplified proceeding to clear the Trademarks Register of dead wood.

Currently, the proceedings are initiated by a request (a letter) made on behalf of any person.

A request for an order directing the Registrar to amend the register to cancel a registration can also be initiated in the Federal Court by any interested party based on grounds that the trade mark was not registrable at the date of registration, is not distinctive, has been abandoned, or non-entitlement of the applicant to registration.

6.3 Statutory Limitation or Time Period
Summary expungement requests under the Act are normally submitted after the three-year period from the registration date. Requests for cancellation are best within five years from the date of registration.

6.4 Initiation of Revocation/Cancellation Proceeding
Any interested person may initiate such proceedings. An interested person is defined in the Act.

6.5 Partial Revocation/Cancellation
The result may be to limit the list of goods and services, or to place geographical limitations. An agreement between multiple entities to divide ownership of a registered mark by voluntary undertaking to refrain from use in different areas of the country may result in de facto dual ownership of a mark.

6.6 Possibilities of Amendment
The Registrar or the Federal Court may order amendment to narrow the scope of a registration. An amendment would not be ordered to widen the scope of a registration. For example, the Registrar may be ordered to delete certain goods and/or services due to non-use.

6.7 Revocation/Cancellation and Infringement
Actions may be heard together, in which case an order for revocation or cancellation may impact on the strength of the plaintiff's infringement case. Otherwise the respective proceedings may follow different timelines in different courts, with the potential for an anomalous result that may require reconsideration.

7. Trial & Settlement

7.1 Special Procedural Provisions
Of particular interest, the parties may refer to a common list of authorities in trade-mark proceedings, concerning confusion, descriptiveness, passing off and use. Fresh evidence may be filed in appeals from a decision of the Registrar.

The Federal Court may hear the proceedings initiated by way of an application or an action. Proceedings may also be initiated in provincial courts on the basis of unregistered rights for passing off. There are no jury trials for trade-mark matters.

Expert evidence may be tendered in various areas. For example, expert evidence may be tendered by linguists on the construction of language, by designers on the impact of design motifs and by marketing professionals on the use of language within a commercial sector.

Trade-mark infringement actions may combine causes of action, with reference to other statutory IP rights, such as copyright and industrial design, and claim recovery for torts such as passing off, unjust enrichment and misleading advertising. The rules of the Federal Court or the rules of the procedure in each of the common law provinces will apply. For actions in the province of Québec, the Québec Civil Code, Civil Code of Procedure and Charter of the French Language should be consulted as well.

7.2 Determination of Cases

Civil trials for trade-mark infringement do not proceed by way of jury.

The parties may influence where the hearing takes place, but not the choice of decision-maker. They may agree on selection of a mediator or arbitrator.

7.3 Possibilities of Settlement

A defendant may make a formal offer to settle, the timing and amount of which may be considered by a court when awarding costs. Mediation is encouraged in all venues and may be mandatory pursuant to the rules of certain provincial courts. Mediation focuses on the interests of the parties. In the Federal Court, mediation services are provided by the associate judges of the Court, called prothonotaries. Pre-trial conferences are also mandatory and will explore possible settlement of disputes.

Alternatively, the parties may have an agreement in place to proceed to arbitration. The details of the arbitration clause may include appointment of an arbitrator and set out the proposed rules and procedures as well as venue.

7.4 Other Court Proceedings

Parallel proceedings in a foreign jurisdiction may influence the outcome in a Canadian court and may provide a reason for a Canadian court to vary a global take-down order.

Within Canada, parallel proceedings may be taken to enforce different types of rights in a brand: registered trade mark, unregistered trade dress and licence, copyright in the trade mark and industrial design in the shape of the product packaging (see below regarding different types of IP rights that may co-exist). A multiplicity of potential causes of action may afford parallel proceedings against someone who is misappropriating a mark, including copyright (logo), industrial design (eye appeal; eg, crisp/product packaging), passing off/misleading advertising (provincial) and the Act. The underlying purpose of each law may differ. As a result, the rights-holders and scope and term of protection may differ. A finding of infringement of one right would not necessarily impact on a claim for infringement of a different co-existing right.

Proceedings regarding counterfeit goods may result in Crown involvement in regard to criminal prosecution. Copyright remedies are both civil and quasi criminal. It may be advisable to refrain from running parallel civil proceedings to avoid interfering with an investigation. However, no damages will be awarded in a criminal proceeding.

A decision of a foreign court, although not binding on a Canadian court, may be informative if counsel explains the relevance, acknowledging the differences in the legal structure, and text of underlying statutory authorities. The English and French language versions of Canadian statutes are given equal weight.

8. Remedies

8.1 Existing Remedies

Where there is a strong resemblance between the plaintiff's mark and the defendant's mark, the plaintiff may sue for injunctive relief, declaratory relief, damages and an accounting of profits, delivery up, destruction and costs.

An injunction may be interim, interlocutory or permanent. An interlocutory injunction requires proof of irreparable harm. A permanent injunction does not require such proof. The burden of proof may be more onerous when seeking a mandatory injunction to follow a course of conduct than to prevent a defendant from taking or continuing with the same course of action. In the case of mandatory injunctions, a court may need to balance the interests in providing adequate and efficient injunctions until trial and the importance of avoiding irreparable damage to the social media presence of the alleged infringer. For example, in the online context, amending a video could entail removal, reposting and loss of all related comments and posts. It may irreversibly truncate conversations under way between consumers and the enjoined party.

The successful plaintiff may elect between damages suffered and an accounting of profits that the infringer made. Also, the court may award punitive damages, delivery up for destruction, seizure of a website, transfer of a domain name and costs. The successful party generally receives an award of legal fees, but less frequently full recovery of all costs incurred. The parties may submit a draft bill of costs for consideration by the court. Judges have wide discretion as to costs. Factors may include complexity of the litigation, difficulties presented by the evidence and whether the newly presented evidence could have been placed before the Registrar.

By combining remedies under the Act with other applicable statutory and common law remedies, it may be possible to recover enhanced damages for wilful infringement and statutory damages.

Additional remedies may be suited to the facts: publication of a notice of culpability for misleading advertising in violation of provincial consumer protection legislation, delivery up and destruction of infringing goods or websites and transfer of domain name pursuant to rules of the domain name registry (which may impose limitations on transfer).

8.2 Rights and Remedies

As a successful party, a defendant may recover all or a portion of its costs. Reimbursement of legal fees on a solicitor and its own client basis is sometimes awarded. A scale is used by the court as a guide unless the parties agree otherwise.

A defendant may seek a declaration of non-infringement (to pre-empt an infringement action) in combination with a Federal Court order directing the Registrar to amend the CIPO federal Trademarks Register. A declaration of non-infringement and challenge to validity of a registration may form part of a counterclaim.

8.3 Different Types of Remedies

Availability of cancellation is not uniform. Examples of exceptions that may apply: trade marks previously registered in Newfoundland, marks that have been on the register for more than five years and marks advertised in the name of a public authority.

Trade marks that are also trade names or domain names may receive protection under the rules of the relevant registries. Proceedings claiming bad faith use of a trade mark as a domain name with a.ca top-level domain can be addressed by the CIRA dispute resolution policy. A domain name registered in the.CA registry cannot be transferred to an entity that does not satisfy the local presence requirements. The Federal Court may order transfer of a domain name on the basis of an in rem action.

9. Appeal

9.1 Special Provisions

An appeal from the trial division of the Federal Court is available as of right within the time set out for filing a notice of appeal, or afterward if leave is granted.

9.2 Factual or Legal Review

The standard of review for trade mark and copyright appeals reflects two approaches: reasonableness and correctness. In the absence of fresh evidence that would have materially affected the decision of the Registrar, the court reviews a decision of the Opposition Board based on the standard of reasonableness. This suggests deference to the expertise of the Registrar. By contrast, a decision of the Copyright Board may be reviewed on the basis of correctness for matters of law over which jurisdiction is shared by the Board and the courts.

9.3 Length of Appeal from Trial Court

The Federal Court website provides a breakdown of the timelines for filing materials, based on which it can be seen that an interval of two years can be estimated between filing of a Notice of Appeal until a Trial Court decision is rendered.

10. Other Trade Mark Issues

10.1 Recognition of Dilution

Non-distinctiveness is a basis for opposing registration and for asserting invalidity of a trade-mark registration on the basis that the mark may not actually (or inherently) distinguish the goods or services allegedly associated with the mark. A mark may lose distinctiveness over time through abandonment, use under licence without adherence to quality control restrictions, or co-existing use of the same or a confusingly similar mark by third parties.

10.2 Protection of Famous Marks

A mark that is famous outside the jurisdiction but not yet used in Canada may be registrable on the basis of proposed use, or making known in Canada, provided that there are no pre-existing marks that are assessed by the Registrar during examination or opposition proceedings as being confusingly similar. Famous or well-known marks may be accorded a broader scope of protection based on notoriety in Canada. Evidence of likelihood of confusion is a requirement for enforcement based on passing off and infringement.

10.3 Special Rules Regarding Geographic Indicators

A trade mark is clearly descriptive of the place of origin if — whether depicted, written or sounded — it is a geographic name and the associated goods or services originate from the location of the geographic name. A trade mark is misdescriptive of origin if the trade mark is a geographic name and the associated goods or services do not originate from the location of the geographic name. If a trade mark is misdescriptive, further analysis is required to determine if it is deceptive. In assessing whether a trade mark is deceptively misdescriptive, it must be determined whether the ordinary consumer would be misled into the belief that the associated goods or services had their origin in the location of the geographic name in the trade mark. A trade mark will be determined to be a geographic name if research shows that the trade mark has no meaning other than as a geographic name. In addition, a trade mark will be determined to be a geographical name if the trade mark, despite having multiple meanings, has a primary or predominant meaning as a geographic name. The primary or predominant meaning is to be determined from the perspective of the ordinary Canadian consumer of the associated goods or services.

If a trade mark is determined to be a geographic name, the actual place of origin of the associated goods or services will be ascertained by way of confirmation provided by the applicant. In determining the place of origin of the associated goods or services, the address of an applicant is irrelevant.

10.4 Special Rules Relating to Surnames

A trade mark is not registrable if it is primarily merely the name or surname of an individual who is living or who has died within the preceding 30 years. By exception, a name that has acquired secondary meaning so as to be distinctive or not without distinctive character is nevertheless registrable. This is demonstrated by evidence of sales, promotion and advertising.

The Actdoes not purport to divest an individual of personal rights in his/her name. Inherent in the right of publicity is the right to use and to control the commercial use of one's own name or likeness. Personality rights survive the death of the rights-holder.

11. Costs

11.1 Costs Before Filing a Lawsuit

Filing a lawsuit is advantageously preceded by verification of the likelihood of a successful outcome. A plaintiff may consult with private investigators, and survey experts to gauge brand awareness, scope of use and likelihood of confusion. Affidavit evidence that describes such investigations and attaches specimens and photos may be tendered in evidence, and the affiant subject to cross-examination. Warning letters may be sent to initiate proceedings and to promote settlement discussions. Injunctions and applications proceed by way of supporting affidavits that show the concerns through evidence that must be notarised.

11.2 Costs Regarding an Infringement Action

The costs of litigation vary depending on many factors, including the complexity, willingness of the parties to resolve before trial, the number of preliminary motions that are initiated, the manner of process (application or ordinary action) and the venue.

Individuals may choose to pare down the costs associated with retaining counsel by (i) civil proceedings in provincial small claims courts, for recovery of less than CAD25,000, or (ii), if appropriate — eg, in the case of counterfeits — through criminal proceedings, should the Crown determine that the facts are warranted.

11.3 Costs of Litigation

Typically, unless the parties can agree on how costs are to be allocated, the losing party will be ordered to pay costs to the prevailing party at a scale set out in the relevant jurisdiction. Indemnification is the primary principle underlying an award of costs, which are awarded in favour of a successful or deserving litigant and payable to the loser, awarded at the conclusion of a proceeding, and taking into account allowable expenses and the nature of the legal representation. The award is within the discretion of the court. In the Ontario Superior Court there are three scales: partial indemnity, substantial indemnity and full indemnity. The conduct of the parties and the complexity of the dispute as well as any uncertainty in the law affecting the issues are factors that are usually taken into account. Formal settlement offers — amount and timing — will generally bear on the quantum of costs awarded.

12. Alternative Dispute Resolution

12.1 Common Way of Settlement

Mediation of opposition proceedings, domain name disputes and judicial disputes is encouraged by the Board and courts, respectively. Providers include those listed with the Intellectual Property Institute of Canada (IPIC), the International Trademark Association (INTA) and the World Intellectual Property Organization (WIPO).

In the Federal Court, prothonotaries (associate judges) act as mediators. Selection of private mediators is at the discretion of the parties in Ontario Supreme Court proceedings. Retired judges frequently serve as mediators and arbitrators. Commercial agreements may contain clauses requiring resolution of trade-mark disputes through ADR. The choice of decision-makers is based on their expertise in the area that is the subject of the dispute or are otherwise qualified in a manner that is acceptable to the parties. Canadian courts generally give deference to the expertise that arbitrators can provide.

13. Trade Marks and Other Intellectual Property

13.1 Protection by Copyright

Reliance on multiple bases of protection can be helpful during enforcement, but pose a challenge during clearance. This is because the bases of protection, identity of rights-holders and standing to initiate enforcement proceedings may differ under different laws and in different jurisdictions.

A trade mark may be protectable as a "work" under the Copyright Act. The Copyright Act covers trade marks and remedies set out in the Copyright Act without distinguishing between types of works. Original jingles should be protectable under both the Copyright Act and the Act. The definition of musical work does not require melody or harmony. As such, pure sound effects may in some cases be protectable not only as trade marks but also as musical works.

Ownership rights in the same content may differ, depending on whether it is the Act or the Copyright Act that is being asserted. Such rights differ in terms of rules (and presumptions) of ownership, duration and criteria used to assess infringement.

Words used in a patent to describe the product manufactured using patented technology may be registrable and enforceable as a trade mark even after the expiry of the patent if at the time of registration they have become the name by which the goods are known. Over time, the words may acquire a secondary meaning to represent the character, quality and place of origin of the goods, so as to distinguish the product of the trade mark-owner. However, trade-mark protection does not extend to functional aspects of a product.

New varieties and strains may be protectable under the Plant Breeders Rights Act. An application to the Canadian Food Inspection Agency may be made for protection of a new "plant variety".

Products and packaging characterised by an original shape, configuration, patent, ornament or combination that is not functional may be protectable if registered under the Industrial Design Act.

An opponent may assert that an applicant for registration of a trade mark is not entitled to registration because the proposed or actual use would not be in compliance with applicable law. In the absence of a finding of infringement of the referenced statute, however, the opposition is unlikely to succeed on this basis because the mandate of the Registrar does not extend to determination of compliance with other legislation.

Blaney McMurtry LLP
2 Queen St. East
Suite 1500
Toronto
ON CANADA

Tel: 416-593-1221
Fax: 416-593-5437
Email: info@blaney.com
Web: www.blaney.com

CHILE

The 'Law & Practice' sections provide easily accessible information on navigating the legal system when conducting business in the jurisdiction. Leading lawyers explain local law and practice at key transactional stages and for crucial aspects of doing business.

Law and Practice

Contributed by Cooper & Cía

CONTENTS

Cooper & Cía is a multidisciplinary Chilean law firm (lawyers, engineers, technicians), specialised in the area of innovation and integral protection of intellectual and industrial property rights, with vast experience in advising corporations, individuals, public institutions and companies, universities and other creative entities. The firm's main practice areas are trade marks, copyright, domain names, patents for inventions, utility models and industrial designs, plant varieties and advertising law. Cooper & Cía has an excellent reputation in litigation, where it has successfully represented trade mark, copyright and patent owners in infringement and anti-counterfeiting cases, obtaining relevant seizure and destruction of products and sanctions against infringers.

Author

Rodrigo Cooper has many years of experience in matters of intellectual property management and technology transfer, regularly advising national and foreign companies on IP matters. The senior partner at Cooper & Cía, he also has a strong reputation in litigation and defence of IP rights. Rodrigo is Professor of Intellectual Property in undergraduate and graduate programmes at the Universidad de Chile, as well as visiting professor at the Pontificia Universidad Católica de Chile and the Heidelberg Centre for Latin America.

1. Types of Trade Marks & Registration

1.1 Types of Trade Marks

The Chilean Industrial Property Law No 19.039, dated September 1991 (with many amendments), provides for trademarking of any sign that is susceptible of graphic representation and capable of distinguishing market products, services or industrial and commercial establishments.

The law also regulates 'geographical indications' and 'denominations of origin'.

No 3D trade marks are recognised.

Trade dress is not recognised under IP Law, and there have been some cases regarding this before the unfair competition courts.

Famous and notorious trade marks are recognised as ground to oppose local piratical applications or to base a cancellation action.

Chilean IP Law recognises certification and collective trade marks, but their requirements of use shall be established by the registered owner, in a private regulation.

All the above is based in statutory law.

1.2 Trade-Mark Rights

The general rule is the "Registration Principle". In order to have rights over a trade mark, prior registration is required.

There are some exceptions in connection with foreign or local trade marks which are not registered in Chile, in cases where another party tries to appropriate it or its good will, in bad faith.

1.3 Standards for Registering

There are no fixed standards for registering trade marks.

Secondary meaning was accepted by law some few years ago; it enables the registration of inherently unregistrable trade marks (generic, descriptive, etc), if the applicant proves that, through wide use in Chile, it has acquired a secondary meaning.

1.4 Trade-Mark Register

There is a Trademark Registry, and it is publicly accessible – for instance, through the internet (www.inapi.cl).

1.5 Types of Registers

In Chile, there are no different types of registers, only one.

Contributed by Cooper & Cía ***Author:*** Rodrigo Cooper

1.6 Searching for Prior Trade Marks

Before applying to register a mark, it is usual to conduct clearance or availability searches, for existing registrations or pending applications.

The Trademark Office website permits identity searches. Law firms have private search engines, allowing phonetical and design searches.

1.7 Registration Requirements

To register a trade mark, an application should be filed at the TMO, specifying the goods or services to be covered by the trade mark.

1.8 Registering a Trade Mark

The law states than anybody may file and register a trade mark, both natural and juridical persons, national or foreign.

1.9 Registering Signs

The law expressly recognises word marks, labels, mixed brands (denomination plus graphic elements), slogans and sound marks. Regarding word marks, labels and mixed brands, they may be simple words, combinations of words and numbers or other graphical elements (for example, 3M).

No 3D trade marks are recognised.

1.10 Other Rights to Signs

Chilean law does not recognise rights to company names nor trade names. However, there is currently a draft in progress which may change this.

Domain names are recognised and registration of them can be obtained through a simple process, online, at the local ICANN Authority (Universidad de Chile).

1.11 Registration Procedure

The application is submitted to a formal examination and then published in abstract in the Official Gazette. From publication there is a term of 30 working days for filing opposition. At the expiry of the term, the application is submitted to the final examination, and may be accepted or rejected by the Registrar, even in a case where no opposition was filed.

Multiclass applications are allowed. We do not recommend them, as an obstacle (eg, an opposition) regarding one class will delay the registration in the other.

1.12 Use in Commerce

Use or non-use is not yet relevant in Chile. Hence, it is not required for any means and a registration may not be challenged on the basis of lack of use.

The draft before Parliament that proposes to change our IP Law will allow the request for the cancellation of a registration if not used within a fixed period.

The law establishes a registration tax of approximately USD250 per class and, in the case of renewal, double that amount.

1.13 Registration of Series Marks

Series trade marks are not recognised under Chilean IP Law.

1.14 Length of Registration Process

Power of attorney is not required, unless to file and reply to oppositions.

If the application suffers no opposition or ex officio objections, the registration process may last approximately nine months. However, if the application is for seeds, in class 31, then it is sent to the agriculture authority for approval. If there is opposition or objection ex officio, the process may take up to 18 months, depending on the activity of the parties.

1.15 Grounds for Refusal

Grounds for refusal include the descriptive character of the mark, lack of distinctiveness, misleading character, applicant acting in bad faith, plus official characters or symbols, flags, colours, technical denominations, commonly used expressions in connection with the goods or services.

1.16 Process for Overcoming Objections

As explained above (see section **1.3 Standards for Registering**), 'secondary meaning' is accepted, but as an exception. Hence, it is up to the applicant to prove emphatically that the expression has acquired distinctiveness through use in Chile.

1.17 Consideration of Prior Rights

The trade mark office only considers the existence of prior rights in the case of an opposition, or when through the examination the Registrar detects an identical or confusingly similar trade mark in a different, but related, class.

1.18 Third-Party Rights

Third parties may file opposition within the term fixed by law. For filing opposition, the third party should be represented by an attorney, as the opposition is considered as a demand, a legal action.

There is no need to prove a specific interest, as the law contains a list of reasons to file the opposition, and they are a prohibition to the Registrar; they are of public interest.

1.19 Revoke, Change, Amend or Correct an Application
It is possible to change an application during the registration process only if the correction is minor and does not affect the trade-mark identity or the description of goods or services. For example, the name and address of the applicant may be corrected.

.

1.20 Assigning an Application or Granting a Licence
It is possible to assign the pending application. In such a case, no recordal tax is imposed. It is also possible to license the pending trade mark but, as no registration exists, it will not be possible to record it.

1.21 Remedies Against the Trade Mark Office
It is possible to file administrative petitions and, if refused, an appeal before the Special Second Instance Industrial Property Court.

1.22 Dividing a Trade Mark
We are not aware that dividing a trade mark has ever happened in our jurisdiction. But, if the application refers to more than one class, we deem it possible to divide it into single classes, before the application is published. It would not be possible to divide it if it has faced opposition, as the opposition is considered a judicial demand and, since its filing, no amendments, apart from limitations, are allowed.

1.23 Length of Term of Protection
The protection term is ten years. The registration may be renewed before its expiry, with a grace period of 30 working days after expiry. In any case, the renewal date will coincide with the prior expiry date.

1.24 Requirements for an Exhaustion
Chilean Law establishes that when a product is put in the market by the registered owner, or with his or her consent (this may be implicit), no further sales may be blocked or conditioned by the trade mark-owner.

1.25 Participation in the Madrid System
Chile is not a member of the Madrid Protocol. No international registrations may be obtained from Chile.

1.26 Consequences for Providing Incorrect Information
If the incorrect information refers to matters of lesser importance, it may be corrected. However, if it refers to legal requirements, the application may be rejected ex officio or, if registration is granted, it may be cancelled, in which case the TMO acts as first-instance court.

1.27 Updating or Refreshing a Design Mark
It is not possible to update or refresh a design mark. For this, a new application should be filed.

1.28 Denotation
No common-law rights are recognised under Chilean law.

The registered trade mark should be used with any of the following indications: "Marca Registrada", "M.R." or ®.

2. Assignment and Licensing

2.1 Assignment Requirements or Restrictions
The assignment should be done in writing, and recorded at the margin of the original registration at the TMO. No approval is required.

2.2 Procedure for Assigning a Trade Mark
It is quite simple: the assignment contract, stating the name of the parties, the indication of the registration being assigned and the price (which may be nominal) is signed by the parties. No solemnities are required. Then, the document is filed at the TMO through an application for recordal. The TMO will verify that the information is correct and, if so, will order the payment of the recordal tax (approximately USD90). Once the payment has been accredited, the recordal takes place and the name of the owner is changed.

2.3 Registering or Recording the Assignment
The law states that the assignment should be recorded, but establishes no penalty in the case of failure. If not recorded, the registration will remain in the name of the prior owner, and the assignment will not be opposable against third parties.

2.4 Trade Marks and Security
As regards trade marks, the rules of general property are applied (ie, a trade mark can be given as a security, be subject to rights in rem, assigned by way of security or levied in execution).

2.5 Licensing Requirements or Restrictions
There are no restrictions or requirements in terms of licensing a trade mark, apart from the basic fact that the licence should be in writing (as for assignments), and recorded. There are no limitations regarding types of licences. Fair competition courts have decided that clauses imposing prices of sale to the licensee are not permitted.

2.6 Procedure for Licensing a Trade Mark
The procedure is the same as for assignment (see **2.2 Procedure for Assigning a Trade Mark**, above).

2.7 Registering or Recording the Licence
The procedure is the same as for **2.3 Registering or Recording the Assignment**, above.

2.8 Reasons to Deny Granting a Perpetual Licence
There is no reason why a trade-mark owner cannot be granted a perpetual licence, but the licensee should be careful to remember to record the licensee against the new registration number, once renewed.

3. Opposition Procedure

3.1 Legal Grounds and Timeframes
Trade mark law states that any opposition should be filed within 30 working days after publication of the application abstract in the Official Gazette.

The Official Gazette publishes trade-mark applications (as well as any other IP right applications), on Fridays. If the Friday is a national holiday, the publication is made the following Monday.

The term is of 30 working days – Saturdays, Sundays and holidays should not be counted.

The law states a list of prohibitions of registration. Although there is no stated distinction, we may say that the prohibitions are usually known as absolute prohibitions and relative prohibitions. For example, it is prohibited to register:

- generic, descriptive and commonly used expressions in connection with the relevant goods or services;
- official names, symbols, national or international;
- colours as such (distinctive combinations are allowed registration);
- technical denominations;
- flags, official seals, etc;
- trade marks equal or confusingly similar to an already registered trade mark in the same or related class;
- trade marks equal or confusingly similar to those registered abroad in the name of a third party, for the same or related goods or services, provided it is famous and notorious;
- trade marks applied in bad faith, and those contrary to good faith and public order, including those against fair competition and commercial ethics.

3.2 Filing an Opposition
Anybody may file an opposition, both natural and juridical persons, either national or juridical. The opponent needs to be represented by an attorney at law. There are no official fees for oppositions. Professional fees usually vary between USD500 and USD600.

3.3 Opposition Procedure
After the opposition is filed, the material file is sent to the Juridical Department at the TMO.

Some weeks after the opposition deadline (there is no fixed term, and it will depend on the TMO's workload), the TMO notifies the applicant with the opposition or oppositions and, if it exists, with any official action. There are cases where there are no oppositions, but the applicant may still receive an official action recommending the refusal of the application. Also, there are cases where an application is opposed, and the TMO also notifies an official action, based on the same trade mark which is mentioned in the application, or on a different trade mark.

Once the applicant is notified, it has 30 working days to reply to the opposition(s) and/or the official action.

Whether the applicant replies or not, some weeks after the 30 days' term, the Registrar will decide if it is or is not necessary to open a probatory term. The parties may also require to open said term.

The probatory term is of 30 working days, extendable for another 30, and any kind of evidence, except for witnesses, may be provided. Documents need not to be legalised, apostilled nor translated.

If no probatory term is open (for example, if the opposition is based on an allegedly similar trade mark, and is only a matter of comparison), or the probatory term has expired, then the TMO will prepare to render its first-instance decision in the case.

Usually, a decision is obtained (depending on the activity of the parties and if a probatory term existed) between 18 and 24 months from the application date.

3.4 Legal Remedies
It is possible for the party that was defeated at first instance to file an appeal before the special Intellectual Property Court, a specialised court that decides in second instance.

If there were two or more parties, the court will decide after oral hearings. If the appeal was filed by the applicant whose application was rejected ex officio, the court will decide without oral hearings.

The appellant has to pay an appeal tax of approximately USD180; this is refunded if the appeal is successful.

Depending on the court's workload, it usually takes between seven and nine months to issue its decision.

4. Initiating a Lawsuit

4.1 Actions to Pursue Infringement
Only registered trade marks are granted legal protection. There is no protection for non-registered trade marks, nor passing off tort. The trade mark-owner may file both civil and criminal action against an infringer.

4.2 Initiating Infringement Proceedings
Civil actions are filed at civil courts, whereas criminal actions should be filed before criminal court.

4.3 Effect of Decisions on Infringement Actions
The Trademark Office does not intervene in infringement action, unless it receives an official requirement from the competent court in charge of the case. For example, any party may require the court to send a petition to the TMO to clarify some aspects of a trade mark registration, such as its specific coverage, if it is in force, etc.

4.4 Declaratory Judgment Proceedings
Declaratory Judgment Proceedings do not exist in Chilean law.

4.5 Jurisdiction of Courts
In terms of which court has jurisdiction, this depends on the type of action. If it is a civil action then it is the court of the defendant's address (ie, their locality). If it is a criminal action then it is the place where the infringement begun – for example, if the infringing goods were imported, the criminal court at the port or city where the goods entered the country.

In both cases, procedural law establishes the superior court to know in second instance, according to hierarchy. In very specific cases, the case may reach the Supreme Court of Justice.

In practice, the vast majority of the cases are settled once seizure of the infringing goods is achieved.

4.6 Prerequisites to Filing a Lawsuit
To establish criminal infringement, the law states that the defendant should have had positive knowledge that he or she was infringing. Hence, usually a warning or cease-and-desist letter is sent through a notary public, informing about the infringement and basic data about the infringed registration. Usually, the defendant is given a short but reasonable term to stop infringement (for example, a week); if infringement continues then the action is filed.

In practice, and in general cases, it is preferable to sue through civil action, where no warning is necessary.

Another scenario is when the action arises from the application of Border Measures. In such cases, we are warned by the Custom Office that some potentially infringing goods have been detected entering the country, and that they have been seized ex officio for the short term stated in the law (between five and ten working days). In such cases, it is more convenient to file the criminal action.

4.7 Representation for Parties
Parties in trade-mark litigation matters must be represented by a lawyer, as in any judicial case.

4.8 Interim or Preliminary Injunctions
Interim or preliminary injunctions are available, although not under said names.

Both civil or criminal courts may issue "Precautionary Measures", such as the seizure of the goods, the closing of places where the infringing goods are manufactured or kept, prohibition to continue selling the goods or rendering the services considered infringement.

Such measures are ordered by courts when they face a prima facie good case, in the sense that, from the information and evidence provided by the plaintiff, it appears reasonable that the goods infringe and there exists a risk that the action will be useless if no immediate seizure and prohibition are ordered. In many cases, the seizure may be ordered before the defendant takes notice of the action.

4.9 Protection for Potential Defendant
If the action is based upon a registration that may be considered to have been obtained by infringing legal prohibitions of registration, the defendant may file an action asking for the cancellation of the registration and claim "litispendencia", asking for the suspension of the infringement case while the cancellation action is decided. That would work if the cancellation case is very well founded.

4.10 Initial Pleading Standards
The action that initiates a civil or criminal action should comply with general basic procedural law. In other words, it shall:

- completely identify the plaintiff and the defendant, with their addresses;
- describe the basic facts that give rise to what is considered infringement;
- provide information about the registration or registrations infringed;
- define articles of IP or other law considered to be infringed (legal basis).

Additionally, it includes concrete petitions to the court, such as the order to seize the infringing goods, to prohibit further commercialisation, the destruction of the relevant goods, the publication of the final decision in a local newspaper at the defendant's cost, and compensation.

4.11 Representative or Collective Actions
In Chile, no collective or class actions are available in TM matters.

4.12 Restrictions on Trade Mark-Owners
If the plaintiff or trade mark-owner is acting in good faith, he or she should fear no actions against him or her. If the action proves to be ill founded and in bad faith, the defendant would be subject to action for damages. Furthermore, if the action is proved to be an anti-competitive action, he or she may also be fined.

5. Infringement

5.1 Action for Infringement
The usual parties to an action for infringement are the trade mark-owner and the infringer. Notwithstanding, the licensee, whether exclusive or not, may file action if the licence was duly recorded at the TMO (otherwise, said licence is not opposable against third parties, in this case, the defendant). However, the licensor may have contractually limited the right of the licensee to initiate action by him or herself.

5.2 Signs and Infringement
The process of determining likelihood of confusion, and hence infringement, is always subjective and depend on many factors. These include: how similar are the trade marks or packaging; whether the goods or services are the same or closely related; how distinctive is the registered trade mark allegedly infringed, both in itself (absolute grounds) and also in comparison to others that may be registered in the same or closely related classes.

It is important to identify if there are signs that the infringer is acting in bad faith – for example, using similar labels, packaging, colours, types of letter, using the same channels of distribution or, alternatively, selling in an informal manner (eg, in flea markets, in the streets, etc).

5.3 Use of a Sign by Defendant
It is necessary to establish that the defendant has used the sign as a trade mark, rather than purely descriptively. If the trade mark upon which the action is based is used (or a confusingly similar one), it is presumed that the intention was to infringe.

In cases where a trade mark has lost a degree of distinctiveness – for example, Scotch (for adhesive tape), Jeep (for vehicles of a certain type) – it is recommendable to send a warning or cease-and-desist letter to the infringer, even for civil cases.

5.4 Defences Against Infringement
There are not many defences against infringement. What is relevant is the registration date, not the priority in the use. However, the non-use may not be used as a defence, as the use is not required by law. Neither the estoppel figure nor the concept of fair use is developed in trade mark matters in this country.

5.5 Role of Experts and/or Surveys
Experts and surveys are very seldom used in trade mark cases. When they are used, it is mainly in matters relating to likelihood of confusion, and they are considered as part of evidence by courts if issued by well-known and respected professionals or companies.

5.6 Administrative or Criminal Offence
As previously stated, trade-mark infringement may constitute civil or criminal offence, not administrative offence.

5.7 Custom Seizures
Chile has a specific law on Border Measures, enacted in 2003. To summarise, Customs may seize counterfeit goods in two cases: (i) when expressly requested by a third party, who provides information that some goods that will be entering the country in an identified vessel, airline, etc, infringe TM Law, and (ii) when, from the examination of the goods by Customs agents, they appear to be probably counterfeits.

For the operation of the latter case (ii), representatives of commonly imitated or infringed trademarks (eg, Apple, Gucci, LV, Hermes, Disney, Nickelodeon, Polo, Lacoste, Prada, etc) send lists to Customs providing the relevant data of said trade marks, and usually advise Customs agents on the most commonly used ports and airports, about the characteristics of the original goods and how to detect fakes.

When goods are seized by Customs, according to either of the above two scenarios, Customs sends an email notification about the seizure resolution to the representative of the trade mark – if it is not in the list, Customs has a link with the TMO – informing that it has a term of between five and ten working days to initiate infringing action before the competent court. In practice, Customs has shown to be very proactive in this matter.

Parallel imports, understood as importation of legitimate products – ie, put in a foreign market by the trade mark-owner or with his or her consent – are allowed in Chile.

6. Revocation/Cancellation

6.1 Remedies and Reasons
TM Law states that a trade-mark registration may be cancelled if it was registered in violation of one or more of the prohibitions established by law.

The general rule is that the cancellation action should be exercised within the period of five years from the registration date. Hence, a cancellation brought after said five-year term is not acceptable.

Notwithstanding, Chile is a member of the Paris Convention. Hence, there is no time limit to ask for the cancellation of a registration that was obtained violating the prohibition to register in the name of a third party a trade mark registered abroad, for the same or related goods or services, provided that trade mark is famous and notorious.

In fact, there have been many cases that cancellations have been obtained after decades of registration and wide use of this type of trade mark (Calvin Klein, Standard & Poor's, Carrefour, Spalding, Iron Maiden, O'Neil, etc).

Also, Chilean TM Law contains a provision stating that there should be no limit term for cancelling a registration obtained in bad faith. This rule has permitted the cancellation of registrations obtained in bad faith by an ex-partner, by a competitor, etc.

6.2 Trade Mark Office and Civil Courts

It is only possible to obtain cancellation action based on the violation of a prohibition of registration. It is not possible to ask for the revocation of the registration based in non-use.

The cancellation action should be brought before the Trademarks Office, which will decide in first instance. It is always possible to file an appeal against the TMO, before the special Second Industrial Property Court.

It may be even possible to go before before the Supreme Court of Justice, through cassation recourse, if the second-instance decision was issued in infraction of the law.

6.3 Statutory Limitation or Time Period

Please see **6.1 Remedies and Reasons** above.

6.4 Initiation of Revocation/Cancellation Proceeding

Any interested party may initiate cancellation proceeding, including the owner of a prior or foreign registration, but not the TMO.

There are no special admissibility rules. Both the TMO and the special second-instance Industrial Property Court have ruled that the plaintiff shall demonstrate any kind of interest, even somehow diffuse.

6.5 Partial Revocation/Cancellation

Partial revocation/cancellation is possible. For example, when the registration is in more than a class and the action is based in a foreign registration in only one class, which is not related to the other classes covered by the registration, or when the prohibition violated refers only to specific goods or services within a wide coverage of the registration.

6.6 Possibilities of Amendment

If during the revocation/cancellation proceedings the parties agree, the defendant may limit its coverage in exchange for the plaintiff desisting from the action. That would be acceptable.

6.7 Revocation/Cancellation and Infringement

Only cancellation actions are possible.

7. Trial & Settlement

7.1 Special Procedural Provisions

TM Law establishes that common rules of civil proceedings – as established in the Civil Procedural Code – shall apply, unless contrary to the special requirements of these type of cases. This means that, although general rules are applicable, some of them, due to the nature of TM cases, are applied in a more flexible manner.

For example, the Chilean Code is very strict regarding evidence. All documents filed as evidence issued abroad should be legalised or apostilled and officially translated. Many decades ago it was accepted (even in rulings by the Supreme Court of Justice) that this is not applicable to TM cases, as it would constitute an exaggerated burden for a foreign plaintiff trying to cancel a local registration to recover his or her trade mark, to be requested to legalise dozens of foreign certificates, evidence of use, etc, and then translate them. Therefore, in this type of case simple copies of foreign documents are allowed as evidence (these can be scanned and printed locally).

Also regarding evidence, in trade-mark cases no witnesses are allowed.

In general terms, both Chilean law and practice are enemies of piracy, so usually the TMO and courts involved in cancellation cases are helpful to the plaintiff, if it has a good case.

7.2 Determination of Cases

Cases are decided by a judge. Cancellation actions are decided by the TMO's Director in first instance, and by a chamber of the special Second Instance Industrial Property Court in second instance. Infringing cases are decided by the judge (civil or criminal) in first instance, and by the competent Court of Appeal in second instance.

7.3 Possibilities of Settlement
There are no fixed or regulated mechanisms such as mediation audiences, but the parties are free to negotiate and settle. The TMO or the competent judge may not mediate.

7.4 Other Court Proceedings
As previously stated, a cancellation action against the registration on which an infringement case is based – if well-founded – may be used to suspend the prosecution of the infringing case, and even the seizure of the goods.

8. Remedies

8.1 Existing Remedies
In a case of infringement, the law states that the plaintiff may require the issuance by the judge of:

- cessation of the infringing acts;
- compensation damages;
- adoption of measures tending to avoid the continuation of the infringement;
- publication of the condemning decision in a newspaper, selected by the plaintiff.

Regarding damages, which under Chilean Law are only compensatory damages, IP Law states that the plaintiff may chose the way to determine them from:

- general procedural rules (needing to prove actual damages and the amount of them);
- profits that the trade mark-owner had ceased to receive as a consequence of the infringement;
- profits obtained by the infringer; or
- price that the offender should have paid the owner of the trade mark for the granting of a licence, taking into account the commercial value of the right infringed and other licences that may have already been granted.

8.2 Rights and Remedies
The rights/remedies for a prevailing defendant are declaration of non-infringement, compensation damages (including attorney's damages), unless the judge rules that the plaintiff had good reasons to sue.

8.3 Different Types of Remedies
There are no different types of remedies for different types of trade mark.

9. Appeal

9.1 Special Provisions
The IP Law establishes a special Second Instance Court for Industrial Property matters – ie, for reviewing first-instance decisions in registration or cancellation cases, issued by the TMO. General procedural rules are applied.

9.2 Factual or Legal Review
The second instance may imply a full review of the facts of the case, of the evidence and of the legal arguments.

9.3 Length of Appeal from Trial Court
The length of time it takes to decide an appeal depends on the current court workload and the activity of the parties, but in a registration (opposition) case or a cancellation case, the special second-instance Industrial Property Court takes approximately eight to ten months.

10. Other Trade Mark Issues

10.1 Recognition of Dilution
Among the facts that are considered when deciding a case is the possibility of dilution.

10.2 Protection of Famous Marks
Chile is a member of the Paris Convention and also has a provision in its IP Law forbidding registration of famous and notorious trade marks registered abroad in the name of its creator, in the same or a related class.

Chilean practice is very strongly against this kind of trademark piracy; hence, the standard of proof required to the foreign-registered owner is not very high.

10.3 Special Rules Regarding Geographic Indicators
Chilean IP Law expressly recognises and regulates Geographical Indicators and Denominations of Origin.

10.4 Special Rules Relating to Surnames
It is forbidden to register a name as a trade mark, unless it is with the consent of the person who bears that name. Even in that case, it is not possible to register it if it is confusingly similar to an already registered trade mark.

11. Costs

11.1 Costs Before Filing a Lawsuit
As in any other country, the costs vary. For a warning letter, a reasonable cost would be of USD150.

11.2 Costs Regarding an Infringement Action
The costs will depend on the kind of action. For example, the place (on many occasions the case should be brought far from Santiago, the capital – for example, in a city port, at the Free Zone at the northern border, etc), and also on the complexity of the case. It is different if it is an infring-

ing action deriving from Custom's application of the Law of Border Measures – the usual fee for which is approximately USD3,500, plus travel expenses) than if it is a complicated case where strong defence is expected (approximately USD8,000 to USD20,000).

11.3 Costs of Litigation

Each party shall pay its fees. Notwithstanding, in the final decision the judge may impose on the losing party the obligation to reimburse the other party's reasonable costs. The problem is that usually the court would fix as "reasonable costs" an amount that is less than the real one.

12. Alternative Dispute Resolution

12.1 Common Way of Settlement

Oppositions and cancellation cases are always decided by the Trademark Office in first instance and by the special Second Industrial Property Court in second instance. Infringement cases are always decided by a court, whether civil or criminal. Alternative dispute resolution does not exist in our jurisdiction.

Cooper & Cía
Alcántara 200 Of. 402, Las Condes
Santiago, 7550159
Chile

Tel: (56) 22245-7171
Email: cooper@cooper.cl
Web: www.cooper.cl

COOPER & CIA
ABOGADOS

13. Trade Marks and Other Intellectual Property

13.1 Protection by Copyright

A label (eg, a character) is usually granted double protection – by trade-mark law, as a label, and through copyright. There is no double protection through patents. Trade dress is not fully recognised, although there exist some decisions regarding this in the area of unfair competition.

CHINA

LAW AND PRACTICE: p.69

Contributed by CCPIT Patent and Trademark Law Office

The 'Law & Practice' sections provide easily accessible information on navigating the legal system when conducting business in the jurisdiction. Leading lawyers explain local law and practice at key transactional stages and for crucial aspects of doing business.

Contributed by CCPIT Patent and Trademark Law Office **Authors:** Mr Bin Zhang, Ms Lei Fu, Ms Lili Wu, Ms Xiaoping Wei

Law and Practice

Contributed by CCPIT Patent and Trademark Law Office

CONTENTS

Contributed by CCPIT Patent and Trademark Law Office **Authors:** Mr Bin Zhang, Ms Lei Fu, Ms Lili Wu, Ms Xiaoping Wei

Contributed by CCPIT Patent and Trademark Law Office ***Authors:*** Mr Bin Zhang, Ms Lei Fu, Ms Lili Wu, Ms Xiaoping Wei

CCPIT Patent and Trademark Law Office is the oldest and one of the largest full-service intellectual property law firms in China. CCPIT provide consultation, prosecution, mediation, administrative enforcement and litigation services relating to patents, trade marks, copyrights, domain names, trade secrets, trade dress, unfair competition and other intellectual property-related matters. The firm's specific trade-marks' work entails: registration consulting; application and review; administrative litigation; disputes concerning trade-mark registration and use; opposition and invalidation; licensing, transfer and contract drafting; renewal; due diligence investigation; search and surveillance; and administrative and judicial enforcement. CCPIT's international trade-mark department is responsible for foreign countries' trademark prosecution and protection in China and has 30 trade-mark professionals with degrees in law and/or language; the domestic trade-mark department serve smainly domestic clients and has ten trade-mark professionals with degrees in law and/or foreign language. Consequently, CCPIT's trade-mark attorneys have established a network with IP professionals at home and abroad, and can assist domestic and foreign clients in obtaining and enforcing trade-mark rights all around the world.

Authors

Mr Bin Zhang is a senior trade-mark attorney and deputy director of CCPIT's patent and trade mark law department. He has successfully handled a great number of IP cases covering trade mark, copyright, licensing, unfair competition, customs protection, trade dress, trade name, cyber-squatting through litigation, and administration or negotiation. Mr Zhang has published many articles in legal periodicals or newspapers and is co-author of the text book Practice of IP Lawyers (2006).

Ms Lei Fu is a trade-mark attorney at the firm who has been working in the IP sector since 2003. Her trade-mark expertise includes legal advice on handling trade-mark infringement and unfair competition acts, customs recordation of IP rights and related legal issues, and domain name registration and disputes. Currently, Ms Fu focuses on trade-mark and copyright infringement and unfair competition cases, including online infringement cases, handling litigations for the above.

Ms Lili Wu has been working as a patent attorney at the firm since 1997. Her practice ranges from patent drafting and prosecuting work to representing clients on invalidation or patent infringement litigation cases before the Patent Re-examination Board and courts. She has extensive experience in helping clients to obtain valuable patents in China and special expertise in consulting clients on strategies of enhancing patent protection in China in software-related fields.

Ms Xiaoping Wei has been working as a trade-mark attorney at CCPIT since 2008. She specialises in trade-mark prosecution, trade-mark search and watch, administrative protection of trade-mark right, opposition, invalidation, litigation, assignment and licensing of trade marks, and providing legal opinion on trade-mark protection strategies. Ms Wei has been providing professional legal services for numerous companies, including large multi-national companies and rising small companies from various industries.

1. Types of Trade Marks & Registration

1.1 Types of Trade Marks

In China's legal system, there are different types of trade marks/service marks, for example, unregistered marks, registered marks, certification marks and collective marks.

According to Article 8 of the China Trademark Law, any sign, capable of distinguishing the goods or services of one natural person, legal person or any other organisation from those of other persons, including words, devices, letters, numerals, three-dimensional signs, a combination of colours, sounds, etc, as well as the combination of such signs, shall be eligible for application for registration as a trade mark.

Trade dress, company names and trade names are not stipulated types of trade marks in accordance with the China Trademark Law, but they can also be protected under certain circumstances, and are mainly protected by Anti-unfair Competition Law.

Contributed by CCPIT Patent and Trademark Law Office ***Authors:*** Mr Bin Zhang, Ms Lei Fu, Ms Lili Wu, Ms Xiaoping Wei

All rights in such trade marks are based on statutory law, rather than case law.

1.2 Trade-Mark Rights

By registering a trade mark with the China Trademark Office (CTMO), the trade mark-owner can enjoy exclusive trade-mark rights over the mark.

Besides registration, the prior use of a trade mark can also be protected in China. For example, a bona fide prior use of an unregistered mark can defend against the tort claim of infringement. An unregistered well-known trade mark can be protected against copy or imitation by a third party on similar goods/services, through oppositions or invalidations, as stipulated by the China Trademark Law. Also, if a mark has prior use and has gained a certain reputation, then a rush-registration of the mark on similar goods/services by a third party is not allowed, as according to Article 32 of the China Trademark Law.

1.3 Standards for Registering

Trade dress is not a stipulated type of trade mark in China. If a trade mark is considered as lack of distinctiveness, by proving that the mark has acquired secondary meaning, the mark can still be approved for registration.

1.4 Trade-Mark Register

Trade-mark applications are filed with the CTMO. The CTMO has an online database which is available to the public. The website is: www.wsjs.saic.gov.cn.

1.5 Types of Registers

In China, there is only one trade-mark register, that is the CTMO.

1.6 Searching for Prior Trade Marks

It is possible to search the database of the CTMO for prior registered marks or marks that are already filed but have not been registered yet, to see whether there is any prior obstacle. But for marks that are already in use but not filed with the CTMO yet, they cannot be located. CCPIT Patent & Trademark Law Office can do such a trade mark search for either word mark or device mark. The information needed includes the trade mark, class and goods/services description to be covered.

1.7 Registration Requirements

The formal requirements to register a trade mark include the following aspects:

- name and address of the applicant;
- clear trade mark sample;
- class and goods/services items covered;
- power of attorney signed by the applicant, if the application is to be filed through a trade-mark agent; and
- a copy of the commercial registry (certificate of good standing) for a company applicant, or a copy of the passport or ID card for an individual applicant.

1.8 Registering a Trade Mark

Any natural person, legal person or other organisation can apply for a trade-mark registration with the CTMO.

1.9 Registering Signs

Any sign, capable of distinguishing the goods or services of one natural person, legal person or any other organisation from those of other persons, including words, devices, letters, numerals, three-dimensional signs, a combination of colours, sounds, etc, as well as the combination of such signs, shall be eligible for the application for registration as a trade mark. A scent cannot be registered as a trade mark yet in China.

1.10 Other Rights to Signs

Apart from trade marks, company names, trade names and a well-known commodity's specific name, packaging and decorating can also be protected, which is mainly stipulated by Anti-unfair Competition Law.

The above-mentioned rights mainly arose from extensive and long-time use and promotion in China.

1.11 Registration Procedure

After an application for registration of a trade mark is filed with the CTMO, the CTMO will conduct a formal examination, especially with respect to goods/services items. If the goods/services items are not standard, the CTMO will issue a notification of amendment and request the applicant to respond within 30 days from receipt of the notification. If the application meets the formal requirements, the CTMO usually issues a filing receipt in about three months. But if there is a notification of amendment, the CTMO will only issue the official filing receipt after the amended goods/services can be accepted. As per current practice, there is only one chance to amend the goods/services. If the goods/services after amendment are still unacceptable, the CTMO may issue an unacceptance notice to the application, without issuing another notification of amendment.

The CTMO then conducts a substantial examination. The legitimate examination limit for a new trade-mark application is nine months. The CTMO shall either refuse a mark or publish it within the examination limit. If there is no opposition within the three-month opposition period, the mark will finally be registered in China.

After the amendment of the China Trademark Law on 1 May 2014, multi-class applications are accepted by the CTMO. There is no cost advantage for multi-class applications compared with that for a separate trade-mark application. After a multi-class application is registered, it is not allowed to be divided. So, if there is an assignment for the mark, all classes for the multi-class application shall be assigned in a lump.

1.12 Use in Commerce

China does not require use in commerce or an intent to use for a trade-mark application.

After registration, a trade mark can be valid for ten years from the registration date of the mark. If the registrant wants to renew the mark for another ten years, a renewal application can be filed within 12 months before the renewal due date or in the grace period of six months after the renewal date.

The official fee for a trade-mark renewal within a renewal due date is CNY1,000 (about USD152). If the renewal application is filed in the grace period, the CTMO will include an additional charge of CNY250 (about USD38).

1.13 Registration of Series Marks

China does not allow for the registration of series marks, ie a number of trade marks within the same application which resemble each other to some respect. Separate trade-mark applications shall be filed with the CTMO if an applicant wants to protect all of the series marks.

1.14 Length of Registration Process

The legitimate examination period for a new trade-mark application is nine months without extension, which means the CTMO will approve or refuse the trade-mark application within nine months from the filing of the application. It takes about one year from filing an application to get a mark registered.

For a Chinese applicant, the application can be filed by the applicant itself or through a trade-mark agent as recorded with the CTMO. But if the applicant is foreign, a trade-mark application must be filed through a trade-mark agent.

The official fee for one trade-mark application in one class with no more than ten items of goods/services is CNY300 (about USD45) for one mark in one class. If the goods/services exceed ten items, the CTMO will charge an additional CNY30 (about USD4.5) for each item from the 11th as official fees.

1.15 Grounds for Refusal

A trade mark will be refused by the CTMO based on absolute grounds, such as the descriptive character of the mark, a lack of distinctiveness or misleading character. An applicant acting in bad faith is not absolute grounds for refusal of a mark by the CTMO in a substantial examination.

The absolute refusal grounds are mainly stipulated in Articles 10, 11 and 12 of the China Trademark Law, as follows:

Article 10

The following signs shall not be used as trade marks:

- those identical with or similar to the state name, national flag, national emblem, national anthem, military flag, army emblem, military anthem, or decorations of the People's Republic of China, etc, and those identical with the name or symbol of a central government department of the state, or with the name of the particular place, or with the name or image of the symbolic building where a central government department of the state is located;
- those identical with or similar to the state name, national flag, national emblem or military flag of a foreign country, etc, unless consent has been given by the government of the country;
- those identical with or similar to the name, flag or emblem of an international intergovernmental organisation, etc, unless consent has been given by the organisation or the public is not likely to be misled by such use;
- those identical with or similar to an official sign or hallmark indicating control and warranty, unless authorisation has been given;
- those identical with or similar to the name or symbol of the Red Cross or the Red Crescent;
- those having the nature of discrimination against any nationality;
- those having the nature of fraud, being liable to mislead the public about the characteristics of the goods such as the quality or the place of origin; or
- those detrimental to socialist morality or customs, or having other unhealthy influences.

The geographical name of an administrative division at or above the county level or a foreign geographical name well-known to the public shall not be used as a trade mark, unless the geographical name has another meaning or the geographical name is used as a component part of a collective mark or a certification mark; registered trade marks consisting of or containing geographical names shall continue to be valid.

Article 11

The following signs shall not be registered as trade marks:

- signs which consist exclusively of the generic names, designs or model numbers of the goods in respect of which the trade mark is used;
- signs which consist exclusively of direct indications of the quality, primary raw material, functions, intended purposes, weight, quantity or other characteristics of goods; or
- other signs which are devoid of any distinctive character.

Signs mentioned in the preceding paragraph may be registered as trade marks if they have acquired distinctive character through use and are capable of being readily identified and distinguished.

Article 12

Where a three-dimensional sign is the subject of an application for registration of a trade mark, the trade mark shall not be registered if it consists exclusively of the shape which results from the nature of the goods themselves, the shape of goods which is necessary to obtain a technical result, or the shape which gives substantial value to the goods.

1.16 Process for Overcoming Objections

If a mark is refused based on absolute grounds, an applicant has the right to file a review on the refusal with the China Trademark Review and Adjudication Board (TRAB) to present arguments and evidence.

If the mark is refused based on a lack of distinctiveness, by claiming acquired distinctiveness, the applicant must file solid evidence to show that the mark has acquired distinctiveness through use.

1.17 Consideration of Prior Rights

In the CTMO's ex-officio examination, the CTMO will not consider the existence of prior rights like trade-name rights, copyright, name rights etc in its examination, instead, it only examines whether the mark shall be refused on absolute grounds and/or whether it is in conflict with prior filed or registered similar trade marks in the name of the other party.

1.18 Third-Party Rights

Third parties cannot file observations during the registration procedure but can file oppositions after the publication of a mark.

Through the substantial examination by the CTMO, if the mark is registrable, the CTMO will publish the mark in the Trademark Gazette.

During the three-month opposition period, any person can file an opposition against a published mark based on absolute grounds. Only prior-right owners or an interested party can file opposition against a published mark if it is based on prior rights. Evidence must be filed along with the opposition to prove the qualification as prior-right owner or interested party.

1.19 Revoke, Change, Amend or Correct an Application

After an application for the registration of a trade mark is filed with the CTMO, an applicant has the right to withdraw the application or remove the registration. Changes or amendments to the trade mark sample during the application process or after the mark is registered are not allowed.

1.20 Assigning an Application or Granting a Licence

A trade mark can be assigned during the application process or after it is registered. For recordal of a licence contract, only a registered mark can be granted a licence.

1.21 Remedies Against the Trade Mark Office

If a mark is refused registration by the CTMO, the only remedy is to file a review on refusal with the TRAB within 15 days from receipt of the refusal.

1.22 Use of a Trade Mark

China adopts a first-to-file principle. It is not required to use a mark before filing.

China encourages the use of a registered trade mark. If a mark is not used for three consecutive years without justified reasons, it is at risk of being cancelled. But the cancellation is initiated by any third party, not on the CTMO's own initiative.

The use of a trade mark, as referred to in the Trademark Law, means the use of a trade mark on goods, packages or containers of the goods or in trading documents, or the use of a trade mark in advertising, exhibition or any other business activities so as to distinguish the origin of goods.

1.23 Dividing a Trade Mark

It is possible to divide a trade-mark application. But a divisional application can only be filed after a mark is partially refused by the CTMO. The divisional application shall be filed with the CTMO within 15 days from receipt of the refusal notification. A divisional application is irrevocable.

1.24 Length of Term of Protection

A registered mark is valid for ten years from the registration date. After the expiry date, a trade mark owner can still file a renewal within the grace period, ie within six months after the expiry date. But if no renewal is filed even in the grace period, the mark will be invalid and the trade mark-owner will have no way to restore it. Instead, a new trade-mark application needs to be filed if the owner still wants to protect the mark in China.

1.25 Requirements for an Exhaustion

China sticks to the principle of territoriality. In accordance with the Trademark Law of the PRC, replacing a registered trade mark without the consent of the trade-mark registrant and putting goods with a substituted trade mark into the market is regarded as trade-mark infringement.

Regarding parallel imports, there is no specific stipulation in China's Trademark Law on whether a parallel import is a trade-mark infringement or not.

1.26 Participation in the Madrid System
China is one of the participating countries in the Madrid System.

There is no procedure for notification of amendment for international trade-mark registration designating China. If the goods/services are not accepted, the CTMO will refuse the mark and there is no review on refusal based on the unacceptance of goods/services description. The applicant has to re-designate the international registration into China.

1.27 Consequences for Providing Incorrect Information
If the information is incorrectly provided, such as a typo in the name or address of an applicant, the applicant can file a recordal of correction with the CTMO to amend it.

But if the information provided for trade-mark filing is by improper means, according to Article 44 of the China Trademark Law, where a trade-mark registration violates the provisions of Articles 10, 11 and 12 of this Law, or the registration of a trade mark was acquired by fraud or any other improper means, the CTMO shall invalidate the registration at issue. Any organisation or individual may request that the TRAB make a ruling to invalidate such a registered trade mark.

1.28 Updating or Refreshing a Design Mark
According to Article 24 of the China Trademark Law, where any word or device of a registered trade mark is to be altered a new application shall be filed.

1.29 Denotation
According to Article 63 of the Implementation Regulation of the China Trademark Law, a registered trade mark can be used on goods, package of goods, illustration books or other attachments. It can be donated as "registered trade mark" or ®.

The sign of TM can also be used to indicate that the sign is used as a trade mark, but it is not a sign indicating that the mark is registered.

2. Assignment and Licensing

2.1 Assignment Requirements or Restrictions
If a trade mark is assigned, the assignor and the assignee shall sign a written assignment contract. The assignment application shall be filed with the CTMO. The assignment application can be filed against registered marks or marks in the process of application. All identical or similar marks in respect of identical or similar goods/services in the name of the assignor shall be assigned together.

The assignment of a mark shall be published after it has been approved by the CTMO. The assignee shall have the exclusive right to use the trade mark from the date of publication.

2.2 Procedure for Assigning a Trade Mark
For filing a recordal of assignment of a trade mark in China, please note the following:

- both the assignor and the assignee shall file the application together.
- documents needed include an application for assignment signed by both parties, powers of attorney signed by both parties and commercial registry or other documents to show the qualification of both parties.
- usually, the assignment contract is not required by the CTMO.

The CTMO usually completes the assignment process in about eight to 12 months.

2.3 Registering or Recording the Assignment
The assignment needs to be recorded with the CTMO. After the approval of the assignment by the CTMO, the CTMO will publish the assignment in the Trademark Gazette. A certificate of assignment will be issued by the CTMO to both the assignor and the assignee.

Only after the approval of the CTMO can the assignee be the trade mark-owner in China. Before the approval of the CTMO, the assignor is still the trade mark-owner of the mark in China.

2.4 Trade Marks and Security
A trade mark is a kind of intellectual property. It can be subject to rights in rem, assigned by way of security, or be levied in execution.

A pledgor and pledgee shall conclude a written contract regarding the pledge of a trade mark which is assignable. The same or similar marks on the same or similar goods/services shall also be included in the pledge contract. Pledge registration shall be filed with the CTMO.

2.5 Licensing Requirements or Restrictions
For recordal purposes, a licence shall be filed against only registered marks, as required by the CTMO.

But for a licence of unregistered marks, there is no specific provision by the China Trademark Law. Usually, a contract between the licensor and the licensee regarding an unregistered mark can also be deemed as valid.

All three types of licences, namely, exclusive licence, non-exclusive licence and sole licence, can be recorded.

2.6 Procedure for Licensing a Trade Mark

The recordal of a licence shall be filed by the licensor.

Documents needed for such a recordal are an application form, power of attorney and commercial registry of both the licensor and the licensee. A licence contract is not required by the CTMO.

Information such as a licensor, licensee, licence term and licensed goods/services shall be clear for recordal.

It takes the CTMO about eight months to approve a licence.

The official fee for a recordal of licence is CNY150 (about USD23).

2.7 Registering or Recording the Licence

A licence contract comes into effect after the execution of the licensor and the licensee. Recordal of a licence with the CTMO is required but not compulsive. A trade-mark licence shall not be used against any bona fide third party, if no record therefore is made.

2.8 Reasons to Deny Granting a Perpetual Licence

A registered trade mark is valid for ten years in China. After renewal, it can be extended for another ten years. A trade-mark licence needs to be within the valid period of the registered trade mark. If a mark is renewed, a new recordal of licence must be filed with the CTMO.

3. Opposition Procedure

3.1 Legal Grounds and Timeframes

The opposition can be filed based on absolute grounds, such as a lack of distinctiveness, misleading as to the characters of the goods/services, having bad social influence etc. The opposition can also be filed based on prior rights like prior trade-mark right, well-known trade mark, prior-use right etc.

An opposition can be filed within three months from the publication of a trade mark. For an international trade mark designating China, the deadline for filing opposition is the last day of the third month from its publication by WIPO.

After the filing of opposition, the CTMO usually issues an official filing receipt in about three months. It takes the CTMO 12 months to make the decision on opposition. The term can be extended for another six months.

3.2 Filing an Opposition

Any person can file opposition based on absolute grounds. Only a prior-right owner or interested party can file opposition based on prior rights, though.

A Chinese opponent can file the opposition either personally or through a trade-mark agent recorded with the CTMO. A foreign opponent must file opposition through a trade-mark agent.

The official fee for filing an opposition is CNY500 (about USD76). An attorney fee is mainly charged depending on the complexity of the case, working hours required etc.

3.3 Opposition Procedure

After an opposition is filed, the CTMO will forward the opposition grounds and evidence to the opposed party and request that the opposed party respond within 30 days from receipt of the notification. There is no evidence-exchange procedure for an opposition. The CTMO will not forward the grounds and evidence filed by the opposed party to the opponent for counter-arguments. Instead, the CTMO will make a decision on an opposition directly.

3.4 Legal Remedies

If the decision on an opposition is made in favour of an opponent and the opposed mark is refused registration, the opposed party has the right to file a review on the opposition with the TRAB within 15 days from receipt of the decision.

If the decision on opposition is not made in favour of the opponent, and the opposed mark is approved for registration, then the mark is registered. The opponent, instead of filing a review on opposition, has to file an invalidation with the TRAB after registration of the opposed mark.

The legitimate examination for a review on an opposition is 12 months and can be extended for another six months.

4. Initiating a Lawsuit

4.1 Actions to Pursue Infringement

A trade-mark registrant can pursue an infringement through legal proceedings in the people's court, or request the local Administration for Industry and Commerce (AIC) to take raid actions against an infringer.

The protections on a registered trade mark compared to an unregistered trade mark is different in the PRC. Unregistered trade marks shall be recognised as "well-known" trade marks in order to be protected in accordance with the Trademark Law of the PRC.

4.2 Initiating Infringement Proceedings

The first instance of trade-mark infringement cases is generally handled by a basic people's court.

There are exceptions. One exception is that the first instance of major foreign-related intellectual property-related cases is handled by an intermediate people's court. Major foreign-related cases refers to cases involving a large amount of subjects, cases with complicated circumstances, cases where one side consists of a large number of parties, and other cases having a major impact. The other exception is for cases involving the recognition of a well-known trade mark, which is handled by an intermediate people's court.

The litigation initiated against a trade-mark infringement is under the jurisdiction of the people's court at the place where the infringement act occurs or at the place of domicile of a defendant. The place where the infringement act occurs includes the place where the infringement act is committed and the place where the result of the infringement occurs.

4.3 Effect of Decisions on Infringement Actions

As unregistered trade marks are recognised as well-known trade marks in order to be protected in accordance with the Trademark Law of the PRC, and most of the infringement actions are initiated based on registered trade marks in the PRC, the CTMO decisions that have influence on the registration status of registered trade marks will have influence on infringement actions.

For example, if the trade mark office issues the decision to cancel a registered trade mark, the CTMO shall publish the cancelled trade mark and the right to use that registered trade mark exclusively shall be terminated from the date of publication. When the registered trade mark is cancelled, the infringement action might not be initiated based on this cancelled registered trade mark.

Another example is the CTMO's decision to declare the invalidation of a registered trade mark. The trade-mark office shall publish registered trade marks declared to be invalid, then the right to use such a registered trade mark exclusively is deemed void at the inception. The CTMO's decision to declare the invalidation of a registered trade mark will not influence the judgment, ruling or consent judgment made and enforced by a people's court in a trade-mark infringement case, nor influence the decision made and enforced by the administration for industry and commerce before the trade mark is declared to be invalid. However, the trade-mark registrant shall compensate others for losses caused by its bad faith.

4.4 Declaratory Judgment Proceedings

An alleged infringer could initiate a lawsuit requesting confirmation on non-infringement. The lawsuit for confirmation of non-infringement can be filed by a specific party which is warned of infringement by an intellectual property right-holder who fails to initiate a lawsuit within a reasonable period of time.

4.5 Jurisdiction of Courts

The people's courts apply a "final after two trials" system. The first instance of trade-mark infringement cases is generally handled by a basic people's court; one exception is that the first instance of the major foreign-related intellectual property-related cases is handled by an intermediate people's court. The second instance is handled by the people's court at the next higher level.

The party who deems that an effective judgment or ruling is erroneous may file a petition for retrial with the people's court at the next higher level.

4.6 Prerequisites to Filing a Lawsuit

There are no prerequisites to filing a lawsuit.

4.7 Representation for Parties

It is not required for the parties in a trade-mark litigation to be represented by a lawyer. According to the regulations of the PRC, parties may retain one or two persons as litigation representatives and the following persons may serve as a litigation representative:

- a lawyer or legal service worker at the basic level;
- a close relative or staff member of a party; and
- a citizen recommended by the community or entity related to a party or a citizen recommended by a social group related to a party.

4.8 Interim or Preliminary Injunctions

Preliminary injunctions are available. When the owner of a registered trade mark or an interested party has evidence proving that another person is engaged in or will soon engage in an act of infringement of the former's exclusive right to use his or her registered trade mark and that, unless the act is stopped in a timely manner, irreparable injury will be caused to his or her legitimate rights and interests, they may, before instituting legal proceedings, apply to the people's court for measures prohibiting the act and preserving the latter's assets in accordance with relevant laws.

The applicant shall provide security, and the amount of security shall equal the amount of property relating to the preservation. After accepting the application, the people's court must issue a ruling within 48 hours and if it rules to take a preliminary injunction/preservative measure, the measure shall be executed immediately. If the applicant fails to initiate an action or apply for arbitration in accordance with the law within 30 days after the people's court takes the preliminary injunction/preservative measure, the people's court shall remove the measures.

4.9 Protection for Potential Defendant

In a trade-mark infringement case, a defendant can initiate a trade-mark cancellation or invalidation action with the CTMO or TRAB against the registered trade mark involved in the trade-mark dispute. In the meantime, the defendant could prepare evidence proving its "fair use" of the relevant trade mark.

4.10 Obtaining Information and Evidence

It is possible for a party to a trade-mark matter to obtain relevant information/evidence from the other or a third party.

In accordance with Article 35 of the Lawyers Law of the PRC, an authorised lawyer may apply to the people's court to gather, investigate and take evidence or apply to the people's court for notifying a witness to testify in court. If a lawyer investigates and takes evidence on his or her own he or she may investigate information related to the legal matter handled by the relevant entity or individual.

In accordance with Article 64 of the Civil Procedure Law of the PRC, a people's court shall investigate and collect evidence which a party and its litigation representative are unable to collect for some objective reason and evidence which the people's court deems necessary for trying a case.

In accordance with Article 67 of the Civil Procedure Law of the PRC, a people's court has the authority to investigate and collect evidence from the relevant entities and individuals, and the relevant entities and individuals shall not refuse such investigation and collection of evidence.

4.11 Initial Pleading Standards

For an action to be initiated it must meet all of the following conditions:

- a plaintiff is a citizen, legal person or any other organisation with a direct interest in the case;
- there is a clear defendant;
- there are specific claims, facts and reasons; and
- the case is within the scope of civil actions accepted by the people's courts and under the jurisdiction of the people's court in which the action is initiated.

There are no special provisions for lawsuits in trade-mark proceedings that differ from non-intellectual property proceedings. Trade-mark infringement litigations are handled in accordance with the Civil Procedure Law of the PRC.

A plaintiff may relinquish or modify its claims.

4.12 Representative or Collective Actions

The Chinese legal system permits representative actions.

If the parties on one side of a joint action are numerous, such parties may recommend a representative or representatives to participate in the action. The litigation conduct of such representatives binds all parties represented; however, to modify or relinquish any claims, admit any claims of an opposing party or reach a settlement, such representatives must obtain consent from the parties represented.

If the subject-matter of action for each party is of the same kind, the parties on one side of an action are numerous, but the exact number of such parties is uncertain when the action is initiated, the people's court may publish a notice to describe the case and claims and notify right-holders to register with the people's court within a certain period of time. The right-holders which have registered with the people's court may recommend a representative or representatives to participate in the litigation; and if no representative is recommended, the people's court may determine a representative or representatives in consultation with right-holders who have registered with the people's court.

4.13 Restrictions on Trade Mark-Owners

If a registered trade mark contains the common name, design or model of goods, or it has direct indications of the quality, main raw materials, functions, uses, weight, quantity and other features of goods, or it contains the place name, the trade mark-owner does not have the right to preclude others from legitimately using the trade mark.

If a three-dimensional registered trade mark comprises a shape resulting from the nature of the goods, a shape of the goods necessary for achieving a technical effect, or a shape to add substantive value to the goods, the trade mark-owner has no right to preclude others from legitimately using such a shape.

If, before a trade-mark registrant applies for trade-mark registration, another party has used an identical or similar trade mark with a certain reputation on identical or similar goods prior to the trade-mark registrant, the trade mark-owner cannot preclude that other party from continuing to use the trade mark for original purposes, but may require the other party to add a distinctive mark.

5. Infringement

5.1 Action for Infringement

A trade mark-owner or interested party can take action against infringement. The interested party can be a licensee for a mark concerned or the legitimate successor of the property rights of a trade mark.

An exclusive licensee can initiate a lawsuit with the courts directly if the registered trade-mark right is infringed upon. A sole licensee can file a lawsuit against an infringement with the trade mark owner, or file the lawsuit itself if the trade mark-owner does not file. With clear authorisation from the trade mark-owner, a non-exclusive licensee can also file a lawsuit against an infringement.

It is suggested that a trade mark-owner takes action to stop infringement after the registration of a trade mark, unless the trade mark-owner has adequate evidence to prove that its trade mark could be recognised as "well-known" by the people's courts in the PRC.

5.2 Signs and Infringement

The following principles are followed while determining whether the use of a sign constitutes trade-mark infringement:

- judging from the common attention of the relevant public;
- not only compare overall appearance, but also the main part of the marks. The objects shall be compared isolated; and
- distinctiveness and reputation are taken into consideration.

Similar goods means the goods are similar in respect of function, usage, manufacturing section, sales channel and consuming target etc or relevant consumers deem they have certain association and are likely to be confused. Similar services means the services are similar in respect of service purposes, content, manner, target etc or consumers deem they have certain association and are likely to be confused.

5.3 Use of a Sign by Defendant

It is necessary to establish that a defendant has used a sign as a trade mark.

In the Trademark Law of the PRC, it is regulated that use of a trade mark means using a trade mark on goods; on the packages or containers of goods; in the trade documents of goods; or for advertisements, exhibitions and other commercial activities for the purpose of identifying the origin of goods. Trade-mark infringement acts are defined based on the use of a trade mark. Therefore, it is necessary to establish that the sign is used as a trade mark. Nominative and descriptive use is a defence for trade mark fair use.

5.4 Defences Against Infringement

Infringement defences can be based on other prior rights, such as trade-name rights, copyright or domain names.

Defences can also be based on the following circumstances:

- if the registered trade mark contains the common name, design or model of goods, or it has direct indications of the quality, main raw materials, functions, uses, weight, quantity and other features of goods, or it contains the place name, the trade mark-owner does not have the right to preclude others from legitimately using the trade mark.
- if a three-dimensional registered trade mark comprises a shape resulting from the nature of the goods, a shape of the goods necessary for achieving a technical effect, or a shape to add substantive value to the goods, the trade mark-owner has no right to preclude others from legitimately using such a shape.
- if, before a trade mark registrant applies for trade-mark registration, another party has used an identical or similar trade mark with a certain reputation on identical or similar goods prior to the trade-mark registrant, the trade mark-owner cannot preclude such other party from continuing to use the trade mark for original purposes, but may require such other party to add a distinctive mark.

5.5 Role of Experts and/or Surveys

According to the regulations, the parties to a trade-mark infringement case may apply to the people's courts to have one or two persons with professional knowledge appear in court to take specialised questions relating to the case. If a people's court approves such applications, the relevant expenses shall be borne by the party that makes the application. The judges and parties concerned may interrogate the persons with professional knowledge that appear in court. Upon approval of the people's courts, the persons with professional knowledge as applied for by each party concerned may cross-examine the issues concerned in the case. The persons with professional knowledge may inquire of the authenticators.

Generally speaking, the experts and/or surveys regarding likelihood of confusion, secondary meaning or genericness are considered ordinary evidence. Other supporting evidences can also be submitted.

5.6 Administrative or Criminal Offence

It is clearly regulated in the Trademark Law of the PRC that the AIC has the authority to investigate and punish, according to the law, any infringement upon the right to use a registered trade mark exclusively; and those suspected of a crime shall be transferred to the judicial authority in a timely manner according to the law.

Regarding an administrative offence, the trade-mark registrant could file a complaint with the local AIC office when trade-mark infringement disputes arise. If the AIC handling the dispute determines that an infringement is constituted, it shall order the immediate cessation of infringement and confiscate and destroy the infringing goods and the tools mainly used for manufacturing the infringing goods and counterfeiting the labels of the registered trade mark. It may also impose a fine of not more than five times the illegal business revenues if the amount of illegal business revenues reaches CNY50,000 or a fine of not more than CNY250,000 if there is no illegal business revenue or the amount of illegal business revenues is less than CNY50,000. If trade-mark infringement has been committed twice or more within five years or there are other serious circumstances, a heavier punishment shall be imposed. If goods infringing the right to use a registered trade mark exclusively are sold without knowledge of such infringement, and the seller is able to prove that the goods are legally acquired and provide the supplier, the AIC shall order the cessation of sales.

Regarding a criminal offence, it includes the following three circumstances:

- without being licensed by the trade mark-owner, a party uses a trade mark identical with the registered trade mark on identical goods, if any crime is constituted, the party shall be subject to criminal liability according to the law in addition to compensating the victim for losses;
- where a party forges or manufactures without authorisation the labels of a registered trade mark of another party or sells the labels of a registered trade mark forged or manufactured without authorisation, if any crime is constituted, the party shall be subject to criminal liability according to the law in addition to compensating the victim for losses; and
- where a party knowingly sells goods on which a registered trade mark is falsely used, if any crime is constituted, the party shall be subject to criminal liability according to the law in addition to compensating the victim for losses.

5.7 Custom Seizures

The Chinese legal system provides for customs seizure of counterfeits. China started to adopt customs' protection of IPRs in 1995. For the purpose of customs' protection, the owner of IPRs which might include trade mark, patent and copyright being already approved, granted or registered by competent state authorities should record its IPRs with China General Administration of Customs on the basis of each certificate for each recordation. If a designated IPR has been successfully recorded with China General Administration of Customs, the information of the IPR is added to the official computer system of China General Administration of Customs and shared by every customs within Chinese territory. When customs officers carry out routine inspections on imported or exported goods, they pay more attention to goods bearing recorded IPRs. If customs suspect some goods have infringed a recorded IPR, it will notify the IPR owner and upon an application filed by the IPR owner with remittance of the required security bond, customs will detain the suspected goods. The security bond will be based on the value of the suspected goods.

6. Revocation/Cancellation

6.1 Remedies and Reasons

Where a registered trade mark has no effectiveness or has bad social influence, or the registration of a trade mark has been acquired by fraud or any other unfair means, the CTMO shall declare the registered trade mark invalid; any other organisation or individual may request the TRAB to declare such a registered trade mark invalid.

Where a registered trade mark is a copy, imitation or translation of a prior well-known trade mark, or it is a misleading geographical indication, or the registrant is an agent or has another relationship with the true owner of the mark, or the registered mark is similar to a prior registered or applied mark on similar goods/services, or it is an infringement of other's prior rights or a copy of other's mark which has been used and has gained a certain reputation, the earlier right-owners or any interested party may, within five years from the date of registration, request the TRAB to declare the registered trade mark invalid. Where the registration has been made in bad faith, the owner of a well-known trade mark shall not be bound by the five-year time limit.

6.2 Trade Mark Office and Civil Courts

Revocation/cancellation can only be brought before the TRAB. If dissatisfied with the decision on revocation/cancellation, an administrative litigation can be filed with the Beijing Intellectual People's Court.

6.3 Statutory Limitation or Time Period

If revocation/cancellation is filed based on absolute grounds, there is no time limit within which the revocation/cancellation has to be filed.

If the revocation/cancellation is filed based on prior rights etc as described in **6.1 Remedies and Reasons**, then the revocation/cancellation shall be filed within five years from registration of the disputed mark.

But if the mark was filed in bad faith, a well-known trade mark-owner is not bound by the five-year limit.

6.4 Initiation of Revocation/Cancellation Proceeding

If a revocation/cancellation is based on absolute grounds, any person can file the revocation with the TRAB. If the revocation is based on relevant grounds (prior well-known trade mark rights, prior similar marks, other prior rights etc), only the prior right-owner or an interested party has the right to file the revocation.

6.5 Partial Revocation/Cancellation

A revocation can be filed against part of the goods/services registered.

6.6 Possibilities of Amendment
After a mark is registered, it is not allowed to be amended. Thus, if a mark is under a revocation/cancellation proceeding, it is not possible to amend the mark. But the applicant/registrant has the right to delete some items of goods/services.

6.7 Revocation/Cancellation and Infringement
Usually, revocation/cancellation is examined case by case. For a revocation with the same nature (the same application, same registrant of the disputed mark, same supporting evidence) and filed at the same time, it is possible to request the examiner to examine them in a lump. But decisions are still made case by case.

Revocation/cancellation and infringement are not heard together. The court for infringement has discretion to determine whether the court will wait for the decision on revocation/cancellation.

7. Trial & Settlement

7.1 Special Procedural Provisions
There are no special provisions for lawsuits in trade-mark proceedings that differ from non-intellectual property proceedings. Trade-mark infringement litigations are handled in accordance with the Civil Procedure Law of the PRC.

7.2 Determination of Cases
The case is determined by a collegial bench. When a people's court tries a first instance civil case, a collegial bench consisting of judges and jurors or consisting of judges only shall be formed. The members of a collegial bench must add up to an odd number. Civil cases tried under a summary procedure shall be tried by a sole judge.

Generally speaking, the parties do not have any influence on who the decision-maker is. However, under certain circumstances, the parties could request disqualification of the judge, court clerk, interpreters, identification or evaluation expert, and surveyor verbally or in writing.

7.3 Possibilities of Settlement
A defendant can file an application for mediation and both sides of a civil action may reach a settlement themselves.

When a people's court conducts mediation, it may be conducted by one judge or by the collegial bench, and mediation shall be conducted on the spot as much as possible. When a mediation agreement is reached, a people's court prepares a consent judgment. A consent judgment states the claims, facts of the case and results of mediation. The judges and court clerk affix their signatures and a people's court its seal to a consent judgment, which shall be served on both sides. Once a consent judgment is signed by both sides, it becomes legally binding.

7.4 Other Court Proceedings
According to the law, if current cases depend on the results of the trial of another case which has not been concluded, the current cases shall be suspended.

In the meantime, the collegial bench of the current proceeding has the right to decide whether to suspend the current case to wait for the result of another proceeding.

8. Remedies

8.1 Existing Remedies
The courts could rule that an infringer bears civil liabilities including stopping the infringement, eliminating negative influence, compensating for the losses etc. The amount of damages for trade-mark infringement is determined according to the actual losses suffered by a trade-mark proprietor. When it is difficult to determine the actual losses, the amount of damages may be determined according to the profits acquired by the infringer. When it is difficult to determine the trade-mark proprietor's losses or the profits acquired by the infringer, the amount of damages may be a reasonable multiple of the royalties. When it is difficult to determine the actual losses of the trade-mark proprietor, the profits acquired by the infringer, or the royalties of the registered trade mark, a people's court may award damages of no more than CNY3 million according to the circumstances of the infringement.

The collegial bench has discretion in ordering remedies.

8.2 Rights and Remedies
Generally speaking, if a defendant prevails in a trade-mark infringement case, the courts will declare that the defendant does not constitute trade-mark infringement. If the defendant would like to request compensation from the plaintiff, the defendant can file a counterclaim or initiate new litigation for compensation.

8.3 Different Types of Remedies
Remedies for different types of trade marks are generally the same.

9. Appeal

9.1 Special Provisions
The appellate procedure of a trade-mark proceeding is generally the same as the appellate procedure for other civil proceedings.

If any party is not satisfied with the judgment of the first instance, it shall have the right to file an appeal with a people's court at the next higher level within 15 days from the date of service of the written judgment. The original trial people's court shall, within five days after receiving a written appeal, serve the copies of the written appeal on the opposing parties, and the opposing parties shall, within 15 days after receiving the copies, submit their written statements of defence. The original trial people's court shall, within five days after receiving the written statements of defence, serve the copies of the written statements of defence on the appellant. After receiving both the written appeal and the written statements of defence, the original trial people's court shall, within five days, transfer them along with the entire case file and evidence to the people's court of second instance.

9.2 Factual or Legal Review

The people's court of second instance shall try a case around a party's claims in appeal. Where a party does not file claims, the people's court shall not try the case, unless the first-instance judgment violates prohibitive provisions in laws or damages the interests of the state, public interests or the legitimate rights and interests of other persons.

9.3 Length of Appeal from Trial Court

According to the Civil Procedure Law of the PRC, a people's court shall complete the trial of an appeal case against a judgment within three months after the appeal is docketed. Any extension of the aforesaid period under special circumstances shall be subject to the approval of the chief justice of the people's court. The above provision applies to the domestic civil lawsuit without involving foreign elements. Actually, there are no specific time limitations for a lawsuit involving foreign elements; however, in practice, the time limitation for a lawsuit involving foreign elements sometimes may refer to that for the lawsuit without involving foreign elements.

A people's court shall issue a final ruling for an appeal case against a ruling within 30 days after the appeal is docketed.

10. Other Trade Mark Issues

10.1 Recognition of Dilution

There is no clear law or regulation against trade-mark dilution in the PRC. However, well-known trade marks may obtain a certain degree of protection against trade-mark dilution, both in trade-mark registration as well as trade-mark infringement cases.

According to the Trademark Law, if a trade mark for registration to be used on different or dissimilar goods is a copy, imitation or translation of a well-known trade mark of another party which has been registered in China; misleads the public; and may cause damage to the interests of the registrant of the well-known trade mark, it will not be registered and will be prohibited from use.

10.2 Protection of Famous Marks

Marks that are famous outside China but are not yet in use or registered in China cannot be protected under the Trademark Law of the PRC.

10.3 Special Rules Regarding Geographic Indicators

Special rules with regard to geographic indicators are included in both the Trademark Law and the Implementing Regulations of the Trademark Law.

If a trade mark contains a geographic indication of the goods but the goods do not originate from the region indicated thereon, thus misleading the public, the trade mark will not be registered and will be prohibited from use; however, those that have been registered in good faith shall continue to be valid. Geographic indicators may be registered upon application as certification marks or collective marks.

10.4 Special Rules Relating to Surnames

There is no special regulation on using one's own surname (or name) as a mark. It is regulated that using the name of a public figure in certain domains to file a trade-mark application is regarded as "having any other adverse effect" which is prohibited from registration in accordance with Article 10 of the trade-mark law.

11. Costs

11.1 Costs Before Filing a Lawsuit

The costs for investigations into a possible defendant as well as the costs for evidence collecting, especially for the notarised preservation of relevant evidence, are the costs that typically arise before a lawsuit.

11.2 Costs Regarding an Infringement Action

In the first instance, typical costs include investigations fees, notarisation fees, translations fees paid to the qualified translation firm (if documents in foreign languages are involved), attorney fees and expenses, and court fees.

11.3 Costs of Litigation

A plaintiff can request that a defendant bear the reasonable costs in a litigation. If the plaintiff wins the case, the judge can request the defendant to bear a certain amount of the reasonable costs including attorney fees. It is at the judge's discretion to decide the amount of reimbursements based on the evidence submitted by the plaintiff.

12. Alternative Dispute Resolution

12.1 Common Way of Settlement

Alternative dispute resolution is not a compulsory element of settling a trade-mark infringement case. In accordance with the Trademark Law of the PRC, when any dispute arises from any infringements upon the right exclusively to use a registered trade mark, the parties concerned shall resolve the dispute through negotiation; and if they are reluctant to resolve the dispute through negotiation or the negotiation fails, the trade-mark registrant or an interested party may initiate an action in a people's court or request the administrative department for industry and commerce to handle the dispute.

For agreements concerning trade-mark matters, if it is agreed in an agreement that the disputes are to be handled through arbitration, then the trade-mark case can be resolved through arbitration.

CCPIT Patent and Trademark Law Office
10/F, Ocean Plaza
158 Fuxingmennei Street
Beijing 100031
China

Tel: +86 10 66412345
Fax: +86 10 66415678
Email: mail@ccpit-patent.com.cn
Web: www.ccpit-patent.com.cn

CCPIT PATENT AND TRADEMARK LAW OFFICE
中国国际贸易促进委员会专利商标事务所

13. Trade Marks and Other Intellectual Property

13.1 Protection by Copyright

A trade mark can also be protected by copyright if it satisfies the requirements of the Copyright Law. If a patent is granted on a trade mark, it could also obtain protection by design patent. The trade dress of a famous product is also under protection in accordance with the Anti-Unfair Competition Law of the PRC.

COSTA RICA

LAW AND PRACTICE: p.87

Contributed by Castro & Pal Abogados

The 'Law & Practice' sections provide easily accessible information on navigating the legal system when conducting business in the jurisdiction. Leading lawyers explain local law and practice at key transactional stages and for crucial aspects of doing business.

Contributed by Castro & Pal Abogados ***Authors:*** Luis Diego Castro, Simon A. Valverde, José Paulo Brenes

Law and Practice

Contributed by Castro & Pal Abogados

CONTENTS

Castro & Pal Abogados has a team of four attorneys and a three-person support staff fully dedicated to trade marks. To help clients obtain and protect their trade-mark rights, Castro & Pal provide services for the registration of trade marks, which includes the preparation, filing and prosecution of Costa Rican and foreign trade-mark applications. The firm also provides services for the protection and enforcement of clients' trade-mark assets in both the courts and before the Costa Rican Trademark Office; the firm's services and experience in this regard extend to all of Latin America. Castro & Pal's trade-marks team is also known for supporting domestic corporations with the complex trade mark-related aspects of their business transactions, and providing expert assistance to companies with their trade-mark election processes.

Authors

Luis Diego Castro is managing partner of Castro & Pal. He specialises in trade-mark law, patent law, trade-secrets law and intellectual property law. He also has particular expertise in terms of technology law, internet and e-commerce issues. Mr Castro served for several years as a member of the intellectual property counsel group for CONCAUSA, a private sector programme supporting the Central American – USA Free Trade Agreement (CAFTA). He is currently a member of the International Association for the Protection of Intellectual Property, the American Intellectual Property Law Association, the International Trademark Association, and the Association of National Professionals in Intellectual Property in Costa Rica.

Simon A. Valverde is a partner at the firm. His practice focuses on trade-mark law, patent law, intellectual property law. He is a member of the Inter-American Association of Intellectual Property, the International Trademark Association, and the Association of National Professional in Intellectual Property in Costa Rica. Simon has written and published extensively on trade-mark issues and is currently a professor of intellectual property courses at post-graduate degree level at Universidad Estatal a Distancia de Costa Rica and Universidad Latina de Costa Rica.

José Paulo Brenes is of counsel at Castro & Pal. He specialises in intellectual property law, IP litigation (civil and criminal) and anti-counterfeiting; he has additional expertise in border measure practice. Jose is a member of the International Trademark Association and the Association of National Professionals in Intellectual Property in Costa Rica. Previously professor of advertisement and IP at Universidad Ulacit (2004/2005), he continues to write and lecture on IP-related matters, including trade marks.

1. Types of Trade Marks & Registration

1.1 Types of Trade Marks
The types of trade marks found under the Costa Rican legal system are the following: trade marks, service marks, trade names, slogans, collective marks, certification marks, appellations of origin and geographical indications.

Rights in such trade marks are based on statutory law.

1.2 Trade-Mark Rights
A trade-mark registration must be obtained in order to have trade-mark rights. Nevertheless, Costa Rica Trademark Law provides for a preferred right to file for the registration of the mark when a third person has been using the same mark at least three months prior to the respective application date.

1.3 Standards for Registering
There are no different standards for registering different types of marks. Further, although secondary meaning is not expressly cited in the law, the Trademark Office and the Administrative Courts have given indirect recognition of its existence.

1.4 Trade-Mark Register
There is a publicly available trade-mark database; however, it is only accessible at the premises of the Trademark Office; it has not yet been made available online.

1.5 Types of Registers
There is a single register for trade marks in Costa Rica; it is formally identified as the Trademark Section of the In-

dustrial Property Registry, but is colloquially known as the Trademark Office or Trademark Registry. The Industrial Property Registry is part of the National Registry, an agency of the Justice Department.

1.6 Searching for Prior Trade Marks

It is a normal practice to search for prior trade-mark registrations at the Trademark Office before applying to register a trade mark. The search needs to be performed at the database of the Trademark Office. Accurate online trade-mark searches are not available in Costa Rica.

1.7 Registration Requirements

To register a trade mark in Costa Rica an application must be filed with the Trademark Office. The application must include the mark with its description, the applicant's name and address, an indication of the international classes in which protection is sought and payment of the filing fee. There is no need to show or claim prior use to apply for a trade-mark registration.

1.8 Registering a Trade Mark

All individuals, foreign and national, as well as any legal entity can file for a trade-mark registration.

1.9 Registering Signs

Words, images, sounds and the shape of the goods, as well as the shape of containers and packages can be registered as trade marks in Costa Rica. The trade dress of a commercial establishment can also be registered as a trade mark.

1.10 Other Rights to Signs

The Costa Rican legal system makes a distinction between trade names and company names. Trade names are signs identifying an open business in a specific location. A company name is the official name given to a corporate entity. Company names are governed by the Registry of Corporations at the Mercantile Registry and are not considered intellectual property rights.

The Costa Rican country code top level domain (ccTLD) is.cr. Top-level (.cr) domains and second-level (.co.cr, .fi.cr, .or.cr, .sa.cr, .ed.cr, ac.cr and go.cr) domains must be obtained at, and are under the administration of, NIC Costa Rica (www.nic.cr), a non-profit organisation and an independent unit of the National Academy of Sciences.

1.11 Registration Procedure

The registration procedure begins when a trade-mark application is filed before the Trademark Office. The application undergoes formal and substantial examination. If approved, the applicant is provided with an advertisement that he or she must publish in the Official Gazette, opening a two-month period to hear any oppositions. If no opposition is filed the trade mark is registered.

Multi-class applications are allowed.

1.12 Use in Commerce

Use in commerce of the applied mark does not have to be demonstrated as of the date of filing the application, but any mark should be used within five years from registration date. Failure to use the mark within five years from registration allows an interested party to file a cancellation action.

1.13 Registration of Series Marks

The Costa Rican trade-mark system does not allow series marks. Any series needs to be filed as a group of individual trade-mark applications.

1.14 Length of Registration Process

The registration process of a trade mark typically lasts four to six months, given no official objections or third party oppositions are received.

Applicants do not need legal representation to initiate a trade-mark registration process. If the application is not filed directly by the applicant him or herself, he or she will be required to have his or her signature notarised, or an attorney's signature showing professional responsibility for the application process.

Official filing fees for a single-word mark application in one class are USD50. Publication fees are not included in the filing fee. Publication costs vary considerably depending of the extension of the publication, but are typically around USD100 for applications with a simple design and short list of goods. Attorney fees are around USD400.

1.15 Grounds for Refusal

Registration of a trade mark may be refused by the Trademark Office when:

- it consists in the usual form of the product or packaging to which it applies;
- it consists in a form which grants a functional or technical advantage to the good or service to which it applies;
- it consists in a sign which is the common designation for the good or service;
- it consists in a sign which may be used to describe a characteristic of the good or service;
- it consists in a colour in itself;
- it consists in a letter or digit in itself, unless it is presented in a special and distinctive form;
- it lacks distinctive character regarding the good or service;
- it is contrary to morality or public order;
- it offends or ridicules people, ideas, religions or national symbols;

- it is misleading;
- it is similar or identical to an expired trade mark in a way which causes confusion, and for the same type of goods or services;
- it replicates a coat of arms, flag or emblem of a state or international organisation;
- it replicates coins, banknotes, seals, stamps;
- it includes or reproduces medals, awards, diplomas or other elements unless these were truly granted;
- it consists in the name of a plant variety protected in Costa Rica or in a state with which a treaty has been signed.

1.16 Process for Overcoming Objections

The typical process to overcome objections raised by the Trademark Office includes either a 15- or 30-working-day period to file a response to the objections. Cancellation or nullity actions against marks that might pose an obstacle for filing the trade mark can be filed as a response to objections raised by the Trademark Office.

1.17 Consideration of Prior Rights

The Trademark Office can refuse registration of a trade mark on the basis of prior rights in the following cases:

- if the sign is similar or identical to a trade mark, a geographical indication or an appellation of origin, registered or pending, protecting similar goods or services;
- if the sign is similar or identical to a trade mark, a geographical indication or an appellation of origin used from an earlier date by a third party for similar goods or services;
- if the sign replicates a trade mark which is well-known in any member state of the Paris Convention;
- if the sign's use affects a third party's personality rights, namely a person's name, title, image or signature;
- if the signs use affects the name rights, image or prestige of a collective entity;
- if the sign replicated a certification mark protected from an earlier date;
- if the sign can infringe a third party's copyright or industrial property right;
- if the sign's registration was requested to perpetrate or consolidate an act of unfair competition.

1.18 Third-Party Rights

Third parties with a legitimate interest have the right to file an opposition against the trade-mark application within two months from the publication of the application in the Official Gazette. The opposing third party may file all evidence in support of its arguments within 30 days from the opposition date. There are no minimum standards to prove legitimate interest. The applicant is then provided with a two-month period to file a response. Finally, the opposition is resolved by the Trademark Office.

1.19 Revoke, Change, Amend or Correct an Application

During prosecution the applicant may revoke, change, amend or correct an application, provided that the modifications are not essential, and the specification of goods or services is not broadened.

1.20 Assigning an Application or Granting a Licence

It is possible to assign an application for a trade mark or grant a licence in relation to it during the application process.

1.21 Remedies Against the Trade Mark Office

When the Trademark Office refuses to register a mark the applicant may file a motion for revocation or an appeal. The motion of revocation is decided by the Trademark Office while the appeal is decided by the Administrative Tribunal for Registry Matters (*Tribunal Registral Administrativo*), which acts as the administrative court of appeals.

1.22 Use of a Trade Mark

The Costa Rican legal system does not require an applicant to have used its trade mark in commerce before registration is issued, but trade-mark use should happen within five years from registration to avoid cancellation.

1.23 Dividing a Trade Mark

A trade-mark application may be divided to separate its original specification of goods or services into two or more registrations. For this purpose a divisional application must be filed and the corresponding fee must be paid.

1.24 Length of Term of Protection

Trade marks are granted in Costa Rica for a ten-year period. The trade mark-owner may renew the trade mark as of one year prior to its expiry date or during a six-month grace period after the date of expiry. An additional fee must be paid for grace period renewals.

1.25 Requirements for an Exhaustion

Trade-mark rights can be terminated if their registration term expires, are annulled or cancelled. Trade marks can be annulled during the four years after their registration if they are proven to have been granted while failing to comply with the basic requirements for registration. Trade marks can be cancelled if they are proven not to have been used for at least five years after their registration. Trade marks can also be cancelled if they become generic.

1.26 Participation in the Madrid System

Costa Rica does not participate in the Madrid System.

1.27 Consequences for Providing Incorrect Information
Trade-mark applications are considered by law a sworn statement. If false information is filed on a bad-faith basis, the applicant may face criminal charges. If the incorrect information was filed unintentionally, then a correction can be filed.

1.28 Updating or Refreshing a Design Mark
Design mark registrations cannot be updated. A new application must be filed.

1.29 Denotation
The use of symbols with marks is not regulated.

2. Assignment and Licensing

2.1 Assignment Requirements or Restrictions
Although it is not mandatory to record a trade-mark assignment before the Trademark Office, it is strongly advisable. As to the requirements, it is necessary to file the written assignment duly legalised, as well as a notarised Power of Attorney either from the assignor or the assignee.

2.2 Procedure for Assigning a Trade Mark
Once the assignment is duly filed, the Trademark Office will review and verify that all formal requirements are met. If the requirements are met, the Trademark Office will issue the certificate of recordal within two to four weeks.

2.3 Registering or Recording the Assignment
As previously indicated, it is not mandatory to register or record the assignment, but it is advisable, since it will be much easier and cost-effective to enforce the mark by the real owner of the mark. There are no major risks if the assignment is not recorded in a timely manner.

2.4 Trade Marks and Security
Marks can be given as securities; in fact, a law enacted two years ago eased the procedure.

2.5 Licensing Requirements or Restrictions
The only requirements for recording a licence are that the document must be in writing and duly legalised and the licensee or the licensor must grant a notarised Power of Attorney to the local attorney. If the licence agreement lacks information, such as the term or the possibility to sub-license, then the Trademark Office will record the licence for all the term of the mark and without possibilities for the assignee to assign the licence or sub-license the mark. Further, the licence can be exclusive, non-exclusive, sole licence. There is no naked licence in Costa Rica.

2.6 Procedure for Licensing a Trade Mark
Once the licence is duly filed, the Trademark Office will review and verify that all formal requirements are met. If the requirements are met, the Trademark Office will issue the certificate of recordal within two to four weeks.

2.7 Registering or Recording the Licence
It is not mandatory to register or record the licence. There are no major risks if the licence is not recorded in a timely manner.

2.8 Reasons to Deny Granting a Perpetual Licence
There are no reasons for a rejection of a perpetual licence. According with Costa Rican law, if there is no term for the licence, then the Trademark Office assumes that it will be valid for the term in which the mark is valid.

3. Opposition Procedure

3.1 Legal Grounds and Timeframes
Any third party that has an interest can file an opposition against a trade mark within two months from publication date. The opponent can argue against the registration of the mark if it is not inherently distinctive, if it is offensive or if its registration jeopardises its prior trade-mark rights, industrial property rights or copyrights.

3.2 Filing an Opposition
Any third party that has an interest can file an opposition. The opponent does not necessarily need representation, but it is advisable. The average office and attorney fees are USD500-800.

3.3 Opposition Procedure
As soon as the opposition is filed, the Trademark Office will normally review it within two weeks to check if it meets the formal requirements. If the formalities are met, the Trademark Office will notify the applicant and provide a one-month period to file any counter arguments. After the applicant files the arguments, the Trademark Office will issue the final resolution usually within six to eight months.

3.4 Legal Remedies
The final resolution issued by the Trademark Office regarding an opposition process can be appealed before the Administrative Courts within five days or appealed before the Judicial Courts within one year.

4. Initiating a Lawsuit

4.1 Actions to Pursue Infringement
Trade mark-owners pursuing infringers may file a civil suit at the judicial courts for trade-mark infringement or unfair

competition. Judicial and administrative actions for trade-mark infringement are only available for owners of registered trade marks. Owners of famous marks, as defined in WIPO's Joint Recommendation Letter 833 of September 1999, have a somewhat restricted ability to prevent trade-mark infringers from taking advantage of the famous trade mark for the same or related goods or services by creating confusion in the consumer.

Criminal actions may also be filed for trade-mark counterfeiting; the sale, offer for sale, storage and importation of counterfeit goods; the acquisition, sale and offer for sale of specimens with reproductions of the mark, such as labels, separated from the goods; the false identification as an authorised distributor and the fraudulent use of appellations of origin. It is required for the trade mark or sign to be duly registered.

4.2 Initiating Infringement Proceedings

Judicial infringement proceedings should be initiated at the civil courts of the jurisdiction where the infringement is taking place, through an abbreviated civil process (*Proceso Abreviado*). A new set of Rules of Civil Procedure will come into effect in October 2018, introducing significant changes to all judicial civil procedures.

4.3 Effect of Decisions on Infringement Actions

Administrative measures taken by the Trademark Office are not available in Costa Rica. Therefore, resolutions regarding oppositions, nullities or cancellation actions can be reverted in a Judicial Court. In some cases, the resolutions issued by the Trademark Office are persuasive but not mandatory. While not mandatory, decisions made by the Trademark Office normally influence the decisions made by the respective judge.

4.4 Declaratory Judgment Proceedings

The alleged infringer may start declaratory judgment proceedings, seeking the nullity or cancellation of the trade-mark registration, provided that the trade mark does not meet the legal requirements to be granted, either due to intrinsic conditions or because it affects third-party rights. Further, the Trademark Law dictates that upon a trade-mark infringement action the nullity action may be filed either as a defence or as a counter-claim against the trade mark-owner. Any nullity action should be filed within four years from the date of the trade-mark registration.

4.5 Jurisdiction of Courts

Civil courts have jurisdiction to resolve trade-mark disputes where the government is not involved. The decision of the civil court may be revised on appeal by the Civil Superior Tribunal. In some instances, depending on the amount of the dispute, the decision of the Civil Superior Tribunal may be revised by the Supreme Court of Justice through an appeal of cassation.

4.6 Prerequisites to Filing a Lawsuit

There are no prerequisites to filing a lawsuit for trade-mark infringement.

4.7 Representation for Parties

Parties in trade-mark litigation matters need to be represented by a lawyer.

4.8 Interim or Preliminary Injunctions

Interim or preliminary injunctions are available in case of trade-mark infringement, either through judicial or administrative authorities. Preliminary injunctions are also available through the criminal courts. For a preliminary injunction to be granted the plaintiff needs to provide evidence of trade-mark registration and ownership and provide evidence, with some degree of plausibility, of the fact that its trade-mark right has been, or is about to be, infringed.

4.9 Protection for Potential Defendant

Potential defendants may require the authorities to require a bond to be posted prior to the injunction. Potential defendants may also initiate a declaratory judgement to annul the trade-mark registration.

4.10 Obtaining Information and Evidence

Costa Rica follows similar rules of evidence in civil procedures to other Latin American countries. Parties are required to file or offer to the court the evidence considered necessary to support their action or defence. All the evidence the parties have filed or offered is obtained and analysed during the disclosing evidence stage of the process, at the beginning of which the judge decides which evidence is admitted. Usually evidence needs to be obtained by the parties, and not through a court order making evidence, or potential evidence, available to the other parties involved.

Technical experts and witnesses are commonly used as evidence.

4.11 Initial Pleading Standards

The initial pleading to initiate a lawsuit is identical to a non-intellectual property proceeding. According to our laws, any lawsuit must indicate detailed facts, evidence, the proper standing that justifies the action and the detailed actions and measures that are requested to the judge.

4.12 Representative or Collective Actions

The Costa Rican legal system does permit representative or collective actions for trade-mark proceedings, but these are very uncommon. There are no specific circumstances for such action except a legal interest of the plaintiff.

4.13 Restrictions on Trade Mark-Owners
Our laws do not have specific provisions regarding this matter, but as in any other lawsuit if there is misuse/abuse of the rights or unfair competition acts, the trade mark-owner's rights can be jeopardised.

5. Infringement

5.1 Action for Infringement
The trade mark-owner would be a necessary party in an infringement action; however, an authorised licensee could also file the infringement action, in lieu of the trade mark-owner or as a co-plaintiff. In the case of criminal actions, the trade mark-owner and any licensee that can prove it is the victim of a trade mark-related crime may file the criminal complaint. It would not be possible for the trade mark-owner to stop infringement before its mark is registered – nevertheless, it would be possible for the owner of a notorious mark to file an infringement action in civil court, even if its mark is not duly registered. In the case of criminal proceedings, it would be required for the mark to be duly registered.

5.2 Signs and Infringement
The general standard to determine if there is trade-mark infringement is the probability or likelihood that a determined use or action causes confusion to the consumer and the following factors or aspects will be taken into consideration:

- identity or similarity between the signs, including graphic, phonetic and meaning similarities;
- the identity, similarity and/or connection or association of the goods/services.

In a case where the mark and the goods/services are identical, Costa Rican Trademark Law considers there is prima facie probability or likelihood of confusion. In the case of criminal actions, the standard for infringement is that marks are identical or substantively identical so that it would deceive consumers and that the goods upon which the mark is used are the same as those included in the registration. In the case of imports, sale and distribution of counterfeit goods, it is also necessary to prove that the defendant knew the goods were fake, in order to obtain a conviction.

5.3 Use of a Sign by Defendant
It is necessary to prove that the mark has been used as a source identifier, as other uses could be deemed to be fair use.

5.4 Defences Against Infringement
The following defences can be filed against an infringement action, in addition to ordinary procedural defences:

- fair use (which includes use of the mark as part of an address), use to indicate a characteristic of the good/service, information as to the use, applicability, availability, compatibility, especially in the case of spare parts;
- Statute of Limitations, which is of four years from the moment the infringing activity ceases;
- cancellation/nullity action – the defendant can file as a defence the fact that the trade-mark registration has been subject of a cancellation/nullity action before the Trademark Office.

Such actions can allege the invalidity of the mark for falling within the prohibitions of the Trademark Law or its cancellation for non-use of the mark. The judge will not render a final decision and normally will suspend procedures until the cancellation/nullity action is resolved. Laches and acquiescence defences are not available in the Costa Rican legal system.

5.5 Role of Experts and/or Surveys
Surveys are allowed and have proven to be very persuasive evidence in proceedings before the Trademark Office and in infringement actions before the courts. As to the role of experts, our code of civil proceedings does not allow as evidence the testimony of an expert witness offered by any of the parties. While parties do file expert reports as evidence, judges are normally reluctant to accept their reports, considering them to be partial and not purely objective. However, the opinion of a court-appointed expert would be highly persuasive. In the case of criminal proceedings, testimony by an expert offered by the trade mark-owner is not only allowed, but required by prosecutors to prove that the questioned or seized goods are counterfeits. Our code of criminal procedures provides all parties the freedom to use any kind of evidence to prove or disprove acts of infringement.

5.6 Administrative or Criminal Offence
The following are considered criminal offences and therefore can be prosecuted in criminal court:

- trade-mark counterfeiting;
- the sale, offer for sale, storage and importation of counterfeit goods;
- the acquisition, sale and offer for sale of specimens with reproductions of the mark, such as labels, separated from the goods;
- the false identification as an authorised distributor and the fraudulent use of appellations of origin.

In order to initiate criminal proceedings, it is required for the trade mark-owner, or any other victim of the crime, to file a complaint before the Prosecutor Office. The criminal action cannot be initiated ex officio. Trade-mark infringement could be considered an administrative offence if it has a negative effect on the consumer. In such a case the offence must be denounced before the Costa Rican Consumer Board, which can apply diverse penalties when the negative effect on the consumer is proven, such as monetary fines and other measures to rectify the effects of the unlawful conduct.

5.7 Custom Seizures

The Costa Rican legal system authorises Customs to retain the release of imported goods that have been deemed to be counterfeits. Such retention or seizure can operate under two circumstances.

- When Customs has reasons to believe that the goods are counterfeit, it will retain the goods ex officio and then must, within a ten-day term, file a criminal complaint before the Prosecutor Office. In order to take action Costa Rican Customs requires that the trade mark-owner inspects the imported goods and file an authenticity report. The trade mark-owner will then have to also file a complaint and assist the prosecutor in proving the goods are counterfeit. The fate of the goods will ultimately be determined by the criminal judge.
- Preliminary Measures – once a trade mark-owner learns of an importation of infringing goods, it can request a civil judge or a criminal judge to order Customs to retain such goods while it files a criminal complaint or a civil law suit. In such cases, the judge normally requests that a guarantee bond is filed. This type of preliminary measures takes a few weeks to be ordered, rendering it an ineffective option for importations.

It is not possible to take legal measures against parallel imports, unless they provoke undue harm on the trade mark-owner.

6. Revocation/Cancellation

6.1 Remedies and Reasons

According to our laws, there are two reasons for filing a cancellation of a trade mark. One reason is due to non-use and the other is if the mark becomes generic. A cancellation due to non-use can be filed if the mark has not been used in a regular manner within five years from the registration date. As to the cancellation for a mark becoming generic, it can be filed at any moment as long as the mark has lost its distinctiveness.

In addition, a nullity action can be filed within four years from the registration date if the mark has not been properly granted due to lack of distinctiveness, or if it jeopardised any prior rights of a trade-mark or copyright-owner.

6.2 Trade Mark Office and Civil Courts

Revocation/cancellation action may be brought either before the Trademark Office or before the civil or criminal courts.

6.3 Statutory Limitation or Time Period

There is no statutory limitation or time period within which to file cancellation actions, but the cancellation for non-use may only be filed if the mark has not been used within five years from registration. There is a four-year statutory limitation for nullity actions.

6.4 Initiation of Revocation/Cancellation Proceeding

Any third party with an interest can file the cancellation actions and any third party, or even the Trademark Office, can file a nullity action. Costa Rican laws – mainly exercised through the Trademark Office and courts – have set a very flexible standard regarding the definition of interest, and therefore the petitioner should not necessarily have a strict legal or commercial interest to file the actions.

6.5 Partial Revocation/Cancellation

A partial cancellation over some goods or services is possible if the owner proves that there is some use of the goods or services.

6.6 Possibilities of Amendment

Amendment is not possible in revocation/cancellation proceedings in Costa Rica.

6.7 Revocation/Cancellation and Infringement

Actions involving revocation/cancellation and infringement are heard together.

7. Trial & Settlement

7.1 Special Procedural Provisions

Unfortunately, there are no special procedural provisions for trade-mark proceedings. All actions are treated equally to any other civil or criminal action.

7.2 Determination of Cases

All cases are determined by legal judges; parties do not have an influence on who is the decision-maker. However, parties may agree to submit the matter to arbitration, in which case they can agree how to select the arbitrator or arbitrators.

7.3 Possibilities of Settlement

A defendant can settle the case at any moment before the issuance of the final resolution. The Costa Rican judicial system encourages the settlement of actions and actually has formal mechanisms during the proceedings, such as a settlement stage with the judge and the parties.

7.4 Other Court Proceedings

If there are several actions filed in different proceedings regarding identical parties and trade mark, then all processes are accumulated into one.

8. Remedies

8.1 Existing Remedies
There are several remedies for a trade mark-owner such as damages, statutory damages if alleged, recovery of attorney's fees, an account of loss of profits and publicity notices. The judge has total discretion in ordering remedies. It is also possible to file for predetermined damages, in which case it is not necessary to prove actual damages.

8.2 Rights and Remedies
A prevailing defendant can have a reimbursement of attorney's fees and a declaration for non/infringement. Further, a publicity notice can be also awarded if requested.

8.3 Different Types of Remedies
All remedies are identical for any type of trade marks.

9. Appeal

9.1 Special Provisions
There are no special provisions concerning the appellate procedure for trade-mark proceedings; actually this is a flaw in the Costa Rican system.

9.2 Factual or Legal Review
The appeal is limited to a legal review rather than a factual review.

9.3 Length of Appeal from Trial Court
An appeal from a trial court decision normally takes 12-18 months.

10. Other Trade Mark Issues

10.1 Recognition of Dilution
The Costa Rican legal system does not recognise dilution, but if the mark is similar to a well-known mark and somehow jeopardises its rights, then an opposition can be filed.

Castro & Pal Abogados
Avenida 18, Calle 37A
Barrio Los Yoses Sur
Oficina esquinera gris
Zapote, 10105
San José
Costa Rica

Tel: +506 22348204
Fax: +506 22348337
Email: info@castropal.com
Web: www.castropal.com

10.2 Protection of Famous Marks
Costa Rica protects marks that are famous overseas but not yet in use locally, as long as the owner proves that the mark is famous. Among the evidence, the owner needs to demonstrate that the mark is considered as famous in any jurisdiction or that local consumers recognise the mark as famous.

10.3 Special Rules Regarding Geographic Indicators
There are no specific rules with regard to geographical indicators other than TRIPS dispositions.

10.4 Special Rules Relating to Surnames
Surnames are registered as any other word; therefore, if there is a pre-existing mark similar or identical to the surname, then the new mark will be rejected.

11. Costs

11.1 Costs Before Filing a Lawsuit
Usually, the costs associated before filing a lawsuit are charged on an hourly basis at an average rate of USD125-200.

11.2 Costs Regarding an Infringement Action
The costs are usually in a range of USD2,500 to USD7,500.

11.3 Costs of Litigation
All costs and fees should be paid by the parties. However, the prevailing party is awarded the right of obtaining reimbursement of attorney fees according to the Costa Rican Bar Association and of all the expenses.

12. Alternative Dispute Resolution

12.1 Common Way of Settlement
Although alternative dispute resolution (ADR) is encouraged by the legal system, it is not a common way to settle trade-mark cases. The most common ADRs processes are arbitration and mediation – these usually are conducted using the rules and before the Costa Rican Commercial Chamber or the America-Costa Rica Chamber of Commerce.

13. Trade Marks and Other Intellectual Property

13.1 Protection by Copyright
A trade mark can be protected by copyright in the case of logos or distinctive typography or numbers in the mark and as industrial designs for trade dress or three-dimensional marks.

ETHIOPIA

LAW AND PRACTICE:

Contributed by Tamrat Assefa Liban Law Offices

The 'Law & Practice' sections provide easily accessible information on navigating the legal system when conducting business in the jurisdiction. Leading lawyers explain local law and practice at key transactional stages and for crucial aspects of doing business.

Law and Practice

Contributed by Tamrat Assefa Liban Law Offices

CONTENTS

Contributed by Tamrat Assefa Liban Law Offices **Authors:** Tamrat Assefa, Marina Bwile

Tamrat Assefa Liban Law Offices has a vibrant practice in trade-mark work and assists major international companies with the prosecution, maintenance and defence of their trade marks. Particular areas of expertise include: trade-mark searches, securing and enforcing trade-mark rights, recording assignment, preventing unauthorised use of trade marks and providing advice on various issues.

Authors

Tamrat Assefa is managing partner and specialises in intellectual property law, foreign investment law, energy and natural resources, labour law, compliance/ regulatory work. He holds a certificate in the WIPO General Course on Intellectual Property.

Marina Bwile is a partner and specialises in intellectual property law, banking and finance, energy and natural resources, civil aviation law. She holds a certificate in the WIPO General Course on Intellectual Property.

1. Types of Trade Marks & Registration

1.1 Types of Trade Marks

Different types of trade marks are recognised in Ethiopia in line with the provisions of Article 2 (12) of the Trade mark Registration and Protection Proclamation No 501/2006, which defines a trade mark as any visible sign capable of distinguishing goods or services of one person from those of other persons, including words, designs, letters, numerals, colours or the shape of goods or their packaging, or the combinations thereof.

On the basis of this provision of law, the Ethiopian Intellectual Property Office (EIPO) registers marks under four categories: figurative marks, word marks, mixed marks and three-dimensional marks.

Collective trade marks are also recognised by the above-mentioned Proclamation, and registered separately under part four (Articles 18-23) of the same.

Rights in these trade marks are based solely on statutory law.

1.2 Trade-Mark Rights

Trade-mark rights are principally obtained through registration.

As an exception to the above, the Proclamation provides that trade marks are accorded protection in Ethiopia if they are entitled to protection as *well-known* trade marks under an international convention to which Ethiopia is a party.

The law permits the acquisition of rights if the trade mark becomes well known in Ethiopia through use. However, in practice, ownership rights of a trade mark are acquired and become binding on third parties only after the mark is registered and a trade mark registration certificate has been granted.

1.3 Standards for Registering

Other than collective marks where a copy of the statute governing its use would be required, the same standards of registration are used to register different types of trademarks, including product configurations.

1.4 Trade-Mark Register

There is a trade-mark register, which is publicly available.

1.5 Types of Registers

Only one type of register is maintained by the Ethiopian Intellectual Property Office.

1.6 Searching for Prior Trade Marks

In Ethiopia, trade-mark rights are not principally acquired by use and, as such, searches are only conducted in the register/database prior to applying to register a mark. It is normal practice to conduct such a search of the register.

Although some protection is accorded to well-known trade marks that are not registered, there is no practical way of conducting a search to find out whether these exist, and it is not normal practice to conduct a search for them.

1.7 Registration Requirements

An application for registration of a trade mark in Ethiopia needs to be made in a prescribed form and filed with the Ethiopian Intellectual Property Office, accompanied by the following:

- payment of the application fee;

- reproductions of the trade mark;
- a list of goods or services for which registration of the mark is requested, and the class numbers of the classification;
- if filed through an agent, a duly authenticated power of attorney granted by the applicant in favour of the agent;
- in the case of a collective mark, a copy of the statute governing its use;
- priority documents, if based on a prior registration outside;
- if it is three-dimensional, a drawing of the mark; and
- a copy of the foreign trade-mark registration certificate or a business licence (or its equivalent) confirming that the applicant is authorised to produce the goods or offer the service for which registration of the mark is sought.

1.8 Registering a Trade Mark

Any natural or juridical person with a legal personality can register a trade mark, except collective marks, which can be registered by trade unions, trade union federations or associations.

To fight against trade-mark squatting, the Intellectual Property Office has introduced rules published in a Directive, requiring applicants to prove that they are engaged in the field of business/activity in which they are seeking to register their trade mark, or alternatively prove that they have registered the trade mark in another country.

1.9 Registering Signs

Any kind of words, designs, letters, numerals or colours, or the shape of goods or their packaging, or any combinations thereof capable of distinguishing the goods or services of one person from those of other persons can be registered as trade marks in Ethiopia.

1.10 Other Rights to Signs

Rights to company names arise from the fact of entry in the Commercial register maintained by the Federal Ministry of Trade and the various State Bureaus of Trade. As a minimum, such registration gives the registrant the right to stop others from registering the same company name.

Although their difference from company names is somehow blurred and they are usually referred to interchangeably, there is a system of protection for Trade Names, laid down by the Commercial Registration and Business Licensing Proclamation No 980/2016. Trade Names have to be published before they are entered into the register and certificates of registration are issued by the Ministry and the various State Bureaux of Trade. The rights obtained upon registration for company and trade names have acquired greater importance since a recent decision passed by the Cassation Bench of the Supreme Court laid down the principle that prior registration in these registers precludes others from registering the same name in the Trademarks register. The decision lays down the rule that the registering authorities also have the obligation to conduct searches into each other's databases before they allow registration of new items into their registers.

In addition to the above, product names to be used in conjunction with pesticides, and other products used in agriculture (referred to as trade names in the particular legislation), are registered with the Ministry of Agriculture in accordance with the provisions of the Pesticide Registration and Control Proclamation No 674/2010.

1.11 Registration Procedure

Multi-class applications are permitted in Ethiopia.

The procedure for registering a mark is as follows:

- compilation of the required documents;
- presenting a filled-out application form along with the required documents to the Ethiopian Intellectual Property Office; there will be an examination and then the Office will send a letter to the Ethiopian Press Agency confirming that it can publish a Cautionary Notice in the local newspapers, in Amharic (Ethiopia's national language), at the client's cost;
- if no opposition is filed within 60 days of the publication of the notices, the trade mark will be registered upon presenting cuttings of the publication and paying the relevant fees.

1.12 Use in Commerce

Use in commerce is not a pre-condition for filing an application to register a trade mark in Ethiopia.

However, non-use for a consecutive period of three years after registration will give rise to a right for any interested party to submit a request for the cancellation of the trade mark. Unless the owner defends him or herself, or itself, by proving that the non-use was due to force majeure, the Intellectual Property office will cancel the trade mark.

Marks are registered in Ethiopia if the applicant can show that it owns the mark in another jurisdiction by providing a certified copy of the foreign registration certificate, or that it is licensed to manufacture the goods or provide the services it seeks to provide under the mark, by producing a certified copy of its business licence (or an equivalent document).

The fees for registering one mark in one class (including an estimate of publication costs, where actual cost depends on the size of the publication) are about ETB6,750 (about USD250), with a 50% increase in the official costs for every additional class.

The validity period for a trade-mark registration is seven years, with the possibility of renewing it for similar periods of time unless the mark becomes generic.

The fees for renewing a trade-mark registration in one class (including an estimate of publication costs, where actual cost depends on the size of the publication) are about ETB4,500 (about USD170), again with a 50% increase in the official costs for every additional class.

1.13 Registration of Series Marks

The registration of series marks as described above is permitted in Ethiopia on the same criteria as other marks. The Intellectual Property Office has introduced a Directive in which it limits the number of trade-marks to be included in one application to five.

1.14 Length of Registration Process

From the receipt of documents required to register a mark in Ethiopia, it takes about 120 days to get the trade mark registered and the trade-mark registration certificate granted.

If the applicant is a foreigner, the law requires them to appoint an agent who is domiciled in Ethiopia, under an authenticated power of attorney. The attorney/agent fees for a single mark in one class depend on the negotiations in a particular case, and range from USD500 to USD800 per mark.

1.15 Grounds for Refusal

The Ethiopian Intellectual Property Office would refuse to register a mark in the following circumstances:

(a) if it consists of sound or smell;
(b) if it is incapable of distinguishing the goods or services of a person from those of other persons;
(c) if it is contrary to public safety or morality;
(d) if it consists exclusively of signs or indications that designate the kind, quality, quantity, intended purpose, value, geographical origin of the goods or services, the time of production of the goods or rendering of the services, or other characteristics of the goods or services;
(e) if it consists exclusively of signs or indications that have become customary in the current language use in relation to such goods or services for which the registration of a trade mark is applied for, or which have become customary in economic and business activities;
(f) if it consists exclusively of a shape that results from the nature of the good itself or that is necessary to obtain a technical result of the good, or that gives substantial value to the good;
(g) if it is likely to mislead the public or the business community, particularly as regards the geographical origin of the goods or services concerned, or their nature or characteristics;
(h) if it is a trade mark that is identical to, an imitation of or contains an armorial bearing, flag or other emblem, a name or abbreviation or initials of the name or official sign or hallmark adopted by any state, intergovernmental organisation, or other organisation created by international conventions, unless authorised by a competent authority;
(i) if it consists exclusively of the surname of the applicant; or
(j) if it consists exclusively of the full name of a living individual without his or her consent.

The restrictions under items (d), (e) and (i) will not be applied if it is certified that, by the date of receipt of an application for registration of a trade mark, the trade mark has become well-known in Ethiopia as a result of its use.

1.16 Process for Overcoming Objections

The applicant is given 90 days to respond to the objection raised by the trade-mark office, with a possibility of extending the period by a further 90 days, twice. Depending on the objection raised, a relevant grounds refusal could be overcome by proving that similar marks are owned by the same entity and that there is no risk of confusing the customer, etc.

Acquired distinctiveness, which is referred to as the mark having become well-known in Ethiopia, is also used to defend against an objection on the basis of absolute grounds of refusal.

1.17 Consideration of Prior Rights

The trade-mark office considers prior rights in its examination of an application for registration, whereby similar marks for similar goods or services applied for or registered before the mark under examination, and found in its database, are given consideration.

1.18 Third-Party Rights

Third parties have the right to oppose an application for registration of a mark once a call for opposition is published in the newspapers, within 60 days of such publication. This time limit can be extended, once, for a further 60 days.

Anyone can bring such an action but, obviously, success at having the application for registration rejected depends on the strength of the rights or arguments raised by the third party.

1.19 Revoke, Change, Amend or Correct an Application

An applicant for registration of a trade mark can withdraw the application at any time while it is pending, or amend its application before the issuance of notice of acceptance for registration and publication for call for opposition by altering the pictorial representation of the trade mark shown in the original application, or reducing the list of goods or services, provided the change is not substantial.

1.20 Assigning an Application or Granting a Licence
It is possible to assign an application for a trade mark or grant a licence in relation to it during the application process.

1.21 Remedies Against the Trade Mark Office
Any person aggrieved by the final decision of the Office on the registration of a trade mark shall have the right to appeal to the court having jurisdiction, within 60 days.

1.22 Use of a Trade Mark
There is no requirement for an applicant to use its mark in commerce before a registration is issued.

1.23 Dividing a Trade Mark
It is possible to divide a trade-mark application into two or more separate applications at any time before registration of the trade mark. The requirements are that the applicant fills out a prescribed form indicating the specification of goods or services for each division, and pays the applicable charges.

Each division is treated as a separate application, with the same filing date as the original application.

1.24 Length of Term of Protection
The term of protection is seven years. The trade-mark owner can renew the trade mark within three months of the term lapsing without any penalty, and within six months thereafter with a penalty (50% of the renewal costs).

The trade-mark owner would be required to fill a prescribed form and file it with the trade-mark office upon paying the prescribed fees, and to publish a renewal notice in the local newspaper. The renewed trade-mark registration certificate can be issued with two months of the date of filing, depending on the backlog at the trade-mark office.

1.25 Requirements for an Exhaustion
Trade-mark legislation in Ethiopia favours international exhaustion of rights, as it provides that "Registration of the mark shall not confer upon the owner the right to preclude third parties from using the trade mark in relation to the goods lawfully sold in any country under that trade mark, provided that these goods have not undergone any change" (Article 27 (1) of the Trade mark Registration and Protection Proclamation No. 501/2006).

In light of the above provision of law, goods bearing the owner's mark must be lawfully sold in the third country in order for there to be an exhaustion of a trade-mark right under the laws of Ethiopia, and the goods must remain the same without any change.

1.26 Participation in the Madrid System
Ethiopia does not participate in the Madrid system.

1.27 Consequences for Providing Incorrect Information
The trade-mark office deals with these issues and would normally ask the applicant to correct the information it has provided when receiving the application from the applicant or at the time of examination, in which case the applicant will be given 90 days within which to comply with the request.

If the provision of incorrect information is discovered after registration and is fundamental to convincing the trade-mark office that the conditions laid down for the registration of trade marks were not initially fulfilled, the registration may be invalidated by the Office, based upon the provisions of Article 36 of the proclamation.

1.28 Updating or Refreshing a Design Mark
Save for minor changes that can be made on a design mark before it is accepted for publication, it is not possible in Ethiopia to update or refresh a design mark at any stage – either during the registration process or after the mark has been registered.

1.29 Denotation
There is no symbol that trade-mark owners should use to denote that a mark is registered.

2. Assignment and Licensing

2.1 Assignment Requirements or Restrictions
A right on a registered trade mark or an application for registration of trade mark may be assigned, or licensed in whole or in part. However, approval by the Intellectual Property Office is required.

The Intellectual Property Office may even reject the transfer if it is convinced that transfer to the new owner will have the effect of somehow confusing the public.

2.2 Procedure for Assigning a Trade Mark
The assignee fills out a prescribed form for the assignment of trade marks, files it with the Ethiopian Intellectual Property Office and pays the applicable fees. The trade-mark office will review the application and the assignment agreement, and thereafter send a notice concerning the assignment to the Ethiopian Press Agency for publication. Once published, a certificate confirming the recordal of assignment will be issued.

2.3 Registering or Recording the Assignment
The assignment needs to be registered with the trade-mark office to enable the assignee to exercise its ownership of the

mark in Ethiopia. If it is not registered, the rights to the trade mark will remain with the previous owner insofar as the authorities in Ethiopia or third parties are concerned. Despite this, there is no time limit for the registration of the transfer, and it may be registered at any time.

2.4 Trade Marks and Security
Trade marks can be given in security, assigned by way of security and levied in execution as part of the business.

2.5 Licensing Requirements or Restrictions
The Trade mark Registration and Protection Proclamation No 501/2006 permits the owner of a trade mark or an applicant for the registration of a mark in Ethiopia to grant any other person a licence to use its mark, by way of a contract.

The preconditions for granting such a contract are as follows:

- it should be made in writing
- it needs to indicate whether it is for all or part of the goods or services for which the mark is registered, or an application for the registration of the mark is filed for; and
- it has to be registered with the Ethiopian Intellectual Property Office.

There are no restrictions under the law on the type of licence an owner of a trade mark can give and, as such, it could be exclusive, non-exclusive, a sole licence, etc. However, a collective trade mark or an application for a collective trade mark may not be licensed.

2.6 Procedure for Licensing a Trade Mark
After the signing of the licence contract, the licensee fills in an application form provided by the trade-mark office, files it together with a copy of the licensing agreement with the trade-mark office, and pays the prescribed fee. The trade-mark office then causes a publication to be made in the local newspaper, following which a certificate confirming the grant of licence is issued to the licensee.

2.7 Registering or Recording the Licence
The licence agreement needs to be filed and registered with the trade-mark office, or it shall have no effect against third parties.

2.8 Reasons to Deny Granting a Perpetual Licence
There are no restrictions on the manner in which a trade-mark owner can grant a licence for use of its mark.

3. Opposition Procedure

3.1 Legal Grounds and Timeframes
The legal grounds under which one can oppose an application for registration of a trade mark, based on its third-party rights, are as follows:

- when the trade mark is identical to an earlier trade mark of another person in respect of the same or closely related goods or services, or if it so nearly resembles such a trade mark as to be likely to deceive or cause confusion;
- when it is identical or confusingly similar to – or contains a translation of – a trade mark that is well-known or established through use in Ethiopia for identical or similar goods or services of another person;
- when it is identical or confusingly similar to – or constitutes a translation of – a trade mark that is registered in Ethiopia for goods or services which are not identical or similar to those in respect of which the registration is applied for, provided that the use of the trade mark in relation to those goods or services would indicate a connection between those goods or services, and that the interest of the owner of the registered trade mark is likely to be damaged by such use; and
- when it contains anything that may be understood as the characteristic of another person's protected literary or artistic rights, or another person's right to a photograph or design without his or her written consent.

Despite the above, there is no clear restriction on the grounds of opposition and it is possible for a person to raise an opposition based on absolute grounds of refusal which were not raised by the Intellectual Property Office against the registration.

An opposition application needs to be filed within 60 days of the publication of the notice in the local newspaper. This timeframe can be extended once for a further 60 days if there are good grounds for seeking such an extension, eg, the client is obtaining the required supporting documents from various sources, and these are filed in good time.

3.2 Filing an Opposition
An opposition application can be filed by any person whose earlier trade-mark rights are likely to be compromised by the registration of the mark that has been advertised. It is understood that, just as in the case of an application for registration, foreign persons need to be represented by a person resident in Ethiopia.

The average office and attorney fees are USD650.

3.3 Opposition Procedure
The opposing party needs to fill in an application form containing clear and comprehensive grounds for opposing the

registration of the mark and file it with the trade-mark office within 60 days of the notice appearing in the local newspaper.

The trade-mark office will then provide a copy of the opposition application to the applicant or its agent in Ethiopia, legally within 30 days of the filing of the opposition, and at the same time inform the applicant of the period within which to respond to the opposition application – legally, a minimum of 90 days. (In practice, the trade-mark office calls the opponents or, if the EIPO officers know the agent of the applicant, serves the person when they appear at EIPO. They do not send any documents by post or employ process servers; this slows down the process because, if the other party does not have available contact details or does not visit EIPO, the proceedings cannot commence until the other party is served with the opposition application.)

If the applicant fails to respond within the time limit of 90 days, its application for the registration of the trade mark will be considered to have been abandoned, and the file marked accordingly.

If the applicant responds, the Trade mark's Directorate at EIPO would be required to render its decision on the opposition within 90 days of filing the response to the opposition.

3.4 Legal Remedies

If any party is dissatisfied with the decision of the Trade mark's Directorate at EIPO, they will have a right to appeal, first to the Appeals Committee within EIPO, within 60 days of the Trademarks Directorate granting its decision. The appeals committee examines the matter and submits a recommendation to the Director General of the EIPO. The decision given by the Director General of the Intellectual Property Office is considered the final decision of the EIPO. The Director General renders a decision within about six months of the appeal being submitted to the appeals committee.

If still dissatisfied with the decision, the person may appeal to the court within 60 days of the Director General granting a decision.

The Federal High Court will give a decision within an estimated period of one year from the submission of the appeal. A second tier appeal to the Federal Supreme Court may occur if the decision of the Intellectual Property Office is reversed, and will also take about a year to reach a decision.

Both sides will have a final recourse to approach the Cassation Bench of the Federal Supreme Court if they believe a fundamental error of law has been made in the decision rendered. It will take about a year and a half for the Cassation Bench to reach a decision.

4. Initiating a Lawsuit

4.1 Actions to Pursue Infringement

An owner of a registered trade mark can take the following actions against an infringer:

- issue a cease-and-desist letter;
- bring an action in a Civil Court with the objective of getting an injunctive order and also compensation; and
- report the matter to the Police with a view to them investigating and passing on their findings to the Attorney General's Office so that criminal action would be filed in court, and the infringing items seized and destroyed.

Provisional measures to stop entry of infringing items through a customs port or otherwise into the market, or to make sure that evidence is preserved, may be taken by court order upon an application by the owner of a registered trade mark. It would be almost impossible for the owner of a trade mark that is not registered to move the authorities and the courts to take the above actions, although theoretically there is protection for well-known trade marks.

An action under the provisions of the Commercial Code and the Trade Competition and Consumers' Protection Proclamation No 813 pertaining to unfair competition may be brought in a civil court or with the tribunals of the Trade Competition and Consumers' Protection Authority as appropriate, by owners of a trade mark that is not registered. This avenue is also available to owners of registered trade marks.

4.2 Initiating Infringement Proceedings

Infringement proceedings are normally initiated before the courts with jurisdiction on the matter, and where unfair competition is a consequence of the infringement before the adjudicative tribunal of the Trade Competition and Consumers' Protection Authority.

4.3 Effect of Decisions on Infringement Actions

The trade-mark office can give opinions to the court or tribunal hearing an infringement action, but it does not make decisions on infringement actions.

4.4 Declaratory Judgment Proceedings

There is no legal framework for declaratory judgments in Ethiopia.

4.5 Jurisdiction of Courts

The courts that have jurisdiction to hear trade-mark matters are as follows:

- First-instance court – for local trade marks;
- High court – appeals from the first-instance courts and initial hearings in respect of foreign trade marks;

- Supreme Court – further appeal (local marks) second instance for foreign-owned marks; and
- Cassation – final appeal.

4.6 Prerequisites to Filing a Lawsuit
Unless it is a claim for damages, it is not necessary for a formal demand letter or warning letter to be issued before filing a law suit, nor is it a requirement to engage in mediation unless there is an agreement requiring that parties attempt to settle their differences amicably before going to court. Mediation and other modes of alternative dispute settlement are not legal prerequisites to filing a lawsuit in Ethiopia.

4.7 Representation for Parties
From a legal point of view, there is no requirement for a lawyer to represent parties in trade-mark litigation matters. However, if the litigation involves foreigners, it may be inevitable that a local lawyer is hired because court proceedings (pleadings and hearing) in Ethiopia are conducted in the local language.

4.8 Interim or Preliminary Injunctions
Interim/preliminary injunctions are available when it can be proved that any property in dispute in the suit is in danger of being wasted, damaged or alienated by any party to the suit, or wrongfully sold in execution of a decree, or if there is a threat of the property being removed or sold with a view to defrauding creditors.

4.9 Protection for Potential Defendant
A potential defendant can ask the court to fix a duration of the injunction, the keeping of an account of any proceeds if it is a business, or the giving of security while the injunction is in force.

4.10 Obtaining Information and Evidence
There are mechanisms through which a party to a trade-mark matter can obtain relevant information and evidence from the other party or a third party. The Ethiopian Civil Procedure Code (CPC) grants authority to the court, either on its own motion or on the application of any of the parties, to send for records that would be useful in resolving the dispute before it.

For the court to grant such an order, an application for the production of records must show how the record is material to the suit in which the application is made, and that the applicant cannot obtain a duly authenticated copy of the record or of such parts thereof as the applicant requires, without unreasonable delay or expense, or that the production of the original is necessary for the purposes of justice. The record to be used in evidence must be admissible in the suit (Article 145 of the CPC).

4.11 Initial Pleading Standards
There are special provisions for lawsuits relating to trade marks that differ from non-intellectual property proceedings.

To commence a suit, the plaintiff/claimant/applicant is required to prepare his or her statement of claim, containing the following:

- the name and place of the court in which the action is brought;
- the title of the action;
- the name, description, place of residence and address for service of the plaintiff and defendant;
- where the plaintiff or defendant is a person under disability, a statement to that effect;
- where the plaintiff is suing in a representative capacity, a statement showing the capacity in which he or she is suing;
- the facts constituting the cause of action, and when and where it arose;
- the facts showing that the court has jurisdiction;
- the facts showing that the defendant is or claims to be interested in the subject-matter and is liable to be called upon to answer the claim; and
- where appropriate, a statement of the value of the subject-matter of the action.

The statement of claim will then be submitted to the Registrar of the court who will check it, open a file and provide it to the judge.

The judge will issue a summons, together with a copy of the statement of claim, to the defendant, requiring the defendant to appear in court on a date set by the judge, with his or her statement of defence, which shall contain the following:

- the name and place of the court in which the defence is filed;
- the number of the suit;
- the facts, if any, showing that the claim is inadmissible on grounds of want of capacity or jurisdiction, or limitation;
- a concise statement of the material facts on which the defendant relies for his or her defence and generally of any ground of defence which, if not raised, would be likely to take the opposite party by surprise or raise issues of fact not arising out of the statement of claim;
- a specific denial of any fact stated in the statement of claim which is not admitted; and
- precise details of the counterclaim, if any.

It is not possible to supplement pleadings with additional documents once they have been filed and accepted by the registrar, except in the case of a counterclaim made in defence, in which case the plaintiff will be permitted to make arguments to counter what has been claimed by the defendant.

4.12 Representative or Collective Actions
Representative or collective actions are permitted in trade-mark proceedings where it can be shown that several persons have the same interest in the suit to be initiated.

4.13 Restrictions on Trade Mark-Owners
A trade-mark owner cannot assert its rights against third parties in relation to goods lawfully sold in any country under his or her trade mark if the goods have not undergone any change, nor to bona fide use of their names, addresses, pseudonyms, a geographical name, or exact indications concerning the kind, quality, quantity, destination, value, place origin, time of production or supply of their goods or services, insofar as such use is for the purpose of information and cannot mislead the public as to the source of the goods or services.

5. Infringement

5.1 Action for Infringement
It is not possible for a third party that cannot demonstrate a right to a trade mark – either as an owner, licensee or assignee – to file an action for infringement.

In accordance with the trade-mark law, infringement proceedings may not be initiated before the date on which the trade mark is in fact registered.

5.2 Signs and Infringement
The factors considered in determining whether a use constitutes trade-mark infringement are:

- if the sign is identical or confusingly similar to – or contains a translation of – a trade mark and is utilised for identical or similar goods or services of the infringed mark;
- where such items are present and there is a likelihood that the use of the infringing mark will cause damage to the trade-mark owner; and
- when it contains anything that may be understood as the characteristic of another person's protected literary or artistic rights, or another person's right to a photograph or design without his or her written consent.

5.3 Use of a Sign by Defendant
It is necessary to establish that the defendant has used the sign as a trade mark in an infringement lawsuit. Authorities in Ethiopia would insist on evidence establishing such use before taking action against the infringer, such as a sample of the items with the sign.

5.4 Defences Against Infringement
Defences against infringement actions in Ethiopia are mainly prior rights and fair use.

5.5 Role of Experts and/or Surveys
The use of experts is not yet common but, where required, courts rely on opinions rendered by the Ethiopian Intellectual Property Office.

5.6 Administrative or Criminal Offence
Trade-mark infringement can constitute a criminal offence.

The activities involved in bringing a criminal action against an infringing person are lodging an accusation with the police, helping them in their investigation (providing proof of ownership of the intellectual property right concerned, usually through providing the certificate and going through additional correspondence with the IP office, making sure that they get proof of the infringing use, providing physical and witness testimony as necessary, locating and apprehending the persons responsible, etc), and then following up on the prosecutor who will handle the case and reporting on the court proceedings as necessary.

It can also constitute an administrative offence where it results in unfair competition.

Unfair competition proceedings are first brought before the adjudicative bench of the Trade Competition and Consumers Protection Authority, with appeals taken to the Federal Appellate Tribunal.

When determining the administrative penalty or measure to take, the adjudicative bench of the Trade Competition and Consumers' Protection Authority will take into account the following factors:

- the nature, duration, gravity and event of the offence;
- the damage suffered as a result of the offence;
- the market circumstances in which commission of the offence took place;
- the benefit derived from the offence;
- the economic status of the offender;
- the degree to which the offender co-operated with the body for the purpose of conducting investigations; and
- the previous behaviour and criminal record of the offender.

5.7 Custom Seizures
If the counterfeit items are all or in part at customs ports and stations, they can be seized and detained by the Ethiopian Revenue and Customs Authority (ERCA).

Under Article 42 (1) of the Trade mark Registration and Protection Proclamation No 501, ERCA is empowered to seize and detain counterfeit goods on the basis of a written application accompanied with a certificate of trade-mark registration and other relevant evidence made by the right-holder, and upon sufficient guarantee provided by the applicant.

It should be noted that this measure is temporary, and ERCA can release the seized and detained goods after crediting the furnished guarantee (to itself), unless the applicant brings a court injunction within ten working days.

Parallel importation is not restricted in Ethiopia and, as long as the product is genuine, authorisation from the owner of the trade mark to use it in Ethiopia is not required. Therefore, it is not possible to remove genuine products along with counterfeits.

6. Revocation/Cancellation

6.1 Remedies and Reasons

A trade mark can be cancelled if it can be demonstrated that the mark has not been in use in Ethiopia.

Under Trade mark Regulation No 273, "use of trade mark" is defined as attaching the trade mark to the goods or packaging or labelling of the goods, displaying the trade mark closely associated with the goods, placing the trade mark in advertising or promotional material for the goods or services, or in any other way establishing a relationship between the trade mark and the goods or services.

6.2 Trade Mark Office and Civil Courts

Cancellation actions are brought before the trade mark office, which adjudicates the case at the preliminary stage and thereafter at the appeal stage through its Appeals Committee. If any of the parties is still not satisfied, they will have the right to appeal to the civil courts.

6.3 Statutory Limitation or Time Period

There is no statutory limitation or time period within which to file revocation or cancellation actions.

6.4 Initiation of Revocation/Cancellation Proceeding

Legally, any interested person can initiate cancellation proceedings. The law requires there to have been continuous non-use for a minimum period of three years, unless the licensee or trade-mark owner proves there were legitimate reasons hindering the use of the mark, or unless there were force majeure events.

6.5 Partial Revocation/Cancellation

Partial cancellation is possible where it is shown that the non-use was in respect of only some of the registered goods.

6.6 Possibilities of Amendment

There are no legal provisions permitting or disallowing the amendment of revocation proceedings; it is at the discretion of the trade mark office.

6.7 Revocation/Cancellation and Infringement

Revocation and infringement cases are not only not held together but they are administered by different entities: cancellation by the trade-mark office and infringement by the courts.

7. Trial & Settlement

7.1 Special Procedural Provisions

Trade-mark proceedings are conducted in the same manner as other civil cases, with no procedural differences.

7.2 Determination of Cases

A normal judge sitting in a commercial bench conducts trade-mark proceedings. Parties have no influence on the appointment of the decision-maker.

7.3 Possibilities of Settlement

There are no formal mechanisms for settling cases, although parties can agree to settle the case out of court by filing a settlement agreement with the judge hearing the case.

7.4 Other Court Proceedings

It is currently unheard of for other court proceedings to have an influence on the current proceedings. A stay in the proceedings would be possible if a party applies to the court hearing the case to have the execution stayed because of a pending appeal.

In principle, no court can try any suit in which the matter at issue is also directly and substantially at issue in a previously instituted civil suit between the same parties, or between parties who claim to be litigating under the same title, where such civil suit is pending in the same or any other court in Ethiopia having jurisdiction to grant the relief claimed.

8. Remedies

8.1 Existing Remedies

The judge orders remedies in line with the applicable laws. The trade-mark law permits the court in a civil action to order an injunction or to order compensation for damages suffered by the claimant – a sum equal to the net profit derived by the defendant from the use or amount of royalty the defendant would have charged for the use of the mark, and legal fees incurred by the claimant.

8.2 Rights and Remedies
Where there was no infringement, the defendant will be entitled to recover the costs incurred in defending the suit.

8.3 Different Types of Remedies
There are no different types of remedies for different types of trade marks.

9. Appeal

9.1 Special Provisions
There are no special provisions concerning the appellate procedure for trade-mark proceedings.

9.2 Factual or Legal Review
The appeal to the Supreme Court and the cassation bench is limited to legal issues, without a review of the facts.

9.3 Length of Appeal from Trial Court
An appeal from a trial court decision will usually take about six months.

10. Other Trade Mark Issues

10.1 Recognition of Dilution
Dilution is recognised in Ethiopia as a ground to oppose a trade-mark registration or to prevent use of a mark in a lawsuit.

10.2 Protection of Famous Marks
There is no protection for marks that are well known outside Ethiopia but are not yet registered in the country; there needs to be use in Ethiopia as well.

10.3 Special Rules Regarding Geographic Indicators
There are no special rules relating to geographic indicators.

10.4 Special Rules Relating to Surnames
The use of a surname as a mark is prohibited; the trade-mark office will not register such marks.

11. Costs

11.1 Costs Before Filing a Lawsuit
The costs would be as follows:

COURT ACTIONS		
A. Civil Claim		
		Official fees (USD)
1	Initial Claim at the High Court	Less than 5, with an additional 1% of the claim if the claim is in excess of ETB200,000
2	Appeal to the Supreme Court	50% of the court fee paid at the High Court
3	Appeal to the Cassation Bench	50% of the court fee paid at the High Court
B. Criminal cases		
		Official fees (USD)
1	Representation in criminal court actions at all levels	0.00
C. Action before the Trade Competition and Consumers' Protection Authority		
		Official fees (USD)
1	Representations at the tribunal	To be paid against invoice / receipt where applicable

11.2 Costs Regarding an Infringement Action
The typical costs for bringing an infringement action to conclusion in the first instance are the same as the costs that arise before filing a lawsuit.

11.3 Costs of Litigation
The losing party usually bears the costs of the suit, unless the circumstances warrant that each party bears its own costs.

12. Alternative Dispute Resolution

12.1 Common Way of Settlement
Informal methods of alternative dispute resolution, including arbitration, mediation and conciliation, are in use and slowly becoming more popular. However, as far as is known, no intellectual property dispute has been settled through ADR, except through direct negotiation by the parties.

13. Trade Marks and Other Intellectual Property

13.1 Protection by Copyright

A trade mark can also be protected by copyright, provided the requirements for filing patents as laid down by the respective legislation are fulfilled, eg novelty and publication.

Tamrat Assefa Liban Law Office
Robel Plaza, 4th Floor, Room 405
Off Africa Avenue, Bole Medhane-alem area
P.O Box 1151 code 1250
Addis Ababa
Ethiopia

Tel: +251 11 667 0506
Fax: +251 11 667 0809
Email: info@ethiolegal.com
Web: www.ethiolegal.com

FRANCE

Contributed by Jacobacci Coralis Harle **Authors:** Séverine Redon, Maria Luisa Arce-Torrecilla, Jean-Mathieu Bertho, Olympe Vanner

Law and Practice

Contributed by Jacobacci Coralis Harle

CONTENTS

Contributed by Jacobacci Coralis Harle ***Authors:*** Séverine Redon, Maria Luisa Arce-Torrecilla, Jean-Mathieu Bertho, Olympe Vanner

Contributed by Jacobacci Coralis Harle ***Authors:*** Séverine Redon, Maria Luisa Arce-Torrecilla, Jean-Mathieu Bertho, Olympe Vanner

Jacobacci Coralis Harle is specialised in patents, trade marks, designs, domain names and copyright. Its main office is located in Paris but it also has offices in Nantes, Lyon and Bordeaux. The firm's key areas of trade-mark practice include: providing advice on the best strategies for protecting trade marks domestically and globally; management of worldwide trade marks portfolios; filing and prosecution of trade-mark applications in France, in the European Union and worldwide; performing searches for interference, identifying possible barriers for registration and advising on the risk of infringing third-party rights; advising on modifications to existing trade-mark portfolios to optimise protection; monitoring/surveillance services; filing and prosecution of oppositions and passive oppositions; drafting contracts (assignments, licences, co-existence agreements). Jacobacci Coralis Harle would like to thank Sandrine Cugini, Sophie Gaillard and Ericka Winogradsky and its trade mark department team for their valuable contribution to this chapter. Jacobacci Avocats was created in 2009 and is a law firm working with the full range of IP rights including trade marks, patents, designs and assists clients in all aspects of the management of those rights: contractual, pre-litigation and litigation. Competence in the area of contract drafting is accompanied by experience in enforcement of the same before national judicial authorities, the European Court of Justice and in multi-jurisdictional disputes. Jacobacci Avocats would like to thank Alexia de Maulde and Aurélie Robert for their valuable contribution to this chapter.

Authors

Séverine Redon has been a partner at Jacobacci Coralis Harle since 2010. Her practice entails: trade marks and designs prosecution; brand selection, portfolio management, IP due diligence; oppositions and cancellation actions; handling of negotiations for settlement agreements of conflict matters. She is experienced in prosecution work and oppositions filed before the European Union Intellectual Property Office (EUIPO), and in co-ordinating trade-mark litigations for clients throughout Europe. Séverine deals especially with the trade mark and design portfolio of companies operating in the fields of fashion, cosmetics, lighting and machinery, foodstuffs, and distribution, providing advice and helping to define strategy to ensure territorial and product protection to clients' brands.

Maria Luisa Arce-Torrecilla is senior trade-mark attorney at Jacobacci Coralis Harle. During her 25 years' experience in the intellectual property field, she has developed a significant expertise related to trade mark and design filing strategies in France and throughout the world, and in the management of trade mark, design and domain name portfolios. The core of her practice is industrial property law (trade marks, designs, indications of origin and geographical indications), copyright law, domain names, unfair competition, EC law, due diligence, Uniform Domain Name Dispute Resolution Policy (UDPR) proceedings, contracts related to Intellectual property rights, litigation in the field of trade marks, designs and unfair competition.

Jean-Mathieu Bertho is co-managing partner at Jacobacci Avocats. His practice focuses on trade-mark enforcement and litigation, patent litigation, copyright and registered design enforcement and litigation, unfair competition matters. Additionally, he has significant knowledge and experience in customs surveillance and e-business, with an extensive practice in competition law and business law. He is a member of APRAM (French association of practitioners in trade marks and registered designs), LES France (French intellectual property association), and of the expert college of UNIFAB (French trade association dedicated to fight against infringement).

Olympe Vanner is co-managing partner at Jacobacci Avocats. She specialises in trade-mark enforcement and litigation, copyright and registered design enforcement and litigation, unfair competition matters, anti-counterfeiting and customs activities, plus IT (in so far as it is related to IP). She is a member of APRAM and UNIFAB.

Contributed by Jacobacci Coralis Harle ***Authors:*** Séverine Redon, Maria Luisa Arce-Torrecilla, Jean-Mathieu Bertho, Olympe Vanner

1. Types of Trade Marks & Registration

1.1 Types of Trade Marks
In France, trade-mark rights are based on statutory law, namely the Intellectual Property Code (IPC), book VII, as interpreted by case law.

A trade-mark right can only be constituted by a registration (Article L.712-1 of the IPC), as French law does not recognise non-registered trade marks. As an exception, the rights arising from a non-registered well-known trade mark are recognised in accordance with Article 6bis of the Paris Convention on the French territory.

French law also provides for collective trade marks and certification trade marks. Collective trade marks can be used by any third party that complies with the regulations of use established by the trade-mark owner. Certification trade marks are a form of collective trade mark that applies to goods/services the characteristics of which are detailed in the regulations of use, and which can be filed and used under more restrictive conditions (Articles L.715-1 to L.715-3 of the IPC).

Other signs are also recognised, such as company names, trade names or shop signs.

1.2 Trade-Mark Rights
It is not possible to acquire trade-mark rights in France without registration.

1.3 Standards for Registering
There are no different standards for registering different types of marks, except for certification trade marks, which are to be filed along with their regulations of use.

1.4 Trade-Mark Register
Pending published trade-mark applications as well as registered trade marks are all recorded on the French trademark register, which also includes all recordals and renewals relating to trade marks. It is administered by the Institut National de la Propriété Industrielle (INPI) and its content is publicly available. The French Trademark Office publishes the Bulletin Officiel de la Propriété Industrielle (BOPI) every week, which provides information on pending trade-mark applications, registrations, deletions, etc.

1.5 Types of Registers
The French Trademark Office has a single register.

1.6 Searching for Prior Trade Marks
The French Trademark Office does not check the existence of prior trade-mark rights, so it is recommended to conduct preliminary availability searches among trade marks and other distinctive signs having effect in France in order to prevent any opposition proceedings or claims from owners of prior rights.

1.7 Registration Requirements
A trade-mark application can be filed with the French Trademark Office by one or several individuals or legal entities having legal capacity.

The application shall be filed in French.

In summary, the application shall include the identity of the applicant, a reproduction of the sign, a list of goods and services for which the protection is claimed and the corresponding classes, and the payment of relevant official taxes.

Specific provisions apply to certification trade marks.

1.8 Registering a Trade Mark
A trade-mark application can be filed in the name of an individual or a legal entity, provided that they have legal capacity. It is also possible to file a trade mark in co-ownership, as long as each of the co-owners has legal capacity.

Regarding certification trade marks, the applicant must be a legal entity that is not the manufacturer, importer or seller of the goods or services covered.

1.9 Registering Signs
According to the current definition provided by Article L.711-1 of the IPC, a trade mark or service mark is a sign capable of graphic representation, such as:

- words, including a simple word, combinations of words, surnames, geographical names, pseudonyms, letters, numerals, abbreviations;
- audible signs such as sounds and musical phrases;
- figurative signs, which can be three-dimensional, such as devices, labels, seals, selvedges, reliefs, holograms, logos, synthesised images, shapes, and arrangements, combinations or shades of colour; and
- combined word/figurative signs.

Moreover, EC Directive 2015/2436 relating to trade marks is to be implemented into French law by 14 January 2019 and no longer refers to the necessity of graphic representation of the trade mark, which will widen the scope of the signs likely to be registered.

1.10 Other Rights to Signs
French law recognises other signs that are not source identifiers by nature but could be used as such, including the following:

- company names – identify a company and are registered with the Trade and Companies Register;
- trade names – identify the specific commercial activity of a company and are registered with the Trade and Companies Register;
- shop signs – identify the location of a business and are registered with the Trade and Companies Register; and
- domain names; and
- geographical indications:
  (a) IGPIA (geographical indications of industrial and handmade products);
  (b) AOC (appellations of origin).

1.11 Registration Procedure
Once a trade-mark application has been filed, the French Trademark Office does the following:

- sends an official receipt with the filing date and the filing number;
- publishes the application in the Trademark Bulletin within six weeks and sends the publication notice;
- examines the application considering the formal requirements and the absolute grounds; and
- notifies opposition and/or possible grounds for refusal.

If all the requirements are met and no opposition is successful, the trade mark is registered and published in the Trademark Bulletin, and the French Trademark Office issues the registration certificate.

Multi-class applications are allowed.

1.12 Use in Commerce
French trade-mark law does not require the use of the sign prior to its filing as a trade mark.

A trade mark may survive on the register indefinitely (provided that it is regularly renewed), even if it is not used. However, a registered trade mark that has not been used for a continuous period of five years may be cancelled (upon the request of an interested party).

1.13 Registration of Series Marks
It is not possible to register series marks in the same application in France: an individual application must be filed for each sign seeking trade-mark protection, even if the signs only differ from the adjunction of non-distinctive elements.

1.14 Length of Registration Process
The applicant must be represented by an attorney if he or she has no establishment or residence within the EEA.

The designation of a representative is also mandatory if the application is filed in co-ownership, in which case the representative should be either one of the applicants or an attorney.

The office fees for a single mark up to three classes are EUR210 (+EUR60 if French Polynesia is included), and an additional EUR42 for each supplementary class.

A trade-mark application is usually registered within approximately five to six months of filing.

1.15 Grounds for Refusal
The registration of a trade mark can be refused by the French Trademark Office on the following absolute grounds:

- if the trade mark is devoid of any distinctive character (and has no distinctiveness acquired by use) with regard to the goods or services claimed in the application – eg, where the sign is, in the common or professional language, exclusively the necessary, common or generic designation of goods or services, or if the sign consists solely of an indication that may, in trade, be used to designate characteristics of goods or services and notably the kind, quality, quantity, destination, value, geographical provenance, time of the production of goods or time of the issuing of services;
- if the sign is constituted exclusively of the form imposed by the nature or function of the goods, or adds substantial value to the goods claimed in the application;
- if the sign is contrary to the public policy or the accepted principles of morality, or if the use of the sign is not legally authorised;
- if the sign is likely to deceive the public – eg, with regard to the nature, quality or geographical origin of the goods or services; and
- if the sign contains a sign excluded by Article 6 ter of the Paris Convention (such as national coats of arms, national flags or other national emblems, designations of international intergovernmental organisations, etc) or by Article 23§2 of annex I C of Agreement establishing the World Trade Organization.

1.16 Process for Overcoming Objections
If an objection is raised by the French Trademark Office against the application, the applicant is entitled to reply within a deadline set by the examiner. The response will be examined and, if it is well-grounded, the examiner will grant the trade-mark registration. However, if the response does not overcome all deficiencies stated in the objection, a decision will be taken to refuse the application, either totally or partially.

Please see **1.21 Remedies Against the Trade Mark Office** regarding the basis of the responses that can be filed by the applicant.

1.17 Consideration of Prior Rights

The French Trademark Office does not consider ex officio the existence of prior rights in its examination of an application for registration; only an interested third party can invoke a prior right through an opposition or observations.

Concerning the prior rights that can be invoked against a trade-mark application, please refer to **3.1 Legal Grounds and Timeframes** regarding the opposition procedure by third parties and legal grounds.

1.18 Third-Party Rights

Third parties may file an opposition or submit observations before the French Trademark Office, within two months of the publication of the trade-mark application.

An opposition may be filed by a limited number of persons, notably by the owner of a prior trade mark with effect in France or the exclusive licensee (under strict conditions). The proceedings are contradictory and lead to a public decision, unless the opposition has been withdrawn.

Any interested party may file observations drawing the attention of the Office to other regulations or facts that may render the trade mark invalid. The observations are transmitted to the applicant, but these proceedings are not contradictory. The Office will not render a decision, but may refuse the trade-mark application or suggest amendments to the applicant as a result of the third party's observations.

1.19 Revoke, Change, Amend or Correct an Application

A trade-mark application can be revoked freely at any time during the registration process. Amendments to the designation of goods or in the form of a limitation can be recorded during the registration process. Material errors can be corrected by the applicant during the registration process but before the beginning of the technical preparations for registration.

However, it is not possible for the applicant to amend the sign that constitutes the trade mark.

1.20 Assigning an Application or Granting a Licence

It is possible to assign a trade mark or grant a trade-mark licence during the registration process, on the condition that the trade-mark application has already been published.

However, there is a risk that the contract of assignment or the licence agreement will be considered null, and that the price will have to be refunded if the registration of the trade mark is finally denied.

1.21 Remedies Against the Trade Mark Office

The applicant is entitled to contest a refusal issued by the French Trademark Office based on absolute grounds. The applicant may submit evidence to the Office and argue against its decision. If the trade mark is refused for lack of distinctive character, then the applicant can provide the Office with evidence of acquired distinctiveness through use. If the trade mark is refused for deceptiveness, the refusal may, in some cases, be overcome by limiting the designation of goods. If the rejection is confirmed, the applicant may contest the decision before French courts.

For refusals based on relative grounds, please see **3 Opposition Procedure**, below.

1.22 Use of a Trade Mark

French trade-mark law does not require the use of a mark before it is registered. However, a registered trade mark that has not been used for a continuous period of five years may be cancelled (upon the request of an interested party).

Such a revocation can be avoided by proving genuine and serious use of the challenged sign for the challenged goods/services covered, with the following stipulations:

- the use must be public;
- the sign must be used in France;
- the sign must be used as a trade mark (and not as a company name, for example); and
- the sign must be used in the form in which it is registered or at least in a form that does not alter the distinctive character of the trade mark.

The courts shall consider all the facts and circumstances establishing the genuine use of the trade mark, particularly the uses in the economic sector concerned, the nature of the goods and services, the market characteristics, and the extent, frequency and duration of use.

1.23 Dividing a Trade Mark

A trade-mark application can be divided before registration. For example, if there is an opposition, or third-party observations, the applicant has the opportunity to divide the trade-mark application in order to obtain its registration for the goods/services that are not affected by the opposition/observation. To this end, the applicant has to file a new trade-mark application and specify in the application form that it is a divisional application. The divisional application has the same filing date as the initial one.

1.24 Length of Term of Protection

In France, a trade mark is protected for ten years from the date of filing, indefinitely renewable for a further term of ten years at a time through the filing of a declaration of renewal. If the term has lapsed, the owner benefits from a grace period of six months to renew its trade mark, for which additional fees are incurred. The renewal can be partial – ie, for some goods and/or services – but the list of goods and/or services cannot be extended.

1.25 Requirements for an Exhaustion

Article L.713-4 of the IPC provides that the owner of a trade mark is not entitled to prohibit the use of the trade mark in relation to goods that have been put on the market in the EEA under that trade mark by the owner, or with their consent.

An exception to this principle applies if the trade-mark owner justifies "legitimate reasons", such as the modification or alteration of the state of the product after it has been put on the market.

The burden of proof of the exhaustion– ie, that the goods have been put on the market in the EEA with the consent of the trade-mark owner – lies with the defendant claiming for it, unless that defendant establishes that there is a risk of market-partitioning.

1.26 Participation in the Madrid System

France joined the Madrid System in 1892. International registrations designating France can be rejected "wholly or partially" by the French Trademark Office within 12 months of the designation.

1.27 Consequences for Providing Incorrect Information

Incorrect information provided with the filing of a trade-mark application can be corrected upon request to the French Trademark Office, on the condition that it is amending purely material errors. If there is a substantial error in the application/registration, the trade mark may not be enforced.

1.28 Updating or Refreshing a Design Mark

An existing figurative trade-mark registration cannot be updated or refreshed; if the sign has evolved and the owner wishes to protect the new sign, a new trade-mark application with the refreshed version must be filed. The new trade-mark application can be filed in association with an anticipated renewal of the initial registration. Both trade marks must be identified in their respective filing forms in order to have the same renewal date in the future.

1.29 Denotation

There is no specific symbol to denote that a sign is a trade mark or that the trade mark is registered.

2. Assignment and Licensing

2.1 Assignment Requirements or Restrictions

The assignment of a trade mark must take the form of a deed between two or more persons (individual or legal) in which the owner of the trade mark transfers ownership to another person, who accepts the transfer. In order to be valid, the assignment must be made in a written contract (L.714-1 of the IPC).

The terms and conditions of the assignment are freely negotiated by the parties.

The trade marks to be assigned must be clearly identified, and the price must be determined by the parties.

The assignment may relate to a trade-mark application or a registered trade mark, and may concern all the designated goods and services or only a part of them. The rights are assigned for the entire territory of France.

Certification trade marks cannot be assigned.

2.2 Procedure for Assigning a Trade Mark

A trade mark must be assigned in writing, and the transfer of ownership may be recorded. Please see **2.3 Registering or Recording the Assignment.**

2.3 Registering or Recording the Assignment

There is no obligation to register the assignment, but it is recommended to record the change of owner before the French Trademark Office in order for it to be enforceable against third parties.

Without registration of the assignment, the assignee cannot take legal action before the courts nor file opposition against other trade marks on the ground of the assigned trade mark.

To register a trade-mark assignment at the French Trademark Office, it is necessary to complete a trade-mark transfer request form, to attach a copy of the deed of assignment and to pay the corresponding taxes.

The recordal request is then examined by the Office from a purely formal standpoint. The Office will not assess the lawfulness or validity of the contract.

2.4 Trade Marks and Security

The trade mark may be given as security, be subject to rights in rem, be assigned by way of security, or be levied in execution. To be valid, a pledge on a trade mark must be made in writing (L.714-1 of the IPC). The rights in rem and the seizure of the trade mark can be registered with the French Trademark Office, but there is no obligation to do so.

Contributed by Jacobacci Coralis Harle ***Authors:*** Séverine Redon, Maria Luisa Arce-Torrecilla, Jean-Mathieu Bertho, Olympe Vanner

Certification trade marks cannot be pledged.

2.5 Licensing Requirements or Restrictions

The licence agreement does not have to be in writing. However, it is recommended that the agreement be concluded in writing to prove the rights and obligations of the parties and to record it on the Trademark Register in order for it to be enforceable against third parties.

The licence may relate to a trade-mark application or to a registered trade mark. The trade marks must be identified. The trade-mark licence may be total or partial (to cover all designated products and services or only a part), may cover the entire territory or only part of it, and may be exclusive or non-exclusive.

2.6 Procedure for Licensing a Trade Mark

The licence agreement is freely negotiated by the parties, with no specific formal requirements. However, it is strongly recommended that a licence agreement is concluded in writing.

2.7 Registering or Recording the Licence

There is no obligation to record the licence agreement at the Trademark Register, but the recordal of the licence agreement has consequences as to the possible courses of action available to the licensee in the event of trade-mark infringement.

Only the recorded exclusive licensee is entitled to file an opposition in order to initiate a trade-mark infringement claim, provided that the licensee agreement does not provide for the contrary and that the trade mark-owner, after formal notice, does not himself or herself bring infringement proceedings within an appropriate period.

However, any licensee (even non-exclusive) is entitled to intervene in trade-mark infringement proceedings initiated by the owner of the trade mark in order to obtain compensation for the damage suffered by him or her.

2.8 Reasons to Deny Granting a Perpetual Licence

A perpetual licence shall be considered null and void, since French law prohibits perpetual undertakings and the validity of the licence is subject to the existence of the trade mark on which the licence is granted.

The licence agreement may be for a fixed or indefinite term, until either party terminates the contract or until the trade-mark registration lapses or is revoked or cancelled.

3. Opposition Procedure

3.1 Legal Grounds and Timeframes

In France, an opposition can be filed within a deadline of two months after the publication of the trade-mark application in the trade-mark bulletin (BOPI).

The opposition can be filed on the basis of the following prior rights:

- a filed or registered trade mark having effect in France;
- a well-known trade mark in France according to Article 6 bis of the Paris Convention;
- geographical indications for industrial and handmade products;
- the name, image or well-known character of a local authority;
- geographical indications for food products regulated by the French Rural and Maritime Fishing Code; or
- a private entity in charge of the defence and management of geographical indications (Article L.721-4 of the IPC).

3.2 Filing an Opposition

An opposition can be filed by the following persons:

- the owner or recorded exclusive licensee of a prior trade mark having effect in France (including the owner of a well-known trade mark according to Article 6 Bis of the Paris convention);
- the organisation in charge of the defence of geographical indications of industrial and handmade products; local authorities whose names are potentially infringed by the contested trade-mark application; and
- the institute in charge of the defence of geographical indications for food products – Institut national de l'origine et de la qualité (INAO).

The opposition may be filed directly by these persons or through a representative.

The designation of a representative is mandatory if the opponent is a foreign resident from outside the EEA. In such a case, the representative must be an attorney.

The designation of a representative is also mandatory if the opposition is filed on the basis of a co-owned prior right. In such a case, the representative should be either one of the applicants or an attorney.

The opposition taxes amount to EUR325.

3.3 Opposition Procedure

The notice of opposition is filed online before the French Trademark Office and must be supported by detailed grounds that develop the opponent's arguments and contain all documents cited.

The Office will notify the applicant of the opposition, and grant the applicant a period of two months to file observations in response.

In the absence of the applicant's observations, the Office will issue a final decision.

If the applicant submits observations, the Office will issue a draft decision. The parties will be given the opportunity to respond with additional observations with the aim of amending the draft decision and, if one of the parties so requests, they may be permitted to submit oral observations. Afterwards, the Office will render a final decision.

3.4 Legal Remedies

An appeal may be filed against the final decision of the Office before the Court of Appeal. The deadline for an appeal is one month from the notification of the decision by the French Trademark Office if the appellant is a French resident, two months if the appellant is a resident of a French overseas territory or department, and three if the appellant is a foreign resident.

4. Initiating a Lawsuit

4.1 Actions to Pursue Infringement

The trade-mark owner may initiate a trade-mark infringement claim before the courts only on the basis of a registered trade mark, within the principle of speciality (or beyond in case of a registered trade mark with a reputation).

By exception, a plaintiff may invoke an unregistered trade mark provided that the trade mark will be considered by French courts to be well-known pursuant to Article 6 bis of the Paris Convention for the Protection of Industrial Property of 20 March 1883.

4.2 Initiating Infringement Proceedings

A trade-mark infringement claim can be brought either before criminal courts (*Tribunal Correctionnel*), which have jurisdiction pursuant to the ordinary rules governing courts' competence, or before one of the ten specialised civil courts of first instance (*Tribunal de Grande Instance*), which have exclusive jurisdiction for trade-mark matters pursuant to Article L.716-3 of the IPC (Paris, Bordeaux, Lille, Lyon, Marseille, Nanterre, Nancy, Rennes, Strasbourg and Fort de France).

The Tribunal de Grande Instance de Paris has exclusive jurisdiction regarding European trade-mark infringement civil claims.

4.3 Effect of Decisions on Infringement Actions

Decisions rendered by trade-mark offices (either in France, at the European level or abroad) that do not affect the existence or the validity of a trade mark do not bind French courts regarding the assessment of infringement of that trade mark.

4.4 Declaratory Judgment Proceedings

Declaratory judgment proceedings are not admitted under French law.

4.5 Jurisdiction of Courts

In civil proceedings, there are ten specialised courts.

In criminal proceedings, the Tribunal Correctionnel is the court of first instance with jurisdiction.

In both criminal and civil proceedings, appeals can be brought before the *Cour d'appel* (court of appeals), which has jurisdiction pursuant to the ordinary rules of competence, and subsequent appeals before the *Cour de cassation* (Supreme Court).

4.6 Prerequisites to Filing a Lawsuit

A plaintiff should make a prior amicable attempt before filing a civil lawsuit, unless there are legitimate grounds resulting from an emergency or from the specificities of the subject under consideration.

This attempt usually consists of the sending of a warning letter.

However, according to the most recent case law rendered by lower courts, non-compliance with this prior amicable duty would not be a sufficient ground to jeopardise the validity of the proceedings.

Such a requirement does not exist before criminal courts.

4.7 Representation for Parties

The parties are required to be represented by a lawyer in trade-mark litigation before civil courts. This requirement does not apply before criminal courts.

4.8 Interim or Preliminary Injunctions

Pursuant to Article L.716-6 of the IPC, a preliminary injunction can be obtained in adversary proceedings before the Juge des référés against the alleged infringer or any intermediary in order to prevent an imminent infringement of a trade mark, or the continuation of it.

The Juge des référés assesses whether the evidence available makes it likely that there is a trade-mark infringement.

In a case of emergency and where required by the circumstances of the case, a preliminary injunction may even be obtained ex parte.

The judge may order appropriate and/or protective measures, such as cessation of the infringement under financial penalty, provisional damages, provisional seizure of assets, communication of evidence from the adverse party or from a third party (right of information), etc.

Subsequent to the issuance of the preliminary injunction, the right-holder must start proceedings on the merits within 20 working days or 31 calendar days (whichever is the longer period), failing which the measures ordered are null and void upon the request of the defendant, and the right-owner could be held liable.

4.9 Protection for Potential Defendant

Whereas no protective brief or declaratory proceedings are admissible under French law, the defendant may, in certain circumstances, require the trade-mark owner to post a bond.

Such a bond could be requested, notably when the right-holder requests a preliminary injunction or proceeds with a saisie-contrefaçon.

Additionally, the defendant may try to paralyse the proceedings of the plaintiff by challenging the validity of the trade mark invoked.

4.10 Obtaining Information and Evidence

There are two mechanisms that enable a party to obtain information from an alleged infringer or even a third party.

The first is the saisie-contrefaçon (Article L.716-7 of the IPC), which is an ex parte order authorising a bailiff to proceed with a seizure of products or documents in the premises of the alleged infringer or any third party.

Such a proceeding is usually used before any action on the merits to evidence the infringement, but could also be used in the course of a pending proceeding.

In particular, the bailiff may be authorised to seize samples of the infringing products in order to evidence the infringement, and to seize all documents relating to the alleged infringement, notably accounting documents (order forms, invoices, catalogues, advertisements, etc) in order to prove the extent, origin and destination of the infringement. The judge may also order the seizure of all the materials used to produce or distribute the alleged infringing products, and of all related documents.

Once a saisie-contrefaçon has been performed, the right-holder must start proceedings on the merits within 20 working days or 31 calendar days (whichever is the longer period), failing which the measures ordered are null and void upon the request of the defendant, and the right-owner-could be held liable.

The second mechanism is the right of information (Article L.716-7-1 of the IPC), which enables the courts to order the disclosure of information on the origin and distribution networks of the alleged infringing goods, possibly under penalty, from the alleged infringer or any third party related to or taking part in the alleged infringement.

This disclosure of information is possible only where there is no legitimate impediment.

The right of information can be enforced in pending proceedings (action on the merits or summary proceeding), and does not require a prior ruling on the infringement.

4.11 Initial Pleading Standards

The burden of proof of the trade-mark infringement lies with the plaintiff, who has to demonstrate the existence of the trade mark and the infringement (usually ascertained by a bailiff report or a saisie-contrefaçon), and of elements relating to the loss suffered in order to obtain damages.

Additionally, in criminal proceedings, the plaintiff has to evidence the bad faith of the infringer – ie, that the infringer knowingly infringed the trade-mark rights. This is not required before civil courts.

In most proceedings, it is possible to file additional written submissions and evidence in the course of the proceedings before the closing of the written phase and the pleading.

4.12 Representative or Collective Actions

Representative or collective actions such as class actions are not possible for trade-mark proceedings.

However, it must be noted that associations or representatives could be authorised to intervene in pending proceedings as amicus curiae.

4.13 Restrictions on Trade Mark-Owners

Several restrictions to the enforcement of a trade-mark infringement may arise, including the abuse of right, where the claims are grounded but the rights are exercised only to cause annoyance, harm or injury to another party.

Other restrictions are linked to competition law pursuant to Articles 36 and 101 of the Treaty on the Functioning of the European Union, according to which trade-mark enforcement shall not constitute a means of arbitrary, discriminatory or disguised restriction on trade between European Union States.

In particular, the rule of exhaustion of trademark rights applies, whereby the trade mark-owner shall not obtain the prohibition of the use of their trade mark in relation to goods that have been put on the market in the EEA under that trade mark by them or with their consent.

More generally, French courts may restrict the enforcement of a trade-mark right when it contradicts other fundamental rights, such as the freedom of speech, public health, etc.

5. Infringement

5.1 Action for Infringement

A trade mark-owner can initiate a trade-mark infringement action against any infringer that reproduces, imitates, uses or affixes the litigious trade mark for identical or similar products or services. Infringing acts include manufacturing, importing, exporting, detaining, promoting, offering for sale and selling of any infringing product.

A trade mark-owner is able to take action to stop infringement before his or her trade mark is registered, provided that the infringing acts intervene after the publishing of the trade-mark application at the Trademark Bulletin; additionally, even before the publishing of the application, the trade mark-owner may pursue any infringing act after sending a copy of the filed trade-mark application to the infringer.

In such cases, the proceedings will be stayed until the publication of the registration of the trade mark.

The registered exclusive licensee is also entitled to initiate trade-mark infringement proceedings (under conditions), and all licensees are entitled to intervene in the trade-mark infringement claim initiated by the trade mark-owner in order to obtain compensation for their own damage.

5.2 Signs and Infringement

There are two kinds of trade-mark infringements: by reproduction or by imitation.

Where the litigious sign identically reproduces a trade mark to cover identical goods or services, it is said to be an infringement by reproduction and the assessment made by the court shall remain limited to the comparison of the signs and goods/services in order to confirm that they are indeed identical.

Where the litigious sign is identical or similar to the trade mark and is used in relation to goods and services that are identical or similar to the goods or services for which the trade mark is registered, it is said to be an infringement by imitation and the court shall determine whether there is a likelihood of confusion on the part of the public because of those similarities.

In making this assessment, the court will take several factors into account, such as the distinctiveness of the prior trade mark or of the part of the sign which is imitated, the reputation of the prior trade mark, and the degree of similarity between the signs and the goods/services concerned.

A high degree of similarity between signs may compensate for a lower degree of similarity between goods/services and vice versa. Additionally, the more distinctive or well-known the prior trade mark is, the more easily the infringement will be admitted.

Infringement by either reproduction or imitation requires evidence that the use of the litigious sign in the course of trade affects one of the trade mark's functions, which are the guarantee of origin ("the essential function of the trade mark"), the guarantee of the quality of the goods or services in question, and the functions of communication, investment or advertising.

5.3 Use of a Sign by Defendant

When ruling on a trade-mark infringement claim, the court will ensure that the litigious sign is used in the course of trade as "a trade mark", ie, for indicating the origin of the good or service.

The mere use of a figurative sign as a decoration or the use of a word in its common sense, even if it is registered as a trade mark, shall not be considered as an infringement as long as it is not perceived by the public as an indication of origin.

5.4 Defences Against Infringement

To challenge the existence of a trade-mark infringement, the means of defence before civil courts are usually as follows:

- invalidity of the trade mark (for fraudulent registration, lack of distinctiveness, lack of descriptiveness, prior rights of the defendant on the sign such as a prior trade mark, a copyright, etc);
- revocation of the trade mark (for non-use, or for becoming generic or deceptive;)
- lapse of time (five years for civil actions, six years for criminal actions);
- tolerance of the use of the litigious sign for five years;
- contradiction with another fundamental right, such as freedom of speech;
- differences between the signs and goods and/or services; and
- lack of use as a trade mark and/or lack of infringement to the trade mark's functions;

The possible good faith of the infringer is not a relevant means of defence before civil courts, unlike criminal courts.

5.5 Role of Experts and/or Surveys

Surveys or an expert's affidavit are admissible as evidence before courts. The affidavits and surveys have to be objective and originate from third parties whose integrity is unquestionable.

French courts strictly control the size and constitution of the panel for surveys, the objective character of the questions, the interpretation of the results, etc.

If the evidence submitted is not sufficiently objective, the court will not consider it.

5.6 Administrative or Criminal Offence

Trade-mark infringement can constitute a criminal offence, which can be pursued before criminal courts.

The proceedings can be initiated either by a complaint filed before the Public Prosecutor, or by a writ of summons directly served to the infringer.

Trade-mark infringement can notably be sanctioned with up to seven years' imprisonment and a fine of up to EUR1.5 million.

5.7 Custom Seizures

European and French laws provide for an efficient system for customs' seizure of counterfeits (which does not apply to parallel imports).

According to the IPC and EC Regulation 608/2013, trade mark-owners can apply for action by the customs authorities against goods suspected of infringing their trade marks.

Customs authorities may detain goods suspected of infringing trade marks for ten days (or three days for perishable goods), so the trade mark-owner may evaluate the genuine character of the goods.

Information regarding the holder/origin/destination of the suspicious goods and their quantities can be disclosed to the trade mark-owner.

If the infringing character of the goods is confirmed, the trade mark-owner may request their destruction (without further court action if the holder does not oppose) and/or initiate a court action.

6. Revocation/Cancellation

6.1 Remedies and Reasons

Any third party that has a legal interest to do so may initiate an action in order to request the cancellation or revocation of a French trade mark.

Whereas revocation applies from the date of the request, a successful claim for invalidity has a retroactive effect as of the date of filing.

A French trade mark may be declared invalid based on absolute grounds as mentioned in **1.15 Grounds for Refusal**, such as lack of distinctive character, genericness, descriptiveness, deceptive character of the trade mark, violation of public policy or accepted principles of morality, etc (L.711-2 and L.711-3 of the IPC). Any trade-mark application fraudulently filed by an applicant acting in bad faith shall also be declared invalid.

Pursuant to Article L.711-4 of the IPC, a French trade mark may also be cancelled based on relative grounds invoked by the concerned third party and, notably, where the trade mark infringes any of the following:

- an earlier mark that has been registered or that is well-known within the meaning of Article 6 bis of the Paris Convention for the Protection of Industrial Property;
- the name or style of a company, where there is a risk of confusion in the public mind;
- a trade name or signboard known throughout the national territory, where there is a risk of confusion in the public mind;
- a protected appellation of origin;
- authors' rights;
- rights deriving from a registered design;
- the personality rights of another person, particularly his or her surname, pseudonym or likeness; or
- the name, image or reputation of a local authority.

The revocation of a trade mark can be requested by any third party that has a legal interest to do so in three circumstances:

- if the trade mark has not been genuinely used for a continuous period of five years following its registration;
- if, as a consequence of acts of the owner, the trade mark has become the common name for a product or service for which it is registered and the proprietor has not taken sufficient measures to prevent this; or
- if, as a consequence of the use made of it by the owner, the trade mark has become misleading as to the nature, quality or geographical origin of the goods and services for which it is registered (L.714-5 and L.714-6 of the IPC).

6.2 Trade Mark Office and Civil Courts
Both cancellation and revocation actions are to be brought before one of the ten specialised civil courts.

6.3 Statutory Limitation or Time Period
A cancellation action can be initiated at any time after the registration of the trade mark, with the following deadlines:

- for a cancellation action based on a well-known trade mark within the meaning of Article 6 bis of the Paris Convention for the Protection of Industrial Property: five years from the registration of the litigious trade mark unless it has been registered in bad faith; and
- for a cancellation action based on any other ground, the lapse of time is five years from the knowledge of the existence of the litigious registration and of the ground for cancellation.

Additionally, the principle of acquiescence will apply for all kinds of cancellation actions (except bad faith of the registrant): if a party fails to initiate a trade-mark infringement claim against another party within five years of gaining knowledge of the use of the trade mark, they shall no longer be entitled to do so.

However, the cancellation of the trade mark can always be invoked by the defendant seeking trade-mark infringement as a means of defence, without any time limit.

6.4 Initiation of Revocation/Cancellation Proceeding
Cancellation and revocation actions can only be initiated by a third party that has a real and present interest in obtaining such a cancellation/revocation.

Courts systematically assess the existence of a real and present interest for the claimant, who has to evidence that the challenged trade mark prevents their use of their own trade mark or the launch of identical/similar goods on the market under the same/similar trade mark.

To bring such evidence, the claimant can file documents in relation to preparation for use of the sign, such as evidence that a logo has been designed and/or market study and/or possible press publishing related to the likely launch of the brand in France, and/or documents that evidence that the claimant already uses a similar sign in other countries and wishes to expand to France, etc.

The Public Prosecutor is also entitled to initiate a revocation action as well as a cancellation action, but only on the grounds of "public interest" (ie, not for infringement to prior rights of third parties); this is very rare in practice.

6.5 Partial Revocation/Cancellation
Partial revocation or cancellation limited to particular goods and services is likely to be ordered when the ground for cancellation/revocation affects only part of the goods and services covered (a trade mark not being used for a few goods, for instance, or if the trade mark is devoid of distinctive character for only part of the services covered, etc).

6.6 Possibilities of Amendment
No amendment is possible in revocation or cancellation proceedings, but the trade-mark owner is always in a position to delete goods and services from its registration in order to limit the risk of litigation, or to negotiate an out-of-court settlement with the claimant.

6.7 Revocation/Cancellation and Infringement
Revocation and cancellation actions can be initiated per se, but most of the time they constitute a defence to a trade-mark infringement claim.

The duration of the proceedings will depend on which court has jurisdiction and the particularities of the case.

7. Trial & Settlement

7.1 Special Procedural Provisions
Trade-mark proceedings shall comply with the general civil (or criminal) procedural rules but there are a few special procedural provisions, notably concerning the saisie contrefaçon, the summary proceeding, the jurisdiction of the specialised civil courts and the right of information.

7.2 Determination of Cases
Trade-mark matters are determined by three professional judges before both civil and criminal courts (in first instance and on appeal).

7.3 Possibilities of Settlement
Unless specific circumstances apply, the plaintiff is required to seek an amicable outcome before initiating a civil action. Most of the time, this involves sending a cease-and-desist letter.

Except the above, and unless the parties are contractually bound to seek an out-of-court settlement or have recourse to mediation or arbitration, there is no formal mechanism for negotiation.

The parties may nonetheless decide to negotiate on their own at any time or request the assistance of the court, which also has a duty to help the parties negotiate.

7.4 Other Court Proceedings

Staying of proceedings can be ordered if another court could render a decision on a question that is likely to affect the case in hand (pursuant to Article 378 of the Civil Procedure Code).

Therefore, for instance, a trade-mark infringement could be stayed pending resolution of a parallel revocation/cancellation of that trade mark in another forum.

The exception of lis pendens could also have an impact when several actions for infringement or a declaration of non-infringement are launched – ie, only the first court seized could have jurisdiction.

8. Remedies

8.1 Existing Remedies

If the infringement is admitted by French courts, the trade mark-owner is likely to obtain the prohibition of use of the litigious sign, financial remedies, the withdrawal and recall of the litigious goods from distribution networks at the expense of the infringer, the destruction of the infringing goods, and the publication of the decision in a newspaper, magazine and/or on the website of the infringer, at the latter's expense.

Financial remedies are assessed by the courts at their own discretion, based on the evidence submitted by the parties. When setting the damages, the court takes into account the negative economic consequences suffered by the owner of the trade mark (including lost profits), profits made by the infringer and moral prejudice caused to the owner of the right because of the infringement.

Alternatively, upon the request of the plaintiff, the court can set the damages as a lump sum, the amount of which must be higher than the royalties that would have been due if the infringer had requested authorisation to use the right at issue.

The court can also order the closing-down of the company (totally or partially, permanently or temporarily) and prohibit it from pursuing the same activities.

8.2 Rights and Remedies

If a trade-mark infringement claim is dismissed, the defendant is entitled to claim reimbursement of their attorney fees, which is usually at least partly granted. If the proceedings were initiated in a culpably thoughtless manner, the plaintiff could be sentenced to pay a fine (maximum EUR10,000), as well as damages to the defendant.

8.3 Different Types of Remedies

All possible remedies are the same, regardless of the type of trade mark.

9. Appeal

9.1 Special Provisions

There are no special provisions concerning the appeal of trade-mark proceedings.

9.2 Factual or Legal Review

The court of appeal will render a ruling on both factual and legal points of view, but limited to the rulings of the judgment against which the parties have filed an appeal.

9.3 Length of Appeal from Trial Court

The appeal proceeding usually lasts 12-24 months.

10. Other Trade Mark Issues

10.1 Recognition of Dilution

Dilution shall not constitute a ground for opposition or for trade-mark infringement per se, but is taken into account in the assessment of the likelihood of confusion and, more importantly, in the assessment of the infringement to a well-reputed trade mark within the meaning of Article L.713-5 of the IPC.

10.2 Protection of Famous Marks

A trade mark that is famous outside France but not in use or registered in France is not entitled to any protection in France.

The only reservation would be fraudulent registration – ie, when a party purposely and fraudulently registers a trade mark in order to prevent its use by another party.

10.3 Special Rules Regarding Geographic Indicators

A geographical indication is a sign that allows the identification of products that have a precise geographical origin and possess qualities, a notoriety or characteristics related to that place of origin.

French law recognises two types of protected geographical indications: those for industrial and handmade products, and those for food products.

The geographical indications for industrial and handmade products are registered with the French Trademark Office. The application must contain certain specifications, describing notably:

- the quality, reputation, traditional know-how or other characteristics of the product concerned that can be attributed essentially to that geographical area or location, and the elements linking the product to the geographical area or the associated determined place;
- the production and processing, including the production or processing operations that must take place in the geographical area or the specific place, and those that guarantee the characteristics of the product;
- the identity of the defence and management body, its statutes, the list of initial operators it represents and the financial arrangements for their participation; and
- the methods and frequency of the controls carried out by the bodies.

The geographical indications for food products are recognised with the Institut national de l'origine et de la qualité (INAO). Applications for recognition of geographical indications for food products must also contain certain specifications, describing notably:

- the geographical area concerned;
- the conditions for the production of the products; and
- the methods and frequency of the controls of the products.

10.4 Special Rules Relating to Surnames

Article L. 713-6 of the IPC provides that the trade-mark right cannot be enforced against the use of one's own surname as a corporate name, a trade name or a shop sign, when that use is made in good faith.

However, this exception does not allow the registration of the surname as a trade mark.

Furthermore, the aforesaid use can be limited or forbidden by the judge when it is prejudicial to the prior trade-mark right or when it does not comply with honest practices in industrial or commercial matters, which is notably the case when proper precautions were not taken to avoid a likelihood of confusion.

As the scope of this derogatory rule is strictly framed, the use of a surname shall therefore not be permitted when it causes harmful confusion with a pre-existing trade mark.

Jacobacci Coralis Harle
32, rue de l'Arcade
75008 Paris
France

JACOBACCI & CORALIS·HARLE

Tel: +33 1 53 04 64 64
Fax: +33 1 53 04 64 00
Email: marks.france@jacobacci.com
Web: www.jacobacci-coralis-harle.com

11. Costs

11.1 Costs Before Filing a Lawsuit

Costs that arise before filing a lawsuit can be estimated at between EUR500 and EUR2,000 for a warning letter, and EUR5,000 for saisie-contrefaçon proceedings.

11.2 Costs Regarding an Infringement Action

The typical costs for bringing an infringement action are EUR5,000-25,000 for summary proceedings, and EUR5,000-40,000 for proceedings before a court of first instance.

11.3 Costs of Litigation

The court may order the losing party to reimburse the legal costs of the winning party, totally or partially, on the ground of Articles 699 and 700 of the French Civil Procedure Code.

Courts are usually reluctant to award the total of the amount requested by the parties, even though they may be more inclined to do so if these amounts are fully justified (for example, by providing the court with invoices).

12. Alternative Dispute Resolution

12.1 Common Way of Settlement

Negotiations are always possible between the parties, and are always encouraged by the courts. Most of the time, these negotiations take place directly between the parties, and ADR is not common in trade-mark matters.

13. Trade Marks and Other Intellectual Property

13.1 Protection by Copyright

A sign registered as a trade mark may also be protected by additional IP rights, such as copyright or even registered design, as long as the conditions of their protection are fulfilled.

GERMANY

LAW AND PRACTICE: p.133

Contributed by SZA Schilling, Zutt & Anschütz

The 'Law & Practice' sections provide easily accessible information on navigating the legal system when conducting business in the jurisdiction. Leading lawyers explain local law and practice at key transactional stages and for crucial aspects of doing business.

Contributed by SZA Schilling, Zutt & Anschütz **Authors:** Thomas Nägele, Steffen Henn, Anke Hofmann, Alexander Stolz

Law and Practice

Contributed by SZA Schilling, Zutt & Anschütz

CONTENTS

Contributed by SZA Schilling, Zutt & Anschütz **Authors:** Thomas Nägele, Steffen Henn, Anke Hofmann, Alexander Stolz

Contributed by SZA Schilling, Zutt & Anschütz **Authors:** Thomas Nägele, Steffen Henn, Anke Hofmann, Alexander Stolz

SZA Schilling, Zutt & Anschütz For almost a century, Schilling, Zutt & Anschütz has been one of the most reputable German corporate law firms and advises domestic and international clients in nearly all areas of corporate and commercial law with currently over 80 attorneys. The IP/IT department of SZA is located in Mannheim and Frankfurt and practises currently with seven attorneys in all areas of Intellectual Property and Information Technology law as well as in the area of Data Protection law. Head of the IP/IT department is Dr Thomas Nägele, a certified Expert Attorney for Intellectual Property Law and author of numerous publications in his respective area. With the establishment of the China Desk SZA provides consultation for Chinese companies regarding investments and business activities in Europe in all fields pertaining to commercial law, especially such as protection of intellectual property, including the registration, defence, judicial and out-of-court enforcement of brands, patents and know-how. Further, in mutual cooperation with leading local law firms, SZA also provides consultation in the field of industrial property rights for European companies regarding their business in China.

Authors

Thomas Nägele is a partner specialising in intellectual property, trade mark & unfair competition, patent litigation, information technology, cyber security and data protection. He is a lecturer at the University of Heidelberg and a member of numerous professional bodies such as the executive committee of IZG - Interdisziplinäres Zentrum für Geistiges Eigentum (Interdisciplinary Centre for Intellectual Property) an der Universität Mannheim e.V. He has contributed a large number of articles to industry publications.

Steffen Henn is of counsel (senior associate). His practice covers copyright, unfair competition law, trade-mark law, information technology law and litigation. He is a member of the Deutsche Vereinigung für gewerblichen Rechtsschutz und Urheberrecht (GRUR) e.V.; Deutsche Gesellschaft für Recht und Informatik. He writes regularly for industry publications.

Anke Hofmann is an associate. Her practice covers copyright, unfair competition law, trade mark law, information technology law and litigation. She has produced numerous articles for industry publications..

Alexander Stolz is an associate specialising in copyright, unfair competition law, trade mark law, information technology law, media law and litigation. He has made several contributions to German law journals.

1. Types of Trade Marks & Registration

1.1 Types of Trade Marks

German trade-mark law has different types of trade marks. Registered trade marks are the most commonly used. However, several unregistered signs – such as unregistered trade marks which acquired protection by extensive use, company designations (eg company names), domains and work titles – and indications of geographical origin are also protected. As Germany has a civil law system, rights in such marks are based on statutory law. However, beyond that, there is a variety of case law, specifying and implementing the statutory law. It is worth noting that such case law is not formally binding but has strong authority in practice.

1.2 Trade-Mark Register

The German trade-mark register is administered by the German Patent and Trademark Office (Deutsches Patent- und Markenamt, located in Munich, hereinafter referred to as "DPMA"). The register, which contains any trade marks applied for, registered, refused or cancelled, is freely available online. Registrations of trade marks are also published in the official electronic Trade Mark Journal (Markenblatt). Not to be confused with the trade-mark register are the German commercial register (Handelsregister), in which companies (including company names) are listed, and the privately organised domain name register for the top level domain ".de".

1.3 Registration Requirements
Protection as a trade mark may accrue from:

- the entry of a sign as a trade mark in the register kept by the DPMA (registered trade mark);
- the use of a sign in the course of trade, insofar as the sign has acquired public recognition as a trade mark within the relevant trading public (trade mark acquired by use); or
- a trade mark constituting a famous mark within the meaning of the Paris Convention for the Protection of Industrial Property (hereinafter referred to as "Paris Convention") (famous trade mark).

An application to enter a trade mark in the register must be submitted to the DPMA and must contain the following:

- information permitting verification of the identity of the applicant;
- a reproduction of the trade mark; and
- a list of the goods and/or services for which registration is sought.

As a general rule, any company, partnership and any private individual can apply for a trade mark for any type of goods or services. A business establishment is not required.

The formal requirements how to submit a trade mark application for the different trade mark types are stipulated in detail in the German Trade Mark Regulation (Markenverordnung).

1.4 Registering Signs
Provided that the sign is appropriate to be distinctive, any type of perceptible sign might be protected as a trade mark. Consequently, besides word marks and figurative marks (which are the most common trade mark types) there are also combined word/figurative marks, sound marks, olfactory marks, colour marks, movement marks, slogans and three-dimensional marks. Combinations of different trade mark types are also possible, for example, three-dimensional signs with a word or image component. However, as a trade mark may only be registered if it is graphically representable under German law, the registration of olfactory marks is currently hardly possible. By contrast, ideas or business concepts are not eligible for trade-mark protection.

1.5 Other Rights to Signs
The right to a name of an individual or an entity is protected under the German Civil Code (Bürgerliches Gesetzbuch, BGB). That means that if the right of a person to use a name is disputed by another person, or if the interest of the person entitled to the name is injured by the unauthorised use of the same name by another person, the entitled person may require the other to remove the infringement.

Moreover, company designations and work titles enjoy protection as commercial designations under the German Trade Mark Act (Markengesetz, MarkenG, hereinafter referred to as "TMA"). Company designations are signs used in the course of trade as a name, company name or special designation of a business operation or an enterprise. Business symbols and other signs intended to distinguish the business operation from other business operations which are regarded as symbols of the business operation within an involved trading community will be deemed equivalent to the special designation of a business operation.

Furthermore, indications of geographical origin are eligible for protection under the TMA which features some special provisions for them.

Internet domains can be registered as a trade mark if they meet the general requirements for trade-mark registration. Internet domains can also be protected as a business designation under the TMA if the general requirements for such protection are met.

1.6 Registration Procedure
After receiving the application and fees, which must be paid within three months after filing the application, the DPMA examines whether the application meets the formal requirements and whether there are absolute grounds for refusal to reject the registration of the trade mark. If the fees are not paid in due time, the application is deemed withdrawn.

If all the requirements are met, the trade mark is registered. The registration of the trade mark is published in the official electronic Trade Mark Journal. On special request, and subject to payment of an additional fee, the application process can be accelerated.

Multi-class applications are allowed. The application fee for up to three classes is EUR300. The class fee upon filing application for the fourth class and for each additional class is EUR100.

1.7 Use in Commerce
German trade-mark law does not require use in commerce of the applied trade mark as of the date of filing of the application. However, the TMA stipulates the "compulsory use" of the trade mark for all goods and services for which the trademark is registered. This means that the trade mark-owner must assiduously use the trade mark in trade for all goods and services for which it is protected in Germany in order to maintain the right to the trade mark. If the trade mark is not

used within a continuous period of more than five years, the trade mark may be cancelled upon request of any third party. For details please see **1.17 Use Requirements**.

1.8 Registration of Series Marks

German trade-mark law allows the registration of series marks, if all applications have the same applicant and the same proposal for the leading class.

1.9 Length of Registration Process

The registration procedure is usually completed within about seven to eight months. It may take longer if the DPMA requires further information from the applicant. The application will be examined faster upon request and subject to payment of a (modest) additional fee.

It is at the applicant's discretion to decide whether to file the application with or without the help of a patent attorney or of an attorney-at-law. However, persons who do not reside in Germany must appoint an attorney in Germany or an attorney established in the European Union (hereinafter referred to as "EU") to act on their behalf in the registration proceedings

1.10 Grounds for Refusal

Absolute grounds for refusal by the trade-mark office to register a trade mark are:

- the trade mark cannot be depicted graphically;
- the form of the trade mark:

(a) results from the very nature of the respective good itself (eg the shape of a pot with a handle as such);

(b) is necessary to obtain a specific technical result (eg the shape of a Lego brick); or

(c) adds substantial value to the respective good (eg the design of a specific pair of jeans);

- the trade mark:

(a)is devoid of any distinctive character with regard to the respective goods or services (eg "soap" for soap). However, this absolute ground of refusal may be repudiated if the trade mark in question has, as a consequence of its use, been established as a distinguishing sign for the goods or services for which it has been filed in the relevant public (ie has acquired a secondary meaning [Verkehrsdurchsetzung]), before the date of the decision on registration; furthermore, this ground for cancellation is applicable only if it is raised within ten years from the registration of the trade mark;

(b) consists solely of signs or indications which may, in trade, be used to designate the kind, quality, quantity, intended purpose, value, geographical origin, or time of production of the respective good or of the rendering of the respective service, or other characteristics of the goods or services (eg "fresh" for vegetables). However, this absolute ground of refusal may be repudiated if the trade mark in question has acquired secondary meaning before the date of the decision on registration;

(c) consists exclusively of signs or indications which have become customary in the current language or in the bona fide and established practices of the trade (eg "Masterbuilder House" ["Baumeister Haus"]) for houses and real estate. However, this absolute ground of refusal may be repudiated if the trade mark in question has acquired secondary meaning before the date of the decision on registration;

(d) is of such a nature as to deceive the public, eg with regard to the nature, quality or geographical origin of the respective good or service (eg "Bolshoi State Ballet" if the applicant has no connection to any institution of the respective state);

(e) is contrary to the ordre public or the accepted principles of morality (eg trade marks which are offensive against minorities);

(f) contains national coats of arms, national flags or other national emblems, or coats of arms of a domestic place, a domestic association of municipalities or of another domestic association of municipal entities (eg the German flag);

(g) contains official approval marks and official marks indicating a warranty and which are excluded from registration as trade marks per notice as published by the Federal Ministry of Justice in the Federal Law Gazette (eg the official approval mark and marks indicating a warranty of the Republic of Cuba for rum);

(h) contains the coats of arms, flags or other signs, seals, or designations, of international intergovernmental organisations and which are excluded from registration as trade marks per notice published by the Federal Ministry of Justice in the Federal Law Gazette (eg the coat of arms of the United Nations);

(i) may evidently be prohibited from use subject to other provisions (ie outside of trade-mark law) in the public interest (eg the English slang-word for marihuana cigarette "reefer" is not eligible for trade- mark protection for tobacco goods because the German Narcotics Act prohibits the advertising of marijuana); or

(j) has been applied for in bad faith.

1.11 Process for Overcoming Objections

If absolute grounds for refusal are identified during the application examination process, the applicant will be notified in writing and will have the opportunity to make a statement. The statement will be examined. If it does not overcome all deficiencies stated in the notification, a decision will be taken to refuse the application (or possibly, part of the application). In this case, the applicant has the opportunity to have this decision reviewed by filing a request for reconsideration (Erinnerung) or appeal proceedings (Beschwerde). For details please see **4.4 Courts with Jurisdiction to Hear Trade Mark Matters**.

1.12 Consideration of Prior Rights

The DPMA does not check the existence of prior rights. Owners of prior rights can initiate opposition proceedings following the registration of the trade mark. For details please see **3 Opposition Procedure**.

1.13 Third Party Rights

Third parties do not have the right to participate during the registration procedure. After the publication of the trade mark in the official electronic Trade Mark Journal, owners of earlier rights have the opportunity to object to the registration. For details please see **3 Opposition Procedure**.

1.14 Revoke, Change, Amend or Correct an Application

After the DPMA has received the application, it is no longer possible to alter the trade mark applied for (even though the information provided is incorrect), except where the amendment relates to the correction of errors of wording or obvious mistakes. However, the applicant can withdraw the application at any time or restrict the contained list of goods and services.

In particular, design marks cannot be updated or refreshed in the course of time. Therefore, a new design usually requires a new trade-mark application.

1.15 Assigning an Application or Granting a Licence

A trade mark application constitutes a right conferring prospective entitlement, which can be assigned and licensed.

1.16 Remedies Against the Trade Mark Office

The registrant can file an objection against the orders of the DPMA and can also file an appeal to the German Federal Patent Court (Bundespatentgericht).

1.17 Use of a Trade Mark

A trade mark is required to be consistently used for the goods or services in respect of which it is registered unless there are legitimate grounds for non-use. The requirements for a serious use of trade mark are as follows:

(1) the use must serve for the purpose of identifying the goods and services covered by the registration. For instance, this is the case when the trade mark is used as a product label;

(2) the use must be made by or with the consent of the proprietor (eg by a licensee);

(3) the use of the trade mark in a form that deviates from the registration is only sufficient insofar as the deviations do not change the distinctive character of the trade mark; and

(4) the use in national territory, also including the affixing of the trade mark on goods or their wrapping or packaging in this country if the goods are exclusively intended for export;

Important indicators for the seriousness of the use are the amount of marketing spendings for the trade mark and the revenue created by the trade mark. After expiry of a grace period (five years) a trade mark which is not seriously used may be cancelled upon request of any third party.

There is no need for a trade mark-owner to use a special symbol (eg TM or ®) to denote that a mark is registered or existing. However, the use of such a symbol might have a positive effect with regard to the mark's distinctiveness in the relevant public in cases in which the mark is rather descriptive.

1.18 Dividing a Trade Mark

The applicant may divide the application by declaring that the application for the trade mark will continue to be dealt with thenceforth as a divisional application for the goods and services listed in the declaration of division. In this case, the seniority of the original application is to be retained for each sub-application. The application documents required (see the first part of **1.3 Registration Requirements**) are to be submitted for the divisional application. If the application documents are not submitted within three months after receipt of the declaration of division, or if the fee in accordance with the Patent Costs Act (Patentkostengesetz) for the division proceedings is not paid within this period, the divisional application is deemed to have been withdrawn. The declaration of division cannot be revoked.

1.19 Length of Term of Protection

The term of protection of a registered trade mark commences on the date of application and ends after ten years on the last day of the month corresponding in name to the month in which the date of application falls. The duration of protection may be extended by terms of ten years each, potentially ad infinitum. The renewal of the trade mark is subject to payment of a renewal fee and, if the renewal is requested for goods and services in more than three classes, also subject to payment of an additional class fee for each further class. A registration may also be extended partially for only some of the classes and goods protected by the respective trade mark.

1.20 Requirements for an Exhaustion

Under the TMA, the proprietor of a trade mark or of a commercial designation is not entitled to prohibit a third party from using the trade mark or the commercial designation for goods which have been put on the market under this trade mark or this commercial designation by him or her or with his or her consent in Germany, in any other of the other Member States of the EU or in any other contracting party to the Agreement on the European Economic Area (hereinafter referred to as "EEA"). This does not apply if the proprietor of the trade mark or of the commercial designation opposes the use of the trade mark or of the commercial designation for legitimate reasons, in particular if the condition of the goods has been changed or impaired after being put on the market.

1.21 Participation in the Madrid System

The TMA shall be applied mutatis mutandis to the international registration of trade marks in accordance with the Madrid Agreement Concerning the International Registration of Marks (Madrid Agreement on Marks, hereinafter referred to as "MMA") and in accordance with the Madrid Protocol of 27 June 1989 Relating to the Madrid Agreement Concerning the International Registration of Marks (Protocol Relating to the Madrid Agreement on Marks, hereinafter referred to as "PMMA").

Under the TMA, the application for the international registration of a trade mark entered in the register in accordance with the MMA or PMMA is to be submitted to the DPMA. Internationally PMMA-registered trade marks are to be examined for absolute grounds for refusal in the same way as German trade marks.

2. Assignment and Licensing

2.1 Assignment Requirements or Restrictions

Trade marks may generally be freely assigned from one owner to another. There are no formal requirements for such an assignment and no approval from the DPMA is required. The (pending) application for the registration of a trade mark as such may also be freely transferred.

2.2 Procedure for Assigning a Trade Mark

A trade mark is assigned by means of a contractual agreement. The further conditions of the agreement are subject to negotiation between the parties. The assignment agreement is not subject to any specific formal requirements; however, it is strongly recommended that such an assignment agreement be concluded in writing for the purpose of preservation of evidence.

2.3 Registering or Recording the Assignment

The parties of a trade-mark assignment are under no obligation to give notice on the change of the owner of the trade mark to the DPMA which administers the German trade-mark register. However, it is recommended that the new owner have the register changed appropriately as the TMA contains a refutable presumption that the registered owner of a trade mark is the actual owner of the trade mark (Section 28 paragraph 1 of the TMA). In particular, if the new owner needs to defend the trade mark, it is considerably easier to raise claims when the new owner is also the registered owner. However, the new owner may have the change of ownership recorded with the DPMA at any time.

2.4 Trade Marks and Security

Trade marks are part of the owner's property and may be subject to rights in rem, assigned by way of security, and may be levied in execution. Rights in rem and actions under levy in execution may be recorded in the German trade mark register. However, it is worth noting that such a recording is just declaratory and does not have a legal effect.

2.5 Licensing Requirements or Restrictions

There are no formal requirements for licence agreements on trade marks. Any trade mark, whether registered or not, may be the subject of a licence agreement. The scope (eg exclusive, non-exclusive, all or part of the services and/or products for which the trade mark is protected, limited in time or perpetual) of the respective licence and further licensing conditions may be freely negotiated between the parties.

2.6 Procedure for Licensing a Trade Mark

A trade mark is licensed by way of contractual agreement between the parties under German law. The further conditions of the agreement are subject to negotiation between the parties. In itself, a licence agreement is not subject to any specific formal requirements. However, it is strongly recommended that a licence agreement be concluded in writing for the purpose of preservation of evidence.

2.7 Registering or Recording the Licence

Unlike in many other countries, a registration of the licence in the German trade-mark register is neither necessary nor possible.

3. Opposition Procedure

3.1 Filing an Opposition

An opposition against a trade-mark registration may be filed in writing within three months after the publication of the registration of a trade mark on the grounds of a risk of confusion with an earlier trade mark, trade-mark application or commercial designation by the owner of such prior right.

According to German case law, an opposition may also be filed by a licensee. A representation of the opponent is not obligatory. The opposition fee amounts to EUR120 and must be paid within the deadline for filing the opposition. Otherwise, the opposition will be deemed as not having been filed. In the case of the involvement of an attorney, the attorney fees depend on the individual agreement between attorney and client.

3.2 Opposition Procedure

Although not mandatory, it is common practice (and to be recommended) to substantiate the opposition in detail. With regard to an opposition based on non-registered trade marks or commercial designations, the opposing party is required to provide evidence with regard to the existence and ownership of such rights. Subsequently, the challenged party will be given the opportunity to respond to the opposition. The filing of a counter-statement is not mandatory. However, it is common practice that the applicant files a counter-statement describing the grounds on which the opposition should be rejected.

The opposition procedure is a summary proceeding. The owner of the challenged trade mark may respond to the opposition by raising the plea of non-use, provided that the earlier trade mark has been registered for at least five years on the date of publication of the contested registration. In that case, the opponent has to substantiate that the trade mark has been used within the relevant five-year period. The DPMA will render a decision on the opposition and either cancel the newly registered trade mark entirely or partly or reject the opposition.

3.3 Legal Remedies

The decision rendered by the DPMA on the opposition may be challenged by the losing party by filing a request for reconsideration (Erinnerung) or an appeal (Beschwerde) to the German Federal Patent Court. Both remedies have to be filed within one month after the contested decision was served upon the respective party.

Whilst the request for reconsideration is only available against a decision rendered by a single member of the DPMA, an appeal may be filed in any case.

The decision process of the DPMA is rather slow; thus, appeal proceedings may easily go on for 12 months or more until a decision is rendered. If an appeal decision of the Federal Patent Court is appealed to the German Supreme Court (Bundesgerichtshof, hereinafter referred to as "BGH"), the duration of the proceedings is considerably longer, being at least a further 24 months.

4. Initiating a Lawsuit

4.1 Actions to Pursue Infringement

Out of court, the owner of a trade mark (or of any other sign protected under the TMA) may send a warning letter to the alleged infringer and demand a declaration of agreement to cease and desist from the respective trade-mark infringement, threatening further legal action in the event of non-compliance. Furthermore, court actions (ie preliminary injunction or regular infringement proceedings) may also be brought before the competent court directly, ie without sending a warning letter first. However, if in such a case the defendant immediately concedes the claims as justified, the trade mark-owner usually has to bear the legal costs of the proceedings.

Before sending a warning letter, in particular in cases when the trade mark infringement is not clear-cut, the trade mark-owner may also send an authorisation inquiry (Berechtigungsanfrage) to the (alleged) infringer first, requesting an explanation why he or she believes they are entitled to use the respective trade mark. An authorisation inquiry, unlike a warning letter, contains neither a request to cease-and-desist from using the trade mark nor a threat of further legal action in case of non-compliance. It serves the purpose of substantiating the suspicion of a trade-mark infringement and does not create the risk of a counter-action because of raising non-existing claims.

Infringement claims may not be raised on the basis of a trade-mark application, but only by the owner of a registered or unregistered trade mark or any other sign protected under the TMA. Licensees might be entitled to raise infringement claims by a respective consent of the trade mark-owner.

4.2 Initiating Infringement Proceedings

With regard to trade-mark infringements, the regional courts (Landgerichte, LG) have exclusive jurisdiction. Furthermore, in each German state there is a limited number of specialised regional courts which deal exclusively with trade-mark cases. Thus, a trade mark-owner would have to review which regional court is competent for the alleged trade-mark infringement in the respective case.

4.3 Effect of Decisions on Infringement Actions

The courts dealing with trade-mark infringement cases are bound by the decisions of the DPMA and the German Federal Patent Court only with respect to the (non-)existence of trade-mark rights. Furthermore, an infringement court cannot completely deny the distinctiveness of an existing trade mark. However, with regard to all other legal questions (eg likelihood of confusion) the court is free to decide.

4.4 Jurisdiction of Courts

Trade-mark matters have to be brought before specific regional courts in the first instance. In the second instance, the higher regional court (Oberlandesgericht, OLG) which is competent for the district of the regional court will decide on an appeal. An appeal decision of a higher regional court may be appealed on points of law only to the BGH and subject to certain conditions (see also **9.1 Special Provisions for Trade Marks**).

4.5 Prerequisites to Filing a Lawsuit

There are no prerequisites with regard to filing a lawsuit. However, an immediate filing of a lawsuit without sending a warning letter might have implications on the obligation to bear the costs if the defendant immediately acknowledges the claims raised as justified.

4.6 Representation for Parties

Due to the exclusive jurisdiction of the regional courts in trade-mark matters, the parties need to be represented by a lawyer.

4.7 Interim or Preliminary Injunctions

The owner of a trade mark or any other sign protected under the TMA may file for a preliminary injunction against the alleged infringer if the prerequisite of urgency is met. This commonly requires that the action for preliminary injunction is filed not later than four weeks after the right-holder became aware of the potential infringement.

4.8 Protection for Potential Defendant

In defence against actions for a preliminary injunction, a potential defendant may proactively file a protective brief (Schutzschrift) substantiating the reasons why an alleged infringement does not exist. A potential defendant may also file an action for declaratory judgment of non-infringement. However, once the trade mark-owner files a counter-claim based on the alleged infringement, there is no justified interest in the declaratory judgment, so that the potential defendant has to withdraw the application for declaratory judgment to avoid unnecessary costs.

4.9 Obtaining Information and Evidence

German (trade mark) law does not provide for disclosure or discovery. However, if (i) the infringement is obvious, or (ii) the owner has already filed an infringement action against the infringer, the owner of a trade mark or commercial designation has a special claim for disclosure of certain information against third parties who, to a commercial extent, possessed infringing goods, used infringing services, rendered services which were used for the infringement or took part in any such action. In addition, during infringement proceedings, the defendant may be ordered to disclose specific information (eg with regard to the revenue generated by the infringing goods or services) to the claimant as part of the infringement claims.

4.10 Initial Pleading Standards

In order to initiate a lawsuit (preliminary and regular proceedings), a statement of claim has to be filed with a court competent for trade-mark matters. The statement of claim has to specify the claims raised, and the facts and grounds on which such claims are based on have to be set out in detail. In a case where the statement of claim is based on more than one trade mark right, according to the most recent jurisprudence the claimant has to specify the order in which the rights shall be considered by the court. Apart from that, trade-mark proceedings follow the applicable rules for non-intellectual property civil law proceedings.

Pleadings in trade mark cases may be supplemented on a case-by-case basis, in particular by claims based on unfair competition and/or tort law.

4.11 Representative or Collective Actions

German trade-mark law does not contain rules for representative or collective actions.

4.12 Restrictions on Trade Mark-Owners

There are restrictions on the trade mark-owner according to specific trade-mark law rules and restrictions based on general principles under German civil law.

German trade-mark law provides that the owner of a trade mark shall not be entitled to prohibit the use of a trade mark with a later time-rank to the extent that they have acquiesced, for a period of five successive years, in the use of this right whilst being aware of such use, unless the third party was acting in bad faith when applying for or acquiring any trade-mark right. Furthermore, the trade mark-owner is not entitled to prohibit any third party from using a trade mark in relation to goods which have been put on the market under that trade mark or commercial designation by the trade mark-owner themselves or with their consent in the Federal Republic of Germany, one of the Member States of the EU or a contracting state of the treaty on the EEA. See also **5.3 Defences Against Infringement Claims.**

With regard to general civil law principles under German law, a trade mark-owner may not assert rights where no legitimate interests can be shown and claims are raised solely in order to harm a third party. German Unfair Competition law may even prevent a trade mark -owner from asserting their rights on the basis of an impediment ban and/or in a case where a trade mark-owner primarily intends to generate legal fees to be paid by third parties.

5. Infringement

5.1 Action for Infringement

Necessary parties to an action for infringement are the trade mark-owner as claimant and at least one third party as alleged infringer(s). A licensee may only bring an action with the approval of the trade mark-owner. Furthermore, a non-licensee or any other party may only bring an action on behalf of the trade mark-owner with the approval of the trade mark-owner and based on their own legitimate interest with regard to the infringement claims raised.

Under German trade-mark law, the filing of an action for infringement based on a trade-mark application is not possible; such action is possible only on the basis of a registered or existing unregistered trade-mark right or commercial designation. On a case-by-case basis, it might be possible to raise claims based on unfair competition or general law principles (eg acting in bad faith) in order to take an action to stop infringement before the registration of a mark.

5.2 Signs and Infringement

In order to find a trade-mark infringement due to a likelihood of confusion with regard to the origin of the goods and services in question, the competing signs need to be compared firstly. The similarity of the signs is examined on the basis of established case law as to whether oral, conceptual or visual similarity exists. Secondly, a comparison of the goods and services for which the respective signs seek protection is conducted in accordance with principles established by case law. Finally, the degree of distinctiveness of the earlier trade mark has to be determined. Then, by conducting an overall assessment of the similarity of the signs and of the goods and services and the distinctiveness of the earlier trade mark, it must be established that these combined factors lead to a likelihood of confusion.

As the use of a sign as a trade mark is a necessary criterion for a trade-mark infringement, the claimant has to establish that the defendant has actually used the sign in such a way and not otherwise (eg purely descriptively).

5.3 Defences Against Infringement

As a defence, a defendant may invoke an earlier right to use a specific sign. A defendant may also refer to the use of their own name or address or the use as an indication concerning the kind, quality, quantity, intended purpose, value, geographical origin, time of production or time of rendering a service or other characteristics of the goods or services as far as the use of the trade mark by a third party is necessary and in accordance with good-faith practices in industrial or commercial matters. Furthermore, a limitation or forfeiture of rights may be invoked as a defence. Forfeiture under trade mark law requires that, after the grace period, the claimant has not used its trade mark for a period of five years. Besides, defences based on general civil law principles are applicable. In this regard, a defendant may argue that the claimant is acting in bad faith when asserting its trade- mark rights due to a lack of a legitimate interest and/or due to the trade mark being acquired in bad faith. See also **4.11 Restrictions on a Trade Mark Owner Asserting Rights**.

5.4 Role of Experts and/or Surveys

Expert statements and/or surveys may be presented by the parties and in particular surveys may constitute a decisive factor for certain issues of a case. However, when presented by one of the parties, the courts will consider expert statements or surveys as part of a party's submissions only and decide whether it is necessary for the court to initiate its own survey or request an expert statement as evidence.

5.5 Administrative or Criminal Offence

Trade-mark infringement may constitute a criminal offence if it is conducted in the course of trade, and may be prosecuted in criminal law proceedings. The initiation of criminal investigations requires the trade mark-owner to file a complaint with the public prosecutor, unless (i) the trade-mark infringer acts systematically for financial gains or (ii) as a member of a criminal organisation; in these cases the public prosecutor may initiate criminal investigations ex officio at any time becoming aware of a trade-mark infringement. Such criminal investigation may eventually lead to criminal proceedings against the alleged infringer. A trade mark-owner may benefit from criminal investigations and proceedings by possibly having the authorities search the premises of the infringer and confiscate goods in a fast and efficient way and due to the possibility of inspecting the files of the authority in order to gain information on the alleged infringer as preparation for a civil law action for damages.

5.6 Custom Seizures

In order to obtain border control actions against potential trade-mark infringements, an application has to be filed with the customs authorities. Once such an obligation has been processed and control measures have been granted, the customs authorities will seize goods entering or leaving the territory of Germany or the EU which are found to be infringing. If the owner of the goods does not oppose to the seizure within two weeks, the goods will be confiscated. In the case of an opposition by the owner of the goods, the trade mark-owner is requested to obtain a court decision confirming an infringement of its trade mark. If infringement cannot be established, the trade mark-owner may be liable for damages. If infringement is established, the trade mark will either be removed from the goods, if possible, or the goods will be destroyed.

6. Revocation/Cancellation

6.1 Remedies and Reasons

German trade mark law contains numerous grounds for the revocation and cancellation of trade marks.

- A trade mark can be subject to cancellation if it was registered in contravention of absolute grounds for refusal in the first place. Absolute grounds for refusal are related to the character of the respective trade mark as such, ie irrespective of any third-party (trade mark) rights. To put it simply: a trade mark which contravenes any absolute ground of refusal is, generally, not eligible for trade mark registration. For details, please see **1.10 Refusal of Registration**.
- Furthermore, a trade mark may be cancelled if it was registered contrary to relative grounds for refusal. In contrast to absolute grounds for refusal (see preceding paragraph), relative grounds for refusal result from the relation of the respective trade mark to earlier pending third-party trade mark registrations and/or earlier registered or unregistered third-party trade marks or other earlier rights. Consequently, a cancellation for relative grounds for refusal is not possible if the owner of the respective earlier right has consented in the registration of the trade mark before the application for cancellation was filed. Relative grounds for refusal apply to trade marks which:

(a) (i) are identical to a pending or registered trade mark with earlier priority (ie which has an earlier application date or, in the case of other rights protected by the TMA, have an earlier date on which they qualified for protection), and

(ii) which are registered for goods or services which are identical to the goods or services for which the pending or registered trade mark with earlier priority seeks or enjoys protection;

(b) (i) due to the identity with, or similarity to, a pending or registered trade mark with an earlier priority, and

(ii) the identity or similarity of the goods or services covered by the respective trade marks, constitute a likelihood of confusion for the general public, including the likelihood of association with the earlier trade mark;

(c) (i) are identical to, or similar to, a pending or registered trade mark with an earlier priority, and

(ii) which have been registered for goods or services which are not similar to the goods or services for which the pending or registered earlier trade mark seeks or enjoys protection,

provided that

(iii) the earlier trade mark is well-known in Germany, and

(iv) the use of the registered younger trade mark would unfairly exploit, or be detrimental to, the distinctive character or the repute of the earlier well-known trade mark without justifiable reason;

(d) (i) are identical with, or similar to, a trade mark with an earlier priority which is famous in Germany in the sense of Article 6 bis of the Paris Convention, and

(ii) if the additional requirements as described in the preceding three items of this list are met, and

(iii) if the application was not authorised by the owner of the well-known trade mark;

(e) has been registered in the name of an agent or representative of the trade mark-owner, without that owner's consent;

(f) could be subject to prohibition of use for the entire state territory of Germany by the owner of

(i) a trade mark acquired by use with an earlier priority, or

(ii) a commercial designation with an earlier priority;

(g) could be subject to prohibition of use for the entire state territory of Germany by the owner of any other right which has not been mentioned in the preceding items and which has an earlier priority than the trade mark (such other rights include in particular, without limitation, rights to a name, the right to one's personal portrayal, copyrights, denominations of variety, indications of geographical origin and other intellectual property rights).

German trade-mark law, however, contains several exceptions to the possibility of cancellation of trade marks for contravention to relative grounds for refusal. With regard to earlier trade marks and commercial designations which have an established reputation, cancellation of the younger trade mark is only possible if those earlier rights are already well-known in respect of the German trade-mark law (see **1.3 Registration Requirements**) on the date which is applicable for the seniority status of the younger trade mark.

Furthermore, a cancellation for contravention to relative grounds for refusal is not possible if the earlier trade mark could itself have been cancelled on the date of the publication of the registration of the younger trade mark because of revocation or contravention to absolute grounds for refusal (see **1.10 Refusal of Registration**).

- Moreover, a trade mark may be revoked at any time as a result of a waiver by the owner.
- The trade mark may also be revoked due to abandonment or lapse because of insufficient use of the trade mark, and because of further reasons which relate to the character of the trade mark, the specific use of the trade mark or the character of the trade mark-owner. In more detail:

(a) A trade mark may be revoked for abandonment or lapse if, within a continuous period of five years starting with the registration date, the trade mark has not been seriously used in the sense of German trade mark law (see **1.17 Use Requirements**). However, that lapse does not occur if at the end of the five-year period and prior to the filing of a cancellation request, the use of the trade mark has started or was resumed. Nevertheless, if this use commences or resumes within three months preceding the filing of the cancellation request, following the expiry of an uninterrupted period of five years of non-use, it will not be taken into account in cases where preparations for the commencement or resumption take place only after the trade-mark holder became aware that the application for cancellation may be filed.

(b) Furthermore, a trade mark may be revoked if:

(i) as a result of acts by, or the inactivity of, the owner, the trade mark became the common name in the trade for the goods or services for which the trade mark is registered;

(ii) as a result of the use of the trade mark by its owner or with the owner's consent, with regard to the goods or services for which it is protected, the trade mark is liable to mislead the general public, in particular, without limitation, as to the nature, quality or geographical origin of the respective goods or services; or

(iii) if the trade mark-owner no longer meets the requirements for being a trade mark-owner as stipulated by the TMA, ie if the trade mark-owner dies (in the case of an individual) or ceases to exist (in the case of a legal entity or a business partnership) without a legal successor which qualifies as a trade mark-owner.

(c) In addition, a trade mark may be cancelled if it was registered in contravention of absolute grounds for refusal (see **1.10 Refusal of Registration**) for an owner who is not eligible for trade-mark ownership (this ground for cancellation is of little practical relevance), or if it contravenes the general prerequisites for the protection of a trade mark as stipulated by the TMA (see **1.10 Refusal of Registration**).

(d) Last but not least, a trade mark may be cancelled because of pre-existing rights of third parties, ie rights with an earlier priority as stipulated by the TMA (on priority, see preceding bullet under (a)).

6.2 Trade Mark Office and Civil Courts

Whether a cancellation action is heard before the DPMA or the civil courts depends on the claimed ground for cancellation.

In the case of cancellation for lapse, the claimant may either file a request for cancellation with the DPMA or directly file a claim for cancellation of the trade mark with the competent civil court. If the owner of the respective trade mark objects within two months after the DPMA has given notice to them with regard to that cancellation request, the claimant needs to file a claim for cancellation with the civil courts if they want to pursue the cancellation further.

If the claimant demands a cancellation for registration in spite of an absolute ground of refusal, it is mandatory to file that complaint with the DPMA. The DPMA's decision may be appealed to the German Federal Patent Court, a special court for, inter alia, specific trade mark cases. The decision of the German Federal Patent Court may, in certain cases, be subject to an appeal on points of law to the BGH.

Claims based on earlier rights of the claimant may not be brought before the DPMA, only before the civil courts.

6.3 Statutory Limitation or Time Period

German trade-mark law stipulates several time limitations for remedies with regard to the different grounds for cancellation.

- Cancellation is only possible if the cause for cancellation still subsists on the date on which the decision on the application for cancellation is handed down, in a case where the reason for cancellation is one of the absolute grounds for refusal described in **1.10 Refusal of Registration** and **6.1 Remedies and Reasons for Revocation/Cancellation.** Furthermore, if the trade mark has been registered in breach of any of the absolute grounds for refusal described in **1.10 Refusal of Registration**, the registration may only be cancelled if the application for cancellation is filed no later than ten years after the respective date of registration.

A cancellation ex officio is only possible with regard to the absolute grounds for refusal outlined in **1.10 Refusal of Registration** above if:

(i) the cancellation proceedings are initiated within a period of two years from the date of registration;

(ii) the absolute ground of refusal still subsists at the time of the decision on the cancellation; and

(iii) the registration has evidently been made in breach of any of the aforementioned absolute grounds for refusal (ie only in clear-cut cases. The DPMA will not conduct a full-scale review of whether the respective ground of refusal is fulfilled in the respective case at hand).

- In the case of relative grounds for refusal (see **6.1 Remedies and Reasons for Revocation/Cancellation**), the registration may not be cancelled because of the registration of a trade mark with earlier seniority where the owner of the earlier trade mark has tolerated the use of the younger trade mark for the goods or services for which it is protected for a period of five consecutive years whilst being aware of such use, unless the application for the registration of the younger trade mark has been made in bad faith. The same applies with regard to the owner of an earlier right to

(i) a trade mark acquired by use (see **1.3 Registration Requirements**),

(ii) a well-known trade mark (see **1.3 Registration Requirements**),

(iii) in a commercial designation (see **1.5 Other Rights to Signs**) or

(iv) in a name of a plant variety.

6.4 Initiation of Revocation/Cancellation Proceeding

Several grounds for cancellation are available to any person, irrespective of whether or not that person has any legal or commercial interest whatsoever in the cancellation of the respective trade mark. This applies with regard to the cancellation for abandonment or lapse (see **6.1 Remedies and Reasons for Revocation/Cancellation**) and the cancellation because of absolute grounds for refusal (see **1.10 Refusal of Registration**).

Furthermore, cancellations because of absolute grounds for refusal may be executed ex officio. However, this is hardly relevant in practice because a cancellation ex officio is subject to strict limitations.

Any cancellation proceedings which are based on earlier third-party rights can only be initiated by the owner of the respective right or persons (ie a licensee) that have been authorised by the owner to initiate cancellation proceedings. In the case of indications of geographical origin, the claim may be made by:

- any competitor of the trade mark-owner;
- certain associations for the promotion of commercial or self-employed interests;
- certain qualified organisations for the protection of interests of customers; and
- the chambers of industry and commerce and the chambers of crafts.

6.5 Partial Revocation/Cancellation

Partial cancellation is possible if the respective reason for cancellation only applies to a part of the goods and/or services for which the respective trade mark is protected.

6.6 Possibilities of Amendment

An amendment of the respective trade mark itself is not possible in cancellation proceedings. However, the owner may restrict the respective trade mark during cancellation cases at any time.

6.7 Revocation/Cancellation and Infringement

Insofar as the civil courts are competent for decisions regarding the cancellation of a trade mark (see **6.2 Where to Bring an Action**), the respective ground for cancellation may generally be introduced into an infringement case before the respective civil court. If the DPMA and German Federal Patent Court have jurisdiction over the cancellation action (see **6.2 Where to Bring an Action**), the infringement trial may be stayed by the respective civil court until the cancellation decision has been reached.

7. Trial & Settlement

7.1 Special Procedural Provisions

Trade-mark proceedings before the civil courts in infringement and cancellation proceedings follow the standard procedural rules as laid down in the German Code on Civil Process (Zivilprozessordnung, ZPO).

Trials before the Federal Patent Court and the BGH in appeal cases (Beschwerden) against decisions of the DPMA in registration proceedings generally also follow these same general rules. However, the TMA stipulates several special provisions for these trials: most notably, the Federal Patent Court investigates the relevant facts of the case ex officio and is not bound by the facts submitted by the participants and the motions of the participants to take evidence. Furthermore, an oral hearing will be held only if:

- any participant requests an oral hearing,
- a taking of evidence is necessary, or
- the Federal Patent Court deems an oral hearing to be useful for the resolution of the case (Sachdienlichkeit).

With regard to the costs of trial, the Federal Patent Court may order that any or part of the necessary legal costs which the participants have incurred for the trial are to be borne by one of the participants for reasons of equity. If the court does not hand down such an order, each participant has to bear their cost alone.

7.2 Determination of Cases

The cases are generally determined by legal judges alone; however, in infringement cases, it is possible to have the case heard by a chamber for commercial matters (Kammer für Handelssachen) at the competent regional court. The case will then be heard by one professional judge and two lay judges with a commercial background. Juries do not exist under German law.

The parties have no direct influence on who hears their case. However, in certain specific cases, they may reject a judge because of concerns of bias. In such a case, the court (without the judge in question) decides whether or not the rejection is justified.

7.3 Possibilities of Settlement

During a pending trial, the parties can settle the case at any time by reaching an agreement. Such a settlement agreement can be made out of court as well as before the court. In the case of the former, the parties need to end the trial (eg by withdrawing the claim etc). The latter ends the trial and – depending on the content of the settlement – provides the parties with an enforceable title. The courts are required by law to seek an amicable solution of the dispute at all times during the proceedings. It is thus not uncommon that the court – usually in an oral hearing – makes a proposal for a settlement agreement. However, the parties are free to follow such a proposal, to amend it or to reject it.

7.4 Other Court Proceedings

An infringement case may be stayed by the court if a parallel cancellation/revocation trial is pending (see **6. Revocation/Cancellation**). However, the infringement court is not obliged to do so.

8. Remedies

8.1 Existing Remedies

Trade mark-owners – whether of a registered trade mark or any other right protected by provisions of the TMA – have a whole bouquet of remedies against infringements. Subject to the respective legal prerequisites, they may apply for (i) (permanent) injunctive relief (meaning an order to refrain from making use of the trade mark or the infringing sign); (ii) disclosure of information on the origin and the distribution channel of infringing goods; (iii) damages; (iv) destruction or recall of infringing goods; and (v) publication of the judgment. Business owners should be aware that they are also liable for the acts of their employees and agents. Besides, apart from the direct infringer, all contributors to a trade-mark infringement are also liable (eg the persons who ordered the infringing goods or devices).

If the trade mark-owner wins the court proceedings, they do not, as a general rule, have to bear any legal expenses, inclusive of their own attorney fees, unless they exceed the statutory fees; however, this is different in proceedings before the DPMA and the German Federal Patent Court (see **7.1 Special Procedural Provisions**).

Any claim for damages requires a culpable infringement ie intent or negligence. Otherwise, monetary claims can only be made based on unjust enrichment. As in other fields of IP in Germany, the calculation basis for damages may be (i) actual damages suffered by the right-holder (including lost profits); (ii) payment of reasonable royalties (fiktive Lizenzgebühr); or (iii) surrender of the profits actually generated by the infringer.

German law does not recognise enhanced damages for intentional infringement. Hence, with regard to the scope of damages there is no difference between intentional or negligent infringement. However, it is worth noting that, unlike negligent acts of infringement, intentional trade-mark infringement may constitute a criminal offence and therefore be prosecuted by the Public Prosecutor's Office, resulting in fines or imprisonment (see **5.5 Administrative or Criminal Offences**).

Even if the focus of trade mark-owners is usually on civil action against infringers, it is worth noting that the initiation of criminal proceedings, depending on the individual case, may be an effective tool to increase the pressure on the infringer (see **5.5 Administrative or Criminal Offences**).

Apart from the aforementioned possible remedies in a main action, a judge may order immediate (preliminary) precautionary measures in cases of infringement or imminent infringement if the trade mark-owner substantially justifies such a request. A preliminary injunction, enforceable by legal process, may include, inter alia, an order to the defendant to refrain from making use of the trade mark or the infringing sign, a request for information, and a sequestration of infringing goods by a bailiff.

Last, but not least, a trade mark-owner may file a request for a seizure of infringing goods with respect to the territory of the EU. The border authorities will seize the goods provided the infringement is obvious (see **5.6 Customs Seizures**).

8.2 Rights and Remedies

For the reimbursement of costs please see the general explanation in **10.3 Responsibility for Paying Costs of Litigation**. In short, if no infringement has occurred, the alleged infringer will not have to bear any attorney costs unless their own attorney costs exceed the statutory fees.

Furthermore, even though a trade-mark infringement has actually occurred, the full cost burden (inclusive of all court and statutory attorney fees) will be ordered to be borne by the trade mark-owner if (i) they fail to send a warning letter to the infringer giving the latter an opportunity to settle before filing an application for injunctive relief; or (ii) the infringer immediately acknowledges the infringement in the court proceedings (ie does not bring forward any arguments against the claim of the trade mark-owner in court). Such an acknowledgment does not, however, affect the validity of damage claims. Thus, to avoid the risk regarding legal costs, a warning letter is highly recommended from the perspective of the trade mark-owner (see **4.1 Actions Available to Pursue Infringement**).

Assuming that a defendant is confronted with an alleged trade mark infringement (eg by receiving a warning letter), and following that, the trade mark owner does not file a lawsuit, the alleged infringer is entitled to file an action for declaration of non-infringement. If the court proceedings lead to the outcome that the allegation was wrongful (so-called "negative declaratory judgment" [negative Feststellungsklage], see **4.7 Protection for the Defendant**), all legal expenses and costs are borne by the trade mark owner.

Independently of any infringement proceedings, the defendant may at any time attack the validity of the trade mark. During revocation proceedings before the Federal Patent Court the civil infringement proceedings may be suspended if there are prospects for success for the invalidity action (see **6. Revocation/Cancellation**).

If it turns out in the further proceedings that an ordered preliminary injunction or border seizure was unjustified, the alleged infringer has a claim for compensation. In particular, the trade mark-owner is liable for loss of profits.

8.3 Different Types of Remedies

As already mentioned, the remedies for the different types of trade mark or other rights obtaining protection under the TMA do not differ (see **8.1 Remedies for the Trade Mark Owner**).

9. Appeal

9.1 Special Provisions

In general, the general civil law rules apply in appellate procedures, with some minor modifications. Appeals against first instance decisions (Berufung) – which will usually be admissible in trade mark cases due to the high value of the amount in dispute (Streitwert) – will be conducted before the higher regional courts. Within one month from service of the full version of the judgment, the appellant must submit a statement of appeal. Within one more month the appellant must submit a statement on the grounds of appeal describing the reasons why they consider the judgment to be erroneous and the significance of these errors for the judgment.

The second appellate level (Revision) before the BGH is subject to explicit permission to appeal being granted. This permission may be granted by the higher regional court or by the BGH after filing a non-admission complaint (Nichtzulassungsbeschwerde) against the denial to grant a second appeal. For the filing of a non-admission complaint and the non-admission complaint respectively, the same deadlines apply as in the first-level appeal (see preceding paragraph). The content requirements are similar, too, whereby it must be submitted by an attorney admitted to practice before the BGH.

9.2 Factual or Legal Review

On the first appellate level, as a general rule, a full review of the facts of the case and on points of law will take place. However, a statement of completely new facts compared to the first-instance proceedings is only permitted subject to certain restrictions.

In contrast, the BGH is bound by the facts found by the first instance and the first appellate level court. Thus, the second level appeal is on points of law only.

10. Other Trade Mark Issues

10.1 Recognition of Dilution

In German Trade Mark Law, the term "dilution" does not exist, which is why a trade mark cannot be opposed or prevented to be used in a lawsuit due to "dilution". However, a trade mark may be contested for the reasons outlined under **6. Revocation/Cancellation**. "Dilution" is rather used synonymously for a detriment to the distinctive character of a well-known trade mark which may cause a trade mark infringement.

10.2 Protection of Famous Marks

Trade marks which are (not yet) registered or in use in Germany can be protected if they are famous marks in the sense of Article 6bis of the Paris Convention (see **1.3 Registration Requirements**).

10.3 Special Rules Relating to Surnames

The owner of a trade mark cannot prohibit someone from using their own surname as a mark in the course of trade. However, the user of a mark with a later priority may be ordered to apply necessary and reasonable measures to prevent confusion.

Contributed by SZA Schilling, Zutt & Anschütz ***Authors:*** Thomas Nägele, Steffen Henn, Anke Hofmann, Alexander Stolz

11. Costs

11.1 Costs Before Filing a Lawsuit

Attorney fees – as well as court fees – are subject to the value of the amount in dispute and the activities of the attorney. Circumstances influencing the value of the amount in dispute are, for example, the reputation of the trade mark, the quantity of infringements, the number of infringers and represented parties, and the complexity of the decisive legal issues. Every activity of the attorney will be remunerated according to the provisions of the German Act on Reimbursement for Lawyers (Rechtsanwaltsvergütungsgesetz). It determines the relevant business fee unit for every legal task and, in an annexed schedule, the applicable fee for the specific amount in dispute.

If the attorney's legal task is limited to the out-of-court assertion of trade mark claims (eg the sending of a warning letter) in a normal case of infringement of a trade mark of average value (where the usual amount in dispute is EUR100,000), the statutory prescribed attorney fee would be EUR1,953.90 plus reasonable expenses and telecommunications costs. Where appropriate, approximately the same costs for an additional patent attorney may be added.

Even if, by law, the statutory legal fees may not be undercut, clients and attorneys are free to agree on a (significantly) higher fee rate by contract which is quite common in IP cases (and in general), at least at well-known law firms. Hourly rates between EUR200 and EUR600, depending on the seniority of the involved counsel, are common practice. Thus, attorney fees usually exceed the amount of the statutory fees by a great deal.

11.2 Costs Regarding an Infringement Action

The aforesaid principles also apply for attorney fees in court proceedings. Assuming an amount in dispute of EUR100,000, after a first-instance proceeding including an oral hearing, attorneys on both sides will each invoice EUR3,757.50 (plus expenses, etc) on the basis of the applicable statutes. Again, due to individual fee agreements the parties' attorney costs may be significantly higher (see **11.1 Typical Costs Before Filing**).

Court fees are calculated in a very similar way according to the Court Fees Act (Gerichtskostengesetz). The value in dispute – which represents the financial interest of the plaintiff – determines the court fee which is multiplied by a number of fee units subject to the court's actions. A normal proceeding with a written judgment amounts to three fee units. Expenses, remuneration of witnesses or experts, cost for service of process or translation costs will be added. A lawsuit with a value of EUR100,000 will thus cause court fees in the amount of EUR3,078 (plus expenses, etc).

11.3 Costs of Litigation

Firstly, the claimant is responsible for paying accrued court fees in order to start the proceedings. During the dispute, expenses incurred for procedural actions are borne by the party which requests them. But ultimately the losing party is required to reimburse the prevailing party for all costs of litigation fees inclusive of court fees, expenses and attorney fees of both parties in the statutory amount; this does not include higher costs due to a fee arrangement (see the last paragraph of **11.1 Typical Costs Before Filing**). The judgment rendered by a court always encompasses a decision on the reimbursement of cost. In the case of a partial win, the statutory amount of the total cost will be split pro rata.

12. Alternative Dispute Resolution

12.1 Common Way of Settlement

In spite of the growing significance of ADR in Germany, it is at present not very common in IP matters, even less in trade mark cases. Apparently, the reason for this is the excellent work of German courts in litigating trade mark and other IP cases. Compared to other countries, the courts work relatively fast and at reasonable cost and usually provide a substantial level of expertise. Thus, it is not necessary for the parties to rely on ADR in order to receive a proper solution of their dispute. Furthermore, a fruitless attempt at ADR is not prerequisite for any court action. Nevertheless, ADR may still be appropriate in cases of long-term and multinational agreements between the parties rather than in infringement cases.

The most common ADR method in IP matters is arbitration. Provided that the parties conclude a valid arbitration agreement in an arbitrable matter (please note: the question of the validity of a granted intellectual property right is not an arbitrable matter), an action before a state court is not admissible. For all arbitrational proceedings conducted in Germany, the 10th Book of the German Code on Civil Procedure (Zivilprozessordnung, Sections 1025 to 1066) applies. The law is based on the UNCITRAL Model Law and Germany is party to various international arbitration treaties such as the New York Convention.

Parties are then free to agree on the language used in the arbitral proceedings, the place of arbitration and the person and the number of arbitrators. Pertaining to the procedural rules, the parties may agree to pre-drafted arbitration rules (eg by the ICC) or leave it to the arbitral tribunal to decide how to approach fact-finding and taking of evidence. In Germany, however, facts and evidence must usually be provided by the parties. "Discovery" rules are not applicable and witnesses are questioned by the judge (no cross-examination). The tribunal's final ruling has the same status as a final court judgment and can be declared enforceable. It includes a decision on the costs, taking into consideration all circumstances of the case, in particular the outcome.

German courts normally do not intervene in a pending arbitration. However, exceptions are made, for instance, for the appointment or challenge of arbitrators if there is no agreement between the parties, interim measures or assistance in taking evidence or enforcement of orders. Moreover, the court can set aside an arbitral tribunal's jurisdiction under specific circumstances if certain essential prerequisites of German Law are not met.

For the sake of completeness, the existing special ADR programmes in domain name disputes deserve to be mentioned as well. Unlike the ICANN UDRP conducted by the WIPO Arbitration and Mediation Centre, inter alia competent for generic top level domains, and the EURid alternative dispute resolution mechanism provided by the Czech Arbitration Court for the top level domain ".eu", the German central registry for the top level domain ".de" (DENIC eG) does not offer an ADR service. There is only the possibility to file a "dispute entry" by which an infringing domain name is transferred to the right-holder after the latter has successfully claimed for a deletion of the domain in court. Thus, domain name disputes usually end up before German courts anyway.

SZA Schilling, Zutt & Anschütz
Otto-Beck-Strasse 11
D-68165 Mannheim

Tel: +49 621 4257 247
Fax: +49 621 4257 286
Email: thomas.naegele@sza.de
Web: www.sza.de

SZA
SCHILLING, ZUTT & ANSCHÜTZ

13. Trade Marks and Other Intellectual Property

13.1 Protection by Copyright

Intellectual property rights are not mutually exclusive. In general, a trade mark might also be protected in parallel by other rights (eg a copyright in the case of a very creative logo), provided that the respective protection requirements are met.

ISRAEL

LAW AND PRACTICE: p.153

Contributed by Yaacov Salomon Lipschutz & Co

The 'Law & Practice' sections provide easily accessible information on navigating the legal system when conducting business in the jurisdiction. Leading lawyers explain local law and practice at key transactional stages and for crucial aspects of doing business.

Law and Practice

Contributed by Yaacov Salomon Lipschutz & Co

CONTENTS

Yaacov Salomon Lipschutz & Co, when it was founded 93 years ago, was one of the first firms in the nascent Israel. From the beginning, the firm's clientele included many of Israel's leading companies and groups in all economic sectors, including banks and financial institutions, energy and utility companies, real estate companies, industrial companies, transportation companies, infrastructure companies, co-operative societies and both local and foreign investors in Israel. Over the years, the firm's practice has developed, along with the development of Israel's economy, to include the high-tech and bio-tech sectors. The firm has offices in Tel-Aviv, Haifa and Jerusalem. The firm's intellectual property group consists of seven practitioners and focuses primarily on technology acquisition and licencing, OEM transactions, IP litigation, trade mark and design prosecution and enforcement and defence of trade secrets and competition law – in all sectors of the economy for the firm's whole range of clients. The IP group also handles customs seizures and domain name disputes.

Authors

Narda Ben Zvi is head of the firm's intellectual property department, co-head of the firm's high-tech department and a partner in the firm's commercial litigation department. Her practice consists of high-value litigations in IP and commercial cases, prosecution proceedings before the registrar of patents, trade marks and designs, service invention enforcement, commercial transactions including structuring and negotiating complex licensing and OEM transactions, joint ventures, co-development and strategic collaboration agreements and transactions involving the licensing or purchase of IP. Narda has over 30 years of experience in the field. She regularly represents domestic and international clients at all levels of the Israeli court system, including the Supreme Court, as well as in arbitrations and mediations. She has special expertise in corporate and intellectual property litigation.

Ori Kasir is a partner at Yaacov Salomon, Lipschütz & Co, in the high-tech and intellectual property group. He specialises in commercial transactions in licensing and transactions in the fields of ad-tech, monetisation, financial technologies and e-commerce. He is also active in IP litigation, with an emphasis on copyrights, design rights, trade marks and passing-off, prosecution proceedings before the registrar of patents, trade marks and designs, and service invention enforcement. Ori has been involved in litigation at all levels of the Israeli court system, including the Israel Supreme Court, as well as in arbitrations and mediations.

Lena Mor is a senior associate and a member of Yaacov Salomon Lipschutz & Co's intellectual property group. Her primary practice focus is IP litigation before courts on all levels, with an emphasis on copyrights, trade-mark infringement and passing-off; commercial transactions and licensing of copyrights, inventions and designs. Lena also advises the firm's clients on consumer protection regulation and compliance, product-labelling and marketing and advertising regulation.

Daniel Sekler is an associate in the firm's intellectual property group. His practice focuses on prosecution and enforcement of trade-mark and industrial design rights, including strategic management of international IP portfolios, customs seizures and domain name disputes, protection and commercialisation of both traditional and digital copyright, trade marks, designs and patents.

Contributed by Yaacov Salomon Lipschutz & Co **Authors:** Narda Ben Zvi, Ori Kasir, Lena Mor, Daniel Sekler

1. Types of Trade Marks & Registration

1.1 Types of Trade Marks
The Israeli legal system (either by statutory law or case law) provides protection to trade marks, service marks, certification marks, collective marks, three-dimensional marks and well-known marks, as well as to trade dress and company names.

1.2 Trade-Mark Rights
Obtaining trade-mark protection in Israel is accomplished via registration with the Israeli Trademark Office. In addition, unregistered "well-known" marks are protected in Israel subject to meeting the criteria set by the Trade Marks Ordinance (eg, the extent to which the mark is recognised in the public circles relating to it, the extent to which the mark is known as a result of marketing efforts, sales, etc). In addition, trade marks used in commerce may be protected through other legal theories such as unjust enrichment, unfair competition and passing-off.

1.3 Standards for Registering
In order for a trade mark to be eligible for registration it must exhibit an inherently distinctive character. Trade marks which are deemed by the Registrar of Trademarks as descriptive of the claimed goods and/or service may be registered provided that the applicant proves acquired secondary meaning through substantial evidence of use. In addition, Israel allows registration of three-dimensional (3D) marks. Israeli case law determined that 3D marks are devoid of distinctive character (in re, CA 11487/03 August Storck KG v Alpha intoit food products Ltd (published 23 March 2008)). An applicant may obtain trade-mark registration for a 3D mark provided that the following conditions are met:

- the applied-for mark is being used as a source to identify goods and services with the applicant;
- the applied-for mark is not intended merely for ornamentation;
- the mark has acquired secondary meaning through use.

1.4 Trade-Mark Register
Israel maintains a publicly accessible Register of Trademarks. In the first quarter of 2017, the Registrar initiated a public file wrapper, enabling the public to retrieve information and documents in a timely manner and free of charge through the online database.

1.5 Types of Registers
Israel maintains a single official trade-mark register – ie, the "Register of Trademarks".

1.6 Searching for Prior Trade Marks
It is normal practice to conduct a preliminary clearance search ahead of applying to register a trade mark in Israel. The clearance search is conducted primarily to reveal previously registered trade marks in the Register of Trademarks which may conflict with the applied-for mark. Nevertheless, in some cases it is advisable to search for non-registered trade marks in order to assess possible third-party oppositions. The preliminary clearance search may be conducted via an official trade mark search carried out by the Registrar or through a private search conducted either by the applicant itself or by a trade-mark professional in the online trade -mark database and other databases and registers.

The standard preliminary clearance search should be conducted in the official trade-mark database and for non-registered trade marks it is advisable to search the official register of corporations and the available domain names with an authorised domain-name registrar.

1.7 Registration Requirements
In order to register a trade mark, the applied-for mark must be eligible for registration under the Trade Marks Ordinance [new version] 1972 (ie, not included in the list of non-registrable marks as described in **1.15 Grounds for Refusal**), exhibit inherent distinctive nature (or acquired secondary meaning), and not conflict with previously registered trade marks. Use in commerce is not a requirement for registration.

1.8 Registering a Trade Mark
In Israel, any legal entity may apply to register a trade mark in its name, as can individuals.

1.9 Registering Signs
Pursuant to the Trade Marks Ordinance, letters, numerals, words, devices, shapes, slogans, colours or combinations thereof, whether two-dimensional or three-dimensional, are eligible for registration, provided they exhibit either inherent or acquired distinctive character.

1.10 Other Rights to Signs
Israel grants protection for domain names through registration with a certified domain name registrar and the Israeli Dispute Resolution Policy. Company names are protected through registration with the Registrar of Companies. Trade dress and packaging may be granted protection via various legal tools including design rights, unjust enrichment, unfair competition regulations, consumer protection acts and passing-off.

1.11 Registration Procedure
A trade-mark application is pending for approximately 18 months following its filing. It is possible to expedite the examination phase by filing a motion for expedited examination supplemented by an affidavit on behalf of the applicant

and subject to payment of expedited examination fees of approximately USD215.

Once the application is examined, the examiner may issue an office action based on either absolute or relative grounds. The issuance of office actions may prolong the registration process for up to 24 months. The deadline to respond to office actions is three months (extendable for another eight months for a prescribed fee). In the event that the response to the office action is accepted, the examiner will publish the application in the Trademark Official Gazette for possible oppositions by third parties. Once the opposition period (three months) lapses with no opposition notice filed, the trade mark will register and an official trade-mark certificate will be issued.

Multi-class applications are available in Israel.

1.12 Use in Commerce

"Use in commerce" is not a condition to register a trade mark in the country.

Trade marks are valid in Israel for a period of ten years from the date of filing the application, thereafter trade marks may be renewed for consecutive periods of ten years each. Trade marks which were filed for registration on or before 6 August 2013 were valid for seven years. Prior to 2010 and Israel's acceptance of the Madrid Protocol, renewals were for consecutive periods of 14 years.

The official fee for renewing a trade mark in one class is approximately USD811. For each additional class the prescribed renewal fee is approximately USD685.

1.13 Registration of Series Marks

Israel does not acknowledge series marks.

1.14 Length of Registration Process

The trade-mark registration process lasts between 18 and 24 months. Representation by an attorney is not compulsory and applicants may apply to register a trade mark independently. However, regarding international designations to Israel by foreign proprietors, if an office action is issued or an opposition notice is filed, the applicant is required to appoint an agent.

The official fee for trade-mark application in one class is approximately USD455. For expedited examination an additional fee of approximately USD214 is required for each class included in the application. Attorney fees vary but will typically be in the range of USD500 to USD1,000 depending on the scope of the goods and services.

1.15 Grounds for Refusal

Refusal on absolute grounds may be evoked in the following circumstances (listed in section 11 of the Trade Marks Ordinance):

- a mark lacking distinctive character;
- a mark affiliated in any manner to the President of the State or to presidential sponsorship or a mark from which any such connection or sponsorship might be inferred;
- flags and emblems of the State or its institutions, flags and emblems of foreign states or international organisations, and any mark resembling any of these;
- public armorial bearings, official signs or seals used by any state to indicate control or warranty, and any signs from which it might be inferred that its proprietor enjoys the sponsorship of or supplies goods or renders services to a head of state or a government, unless it is proved to the Registrar that the proprietor of the mark is entitled to use it;
- a mark in which any of the following words appear: "Patent", "Patented", "By Royal Letters Patent", "Registered", "Registered Design", "Copyright", "To counterfeit this is forgery" or words to like effect;
- a mark which is or may be injurious to public policy or morality;
- a mark likely to deceive the public, a mark which contains a false indication of origin, and marks which encourage unfair trade competition;
- a mark containing a geographical indication in relation to goods that do not originate in the geographical area indicated, or a geographical marking that could be misleading in relation to the genuine geographical area of the origin of the goods;
- a mark containing a geographical marking that is verbally correct but contains a false representation to the effect that the goods originate in another geographical area;
- a mark identical with or similar to emblems of exclusively religious significance;
- a mark on which the representation of a person appears, unless the consent of that person has been obtained; in the case of representation of a deceased person, the Registrar shall request the consent of his or her survivors unless, in their opinion, reasonable grounds exist for not doing so;
- a mark consisting of numerals, letters or words which are in common use in trade, to distinguish or describe goods or classes of goods or which bear direct reference to their character or quality, unless the mark has a distinctive character within the meaning of section 8(b) or 9 of the Ordinance;
- a mark whose ordinary significance is geographical or a surname, unless represented in a special manner or unless having a distinctive character within the meaning of section 8 (b) or 9 [of the Ordinance];

A mark that identifies wine or an alcoholic drink containing a geographical signification, if the origin of the wine or alcoholic drink is not in that same geographical area.

1.16 Process for Overcoming Objections

In order to overcome a refusal based on absolute grounds, the applicant may opt to file written arguments in support of the mark in response to the grounds of refusal. For proprietors domiciled in or maintaining a principal business in countries outside of Israel where they obtained a corresponding trade-mark registration, it is possible to motion to base the Israeli application on the applicant's domicile registration in order to overcome a refusal on absolute grounds. Furthermore, various grounds of refusals may be overcome by substantiating acquired distinctiveness by submitting an affidavit and supporting evidence. In addition, applicants may request to conduct a unilateral hearing before the Registrar in order to outline their arguments orally and attempt to persuade the Registrar to allow registration of the applied-for mark.

In the case of a refusal on relative grounds, the applicant may assert the differences between the cited marks and claim eligibility for co-existence; obtain a letter of consent or reach a co-existence agreement with the owner of the cited mark, the acceptance of which is at the discretion of the Registrar; lodge a cancellation action against the cited mark.

1.17 Consideration of Prior Rights

The Registrar considers the existence of prior rights when examining an application for registration and may refuse registration of an application which it deems likely to create confusion with a prior registered mark and/or an unregistered well-known trade mark.

Furthermore, the Trade Marks Ordinance provides the practice of interference proceedings. In the event that two or more pending applications are deemed similar in their overall appearance, sound, and apply to similar consumer crowds, the Registrar may initiate interference proceedings (also known as "competing application procedure") during which each party will be requested to submit its evidence and shall maintain the right to cross-examine affiants. The Registrar will determine which of the parties' marks is favourable for registration over its counterpart in accordance with three principles: the bona fide intention of each party in choosing the mark; the duration and scope of use of each party in its mark; and the date of filing of the application. It is notable that the Registrar maintains full discretion to declare concurrent registration of the parties' marks.

1.18 Third-Party Rights

Third parties have the right to file observations during examination as well as an opposition against registration of a trade mark.

In the event that a third party submits an observation during the examination of the application, the Registrar will issue an office action requiring the applicant to respond within three months (extendable for up to eight months) either by filing written arguments or motioning for a hearing before the Registrar.

In addition, third parties may file an opposition notice within three months (non-extendable) of the date of publication of the trade mark in the Trademark Official Gazette.

Any third party may file an opposition, and proof of standing or commercial interest is not required.

1.19 Revoke, Change, Amend or Correct an Application

Applicants may revoke a trade-mark application at any time. Applicants may also file for an amendment of the mark itself. However, amendments to the mark are permitted solely if they do not materially alter the applied-for mark and are subject to the discretion of the examiner. In addition, it is possible to amend the specification of goods and/or services provided that the amendments narrow, but not broaden, the scope of the originally filed list of goods and services. Such an amendment is also subject to the discretion of the Registrar.

1.20 Assigning an Application or Granting a Licence

The Registrar allows assignment of an application during the registration process. Licensing is available only for registered marks.

1.21 Remedies Against the Trade Mark Office

The refused applicant may motion for a unilateral hearing before the Registrar. In addition, an applicant maintains the right to appeal the Registrar's decision to the District Court.

1.22 Use of a Trade Mark

"Use in Commerce" is not a condition for trade-mark registration in Israel.

1.23 Dividing a Trade Mark

It is possible to divide a multi-class trade-mark application by submitting a corresponding motion to the Registrar. In addition, it is possible to consolidate two or more trade-mark applications for the same mark with the same filing date to a multi-class registration. This is performed by submitting a corresponding motion and remitting the applicable official fees.

1.24 Length of Term of Protection

Trade marks are granted protection for a period of ten years, from the date of filing the application. Trade mark-owners may renew their registration indefinitely, for consecutive terms of ten years each. In order to renew the registration of a trade mark the owner must remit the applicable office fees in conjunction with a motion to renew the trade mark.

The Trade Marks Ordinance grants a grace period of six months for renewal. However, renewal of a trade mark during the grace period incurs a surcharge in the official fees for each month of delay. If a trade mark is not renewed during the grace period, the owner is granted a one-year period to reinstate the registration, subject to the discretion of the Registrar. Though the trade mark's status during this one-year period is "abandoned due to non-payment", the Office will continue to cite the trade mark in case a similar application is submitted during the one-year reinstatement period. If the trade-mark owner refrains from renewing or reinstating the registration, the trade mark will be permanently cancelled.

1.25 Requirements for an Exhaustion

Trade mark rights may be exhausted when registration is not renewed as described in the section above. Furthermore, a trade mark may be effectively exhausted in the event of parallel import of goods. The right for parallel import was recognised under the Supreme Court Ruling in re, PCA 371/89 Illan Leibowitz v. A. & Y. Eliyahu Ltd, and affirmed by contemporary ruling of the Supreme Court in re, CA 7629/12 Elad Menahem Swisa et al v. Tommy Hilfiger Licensing LLC et al (Published 16 November 2014) (Tommy Hilfiger). In Tommy Hilfiger, the Supreme Court thoroughly discussed the relations between parallel import and trade mark rights and determined that parallel import is a legitimate action, not infringing trade-mark rights subject to certain restrictions determined by the court.

1.26 Participation in the Madrid System

Israel is a member of the Madrid Protocol since 2010. Designations under the Madrid Protocol to Israel are scheduled for publication in the Trademark Official Gazette within 18 months of the IR's application date (assuming no office actions are issued). Nevertheless, the Registrar maintains discretion to extend the 18-month period with prior notice to the applicant. The only requirement from foreign applicants under the Madrid Protocol is to appoint an agent in cases where an office action or an opposition notice is issued.

1.27 Consequences for Providing Incorrect Information

Knowingly providing incorrect information to the Registrar is a criminal offence subject to one year's imprisonment. An applicant is required to disclose full and correct information in a trade-mark application and during the prosecution of a trade mark and to conduct judicial procedures in good faith (section 61(b) Contracts Law (general provisions), 1973). In addition, violating the duty to conduct judicial procedures in good faith may result in revocation of the application or registration. Such determination can be made by the Registrar when residing as an adjudicator.

1.28 Updating or Refreshing a Design Mark

The Registrar prohibits updating or refreshing a design mark. In cases of material amendments to a proprietor's design, a fresh application is required.

1.29 Denotation

Use of the symbol ® is allowed solely with respect to registered trade marks. Trade mark-owners may assert common-law rights in non-registered trade marks by using the symbol.

2. Assignment and Licensing

2.1 Assignment Requirements or Restrictions

An assignment of a trade mark, registered or pending, is available by submitting a motion for assignment in which the parties are required to declare that no consumer confusion will arise due to the assignment. The motion for assignment must be supplemented by a written agreement or deed of assignment executed by both parties as well as a power of attorney. In addition, the parties are required to remit the official fees prescribed for assignment. The Registrar may refuse to approve the assignment on grounds that the use of the assigned mark by the assignee will create consumer confusion or if the assignment is adverse to public policy.

2.2 Procedure for Assigning a Trade Mark

The owner of the assigned mark is required to submit to the Trademark Office a motion of assignment according to the requirements of the Trademark Regulations, 1940, supplemented by a deed of assignment executed by both parties, a power of attorney, and remittance of the official fee. The Registrar will examine the motion and the supplemented documents and determine whether or not to approve and record the assignment.

2.3 Registering or Recording the Assignment

An assignment of a trade mark is required to be recorded in the Register of Trademarks as aforementioned. If the assignment is not recorded at all in the Register, the goodwill in the mark and the underlying use following the assignment will not be attributed to the assignee, which may expose the trade mark to cancellation actions on grounds of non-use.

2.4 Trade Marks and Security

Israel recognises rights in rem to a registered trade mark as well as to well-known trade marks. Registered trade marks may be granted as securities or levied in execution. In order to effect a registered trade mark properly as security, it is required to record the beneficiary of the security in the Register of Trademarks.

2.5 Licensing Requirements or Restrictions
A registered trade mark may be licensed. A trade-mark licence requires a written agreement and the recording of the licence with the Registrar. The Registrar maintains the discretion whether or not to authorise the licence as well as to issue orders or prescribe specific terms for the licence agreement. Israel recognises any kind of licence – eg, exclusive licence, non-exclusive licence, sole licence, perpetual licence – subject to the discretion of the Registrar.

2.6 Procedure for Licensing a Trade Mark
To license a trade mark the parties are required to submit a motion to record a licence supplemented by the licence agreement, a power of attorney (no notarisation or legalisation required) and remit the applicable office fees. In the motion (or in the licence agreement itself) the parties are required to detail:

- the relationship between the licensor and the licensee;
- any limitations on the licensee;
- the supervision of the licensor's use of the trade mark;
- the goods and/or services subject to the licence;
- the period for which the licence is given;
- a declaration that, to the best of their knowledge, no consumer confusion will arise as a result of the licence.

The Registrar may request additional information and may approve the licence if it does not contradict public policy and will not cause consumer confusion.

2.7 Registering or Recording the Licence
For a licence agreement to enter into effect, the licence is required to be recorded in the Register of Trademarks. If there is no such record, the use of the trade mark by the licensee and the good will of the trade mark will not be attributed to the licensee and the trade mark will be vulnerable to cancellation actions on non-use grounds.

2.8 Reasons to Deny Granting a Perpetual Licence
The Registrar may refuse to record a perpetual licence (as well as any kind of licence) if it is found either to mislead consumers, negate the public policy or induce unfair competition.

3. Opposition Procedure

3.1 Legal Grounds and Timeframes
A third party that finds itself injured or otherwise harmed by a trade-mark application may lodge an opposition action within three months of the publication date of the opposed trade mark. The three-month publication period is non-extendable.

Opposition proceedings may be filed on any grounds for which the Registrar of Trademarks may refuse registration of a trade mark, and which are prescribed throughout the Trade Marks Ordinance.

3.2 Filing an Opposition
Any interested third party, as well as any party claiming ownership in the mark itself, may lodge an opposition on grounds indicated in the Trade Marks Ordinance. Parties domiciled in Israel are not required to appoint an agent. Owners of international designations to Israel, however, are required to appoint an agent in accordance with the Madrid Protocol. The fee for lodging an opposition notice is approximately USD230 per opposition submitted. Due to the litigious nature of opposition procedures, the professional fees vary between cases, while the customary fee is on a time-spent basis.

3.3 Opposition Procedure
Oppositions are lodged by filing an opposition notice with the Registrar. The Registrar notifies the owner of the applied-for mark of the opposition notice and the applicant is entitled to file a notice in response to the opposition within two months. Should the application owner fail to submit a notice in response in a timely manner or apply to extend the deadline, the trade mark will be deemed withdrawn. Once both parties have filed their statements, each party is required to file its evidence in the form of an affidavit supported by all evidence it wishes to submit as proof of its position. Each party may subsequently file evidence in response and the Registrar will schedule a hearing during which the affiants of both parties will be cross-examined on their affidavits. Thereafter, the parties will submit written summations (the Registrar may also order oral summations) and the Registrar will render its resolution.

3.4 Legal Remedies
The Registrar's resolution in an opposition procedure may be appealed "by right" (ie, no request for permission to appeal is required) within 30 days of the resolution's date to either the Tel Aviv District Court or to the Jerusalem District Court, at the appellant's discretion. The decision of the District Court may be appealed to the Supreme Court within 30 days – solely if permission to appeal is granted.

4. Initiating a Lawsuit

4.1 Actions to Pursue Infringement
A trade mark-owner may pursue infringement either by filing a civil action or by filing a criminal complaint (in the appropriate cases). A civil action may be submitted for infringement of either a registered or non-registered well-known mark, for trade-mark infringement, passing-off, unjust enrichment and possibly additional causes of actions,

based on circumstances. In addition, a trade mark-owner may initiate customs seizure proceedings to counter counterfeit goods.

4.2 Initiating Infringement Proceedings
A trade mark-owner may initiate an infringement action in either the District Court or the Magistrates' Court, depending on the relief requested. If the plaintiff seeks an injunction or his or her claimed monetary relief is of or above NIS2.5 Million, he or she should apply to the District Court; otherwise, they should apply to the Magistrates' Court.

4.3 Effect of Decisions on Infringement Actions
The Trademark Office acts as a judicial tribunal as well as an administrative instance. The ruling of the Registrar in his or her judicial capacity, such as decisions regarding similarity of marks or the likelihood of confusion, may be used in any civil case between the parties. However, these are not conclusive and the court may reach different conclusions.

4.4 Declaratory Judgment Proceedings
An alleged infringer may initiate declaratory judgment proceedings for a ruling of non-infringement after receipt of a cease-and-desist letter.

4.5 Jurisdiction of Courts
The majority of trade-mark infringement cases are heard before the District Courts, in accordance with the applicable rules of venue. However, as aforementioned, cases which do not involve a claim for injunction and/or seek monetary relief of less than NIS2.5 million will be heard before the Magistrates' Court. An appeal on the ruling of the first instance is granted by right to a higher court (either District or Supreme Court). An appeal on the ruling of the second instance requires permission to appeal. If the second instance is the Supreme Court, there is no right of a third-round appeal. An appeal on the Registrar's ruling is heard before the District Court and the decision of the District Court may be appealed to the Supreme Court – if permission to appeal is granted.

4.6 Prerequisites to Filing a Lawsuit
There are no prerequisites for filing a lawsuit in Israel. However, it is customary to send a cease-and-desist notice prior to lodging an action.

4.7 Representation for Parties
Parties which are engaged in infringement actions before a court are not required to appoint representation. However, it is highly advisable to retain an intellectual property professional to conduct litigation.

4.8 Interim or Preliminary Injunctions
Interim and preliminary injunctions are available either through inter parte or ex parte proceedings. In order to receive interim relief, the plaintiff is required (i) to provide prima facie evidence and substantiate its cause of action and (ii) to prove that the interim relief is urgently required, and that the balance between the damages that may be inflicted on the respondent as a result of granting the injunction, and the prospective damages to the plaintiff should an interim relief be refused, leans towards the plaintiff and justifies granting the injunction. Furthermore, in order to receive an injunction, the claimant must submit its claim in good faith, act expediently and without delay. If the court finds that the motion suffers from unreasonable delay (laches), this serves as sufficient cause to reject the motion for injunction.

4.9 Protection for Potential Defendant
The measures that may be taken by a potential plaintiff will naturally vary from case to case, based on circumstances. Other measures may include initiating declaratory judgment proceedings for a ruling of non-infringement and applying to the Registrar to revoke the subject-matter trade mark; also, in the event that the action was already filed, requesting that the claimant submit a bond to secure the defendant's expenses.

4.10 Obtaining Information and Evidence
The Israeli legal system has implemented disclosure and discovery mechanisms as preliminary proceedings between or among parties to litigation proceedings conducted in court in accordance with the Civil Procedure Rules,1984. In addition to disclosure and discovery proceedings, the rules of procedure allow for sending a questionnaire to the counter party. Disclosures and discoveries are facilitated by the parties themselves and are scheduled to be completed within 30 days (extendable) from submission of the last statement of response on behalf of the plaintiff. During the disclosure and discovery process, the parties exchange disclosure affidavits which detail each party's documents relevant to the dispute, provide copies of documents, and submit an affidavit in response to the questionnaire. A party that fails to disclose a document or evidence may not rely on it to corroborate its claims and may be subject to sanctions imposed by the court.

Litigation proceedings before the Registrar do not entail disclosure and discovery proceedings as detailed above. The Registrar is authorised to instruct the parties to conduct general discoveries or specific ones but those, if conducted, will be of a much smaller scale.

4.11 Initial Pleading Standards
Any legal proceedings initiated in the Israeli court system (as opposed to the proceedings before the Registrar) are governed by the Civil Procedure Rules mentioned above. There are no special or specific instructions as to the scope of the pleadings other than the requirement that the court pleadings sufficiently detail the causes of action and include all relevant information and documents required for the

subject-matter. Pleadings may include all relevant causes of action such as trade-mark infringement, unjust enrichment, passing-off and any other cause of action arising from the circumstances. There are no special provisions concerning trade-mark actions.

4.12 Representative or Collective Actions
Israel allows collective actions as class actions. Class actions may be filed for specific causes of action, prescribed by the second addendum to the Class Action Act, 2006. The Class Action Act, 2006, does not include the violation of the Trade Marks Ordinance as grounds for a class action; however, one of the provisions of the second addendum empowers consumers to file class actions on grounds of consumer misleading or deceit, contrary to the provisions of the Consumer Protection Act, 1981. Therefore, if a vendor uses a trade mark in a misleading manner, that action may be considered a violation of the Consumer Protection Act and, thereby, grant consumers a cause for class action. To date, there has not been a class action suit involving the misleading of consumers with regard to a trade mark's source.

4.13 Restrictions on Trade Mark-Owners
When asserting their rights, trade mark-owners are required to exercise their rights in accordance with general principles of the law – such as the requirement to exercise their rights in good faith – and may be subject to restrictions under competition law, depending on the circumstances.

5. Infringement

5.1 Action for Infringement
The owner of the trade mark is a required party for any trade-mark infringement action. In addition, any relevant party whose rights may be affected from a judicial decision on the case should be included as a party. Therefore, a licensee will most likely be a party to an infringement case. Israel allows trade mark-owners to pursue their rights even before obtaining trade-mark registration through passing-off, well-known mark, unjust enrichment and product-labelling regulations. It is notable that in infringement cases which do not rely on a registered trade mark, the plaintiff is required to establish good will in the mark through substantial evidence.

5.2 Signs and Infringement
Israeli courts have adopted the triangular test to determine whether use of a sign is likely to create consumer confusion and therefore constitute infringement (CA 261/64 Pro-Pro Biscuit Ltd v L. Frumin and sons Ltd, published 15 September 1964). The plaintiff carries the burden of substantiating the likelihood of confusion by applying the triangular test. The triangular test consists of the following considerations: (i) similarity in sound and appearance; (ii) similarity in goods and services and similarity in the designated consumer crowds; (iii) further factual considerations, applicable on a case-by-case basis.

In the case of a claim for infringement of a non-registered trade mark, the plaintiff is required to establish good will in the mark, as well as likelihood of confusion pursuant to the triangular test.

5.3 Use of a Sign by Defendant
The test case for trade-mark infringement is likelihood of confusion pursuant to the triangular test. Nevertheless, defendants may assert nominative fair-use and descriptive fair-use defences which are applicable in instances where the use of the trade mark by a person or entity other than the proprietor was intended to describe the goods covered by the trade mark without creating an association or sponsorship between the defendant and the plaintiff. In such cases, and pursuant to good-faith standards and considerations of likelihood of confusion, the use of a trade mark by another may be allowed.

5.4 Defences Against Infringement
The Trade Marks Ordinance provides for specific defences such as nominative fair use, descriptive fair use, and non-distinctiveness claim. In addition, the Trade Marks Ordinance allows an individual or legal entity, under certain circumstances, to use a trade mark if it consists of their given name or business name. Fair-use defence is subject to standards of good faith and likelihood of confusion.

In addition, a defendant in a trade-mark infringement case can apply general defences such as equitable estoppel, bad faith, submission of a request to revoke or cancel the trade mark, etc.

5.5 Role of Experts and/or Surveys
Attesting experts is common practice and usually serves as a persuasive measure to establish either distinctiveness (or non-distinctiveness) or likelihood of confusion. Consumer surveys are an important tool for establishing good will (or lack thereof) and likelihood of confusion or distinctiveness. The courts have determined that the use of consumer surveys, although not mandatory, is a highly important indicator in trade-mark infringement cases (in re, CA 4410/06 N.R.G Energy international Ltd. v Texaco Inc, published 31 August 2010).

5.6 Administrative or Criminal Offence
Trade-mark infringement may constitute either an administrative offence or a criminal offence. Administrative procedures are executed by the Israeli Customs Administration pursuant to importation of counterfeit goods into Israel.

With respect to criminal procedures – infringement of a registered trade mark is a penalty punishable by up to three years' imprisonment or a fine of up to USD450,000.

A criminal procedure is administered by the State Attorney's Office. The prosecution carries the burden to prove the defendant's guilt beyond any reasonable doubt. In addition, trade mark-owners may lodge a private criminal action in the event that the State Attorney's Office does not move forward with an investigation.

5.7 Custom Seizures

Counterfeit goods imported into Israel (as opposed to parallel import of genuine goods) are intercepted by the Israeli Customs Administration. It is possible for trade mark-owners to record their registered trade marks with the customs agency for the purpose of monitoring possible infringements. Once the goods are seized (either by prior request of the proprietor or by routine customs operations), the Customs Administration will contact the proprietor and condition the detainment of the goods by the deposit of a bank guarantee to secure possible financial damages to the importer should the goods eventually be released to its custody, or to cover storage and destruction expenses.

Customs seizure is divided into two separate procedures: a short procedure and a long procedure. A short procedure is initiated in such cases where customs intercept small-scale shipments, a shipment suspected of violating local import regulations, goods entering the country via parcel or private package, or small-scale shipments consisting of several different trade marks. Under the short procedure, the owner is granted three business days (extendable at the discretion of the Customs Administration) to submit a written opinion detailing why the goods are believed to be counterfeit, authorise the destruction of the goods, and stipulate to join Customs as a party in case a lawsuit is filed by the importer. Under the short procedure, the trade mark-owner will not receive the details and contact information of the importer.

A long procedure is initiated in cases of interception of a large shipment or when the goods are of high monetary value. In the long procedure the trade mark-owner is granted three business days (extendable at the discretion of the Custom's Administration) to submit a bank guarantee, and an opinion detailing why the goods are counterfeit. Under the long procedure, the trade mark-owner receives the details of the importer and is compelled, in return, either to settle with the importer or to file a lawsuit within ten business days of receipt of the specimens of the counterfeit goods, (a period extendable at the discretion of the Customs Administration).

It is notable that, while in the short procedure the trade mark-owner is not informed of the importer's details, owners may opt to initiate a long procedure in order to receive the importer's information and pursue their damages and enforce their rights.

6. Revocation/Cancellation

6.1 Remedies and Reasons

Revocation actions may be based on three types of grounds: (i) non-use, (ii) absolute or relative grounds making the registered trade mark non-eligible for registration, as indicated by the Trade Marks Ordinance, and (iii) registration in bad faith.

Non-use revocation actions may be filed by any interested party, based on the claim that during the three years preceding the revocation application the trade mark was not used in Israel.

Revocation actions on relative or absolute grounds may be filed up to five years from the official registration date by any party finding itself injured by the registration. Such revocation actions may be based either on grounds that the petitioner claims to be the true owner of the trade mark or based on the prescribed grounds in clauses 8-11 in the Trade Marks Ordinance (see section **1.Types of Trade Mark and Regulations**).

Revocation actions based on registration in bad faith may be filed at any time by any party finding itself injured by the registration. The term "any time" was recently interpreted as "without any time limitations" and the court cancelled a trade mark that was registered for 40 years on the grounds that it was registered in bad faith (in re C.A 29227-13-16 Habitat Ltd et al v CAFMO et al, published 13 November 2016). For trade marks owned by non-Israeli proprietors that are also registered in their domicile, a trade mark will not be cancelled on grounds of registration in bad faith providing the original registration in the proprietor's country of origin is validly registered.

6.2 Trade Mark Office and Civil Courts

Revocation and cancellation actions should be brought before the Trademark Office, which has exclusive authority on the subject matter. The District Court is authorised to rule on cancellation or revocation of trade marks as an appellate court.

6.3 Statutory Limitation or Time Period

Non-use actions may be filed only if at least three years have elapsed from the official date of registration of the trade mark.

Revocation actions on grounds of relative or absolute grounds may be filed up to five years from the official date of registration.

Revocation actions based on a claim of bad faith in registration may be filed at any time (see section **6.1 Remedies and Reasons** above).

6.4 Initiation of Revocation/Cancellation Proceeding

Revocation actions may be filed by any person (including legal entities) injured by the registration, such as competitors, third parties claiming ownership of the trade mark or a similar mark, etc. There are no admissibility or standing requirements, other than being injured by the challenged registration. The Trademark Office will not initiate independent revocation proceedings.

6.5 Partial Revocation/Cancellation

Partial revocation/cancellation is possible in cases when the revocation application pertains to only some of the goods and/or services or to some of the classes in respect of which the trade mark is registered.

6.6 Possibilities of Amendment

Amendment to the scope or the description of goods and services is possible in revocation proceedings, either by order of the Registrar or by request of the parties. An amendment to the scope or the description of goods and services will be granted only if it narrows the scope of protection of the list of goods and services.

6.7 Revocation/Cancellation and Infringement

Infringement actions are heard before a competent court while revocation actions are heard before the Registrar. As the Registrar has exclusive authority to revoke or cancel a trade mark (as a first instance), it is often the case that soon after an infringement action is brought before a competent court, a revocation action is submitted to the Registrar. Although the proceedings before the court and the Registrar may be conducted in parallel, it is likely the infringement action will be stayed until resolution in the revocation action.

7. Trial & Settlement

7.1 Special Procedural Provisions

Proceedings conducted before the Registrar are subject to a special procedure determined by the Trade Marks Ordinance and Trademark Regulations. This procedure is less structured, granting more discretion to the Registrar and providing fewer procedural measures than the procedure which applies to legal proceedings in the court system – for example, the disclosure proceedings allowed in proceedings before the Registrar, if allowed at all, are very limited. Provided, however, that where the specific trade-mark procedural provisions are silent, the civil procedure rules will apply.

In trade-mark cases adjudicated before the civil court system, the general rules of civil procedure apply and there are no specific rules for trade-mark cases.

7.2 Determination of Cases

Trade-mark infringement cases are heard before a judge assigned to the case by the court, without necessarily having trade mark or intellectual property expertise or experience. The parties do not have any influence on the identity of the decision-maker.

7.3 Possibilities of Settlement

A defendant may attempt to settle the case at any stage of the trial by proposing a settlement to its counterparty. The court itself will not take part in such negotiations. Nevertheless, Civil Procedure Rules impose mandatory mediation between or among the parties before the trial proceeds to the stage of evidence.

The mandatory mediation is conducted before a mediator appointed by the court or chosen by the parties.

7.4 Other Court Proceedings

The rule of lis alibi pendens applies in the Israeli legal system and judicial tribunals will attempt to avoid parallel proceedings. Therefore, if revocation proceedings are initiated parallel to an infringement action, the infringement action will probably be stayed until final resolution is rendered by the Registrar in the revocation action.

8. Remedies

8.1 Existing Remedies

A trade mark-owner may receive any or all of the remedies available to a plaintiff under the Israeli law, which include:

- interim and permanent injunctions;
- actual damages suffered as a result of the infringement or statutory damages under certain causes of action (other than trade-mark infringement under the Ordinance);
- punitive damages for wilful infringement;
- account of profits – in order to allow the plaintiff to substantiate the actual damages sustained by the infringement of the trade mark;
- reimbursement of legal expenditures and attorney fees to the prevailing party – in the majority of cases, the prescribed expenditures and legal expenses do not cover the actual expenses.

In addition, the court may order the destruction of the infringing goods and transfer of ownership of the infringing goods to the plaintiff in consideration of their value.

All remedies are subject to the discretion of the court. In addition, the court may issue any other order it sees fit.

8.2 Rights and Remedies

A defendant that successfully countered an infringement action is eligible for reimbursement of legal expenditures and attorney fees. In the majority of cases, the reimbursed expenditures and legal expenses do not cover the actual expenses. Defendants may request that the court issue a brief of judgment for non-infringement based on the judgment.

All remedies are subject to the discretion of the court. In addition, the court may issue any other order it sees fit.

8.3 Different Types of Remedies

All types of trade marks are afforded the same scope of remedies available under the Ordinance.

9. Appeal

9.1 Special Provisions

The provisions regarding the appellate procedure for trade-mark proceedings conducted before a competent court in the civil court system are identical to those that apply to any other court case.

The provisions regarding the appellate procedure for trade-mark proceedings conducted before the Registrar are of the same nature as those prescribed for other civil cases with two exceptions: (i) an appeal on the ruling of the Registrar should be submitted to either the Tel-Aviv District Court or the Jerusalem District Court; (ii) in order to appeal the District Court of Appeals' ruling (second-round appeal) to the Supreme Court, a permission to appeal is required and an application for such permission should be filed with the Supreme Court within 30 days of the District Court's ruling.

9.2 Factual or Legal Review

The Court of Appeals does not interfere with the factual findings of the lower instance other than in extraordinary circumstances, such as a material error in the findings. By rule of thumb, courts of appeal review legal claims.

9.3 Length of Appeal from Trial Court

The timeframe for a decision in an appeal varies between the courts and is dependent on each court's workload and the conduct of the parties themselves. The average appeal case is resolved within 12–18 months.

10. Other Trade Mark Issues

10.1 Recognition of Dilution

Dilution has been recognised as a valid cause of action by the Israeli courts in connection to unfair competition (in re, CA 6181/96 Cardini v Bacardi & Company Limited, published 19 July 1998). To establish dilution, the plaintiff must substantiate that its trade mark has become a well-known trade mark. Dilution is a valid ground to oppose a trade-mark registration under section 11(13)–(14) to the Trade Marks Ordinance, with regard to well-known trade marks.

10.2 Protection of Famous Marks

Israel recognises the protection of famous trade marks outside of its jurisdiction through the "well-known trade mark" doctrine, even if that trade mark is not registered or in use in Israel.

10.3 Special Rules Regarding Geographic Indicators

Geographical indicators and appellation of origins are ineligible for registration as trade marks unless they have acquired secondary meaning and will not mislead consumers as to the origin of the goods. Registration of geographical indicators or appellation of origin is possible through the Appellations of Origin and Geographical Indications (Protection) Act, 1965, via a separate procedure.

10.4 Special Rules Relating to Surnames

The Trade Marks Ordinance grants protection to the use of one's own surname which conflicts with a registered trade mark. In such cases, the defendant may enjoy the defence of nominative fair use, subject to considerations of likelihood of confusion.

11. Costs

11.1 Costs Before Filing a Lawsuit

The costs for preparing a lawsuit will vary based on the complexity of the circumstances, and whether or not it will be required to conduct a survey, submit an expert opinion, translate or notarise evidence, etc. Such costs may range from a couple of thousands of dollars in a simple case to approximately USD15,000 in complex cases. One needs to take into account a court fee of 2.5% of the amount claimed (of which 1.25% is required to be paid upon submission of the statement of claim), and a guarantee (such as either a bank guarantee, or cash deposit as well as a personal guarantee) is required if an interim relief is requested.

11.2 Costs Regarding an Infringement Action

As the scope of infringement actions is dependent on the facts and specific circumstances, the cost of litigating each case varies respectively. Litigation cases are normally charged on a time-spent basis.

11.3 Costs of Litigation

The official court fees are first remitted by the plaintiff. The judgment of the court will typically include an order in respect of costs and regarding legal fees and is at the discretion of the judge. In most cases, the judge will grant the prevailing party a certain award of costs (ranging from actual cost of litigation based on receipts for amounts spent, to a fixed amount set by the judge) and attorneys' fees at an amount which is much lower than the amount actually spent by the prevailing party.

12. Alternative Dispute Resolution

12.1 Common Way of Settlement

Alternative dispute resolution proceedings are common and are advised for settling disputes. The Israeli Civil Procedure Rules impose mandatory mediation before a court-appointed mediator as a preliminary measure to resolve disputes – after a lawsuit is filed. In general, resorting to mediation or binding arbitration is common in Israel, and the tendency of parties to resort to mediation or arbitration is increasing in light of the overload of the court system, and the long period of litigation.

The most common ADR is mediation, since it is quick, inexpensive and the resolution of the dispute is dependent on both parties' consent. The mediator can only recommend a resolution and does not bind the parties. The mediation is confidential and neither party may cite or rely upon statements given during the mediation.

Arbitration is more similar to a litigation process and the arbitrator renders a resolution that is binding on the parties. Therefore, the parties will typically execute an arbitration agreement, an agreement that includes the agreed-upon rules and procedures of the arbitration (for example, provisions regarding appealing the arbitrator's judgment, whether the arbitration will be heard according to the rules of evidence and procedure in civil courts, etc). The prevailing party is required to affirm the judgment before a competent district court and the losing party may motion to cancel the judgment solely on grounds prescribed in the Arbitration Act, 1968; however, such a motion is rarely accepted.

In addition to arbitration and mediation procedures, parties may resolve their dispute via an amicable out-of-court settlement agreement.

13. Trade Marks and Other Intellectual Property

13.1 Protection by Copyright

A designed trade mark may be protected by copyright law provided that the plaintiff substantiates that the trade mark qualifies as a protected work of art and that he or she is the original creator of the work. In addition, proprietary rights in trade dress may be protected by a registered design.

Yaacov Salomon, Lipschütz & Co.
'Beit Silver'
7, Abba Hillel Silver st.
P.O.B 3424 Ramat-Gan
Israel 5213602

Tel: 972-3-5757712
Fax: 972-3-5757725
Email: office-tel-aviv@ysl-law.com
Web: www.ysl-law.com

Yaacov Salomon, Lipschütz & Co.
LAW OFFICES & NOTARIES

ITALY

LAW AND PRACTICE: p.169

Contributed by Clifford Chance Studio Legale Associato

The 'Law & Practice' sections provide easily accessible information on navigating the legal system when conducting business in the jurisdiction. Leading lawyers explain local law and practice at key transactional stages and for crucial aspects of doing business.

Law and Practice

Contributed by Clifford Chance Studio Legale Associato

CONTENTS

Clifford Chance Studio Legale Associato is a single partnership operating through an integrated network founded on a 'one firm' approach. Creating an environment where lawyers work closely with colleagues from our 32 offices (and local 'best friend' firms where we have strong relationships) is critical to the success of delivering a first-rate service. The team has an in-depth knowledge of the IP sector with close links to trade associations, speak regularly at industry-specific conferences and often author industry-related articles in legal and trade journals. Expertise includes legal advice prior to the use of any kind of trade marks; enforcement of claims arising from trademark and copyright laws and defence against third party attack.

Author

Monica Rivas is a Counsel is the head of the Intellectual Property practice (part of the Litigation & Dispute Resolution department). She advises national and international clients in the field of intellectual property, including patent, know-how, trademark, design, copyright and related competition. She regularly contributes to industry publications and is a regular speaker on IP matters.

1. Types of Trade Marks & Registration

1.1 Types of Trade Marks

Marks, business names and trade names are the typical forms of distinctive sign in the Italian legal system (segni tipici).

There are also distinctive signs that are non-typical (segni atipici) but nonetheless have the function of identifying the business and communicating, including advertising slogans, trade dress and domain names.

With specific respect to trade marks, there are various categories, which differ based on the nature of the sign.

Using the list set out in the law as a reference and in particular in Italian Legislative Decree No 30/2005 and further amendments (the Italian Code of Intellectual Property Code, the "IP Code"), a trade mark can be comprised of (i) words, be they actual or fanciful, or (ii) drawings. Typically, trade marks are classified, in the first case, as word trade marks and in the latter case as figurative trade marks.

Trade marks comprised of both words and images, on the other hand, are typically classified as complex trade marks. The complex marks are typically made up of a distinctive core and further secondary elements (marchi complessi). There are also marks that combine elements that would not be distinctive when taken alone (marchi d'insieme).

A trade mark can also be a person's name, in which case it is classified as a patronymic trade mark.

In addition to words and images, the law also allows registration as trade marks of numbers and letters in the alphabet.

It is also possible to register as trade marks the following: graphically represented sounds, the shape of a product or the product's packaging and the colour combination or colour shades of a product.

The IP Code does not expressly mention the possibility for the applicant to file a trade-mark application for other types of signs, such as smell, position, movement, tactile and gustative marks. Despite this fact, Italian undertakings are increasingly focusing their attention on these kind of signs as trade marks.

Nowadays, amongst the elements that can be granted trademark protection, especially in the fashion industry, there are some elements of the products. These elements, originally created as decorative or merely aesthetic signs, are becoming a symbol, like the essence of the "exclusive style" of a certain brand.

Among these elements there are also some signs that cannot be easily specified in a single element (because they are susceptible to innumerable variations; all, however, referable to a common denominator or style).

The Italian courts classify word marks as strong or weak (marchi forti e deboli) depending upon the strength of their distinctiveness.

Strong word marks are often made-up words regarding a name that has no conceptual relationship to the product or service in connection with which it is used.

Marks may also be classified as ordinary marks, or as marks that have a reputation (marchi di rinomanza), and thus enjoy protection beyond particular categories of goods and services, on a basis that proceeds from issues other than a risk of confusion.

Collective trade marks have instead the function of guaranteeing the origin, nature or quality of certain goods or services and can be registered only by entities that guarantee compliance with this function (eg, consortiums). All the subjects that respect the requirements to use collective trade marks are allowed to use them.

1.2 Trade-Mark Rights

The Italian system recognises registered and unregistered trade marks (or de facto trade marks).

The fundamental condition to be met to obtain trade-mark protection for unregistered trade marks, but also to ground an unfair competition claim, is to demonstrate that the unregistered mark is perceived by the general public as an indication of the origin of the product or, alternatively, has become well known/notorious in the relevant market.

This burden of proof is up to the unregistered trade mark owner and it is not always an easy proof.

If the unregistered trade mark is known only at a local level, the registration of a following identical trade mark is permitted, but the owner of the previous unregistered trade mark is always allowed to continue the use of the sign within the limits of such use (so-called diritto di preuso).

1.3 Standards for Registering

Under Italian law, a trade mark is capable of registration where it has the essential function of acting as a source indicator and it has distinctiveness.

Under Article 13(2) of the IP Code, "A trade mark that prior to the application for registration has following its use acquired distinctiveness may be the subject of registration." Besides, under Article 13(3), "A trade mark may not be declared or considered null and void if prior to the submission of the application for annulment or the defence of annulment the trade mark in question has following its use acquired distinctiveness."

This rule represents an exception to the general prohibition on registering trade marks that are merely descriptive or that lack distinctiveness and a defence to an application for annulment of a registered trade mark.

The rule introduced in Italy at the time that European Directive 89/104/EEC was implemented incorporates a principle that had already been affirmed in Italian case law. It is based upon the doctrine of "secondary meaning", that a trade mark that originally lacked distinctiveness as a result of non-specificity, mere descriptiveness or a lack of originality may later acquire that distinctiveness. In doing so, it acquires a secondary, additional meaning, in its ability to identify an enterprise; that is, to act as a source indicator.

The doctrine enables developments in a mark's distinctiveness to be better exploited. It comes into play where a trade mark that was merely descriptive, and thus essentially void, subsequently becomes distinctive through use.

Typically, this will be the result of large, targeted investments in marketing, which may lead to a radical transformation in the distinctiveness with which a mark is perceived within its market.

1.4 Trade-Mark Register

The Italian Patents and Trade Marks Office is the Ufficio Italiano Brevetti e Marchi (UIBM) and it keeps the trade-marks register.

All information related to filing applications of trade marks, including any relevant form, is stored there.

The register is publicly and freely available on UIBM's website at the following address: https://ww.uibm.gov.it/. Through this site, it is possible to do researches of novelty.

1.5 Types of Registers

In Italy there is just one trade-mark register.

1.6 Searching for Prior Trade Marks

It is normal practice to search for prior trade marks. Trade mark attorneys carry out this type of search for previous registered rights before filing (also on professional databases). They provide the applicant with the most relevant results, pointing out — based on pre-established parameters — the criteria in the decision to continue or not with the registration of a trade mark.

It is obviously more difficult to search for unregistered trade marks; because of their nature, there is no register or database for non-registered trade marks.

1.7 Registration Requirements

The requirements for the valid registration of a trade mark are:

- the graphical reproduction of the trade mark, which is an essential condition of the existence of the trade mark in

order to ensure its basic function, which is to differentiate the origin of products and services (Article 7 IP Code);
- the novelty, ie, the sign shall not be identical or similar to previous registered or unregistered trade marks (Article 12 IP Code);
- the distinctive character, ie, the sign shall be capable to act as a source indicator distinguishing products and services of a specific business (Article 13 IP Code); purely descriptive marks are unsuitable for registration as a trade mark; and
- the lawfulness, ie, the sign shall not be contrary to law, public order and morality, and shall not mislead consumers as to the geographical origin, characteristics and quality of the relative products and services for which the trade mark has been registered (Article 14 IP Code).

Pursuant to Article 9 of the IP Code, a sign cannot be registered as a trade mark if it is constituted exclusively by the product's shape, which is (i) necessary to obtain a technical result, (ii) crucial for the product's value, or (iii) imposed by the nature itself of the product.

1.8 Registering a Trade Mark

According to Article 19 IP Code, a registration of a trade mark can be obtained by anyone making use, or proposing to make use, of it for manufacturing or trading products, or for rendering services of his or her own enterprise, or of enterprises under her or his control, or using the trade mark with his or her consent.

Not only individuals or private entities, but also public entities are therefore entitled to register a trade mark.

1.9 Registering Signs

Under Article 7 IP Code, any sign capable of being represented graphically, in particular words, including personal names, designs, letters, figures, sounds, the shapes of goods or their packaging, the combinations or chromatic shades may be the subject of registration as a trade mark, provided that such signs are capable of distinguishing goods or services of one enterprise from those of other enterprises.

1.10 Other Rights to Signs

The Italian legal system recognises other rights to signs or source identifiers besides trade marks, which include company names, trade names and domain names.

Company names are regulated by Article 2567 of the Italian Civil Code (ICC). They are the names of the business entities and are protected against following confusingly similar company names of other business entities.

Trade names are regulated by Article 2563 ICC. They shall include at least the surname or the initials of the entrepreneurs. According to case law, the right arises from the use per se, whilst the registration in the company register can establish a data certa (certain date).

The domain name is the sign associated to an IP address. The exclusive rights of a domain name derive from the registration of the domain name on a first-come, first-served basis. The IP Code has recognised the domain name as a distinctive sign in its own right; therefore, if certain conditions are met, the previous domain is able to invalidate the registration of subsequent marks identical to it.

Under Italian law, IP rights constitute in general a unified law sector (so-called principio di unitarietà dei segni distintivi). As a result, a registered and currently valid trade mark would enable the owner also to use it as a company name, trade name and domain name.

1.11 Registration Procedure

An application for a trade mark can be filed before any Italian Chamber of Commerce or the UIBM and shall contain information regarding the applicant and his or her representative, if any, as well as a specimen of the trade mark.

Multi-class applications are permitted, but the applicant has to claim specific products and services within the relevant class/classes in the application form.

Once filed, the UIBM checks the formal validity of the trade mark application and carries out its examination on the absolute grounds of refusal set by Article 170 IP Code (graphical representation, distinctiveness, lawfulness).

After this check, the application for registration is published in the Official Gazette of the UIBM.

According to Article 175 IP Code, any third party can send written remarks to the UIBM, without assuming the status of party in the registration procedure. The UIBM can consider the observations relevant and in that case assign to the applicant a term to reply.

If no relevant objections are raised, the trade mark application is published in the National Trade Marks Bulletin.

A three-month period is then given for any third party to present opposition based on any of the relative grounds for refusal provided by Article 12 of the IP Code (novelty).

In the event that no oppositions are filed (or they have been rejected by the Office) and no observations have been considered relevant by the UIBM, the trade mark is registered. Exclusive rights arise from the registration, but the effects of registration run retroactively from the date of filing of the application and may be enforced against third parties from the date of publication of the application.

1.12 Use in Commerce
Italian legislation does not require the effective use of the sign in commerce as a condition for the registration of the trade mark.

If a trade mark has not been the object of genuine use for a period of five years since the registration, in connection with products and services claimed in the registration, any third party could raise the non-use objection in any court proceedings and/or could start an action aimed at obtaining the annulment of the trade mark as a result of its non-use according to Article 24 IP Code.

The duration of protection of a registered trade mark lasts ten years.

The owner can apply for a renewal. The duration of the trade mark is therefore potentially unlimited.

The Office fees for filing a single-word mark in one class amount roughly to EUR160 and representative fees generally amount roughly to EUR500/600.

Taxes for renewal are, in 2018, the following:

- EUR16 for the revenue stamp;
- EUR67 renewal fee including one class (EUR34 for each added class); and
- EUR202 renewal fee for collective marks for one or more classes.

1.13 Registration of Series Marks
In principle, Italy does not allow for registration of series marks. Separate trade-mark applications shall be filed with the UIBM if the applicant wants to protect all of the series marks. Using these separate filings, defensive trade marks can be registered. A defensive trade mark is a trade mark — similar to the "principal" trade mark in relation to which the owner has a direct commercial interest – registered for strengthening the protection for the principal trade mark.

A defensive trade mark, also called a "protective" trade mark, does not expire for lack of use, as long as (i) the main trade mark is effective, (ii) it is registered for the same classes of products or services as the main trade mark and (iii) the defensive trade mark and the principal trade mark are registered in the name of the same owner.

A substantial number of Italian court decisions have held that the defensive trade mark offers a sphere of protection that is independent from, or reinforcement of the protection available to, the main trade mark.

Although certain opposite minority opinions exist, the leading position is that a defensive trade mark must be similar to the main trade mark, but similarity does not mean that there must be a likelihood of confusion between the defensive trade mark and the principal trade mark; otherwise its role as defensive trade mark would cease to exist. A defensive trade mark is what prevents third parties from "coming near" the main trade mark, even to an extent that would otherwise be lawful.

1.14 Length of Registration Process
The procedure to register a trade mark before the UIBM lasts roughly 15/18 months.

Representation by an Italian attorney is not mandatory. Applicants may only be represented professionally by qualified trade-mark attorneys holding membership in the Italian Industrial Property Consultants Institute, or by attorneys (avvocati).

In the case of opposition, the registration process is stayed until the Opposition Division or, if applicable, the Appeal Commission grant their final decision. For the fees and taxes to pay, see **1.11 Registration Procedure**.

1.15 Grounds for Refusal
The UIBM carries out the assessment of the "absolute grounds of refusal". Particularly, the UIBM may refuse the registration of a trade mark application for the following reasons.

- The sign cannot be graphically represented (Article 7 IP Code). This condition is required mainly to allow easier and quick consultation of the trade-mark register by the interested parties. These parties should be able to verify the nature and object of the signs previously registered by other applicants whom they are requested to confront. From a different point of view, a clear and precise graphic representation of the mark allows the trade-mark office in charge of the registration procedure to take charge of the related application.
- The signs have become of common use in the current language or in the practice of the trade, or if the signs consist merely of the generic names of products/services or of any related descriptive indications (Article 13 (1) IP Code).
- If the subject of the application is a shape mark, it cannot consist exclusively of a shape that results from the nature of the goods themselves, or a shape that is necessary to obtain a technical result, or a shape that gives substantial value to the products (Article 9 IPC).
- The subject of a trade mark consists of symbols, emblems and flags protected by international treaties or of public interest, unless authorised by the competent authorities (Article 10 IPC).
- The trade mark is contrary to the law, public policy or morality and is able to deceive the public; for example, as to

the nature, quality or geographical origin of goods/services (Article 14 (1) letters (a) and (b) IPC).

1.16 Process for Overcoming Objections
See **1.11 Registration Procedure**.

1.17 Consideration of Prior Rights
The UIBM does not consider the existence of prior rights like trade-name right, copyright and name right as it only examines whether the mark shall be refused by absolute grounds of refusal.

The UIBM examines, however, compliance with Article 8 of the IPC, which concerns, to some extent, relative grounds for refusal.

According to this provision:

- people's portraits cannot be registered as trade marks without the consent of the related people or their relatives;
- people's names that do not belong to the applicant can be registered, provided that their use does not damage the reputation of the owner; and
- if notorious, people's names and signs used in artistic, literary, scientific, political and sports fields, and names of slogans/events/non-profit organisations and their emblems, can be registered or used as trade marks only by the rights-holders or with their permission.

1.18 Third-Party Rights
See **1.11 Registration Procedure**.

1.19 Revoke, Change, Amend or Correct an Application
According to Article 172 IP Code, the applicant may (i) revoke its trade-mark application, (ii) amend or correct non-substantial aspects of the trade-mark application before the UIBM makes a decision and (iii) complete or add documents if requested from the UIBM. After registration, no amendments/corrections/extensions can be made, albeit it is always possible to exclude specific classes from protection (for example, in the case of a court ascertaining a partial annulment for lack of genuine use).

1.20 Assigning an Application or Granting a Licence
The assignment of the application for the registration of a trade mark is always allowed and shall be notified to the UIBM pursuant Article 172 (2) IP Code.

1.21 Remedies Against the Trade Mark Office
The decisions of the UIBM can be appealed before the Board of Appeal (Commissione dei ricorsi) within 60 days.

Board of Appeal decisions can be appealed before the Italian Court of Cassation only for violation of law according to Article 111 of the Italian Constitution.

1.22 Use of a Trade Mark
Italian legislation does not require the effective use of the sign in commerce as a condition for the registration of the trade mark.

Indeed, according to Article 19 IP Code, the applicant may obtain the registration of the sign, which is merely intended to be used in the course of trade.

Genuine use must be in place within five years from the registration; after that, the use must not be interrupted for an additional five-year period. According to Italian prevailing case law, genuine use is a use that could be regarded as non-nominal use (uso non simbolico) and, therefore, a use that is able to reach a minimum quantitative decree in terms of sales figures.

The exact decisive threshold proving genuine use cannot be defined out of context according to Italian case law and a precise guideline is missing.

The evaluation basically depends on the circumstances of the single case, the evaluation of the submitted evidence in its entirety, the nature and characteristics of the goods or services, the particular area of business, etc.

According to a different thesis, genuine use would not be strictly related to a specific quantitative threshold, but would be any use that is able to provoke a notoriety of the sign in the relevant market.

1.23 Dividing a Trade Mark
Article 158 (1) IP Code expressly states that every trade-mark application must concern one sign only; therefore, if the application regards more than one sign, the UIBM will assign a term to the applicant to divide the application.

Besides, in the case that the application regards more than one class of goods or services for which the trade mark is sought to be registered, the applicant may choose to divide the application in several partial applications (i) before the UIBM decides the trade-mark application procedure, (ii) during the opposition procedure before the UIBM, or (iii) during every appeal proceeding regarding the registration of the trade mark.

1.24 Length of Term of Protection
According to Article 15 IP Code, the registered trade mark is protected for ten years starting from the application date and can be renewed with respect to the same sign and the same

products and services for ten-year periods, for an indefinite number of times.

The renewal must be requested within twelve months before the expiry date of the ten-year period, or within six months after the expiry date. In the second case, however, an additional fee must be paid. If the delay in payment exceeds six months, the trade mark at issue expires.

1.25 Requirements for an Exhaustion

According to Article 5 IP Code, "the exclusive rights conferred to the holder of an industrial property right by the Code are exhausted once the products covered by an IPR are put into the market by the holder or with his consent, within the territory of the State or the territory of a Member State of the European Community or the European Economic Area."

The trade-mark holder can therefore no longer exercise control over goods that were first launched on the market with its consent, unless there are legitimate reasons for the holder to oppose further commercialisation of these goods, especially where the condition of the goods is changed or impaired after they have been put on the market.

1.26 Participation in the Madrid System

Italy participates in the Madrid System.

Article 171 IP Code states that the UIBM will examine the international application designating Italy according to the same rules valid for national trade marks.

1.27 Consequences for Providing Incorrect Information

In the case of incorrect information regarding an "absolute grounds of refusal", the error could be declared in the ex officio examination carried out by the UIBM; after the registration, the same error could be raised by the interested party before the competent court. Instead, in the case of errors regarding "relative grounds of refusal", the error could be invoked by the interested party in the opposition procedure or, later, before the competent court.

Eventually, if the incorrect information constitutes a mere material error (not relevant for the validity requirements of the trade mark), it is possible to request an errata corrige to the UIBM. The request shall be submitted by the owner or their representative containing the error to be corrected and an exact indication of the requested correction and/or the place where the error is reported (UIBM database, official bulletin, etc).

1.28 Updating or Refreshing a Design Mark

There are no specific rules for design marks.

1.29 Denotation

It is neither necessary nor mandatory for the trade mark-owners to use symbols such as ®, or TM. However, it is quite common in the course of trade to use them to denote that the trade mark has been registered and that it is valid and effective.

2. Assignment and Licensing

2.1 Assignment Requirements or Restrictions

According to Article 2573 ICC and Article 23 IP Code, the trade mark can be assigned upon consideration or for free for all or for part of the goods and services for which it has been registered. The assignment of a trade mark can be made separately from the going concern.

The assignment of the trade mark must not result in misrepresentation as to the characteristics of the products or services, which are essential in the public's appreciation. In other words, a change in owner of the assigned trade mark must not result in misrepresention for the public.

The assignment of a trade mark is not subject to any specific formal requirement, but is typically made in writing, also for the purpose of evidence.

2.2 Procedure for Assigning a Trade Mark

Italian law does not require a specific procedure to assign a trade mark.

2.3 Registering or Recording the Assignment

According to Article 138 IP Code, any trade-mark assignment concerning Italian trade marks (and therefore also the Italian portion of WIPO trade marks) must be recorded with the UIBM.

Without recording (at least according to the main interpretation), any agreement is enforceable and binding for the signing parties, but the record is required in order to be the assignee capable to exercise the rights arising under the trade mark also against third parties. Registration is therefore strongly recommended in any scenario of trade0mark assignment.

The recording procedure has become easier (in connection with the assignment agreements) under the IP Code.

Under the standard provision, it was necessary to have a copy of the agreement, containing at least the trade mark's number, a mention of the assignment and the date from which the rights have been assigned. The agreement must be signed by the parties with a public notary in their own country and subsequently legalised. The involvement of the public notary is necessary only to certifify that the signatures of the parties are true (it is not a public deed). It was also necessary to have a sworn translation of the agreement.

Under the IP Code, as a fall-back option it is possible to file a declaration in place of filing a copy of the agreement (dichiarazione di avvenuta cessione), even though the UIBM may also require that the declaration is notarised by a public notary and subsequently legalised.

2.4 Trade Marks and Security

Article 140 IP Code provides that security rights over IP can be created only for cash receivables and Article 138 of the IP Code also requires inter vivos deeds that "create, amend or transfer [...] special privileges or security rights created under Article 140" over IP to be registered formally with the UIBM.

Article 138 of the IP Code speaks in relation to industrial inventions, trade marks and all other IP rights (except copyright), which are all subject to the same law for this purpose. If more than one security right is registered, they will be ranked accordingly to the transcription date.

Security rights that are not transcribed will be unenforceable towards third-party purchasers, creditors and also any trustees in bankruptcy.

The issue of what the nature of such security is — ie, whether a pledge or a mortgage — remains opens under Italian law.

According to the prevailing Italian jurisprudence, real rights of security over IP should be deemed to be a pledge and specifically the special type of pledge over "rights other than receivables" (diritti diversi dai crediti) envisaged under Article 2806 of the ICC.

A different current of jurisprudence, however, underscores that the legal framework applicable to pledges over IP is closer to the legal framework applicable to mortgages over personal property, which must be registered to be effective.

According to supporters of the first view, the reference to "special laws" in Article 2806 of the ICC, and therefore in the IP Code, would allow derogation from the provisions of the ICC that govern the ordinary creation of a pledge, namely the delivery of physical possession. This works to allow the creation of a pledge over IP rights by way of transcription and without any transfer of physical possession.

Supporters of the second view, however, see the requirement for transcription in the public records (also with different rankings) as an element that renders security over IP rights more similar to mortgages than to traditional pledges (which is based on transfer of physical possession).

Thus, if it is a pledge, it is an "anomalous" pledge and it is especially a "transcribed" pledge that, in terms of formalities requested and rights attributed to creditors, is in practice very similar to a mortgage over personal property.

In conclusion, it is indeed clear that such security is atypical and sui generis, for which gaps in the applicable law will need to be addressed from time to time, applying by analogy the rules and principles of the ICC to the extent compatible.

2.5 Licensing Requirements or Restrictions

The rules on the registration of trade-mark assignments also apply to licences.

According to Art 23 (2) IP Code, a trade mark may be licensed, also on a non-exclusive basis, for all or part of the products or services for which it is registered and for the whole or part of the territory of the country, provided that, in the case of a non-exclusive licence, the licensee expressly undertakes to use the trade marks to distinguish the products or services equal to those traded or rendered in the territory of the country with the same trade mark by the holder or any other licensees. Licences must not result in deception with regard to characteristics of the products and/or services that are widely considered to be essential.

Article 23, (3) IP Code also states that "the owner of a trade mark may invoke the rights conferred by that trade mark against a licensee who contravenes any provision in his licensing contract with regard to its duration, the manner of the trade mark's use, the scope of the goods or services for which the licence is granted, the territory in which the trade mark may be used, or the quality of the goods manufactured or of the services provided by the licensee." This provision of law implements the corresponding provision in Directive 89/104/EEC, Article 8, (2), which is very similarly worded.

The protection granted by Article 23, (3) IP Code allows the owner of the trade mark to benefit from a further defence, symmetrical and parallel to the contractual one, which is infringement action (including related precautionary measures).

2.6 Procedure for Licensing a Trade Mark

See **2.3 Registering or Recording the Assignment**.

2.7 Registering or Recording the Licence

As with an assignment, a licence is subject to Article 138 of the IP Code and to the effects of registration determined by Article 139 of the IP Code.

2.8 Reasons to Deny Granting a Perpetual Licence

A 'perpetual' licence, while held to be of indefinite duration, could be found to be terminable according to the general principles of the ICC. If the parties intend that the licence should not be capable of termination (at least for a specific period) then this should be stated expressly.

3. Opposition Procedure

3.1 Legal Grounds and Timeframes

In receiving the application for registration of a trade mark, the UIBM examines the formal and substantive requirements set by Articles 7, 8, 9, 10, 11, 13 (1), 14 (1) let. (a) and (b) of the IP Code (the "absolute grounds of refusal"). The UIBM does not carry out the examination in relation to novelty and prior rights of third parties (the "relative grounds of refusal"), which shall be invoked directly by the right-holder in the opposition procedure.

Particularly, Article 176 (5) of the IP Code states legal grounds for the opposition as:

- the rights deriving from the registration of a national trade mark or a foreign trade mark with effect in Italy that is identical to the trade mark to be opposed and registered for identical products and services (Article 12 (1) let. (c) of the IP Code);
- the rights deriving from the registration of a national trade mark or a foreign trade mark with effect in Italy that is similar and registered for identical or similar products and services (Article 12 (1) let. (d) of the IP Code); or
- the lack of consensus by the natural or legal person entitled to the name, surname or personal image, in the case of registration of a trade mark of a name, surname or image belonging to person different to the registrant (Article 8 of the IP Code).

The deed of objection must be filed before the UIBM within three months from:

- the date of publication in the official gazette of company trade marks of the application for registration of a trade mark considered recordable by the UIBM (Article 170 let. (a) of the IP Code);
- the date of publication in the official gazette of company trade marks of registration of a trade mark, the application of which has not been published (Article 179 (2) of the IP Code); or
- the first day of the month following the publication in the WIPO international trade mark gazette of the registration of the international trade mark.

The deed opens the administrative proceedings before the UIBM, which lasts from 24 to 36 months.

After expiry of the above delay for filing an opposition before the UIBM, the same legal grounds could be invoked in an ordinary legal action before the judicial authority. The legal action before the judicial authority is instead mandatory to invoke an absolute ground of refusal (not considered by the UIBM) or the rights deriving from prior non-registered trade marks (Article 12 (1) let. (a) and (b) of the IP Code) or from well-known trade marks (Article 12 (1) let. (e) and (f) of the IP Code). However, such legal action is not an opposition procedure but a claim of nullity of a registered trade mark.

3.2 Filing an Opposition

Article 177 of the IP Code sets the following list of parties legitimate to file the opposition:

- the holder of a prior trade mark registered in Italy or with validity in Italy (eg, the European trade mark);
- the applicant for a registration of a national trade mark, if the application has been submitted before the application of the trade mark opposed, or the applicant for the extension of a foreign trade mark in Italy, if the priority of the foreign trade mark is precedent to the application of the trade mark opposed;
- the licensee of the exclusive sign to be registered; and
- the natural or legal person entitled to the name, surname or personal image, in the case of registration of a trade mark of a name, surname or image belonging to a person different to the registrant (Article 8 IP Code).

If the opposing party is not established in Italy, the appointment of a representative domiciled in Italy for the procedure (trade-mark attorney or lawyer) is mandatory. In other cases, the appointment is facultative (although it is very frequent).

As far as the costs are concerned, the average office duties are around EUR300. As far as the attorney fees are concerned, there is no official table of tariff for the sector; therefore the fees are agreed directly by the parties.

3.3 Opposition Procedure

The opposition procedure is regulated by Articles 174 and following of the IP Code, and could be divided into five phases.

Deed of Opposition

The procedure starts with the deed of opposition, to be filed before the UIBM within three months from the date of publication of the registration (or from the equivalent publications set in Article 176 IP Code). The deed shall be in Italian and must contain:

- the references of the registration of the trade mark to be opposed (applicant, number and date of the request of registration, products and services for which the opposition is requested);
- the references of the rights that ground the opposition (prior trade mark or trade marks; products and services

for which the opposition is requested; the name, surname or image according to Article 8 of the IP Code); and
- the legal arguments of the opposition.

The opponent shall pay the office duties, the lack of which implies the renouncement of the opposition.

Notification of the Opposition
Within two months from the delay for filing the opposition, the UIBM examines the formal requirements of the opposition and notifies the opposition to the applicant for the registration of the trade mark opposed.

Cooling-off Period
After the notification of the opposition, the parties have two months to reach an agreement; before that the UIBM examines the merit of the opposition ("cooling-off period"). The cooling-off period could be extended until twelve months upon joint request of the parties (Article 178 IP Code).

Procedural Phase
In the case that the parties do not reach any agreement, the opponent within two months from the end of the cooling-off period shall file the documents set by Article 176 (4) IP Code, ie:

- a copy of the application or certificate of registration of the trade mark on which the opposition is based, except for national applications or certificates, and, if it is the case, the documentation relating to the priority right or pre-existence of which it benefits, as well as their translation into Italian, if applicable;
- any other documentation to prove the alleged facts;
- the documentation required to prove the legitimacy to file the objection, should the prior trade mark not be in its name on the register held by the UIBM; and
- the deed of appointment of the representative, if applicable.

The applicant for the registration of the trade mark opposed can lodge, within 60 days from the receipt of the above documentation from the opponent, a brief with the arguments that ground the rejection of the opposition and the eventual relative documentation. In the same brief the applicant could ask for proof of the effective use by the opponent of the trade mark that grounds the opposition (Article 178 (4) IP Code), to be filed within 60 days from the notification of such request.

Decision
After the delays for the above filings, the UIBM decides the opposition and, consequently, the registration of the trade mark opposed shall be confirmed or rejected (even only partially, for some of the products and services for which the registration was requested).

3.4 Legal Remedies
The decision of the UIBM could be appealed before the Board of Appeals within 60 days from the communication of the decision (Article 182 IP Code).

The Board of Appeals is the body of second instance in the UIBM formed by ten members chosen from judges of the Italian Court of Appeals and professors of law in Italian universities (Article 135 IP Code).

The procedure before the Board of Appeals is regulated by Article 136 IP Code. The parties each have 60 days to file the briefs and replies, with the relative documentation. The parties can ask to discuss orally the case at the hearing before the Board of Appeals (Article 136 (10) IP Code). The proceedings of the second instance is competent also in the merit of the decision of the first instance and the Board of Appeals can issue provisional measures in the case of serious and irreparable harm (Article 136 (17) IP Code).

4. Initiating a Lawsuit

4.1 Actions to Pursue Infringement
The owner has several options to react against trade-mark infringement depending on the scale and type of infringement, and the value of the infringed trade mark. The owner might commence civil and/or criminal proceedings, and can alert the customs authorities in the case of counterfeiting.

A range of interim measures is available in civil proceedings.

In proceedings on the merits, the right-holder can request declaratory judgment, definitive injunction, definitive removal from the market of the counterfeit goods, their destruction, assignment of infringing goods, publication of the judgment and award of damages.

No substantial difference exists between registered or unregistered trade marks in this respect, albeit unregistered trade marks are more often enforced though unfair completion claims and the burden of proof to enforce unregistered trade marks is more difficult.

4.2 Initiating Infringement Proceedings
As from 1 July 2003, specialised divisions, spread all over the Italian territory, have exclusive jurisdiction on IP matters. Article 2 of the Law Decree No 1 of 24 January 2012 renames the Special Section in Industrial and Intellectual Property as the Special Section for Enterprises (Sezioni per le Imprese).

Infringement proceedings can be established before the forum of the alleged infringer (forum rei) or before the court where the infringement has occurred (forum commissi delicti).

4.3 Effect of Decisions on Infringement Actions

Article 120 (1) IP Code expressly states that actions of nullity and/or infringement that are filed when the procedure of registration is still pending shall be suspended by the court until the UIBM issues the decision on the registration.

4.4 Declaratory Judgment Proceedings

The alleged infringer is entitled to start a declaratory non-infringement action once the alleged infringer has received at least a cease-and-desist letter from the trade mark-owner. The declaratory non-infringement action can be commenced in interim proceedings (Article 120(6bis) IP Code).

4.5 Jurisdiction of Courts

Article 120 (2) IP Code provides that the proceedings on the validity of the trade mark shall be brought before the court where (i) the defendant has its residence or domicile; if not applicable, where (ii) the plaintiff has its residence or domicile; or, if not applicable, (iii) before the Court of Rome. The domicile could be determined considering the domicile indicated in the trade-mark registration form. In the case of claim of infringement, the proceedings can also be brought before the court where the infringement occurred.

The decision of first instance can be appealed before the competent Court of Appeal, which also has full authority to revoke the first decision on the merits.

The decisions of the Court of Appeal can be appealed before the Italian Court of Cassation only on certain grounds, therefore it is excluded a new scrutiny on the factual background of the dispute.

4.6 Prerequisites to Filing a Lawsuit

Although Italian law does not require the plaintiff to adopt formal conditions before a trade mark-related lawsuit (ie, a formal demand letter, warning letters, engaging in mediation), the plaintiff frequently sends a cease-and-desist letter.

4.7 Representation for Parties

The fighting parties in a trade-mark dispute shall be represented by an attorney-at-law admitted to the Italian Bar. The only exception relates to proceedings before the Italian Court of Cassation, for which a specific qualification (cassazionista) is required. This qualification can now be obtained through an examination after accruing at least five years' experience as a lawyer.

4.8 Interim or Preliminary Injunctions

According to Articles 129 and 131 of the IP Code and in compliance with the rules of the Italian Code of Civil Procedure concerning precautionary proceedings, a registered trade mark-owner could request:

- the measure of injunction from manufacturing, trading and using anything infringing the right;
- the seizure of any infringing goods; and
- an order to recall of any of the same infringing goods.

The granting of preliminary measures requires two fundamental conditions. Firstly, "fumus boni iuris", which implies, on the balance of probabilities, the existence of infringement and "apparent" IP right validity. In other words, full evidence of the infringement is not requested; in fact, "fumus boni iuris" implies that the claimant has to prove that he or she is entitled to enforce his or her alleged rights and that there are good reasons to believe that these rights are indeed being infringed by the defendant. Secondly, "periculum in mora" (urgency) needs a demonstration that the delay incurred in ordinary litigation will generate an "irretrievable loss". According to certain case law, periculum is in re ipsa whenever the infringement implies a concrete risk of passing offpotentially irreversible and, at the same time, damage quantification is difficult.

According to general Italian civil proceeding law, the content of certain precautionary judgments can become stable without the need to start an action on the merits, upon the condition that the precautionary judgment is suitable to anticipate the content of the hypothetical final decision to be delivered by the judge at the end of a proceeding on the merits (Article 669-octies (6), (7) and (8) of the Italian Civil Proceeding Code).

With specific reference to Italian IP legislation, according to some scholars, the interim injunction (which prevents an entity from keeping an unlawful behaviour concerning an IP right) falls within the scopes of application of the abovementioned rule set forth by Article 669-octies (6), (7) and (8) of the Italian Civil Proceeding Code. In particular, the content of an interim injunction (ie, the order to stop a determined behaviour) is mostly the same as one of an injunction ordered at the end of an action on the merits and, therefore, if none of the parties starts the action on the merit, the effects of the interim injunction remain stable, as confirmed by Article 131 (1-quarter) of the IP Code.

On the other hand, a different doctrine retains that the abovementioned rule contained in the IP Code breaches the principles set forth in the TRIPs Agreement, where it is stated that measures taken on an interim basis shall "cease to have effect, if proceedings leading to a decision on the merits of the case are not initiated within a reasonable period, to be determined by the judicial authority ordering the measures where a Member's law so permits or, in the absence of such a determination, not to exceed 20 working days or 31 calendar days, whichever is the longer" (Article 50 (6) TRIPs Agreement). Therefore, on the basis of the here mentioned theory, the party that obtained an IP interim injunction should go on the merits in order to try to stabilise the effects of the same injunction, in order to comply fully with the provisions of the TRIPs Agreement.

4.9 Protection for Potential Defendant

Italian procedural law does not provide for the option of filing protective briefs. A potential defendant may consider starting interim proceedings or proceedings on the merits requesting a preliminary declaration of non-infringement (or filing a revocation action for lack of genuine use).

When proceedings are pending and orders have been granted against the potential infringer, it may request the court to order a bond to be posted by the trade mark-owner for compensation for potential damages.

4.10 Obtaining Information and Evidence

Article 129 IP Code provides the search order (descrizione) in order to collect evidence before trial. The search order can be asked for as an interim measure, before the opening of the ordinary proceedings, or during the ordinary proceedings of infringement. The disclosure/discovery is enforced with a clerk of the court and a court's expert appointed by the judge. The disclosure/discovery order shall be confirmed by the judge in following a hearing with all the parties involved.

With main proceedings pending, the trade mark-owner is entitled to request the infringer to disclose any information on the origin and distribution networks of the infringing goods or services advertised/marketed/sold ("right of information"). Such information might include the names and addresses of the producers, manufacturers, distributors, suppliers and other previous holders of the goods or services, as well as the intended wholesalers and retailers, and information on the quantities produced, manufactured, delivered, received or ordered, in addition to the price obtained for the goods or services thereof.

4.11 Initial Pleading Standards

The claimant, in order to bring an action, has to serve upon the counterparty a writ of summons (atto di citazione).

The writ of summons is drafted and signed by legal counsel with authority (by power of attorney) to sign on behalf of his or her client.

The writ of summons must contain all the elements necessary to identify the claim and causes of action, and must contain the vocatio in ius (summons to court).

Between service of the writ of summons and the date given for the first hearing, the defendant has at least 90 days (or 150 days in the case of a defendant residing abroad) to prepare its defence.

The writ of summons must be filed at the court after service in order for the case to be entered on the court register and assigned to a specific judge.

Italian ordinary civil proceedings are essentially "written", based on the filing of pleadings exchanged between the parties and made up of a number of hearings fixed by law, each devoted to certain activities, which are outlined below.

After the statement of the defendant, the plaintiff can slightly modify or amend his or her claims, in the light of the objections and possible counterclaim raised by the defendant; however, the plaintiff cannot submit a completely new claim (so-called mutatio libelli is forbidden).

4.12 Representative or Collective Actions

The Italian legal system does not permit collective actions for trade-mark proceedings.

4.13 Restrictions on Trade Mark-Owners

There is case law in Italy in relation to right abuse and sham litigation, especially when the IP right is found null and void during the litigation itself. There is case law according to which sending a letter requiring the recipient not to put a product on the market may give rise to issues under Article 2598 of the ICC (ie, the unfair competition law), given that a threat of litigation that is made in bad faith, or negligently in ignorance of a trade mark's invalidity, constitutes an unacceptable attempt to disrupt a market. In competition terms, a notice sent to a competitor's clients seeking to enforce IP rights that are subsequently declared void is considered automatically unfair competitive practice. This should not be automatically the case where the communication is not disclosed to third parties or where it is disclosed to third parties by the receiving party itself.

5. Infringement

5.1 Action for Infringement

The necessary parties to an action for infringement are the trade mark-owner (and other parties that appear in the trade-marks registration, if any) and the alleged infringer.

The lawsuit can be started by the trade mark-owner and/or its exclusive licensee. The trade mark-owner can commence the action also enforcing the trade-mark application.

5.2 Signs and Infringement

Pursuant to the IP Code, the owner of an earlier trade mark, which has validity in Italy, is entitled to prohibit third parties to adopt a sign:

- that is identical and is used for identical products and/or services (this is the case referred to as "identical-identical",

where the infringement test is solely based on the identity of the signs and of the product/services, without any need to assess whether there is any likelihood of confusion);
- that is identical or similar and is used for identical or similar products and/or services, if, due to the identity or the similarity of the signs or products, there is likelihood of confusion in the relevant public, which may consist of the likelihood of 'association' of the two signs; or
- when the earlier trade mark is a renewed trade mark within Italy and the subsequent user is infringing the earlier rights, even if the subsequent trade mark is used for dissimilar products and/or services, if the use of the subsequent trade mark would take unfair advantage of, or be detrimental to, the distinctive character or the reputation of the earlier trade mark.

5.3 Use of a Sign by Defendant
Purely descriptive use is allowed in Italy according to Article 21 of the IP Code.

In this kind of use, the sign is used as a trade mark, eliminating or at least reducing the chances of the use being found to be trade mark infringement. Under this principle, a party, even a direct competitor, may use another party's trade mark to describe their own product or services. This typically happens in the case of patronymic trade marks that cannot prevent the use of the name of the competitor (if identical to the trade mark) in compliance with the principle of professional fairness in the market. In certain cases, it is not easy to draw a line between lawful and infringing uses.

5.4 Defences Against Infringement
The defendant can first try to deny the existence of a likelihood of confusion or prejudice to the notoriety of the well-known trade mark.

Besides, the defendant can allege that its use is purely descriptive according to Article 21 of the IP Code (eg, corresponding the trade mark to his or her personal name).

The defendant can also react with a counterclaim. The defendant can in particular object in relation to the plaintiffs' trade mark respectively:

- the nullity and/or the weakness;
- the lack of genuine use; and
- the fact that its filing has been made in bad faith. Under Italian law, registration of a trade mark in bad faith is prohibited. According to Italian scholars and case law, there is a lack of clear criteria for what constitutes bad faith. However, opinions suggest that trade marks may be considered to be made in bad faith if they are not used but obstruct the registration of a third-party trade mark.

In interim proceedings, the defendant can also deny the existence of the periculum in mora.

5.5 Role of Experts and/or Surveys
Contrary to patent litigation, the role of experts in trade mark litigation is limited.

Frequently, however, market research by the parties is presented as evidence of consumer perceptions of the strength of the trade mark or the existence of the likelihood of confusion, but its usefulness may be called into question. Such evidence is commonly admitted by the courts, although the courts are not bound to follow the conclusions the research draws, not least because the questions posed are often fraught with bias. As a result, the courts will on occasion simply ignore such evidence.

5.6 Administrative or Criminal Offence
There are few provisions related to criminal enforcement as the infringement of a trade mark, under certain circumstances, is subject to criminal and administrative sanctions,

The main rules are Articles 473 and 474 of the Italian Criminal Code and Article 127 of the IP Code.

If the infringement is particularly serious, criminal action based on these provisions may be brought by the Public Prosecutor, ie, without private prosecution. The criminal route is frequently invoked in Italy to induce a deterrent effect against the infringement.

The role of the Public Prosecutor is fundamental in the management of the case. In fact, the trade mark-holder can only submit his or hercomplaint before the Public Prosecutor, who is free to decide what action should be taken. Besides, the Public Prosecutor can order special initiatives involving the criminal police in order to collect any sort of evidence by any legal means, in any place and at any time.

In certain circumstances, however, the infringement cannot imply a criminal condemnation for lack of willingness.

5.7 Custom Seizures
The trade mark-owner may seek the assistance of the Italian customs authority to prevent the importation of counterfeit products.

With a view to eliminating international trade in goods infringing IP rights, the European Parliament and the Council have introduced Reg. 608/2013/EU repealing the earlier Reg. 1383/2003/CE. The new Regulation, which took effect on 1 January 2014, creates procedural rules for customs authorities to detain counterfeit or pirated goods.

6. Revocation/Cancellation

6.1 Remedies and Reasons
The IP Code sets forth the actions for obtaining special remedies named "nullità" (nullity) and "decadenza" (revocation/cancellation) of the trade mark.

These kind of decisions are absolute and once the trade mark is finally declared null or cancelled, the judgment is binding erga omnes (when registered with the UIMB). Relative and absolute grounds for refusal correspond to the grounds for these kind of actions. Non-use may be raised as a ground in cancellation proceedings. Besides, deceiving trade marks can be cancelled.

6.2 Trade Mark Office and Civil Courts
The actions of cancellation and/or revocation can be brought only before the ordinary judicial authority.

6.3 Statutory Limitation or Time Period
The IP Code (Article 28) provides for the possibility of declaring an action seeking the nullity of a later trade mark to be time-barred when the owner of the earlier trade mark on which the application is based has been aware of the use of the later trade mark in the marketplace and has consented to its use for at least five years (convalida).

6.4 Initiation of Revocation/Cancellation Proceeding
The grounds of cancellation are distinguished between absolute and relative grounds.

Absolute grounds of cancellation are ones in which there are no prior private rights or interests violated by the registration of the trade mark. According to Article 122 (1) IP Code, absolute grounds of cancellation could be invoked by everyone with a legitimate interest (eg, a competitor in the case of a deceptive trade mark) and by the Public Prosecutor.

Relative grounds of cancellation concern a prior rights owned by a third party (eg, prior registered or non-registered trade mark). In those cases, the claim could be made only by the right-holder (Article 122 (2) IP Code).

The grounds of revocation are considered absolute grounds and therefore could be invoked by everyone with a legitimate interest and by the Public Prosecutor (Article 122 (1) IP Code).

6.5 Partial Revocation/Cancellation
According to Article 27 IP Code, the cancellation and revocation could be declared for part of the products or services to which the trade mark was registered.

In particular, a trade mark could be partially cancelled if it is used in relation to certain products or services, whilst it is not used for other products or services.

According to certain Italian case law, however, a trade mark cannot be cancelled, even partially, if it is used for similar products, whilst the use in relation to certain products only might not take the trade mark alive for non-similar products. Where a trade mark has been registered for more than one product or service and it is not in practice used for all of these, it may be deemed to be registered in respect only of these for which it has been used.

By contrast to the Community law, the Italian courts have tended to find that such deemed non-registration never regards products and services that are similar to those for which the trade mark has seen genuine use, even if the classes of goods are drawn very widely. Where the trade mark is well-known, the courts go much further. In such cases, use of the trade mark means the registration is not susceptible to revocation not only for the products or services for which it has been registered, but also for dissimilar products and services.

As a result, a well-known trade mark risks being considered capable of revocation, for any of its registered classes, only if its use has ceased completely in relation to all classes. Leading Italian academic authorities consider that harmonisation with Community trade mark law means that while well-known trade marks are afforded greater protection, that should not mean they are not susceptible to being deemed non-registration for particular classes, but only to enjoy a greater protection in the case of infringement if the conditions of the broader protections are satisfied.

6.6 Possibilities of Amendment
After a mark is registered, it is not allowed to be amended. Therefore, if a mark is under revocation/cancellation proceedings, amendments are not allowed. However, it remains possible to delete some items of goods/services.

6.7 Revocation/Cancellation and Infringement
Actions involving revocation/cancellation and infringement can be heard together before Italian courts.

7. Trial & Settlement

7.1 Special Procedural Provisions
Generally, the proceedings of the disputes related to trade marks are regulated by ordinary provisions of the Italian Code of Civil Proceedings.

Notwithstanding, Chapter III, Section I of the IP Code provides some special rules applicable only to IP-related disputes (included trade marks). See the previous answers re competent courts, jurisdictions and discovery.

7.2 Determination of Cases
Legal judges decide IP disputes and decisions are based only on the evidence before them.

7.3 Possibilities of Settlement
The parties can settle the case at any stage and phase of the proceedings. The settlement could be reached before (in order to avoid the litigation) or after the decision (in order to avoid or modify the enforcement of the decision).

Generally, the settlement is reached through negotiations, also amongst lawyers. It is forbidden to disclose in court communications between lawyers concerning discussions on out-of-court settlement.

Alternatively, the parties can opt for a mediation through the service rendered by ADR entities. In the context of a legal dispute, the judge has the power to invite the parties to settle the case and can schedule a specific hearing for this purpose.

7.4 Other Court Proceedings
An infringement case can be stayed pending resolution of a validity attack in another forum (Article 295 of the Italian Code of Civil Proceedings).

8. Remedies

8.1 Existing Remedies
The remedies are regulated by Articles 124-127 IP Code and they include (i) final injunctive relief and/or withdrawal from the market of the products with the infringing sign, with possible penalty for each day of delay in the enforcement of the measure; (ii) seizure or destruction of the counterfeiting products; and (iii) publication of the decision in the Italian press.

The owner may claim for damages. They can include the actual damage and the loss of profits, and could be quantified in three alternatives as follows:

- damages award to be evaluated (often after appointment of a court expert) on the basis of the following criteria (or combination of them): all negative economic consequences, including loss of profits suffered by the right-holder; counterfeiter's profits and benefits; and, in appropriate cases, non-economic factors, such as moral damages;
- as an alternative, a lump sum based on equity (without the appointment of a court expert), but an award for loss of profits cannot be lower than a reasonable royalty; and
- in any event, a trade mark-owner's right to ask for the full recovery of the counterfeiter's profits instead of compensation for damages (for loss of profits) or to the extent to which they exceed such damages.

8.2 Rights and Remedies
In principle, the unsuccessful party shall be ordered to pay all costs.

8.3 Different Types of Remedies
The possible remedies do not vary depending on the types of different trade marks.

9. Appeal

9.1 Special Provisions
The proceedings of appeal in IP-related disputes are regulated by the general provision governing ordinary civil proceedings (Articles 323-359 of the Italian Code of Civil Procedure). The IP Code does not contain any special or derogatory rules.

9.2 Factual or Legal Review
In the Italian civil procedural system, the proceedings of second instance are a full-review appeal; therefore, the Court of Appeal can review the facts of the case, reopen the phase of discovery and proof (if strictly necessary), and revert the decision on the merit of the case or the interpretation/application of the law invoked.

9.3 Length of Appeal from Trial Court
There is not a timeframe fixed by statutory provisions.

The timing to reach a decision in second instance varies according to the complexity of the case, the possible reopening of the phase of proof and discovery, and the agenda of the judges. Generally, appeal proceedings last from two to four years.

10. Other Trade Mark Issues

10.1 Recognition of Dilution
Article 13 (4) IP Code provides that dilution — ie, the loss of distinctiveness of the trade mark that became the generic name of the product, as a result of the trade mark-owner's conduct or inaction — could cause the revocation of the trade mark (Article 26 of the IP Code).

10.2 Protection of Famous Marks
Regardless of genuine use, the holder may rely on the protection of well-known marks. This is used in principle by reference to Article 6-bis of the Paris Convention, referring to those marks that are known, regardless of their use in the country, to a large number of those involved in the production or trade or use of the goods concerned and is clearly associated with goods coming from a particular source. According to Article 12 (1) let. (b) of the IP Code, a trade mark that within the meaning of Article 6-bis of the Paris Convention is well-known to the interested public, also due

to the reputation acquired throughout the country through the promotion of a trade mark, shall also be considered as known in Italy. No specific threshold needs are to be met, neither in terms of percentage of population awareness, nor in terms of widespread recognition across the country. Nevertheless, to enjoy sufficient reputation a trade mark needs to be known by a significant section of the public concerned with the products or services that it covers, in a substantial part of the territory in which it is registered or used.

10.3 Special Rules Regarding Geographic Indicators

Special rules concerning geographical indications are set forth in Articles 29-30 IP Code.

Article 21 (1) let. (b) of the IP Code provides that geographic indicators (relating to specimen, quality, quantity, destination, value, geographical provenance, period of fabrication of the product or of rendering of the service and other characteristics of the product or service) shall not be restricted by the trade-mark rights if their use is compliant with the principles of fair practices.

10.4 Special Rules Relating to Surnames

The use of one's own name or surname is allowed according to Article 21 (1) let. (a) IP Code and shall not be restricted by a third party's exclusive right in so far as such use is compliant with the principles of fair practices.

11. Costs

11.1 Costs Before Filing a Lawsuit

Typically the costs arising before the lawsuit are related to the collection of evidence, the warning letter and the eventual urgent proceedings before the ordinary lawsuit to obtain a relief or to conduct the discovery against the infringer.

11.2 Costs Regarding an Infringement Action

In principle, lawyers and their clients can agree in writing different legal fees.

The most common legal fee structures are hourly rates, estimated fees with a cap and flat fees.

If no agreement has been reached, Italian law provides for a mandatory fixed tariff system, which sets out the amount of fees due by the client for every stage of the proceedings.

11.3 Costs of Litigation

According to Article 91 of the Italian Code of Civil Procedure, the judge in the sentence condemns the losing party to reimburse the legal fees of the prevailing party. In the case that the judge held only in part or rejected reciprocal claims, the fees could be declared reciprocally compensated.

12. Alternative Dispute Resolution

12.1 Common Way of Settlement

The parties of a dispute can opt for mediation through the service rendered by ADR entities. A mediation clause could also be inserted in a previous agreement concerning the licence or the assignment of a trade mark. Furthermore, in the context of a legal dispute, the judge can suspend the proceedings, ordering the party to attempt a mediation.

Currently, the predominant view that disputes concerning Italian intellectual and industrial property rights, including trade marks, can be resolved by way of arbitration finds its bases in Italian law. This is namely the notion that IP rights are disposable and, following a recent change in law, that IP disputes no longer require the involvement of the public prosecutor.

It is also possible to defer to arbitration matters involving liability in tort, subject to an agreement including a specific covenant that expressly provides that "future disputes relating to one or more specific non-contractual relationships will be deferred to arbitration." Often, however, the above wording is not included in arbitration clauses that govern trade mark licence agreements, which provide for arbitration exclusively in the case of disputes arising from the licence agreement.

13. Trade Marks and Other Intellectual Property

13.1 Protection by Copyright

The duplication of legal protections is a very complex issue pursuant to Italian law.

According to prevailing opinion, the same item may be protected at the same time as industrial design, copyright, unfair competition, trade marks and even as patents or utility models, if the necessary requirements are met.

One of the main effects of this potential duplication of legal protection consists of extending the duration of protection.

Clifford Chance
Piazzetta Maurilio Bossi
3- 20121 Milan
Italy

CLIFFORD CHANCE

Tel: +39 02806341
Fax: +39 0280634200
Email: cliffordchanceitaly@cliffordchance.com
Web: www.cliffordchance.com/home.html

JAPAN

LAW AND PRACTICE: p.189

Contributed by TMI Associates

The 'Law & Practice' sections provide easily accessible information on navigating the legal system when conducting business in the jurisdiction. Leading lawyers explain local law and practice at key transactional stages and for crucial aspects of doing business.

Contributed by TMI Associates **Authors:** Mitsuko Miyagawa, Takeshi Hironaka, Seiro Hatano, Seiji Kurishita

Law and Practice

Contributed by TMI Associates

CONTENTS

Contributed by TMI Associates ***Authors:*** Mitsuko Miyagawa, Takeshi Hironaka, Seiro Hatano, Seiji Kurishita

TMI Associates' intellectual property practice – which includes trade marks and patents – has been an integral part of the firm since its establishment in 1990, and TMI Associates possess considerable experience and expertise in this area. Lawyers and patent/trade-mark attorneys and paralegals comprise a unique organisational structure that enables the team to respond in a highly effective and efficient manner to the needs of clients across a wide variety of businesses and technologies from all around the globe. The team of IP lawyers and patent/trade-mark attorneys work together on all aspects of intellectual property law, including patent/trade-mark prosecution, trials before the Japan Patent Office, infringement litigation, IP due diligence, and import suspension applications at customs.

Authors

Mitsuko Miyagawa is a partner in TMI Associates' IP practice group, an attorney-at-law admitted in Japan (1986) and the State of New York, USA. She is a specialist in the field of both prosecution and enforcement of intellectual property rights, and especially renowned for her legal services in relation to brand protection and IP-related business transactions. She has served as a member on several governmental committees related to intellectual property rights, and in 2013 was appointed by Prime Minister Shinzo Abe. A board member of The Japan Trademark Association and Vice-Chairperson of the IP Center of The Japan Federation of Bar Associations, Mitsuko is also a lecturer on IP Law at Keio Law School.

Takeshi Hironaka is an international patent/trade-mark attorney. After qualifying in Japan he subsequently worked for a Barcelona-based Japanese/US joint legal venture for eight years. A partner at the firm, Takeshi assists both domestic and foreign brand-owners with trade-mark matters, helping them to build and organise global trade-mark portfolios, and assisting with domestic and overseas prosecutions, cancellation and invalidation actions, in addition to complex litigations, defending and enforcing his clients' trade marks. He is a member of the Japan Patent Attorneys Association and has written several articles for legal publications.

Seiro Hatano is a partner at TMI Associates, whose practice covers the full range of contentious and non-contentious IP-related work with particular focus on trade mark and unfair competition. He has considerable experience with contentious works regarding trade marks and unfair competition, including litigation representing foreign-based clients. In addition, he has expertise in intellectual property transactions for brand management through, among others, licensing and M&A. Mr Hatano specialises in trade-secrets and copyright disputes; his wider work covers a range of sectors, including the TMT sector. He also has experience working at the Intellectual Property Policy Office of the Ministry of Economy, Trade and Industry of the Japanese Government.

Seiji Kurishita is a senior associate at the firm. A specialist in the field of trade marks, with more than ten years of experience in trade-mark prosecution and litigation in Japan, he assists both domestic and foreign clients with protecting and structuring stronger trade-mark portfolios around the world. His practice covers all aspects of trade-mark law, including trade-mark searches, prosecution, trial, litigation and licensing. Seiji has a broad range of industry experience such as apparel, food and beverage, chemicals and information technology. He is a member of the Japan Patent Attorneys Association.

1. Types of Trade Marks & Registration

1.1 Types of Trade Marks

In Japan, "trade marks," "collective trade marks," "regional collective trade marks" and "defensive marks" can be registered under the Trademark Act. "Trade marks" can be registered in relation to services as well as goods (Article 2). "Collective trade marks" can be registered so as to be used by members of business co-operatives and associations (Article 7). "Regional collective trade marks" consist of a region's name and the name of the particular goods or services (eg, Tokyo Silverware or Kyoto Pickled Vegetables), and can be registered so as to be used by members of business co-operatives and associations (Article 7-2). "Defensive marks" can extend the protection of a famous mark to cover goods and services for which the applicant does not intend to use the mark (Article 64).

Trade dress – such as the shape of the container of a product – can be protected as a three-dimensional trade mark or under the Unfair Competition Prevention Act. It should be noted, however, that a trade dress such as a basic-shape product container without any distinctive word, mark or sign on it is often deemed indistinctive and cannot be registered unless acquisition of a secondary meaning is proven. Furthermore, to qualify for protection under the Unfair Competition Prevention Act, it must be shown that the trade dress is well-known and that there is likelihood of confusion.

Any newly established company must record its trade name on the company register, but this only means that no other company can register the same company name with the same address; another party may record the same company name if its corporate address is different. It is possible to obtain broader protection by registering the company name as a trade mark on the trade-mark register, provided that the company name satisfies all the requirements for registration as provided under the Trademark Law. The Companies Act also provides that no one can use any company name or trade name that is likely to cause confusion with another company, and any person whose business is damaged by such an act, among others, may seek injunctions against such use.

Rights in trade marks are granted based on statutory law upon successful registration of the trade mark on the Trademark Register.

1.2 Trade-Mark Rights
We must obtain a trade-mark registration in order to have trade-mark rights in Japan. We cannot acquire trade-mark right merely by using the mark.

1.3 Standards for Registering
Under Article 3 of the Japanese Trademark Act, an indistinctive mark, including a common name of goods, a mark consisting solely of the place of origin, and a product configuration cannot be registered. However, that indistinctive mark can be registered if the trade-mark applicant successfully proves that it has acquired a secondary meaning as the result of continuous and extensive use. Typically, the applicant is required to show that the trade mark in question is well-known throughout Japan.

For a colour trade mark, similarly, the applicant is required to show acquisition of secondary meaning through actual use.

1.4 Trade-Mark Register
The following matters are recorded in a trade-mark register (Article 71):

- the establishment, renewal of the duration, division, transfer, modification, extinguishment, restoration or restriction on disposition of a trade-mark right;
- the establishment, renewal of the duration, transfer or extinguishment of rights based on a defensive mark registration;
- the establishment, maintenance, transfer, modification, extinguishment or restriction on disposition of an exclusive right to use or a non-exclusive right to use; and
- the establishment, transfer, modification, extinguishment or restriction on disposition of a right of pledge on a trade-mark right, an exclusive right to use or a non-exclusive right to use.

Any person may file a request for the issuance of documents whose contents are registered in a trade-mark register (Article 72). In this regard, some of the above matters are also confirmed by using the free "J-Plat Pat" database.

1.5 Types of Registers
There is only one trade-mark register in Japan. Unlike the US, Japan does not have a supplementary register on which descriptive marks are registrable.

1.6 Searching for Prior Trade Marks
It is normal practice to search for prior trade marks before applying to register a mark in Japan. The search is usually conducted by using "J-Plat Pat", which includes the marks applied with and registered by the Japan Patent Office ("JPO"). Unlike the US, since no trade-mark right will arise unless it is registered, the search does not generally cover marks in use but not applied or registered.

1.7 Registration Requirements
Any person seeking to register a trade mark shall submit an application to the Commissioner of the JPO accompanied by the required documents (Article 5). The application must include:

- the applicant's name and address;
- the trade mark to be registered; and
- the designated goods and/or services.

No trade-mark right will arise unless and until such an application is filed, examined by the JPO, and matures into registration on the trade-mark register. A trade-mark right will arise upon registration of the establishment of such right (Article 18 (1)).

Contributed by TMI Associates ***Authors:*** Mitsuko Miyagawa, Takeshi Hironaka, Seiro Hatano, Seiji Kurishita

1.8 Registering a Trade Mark

Any entities with the legal capacity to hold rights can register a trade mark. Such entities include individuals, legal entities and trade bodies, but not unincorporated associations (eg, a sports club or residents' association).

1.9 Registering Signs

Article 2 of the Trademark Act defines a "trade mark" as any character(s), figure(s), sign(s), three-dimensional shape(s), sound(s) or colour(s), or any combination thereof, specified by a Cabinet Order, which an individual could recognise as being:

- used in connection with the goods of a person who produces, certifies or assigns the goods as a business; or
- used in connection with the services of a person who provides or certifies the services as a business (except for those provided for in the preceding item).

"Services" includes retail services and wholesale services – namely, the provision of benefits for customers conducted in the course of retail and wholesale business.

On 1 April 2015, Japan expanded trade-mark protection to cover a further five categories of non-traditional trade marks, as follows:

- motion marks;
- hologram marks;
- colour marks;
- sound marks; and
- position marks.

1.10 Other Rights to Signs

The Japanese legal system recognises other rights to signs or source-identifiers besides trade marks. Under the Unfair Competition Prevention Act ("UCPA"), the act of using an indication of goods or business that is identical or similar to a well-known mark that causes a likelihood of confusion (Article 2.1.1) and the act of using an indication of goods or business that is identical or similar to a famous mark as one's own indication, regardless of the likelihood of confusion (Article 2.1.2), will constitute unfair competition; any person whose business is damaged by such unfair competition may seek damages and injunctions against the infringer. Such indication includes company names, trade names and trade marks. In addition, under the UCPA, the act of obtaining or using a domain name that is identical or similar to an indication with wrongful purposes, or for the purpose of acquiring a wrongful benefit or harming another person, will also constitute unfair competition (Article 2.1.13). The company name can be protected under the Companies Act.

1.11 Registration Procedure

The registration procedure for a trade mark in Japan is as follows.

- Application – the person wishing to register a trade mark needs to submit an application with the JPO (Article 5). The applicant can file multi-class applications. The contents of the application will be published (Article 12-2).

- Examination – if the application meets the requirements, a substantive examination will be conducted by the JPO (Article 14). If the application fails to meet the substantive requirements, a notification of reasons for refusal will be sent to the applicant (Article 15-2). The applicant is entitled to file an Argument and Amendment in response to such notification (Article 15-2 and Article 68-40).

- Registration – if the application meets the substantive requirements, a decision to register a trade mark will be made (Article 16). In Japan, the trade-mark applicant is required to pay the official registration fee to register the trade mark after the decision of registration is granted. Subject to the payment of the registration fee, the registration of the trade-mark right will take place and the trade-mark right will come into force (Article 18).

- Publication – Japan adopts a "post-registration" opposition system. Once the trade mark is registered, the contents of the trade-mark registration are published on the trade-mark gazette (Article 18). Any person may file an opposition against the registered trade mark within two months of the publication (Article 43-2).

1.12 Use in Commerce

Use in commerce is not required for filing, registering or renewing a trade mark.

The trade-mark applicant's intention to use the trade mark is sufficient for the JPO to register the trade mark and, in principle, the trade-mark applicant is not required to submit a declaration of intent to use or any similar documentary proof of its intent to use. However, if the JPO finds the scope of the goods and/or services claimed in a trade-mark application to be overly broad, it will require the applicant to submit documentary evidence to show that it has a bona fide intent to use the trade mark in Japan by way of evidence showing that the trade-mark applicant is actually providing all the goods and services designated in the application, or by way of a declaration of the intent to use together with a simple business plan.

1.13 Registration of Series Marks

Japan does not allow the registration of series marks.

Contributed by TMI Associates **Authors:** Mitsuko Miyagawa, Takeshi Hironaka, Seiro Hatano, Seiji Kurishita

1.14 Length of Registration Process

If a trade-mark application proceeds smoothly, it will take six to 12 months from filing to registration. If the trade-mark applicant is a resident in Japan, representation is not necessary to initiate the registration procedure. If the applicant is not a resident in Japan, the trade-mark application needs to be filed by an attorney with a domicile in Japan. The typical cost for filing and registering a single-word mark in one class is about JPY179,600, comprising JPY49,600 for the official fee and JPY130,000 for the attorney fees.

1.15 Grounds for Refusal

The JPO refuses the registration of trade marks that do not enable consumers to differentiate the applicant's goods or services from those belonging to other parties (Article 3). According to Article 3, Paragraph 1, the trade mark will be refused if it:

- consists solely of a mark indicating, in a common manner, the common name of the goods or services;
- is customarily used in connection with the goods or services;
- consists solely of a mark indicating, in a common manner, in the case of goods, the place of origin, place of sale, quality, raw materials, efficacy, intended purpose, quantity, shape (including shape of packages), price, method or time of production or use, or, in the case of services, the location of provision, quality, articles to be used in such provision, efficacy, intended purpose, quantity, modes, price or method or time of provision;
- consists solely of a mark indicating, in a common manner, a common surname or a common name of a juridical person;
- consists solely of a very simple and common mark; or
- does not enable consumers to recognise the goods or services as those pertaining to a business of a particular person.

The JPO can also refuse the registration of trade marks in terms of public interest (Article 4). According to Article 4, Paragraph 1, Items 1 to 7, 9, 16 and 18, the trade mark will be refused if it:

- is identical or similar to the national flag, the imperial chrysanthemum crest, a decoration, a medal or a foreign national flag;
- is identical or similar to the coat of arms or any other State emblems (except national flags of any country of the Union to the Paris Convention, any member of the World Trade Organization or any Contracting Party to the Trademark Law Treaty) of a country of the Union to the Paris Convention (refers to the Paris Convention for the Protection of Industrial Property of 20 March 1883, as revised at Brussels on 14 December 1900, at Washington on 2 June 1911, at the Hague on 6 November, 1925, at London on 2 June 1934, at Lisbon on 31 October 1958 and at Stockholm on 14 July 1967; the same shall apply hereinafter), a member of the World Trade Organization or a Contracting Party to the Trademark Law Treaty designated by the Minister of Economy, Trade and Industry;
- is identical or similar to a mark indicating the United Nations or any other international organisation that has been designated by the Minister of Economy, Trade and Industry;
- is identical or similar to the emblems or titles in Article 1 of the Act Concerning Restriction on the Use of Emblems and Titles of the Red Cross and Others (Act No 159 of 1947) or the distinctive emblem in Article 158(1) of the Act Concerning Measures to Protect Japanese Citizens During Armed Attacks and Others (Act No 112 of 2004);
- is comprised of a mark identical or similar to an official hallmark or sign indicating control or warranty by the national or a local government of Japan, a country of the Union to the Paris Convention, a member of the World Trade Organization or a Contracting Party to the Trademark Law Treaty which has been designated by the Minister of Economy, Trade and Industry, if such trade mark is used in connection with goods or services identical or similar to the goods or services in connection with which the hallmark or sign is used;
- is identical or similar to a famous mark indicating the State, a local government, an agency thereof, a non-profit organisation undertaking a business for public interest, or a non-profit enterprise undertaking a business for public interest;
- is likely to cause damage to public order or morality;
- is comprised of a mark identical or similar to a prize awarded at an exhibition held by the national or a local government (hereinafter referred to as the "Government, etc") or by those who are not the Government, etc, that conforms to the standards specified by the Commissioner of the JPO, or at an international exhibition held in a foreign country by the Government, etc, of the foreign country or those authorised thereby (except those used by the recipient of such a prize as part of his or her own trade mark);
- is likely to mislead regarding the quality of the goods or services;
- consists solely of a three-dimensional shape of goods or their packaging, which is indispensable for such goods or their packaging to function properly.

Furthermore, an application for a mark identical or similar to another's trade mark that is well known in or outside Japan can be refused under Article 4, Item 1, Paragraph 19.

1.16 Process for Overcoming Objections

Objections raised by the JPO regarding lack of distinctiveness may be overcome by claiming acquired distinctiveness (Article 3, Paragraph 2).

Contributed by TMI Associates ***Authors:*** Mitsuko Miyagawa, Takeshi Hironaka, Seiro Hatano, Seiji Kurishita

1.17 Consideration of Prior Rights

The JPO refuses the registration of trade marks due to the existence of prior rights (Article 4). According to Article 4, Paragraph 1, Items 8, 10 to 15, 17 and 19, the trade mark will be refused if it:

- contains the portrait of another person, or the name, famous pseudonym, professional name or pen name of another person, or a famous abbreviation thereof (except those for which the registration has been approved by the person concerned);
- is identical or similar to another person's trade mark that is well known among consumers as indicating goods or services in connection with the person's business, if such a trade mark is used in connection with such goods or services, or with goods or services similar thereto;
- is identical or similar to another person's registered trade mark which has been filed prior to the filing date of an application for registration of said trade mark, if such trade mark is used in connection with the designated goods or designated services relating to said registered trade mark (referring to goods or services designated in accordance with Article 6(1) – including cases where it is applied mutatis mutandis pursuant to Article 68(1); the same shall apply hereinafter), or goods or services similar thereto;
- is identical to a registered defensive mark of another person (referring to a mark registered as a defensive mark; the same shall apply hereinafter), if such trade mark is used in connection with designated goods or designated services relating to the defensive mark;
- is identical or similar to the name of a variety registered in accordance with Article 18(1) of the Plant Variety Protection and Seed Act (Act No 83 of 1998), if such trade mark is used in connection with seeds and seedlings of the variety or goods or services similar thereto;
- is likely to cause confusion in connection with the goods or services pertaining to a business of another person (aside from those listed above);
- is comprised of a mark indicating the place of origin of wines or spirits of Japan that has been designated by the Commissioner of the JPO, or a mark indicating the place of origin of wines or spirits of a member of the World Trade Organization which is prohibited by said member from being used on wines or spirits not originating from the region of said member, if such a trade mark is used in connection with wines or spirits not originating from the region in Japan or from the said member; or
- is identical or similar to a trade mark that is well known among consumers in Japan or abroad to indicate goods or services pertaining to a business of another person, if such trade mark is used for unfair purposes (ie, gaining unfair profits, causing damage to the other person, or any other unfair purposes) (except those provided for in each of the preceding items).

1.18 Third-Party Rights

Any person can provide useful information for the examination if they believe an applied-for trade mark does not meet the substantive requirements for registration (Enforcement Regulations of the Trademark Act, Article 19). Specifically, anyone is permitted to submit information about an earlier-registered or unregistered trade mark which they believe should be cited as a bar to registration of the trade-mark application under examination. The JPO Examiner can decide whether or not to refuse the application based on the information submitted.

In addition, any person can file an opposition to a registration within two months of the date of publication (Article 43-2).

1.19 Revoke, Change, Amend or Correct an Application

The applicant can make amendments to its application when the case is pending examination, examination on opposition to registration, trial or retrial (Article 68-40). It is very common for the applicant to amend the description of the goods and services at the request of the JPO Examiner. Amendment of the trade mark itself is usually not permitted.

1.20 Assigning an Application or Granting a Licence

An application can be assigned while it is pending examination (Article 33, Paragraph 1 of the Patent Act as applied under Article 13 of the Trademark Act). However, a licence for a trade-mark right can only be granted after such right is established by the registration.

1.21 Remedies Against the Trade Mark Office

An applicant who is dissatisfied with the JPO's decision of refusal may appeal such decision within three months of the date on which a certified copy of the decision is received (Article 44). If the applicant is dissatisfied with an appeal decision made by the JPO, it may appeal to the Intellectual Property High Court ("IP High Court") within 30 days of the date on which a certified copy of the decision is received (Article 178 of the Patent Act as applied under Article 63 of the Trademark Act).

1.22 Use of a Trade Mark

Use of a trade mark is not necessary in order to maintain a registered trade mark, so the owner of the registration does not need to file any proof of use when renewing the trade-mark right. However, if a third party files a cancellation action against the registration based on non-use, the owner of the registration needs to prove use of the trade mark during the three years prior to the registration of the request for the trial (Article 50).

Contributed by TMI Associates ***Authors:*** Mitsuko Miyagawa, Takeshi Hironaka, Seiro Hatano, Seiji Kurishita

1.23 Dividing a Trade Mark

The applicant is permitted to divide a trade-mark application (Article 10), provided that the application is pending in examination, trial or retrial, or if a suit against a trial decision to refuse the application is pending in court. Since the application should be divided per designated goods or services, the original application should include two or more designated goods or services to divide the application.

1.24 Length of Term of Protection

The duration of a trade-mark right expires ten years after the date of registration (Article 19). The owner can file a renewal application during the six months preceding the expiration of the trade-mark right (Article 19 and Article 20, Paragraph 2). Within six months of the expiry date (the grace period), the owner may file a renewal application by paying double the official fees as a bail-out measure (Article 20, Paragraph 3).

1.25 Requirements for an Exhaustion

The Japanese Trademark Act contains no provision for exhaustion of trade-mark rights. Nevertheless, in accordance with the precedents, it is generally considered that, once goods with the registered trade mark are put on the market subject to the consent of the trade mark-owner, further distribution of the goods as they are by any third party will not be considered to constitute trade-mark infringement.

1.26 Participation in the Madrid System

Japan participates in the Madrid System and adopts a two-part payment of individual fees, with the second part of the individual fees needing to be paid directly to the International Bureau after the decision of registration is made by the JPO.

1.27 Consequences for Providing Incorrect Information

If a trade mark application includes incorrect information, such as typos in the applicant name and descriptions of the goods and services, the JPO issues an Office Action requesting the applicant to correct such information. When the typos are very minor, the JPO tends to correct them by their own authority.

1.28 Updating or Refreshing a Design Mark

Updating or refreshing a design mark is not allowed in Japan.

1.29 Denotation

Although it is not mandatory, it is encouraged to denote that a mark is registered in Japan. No symbol is provided in Japanese trade-mark law, but indications such as ® and "a registered trade mark" are widely used for registered trade marks in Japan. We do not have a concept of "common-law rights" in Japan.

2. Assignment and Licensing

2.1 Assignment Requirements or Restrictions

A trade mark can be assigned before and after registration (Article 24-2 and Article 33, Paragraph 1 of the Patent Act as applied under Article 13 of the Trademark Act).

A trade mark owned by the state, a local government, an agency thereof, or a non-profit organisation undertaking a business for public interest may not be assigned (Article 24-2, Paragraph 2).

A trade mark owned by a non-profit enterprise undertaking a business for public interest may not be transferred unless the business is transferred together with such a right (Article 24-2, Paragraph 3). A regional collective trade mark may not be assigned (Article 24-2, Paragraph 4). Where the owner of a collective trade mark wishes to transfer the collective trade mark as a collective trade mark, they should submit certain documents to the JPO. The documents need to state that the collective trade mark should be transferred as a collective trade mark, and must prove that the assignee is the proper entity entitled to own the collective trade mark (Article 24-3, Paragraph 2).

2.2 Procedure for Assigning a Trade Mark

In order to register the assignment of a registered trade mark, an application for recordal of assignment has to be filed with the JPO. Typically, an Assignment Deed specifying the subject trade mark by its application/registration number, the consent by the assignor for the assignee to take the steps to record the assignment and a signature by the assignor are required, along with a power of attorney by the assignee. The assignment is then recorded on the trade-mark register (Article 71).

It is also possible to assign a pending application before registration, in which case the documents listed above are typically required.

2.3 Registering or Recording the Assignment

The assignment of a trade-mark right needs to be registered (Article 98, Paragraph 1 of the Patent Act as applied under Article 35 of the Trademark Act), and takes effect only upon recordation on the trade-mark register. If it is not registered, the assignment may be deemed invalid. Therefore, once the trade mark-owner and the assignee agree that a trade-mark right is assigned, the assignee must promptly record the assignment with the JPO. If a third party subsequently acquires the trade-mark right from the trade mark-owner and successfully records such acquisition before the previous assignment is recorded on the trade-mark register, that third party may acquire the trade-mark right (in this case, the assignee would need to institute a lawsuit against the assignor for breach of contract).

However, if a transfer of a trade-mark right occurs as the result of a general succession (eg, a merger of a company or inheritance), the transfer takes effect when such general succession occurred, but the transferee is encouraged to record such transfer to keep the record up to date (Article 98, Paragraph 2 of the Patent Act applied under Article 35 of the Trademark Act).

2.4 Trade Marks and Security

A trade mark can be subject to pledge and assigned by way of security. In the case of compulsory execution, a trade mark may be subject to seizure and auctioned as part of the property of the obliger.

2.5 Licensing Requirements or Restrictions

Under the Japanese Trademark Act, a licence can be granted with regard to a registered trade mark. There are two types of licences under the Japanese Trademark Act: an exclusive licence (SENYO SHIYOKEN) and a non-exclusive licence (TSUJO SHIYOKEN) (Articles 30 and 31). Under Article 30 of the Japanese Trademark Act, an exclusive licence is a very strong right for the licensee. Once an exclusive licence is established under such article (which requires the licence to be recorded at the JPO), the trade mark-owner (Licensor) is prohibited from using the trade mark without authorisation from the exclusive licensee. An exclusive licence cannot be established in connection with a trade mark owned by the state or a local government, an agency thereof, a non-profit organisation undertaking a business for public interest, or a person undertaking a non-profit activity for public interest or a regional collective trade mark (Article 30, Paragraph 1). A non-exclusive licence cannot be established in connection with a trade mark owned by the state or a local government, an agency thereof, a non-profit organisation undertaking a business for public interest, or a person undertaking a non-profit activity for public interest (Article 31, Paragraph 1). However, a trade mark-owner can grant either an exclusive or a non-exclusive licence based on a licence agreement. Such licence is considered a contractual right, which comes into existence by agreement of the parties, and is not eligible for registration of a licence under the Japanese Trademark Act.

2.6 Procedure for Licensing a Trade Mark

In order to register a trade-mark licence (SENYO SHIYOKEN or TSUJO SHIYOKEN) under the Japanese Trademark Act, an application for the recordal of such licence may be filed with the JPO (Article 71). Typically, a deed of licence specifying the subject trade mark by its application/registration number and the content of the licence to be granted, the consent of the licensor for the licensee to take the steps to record the licence and a signature by the licensor are required, along with a power of attorney by the licensee. The financial conditions of the licence agreement do not need to be disclosed, and it is not necessary to file the original licence agreement. If all the formalities are fulfilled, the licence is recorded on the trade-mark register.

2.7 Registering or Recording the Licence

Under the Japanese Trademark Act, an exclusive licence (SENYO SHIYOKEN) must be registered in order to take effect (Article 98, Paragraph 2 of the Patent Act as applied mutatis mutandis under Article 30 of the Trademark Act).

On the other hand, it is not mandatory to register a non-exclusive licence (TSUJO SHIYOKEN) under the Japanese Trademark Act in order for such licence to take effect. However, if the non-exclusive licence has not been registered, the licensee cannot assert its licence against the third party. Therefore, if the trade-mark right is assigned by the trade mark-owner to a third party, then the licensee of a non-exclusive licence that has not been recorded may lose its licence (Article 31, Paragraph 4).

If there is a gap between the licence being entered into and its registration on the trade-mark register, the licensee can only claim its licence and other rights against the trade mark-owner based on the contract (licence agreement) vis-à-vis the trade mark-owner. Without recordation on the trade-mark register, the licensee cannot claim its licence against third parties.

2.8 Reasons to Deny Granting a Perpetual Licence

There is no reason to prohibit a trade mark-owner from granting a perpetual licence in Japan. In other words, setting the term of the licence perpetual does not necessarily render the licence agreement invalid or unenforceable. However, the trade-mark right must be renewed every ten years and if the underlying trade-mark right is not renewed, the licence may be lost as a consequence of such failure of renewal.

3. Opposition Procedure

3.1 Legal Grounds and Timeframes

An opposition may be filed based on the following grounds (Article 43-2):

- lack of distinctiveness (Article 3);
- unregistrability (Article 4, Paragraph 1). Most notably, an opposition can be filed based on relative grounds for refusal (ie, the published mark is identical or similar to an earlier trade mark and used for the same or similar goods/services);
- violation of requirements for a collective mark (Article 7-2, Paragraph 1);
- violation of the first-to-file rule (Article 8, Paragraph 1, 2 and 5);

- violation of provisions prohibiting re-registration of cancelled trade marks (Article 51, Paragraph 2, Article 52-2, Paragraph 2 and Article 53, Paragraph 2);
- violation of the enjoyment of trade-mark rights by foreign nationals (Article 25 of the Patent Act as applied under Article 77, Paragraph 3 of the Trademark Act);
- infringement of the provisions of the Trademark Law Treaty, Paris Convention, and relevant treaties; and
- violation of requirement for explanation of the trade mark (Article 5, Paragraph 5)

It usually takes about one year for a decision to be issued following the filing of an opposition.

3.2 Filing an Opposition

Any person can file an opposition (Article 43-2). Representation is not necessary. The average cost for opposing a registration in one class is about JPY311,000, comprising JPY11,000 for the official fee and JPY300,000 for the attorney fees.

3.3 Opposition Procedure

An opposition to a trade-mark registration can be filed with the JPO for each or all of the designated goods and services, within two months of the publication (Article 43-2, Paragraph 1); the opposition deadline is not extendable. Once a bare-bones notice of opposition is filed, the opponent can supplement detailed grounds and supporting evidence within 30 days if they are a resident in Japan, or within 90 days if they are not a resident in Japan. The examination of the opposition is conducted by a collegial body of trial examiners (Article 43-3, Paragraph 1). In principle, the examination of the opposition is conducted on the basis of documents, but oral examination may sometimes be conducted under the chief trial examiner's authority (Article 43-6). When the chief trial examiner intends to render a rescission decision, he or she shall notify the owner of the trade-mark right and give such owner the opportunity to submit an argument within an adequate period of time (Article 43-12). When a decision has been rendered, the Commissioner of the JPO shall serve a transcript of the decision on the owner of the trade-mark right and the opponent (Article 43-13).

3.4 Legal Remedies

If the collegial body of trial examiners renders a decision to maintain the trade-mark registration and dismisses the opposition, such decision cannot be appealed. However, if the opponent is dissatisfied with such dismissal, it is possible to file an invalidation action for the same grounds. If the trial examiners render a rescission decision with which the owner of the trade mark is dissatisfied, it may appeal to the IP High Court within 30 days of the date on which a certified copy of the decision is served (Article 178 of the Patent Act as applied under Article 63 of the Trademark Act). The chief trial examiner may ex officio designate an additional period extending the above time period for a person in a remote area or an area with transportation difficulties (eg, a foreign resident) (Article 178 of the Patent Act as applied under Article 63 of the Trademark Act). It usually takes about eight months from the filing of an appeal for a court to make a decision.

4. Initiating a Lawsuit

4.1 Actions to Pursue Infringement

The trade mark-owner may claim damages or injunction (including a preliminary injunction) against the infringement of a trade-mark right through infringement litigation. Under the Japanese Trademark Act, a trade-mark right comes into existence upon registration at the JPO (Article 19, Paragraph 1 of the Trademark Act). Therefore, the owner of an unregistered trade mark cannot enjoy protection against infringement of a trade-mark right under the Trademark Act, although unregistered marks can be protected under the Unfair Competition Prevention Act (UCPA) if the mark is well-known or famous as an indicator of origin and satisfies other requirements of protection under the UCPA. In addition, if the infringing goods are imported, the owner of a registered and/or well-known/famous trade mark may file an import suspension application with the Customs Office. Furthermore, the trade mark-owner may use alternative dispute resolution proceedings, such as mediation or arbitration, if the other party agrees to it. Those other actions are also available to the claim under the UCPA.

4.2 Initiating Infringement Proceedings

The trade mark-owner may file a lawsuit before the court that has jurisdiction over the location of the infringing act or defendant. In addition, with respect to a claim for damages, the court that has jurisdiction over the location of the plaintiff can hear the case. Further, for a trade-mark infringement case, the plaintiff may select the Tokyo District Court at its option if a district court located within the jurisdictional district of any of the High Courts in the east part of Japan, (ie, the Tokyo High Court, the Nagoya High Court, the Sendai High Court or the Sapporo High Court), or may select the Osaka District Court at its option if a district court located within the jurisdictional district of any of the High Court in the west part of Japan (ie, Osaka High Court, the Hiroshima High Court, the Fukuoka High Court or the Takamatsu High Court). It should be noted, however, that the court can transfer the case to another court with jurisdiction if necessary to avoid undue delay of the procedure or to ensure equity between the parties.

4.3 Effect of Decisions on Infringement Actions

Once the decision of the JPO becomes final, then the effect caused by the decision would be binding on any persons and thus such decision could legally affect the infringement actions in case the JPO decision is to invalidate or cancel the trade-mark registration which is the basis of the infringement action. However, until the decision becomes final, the decision will not be legally binding and thus technically has no effect on infringement actions, although it might affect the perception of the court in practice.

4.4 Declaratory Judgment Proceedings

The alleged infringer can initiate a lawsuit for declaratory judgment to confirm that there is no trade-mark infringement and that the trade mark-owner therefore has no right to seek an injunction. When the trade mark-owner initiates a lawsuit for trade-mark infringement, the defendant can still initiate a lawsuit for declaratory judgement for the same trade mark, but the claim will be dismissed due to lack of benefit of suit.

4.5 Jurisdiction of Courts

The district court or the summary court will have jurisdiction to hear trade-mark matters in the first instance, although the summary court will only deal with cases whose jurisdictional amount is less than JPY1.4 million.

Where the district court is the court of first instance, the appeal court will be the relevant high court with jurisdiction over the case heard by the district court, and the parties may appeal decisions of the high court to the Supreme Court as the court of third and final instance.

Where the summary court is the court of the first instance, the appeal court will be the district court and the parties may appeal decisions of the district court to the high court as the court of third and final instance. It should be noted, however, that it is not common for the summary court to deal with trade-mark matters.

4.6 Prerequisites to Filing a Lawsuit

There are no such prerequisites.

4.7 Representation for Parties

In Japan, a party may choose whether or not to be represented by a lawyer, although it is common for lawyers to represent the parties in trade-mark litigation matters. A patent attorney (benrishi) – which is a different profession from a lawyer (bengoshi) – can also represent a party in trade-mark litigation matters under certain conditions.

4.8 Interim or Preliminary Injunctions

Preliminary injunctions are available under the Civil Preservation Act if they are necessary in order for a rights owner to avoid any substantial detriment or imminent danger with respect to the trade-mark rights in dispute.

4.9 Protection for Potential Defendant

A potential defendant can file a request for a trade-mark invalidation trial before the JPO and/or initiate a lawsuit for declaratory judgment to confirm the absence of the right to demand an injunction, etc. There is no need for a potential opponent to lodge a protective brief to take these actions. It should be noted that, if a trade mark-owner starts the proceeding for a preliminary injunction under the Civil Preservation Act, the respondent/a potential defendant in the formal litigation is not entitled to require a bond to be posted by the trade mark-owner under the Civil Preservation Act, while a court usually orders the owner to deposit a certain amount of money as a security when issuing an interim injunction order.

4.10 Obtaining Information and Evidence

Although there is no discovery procedure in Japan, the Trademark Act provides that a court can order a party to produce documents upon the other party's request for the purpose of proving infringement activities or calculating damages; however, this does not apply where there are reasonable grounds for the alleged infringer to refuse production of the documents.

4.11 Initial Pleading Standards

A complaint must identify the names and addresses of the plaintiff and defendant (and the plaintiff's attorneys' names and addresses, if appointed), as well as the gist of the demand and the grounds for the demand. In particular, the infringing goods or services and the infringing acts must be specified in detail. To identify those facts, a trade mark-owner is expected to conduct a sufficiently detailed investigation and analysis on the case before initiating the lawsuit.

There are no special provisions for lawsuits in trade-mark proceedings that differ from non-intellectual property proceedings.

Supplementing pleadings with additional arguments is acceptable. The court examines the case through periodic hearing procedures (generally once a month), and each party is allowed to add its legal/factual arguments or evidence in the course of those procedures. The plaintiff may even expand or amend the claim or statement of claim until the oral argument is concluded. However, the court may limit such additional arguments or evidence if it considers that they would substantially delay the court proceedings.

4.12 Representative or Collective Actions

There is no legal system that allows for representative or collective actions for trade-mark proceedings; however, if the subject matter of the suits is common to two or more persons or is based on the same factual or statutory cause, these persons may sue or be sued as co-parties.

4.13 Restrictions on Trade Mark-Owners
Abuse of rights is restricted under the Civil Code. For example, if a trade-mark registration has grounds for invalidation, that patent right may not be exercised even before the trade-mark right is actually cancelled on the ground that the exercise of the right is considered to be an abuse of that right. Moreover, the act of filing a lawsuit may cause tort liability where the allegation of the infringement is entirely baseless and the owner of the trade-mark right is fully aware of the lack of legal grounds and that such litigation is unreasonable. Even without filing a lawsuit, a groundless threat of trade-mark infringement may be considered an act of obstruction of business and cause tort liability, or could even constitute criminal liability.

In addition, according to the competition law guidelines provided by the Japan Fair Trade Commission (JFTC), interference with legitimate parallel importation by a trade mark-owner may be considered a violation of competition law and may even be considered to constitute a tort against the parallel importers.

Furthermore, if the owner of the trade-mark right makes or disseminates a false allegation of infringement of that trade-mark right, this could constitute an act of unfair competition under the Unfair Competition Prevention Act, and the owner of the trade-mark right may be subject to a claim for injunction and/or damages.

5. Infringement

5.1 Action for Infringement
The necessary parties to patent infringement litigation are the plaintiff (ie, trade mark-owner) and the defendant (ie, alleged infringer). A registered exclusive licensee is entitled to file an action based on infringement of the registered exclusive licence (SENYO SHIYOKEN), seeking the same remedies as the trade mark-owner. In this regard, there are arguments over whether or not non-registered exclusive licensees or non-exclusive licensees can initiate an action for infringement. With regard to injunctions, it is generally considered that neither a non-registered exclusive licensee nor a non-exclusive licensee is entitled to claim for an injunction, whereas, with respect to a claim for damages, a non-registered exclusive licensee may claim for damages, although a non-exclusive licensee is not permitted to claim for damages.

5.2 Signs and Infringement
The plaintiff must prove the existence of the trade-mark registration, the similarity between the registered trade mark and the mark at issue, and the similarity between the designated goods/services and the goods/services at issue. The distinctiveness of the registered mark is presumed, and it is the defendant who has the burden of proving lack of distinctiveness as its defence. The similarity of the marks is determined through taking into account the similarity in terms of appearance, connotation and pronunciation between the marks, as well as the likelihood of confusion.

5.3 Use of a Sign by Defendant
It is necessary to establish that the defendant has used the sign as a trade mark, ie as a source indicator of origin for the designated goods and/or services. If the defendant successfully proves that the sign has not been used as a source indicator, trade-mark infringement will not be established.

5.4 Defences Against Infringement
If the defendant has used a mark and the mark has become famous prior to the registration of the trade mark at issue, the defendant can claim "prior use" as a defence.

The defendant may also claim, as their defence, that a trade mark is a generic term or that the use thereof is only descriptive (ie, indicating the contents, quality, origin, shape, or materials, etc). In addition, the defendant may also claim, as their defence, that the defendant's mark is not being used as an indicator of origin (ie, a "trade-mark use").

The defendant may also claim abuse of trade-mark rights if there is any ground for invalidation or cancellation of the trade-mark registration.

Non-use of a trade mark cannot be claimed directly as a defence. Nevertheless, non-use of a trade mark for a continuous period of three years or more could be grounds for cancellation of the trade-mark registration and, therefore, the defendant may claim abuse of rights on the grounds of non-use for such period.

As to the statute of limitations, the trade mark-owner cannot claim damages for an infringement when more than three years have passed since the trade mark-owner became aware of the infringement and of the identity of the infringer that caused the damage, and there is an overall limit of ten years from the act of infringement.

5.5 Role of Experts and/or Surveys
Expert opinions and surveys can be used as substantive evidence for certain legal issues, such as the likelihood of confusion, secondary meaning or genericness. However, given that the court may consider it to be somehow partial or biased, such evidence is unlikely to be decisive, and thus the court will determine the case taking into account all the other evidence as well.

5.6 Administrative or Criminal Offence
Trade-mark infringement can constitute a criminal offence, but there is no such administrative offence under Japanese law. The criminal offence of trade-mark infringement by way

of using a mark identical to the registered trade mark for the designated goods or services carries a penalty of up to ten years' imprisonment and a fine of up to JPY10 million for those infringing upon the trade mark, whereas the criminal offence of trade-mark infringement by way of using a mark similar to the registered trade mark for the designated goods or services – or using a mark identical or similar to the registered trade mark for goods or services similar to the designated goods or services – carries a penalty of up to five years' imprisonment and a fine of up to JPY5 million.

5.7 Custom Seizures

Japan Customs seizes counterfeit goods upon request from the owner of a registered and/or well-known/famous trade mark, or at Customs' discretion.

Parallel imports will not be subject to customs seizure if they are considered to be the parallel importation of genuine goods. According to the precedents, parallel imports will not be considered as infringement if:

- the trade mark on the parallel imported goods is duly affixed under the authorisation of the trade mark-owner or its licensee in a foreign jurisdiction;
- the trade mark on the parallel imported goods indicates the same origin as that of the Japanese registered trade mark, on the grounds that the trade mark-owner in the foreign jurisdiction is the same as that in Japan, or the trade mark-owners in both jurisdictions have so close a relationship that they could be legally or economically treated as the same person; and
- the trade mark guarantees no substantial difference in quality between the parallel imported goods and the products to which the trade mark was attached by the Japanese trade mark-owner.

The trade mark-owner submits a written request for the seizure of certain counterfeit goods to Japan Customs, which will seize those goods. Meanwhile, if Japan Customs finds any suspicious goods itself, it will contact the trade mark-owner to confirm if the goods are counterfeit and, upon receiving confirmation from the trade mark-owner, may seize the goods at its discretion.

6. Revocation/Cancellation

6.1 Remedies and Reasons

Cancellation Action Based on Non-Use

Any person may file a request for a trial for cancellation of a trade mark if the trade mark has not been used for three years or longer (Article 50, Paragraph 1). Where such a request is filed, the burden of proof of use is on the owner (Article 50, Paragraph 2). The use of the mark within the three months before the filing of the request cannot be a defence if the person requesting cancellation can prove that the owner knew the cancellation action was likely to be filed (Article 50, Paragraph 3).

Cancellation Action Due to Misuse

Any person may file a request for a trial for cancellation of a trade mark where the use of the trade mark misleads the consumers as to the nature of the goods/services or causes confusion with the goods/services of another person (Article 51, Article 52-2 and Article 53).

Cancellation Action Against a Trade mark Registered Without Approval

A person who has the right pertaining to the trade mark in a foreign member country of the Paris Convention, WTO or Trademark Treaty may file a request for a trial for cancellation of a trade mark if the application for trade-mark registration was filed by their agent or representative without their approval (Article 53-2).

Invalidation

A person who has a legal interest in invalidating the trade mark at issue may appeal for invalidation of the trade mark based on the following grounds (Article 46):

- lack of distinctiveness (Article 3);
- violation due to unregistrability (Article 4, Paragraph 1). Most notably, an invalidation action can be filed based on the relative grounds for refusal (ie, the trade mark in question is identical or similar to an earlier trade mark and is used for the same or similar goods/services);
- violation of requirements to be a collective mark (Article 7-2, Paragraph 1);
- violation of the first-to-file rule (Article 8, Paragraphs 1, 2 and 5);
- violation of provisions prohibiting re-registration of cancelled trade marks (Article 51, Paragraph 2, Article 52-2, Paragraph 2 and Article 53, Paragraph 2);
- violation of the enjoyment of trade-mark rights by foreign nationals (Article 25 of the Patent Act applied under Article 77, Paragraph 3 of the Trademark Act);
- infringement of the provisions of the Trademark Law Treaty, Paris Convention, and relevant treaties;
- violation of the requirement of explanation of the trade mark (Article 5, Paragraph 5);
- misappropriated application; and
- other subsequent grounds.

6.2 Trade Mark Office and Civil Courts

Cancellation actions and invalidations must be filed with the JPO.

6.3 Statutory Limitation or Time Period

The time period of five years applies for cancellation actions due to misuse, or against trade marks registered without approval (Article 52, Article 53, Paragraph 2 and Article 53-3).

The same time period also applies for invalidations, depending on the grounds for invalidation (Article 47). Most notably, invalidation actions based on absolute grounds for refusal and relative grounds for refusal are time barred, except for cases of trade marks filed in bad faith or for the purposes of unfair competition.

6.4 Initiation of Revocation/Cancellation Proceeding

Any person may request a trial for a cancellation action, except for a cancellation action based on Article 53-2 (a registration obtained by an agent or representative without authorisation), which must be filed by the owner of the right pertaining to the trade mark in the foreign member country of the Paris Convention, WTO or Trademark Treaty.

An invalidation action needs to be filed by a person who has a legal interest in invalidating the trade mark at issue, such as an applicant who received an official action from the JPO citing the trade mark at issue as an obstacle against their application.

6.5 Partial Revocation/Cancellation

Cancellation actions based on non-use and invalidation can be filed in a partial manner, specifying certain designated goods/services. It is not permitted to seek partial cancellation in a cancellation action for misuse or in a cancellation action for unauthorised registration by an agent or representative.

6.6 Possibilities of Amendment

The owner of the trade mark cannot make amendments in cancellation/invalidation proceedings if such amendments alter the situation. For example, it is not permitted to add cited trade marks or to expand the scope of the goods and services attacked in the cancellation action/invalidation actions. Filing additional evidence may not be allowed if such evidence involves a new legal argument and necessitates a defence by the defending party that was not expected when the action was originally filed.

6.7 Revocation/Cancellation and Infringement

Revocation/cancellation of the trade-mark registration is separate from the infringement procedure. Nevertheless, the court may dismiss the claim of infringement if it believes that the trade-mark registration should be revoked or cancelled. In such an event in an infringement case, the registration of the trade mark at issue will remain until it is revoked or cancelled in a separate cancellation/revocation procedure at the JPO.

7. Trial & Settlement

7.1 Special Procedural Provisions

There are no provisions specifically applicable to trial and settlement for trade-mark rights proceedings. However, in practice, the trial will be divided into two parts. First, the court focuses on determining whether the infringement of the trade-mark rights is established; after the court tentatively concludes the establishment of the infringement, it will assess the damages incurred by the plaintiff.

7.2 Determination of Cases

The case is determined solely by a legal judge. The Japanese legal system has neither technical judges nor jury trials for intellectual property cases.

There are special divisions for intellectual property matters in the Tokyo District Court and the Osaka District Court (four divisions at the Tokyo District Court and two divisions at the Osaka District Court), where judges who are experienced in intellectual property matters will hear and decide the cases.

The judges in these courts and the IP High Court rarely have technical backgrounds. Technical advisers may be appointed to support the judge on advanced or complicated technical issues, and to conduct research into highly advanced issues (including intellectual property issues and patent issues) on the judge's behalf. The parties cannot influence who will judge the case, except that a party can request to avoid a certain judge if they have reason to believe that said judge cannot be impartial due to a certain relationship with the other party (eg, if the judge is a relative of one party).

7.3 Possibilities of Settlement

The judge usually takes the initiative on settlement negotiations, unless the parties clearly refuse to settle the case. In no event will the defendant be obliged to settle the case. Generally speaking, the court prefers to resolve cases via settlements rather than judgments. The judge may disclose or imply to the parties (or even to only one party) their unofficial opinion on the case in order to facilitate the settlement negotiations. The judge will cease settlement negotiations if one party decides that they require a court decision rather than a settlement.

7.4 Other Court Proceedings

Even if there are any pending parallel revocation or infringement proceedings, the current proceedings will not normally be stayed, and the court will separately and independently make the judgment for the case. The court can even dismiss the claim for infringement on the grounds that the patent at issue is invalid, without the need to conduct a revocation proceeding. This means that it is possible for there to be a contradiction between two cases on the same subject matter.

However, in practice, the High Court, as the court of second instance, will make consistent judgments with those cases so that any such contradiction in the first instance will be resolved.

8. Remedies

8.1 Existing Remedies
The remedies available for a trade mark-owner are injunctive relief. Damages or an account of profit is available as a remedy for trade-mark infringement under the Civil Code. In addition, the court may order the defendant to take measures necessary to restore the business credibility of the trade mark-owner, such as publication of an apology. As part of the injunctive relief, the trade mark-owner can also seek disposal of the infringing goods. Attorney's fees can be recovered as part of the damages, although the recovery thereof is very limited (in practice, around 10% of the total amount of damages is admitted as the amount of reasonable attorney fees by the court). A trade mark-owner can only seek compensatory damages. Claims for enhanced damages, such as punitive damages, are not eligible even in cases of wilful infringement. The Trademark Act provides for certain presumptions of the damages that are to be calculated based on the profit from the infringement or the assumed royalties. The judge has discretion to determine the appropriate remedies or amount of damages provided that such discretion is only within the scope of claims sought by the plaintiff (ie if the plaintiff does not seek an injunctive relief, the judge cannot order such relief) and within the amount of the claim made by the plaintiff. In addition, a trade mark-owner may request banks to freeze the bank accounts which infringers have used to receive payments for counterfeit goods.

8.2 Rights and Remedies
If the defendant prevails, the court can order the plaintiff to pay the court costs (such as transportation fees to attend court hearings and daily allowances for witnesses), but not the defendant's attorney fees or other costs incurred by the defendant in the course of the procedure. There is no right of, or remedy for, a prevailing defendant to recover their own costs.

The prevailing defendant may seek damages arising out of the infringement litigation, including their attorney fees, if the litigation itself is considered to constitute a tort on the grounds that:

- an allegation of trade-mark infringement is entirely baseless and the patentee is fully aware of the lack of legal grounds;
- such litigation is quite unreasonable; and
- the lawsuit itself should therefore be considered to constitute a tort.

However, the courts rarely accept such claims.

8.3 Different Types of Remedies
There are no different remedies for different types of trade marks.

9. Appeal

9.1 Special Provisions
Generally speaking, there is no special provision concerning the appellate procedure for trade-mark proceedings.

It should be noted, however, that the appeal court for a trade-mark case will be the IP High Court, which specialises in intellectual property matters, if the district court of first instance is located within the jurisdictional district of the Tokyo High Courts.

9.2 Factual or Legal Review
As the court of second instance, the high court undertakes not only a legal review of the facts of the case, but also a full review of the decisions made by district courts in the first instance. The high court can also conduct factual findings on its own. A party may submit additional legal arguments, facts or evidence to the appeal court, unless such an additional claim is considered to cause delay to the procedure due to that party's fault. The Supreme Court, however, as the court of third instance, only reviews the legal issues of the case.

9.3 Length of Appeal from Trial Court
It would depend on the case but, according to the report published by the IP High Court, the recent average period for the trial of an intellectual property-related case in the appeal court is less than eight months.

10. Other Trade Mark Issues

10.1 Recognition of Dilution
Dilution is not explicitly recognised as a ground to oppose a trade-mark registration, but Article 4, Item 1, Paragraph 19 of the Trademark Act may be a ground to oppose a trade mark that causes dilution of a famous trade mark (please see **1.17 Consideration of Prior Rights**). In addition, dilution is not explicitly recognised as a ground to prevent use of a mark in a lawsuit, whereas it could be taken into account in a decision of likelihood of confusion with respect to the claim under Article 2.1.1 of the Unfair Competition Prevention Act if the mark is well-known among customers (please see **1.10 Other Rights to Signs**).

Contributed by TMI Associates **Authors:** Mitsuko Miyagawa, Takeshi Hironaka, Seiro Hatano, Seiji Kurishita

10.2 Protection of Famous Marks
Marks that are famous outside Japan are not directly protected under Japanese law. However, the Japanese Trademark Act provides that an application for registration shall be rejected or a registration of a trade mark shall be invalidated if it is identical or similar to a trade mark that is well-known among consumers outside Japan to indicate goods or services pertaining to a business of another person, and if such a trade mark is used for unfair purposes (eg, gaining unfair profits or causing damage to the other person).

10.3 Special Rules Regarding Geographic Indicators
Japan has the Geographical Indication (GI) protection system, under which names of regional brand products that have obtained a reputation as a result of unique production methods and natural characteristics such as regional climate and soil conditions are registered by Ministry of Agriculture, Forestry and Fisheries and protected as Intellectual Property. In addition, if geographic indicators are to be used by members of business co-operatives and associations, and are well-known among consumers, they may be registered by the JPO and protected as "regional collective trade marks."

10.4 Special Rules Relating to Surnames
There are no special rules that would allow an individual to use his or her own surname as a trade mark, even though such use could cause confusion with a pre-existing mark, and constitute unfair competition. Furthermore, if the surname is registered as a trade mark, the use of the same surname as a trade mark by others would constitute a trade-mark infringement. That said, given that a surname is frequently indistinctive unless it is very uncommon and rare, in reality, it would be quite exceptional for use of one's surname actually to cause confusion. In addition, the Trademark Act provides that a common surname may not be registered because a common surname is indistinctive.

A common surname can be registered as a trade mark if it has acquired a secondary meaning as the result of actual use. TOYOTA and HONDA are good examples of such registered trademarks composed of a surname. Further, an uncommon surname can be registered as a trade mark. If a surname is registered as a trade mark (either because it is a common surname but has acquired a secondary meaning or because it is deemed an uncommon or rare surname), the use of the same surname by others as a trade mark for the goods or services for which the surname trade mark is registered would infringe upon such registered trade mark. For the avoidance of doubt, use of a person's surname just as his or her own surname (and not as a trade mark) would not be restricted under the Unfair Competition Law or the Trademark Act.

11. Costs

11.1 Costs Before Filing a Lawsuit
With respect to trade-mark infringement litigation, costs that typically arise before filing a lawsuit would be for investigating the accused products or services, sending warning letters, and preparing for the litigation.

11.2 Costs Regarding an Infringement Action
For filing litigation, a stamp fee will be incurred, the amount of which will vary depending on the amount of the claim. Other costs are mainly attorney fees and are dependent on the case and the individual attorney's fee structure. Generally speaking, the costs for trade-mark infringement cases would be lower than those for patent cases.

11.3 Costs of Litigation
In general, court costs are borne by the losing party. However, the proportion of the responsibility for the court costs is left up to the court's discretion, and the court may allocate the responsibility of the court costs to the prevailing party in proportion to the part of its claim not accepted by the court.

Note: the court costs do not include attorney fees and thus, generally speaking, each party must bear their own attorney's fee. The plaintiff may seek compensation for their attorney's fees as part of the damages but the recovery rate is left up to the court's discretion and is usually quite limited, even if the plaintiff wins the case (in practice, approximately 10% of the total amount of damages admitted by the court).

12. Alternative Dispute Resolution

12.1 Common Way of Settlement
Alternative dispute resolution is not a common way to settle trade-mark cases in Japan. However, methods such as mediation or arbitration are is available, with the Japan Intel-

TMI Associates
23rd Floor, Roppongi Hills Mori Tower
6-10-1 Roppongi
Minato-ku
Tokyo
Tokyo-to
Japan
106-6123

Tel: +81 3 6438 5511
Fax: +81 3 6438 5522
Email: info_general@tmi.gr.jp
Web: www.tmi.gr.jp

TMI Associates

lectual Property Arbitration Centre (JIPAC) being the sole ADR organisation that provides for dispute resolution in the field of intellectual property.

13. Trade Marks and Other Intellectual Property

13.1 Protection by Copyright

Technically speaking, if a trade mark is so creative as to be considered as "copyrighted work" under the Copyright Act (such as a unique device mark), it can be protected by copyright; however, in practice, a trade mark is often considered insufficiently creative, especially those consisting only of characters. A trade mark can also be protected as a design patent if its design (typically its shape) is registered as such. The trade mark could be protected as trade dress under the Unfair Competition Prevention Act (please see **1.1 Types of Trade Marks**).

MACAU

LAW AND PRACTICE: p.209

Contributed by DSL Lawyers

The 'Law & Practice' sections provide easily accessible information on navigating the legal system when conducting business in the jurisdiction. Leading lawyers explain local law and practice at key transactional stages and for crucial aspects of doing business.

Law and Practice

Contributed by DSL Lawyers

CONTENTS

Contributed by DSL Lawyers ***Author:*** Carlos D Simões

DSL Lawyers is a leading intellectual property firm in Macau, with lawyers that pioneered this area in Macau, being responsible for setting up some of the largest IP portfolios in the jurisdiction. The main industries of focus in Macau are consumer goods, luxury and fashion items, hospitality and gaming services. Through the firm's extensive network of associates, the IP team works often on matters covering several jurisdictions and countries. DSL's IP practice covers trade marks, patents, designs and copyrights. The firm's wider IP practice includes such issues as domain names and e-commerce, licensing agreements and franchise, plus litigation and anti-counterfeiting enforcement, including oppositions and administrative disputes. DSL is also a member of international associations such as the International Trademark Association (INTA) and the Asian Patent Attorneys Association (APAA).

Author

Carlos D Simões' practice covers both prosecution and litigation. He manages the portfolio of various multinationals in Macau, being retained on a regular basis to advise on strategies for new trade marks and on disputes amongst trade-mark owners. As a litigator, Carlos is experienced in the local appeal system both at administrative level and with Macau courts. He has successfully litigated for various companies and entrepreneurs in Macau, securing their rights locally – either against competitors with similar or conflicting trade marks or against squatters attempting to take advantage of unregistered trade marks or notorious trade marks.

1. Types of Trade Marks & Registration

1.1 Types of Trade Marks

In Macau it is currently possible to apply for registration of (i) service marks, (ii) products marks, (iii) certification marks and (iv) collective marks. All these types are governed by statutory law, as case law is not relevant for these purposes.

1.2 Trade-Mark Rights

In Macau only registrations will secure trade-mark rights (Section 6, IPC). Use is only relevant to support a priority claim (based on use) if the use of the mark started within six months prior to the application date (Section 202, IPC).

1.3 Standards for Registering

Trade dress in Macau could secure registrations as a 3D trade mark (Section 197, IPC) as there is no specific trade mark for trade dress. In general, there are no different standards for registration of different types of marks (only different formalities, namely for certification of marks and collective marks).

1.4 Trade Mark Register

The trade-mark register is available at: www.economia.gov.mo/en.

1.5 Types of Registers

There are no different types of registers for trade marks, all registrations are made at the same level.

1.6 Searching for Prior Trade Marks

It is normal practice to search for prior trade marks, but only forward marks. The online database is not searchable in a reliable way for logo/mixed trade marks. Trade-mark searches can serve to provide information on trade marks registered in Macau. This helps to find out if there are any marks in the trade-mark register that are similar to the one intended to be filed for registration. Therefore, using trade-mark search appropriately can minimise the risks of refusal of the trade-mark applications.

1.7 Registration Requirements

The formal requirements for registration of trade marks are: (i) one JPEG sample image of the trade mark; (ii) classes and specifications of goods; (iii) name and address of applicant; (iv) original PoA as executed by applicant.

1.8 Registering a Trade Mark

Any party may apply for trade-mark registration, provided the applicant has been legally incorporated – natural persons, corporations, companies, societies, etc (Section 187, IPC).

1.9 Registering Signs
Most types of signs can be registered as trade marks in Macau, in particular: words, images, shapes, sounds and colours. Registration of scents is not available in Macau.

1.10 Other Rights to Signs
In Macau there are separate registration systems to protect the parties entitlements to (i) company names, (ii) business or trade names, (iii) domain names and (iv) geographic denominations.

1.11 Registration Procedure
Multi-class applications are not available. Once the application is filed there is (i) a formal examination, to confirm that all requirements have been met, followed by (ii) publication in the Official Gazette, (iii) and an opportunity for third parties to submit oppositions within 60 days. Once this period has elapsed, the application will be subject to (iv) material examination, which will also include a decision on the opposition, if any. The final step is (v) registration, which is also subject to publication in the Official Gazette.

1.12 Use in Commerce
In Macau use of the trade mark is not relevant at the time of the application. Use is only required to avoid cancellation for non-use, as once three years have elapsed since registration, the trade mark will become vulnerable to the said cancellation (Section 232, No 2, IPC). Trade-mark registrations are renewable for successive periods of seven years (Sections 218, IPC), upon payment of renewal fees.

1.13 Registration of Series Marks
Series of trade marks are not available in Macau and the trade mark must be used as registered.

1.14 Length of Registration Process
The average turnaround time of a trade-mark application in Macau is ten months, but this may change from year to year. The application is to be supported by a Power of Attorney, because only local entities (Macau residents and companies incorporated in Macau) do not require an agent in Macau. The standard official fees are USD125 and the average agent fees USD400.

1.15 Grounds for Refusal
The grounds for refusal of a trade mark are listed under Section 9, No 214, IPC and include (i) descriptive character of the mark, (ii) lack of distinctiveness, (iii) misleading character and (iv) bad faith of applicant.

1.16 Process for Overcoming Objections
The practice of the IP office is to raise citations (ie, prior to the final decisions being made) in very few cases and almost exclusively in relation to prior rights (and a declaration of consent being required thereon). In most cases, the applicant becomes aware of the objections upon the decision being made and thus may only react within appeal proceedings (as per answer to **1.21 Remedies Against the Trade Mark Office**, below).

1.17 Consideration of Prior Rights
The IP Office is entitled to make a decision based on the existence of registered prior rights (relative grounds, as per Section 214, IPC). In these cases (refusal due to prior rights), only registered prior rights are relevant.

1.18 Third Party Rights
There is a term of 60 days for opposition purposes, which runs prior to the examination being made. If an opposition is filed, there will an additional term of 30 days to submit supplementary evidence (as per Section 211, IPC) and the applicant is also entitled to file a reply to the opposition. The process is exclusively handled in writing as only documentary evidence is admitted and no witnesses are heard. The written submissions made by either or both parties (applicant/opponent) will be decided as part of the material examination of the application and not as a separate decision. Only parties (natural or legal persons) that show an interest (usually, prior or conflicting rights) will be admitted to submit an opposition.

1.19 Revoke, Change, Amend or Correct an Application
Any changes (including amendments or corrections) to the trade mark are only admissible until the application is granted registration (as per Section 224, IPC). Once registration is granted, only voluntary cancellation of registration or the addition of colour claim will be admissible changes.

1.20 Assigning an Application or Granting a Licence
There are no restrictions to the assignment or licensing of a pending application (ie, not yet granted registration). However, if the application is refused, these recordals (assignment or licensing) will be forfeit.

1.21 Remedies Against the Trade Mark Office
The decision of approval or refusal of a trade-mark registration is published in the Macau Official Gazette. According to Item (a) of Section 275, IPC, an appeal against that decision should be lodged with the Court of First Instance, within one month of the date of publication (Section 277, IPC).

1.22 Use of a Trade Mark
There is no requirement of use in commerce, as explained above under **1.2 Trade-Mark Rights**.

1.23 Dividing a Trade Mark
Under Section 208, IPC, the division of a pending application is only admissible when certain goods or services of its specification belong to a class other than the one applied for originally (namely to preserve the priority claim).

1.24 Length of Term of Protection
The term of protection is seven years, subject to successive and indefinite renewals (of seven years terms) – see Section 218 No 1 IPC.

1.25 Requirements for an Exhaustion
In Macau there is no concept of exhaustion, as such, but instead there is the concept of "preclusion for tolerance" – this means that a trade mark-owner cannot react against a competing or conflicting trade mark if no action was taken for a period of over three years, unless bad faith is involved (Section 221, IPC).

1.26 Participation in the Madrid System
Macau is not part of the Madrid system.

1.27 Consequences for Providing Incorrect Information
If the details provided by the applicant are incorrect this could ultimately lead to the application being refused (if no remedy is provided). Such incorrect information, if deemed material, could also be argued by a third party as grounds to cancel the registration.

1.28 Updating or Refreshing a Design Mark
Updating or refreshing a design mark is not admissible, as changes are only possible before registration is granted.

1.29 Denotation
The usual symbol ® is available in Macau (as well as "Registered Trademark" and "TM", in English), as per section 225, IPC.

2. Assignment and Licensing

2.1 Assignment Requirements or Restrictions
For an assignment to be admissible it is necessary to have a written assignment agreement and a power of attorney from either assignee or assignor (the original registration certificate is not necessary).

2.2 Procedure for Assigning a Trade Mark
The recordal of assignment is mandatory and must be required at the IP Office. The required application must be filed with the IP Office and it will be subject to a formal decision, followed by publication in the Macau Official Gazette. The entire process will take three to four months.

2.3 Registering or Recording the Assignment
The assignment of a trade mark is subject to registration and publication (as per Sections 10 and 11, IPC). The assignment will be valid amongst the signing parties from the date it is signed and against third parties from the moment it is published.

2.4 Trade Marks and Security
A trade mark, as any other registered right in Macau, can be offered in security, subject to rights in rem and levied in execution (Section 14, IPC).

2.5 Licensing Requirements or Restrictions
The licence of a trade mark can be recorded while the same is pending or after it has been registered. It is subject to written form and it may be exclusive or non-exclusive (in the absence of any provision, the law assumes the same is non-exclusive – see Section 13, No 2, IPC). The licence should be recorded with the IP Office and such recordal is subject to (i) formal decision of IP Office and (ii) publication in Official Gazette.

2.6 Procedure for Licensing a Trade Mark
The licensing of a trade mark requires a written agreement and is valid for the term agreed by the parties (licensor/licensee) or, if shorter, the term of the trade mark (Section 12, IPC). The licensee is always entitled to certain rights, as provided by statute (Section 13, IPC).

2.7 Registering or Recording the Licence
As mentioned, if the licence is not recorded the licencee will not be admitted to use or enforce the rights provided for in the agreement and by statute.

2.8 Reasons to Deny Granting a Perpetual Licence
Although in Macau there is no statutory restriction to a perpetual licence, in general the Macau system is shy of perpetual arrangements and the licence would be limited by the duration of the licensed trade mark.

3. Opposition Procedure

3.1 Legal Grounds and Timeframes
According to Section 211, No 1, IPC, the term for opposition is 60 days from publication of the application in the Official Gazette. The opponent is allowed to argue any relative or absolute grounds of refusal (as per Section 9.214 and 215, IPC).

3.2 Filing an Opposition

Any party that shows an interest in the refusal of application will be admitted to file an opposition. The appointment of an attorney is mandatory; the government fees payable for the opposition are around USD100.

3.3 Opposition Procedure

As explained above under **1.11 Registration Procedure**, the opposition procedures are deemed part of the application proper. Once the opposition has been filed (i) the applicant will have a 30-day term to reply, and (ii) the opponent may ask for an additional submission within 30 days, limited to supplementary evidence. Once all the written submissions have been filed together with documentary evidence deemed relevant (there are no depositions of witnesses), the entire process will move forward for a final decision, which will also contain the material examination of the trade mark (combined decision for both matters).

3.4 Legal Remedies

Either party may react against the decision made by filing a subsequent appeal, within 30 days, to the Court of First Instance. The usual turnaround time for this type of appeal (which typically does not involve a hearing) is eight to 12 months.

4. Initiating a Lawsuit

4.1 Actions to Pursue Infringement

Macau being a civil law jurisdiction, unregistered trade marks are not admissible and registration is necessary to secure protection – only registered trade marks will entitle its owner to file infringement claims. The trade mark-owner has usually two options to react against infringers: civil or criminal procedures. Criminal proceedings are the preferred option (namely against counterfeiters) as within the same Macau customs will handle the investigation and seize the infringing products.

4.2 Initiating Infringement Proceedings

Civil proceedings have to be filed with the Court of First Instance and criminal proceedings with the Macau Criminal Courts. In Macau there is no specialised jurisdiction for IP matters.

4.3 Effect of Decisions on Infringement Actions

Infringement actions are based on the assumption that the trade mark is valid and effective. If the trade mark is deemed invalid by the IP Office, the infringement proceedings will come to a halt.

4.4 Declaratory Judgment Proceedings

In Macau it is possible for the infringer to start declaratory infringement proceedings in the courts and to seek a decision to confirm that there is no infringement attached to his or her actions as infringer.

4.5 Jurisdiction of Courts

In Macau, the courts that have jurisdiction to decide trade-mark matters are the general courts, with jurisdiction over civil matters. These are the Court of First Instance, the Court of Appeal and the Court of Last Appeal.

4.6 Prerequisites to Filing a Lawsuit

In Macau there are no pre-requisites to file a lawsuit (eg, requisites of a prior demand letter or mediation).

4.7 Representation for Parties

In Macau the representation by a lawyer is mandatory for court matters (except for claims with the Court of Small Claims).

4.8 Interim or Preliminary Injunctions

Both preliminary and interim injunctions are available in Macau, and subject to the same material requirements:

- right of the plaintiff requiring protection;
- imminent danger or loss to such right if such an injunction is not obtained;
- the gain obtained though the infraction must be thought greater than the loss it causes.

The injunction may be decided ex parte (in the absence of the defendant), or with both parties attending.

4.9 Protection for Potential Defendant

In Macau the usual method for a defendant to protect itself is to file a counter-claim, either in the same proceedings or in separate proceedings. It is not possible to require bond from the plaintiff or to file protective briefs.

4.10 Obtaining Information and Evidence

The Macau courts may, if requested by any of the parties in the proceedings, order a third party to disclose information or provide documentation to the court. The parties requesting such a discovery order must provide reasonable evidence that the third party holds such information or document and, based on such evidence, the court may apply a fine to the party refusing to disclose the information or document; alternatively, the courts, when making the final decision, may give weight to such refusal.

4.11 Initial Pleading Standards

The proceedings on trade-mark matters follow the general procedural rules of any other civil claim. The initial writs must contain:

- a full description of all facts relevant for the material decision to be made;

- the arguments of law that support the request made;
- all the evidence available to support the claim.

Although it is possible to make supplemental submissions to file additional documentary evidence, the general standard is that the initial writs must have a very high degree of completeness (unlike other jurisdictions, namely in common-law systems).

4.12 Representative or Collective Actions
In Macau, there is no concept of class actions or collective actions, although under procedural laws different plaintiffs may join efforts to sue the same defendant in the same case (for identical claims only).

4.13 Restrictions on Trade Mark-Owners
In general, there are not many statutory restrictions against the holder of a right making groundless threats or filing necessary claims. The judges are entitled to strike down a claim if they deem it abusive or groundless; if such conclusion is only made at a later stage of the proceedings, the judges may apply a fine to the plaintiff.

5. Infringement

5.1 Action for Infringement
Infringement actions may only be initiated by the trade mark-owner or a party appointed by the same. A licensee may only start infringement actions if the relevant licence has been recorded with the IP Office (as per Section 13, IPC). It is also possible for the applicant to start a court action before the registration is granted, but in these cases there will be no decision made by the courts until registration is granted (Section 7, IPC).

5.2 Signs and Infringement
In our experience the main tests made by the courts in assessing trade-mark infringement are the degree of similarity between signs or words (from the perspective of the averagely attentive consumer) and of the goods or services to which the same is being applied.

5.3 Use of a Sign by Defendant
We confirm that to claim infringement it is a requirement that the infringer (defendant) used the trade mark with a commercial benefit (as a trade mark).

5.4 Defences Against Infringement
In general, the defendant would be allowed to use all the relevant arguments that are deemed applicable to the specific situation, including prior rights, owner-name defence, fair use and unwilful use. Limitations and forfeiture may also be argued, as the limitation are relatively short (three years) for non-contractual liability.

5.5 Role of Experts and/or Surveys
The local courts are usually open to the use of any documentary evidence (including market and consumer surveys on secondary meaning, trade-mark recognition, etc). However it is uncommon for the courts to rely on experts in making such assessment, as this arrangement (appointment of experts) is usually time-consuming.

5.6 Administrative or Criminal Offence
As explained in **4.1 Actions to Pursue Infringement**, criminal claims are a common arrangement for trade mark-owners to seek protection against infringers. This option starts with a claim being filed with Macau Customs (a police force that has jurisdiction over IP matters). Macau Customs ("MC") will act on such claim, making the necessary investigation visit to the infringer premises and possible seizure of infringing goods. Once the investigation is completed, and assuming that sound evidence of trade-mark infringement was obtained at that stage, the matter will be passed to the Public Attorney ("PA") for indictment purposes. The PA will be in charge of the matter throughout the trial and until a conviction has been secured.

5.7 Custom Seizures
As explained, seizure of counterfeits by MC are fairly common in Macau. However, the owner of trade marks may not take action against parallel imports and may not prevent parallel imports from entering the market.

6. Revocation/Cancellation

6.1 Remedies and Reasons
Under Section 231, IPC, a trade mark will be cancelled in the case of (i) non-use for a period of over three years, (ii) substantial changes, or (iii) lack of renewal. Additionally, under Sections 229 & 230, a trade mark may still be revoked if it was granted in violation of the rules that govern the granting of registrations and/or against public order. In these cases the revocation can only be decided by the Macau courts.

6.2 Trade Mark Office and Civil Courts
If dealing with the causes of cancellation provided for in Sections 51, No 1 and 231, No 1, IPC (non-renewal, lack of payment of renewal fees, withdrawal by owner, change of trade mark and non-use for a period of three years), the application will be decided by the IP Office. For all other causes of revocation (detailed in Sections 229 and 230, IPC), the decision must be taken by the Macau courts.

6.3 Statutory Limitation or Time Period
There is only a time bar for annulment decisions (as governed by Section 230, IPC) which is five years from the date of registration. For all the other causes of revocation or cancellation, there is no time bar.

6.4 Initiation of Revocation/Cancellation Proceeding

For the actions to be decided by the IP Office, the plaintiff must argue and show an interest in the decision requested. For claims of annulment to protect notorious marks, the plaintiff must apply for the relevant trade-mark registration in Macau as a prerequisite to file the claim (Section 230, No 2, IPC). For claims requesting a trade mark to be declared null and void (Sections 47 and 227, IPC) any party may apply for the same at any given time.

6.5 Partial Revocation/Cancellation

Under Sections 231 and 216, IPC, the revocation or cancellation decision may be partial.

6.6 Possibilities of Amendment

An amendment is possible within revocation or cancellation proceedings, provided the counterparty has not been served yet. If the counterparty has been served, it must agree to the amendment.

6.7 Revocation/Cancellation and Infringement

The cases where infringement revocation or cancellation are decided at the same time (decision) are those ones in which the latter (revocation/cancellation) is part of a counter-claim of the defendant in the infringement proceedings. Outside these exceptional cases, if the claims were filed separately, in different cases, they will be heard and decided separately.

7. Trial & Settlement

7.1 Special Procedural Provisions

There are only special procedures for trade-mark proceedings when the proceedings are appeals from decisions made by the IP Office (either for refusing, granting or cancelling a trade mark). In these cases the appeals to a Macau court are akin to administrative appeals and are exclusively processed by documents. For the other types of claims, such as a claim for trade-mark annulment or for a trade mark to be declared null and void, the civil proceedings are followed and are fairly wide and open and subject to full trial.

7.2 Determination of Cases

In Macau there is no jury system, all cases are decided by judges.

7.3 Possibilities of Settlement

The chances of a defendant getting a settlement are exclusively a result of his or her private discussions or negotiations with the plaintiff. Although there are usually "conciliation" conferences or hearings, neither the judges nor the PA will make a push for a settlement.

7.4 Other Court Proceedings

Any party to a court case can request a stay on the grounds that there is a previous case to be decided which will likely have an influence on the outcome of the case being stayed. However, the judge has absolute discretion in deciding whether to stay the proceedings or not, so the party must explain carefully and in detail the relationship between the two cases.

8. Remedies

8.1 Existing Remedies

A Macau judge has wide discretion in ordering remedies, there being some that are fairly common – damages, including for past losses and future profits – and infringement relief. It is very rare – indeed, almost unheard of – to have the local courts deciding remedies such as (i) publicity notices, (ii) freezing of bank accounts or (iii) an account of profits.

8.2 Rights and Remedies

There are very few remedies available for prevailing defendants and those are normally limited to declaration of non-infringement and recovery of courts costs.

8.3 Different Types of Remedies

In Macau there are no different remedies for different types of trade marks.

9. Appeal

9.1 Special Provisions

The only relevant provision to consider for Macau appeals is that the Macau Court of Appeal will only take an appeal if the amount of the claim is higher than MOP1,000,001.

9.2 Factual or Legal Review

Appeals are mostly lodged and decided on legal arguments. However, an appellant may also ask for a review of the facts, if it is argued that they were poorly decided or wrongly considered.

9.3 Length of Appeal from Trial Court

An appeal decision from the Court of Appeal will take at last one year, from the filing date of appeal, to be decided.

10. Other Trade Mark Issues

10.1 Recognition of Dilution

Under Section 231, IPC, a party may argue that a trade mark lost distinctiveness because it became a common denomination, in the market place, to designate a certain type of product or service. However, this type of defence, to be admissible, would necessarily entail that the defendant files a counter-claim requesting that a certain trade mark be cancelled.

10.2 Protection of Famous Marks

In Macau the notorious trade marks are all protected in the same circumstances as provided under Section 6-bis of the Paris Convention, which is applicable in Macau.

10.3 Special Rules Regarding Geographic Indicators

In Macau "geographic denominations" are subject to a separate registration system that is governed by Sections 254 to 262, IPC.

10.4 Special Rules Relating to Surnames

In Macau there are no special rules to protect the use of one's surname as a trade mark against a pre-existing trade mark. Instead, there are rules providing that if a trade mark is obviously an individual's surname, that individual shall give his or her consent to the registration of a trade mark that is identical to his or her surname. Also, the registration of trade marks will not override the individual's entitlement to his or her surname, if identical to the trade mark.

DSL Lawyers
Av. da Praia Grande 409
16/F China Law Building
Macau

Tel: (853) 2822 3355
Fax: (853) 2872 5588
Email: cdsimoes@dsl-lawyers.com
Web: www.dsl-lawyers.com

11. Costs

11.1 Costs Before Filing a Lawsuit

The costs of filing a lawsuit are those common to many other jurisdictions: lawyers' fees (the bulk of costs), court costs (usually not very high) and various types of disbursements (translation, registration fees, etc).

11.2 Costs Regarding an Infringement Action

The costs involved in a infringement action could vary significantly, but would be usually in the range of USD3,750 to USD6,750.

11.3 Costs of Litigation

The losing party shall pay all the expenses of the lawsuit except lawyers' fees. On this topic the Macau courts are very conservative – less than 10% can be recovered by the winning party.

12. Alternative Dispute Resolution

12.1 Common Way of Settlement

In Macau the use of ADR to address trade-mark disputes is very uncommon.

13. Trade Marks and Other Intellectual Property

13.1 Protection by Copyright

In Macau it is common to have trade-mark matters subject to copyright protection, but it is less common to have it protected by design patents.

MALAYSIA

LAW AND PRACTICE: p.221

Contributed by Lee Hishammuddin Allen & Gledhill

The 'Law & Practice' sections provide easily accessible information on navigating the legal system when conducting business in the jurisdiction. Leading lawyers explain local law and practice at key transactional stages and for crucial aspects of doing business.

Law and Practice

Contributed by Lee Hishammuddin Allen & Gledhill

CONTENTS

Lee Hishammuddin Allen & Gledhill is a full-service law firm housing various practice groups, including dispute resolution, arbitration, financial services, Islamic finance, corporate and commercial, employment and industrial relations, insolvency, insurance, IP and TMT, real property, regulatory and compliance, and tax. The firm's trade-marks practice is part of its wider IP and TMT department; its seasoned team of trade-mark, industrial design and patent agents, litigators and commercial lawyers work closely with in-house counsel to protect intellectual properties, innovation and creativity. LHAG has more than 100 lawyers with offices in Kuala Lumpur, Penang and Johor Bahru; clients include top-ranked local conglomerates and multinational companies spanning industries such as IT, e-commerce, telecommunications, biotechnology, healthcare, entertainment and FMCG (fast moving consumer goods).

Authors

Bahari Yeow is head of IP & TMT at LHAG. Bahari's broad practice includes IP litigation as well as trade-mark prosecution, brand protection and anti-counterfeiting. He is a qualified patent, trade-mark and industrial design agent who acts for owners of well-known brands, characters and trade marks. He currently serves as a member of the Group Standing Committee for Copyright (2015-2018) of the Asian Patent Attorney Association (APAA) Malaysia.

Lim Zhi Jian is a senior associate at LHAG. He advises clients on all aspects of IP concerning strategy in protection of trade-secret and confidential information, and enforcement of trade marks, copyright, patents and design. Jian has represented a wide range of local and international clients in a multitude of contentious matters including expungement of registered marks, procuring trade-description orders, search-and-seizure orders, injunctions, advising on free-trade zones and jurisdictional matters, and procuring judicial assignments of patent. He has assisted clients in actions for breach of confidentiality or trade secrets, anti-counterfeiting, infringements and prosecution (trade mark, copyright, industrial design and patent) and domain name disputes. Experienced in all stages of litigation, Jian regularly appears in the courts for various processes including full trials, applications, interlocutory proceedings and appeals.

1. Types of Trade Marks & Registration

1.1 Types of Trade Marks
The different types of trade marks in Malaysia include standard trade marks, certification trade marks and defensive trade marks.

The rights in such trade marks are based on the **Trade Marks Act 1976** ("TMA"), the relevant provisions of which are supported and explained in greater detail by case law.

1.2 Trade-Mark Rights
A person can acquire rights merely by using a mark, because the first user of a mark in the course of trade is considered the owner of the trade mark. However, a trade mark obtains proprietary character once it has been registered, and as a result the registered proprietor has the exclusive right to use the registered mark in relation to their goods or services.

1.3 Standards for Registering
There are different standards for registering certification and defensive trade marks.

For certification trade marks, it must be shown that the goods or services possess certain standards in relation to their origin, material, quality, accuracy or other characteristics before the mark can be registered.

Defensive trade marks must consist of an invented word or words, and are designed to minimise consumer confusion if a business attempts to use a well-known mark in unrelated classes of products or services.

1.4 Trade-Mark Register
The Malaysian Register of Trade Marks is publicly accessible.

1.5 Types of Registers
There is only one Register of Trade Marks in Malaysia.

1.6 Searching for Prior Trade Marks
It is common practice to search for prior registered trade marks before applying to register a mark. This includes a computer search or manual search of all applications filed and registrations disclosed in the public records, available at the Intellectual Property Corporation of Malaysia (" MyIPO "). The results of the search may give applicants a better view on the likelihood of their application facing objection during the registration process.

1.7 Registration Requirements
A mark must fall within the statutory definition of a 'trade mark' under the Trade Marks Act in order to be registered. It must constitute a registrable mark, and must satisfy at least one of the following requirements under s.10(1) of the TMA :

- the name of an individual, company or firm represented in a special or particular manner;
- the signature of an applicant for registration or of some predecessors in his or her business;
- an invented word or words;
- a word having no direct reference to the character or quality of the goods or services, not being a geographical name or surname, according to its ordinary meaning; or
- any other distinctive mark.

The mark must also not be a prohibited mark as defined under statute, nor a mark that has been expressly excluded from registration.

1.8 Registering a Trade Mark
Only the proprietor of a trade mark can register that mark.

1.9 Registering Signs
The types of marks that can be registered as a trade mark include any brand, heading, label, ticket, name, signature, word, letter, numeral and device, according to s. 3 of the TMA. This would include any word marks, slogans, signs, symbols, numbers and packaging trade dress, amongst others.

In **Kraft Foods Schweiz Holdings GmbH v. Pendaftar Cap Dagangan** [2016] 9 CLJ 558, Wong Kian Kheong JC held that a 3D mark falls within the meaning of a "mark" in s. 3(1) of the TMA and is registrable in Malaysia as a trade mark.

1.10 Other Rights to Signs
Domain names must be registered with the Malaysian Network Information Centre (MYNIC), and can only be registered if there are no other identical pre-existing domain names. The success of the registration will depend on who applies to register the domain name first.

Organisations are permitted to apply for domain names including .com.my,. net.my and .org.my, whilst Malaysian individuals (ie, holding a Malaysian National Registration Identity Card – NRIC) aged 18 and above can apply for personal domain names (.name.my). Both organisations and individuals are able to apply for a second level domain name (.my). Only certified agencies within the education, military and government sectors can apply for .edu.my mil.my and gov.my. All applicants must provide the proper documentation and supporting documents in their application. If the applicant is not a Malaysian, they must provide valid proof of residing in Malaysia, have a valid passport and be 18 and above. Companies must have a presence in Malaysia to register a domain name.

1.11 Registration Procedure
An application must be filed with the Malaysian Intellectual Property Office (Intellectual Property Corporation of Malaysia). The application is to be amended in the event of any non-compliance. The Trademark Registrar will formally check whether the application complies with relevant statutory requirements (along with issuing amendment requirements if necessary). A search for prior marks and an examination as to the mark's registrability will be conducted. The Trademark Registrar may issue an objection, and require the applicant to make necessary submissions to waive that objection. The Mark will then be gazetted and advertised for opposition upon acceptance by the Registrar. Where there are no oppositions, the Certificate of Registration will be issued.

Multi-class applications are not available in Malaysia; single applications must be filed for each class.

1.12 Use in Commerce
The Malaysian trade-mark registration system requires that the mark is to be used or at the minimum proposed to be used by the applicant in relation to the goods or services for which it is to be registered.

Therefore, a mark is registrable even if it has yet to be used, as long as the applicant intends to use the mark in Malaysia. After registration, use of the mark must be shown or the registration is liable to be expunged based on non-use upon application by an 'aggrieved person' pursuant to s. 46 of the TMA.

1.13 Registration of Series Marks
The Malaysian registration system allows for the registration of series marks.

1.14 Length of Registration Process
Normal Examination Process
The registration procedure usually takes 12 to 18 months, but is quicker in some instances.

The applicant does not need representation such as an attorney in order to initiate the registration procedure, but it is common to employ trade-mark agents to assist with registering a mark.

The current Official Fee is MYR1,065 for a single word mark in one class, assuming the registration is straightforward. Attorney or agent fees would vary.

Expedited Examination Process
Pursuant to regulation 18A of the **Trade Marks Regulations 1997** ("TMR"), an applicant may request an expedited examination of their application. The request can be made within four months of the date of filing the application, by filing form TM 5A. If the request is accepted by the Registrar, the applicant has to file TM 5B within five working days of the Registrar's decision.

The request for expedited examination must be supported by statutory declaration. The decision to accept or refuse the request will be based on the reason stated by that applicant. Regulation 18A(3) provides as follows:

"If an applicant has requested an expedited examination, the Registrar may do so if the Registrar is reasonably satisfied that—

(a) the request is in the national or public interest;
(b) there are infringement proceedings taking place or evidence showing potential infringement in respect of the trade mark applied for under regulation 18;
(c) registration of the trade mark is a condition to obtain monetary benefits from the Government or institutions recognised by the Registrar; or
(d) there are other reasonable grounds which support the request" (emphasis added).

1.15 Grounds for Refusal

Registration of a trade mark can be refused in the following circumstances:

- if the mark does not fulfil at least one of the criteria set out in s. 10(1) of the TMA. For easy reference, s. 10(1) of the TMA provides that a mark is registrable if it is:
  - (a) the name of an individual, company or firm represented in a special or particular manner;
  - (b) the signature of an applicant for registration or of some predecessors in his or herbusiness;
  - (c) an invented word or words;
  - (d) a word having no direct reference to the character or quality of the goods or services, not being a geographical name or surname, according to its ordinary meaning; or
  - (e) any other distinctive mark;
- if the mark is identical to a trade mark belonging to a different proprietor or so nearly resembles such a trade mark that it is likely to deceive or cause confusion: s. 19(1) and (2) of the TMA;
- where separate applications are made by different persons to be registered as proprietors respectively of trade marks that are identical or so nearly resemble each other that they are likely to deceive or cause confusion: s. 19(3) and (4) of the TMA;
- if the mark is likely to deceive or cause confusion to the public, or would be contrary to law: s. 14(1)(a) of the TMA;
- if the mark contains or comprises any scandalous or offensive matter or would not be afforded court protection: s. 14(1)(b) of the TMA;
- if the mark contains any matter that the Registrar believes may be prejudicial to the nation's interest or security: s. 14(1)(c) of the TMA;
- if the mark is similar or identical to other mark(s) belonging to different proprietor(s) that are well known in Malaysia for the same goods or services: s. 14(1)(d) of the TMA;
- if the mark is well known and registered in Malaysia for goods or services that are not the same as those in respect of which registration has been applied for: s. 14(1)(e) of the TMA;
- if the mark contains or consists of a geographical indication with respect to goods not originating in the territory indicated, if use of the indication in the mark for such goods in Malaysia is of a nature that would mislead the public as to the true place of origin of the goods: s. 14(1)(f) of the TMA;
- if the markcontains or consists of a geographical indication identifying wines or spirits that do not originate in the place indicated by the geographical indication in question: s. 14(1)(g) of the TMA;
- if the mark is declared as protected by the Ministry, eg representation referring to a name, crest or flag of an international organisation or a city: s. 15 of the TMA.

1.16 Process for Overcoming Objections

If MyIPO objects to the trade-mark application, the applicant may appeal to MyIPO to waive its objection by filing a written submission. If the Registrar maintains its objection, the applicant may appeal to MyIPO by requesting an ex-parte hearing. If MyIPO continues to object after such hearing, an appeal can be made to the High Court, and subsequently to the Court of Appeal and the Federal Court: s. 25(3) of the TMA; Yong Teng Hing v. Walton International Ltd; Pendaftar Cap Dagang, Malaysia (Interested Party) [2011] 7 CLJ 401, Federal Court (c/f Tio Chee Hing v. United Overseas Bank (Malaysia) Bhd [2013] 2 CLJ 910, Federal Court).

The reasoning will depend on the basis for objection, but can include claiming that the mark consists of invented word(s), that the mark has no direct reference to the character or quality of the goods/services, and that the mark is distinctive.

1.17 Consideration of Prior Rights

The examination of prior rights includes assessing the prior marks filed and/or registered in Malaysia.

The law governing the foundation that led to common law proprietorship over a trade mark or source identifier has been well settled. The legal position under common law that the first user of a mark is lawfully entitled to use said mark has been established in Mesuma Sports Sdn Bhd v. Majlis Sukan Negara Malaysia; Pendaftar Cap Dagangan Malaysia (Interested Party) [2015] 9 CLJ 125, Federal Court.

Whoever first uses a trade mark owns that trade mark under common law, and such common law ownership would in turn entitle him or her to file for trade-mark application as a bona fide applicant, pursuant to s. 25(1) of the TMA. Thus, the Registrar may raise objection if there is evidence to suggest that the applicant is not the bona fide applicant pursuant to s. 25(1) of the TMA.

It may be necessary to show factual distinctiveness as opposed to inherent distinctiveness, which is relevant in determining whether the mark is registrable.

It has been suggested that it is possible to appeal an objection of the Registrar to a trade mark that is identical to or very nearly resembles another trade mark in the Register if the applicant or their predecessor in business has continuously used that trade mark from a date *before* the use of the other trade mark by the registered proprietor.

1.18 Third-Party Rights

Third parties have the right to participate during the registration procedure by initiating opposition proceedings when the mark is published for opposition. Any person may initiate opposition proceedings. The third party may file the requisite opposition forms and submissions to the Registrar where there may be an inter-partehearing.

If the opposition is accepted by the Registrar, a refusal will be issued.

If the opposition is refused by the Registrar, the mark will proceed for registration.

An appeal can be made against the decision of the Registrar to the High Court, and later the Court of Appeal and the Federal Court: Yong Teng Hing v. Walton International Ltd; Pendaftar Cap Dagang, Malaysia (Interested Party) [2011] 7 CLJ 401, Federal Court (c/f Tio Chee Hing v. United Overseas Bank (Malaysia) Bhd [2013] 2 CLJ 910, Federal Court).

1.19 Revoke, Change, Amend or Correct an Application

It is possible to revoke, change, amend or correct an application for a trade mark during the process of registration, eg, in order to correct a clerical error or an obvious mistake: s. 74(1) of the TMA.

Before registration, an applicant may alter his or her mark only with the permission of the Registrar. In some instances, the applicant may be permitted to amend his or her mark before it is advertised, which may be an option to overcome an objection to it. For example, extraneous and non-trade mark matter on a label mark may be removed, or a slight amendment may be allowed in order to avoid a citation. Amendment of the mark may be allowed if the alteration does not substantially affect the identity of the mark (s. 74(2) of the TMA), or the change may simply be to supply better representations, such as if coloured ones were submitted in error.

The applicant may not be permitted to amend his or her mark after it has been advertised and before it is registered, even in opposition proceedings.

Amendments of specifications or class numbers may be allowed, but the applicant is not allowed to enlarge the specification of his or her original claim under any circumstances. In particular, transfer of goods or services between filed applications on different dates is not permitted even if the marks are identical: MyIPO Manual at para 9.14.

1.20 Assigning an Application or Granting a Licence

The assignment may be filed during the application process; however, in practice, it will only be processed after registration has been granted.

1.21 Remedies Against the Trade Mark Office

It is possible for the applicant to make an appeal to the High Court and subsequently the Court of Appeal and the Federal Court where the trade-mark office issues a refusal to register a trade mark.

Upon receipt of the notice of the Order of the Court, the Registrar rectify the Register or give effect to the Order of the Court: s. 45(1)(d) of the TMA.

Where the appeal is successful, costs may be awarded in favour of the applicant. However, in some instances, the Court may allow the appeal of the applicant against the decision of the Registrar with no order as to costs: Illinois Tool Works, Inc v. Pendaftar Cap Dagangan, Malaysia [2010] 3 CLJ 837; Cargill, Incorporated v. Pendaftar Cap Dagangan [2013] 10 CLJ 144.

1.22 Use of a Trade Mark

There is no requirement for an applicant to use its mark in commerce before registration is issued, but there must be an intention to use the mark.

In Jost Cranes GmbH & Co. KG v. Jost Cranes Sdn Bhd [2010] 4 MLJ 191 (Azahar Mohamed J (now FCJ)) and Tokai Corporation v. DKSH Malaysia Sdn Bhd [2016] 1 LNS 1092 (Wong Kian Kheong JC), the Malaysian Court adopted the principle in the case of Daimler AG v. Sany Group Co Ltd [2009] EWHC 1003 (Ch). Based on these authorities, the following principles may be derived with regards to the meaning of genuine use:

- Genuine use is a qualitative and not a quantitative criterion.
- The use has to be consistent with the essential function of the trade mark, which is to guarantee the identity of the origin of the goods or services to the customer or end users.
- The use has to be on the market by the proprietor or an authorised third party and not just internal use by the undertaking concerned.
- The use has to be to maintain or create a share in the market for the goods or services protected by the mark.
- The court has to take into consideration all the facts and circumstances relevant to establishing whether the commercial exploitation of the mark has been real and, in particular, whether such use would be viewed as warranted in the trade sector concerned to maintain or create a share in the market for the relevant goods or services protected by the mark.
- The nature of the goods in issue have to be taken into account, such as the characteristics of the market concerned and the scale and frequency of the use of the mark.

In Abercrombie & Fitch Co. & Anor v. Fashion Factory Outlet KL Sdn Bhd & Ors [2008] 7 CLJ 413, Ramly Ali J (now FCJ) held that the sale of goods bearing a trade mark over the internet or via a website has been recognised as a use of the trade mark. The court may take into consideration the intention and purpose for putting up the website. If the website is intended to be used to seek worldwide trade with a view towards commercial gain, its activities fall squarely within the category of 'doing business over the internet' and may constitute 'use' for the purpose of trade-mark proceedings.

1.23 Dividing a Trade Mark

Where a single registration is split between two persons as a result of a part assignment, whether by division of markets or division by goods or services, the registrations may be separated: reg. 68 of the TMR.

If a part assignment results in a complete separation of markets, it is permitted. A single registration may be split into different export markets, but an assignment that would result in an exclusive right in the same mark for the same goods or services being held separately for different part of Malaysia will usually not be permitted: MyIPO Manual, para 18.15.

The more usual type of part assignment involves splitting the goods or services of a single registration. This is permitted if the Registrar is satisfied that the two resultant registrations do not contain goods or services of the same description: MyIPO Manual, para 18.54.

A part assignment is usually accompanied by a part cancellation of goods or services, as the case may be. The Registrar is concerned with matters of registration of trade marks and the protection of the public from the likelihood of confusion or deception that might result from the action of the parties: MyIPO Manual, para 18.61 and 18.65.

1.24 Length of Term of Protection

The term of protection for a registered trade mark is ten years from its application. The mark is renewable every ten years after it has lapsed, with a grace period of one year after the expiry date. The applicant must file the requisite renewal forms with the Registrar. There is also an option to restore the registration.

1.25 Requirements for an Exhaustion

The exhaustion of intellectual property rights constitutes one of the limits of IP rights.

TMA

In Malaysia, trade-mark owners' rights are well protected under the TMA. In Low Chi Yong v. Low Chi Hong and another (Civil Appeal No 02(f)-16-03/2017(K), the issue before the Federal Court was whether the proprietor would be considered to have abandoned his or her exclusive right to the trade mark in perpetuity by giving his or her consent to the use of the registered trade mark to a company or a firm of which he or she is still a shareholder/director or partner, even if he or she does not derive any benefit therefrom (and has withdrawn from the company), and also be said to be guilty of estoppel, acquiescence or laches.

The Federal Court held at para 56:

"In light of the clear provisions of the TMA 1976, where the protection given to ... the registered owner of the trade mark [is] clearly spelt out, and as consent was never given by him to the respondents after leaving the 2nd respondent (and any assignment was never established), let alone the collective exceptions to the infringement in the TMA 1976, the principles of abandonment, estoppel, acquiescence and laches were never proved, the position of the respondents was therefore untenable."

Prima Facie and Conclusive Evidence of Validity of Registration
In all legal proceedings relating to a registered trade mark, the fact that a person is registered as the proprietor of the trade mark shall be prima facie evidence of the validity of the original registration of the trade mark and of all subsequent assignments and transmissions thereof: s. 36 of the TMA.

After the expiry of seven years from the date thereof, the original registration of the trade mark under TMA shall be taken to be valid in all respects unless it is shown that the original registration was obtained by fraud, that the trade mark offends against section 14, or that the trade mark was not, at the commencement of the proceedings, distinctive of the goods or services of the registered proprietor: s. 37 of the TMA.

Exhaustion
A mark may be expunged when it became generic or is deemed to have lost its distinctiveness.

When a rectification of the Register is made and a mark is expunged, the mark is deemed to have never been registered, thus exhausting any trade-mark rights in regard to that registered mark.

Where a mark is assigned from the assignor to the assignee, the assignor is stripped of all legal rights over the trade mark, as an assignment is essentially transferring the ownership in the trade mark to the assignee.

Trade mark rights are also exhausted where the trade mark is not renewed by providing payment of the renewal fee when it is due for renewal, and the grace period has expired.

Parallel Import
In general, "parallel importation" is not trade mark infringement as the mark is being used to indicate the registered proprietor's own products: Hai-O Enterprose Bhd v. Nguang Chan @ Nguang Chan Liquor Trader [1993] 1 BLJ 53.

Generally speaking, parallel imports refer to goods that are lawfully manufactured overseas but imported and distributed in Malaysia by a person other than the registered proprietor of the trade mark. Parallel imports benefit consumers as the goods may be sold at lower prices in the domestic market due, for example, to fluctuations in currencies, market strategy, trade policy and distribution costs. Parallel imports are sometimes referred to as 'grey market' goods because, even though they are legitimately manufactured and marketed abroad, problems crop up time and again, such as whether the goods may be legitimately imported and distributed in Malaysia: Tien Ying Hong Enterprise Sdn Bhd v. Beenion Sdn Bhd [2011] 2 CLJ 469. In Tien Yong Hong, supra, the court made a clear distinction between parallel imports and "pirated" goods; the former are legitimately manufactured genuine goods whilst the latter are imitation or counterfeit goods. Azahar Mohamed J (now FCJ) held:

"[14] On the other hand, it seems to me that **our laws do not expressly forbid the importation of parallel goods into Malaysia** ; it is a lawful international business. Nevertheless, **there is this very important qualification to be made. Not all parallel imports are permitted under the Act for the reason that by virtue of s. 35 of the Act the registered proprietor of the trade mark has the exclusive right to the use of the trademark in relation to those goods**. It seems to me clear on principle and on authority that our trade-mark law is territorial in nature. That this principle has been firmly laid down can be seen in our Court of Appeal in *Lim Yew Sing v. Hummel International Sports & Leisure A/S [1996] 4 CLJ 784.*

...

[17] In the first place, I find it useful to refer to *Trade Marks Law in Malaysia, Cases and Commentary* by Dr Ida Madieha bt Abdul Ghani Azmi, where in commenting s. 40(1)(d) of the Act, the learned author summarises the principle as follows:

With regard to subsection (d), **the element of consent must exist**. This **provision indirectly covers parallel imports, as this is where the issue of implicit consent appears**.

[18] The above summary captures the essence of the point that I want to make. The reading of the **provision therefore made it possible for a valid registered trademark owner in Malaysia to put a stop to parallel imports of the goods bearing a similar trade mark from overseas**. Therefore, in the context of our present case, parallel imports of the batteries bearing the SEZAIKEN trade mark are permitted under the Act if and only if the plaintiff must be taken to have consented to their importation, distribution and sale in Malaysia." (Emphasis added)

1.26 Participation in the Madrid System
Malaysia deposited the Madrid Protocol accession instrument in Washington DC on 15 August 2016. The Protocol became binding on Malaysia on 15 September 2016.

Malaysia does not participate in the Madrid system, but it is likely to be implemented in the near future.

1.27 Consequences for Providing Incorrect Information
The consequences of providing incorrect information would depend on the nature of the information, and at what stage the incorrect information was discovered. At the application stage, amendments are possible at the direction of the Registrar or upon application by the applicant.

Every person who makes a false entry or causes a false entry to be made in the Register or in any certified copy of the Register, or who produces or tenders evidence or documents that they know to be false, may be guilty of an offence and is liable, on conviction, to a fine not exceeding MYR5,000 or to a term of imprisonment not exceeding five years, or both: s. 9 of TMA.

Furthermore, all applications for trade-mark registration will need to be supported by a statutory declaration. Any statutory declarations required under TMA shall be made in accordance with the Statutory Declaration Act 1960.

Declarations made by virtue of the provisions of the Statutory Declaration Act 1960 shall be deemed to be such declarations referred to in s. 199 and 200 of the Penal Code.

S. 199 of the Penal Code provides:

"Whoever, in any declaration made or subscribed by him, which declaration any Court, or any public servant or other person, is bound or authorised by law to receive as evidence of any fact, makes any statement which is false, and which he either knows or believes to be false or does not believe to be true, touching any point material to the object for which the declaration is made or used, shall be punished in the same manner as if he gave false evidence."

S. 200 of the Penal Code provides:

"Whoever corruptly uses or attempts to use as true any such declaration knowing the same to be false in any material point, shall be punished in the same manner as if he gave false evidence."

After registration, the mark is liable to be expunged or varied upon application to the court by a 'person aggrieved' where it is proven that the entry made in the register is without sufficient cause, that the entry is wrongfully remaining in the Register or due to any error or defect in any entry in the Register, as a result of the incorrect information provided.

1.28 Updating or Refreshing a Design Mark

A design mark as a form of trade mark can be amended before advertisement of the mark during the registration process with the Registrar's permission, and the modification cannot substantially affect the identity of the mark under the application. This is usually in the context where an objection is issued on the basis that the mark is not distinctive or not capable of distinguishing, hence the requirement to modify the mark.

After registration of the mark, additions or alterations can only be made upon application to the Registrar for leave to make the addition or alteration, which does not substantially affect the identity of the mark, and this is judged qualitatively. The Registrar has the discretion to refuse leave or to impose any terms or limitations upon the grant of leave.

1.29 Denotation

Trade-mark owners may use the symbol ® to denote that the mark is registered. The TM symbol can be used to show that the rights in the trade mark are being claimed by the owner.

It should be noted that individuals making the following representations will be found guilty of an offence and be liable, on conviction, to a fine not exceeding MYR500 or to a term of imprisonment not exceeding two months, or to both, under s. 81(1) of TMA1:

- with respect to a mark that is not a registered trade mark, to the effect that it is a registered trade mark;
- with respect to a part of a registered trade mark that is not a part separately registered on a trade mark, to the effect that it is so registered;
- to the effect that a registered trade mark is registered in respect of goods or services in respect of which it is not registered; or
- to the effect that the registration of a trade mark gives a right to the exclusive use of the trade mark in circumstances in which, having regard to conditions or limitations entered on the Register, the registration does not give such right.

2. Assignment and Licensing

2.1 Assignment Requirements or Restrictions

A deed of assignment is required to assign ownership of a trade mark. The terms of the deed of assignment must clearly provide that the assignment must be for valuable consideration, and whether the assignment is absolute and with or without goodwill, for example.

In GS Yuasa Corp v. GBI Marketing Malaysia Sdn Bhd [2017] 8 MLJ 166, at paragraph 35(a), the court held that an assignment of two valuable trade marks for only MYR10 was a sham. The decision has been affirmed by the Court of Appeal.

A mark may be assigned to the assignee at any stage. However, the recordal of assignment may only be processed by the trade-mark office upon registration of the mark.

When the Registrar is satisfied as to the title of the assignee, he or she shall cause the assignee to be registered as the proprietor of the trade mark: reg. 67 of TMR.

2.2 Procedure for Assigning a Trade Mark

An assignee shall make an application to register his or her title by filing Form TM 15, accompanied by the prescribed fee: reg. 63(1) of TMR. Application may be made jointly with the registered proprietor: reg. 63(2) of TMR.

The application shall contain the full name and trade or business address of the applicant and, if the applicant is a partnership, the full names of all the partners: reg. 64(1) of TMR.

An attested copy of the instrument evidencing the assignment (eg, the deed of assignment) shall be filed together with the Application: reg. 64(2) of TMR.

At any time, the Registrar may require the applicant to produce for inspection any instrument of which an attested copy has been filed, by notice in writing sent to the applicant: reg. 64(3) of TMR. This instrument is not open for public inspection: reg. 64(4) of TMR. The Registrar may call for such proof or additional proof of title: reg. 65 of TMR.

Where an applicant does not claim under any instrument which is capable in itself of furnishing documentary proof of his or her title, he or she shall file with the application a statement of case setting forth the full particulars of the facts upon which the claim to be the proprietor of the mark in question is based, and showing that it has been assigned or transmitted to him or her, and, if the Registrar so requires, the case shall be verified by statutory declaration: reg. 64(5) of TMR.

Where the assignment is made without goodwill, the assignment shall be advertised in prominent newspapers or other publications approved by the Registrar in any particular case, and the advertisement shall state that the assignment was otherwise than in connection with the goodwill of the business concerned (reg. 66(1) of TMR), and the copy of the advertisement shall be filed with the Registrar; until this has been done, the assignment shall be deemed not to have taken effect: reg. 66(2) of TMR.

2.3 Registering or Recording the Assignment

Assignment or transmission must be recorded in the Register of Trade Marks, upon application to the Registrar. Even though the validity of a mark is not affected by the assignment not being registered, if the assignment is not recorded in the Register of the Trade Mark Office, the assignee may not be able to establish its exclusive rights afforded under TMA to initiate any trade-mark infringement against the infringer.

The assignment takes effect on the effective date as provided in the deed of assignment.

2.4 Trade Marks and Security

Powers of a registered proprietor include enforcing equities in respect of a trade mark as they would any other personal property. It is possible to use a trade mark as security.

2.5 Licensing Requirements or Restrictions

The registered proprietor of a trade mark may grant, by lawful contract, a right to a licensee to use the trade mark for all or any of the goods or services: s. 48(1) of TMA.

The licensee may be entered on the Register as a registered user of the mark, with or without any conditions or restrictions, provided that it shall be a condition of any such registration that the registered proprietor shall retain and exercise control over the use of the trade mark and over the quality of the goods or services provided by the registered user in connection with that trade mark: s. 48(1) of TMA.

A licence may be exclusive, non-exclusive, a sole licence, or it may be for a limited duration or otherwise.

A licensing agreement must be signed by both the licensor/registered proprietor and the licensee. It may lay down the agreed terms and conditions, including a clause authorising the use of the mark by the licensee, a quality control clause and a clause identifying that the licensee acknowledges that they are the sole and exclusive licensee of all right, title and interest in the trade mark, and all goodwill is to be associated with the licensor and any goodwill generated by the licensee is to be for the benefit and on behalf of the licensor.

It is not mandatory for the registered proprietor to file a recordal of registered user, and parties are bound by the licensing agreement entered between them even when there is no the recordal of registered user: McLaren International Ltd v. Lim Yat Meen [2008] 1 CLJ 613, Court of Appeal.

If an application for registered user is filed, the effective date of the registered user shall be based on the effective or permitted date as set out in the licensing agreement. The courts have recognised that the effective period of use for a mark by a registered user may pre-date the date of application for registration. There is nothing in s. 46 of the Act or reg. 81(2) TMR that could be read to preclude the use of a trade mark by a registered user to be in force retrospectively before the date of application to register: LB (Lian Bee) Confectionery Sdn Bhd v. QAF Ltd [2012] 3 CLJ 661, Federal Court.

The recordal of registered user shall cease to have effect in the following circumstances:

- if the trade mark ceases to be a registered trade mark;
- if the goods or services for which the trade mark is registered are subsequently limited so as to exclude any or all of

the goods or services in respect of which the registration of the registered user has been made;
- if the registered proprietor ceases to exercise control over the use of the trade mark and over the quality of the goods or services provided by the registered user concerned in relation to that trade mark;
- at the date of expiry of the last registration of the trade mark, unless a fresh application accompanies any application for renewal of the registration of that trade mark; or
- at the date of any assignment or transmission of the registered trade mark, unless and until the devolution of title is recorded on the Register in accordance with the provisions of this Act and the subsequent proprietor of the registered trade mark makes a fresh application: s. 48(6) of TMA.

The registration of a person as a registered user may be cancelled by the Registrar on the application of the registered proprietor, and the Registrar may at any time cancel the registration of a person as a registered user of a trade mark for any goods or services in respect of which the trade mark is no longer registered: s. 49 of the TMA.

2.6 Procedure for Licensing a Trade Mark

Where it is proposed that a licensee shall be registered as a registered user of a trade mark, the registered proprietor shall submit an application to the Registrar for the registration of that person as a registered user of the trade mark, and such application shall be accompanied by the prescribed fee and the following information:

- the representation of the registered trade mark;
- the names, addresses, and addresses for service of the parties;
- the goods or services in respect of which the registration is proposed;
- any conditions (eg, sole licence, an exclusive licence or a non-exclusive licence) or restrictions proposed with respect to the characteristics of the goods or services, to the mode or place of permitted use or to any other matter; and
- whether the permitted use is to be for a period or without limit of period, and the duration of such period if there is one: s. 48(2) of TMA.

The registered proprietor shall furnish the Registrar with such further documents, information or evidence as the Registrar may require: s. 48(3) of TMA.

On receipt of an application for registration of a person as a registered user of a trade mark, the Registrar shall enter on the Register all the particulars required to be provided thereunder: s. 48(4) of TMA.

2.7 Registering or Recording the Licence

It is not mandatory to register a licensee as a registered user: McLaren International Ltd v. Lim Yat Meen [2008] 1 CLJ 613, Court of Appeal. Section 48 of the TMA was permissive rather than mandatory.

However, if the registered proprietor does not use the registered mark in Malaysia, and the registered mark is only used by the licensee in Malaysia, it is important to file a recordal of registered user to minimise the risk of expungement of the registered mark on the basis of non-use under s. 46 of the TMA.

According to s. 46 of TMA, the Court may order the registered mark to be removed from the register if, for a certain period, there was no use in good faith of that trade mark by the registered proprietor or by the registered user of the trade mark: McLaren International Ltd v. Lim Yat Meen [2009] 4 CLJ 749, Federal Court. Thus, if the registered proprietor does not use the mark itself in Malaysia, and all the use is by the licensee, it is important that the licensee is recorded as registered user.

Where a person has been registered as a registered user of a trade mark, the use of that trade mark by the registered user within the limits of his or her registration shall be deemed to be use by the registered proprietor of the trade mark to the same extent as the use of the trade mark by the registered user, and shall be deemed not to be used by any other person: s. 48(5) of TMA.

2.8 Reasons to Deny Granting a Perpetual Licence

Based on s. 48 of the TMA, an application by the registered proprietor to register a person as a registered user can specify whether the use by the registered user is to be for a period or without time limit.

Whilst the licensor may grant a perpetual licence to the licensee, the licensor may be bound by the terms of the agreement. In the event of any dispute between the licensor and the licensee, the perpetual term of the licence may be a relevant factor to be considered by the Court in granting an interim injunction to restrain the termination pending the disposal of the action.

3. Opposition Procedure

3.1 Legal Grounds and Timeframes

The legal grounds for opposition may include:

- that the applicant is not the lawful proprietor of the opposed mark;
- that the opposed mark is likely to deceive or cause confusion to the public or would be contrary to law;
- that there is a conflict with the opposed mark and an application pending registration, or that the tort of passing-

off would arise due to the use of the opposed mark (and therefore is not entitled to protection by any court of law);
- unlawful use of the opposed mark due to its infringement of copyright law and other laws;
- that the opposed mark is scandalous or offensive, or would otherwise not be entitled to protection by any court of law;
- that the opposed mark does not meet the criteria for registration;
- that the opposed mark is identical to or very closely resembles the opponent's mark; and
- that the opposed mark is identical to or very closely resembles a well-known mark.

In Yong Teng Hing B/S Hong Kong Trading Co. v. Walton International Ltd [2012] 6 CLJ 337, the Malaysian Federal Court held that use of the mark in relation to goods in one class may lead to deception or confusion to the public under s. 14(1)(a) of the TMA, by reason only of the goodwill and reputation in respect of another mark in relation to goods in another class.

Within two months of the date of any advertisement in the *Gazette* of an application for registration of a mark, any person may give notice in writing to the Registrar on Form TM 7 –, accompanied by the prescribed fee – of opposition to the registration, and at the same time send a copy of the notice to the applicant: reg. 37 of TMR.

3.2 Filing an Opposition

Any person may file an opposition: s. 28 of TMA.

The opponent does not necessarily need representation by an attorney or trade-mark agent. However, where the opponent does not reside or carry on business in Malaysia, he should appoint a trade-mark agent: s. 79(1), s. 80(1) of TMA and reg. 10(1) of TMR.

The average office and attorney fees vary but can cost in the range of MYR5,300 to MYR6,500 (approximately USD1,190 to USD1,450).

3.3 Opposition Procedure

Within two months of the date of any advertisement in the *Gazette* of an application for registration, any person may give notice in Form TM 7 – accompanied by the prescribed fee – and at the same time send a copy of the notice to the applicant: reg. 37 of TMR. A notice of opposition shall include a statement of the grounds of opposition: reg. 38(1) of TMR.

If registration is opposed on the ground that the mark resembles another mark already on the Register, or the registration of which is the subject of a current application, the number and class of that other mark and, except in the case of an application not yet advertised, the number of the *Gazette* in which it has been advertised shall be set out in the notice: reg. 38(2) of TMR.

Within two months of the receipt of a notice of opposition, the applicant may file a counter-statement on Form TM 8 setting out the grounds supporting his or her application and the facts, if any, alleged in the notice of opposition which he or she admits, and at the same time send a copy of the counter-statement to the opponent: reg. 39(1) of TMR. If no counter-statement is filed within the time period or if there is no extension of time granted, the application shall be deemed abandoned: reg. 39(2) of TMR.

Within two months of the receipt of the counter-statement, the opponent shall file with the Registrar such evidence by way of statutory declaration in support of his or her opposition, and at the same time send a copy of that evidence to the applicant: reg. 40(1) of TMR. If no evidence is filed within the time period or if there is no extension of time granted, the opposition shall be deemed abandoned: reg. 40(2) of TMR.

Within two months of the receipt of the opponent's evidence, the applicant shall file with the Registrar such evidence by way of statutory declaration in support of his or her application and at the same time send a copy of that evidence to the opponent: reg. 41(1) of TMR. If no evidence is filed within the time period or if there is no extension of time granted, the application shall be deemed abandoned: reg. 41(2) of TMR.

Within two months from the receipt of the copies of the applicant's evidence, the opponent may file evidence in reply by way of statutory declaration, and at the same time send a copy of that evidence to the applicant: reg. 42(1) of TMR.

Evidence in reply shall be confined to matters strictly in reply to the applicant's evidence: reg. 42(2) of TMR.

No further evidence may be filed by either side, unless the Registrar gives leave to either party to file such further evidence upon such terms as to costs or otherwise as he or she may think fit: reg. 43 of TMR.

Upon completion of the evidence, the Registrar shall give notice to the parties of a date by which they may send to him or her any arguments or submissions in writing: reg. 46(1) of TMR. The date shall be at least one month after the date of receipt by the parties of the notice given by the Registrar: reg. 46(2) of TMR.

As soon as may be after the expiry of the period notified, the Registrar shall consider the evidence and any written submissions or arguments, and shall communicate to the parties in writing his or her decision on the matter and the grounds of his or her decision, within two months: reg. 47 of TMR.

3.4 Legal Remedies

The decision of the Registrar can be appealed to the High Court.

Based on O. 87 r. 3 of the **Rules of Court 2012** ("ROC "), any party may appeal against the Registrar's decision by way of Originating Summons ("OS"), which shall be brought within one calendar month from the date of the decision appealed against: s. 28(5) and s. 28(6) of TMA.

In **Kraft Foods Schweiz Holding GmbH v. Pendaftar Cap Dagangan** [2016] 9 CLJ 558, Wong Kian Kheong JC held:

"Although parties may consent to an extension of time in writing under O. 3 r. 5(3) of the ROC, such a provision does not apply to this OS because O. 3 r. 5(3) only allows parties to consent in writing to an extension of time to serve, file or amend any pleading or other document beyond a time period, as stipulated in the ROC. Order 3 r. 5(3) of the ROC could not authorise an extension of time to file an action, especially when there is a specific time period to file this OS, as provided in O. 87 r. 3 of the ROC. If this OS is time-barred under O. 87 rr. 3 and 8, despite the Registrar's extension, **the court has no jurisdiction or competence to hear this OS and the parties' consent, election, waiver or acquiescence could not confer jurisdiction or competence for the court to hear the OS.**" (Emphasis added)

4. Initiating a Lawsuit

4.1 Actions to Pursue Infringement

For a registered mark, the registered proprietor may initiate an action against the infringer based on trade-mark infringement: s. 38 of TMA.

For a mark that is not registered, the proprietor may initiate an action against the infringer based on the tort of passing off.

Action for infringement can be initiated where a person who is neither the registered proprietor nor registered user of the trade mark uses a mark that is identical to or so closely resembles the registered mark that it is likely to deceive or cause confusion in the course of trade in relation to goods or services in respect of which the trade mark is registered, in a manner that would render use of the mark likely to be taken as being use as a trade mark, or using a mark in relation to goods or services to import a reference that the person has a right either as registered proprietor or as registered user to use the trade mark or to goods/services with which the person is connected in the course of trade: Tohtonku Sdn Bhd v. Superace (M) Sdn Bhd [1992] 2 CLJ 1153; [1992] 1 CLJ Rep 344, Supreme Court; Acushnet Company v. Metro Golf Manufacturing Sdn Bhd [2006] 7 CLJ 557; Philip Morris Products SA v. Ong Kien Hoe [2016] 2 CLJ 106.

Where an owner of certain goods does certain acts or authorises acts that the registered proprietor or registered user has prohibited via a statement in a notice upon the goods to be done, in relation to the goods in the course of trade or with a view to dealing with the goods in the course of trade, it is deemed to infringe the trade mark, unless certain exceptions apply.

Trade-Mark Infringement

In order to succeed in an action for trade-mark infringement, the plaintiff is required to establish:

- that the defendant is neither the registered proprietor nor the registered user of the trade mark;
- that the defendant used a mark identical to or so closely resembling the plaintiff's registered trade mark that it is likely to deceive or cause confusion;
- that the defendant was using the offending mark in the course of trade;
- that the defendant was using the offending mark in relation to goods or services within the scope of the registration; and
- that the defendant used the offending mark in such a manner as to render the use likely to be taken either as being used as a trade mark or as importing a reference to the registered proprietor or the registered user or to their goods or services: Fabrique Ebel Societe Anonyme v. Sykt Perniagaan Tukang Jam City Port & Ors [1989] 1 CLJ (Rep) 537, 540 & 541; A Clouet & Co Pte Ltd v. Maya Toba Sdn Bhd [1996] 1 BLJ 239; Leo Pharmaceutical Products Ltd AS (Lovens Kemiske Fabrk Produktionsaktieselskab) v. Kotra Pharma (M) Sdn Bhd (No 2) [2012] 10 CLJ 507, at para 83 and 84.

Tort of Passing Off

In an action based on the tort of passing-off, the plaintiff is required to establish:

- that there is misrepresentation by a defendant;
- that the defendant's misrepresentation is made in the course of trade;
- that the defendant's misrepresentation is made to prospective or ultimate consumers of goods or services supplied by defendant;
- that the defendant's misrepresentation is calculated to injure the plaintiff's business or goodwill in the sense that this is a reasonably foreseeable consequence; and
- that the defendant's misrepresentation causes actual damage to the plaintiff's business or good will: Seet Chuan Seng

& Anor v. Tee Yih Jia Food Manufacturing Pte Ltd [1994] 3 CLJ 7, Supreme Court.

The test of passing off as set out in the House of Lords in Reckitt & Colman Products Ltd v. Borden Inc & Ors [1990] 1 All ER 873, at 880 is as follows:-

- the plaintiff has goodwill or reputation attached to the goods or services which the plaintiff supplies in the mind of the purchasing public by association with the get-up, brand name, trade description or features of labelling or packaging (which is distinctive of the plaintiff's goods or services);
- the defendant has misrepresented to the public, which leads or is likely to lead the public to believe that the defendant's goods or services are the goods or services of the plaintiff; and
- the plaintiff must prove that he or she suffers or, in a quia timetaction, is likely to suffer damage by reason of the defendant's misrepresentation: Sinma Medical Products (M) Sdn Bhd v. Yomeishu Seizo Co Ltd & Ors [2004] 4 MLJ 358, Court of Appeal.

4.2 Initiating Infringement Proceedings
A trade-mark owner may initiate infringement proceedings in the High Court.

4.3 Effect of Decisions on Infringement Actions
The decision of the trade-mark office to register a mark will give rise to statutory rights for the registered proprietor to initiate infringement proceedings against an alleged infringer of their registered trade mark.

4.4 Declaratory Judgment Proceedings
Any person may institute declaratory judgment proceedings if they are entitled to any legal character or to any right as to any property, and the court has the discretion whether to make a declaration or otherwise. The court's jurisdiction to make a declaratory order is unlimited, subject only to its own discretion. An exception is that the court will not make a declaration where the person is able to seek other relief than a mere declaration or title but does not do so.

In Dato' Raja Ideris bin Raja Ahmad & Ors v. Teng Chang Khim (Chairman of the select Committee on Competence, Accountability and Transparency and the Chairman of the Committee of Rights and Privileges State Legislative Assembly of Selangor) & Ors [2012] 5 MLJ 490, the Court of Appeal held at 498 and 499-500:

"[25] The question raised in the aforesaid submissions may be formulated as follows:

Upon a true construction of s. 41 [SRA] and O. 15 r. 16, where the OS prays for a declaratory judgment in the form of declarations, is it proper to strike out the OS on the ground that it discloses no reasonable cause of action?

...

[28] **A declaratory judgment merely states the rights or legal position of the parties as they stand without altering them in any way**: see **Gan Hwa Kian & Anor v. Shencourt Sdn Bhd** [2007] 4 MLJ 554. **'A declaration can be used to ascertain and determine the legal rights of parties or to determine a point of law'**: Brett Andrew Macnamara v. Kam Lee Kuan [2008] 7 CLJ 625; [2008] 2 MLJ 450 at p 459 per Balia Yusof J (now JCA). **By virtue of s. 41 and O. 15 r. 16, the court's jurisdiction to make a declaratory order is unlimited, subject only to its own discretion. The court has power to grant a declaration irrespective of whether an application has a cause of action or not and even if a cause of action does not exist at the time of the filing of an application** ...

[29] **The jurisdiction to make a declaration under the rule is not confined to cases in which the plaintiff has a complete and subsisting cause of action: Guaranty Trust Co of New York v. Hannay** [1915] 2 KB 536 (CA) (Eng); Dewan Singh v. M Thynappa Ltd & Yeo Teck Cmhiang [1939] 1 LNS 20; [1939] MLJ 278; **Haji Hussin bin Haji Ali & Ors v. Datuk Haji Mohamed bin Yaacob & Ors and connected cases** [1983] 2 MLJ 227 (FC); Karpal Singh v. Sultan of Selangor [1987] CLJ Rep 686; [1988] 1 MLJ 64; and Tengku Mariam binte Tengku Sri Wa Raja & Anor v. Commissioner for Religious Affairs, Terengganu & Ors [1968] 1 LNS 156; [1969] 1 MLJ 110. **Our answer to the question set out in para** [25] is in the negative."

4.5 Jurisdiction of Courts
The High Court has jurisdiction to hear trade-mark matters.

An appeal may be made to the Court of Appeal.

Parties may appeal to the Federal Court against the decision of the Court of Appeal, but must first obtain leave to appeal to the Federal Court. Based on s. 96(a) of the Courts of Judicature Act 1964, an appeal shall lie from the Court of Appeal to the Federal Court with the leave of the Federal Court if there is a judgment or order of the Court of Appeal in respect of any civil cause or matter decided by the High Court in the exercise of its original jurisdiction, and

- the case involves a question of general principle decided for the first time or a question or questions of importance upon which further argument and a decision of the Federal Court would be to the public advantage.

4.6 Prerequisites to Filing a Lawsuit

Parties may issue a letter of demand or a cease-and-desist letter for the infringer to cease their act of infringement.

However, there is no prerequisite to issue a formal demand letter or warning letter, nor to engage in any mediation prior to filing a lawsuit.

4.7 Representation for Parties

Subject to the following, parties may sue or carry on proceedings in Court through a solicitor or in person: O. 5 r. 6(1) of the Rules of Court 2012.

A body corporate or company may not begin or carry on any proceedings other than through a solicitor: O. 5 r. 6(2) of the Rules of Court 2012.

A person under disability may not bring, make a claim in, defend, make a counterclaim in or appear in any proceedings except through his litigation representative: O. 76 r. 2 of the Rules of Court 2012.

4.8 Interim or Preliminary Injunctions

Interlocutory injunctions are available.

In order to succeed in an application for an interlocutory injunction, the plaintiff is required to establish the following:

- that there is a bona fide serious issue to be tried;
- that the balance of convenience has tilted in favour of the grant of the interlocutory injunction, ie the plaintiff would suffer greater injustice if relief is withheld; and
- that damages is not an adequate remedy, ie an award of monetary compensation would be inadequate in the event that the plaintiff succeeds in establishing his or her claim at trial: Keet Gerald Francis Noel John v Mohd Noor bin Abdullah & Ors [1995] 1 MLJ 193.

The court may also take into account factors such as:

- the justice of the case;
- the practical realities of the case;
- the plaintiff's ability to meet his or her undertaking in damages should the suit fail, and, in appropriate cases, may require the plaintiff to secure his or her undertaking, for example, by providing a bank guarantee. Of course, cases may arise where the injustice to the plaintiff is so manifest that the Judge would be entitled to dispense with the usual undertaking as to damages: Cheng Hang Guan v. Perumahan Farlim (Penang) Sdn. Bhd. [1988] 1 CLJ 435 (Rep);[1988] 3 MLJ 90);
- whether there is any delay in the making of the application; and
- public interest in appropriate cases.

4.9 Protection for Potential Defendant

The validity of the plaintiff's trade-mark registration may be challenged by a potential defendant to protect itself, for example by asserting that the trade mark should not have been registered.

- In all legal proceedings relating to a registered trade mark, the fact that a person is registered as proprietor of the trade mark shall be prima facie evidence of the validity of the original registration of the trade mark: s. 36 of the TMA.

In all legal proceedings relating to a trade mark registered in the Register, the original registration of the trade mark shall be taken to be valid after the expiry of seven years from the date thereof, in all respects unless it is shown:

- that the original registration was obtained by fraud;
- that the trade mark offends against s. 14 of TMA; or
- that the trade mark was not, at the commencement of the proceedings, distinctive of the goods or services of the registered proprietor: s. 37 of TMA.

In order for a potential defendant to expunge a registered mark, whether based on s. 45 of TMA or s. 46 of TMA (ie, on the basis of non-use), they must first establish that they are an "aggrieved person". In LB (Lian Bee) Confectionary Sdn Bhd v. QAF Ltd [2012] 3 CLJ 661, the Malaysian Federal Court held at para 18:

"In accordance with the principle of construction in bonam partem, it is noted that the learned trial judge had found that the appellant had been infringing the Registered Trade Mark "Squiggles" since 2007. The Registered Trade Mark "Squiggles" was registered on 20 August 2004. Until its expungement, the registered trade mark remains a registered trade mark. In this case, even before the application for expungement, the appellant had unlawfully been using the Infringing Mark "Squiggle" which is confusingly similar to the Registered Trade Mark. **Applying the principle of construction in bonam partem, the appellant cannot be regarded as being a bona fide "person aggrieved" or a person who is lawfully aggrieved for the purposes of s. 46(1)(b) of the** TMA. Furthermore, **if the appellant is to be regarded as a "person aggrieved" for the purposes of s. 46(1)(b) of the** TMA, **it would mean that all infringers may apply to expunge the very trade mark they have been infringing and this would be contrary to the time-honoured principle of not allowing them to benefit from their very own wrong or unlawful act**." (Emphasis added).

4.10 Obtaining Information and Evidence

A discovery process is available, provided by the Rules of Court 2012.

Discovery applications are made after the close of pleadings but before trial starts. There are three stages in which discovery would apply: disclosure of a list of documents, where copies of documents are inspected and taken, and production of the documents.

4.11 Initial Pleading Standards

A lawsuit is initiated by filing a Writ and Statement of Claim, or Originating Summons, whichever is appropriate, in which the defendant is informed of the plaintiff's claim and the material facts on which they are based, and of the relief claimed by the plaintiff. The remedy or relief being sought must be specified. The plaintiff does not plead law or evidence in the statement of claim.

The particulars of the plaintiff(s) and defendant(s) shall be stated in the Statement of Claim O. 18 r. 6(4) of Rules of Court 2012.

Every pleading shall contain only a statement in a summary form of the material facts on which the party pleading relies for his or her claim or defence, as the case may be, but not the evidence by which those facts are to be proved, and the statement shall be as brief as the nature of the case admits: O. 18 r. 7 (1) of the Rules of Court 2012.

The effect of any document or the purpose of any conversation referred to in the pleading shall, if material, be briefly stated, and the precise words of the document or conversation shall not be stated, except insofar as those words are themselves material: O. 18 r. 7 (2) of the Rules of Court 2012.

In any pleading subsequent to a statement of claim, a party shall plead specifically any matter, for example, performance, release, any relevant statute of limitation, fraud or any fact showing illegality:

- which he or she alleges makes any claim or defence of the opposite party not maintainable;
- which, if not specifically pleaded, might take the opposite party by surprise; or
- which raises issues of fact not arising out of the preceding pleading: O. 18 r. 8 of the Rules of Court 2012.

In any pleading, a party may plead any matter that has arisen at any time, whether before or since the issue of the writ: O. 18 r. 9 of the Rules of Court 2012.

In any pleading, a party shall not make an allegation of fact or raise any new ground or claim that is inconsistent with a previous pleading: O. 18 r. 10 of the Rules of Court 2012.

A party may raise any point of law by his or her pleading: O. 18 r. 11 of the Rules of Court 2012.

Every pleading shall contain the necessary particulars of any claim, defence or other matter pleaded, including:

- particulars of any misrepresentation, fraud, breach of trust, wilful default or undue influence on which the pleading party relies; and
- where a pleading party alleges any condition of the mind of any person, whether any disorder or disability of mind or any malice, fraudulent intention or other condition of mind except knowledge, particulars of the facts on which the party relies: O. 18 r. 12(1) of the Rules of Court 2012.

No party shall quantify any claim or counterclaim for general damages: O. 18 r. 12(1A) of the Rules of Court 2012.

A statement of claim shall state specifically the relief or remedy which the plaintiff claims, but costs do not need to be specifically claimed: O 18 r. 15(1) of the Rules of Court 2012.

In trade-mark proceedings, the Registrar may be directed by the court or has the right to appear and be heard, and shall appear if the Court so directs, where the relief sought includes alteration or rectification of the Register: Ho Tack Sien v Rotta Research Laboratorium S.p.A. [2015] 4 CLJ 20, Federal Court.

The Registrar may submit a signed written statement to the court within his or her knowledge as they think fit, which will be deemed to form part of the evidence in the proceedings. This includes giving particulars of the proceedings before him or her in relation to the matter at issue, the grounds of any decision given by him or her affecting the matter in issue, the practice of the office in similar cases or any other matters relevant to the issues.

Amendments to pleadings can be made at any stage of the proceedings, but should be made as early as possible and should not cause injustice to the other party.

Amendment of pleading may be made without leave of the court before the pleadings are deemed to be closed: O. 20 r. 3(1) of the Rules of Court 2012. After the close of pleadings, amendments may be made with leave of the court, provided that:

- the application for amendment is bona fide ;
- there is no prejudice caused to the other side which cannot be compensated by costs; and
- the amendments would not in effect turn the suit from one character into a suit of another and inconsistent character: Yamaha Motor Co Ltd v. Yamaha (M) Sdn Bhd & Ors [1983] 1 MLJ 213, Federal Court.

In Hong Leong Finance Bhd v. Low Thiam Hoe [2015] 8 CLJ 1, the Federal Court held as follows:

- when dealing with an application to amend the pleadings that would introduce a new case in the claim or defence on the eve of the trial, the principles in Yamaha Motor are not the sole considerations;
- the principles in Yamaha Motor apply to cases where the application to amend the pleadings is made at an early stage of the proceedings;
- there has to be a cogent and reasonable explanation in the applicant's affidavit as to why the application was filed late;
- the application to amend the pleadings is not a tactical manoeuvre;
- the proposed amendment must disclose full particulars for the court to ascertain if there is a real prospect of success in proving the same; and
- lateness in the application to amend the pleadings cannot necessarily be compensated by payment of costs.

4.12 Representative or Collective Actions

In Malaysia, three requirements must be satisfied to be able to take a representative action, as per the case *Duke of Bedford v Ellis* [1901] AC 1:

- the plaintiff and those represented by him or her are members of a class and have a common interest;
- they must have a common grievance; and
- the nature of relief sought is beneficial to all.

A representative action for trade-mark proceedings is possible if the above requirements are met.

4.13 Restrictions on Trade Mark-Owners

After an action is initiated by a trade-mark owner, the other party may apply to strike out the claim on the following grounds:

- it discloses no reasonable cause of action;
- it is scandalous, frivolous or vexatious;
- it may prejudice, embarrass or delay the fair trial of the action; or
- it is otherwise an abuse of the process of the court: Order 18 rule 19 of the Rules of Court 2012.

The court may also strike out a claim when the purpose for initiating the process is other than to obtain genuine redress offered by the process. In other words, the dominant purpose for which the process was invoked is collateral, that is to say, aimed at producing a result not intended by the invocation of the process: Malaysia Building Society Bhd v. Tan Sri General Ungku Nazaruddin Ungku Mohamed b [1998] 2 CLJ 340, Court of Appeal.

The principles upon which the court acts in exercising its power under any of the four limbs of O. 18 r. 19 of the Rules of Court are well settled. It is only in plain and obvious cases that recourse should be had to the summary process under this rule, and this summary procedure can only be adopted when it can clearly be seen that a claim or answer is on the face of it "obviously unsustainable". It cannot be exercised by a minute examination of the documents and facts of the case, in order to see whether the party has a cause of action or a defence. The court must be satisfied that there is no reasonable cause of action or that the claims are frivolous or vexatious or that the defences raised are not arguable. As long as the pleadings disclose some course of action or raise some question fit to be decided by the Judge, the mere fact that the case is weak and not likely to succeed at the trial is no grounds for the pleadings to be struck out: Bandar Builder Sdn Bhd v. United Malayan Banking Corporation Bhd [1993] 4 CLJ 7, Supreme Court.

5. Infringement

5.1 Action for Infringement

The necessary parties to an action for infringement are the registered proprietor and the person whom an infringement proceedings are being initiated against. Joint proprietors can bring a proceeding in their own names.

A registered user can also be a party to an action for infringement and institute proceedings in their own name where the registered proprietor fails to commence proceedings for infringement within two months of being called upon to do so by the registered user: s. 51(1) of TMA. In this case, the registered proprietor will be a defendant in the proceedings: s. 51(2) of TMA.

A third party who is not the trade-mark owner cannot file an action for infringement.

A trade-mark owner may take action to stop infringement before its mark is registered by initiating an action based on the tort of passing-off.

5.2 Signs and Infringement

A registered trade mark is infringed by a person who is not the registered proprietor of the trade mark nor the registered user of the trade mark using a mark that is identical to it or that so closely resembles it that it is likely to deceive or cause confusion in the course of trade in relation to goods or services in respect of which the trade mark is registered in such a manner as to render the use of the mark likely to be taken either:

- as being used as a trade mark; or

- the defendant's use of the plaintiff's mark in an advertising circular or other advertisement, which is likely to be taken as importing a reference to the defendant having the right as either the registered proprietor or the registered user to use the mark or to goods/services with which the proprietor or registered user is connected in the course of trade: s. 38 of TMA.

Under s. 38 of the TMA, a registered trade mark is infringed by a person who uses a mark that:

- is identical to it; or
- so closely resembles it that it is likely to deceive; or
- so closely resembles it that it is likely to cause confusion: Tohtonku Sdn Bhd v. Superace (M) Sdn Bhd [1992] 1 CLJ Rep 344.

In considering whether there is confusion and deception to the public by the existence of two similar trade marks, the factors to be taken into account may be summarised as follows:

- the idea of the mark is to be regarded;
- the elements of the mark must be taken as a whole;
- imperfect recollection of the mark by customers or purchasers should be taken into account;
- the aural as well as the visual aspect of a customer towards the mark is relevant; and
- all the circumstances of the trade are to be considered: Bata Ltd v. Sim Ah Ba [2006] 3 CLJ 393, Court of Appeal.

The tests and principles of comparison that are widely accepted and applied may be summarised as follows:

- the idea conveyed by both trade marks must be compared;
- the marks as a whole must be compared;
- the 1st syllable of the trade marks is of importance;
- the ear as well as the eye must be considered;
- the imperfect recollection of customers/potential customers must be considered; and
- the essential features of the trade marks must also be compared: Consitex SA v. TCL Marketing Sdn Bhd [2008] 8 CLJ 444.

5.3 Use of a Sign by Defendant

The registered trade mark has been infringed if the defendant has used the registered trade mark in the course of trade.

To constitute trade mark infringement, the mark has to be used in a way that would indicate the origin of the goods and/or services, in the course of trade and in relation to the goods or services registered.

TMA does not define the phrase "in the course of trade" in relation to goods: s. 3(1) TMA only defines it in relation to the provision of services: Philip Morris Brands Sarl v. Goodness for Import and Export [2017] 1 LNS 966.

In Mesuma Sports Sdn Bhd v. Majlis Sukan Negara, Malaysia (Pendaftar Cap Dagangan, Malaysia, interested party) [2015] 2 MLJ 176, the Court of Appeal held at paragraph 33 as follows:

"A further word on the 'use in the course of trade' argument. We are of the view that **the respondent need not be a 'commercial entity' before it can be said that the respondent had used the design 'in the course of trade'**. The respondent need not be a commercial entity to manufacture and sell sporting goods bearing the design before it can be said that it was using the design in the course of trade. **The respondent by using the design owns the goodwill generated thereby in relation to the mark. The respondent in using the design for purposes of branding can be deemed to be using the mark in the course of trade.**" (Emphasis added).

The Court of Appeal's decision in Mesuma Sports has been affirmed by the Federal Court. In the Federal Court in Mesuma Sports [2015] 6 MLJ 465, at paragraphs 52, 53 and 66, Azahar Mohamed FCJ held:

"[52] The operative words are **'in the course of the trade'; the mark must be used in the course of trade to indicate that the goods bearing the same mark originate from the same source**. These are **undeniably very wide-ranging words. The term 'trade' is very wide. The word 'trade' used in the provision is not defined.** In constructing and interpreting the meaning of a word used in the Act, the ordinary meaning of the work must be applied unless there is a clear ambiguity (see Dupont Steels Ltd v. Sirs [1980] 1 WLR 142). We do not see anything ambiguous in the provision. The word in question therefore should be given its plain and ordinary meaning (see Chin Choy & Ors v. Collector of Stamp Duties [1978] 1 LNS 26; [1979] 1 MLJ 69 and Calamas Sdn Bhd v. Pentadbir Tanah Batang Padang [2011] 5 CLJ 125). Its scope of meaning and application can be seen by referring to the Concise Oxford Dictionary (9thEd): Trade is defined as, among others, business conducted for profit, business of a specified nature, a transaction with a person for a thing. In Aristoc Ltd v. Rysta Ltd [1944] 62 RPC 65, Lord MacMillan in the course of his judgment said 'trade' is no doubt a wide word but its meaning must vary with and be controlled by its context.

[53] In asserting its position that the plaintiff was not first in time to use the tiger-stripes design as a trade mark in the course of trade, the main thrust of the arguments of the defendant's learned counsel was grounded on the basis that the plaintiff was not a profit-making organisation; hence the plaintiff was not an entity connected in the course of trade... He relied on the provisions of s. 3 [TMA] to support the

argument that the mark must be used in the course of trade to connect the goods with that mark. He contended that the use in 'a trade mark sense' can only be achieved through the manufacturing and sale of goods with the tiger-stripes design embodied, and goodwill can only be achieved through business activities such as 'manufacturing, supplying and selling' the sports attire it had produced.

[66] The plain and natural interpretation of the phrase 'in the course of trade' does not bear out the proposition advanced by learned counsel for the defendant that the use in 'a trade mark sense' can only be achieved through the manufacturing and sale of sports attire with the tiger-stripes design embodied, and goodwill can only be achieved through such business activities. We are quite unable to agree with his contention. From a perusal of the provisions of s. 3 [TMA], we can find not a word in it to support the restrictive interpretation of learned counsel. An implication of learned counsel's contention, as pointed out by the Court of Appeal in the present case, and we respectfully agree, would mean disregarding other forms of use in the course of trade, such as obtaining sponsorships, granting merchandising rights and other licensing rights over the use of the tiger stripes design. With respect, we would be wrong if we were to hold so." (Emphasis added)

5.4 Defences Against Infringement

Defences against infringement include:

- the use in good faith by a person of his or her own name or the name of his or her, or their predecessor's business;
- the use in good faith by a person of a description of the character or quality of his or her goods or services, where the description is not importing a reference to the trade mark of another trader;
- the owner or his or her predecessors in business continuously using his or her trade mark from a date before the use of the registered trade mark by the registered proprietor (or their predecessor in business) or by a registered user of the mark or before registration of the trade mark, whichever is earlier;
- the registered proprietor or registered user has applied the trade mark on the goods in the course of trade and has not subsequently removed or obliterated it;
- a person uses a trade mark in relation to goods or services where the registered proprietor or registered user has expressly or impliedly consented to;
- the use of the trade mark by a person in relation to goods or services adapted to form part of or be accessory to other goods or services in relation to which the trade mark has been used without infringement of the right given or might for the time being be so used, if the use of the trade mark is reasonably necessary in order to indicate that the goods or services are adapted as such; and
- the registered trade mark being used by concurrent proprietors: s. 40 of the TMA.

5.5 Role of Experts and/or Surveys

Expungement of a mark by a third party can be based on non-use of a mark. The third party applying to expunge the mark must prove a prima faciecase of non-use. The most common way of doing this is via a survey or market research report. Where a market survey is submitted in court to show that a mark has not been used during the relevant statutory period, and where this is not rebutted by the defendant, the plaintiff would establish a prima facie case of non-use, which will shift the burden to the defendant to establish use of its trade mark.

5.6 Administrative or Criminal Offence

Under the Trade Descriptions Act 2011 (" **TDA** "), a penalty will be imposed for using a false trade description relating to a trade mark. The Public Prosecutor has the discretion as to whether prosecution is to be initiated.

A trade description order can be applied for via filing an originating summons supported by an affidavit, on an ex partebasis. Where a trade description order is obtained, it declares that an infringing trade mark is a false trade-description in relation to any of the goods that it applies to, as is specified in the order, and therefore would enable the offence to be prosecuted under the TDA. Infringement of trade mark or passing-off must be proven by the applicant for a trade-descriptions order.

In Tan Kim Hock Product Centre Sdn Bhd v. Tan Kim Hock Tong Seng Food Industry Sdn Bhd [2017] 7 CLJ 191, the Court of Appeal held:

"[18] Further, **the law recognised that a trade description order could be applied for ex parte from the court.** (In-Comix Food Industries Sdn Bhd v. A. Clouet & Co (KL) Sdn Bhd [1996] 2 BLJ 543; MajuPerak Tepung Beras Sdn Bhd v. Tiga Gajah Cho Heng Sdn Bhd [2001] 3 CLJ 241). The purpose of such order was to have it declared by the court, on evidence shown, **that the trade-mark rights of the registered owner, or such interested person, had been infringed by imitation or that counterfeits goods have been found in the market**. It was also to assist and move the relevant machinery in the area of criminal law to counter such infringements (see *In-Comix Food Industry, supra*) and further to prevent the public from being confused or misled by products or goods bearing a false trade-description.

[41] We have already expressed our views as to the tenor and purport of s. 9 of the Act and the nature of the trade-description order that might be granted by the court upon the application of the proprietor of a registered trade mark. **We found nothing in that section that required the applicant**

to resort to any other measure or prerequisite proceeding before seeking the order thereunder. It was also not reasonable to impose such a condition or make the proprietor of a registered trade mark wait, once it was established on evidence that there were counterfeits or products with false trade-description or marks in the market, threatening the trade-mark owner's commercial interests. It was also in the interest of the general public that a trade-description order should be issued expeditiously in such circumstances." (Emphasis added)

A Controller, Deputy Controller and/or Assistant Controllers of Trade Descriptions may be appointed, with the power to (a) purchase goods to ascertain whether the TDA is being complied with; (b) arrest anyone believed to have committed an offence under the TDA without warrant; (c) prosecute anyone committing an offence under the TDA; and (d) compound offences.

5.7 Custom Seizures

For parallel import, please refer to **1.25 Requirements for an Exhaustion**.

Part XIV A of TMA (ie Border Measures) states that a trade-mark owner may apply to the Registrar of Trade Marks for counterfeit trade-mark goods to be prohibited from being imported into Malaysia, where the trade-mark owner is aware that counterfeit trade-mark goods are to be imported into Malaysia for sale.

Upon approval, an officer will be appointed in Customs by the Registrar of Trade Marks, who will seize and detain goods within 60 days of the date of approval.

The trade-mark owner must provide a security deposit to the Registrar to cover the Registrar's expenses, prevent abuse and provide compensation to the importer if it is ordered to do so.

After the goods are seized, the trade-mark owner must begin an infringement action and obtain a court order to prevent the goods from being released. Where successful, the seized goods will be ordered to be forfeited and disposed of as per the court's directions.

Where the action fails, the trade-mark owner may be required to pay compensation if the importer can show loss or damage suffered.

6. Revocation/Cancellation

6.1 Remedies and Reasons

The cancellation of an entry of a trade mark, the correction of error or the amendment of the specification of goods or services in the Register may be made by the registered proprietor pursuant to s. 43(1)(b) of the TMA.

An application for rectification of a trade mark can be made pursuant to ss. 45 and 46 of the TMA.

Section 45 of the TMA provides that the court may make such order for making, expunging or varying such entry as it thinks fit, on the application in the prescribed manner of any person aggrieved by the non-insertion in or omission from the Register of any entry, or by any entry made in the register without sufficient cause, or by any entry wrongfully remaining in the Register, or by any error or defect in any entry in the Register.

Section 46 of TMA provides that an aggrieved person may apply for the court to order a trade mark to be removed from the Register based on non-use of the mark.

An application to expunge a trade mark via rectification is commonly used by the defendant as a counterclaim, as it provides a defence to an infringement action, whereby the registration is deemed to have never been made.

Third parties may apply for rectification in attempts to remove a registered mark from the Register on the grounds that it is wrongfully remaining in the Register.

Furthermore, rectification is a method to allow third parties to take over other trade marks, for instance, in situations where there is interest in a particular registered mark owned by a different proprietor, where a trade-mark owner has commenced a business using a mark, not realising that another proprietor has registered the same mark, protecting existing marks from encroaching marks, or where there is interest to venture into other areas using the same mark but another proprietor has registered the mark.

6.2 Statutory Limitation or Time Period

Any application for expungement or revocation under s. 45 of TMA ought to be made within seven years of the date of registration of the mark.

After the expiry of seven years from the date thereof, the original registration of the trade mark under TMA shall be taken to be valid in all respects, unless it is shown:

- that the original registration was obtained by fraud;
- that the trade mark offends against section 14; or
- that the trade mark was not, at the commencement of the proceedings, distinctive of the goods or services of the registered proprietor: s. 37 of the TMA.

For s. 46 of the TMA – ie, expungement on the basis of non-use of the trade mark – the applicant must show either that:

- the trade mark was registered without an intention in good faith to use it in relation to those goods or services and no actual subsequent use in good faith in relation to those goods or services up to one month before the date of the application for removal; or up to one month before applying to remove the trade mark, there was no use in good faith for a continuous period of at least three years in relation to those goods or services for which the trade mark had been registered.

6.3 Initiation of Revocation/Cancellation Proceeding

Only a 'person aggrieved' as laid down in ss. 45 and 46 of the TMA can apply for rectification of trade marks.

In McLaren International Ltd v Lim Yat Meen [2009] 5 MLJ 741, a 'person aggrieved' is defined as a person who has used his or her mark as a trade mark, or a person who has a genuine and present intention to use his or her mark as a trade mark in the course of trade that is the same or similar to that of the registered mark the person wishes to remove, and cannot be a mere 'busybody'.

In Mesuma Sports Sdn Bhd v Majlis Sukan Negara Malaysia (Pendaftar Cap Dagangan Malaysia, interested party) [2015] 6 MLJ 465, the person must have a legal interest, right or legitimate expectation in their own mark that is substantially affected by the presence of the registered mark.

In LB (Lian Bee) Confectionery Sdn Bhd v QAF Ltd [2012] 4 MLJ 20, this may include a person with a bona fideintention to use a trade mark that is registered but has not been continuously used by the registered proprietor for at least three years.

6.4 Partial Revocation/Cancellation

Partial revocation/cancellation is possible under ss. 45 and 46 of TMA.

For example, the court may have the power to rectify part of the registration, ie, for the purpose of correcting any error or defect in the entry in the Register: s. 45 of TMA.

Similarly, if a registered mark is for a range of goods and the proprietor uses part of those goods and did not use other goods as set out in the specification, the court may expunge the mark in relation of those goods or may direct that the registration be subjected to such conditions, amendments, modification or limitations as the court thinks proper: s. 46(3) of TMA.

6.5 Possibilities of Amendment

A mark can be varied pursuant to s. 45 of TMA, for example, to ensure that all the error or defects are duly rectified in the Register.

6.6 Revocation/Cancellation and Infringement

Any party may apply to consolidate both infringement and revocation matters so that they will be heard together. A court has the discretion and power to direct if the court is to hear the revocation proceedings first, or simultaneously.

Revocation/cancellation can also be used by the defendant in a counterclaim to an infringement action.

7. Trial & Settlement

7.1 Special Procedural Provisions

Under s. 62(3) of the TMA, in any action or proceeding relating to a trade mark or trade name, the Registrar or the court shall admit evidence of the usages of the trade concerned or evidence of business usages in the provision of the services in question, and evidence of any relevant trade marks, trade names, business names or get-ups legitimately used by other persons.

Section 64(1) of the TMA provides that printed or written copies or extracts of or from the Register purporting to be certified by the Registrar and sealed with his or her seal shall be admissible as evidence in any proceedings before any court of law without further proof or production of the originals. Furthermore, s. 64(2) of the TMA states that a certificate purporting to be under the hand of the Registrar as to any act which he or she is authorised under the TMA to perform and which has or has not been performed, as the case may be, shall be prima facie evidence in any proceedings before any court of law having or not having performed the act.

In any legal proceedings in which the relief sought includes alteration or rectification of the Register, the Registrar shall have the right to appear and be heard, and shall appear if so directed by the court: s. 65(1) of TMA. Furthermore, under s. 65(2) of the TMA, unless otherwise directed by the court, the Registrar, in lieu of appearing and being heard, may submit to the court a statement in writing signed by him or her, giving particulars of the proceedings before him or her in relation to the matter at issue or on the grounds of any decision given by him or her affecting the matter at issue or the practice of the office in like cases, or of such other matters relevant to the issues, and within his or her knowledge as Registrar, as he or she thinks fit, and such statement shall be deemed to form part of the evidence in the proceedings.

7.2 Determination of Cases

In Malaysia, there is a specialised Intellectual Property High Court in the High Court of Malaya at Kuala Lumpur, which hears all intellectual property disputes.

Both parties will have the right to present the facts and evidence before the Court.

7.3 Possibilities of Settlement

A defendant can make an offer to settle the matter at any time after the commencement of action and before the court disposes of the matter: O. 22B of the Rules of Court 2012.

7.4 Other Court Proceedings

A defendant may file a counterclaim for revocation when being sued for infringement. The party may apply to consolidate both matters so that they will be heard together. A court may hear the revocation proceedings first, or simultaneously.

8. Remedies

8.1 Existing Remedies

Remedies for trade-mark owners include injunctions, order for delivery up or obliteration of the offending trade mark, damages, account of profits, declaration of infringement by defendant, and costs (partial).

The court has discretion to grant injunction, delivery up, account of profits, declaration of infringement, and costs or such other relief as it deems fit.

8.2 Rights and Remedies

Costs may be awarded in favour of a prevailing defendant.

8.3 Different Types of Remedies

The type of remedy sought would depend on the facts of each case.

9. Appeal

9.1 Special Provisions

The appellate procedure for trade-mark proceedings is the same as all appellate civil disputes.

9.2 Factual or Legal Review

Appeals to the Court of Appeal involve a re-hearing of the case, which includes a review of both facts and law.

Appeals to the Federal Court are limited to a review of the law involved in the case.

9.3 Length of Appeal from Trial Court

The trial Court may dispose of the disputes within nine months from the date of commencement of the action.

An appeal from a trial Court may be disposed of within six to nine months.

10. Other Trade Mark Issues

10.1 Recognition of Dilution

The Court in Malaysia recognises the principle of dilution, and this may be a factor to be relied upon in opposition to a trade-mark registration, or to present use of an infringing mark.

10.2 Protection of Famous Marks

Foreign Mark

Trade-mark laws are territorial in nature. In **McLaren**, *supra*, the Court of Appeal held at para 15:

"To add to the above list, it must be understood **that even if the respondent had appropriated the appellant's mark knowingly when filing the trade mark in 1992, that move broke no law**. So long as the appellant had yet to use it here prior to the respondent's registration he had every right to act as he did. There was no necessity for the respondent to do the impracticable like scouring the globe and enquiring from those carrying that name or trade name whether they intended to come to Malaysia and register the mark here. A faultless respondent need not have to step aside and fold up his business, merely because some foreign company had made radical demands on the Registrar of Trade Marks."

However, the principle has been clarified by the Federal Court in Yong Teng Hing B/S Hong Kong Trading Co. v Walton International Ltd [2012] 6 CLJ 337, where the Federal Court held:

"We are of the view that the principles in the *Hummel* case would apply if there had been no use of the foreign trade mark at all in Malaysia. It is very clear that the principles laid down in *Hummel* have no application to the facts of the present case. We noted that it is for this reason the Court of Appeal in the present case had rightly distinguished the *Hummel* case wherein at p. 20 of the judgment it had this to say:

In *Lim Yew Sing v. Hummel International Sports & Leisure A/S [1996] 4 CLJ 784* ; [1996] 3 MLJ 7, **the Court of Appeal had decided that a Malaysian trader could only become the registered proprietor of a foreign trade mark used for similar goods if the foreign trade mark has not been used at all in Malaysia**. In the present case it is clear from the unchallenged evidence that the appellant's predecessor, **Giordano Limited Hong Kong**, is the first user of the GIORDANO trade mark in relation to, amongst others, articles of clothing, leather belts, bags, wallets and umbrellas in Malaysia since as early as the year 1990, before the filing date of the respondent's application for registration."

Well Known Marks

A well-known trade mark in Malaysia (ie, the Malaysian public is familiar with the mark because it is famous and well established among Malaysians) is accorded protection in Malaysia even though the owner of the mark has not used the mark in Malaysia.

10.3 Special Rules Regarding Geographic Indicators

Based on s. 5(1) of the Geographical Indications Act 2000, the Court may grant an injunction to prevent any unlawful use of a geographical indication, and may award any damages and any other legal remedy or relief as it deems fit, where an 'interested person' (which the Act defines as including individual consumers of goods bearing a false or misleading geographical indication) institutes proceedings in the Court to prevent, in respect of geographical indications:

- the use in the course of trade of any means in the designation or presentation of any goods that indicates or suggests, in a manner that misleads the public, that the goods in question originate in a geographical area other than the true place of origin;
- any use in the course of trade that constitutes an act of unfair competition within the meaning of the Paris Convention;
- any use in the course of trade of a geographical indication which, although literally true as to the country, territory, region or locality in which the goods originate, falsely represents to the public that the goods originate in another country, territory, region or locality; or
- any use in the course of trade of a geographical indication identifying wines or spirits not originating in the place indicated by the geographical indication in question, even where the true origin of the wines or spirits is indicated or the geographical indication is used accompanied by expressions such as "kind", "type", "style" or "imitation".

10.4 Special Rules Relating to Surnames

For a mark to be registrable, it cannot have a direct reference to, nor be descriptive of, a surname.

Lee Hishammuddin Allen & Gledhill
Level 6, Menara 1 Dutamas
Solaris Dutamas
No. 1, Jalan Dutamas 1
50480 Kuala Lumpur
Malaysia

Tel: +603 6208 5888
Fax: +603 6201 0122
Email: lzj@lh-ag.com
Web: www.lh-ag.com

LH AG Advocates and Solicitors
Lee Hishammuddin Allen & Gledhill

11. Costs

11.1 Costs Before Filing a Lawsuit

The costs that typically arise before filing a lawsuit include a 'getting-up fee', which takes into account whether the advocate or solicitor has acted reasonably and properly in getting up his or her client's case in preparation for the trial. In this case, work done before the action is initiated may be taken into account.

11.2 Costs Regarding an Infringement Action

Costs are not fixed, and depend on the enforcement type and manner.

11.3 Costs of Litigation

Generally, the losing party must pay costs to the winning party. However, whether costs are awarded depends on the court exercising its discretion.

12. Alternative Dispute Resolution

12.1 Common Way of Settlement

Alternative dispute resolution (ADR) is available to resolve a trade-mark case.

13. Trade Marks and Other Intellectual Property

13.1 Protection by Copyright

A trade mark may also be protected under copyright law, provided that it is one of the category of works eligible for copyright protection, such as artistic works. Logos are a form of 'graphic works', and are considered artistic works under the Copyright Act 1987.

NORWAY

LAW AND PRACTICE: p.247

Contributed by Kvale Advokatfirma DA

The 'Law & Practice' sections provide easily accessible information on navigating the legal system when conducting business in the jurisdiction. Leading lawyers explain local law and practice at key transactional stages and for crucial aspects of doing business.

Contributed by Kvale Advokatfirma DA **Authors:** Marie Vaale-Hallberg, Lars Trygve Jenssen, Kaia Bugge Fougner, Tarje Neergaard

Law and Practice

Contributed by Kvale Advokatfirma DA

CONTENTS

Contributed by Kvale Advokatfirma DA **Authors:** Marie Vaale-Hallberg, Lars Trygve Jenssen, Kaia Bugge Fougner, Tarje Neergaard

Contributed by Kvale Advokatfirma DA ***Authors:*** Marie Vaale-Hallberg, Lars Trygve Jenssen, Kaia Bugge Fougner, Tarje Neergaard

Kvale Advokatfirma DA advises on all aspects of ownership, protection, exploitation and enforcement of trade marks in a wide range of industries. This includes particular notable strength in matters related to fast-moving consumer goods (FMCG), telecom, oil/gas, luxury goods, digitalisation/industry 4.0, online use/e-commerce, new technology, licensing, and dispute resolution. Trade-mark matters are handled in Kvale's seven-partner IP/TMT department. Advising a diverse and high-profile list of clients, the firm undertake a comprehensive range of advice including all aspects of the life cycle of the trade marks, including, but not limited to IP strategy, national and international registrations, portfolio management services, non-use and cancellation, transfer, licensing and collaboration arrangements in relation to a wide range of industries, conflict-handling and litigation. Kvale conduct detailed M&A due diligence and have considerable experience of drafting and negotiating contracts such as global cross-licensing and co-existence agreements.

Authors

Marie Vaale-Hallberg is one of Kvale's specialised IP partners, working with trade mark and marketing law matters in particular. She works with major international and national brands, both with enforcement and prosecution as well as undertaking contractual work. Marie has a strong commercial focus and offers detailed insight into the Norwegian retail market, and she stands out for her particular knowledge of regulatory law within the food and beverages sector; Marie is a member of Food Lawyers Network. She has broad IP judicial practice, involving research and development agreements, protection and enforcement of trade marks, patents and designs, IP strategies and marketing law. She is frequently invited to lecture on IP and other legal subjects in Norway and abroad.

Lars Trygve Jenssen started Kvale's IP department in 2004 and has played a central role in building it into today's highly regarded practice. A partner at the firm, he is a highly experienced intellectual property lawyer and trusted adviser, particularly within the fields of trade marks, copyright, IT/digitalisation and licensing. Lars actively leads trade-mark work for a range of top-tier clients such as Telia, L'Occitane, Land Rover Jaguar, Dixons Phonehouse and The Norwegian National Museum. He also has considerable experience with corporate law and M&A, often advising companies in the IP/TMT sectors.

Kaia Bugge Fougner is a senior lawyer who has specialised in intellectual property law and marketing law for over ten years. She has a broad marketing and IP law practice, including copyright, protection and enforcement of trade marks and design rights, the development of IP strategies and drafting different types of contracts. Kaia has extensive trade-mark experience from working not only for different law firms, but also for the Norwegian Board of Appeal for Industrial Property Rights (KFIR); she worked in KFIR as a trade-mark expert, making decisions concerning trade marks and company names. Kaia has also worked several years as an in-house lawyer for a multinational corporation, taking care of all Norwegian legal issues, including in particular contract, trade-mark and marketing matters. Kaia speaks regularly at conferences and seminars, has served as an external examiner at the University of Oslo and the University of Bergen, and is the author of several publications.

Tarje Neergaard joined Kvale as an associate in 2017. He specialises in intellectual property law and data protection law. Although his key focus is trade-mark matters, he also shows a keen interest in patent infringement cases, as well as in preparing compliance standards and contracts regulating the rights of commercial actors to intellectual property. He is a member of the Norwegian Bar Association. Prior to joining the firm, he was situated at the Fridtjof Nansen Institute working on a book project based on his Master's thesis entitled Human Genetic Resources as Property.

Contributed by Kvale Advokatfirma DA ***Authors:*** Marie Vaale-Hallberg, Lars Trygve Jenssen, Kaia Bugge Fougner, Tarje Neergaard

1. Types of Trade Marks & Registration

1.1 Types of Trade Marks

The Norwegian Trademarks Act of 26 March 2010, in principle, gives protection to all signs capable of distinguishing an entity's goods or services from others, such as words (including slogans), numbers, figures and images, trade dress and packaging.

The Norwegian Trademark Act establishes that "collective trade marks" may be protected, that is, trade marks pertaining to a society or organisation to be used by its members. A sub-category of the "collective trade mark" is the so-called guarantee or certification mark, which is used by agencies, foundations, companies or other associations to demonstrate that certain standards or controls to which the marks relate are met (see section 1, first and second para and section 2, first para).

1.2 Trade-Mark Rights

The Norwegian Trademark Act establishes the so-called "two-track" system by which protection can be obtained by registration and/or by use.

Applications are sent to the Norwegian Industrial Property Office ("NIPO") and can be either national or international, asserting the Madrid System.

A trade mark is established by use when and for as long as it is well known in the circle of trade in Norway for the relevant goods and/or services as someone's sign. Obtaining exclusivity without registration is more time- and cost-efficient, but less predictable in terms of protection. In addition, the latter type only provides protection in the geographical area where the trade mark is used or branded, etc. One would therefore be advised to register the trade mark.

Both types of protection have their legal basis in section 3.

1.3 Standards for Registering

The legal requirements for registering different types of marks are the same.

1.4 Trade-Mark Register

Norway has a trade-mark register, which is publicly available.

The NIPO is established as the governing body responsible for registering all registrable industrial rights, including trade marks. Every national and international trade-mark application that designates Norway may be found online in the NIPO's database. Applications leading to registrations are registered by the NIPO in the Norwegian Trademark Register ("det norske varemerkeregisteret") and then published in the Norwegian Official Trademarks Gazette ("Norske varemerketidende") (see section 22, first para).

1.5 Types of Registers

The Norwegian legal system does not operate with different types of registers, eg, principal and supplemental registers.

1.6 Searching for Prior Trade Marks

Although there is no legal requirement to do so, performing a search in the NIPO's registers as well as checking whether there are confusingly similar or identical brands in use is recommended and considered normal practice.

1.7 Registration Requirements

A trade mark may be registered if it is capable of being represented graphically, provided that such signs are capable of distinguishing the goods or services of one undertaking from those of other undertakings.

Marks that merely state the nature or specific properties of the goods or services are not eligible for trade-mark registration; descriptive marks, such as "rye bread" for bread or "dark chocolate" for chocolate, are therefore ineligible for registration (see section 2, cf. section 14).

1.8 Registering a Trade Mark

An exclusive right to a trade mark may be acquired by any natural or legal person as a distinctive sign for goods or services in an industrial or commercial undertaking. This applies to both registered and unregistered trade marks (see section 1, first and second para).

1.9 Registering Signs

Any sign capable of distinguishing the goods or services of one undertaking from those of another may constitute a trade mark. The term "sign" shall be interpreted widely, thus including numerals, figures, pictures, the shape or get-up of the goods, the packaging, words and combinations of words, sounds, colours and scents, insofar as the sign may be graphically presented. Sounds, colours and scents are therefore not ineligible for trade-mark protection per se, but the requirement related to graphical presentation will, in many cases, constitute an obstacle. A relevant example to this end is the decision by the Norwegian Supreme Court (HR-2017-2356-A) that addressed whether a colour could be established as a trade mark by use. The Supreme Court confirmed that a colour may constitute a mark, as it may be graphically presented. However, the condition to establish the trade mark by use was not met, as the producer of the pharmaceutical had used several different nuances of the colour, which suggested that the incorporation of the nuance as a trade mark was undeliberate (see sections 2 and 14 of the Trademark Act).

1.10 Other Rights to Signs

Norwegian legislation recognises other rights to signs or source-identifiers besides trade marks, such as rights to company names, trade names and domain names.

Contributed by Kvale Advokatfirma DA **Authors:** Marie Vaale-Hallberg, Lars Trygve Jenssen, Kaia Bugge Fougner, Tarje Neergaard

The rights to company names and secondary trade names are outlined in the Company Name Register Act. Any company name that is not identical to another company name already registered or in the process of being registered may be registered at the Brønnøysund Register Centre ("Brønnøysund registeret"). In order for the company name to be protected against confusingly similar trade marks, it must meet the same requirements of distinctiveness as trade marks. Additional legal protection may be provided by the Marketing Control Act and the posed requirement of "good business practice" in businesses' transactions with one another (see section 1, cf section 8).

The rights to secondary trade names are established by use, which is considered to be when and for as long as it is well-known as someone's trade name in the circle of trade in Norway for the relevant goods and services (see the Company Name Register Act section 1-1, third para).

There are currently no Norwegian laws that regulate rights to domain names specifically. Domain names under the domain ".no" are registered at the Norwegian service for registration of internet domain names ("Norid") in accordance with Norid's guidelines. According to appendix H of said guidelines, the rights-holder of a trade mark or a company name may, in the event of conflict, demand that Norid deletes or transfers conflicting domain names under the domain ".no".

Applications for company names, domain names and trade names must be filed separately as the governing bodies have different areas of competence and expertise in terms of registration.

1.11 Registration Procedure

Trade-mark applications may be filed online via the public service centre "altinn.no", or via paper application. If the trade-mark application is to be filed online, the applicant must have a Norwegian national identity number. All trade-mark applications will be received and processed by the NIPO.

The application must include the name and address of the applicant, a representation of the trade mark, and a list of the goods or services in respect of which the registration is requested; hence, multi-class applications are allowed (see section 12, second para).

There is an application fee when applying for a trade mark, and the NIPO will send an invoice to the applicant for the fee, which is currently NOK2,900 (approximately EUR300) and covers registration for up to three classes. Each extra class incurs an additional fee, currently at the rate of NOK750 (approximately EUR80). The same system applies to collective marks, but the rates are higher.

If the payable fee is not paid in due time, the applicant may risk dismissal of the application or registration (see section 12, third para).

During the case proceedings, the NIPO will examine whether there are any obstacles to the registration. Should such obstacles be observed, the applicant will be informed within three to six months of the filing of the application. The letter received by the applicant from the NIPO constitutes a so-called written opinion, whereinafter the applicant shall be given the possibility to respond in writing or during oral proceedings if requested (see section 23).

If the trade mark is not approved for registration, the applicant may choose to pursue the decision at the Norwegian Board of Appeal for Industrial Property Rights ("KFIR"). Such action must be made no later than two months after the NIPO's decision. See section 49.

Should the KFIR uphold the NIPO's decision, the applicant may pursue the matter in court (see section 52).

1.12 Use in Commerce

There are no formal requirements under Norwegian law for an application to demonstrate or document use in commerce of a trade mark. If the trade mark lacks distinctiveness, however, the NIPO may require the applicant to provide documentation proving acquired distinctiveness through use.

1.13 Registration of Series Marks

The Norwegian system does not allow the registration of series marks. If the applicant wishes to register multiple trade marks at the same time, they must do so by filing several applications, ie, one for each trade mark. The same applies if the applicant wishes to register multiple variations of the same mark.

1.14 Length of Registration Process

Assuming the application does not contain errors or deficiencies, and that the NIPO finds no obstacles in terms of being able to register the trade mark, registration will normally occur within three to six months from the time of filing.

The applicant does not need representation during the application and registration procedure. Should the applicant choose to seek representation, as would be advised, such representation for a single word mark in one class would cost the applicant approximately NOK6,000 (approximately EUR600), but the prices vary considerably.

1.15 Grounds for Refusal

According to section 14, a trade mark cannot be registered if it exclusively or with only insignificant changes or additions consists of signs or indications that:

- indicate the kind, quality, quantity, intended purpose, value or geographical origin of the goods or services, the time of production of the goods or the rendering of the services or other characteristics of the goods or services; or
- constitute customary designations for the goods or services according to normal linguistic usage or loyal, established business practice.

Section 15 states that a mark cannot be registered if it:

- is contrary to law or public order, or liable to cause offence;
- is liable to deceive, for example in respect of the nature, quality or geographical origin of the goods or services;
- contains unauthorised escutcheons or other signs covered by Section 165, letter b and Section 166 of the Norwegian Penal Code, or a national flag or anything that is liable to be understood as a sign or flag; or
- for wine and spirits, consists of or contains anything that is liable to be understood as a geographical indication of origin, unless the geographical origin of the goods is in accordance with the indication.

Section 16 states that a mark cannot be registered in the following circumstances, without the consent of the relevant owner:

- use of the trade mark would infringe the right of another in this country to a trade mark or business name or another business sign;
- the trade mark is liable to be confused with a trade mark, business name or other business sign that someone else started to use before the applicant as a distinctive sign for goods or services and is still using, and the applicant was aware of this use when the application for registration was filed, in such a way that the filing shall be considered to have taken place in conflict with honest practices in industrial or commercial matters;
- the trade mark contains something that is liable to be perceived as another person's name, stage name or portrait, unless it obviously refers to a person who is long dead;
- the trade mark contains something that is liable to be perceived as the distinctive title of another's protected creative or intellectual work, or infringes another's right in Norway to a creative or intellectual work or photography or design; or
- the trade mark infringes another's right in Norway to a designation protected in regulations pursuant to Act No 6 of 17 June 1932 on Quality Control of Agricultural Goods, etc. or Act No 124 of 19 December 2003 on Food Production and Food Safety, etc.

These are regarded as absolute grounds for refusal.

1.16 Process for Overcoming Objections

The NIPO will send a letter to the applicant within three to six months (written opinion) concerning either the approval of an application for registration or an assessment of the obstacles hindering approval. In the written reply or during the oral proceedings, the applicant can claim acquired distinctiveness through use, etc. Additional letters may be exchanged thereafter until the NIPO finds that the application is ready for a final assessment.

In the event of an older registration that constitutes a hindrance for registration but has not been in use during the preceding five years, the applicant may initiate a cancellation process. Pending the outcome of the cancellation process, the NIPO will normally place the application process on hold (see section 37).

Another way to overcome a registration obstacle due to an older mark is to provide a confirmation from the older right-holder that the trade marks may co-exist (see section 16).

1.17 Consideration of Prior Rights

The NIPO shall ensure that there are no registered trade marks or applications for registration that constitute obstacles to the registration of the trade mark being applied for, but does not examine whether there are other obstacles that may prevent registration, unless it has been made aware of these obstacles. Potential obstacles that are not examined on the NIPO's own initiative are, inter alia, company names, trade names, unregistered trade marks, other persons' names, stage names, portraits, titles of protected creative or intellectual work, photographs, designs or protected designations (see section 20).

1.18 Third-Party Rights

Third parties have the right to participate during the registration process by filing protests prior to the registration. There is no requirement for any sort of commercial interest when protesting a trade-mark application. A protest will typically be filed by a third party who disapproves of the potential registration of a descriptive word that should be non-exclusive and available to everyone, or by a third party holding the rights to a trade mark that is liable to be confused with a trade mark that is subject to registration.

If a third party wishes to protest prior to the registration of the application for a trade mark, they should file an informal written protest to the NIPO, including the grounds for the protest. Informal protests do not grant the third party the rights of a party to a case, as they lack a formal legal basis in Norwegian legislation. However, there is nothing to hinder the NIPO taking the protest into consideration (for the formal opposition procedure, see below).

1.19 Revoke, Change, Amend or Correct an Application

The application for a trade mark can always be revoked by the applicant. As long as the overall impression of the trade mark stays the same, insignificant/insubstantial changes may be made to a trade mark for which an application has been filed for registration (see section 13, first para).

Furthermore, and according to section 13, second para, the applicant may also choose to limit the list of goods or services for which application is made for registration of a trade mark, thus allowing the applicant to revoke an application in part if they so choose.

1.20 Assigning an Application or Granting a Licence

Norwegian legislation does not restrict either transferral of rights or licensing during the application process; parties are free to enter into such agreements if they so desire.

1.21 Remedies Against the Trade Mark Office

If the registration of a trade mark has been denied by the NIPO, the applicant may choose to pursue the decision at the KFIR. Such action must be made no later than two months after the NIPO's decision (see section 49, first para and section 50, first para).

Should the KFIR uphold the decision of the NIPO, the applicant may pursue the matter in court (see section 52).

1.22 Use of a Trade Mark

There is no requirement in the Norwegian legal system for an applicant to make use of its mark in commerce before the registration is issued.

1.23 Dividing a Trade Mark

An applicant may request that the application is divided into two or more applications. A split is particularly relevant when it is not possible to register the application for certain goods on the list, etc (see section 82 and the appurtenant regulation sections 17 ff).

1.24 Length of Term of Protection

The protection provided by registration is ten years from the application date and, insofar as the trade-mark owner has requested a renewal, ten years from the expiry of the previous period. There are no limitations on how many times a trade mark can be renewed.

The request for renewal must be filed in writing no earlier than one year before and no later than six months after the expiry of the registration period (see sections 32 and 33).

1.25 Requirements for an Exhaustion

In Norway, and in accordance with 2008/95/EC, a trade-mark right is exhausted when the trade-mark owner – or another party with the owner's consent – has consented to put goods under a certain trade mark on the market within the EU/EEA. Consequently, a trade-mark owner cannot prevent parallel import of its goods from a country within the EU/EEA if they have already consented to put their goods under a certain trade mark on that market. This does not apply, however, if the owner of the trade mark has legitimate reasons to oppose further commercialisation of the goods, for example if the condition of the goods has changed or been impaired after they were put on the market; in the latter situation, re-packaging may therefore be prohibited (see the Trademarks Act section 6). As Norway is part of the EEA Agreement, however, the re-packaging of products – which may be a prerequisite to meet different national requirements, as is often the case for pharmaceuticals – cannot be prohibited if it is necessary to obtain effective access to the relevant market.

1.26 Participation in the Madrid System

An applicant that aims to obtain an international trade-mark registration can assert the Madrid System, to which Norway is party, by applying to the NIPO and designating the respective countries in the application.

In order to be eligible to file an international application, the applicant must have filed for or previously been granted registration of a trade mark in Norway. The applicant must also be either a Norwegian citizen, domiciled in Norway, or operating an industrial or commercial establishment in Norway.

The application shall be filed in English and include the following information:

- the name and address of the applicant;
- the numbers and dates of the Norwegian trade-mark registrations or applications on which the international registration is to be based;
- a representation of the trade mark;
- a list of the goods or services for which the trade mark is to be registered; and
- a list of the designated countries or international organisations for which registration is requested (see sections 66 and 67 of the Trademarks Act).

1.27 Consequences for Providing Incorrect Information

The NIPO will notify an applicant if they provide the NIPO with incorrect or insufficient information that hinders the registration of an applied trade mark. The applicant shall be given a reasonable time limit to respond and, if possible, remedy the deficiencies.

The NIPO may cancel the registration in part or in full if a person has filed an opposition in accordance with section 26, or if a party with a legal interest has required an administrative review in accordance with section 40. The grounds for filing an opposition or requesting a revocation/cancellation will typically be if the application and/or registration builds on incorrect information.

The NIPO may also cancel the registration on its own initiative, but only if the registration of a trade mark, a renewal or the alteration of a registration has taken place by obvious mistake (see section 45, first para).

Wrongful acts, such as forgery of a trade-mark owner's consent, etc, may be reported to the authorities, whereinafter the applicant may be subject to criminal liability.

1.28 Updating or Refreshing a Design Mark

As is the case for other trade marks, design marks are eligible for updates or refreshments, as long as the overall impression stays the same. Insignificant/insubstantial changes are therefore allowed without having to file a new application for registration (see section 13, first para).

1.29 Denotation

Symbols denoting that a mark is registered have no legal status in Norway, although many trade-mark holders have chosen to use these symbols on the Norwegian market for practical purposes, eg, if multinational packages are used, or for protective purposes.

2. Assignment and Licensing

2.1 Assignment Requirements or Restrictions

Trade marks, trade names and company names may be transferred under the basic principles of Norwegian contract law, either alone or together with the company to which the trade mark is registered. If a company changes ownership, its trade marks and trade names are transferred alongside the company, unless otherwise agreed (see sections 53, first and second para of the Trademarks Act and 4-3 of the Company Name Register Act). International trade-mark registrations can also be assigned. Unlike the assignment of a right to a national trade-mark registration, assignment of a right to an international trade-mark registration requires notification to the International Bureau (see section 72, fourth para of the Trademarks Act).

Company names may be transferred alongside the company's operations or substantial parts of the operations. If the company or a substantial part of the company is transferred, the right to the company name will be transferred to the new owner, unless otherwise agreed. If the company holds the name of the transferee, the right to the company name will only be transferred alongside the company if there is an explicit agreement between the parties (see section 4-1 of the Company Name Register Act).

2.2 Procedure for Assigning a Trade Mark

No standard procedures apply to the assignment of a trade mark, so an assignment may, in principle, be completed in both oral and written form. Should the parties wish for the assignment to be registered by the NIPO and taken into the Norwegian Trademark Register, which is the preferred alternative, the assignment must be done in writing and undersigned by both parties.

2.3 Registering or Recording the Assignment

The parties may agree to register the assignment of a registered trade mark in the trade-mark register, but there is no obligation to do so, unless one of the parties requests such recording (see section 56, second para).

The new owner carries the burden of proof as to whether the assignment/transfer has actually taken place. The person that is registered as the owner will, at any time, carry the risk in case of legal proceedings concerning the trade mark, eg related to a trade-mark infringement claim (see section 56, first para).

2.4 Trade Marks and Security

A trade mark can constitute a non-possessory security interest for a debt, a distraint to cover a debt past due or, in the event of bankruptcy, part of the satisfaction of a claim.

In order for a trade mark to constitute a security interest, a non-possessory mortgage must be created. To obtain legal protection, the action must be registered on either of the parties' section sheets in the Movables register (see sections 3-4 and 3-6 of the Mortgage Act).

If a creditor obtains a security interest created by distraint levied by the seizure authorities, the creditor must be entered on the distrainee's sheet in the movable register in order to obtain legal protection for the security interest (see section 5-9 of the Mortgage Act).

If a creditor wishes to seek satisfaction in a trade mark in the event of a bankruptcy, the trade mark in question must belong to the debtor and have a financial value, ie, be eligible to be converted into money (see section 2-2 of the Satisfaction of Claims Act).

2.5 Licensing Requirements or Restrictions

It is possible to license a trade mark in the Norwegian legal system. A licence may be assigned from A to B as a consequence of the trade-mark owner's right of freedom to contract with another party, ie a licensee/contracting party. As part of the contract, the contracting party may use the trade mark in an industrial or commercial setting but may not license their right further, unless this has been agreed upon by the parties to the licence agreement (see section 54 of the Trademarks Act).

Registration and approval from the NIPO is not an absolute requirement but, if requested by either of the parties, the assignment of the registered trade mark shall be entered in the register and published in the same manner as applied to assignments (see section 56, second para).

The contracting parties may regulate the use of the trade mark (licence) via the licence agreement. The trade-mark owner may invoke certain actions if the licensee fails to comply with the following provisions of the licence agreement:

- the duration of the licence;
- the form in which the trade mark may be used, and the goods or services for which it may be used;
- the geographical territory in which the trade mark may be used; or

the quality of the goods or services for which the trade mark may be used (see section 54, second para).

Although the Trademarks Act does not explicitly regulate different types of licence agreements, it is stressed in the preliminary works that 2008/95/EC ("Directive") applies in a Norwegian context. Thus, a licence may be exclusive and/or non-exclusive, cf Article 8 of the Directive.

There is generally nothing to prevent the parties agreeing upon the terms and conditions regulating the licence agreement, as they consider appropriate, but competition law may be asserted if the agreement aims to prevent, restrict or distort competition, eg, by fixed pricing or market-sharing. The parties to the licence agreement would therefore be advised to consider the principles relating to competition law before preparing and carrying out the agreement (see section 10 of the Competition Act).

2.6 Procedure for Licensing a Trade Mark

The contracting parties – ie, the owner and the licensee – will establish the rules and principles relating to the use of the trade mark in the licence agreement. The contract shall be in writing if any of the parties requires it to be so, although such requirement only applies if the licence is to be registered in the trade-mark register.

The rules and principles carried out in the agreement are subject to revision under the applicable principles in Norwegian contract law.

2.7 Registering or Recording the Licence

Norwegian legislation does not require registration of the licence agreement at the NIPO, but registration is possible.

However, insofar as the licence agreement has not been registered, the trade-mark owner will always run the risk of legal proceedings concerning the trade mark, as well as receiving any notifications relating to the trade mark from the NIPO (see section 56).

2.8 Reasons to Deny Granting a Perpetual Licence

It is possible to grant a perpetual licence in the Norwegian legal system. The trade mark must be renewed every ten years, but there are no limitations on how many times it can be renewed.

3. Opposition Procedure

3.1 Legal Grounds and Timeframes

The registration of a trade mark can be opposed by a third party if it:

- lacks distinctiveness as a sign for the relevant goods or services, or is incapable of being represented graphically;
- conflicts with public interests;
- conflicts with existing rights, without the consent of the rights-holder; or
- has been registered with the wrong person (see the Trademarks Act sections 14, 15, 16 and 21).

The opposition must be filed no later than three months after the day of publication in the Norwegian Official Trademarks Gazette (see section 26, first para).

3.2 Filing an Opposition

Anyone may file an opposition to the registration of a trade mark. In accordance with section 26 of the Trademarks Act, an opposition shall be filed in writing and include the following information:

- the name and address of the person filing the opposition;
- a specification of the registration to which the opposition applies;
- the grounds on which the opposition is based; and
- necessary documentation of circumstances invoked in support of the opposition.

The opponent does not need to be represented by an attorney, but it is advisable in most cases and particularly when the opposition relates to the material requirements set out in the Trademark Act, such as distinctiveness and graphical reproduction.

Contributed by Kvale Advokatfirma DA **Authors:** Marie Vaale-Hallberg, Lars Trygve Jenssen, Kaia Bugge Fougner, Tarje Neergaard

Depending on the complexity of the case, average office fees and attorney fees may be in the range of NOK5,000-15,000 in less complex cases, and between NOK50,000 and NOK100,000 in more complex cases.

3.3 Opposition Procedure

Official objections may be filed no later than three months after the trade mark has been approved for registration and published in the Norwegian Official Trademark Gazette (see section 26).

As soon as possible after the opposition procedure has commenced, the applicant shall receive a notice from the NIPO explaining why the registration has been opposed by the third party. The applicant will then be given the opportunity to contradict the grounds on which the opposition is based. The NIPO shall only consider factors invoked in the opposition procedure (see section 27). Once the NIPO has sufficient information available, it shall make a decision on the matter within two months.

If the NIPO finds that the trade mark was registered in contravention of sections 14, 15 and 16, and the obstacles to register the trade mark still exist, the registration of the trademark shall be cancelled in full or in part. If there are no obstacles to registering the trade mark, however, or if such obstacles no longer exist, the opposition shall be dismissed. The owner and the opponent shall then receive a notification from the NIPO regarding the outcome of the opposition case (see section 29).

The decision in an opposition case may be appealed to the KFIR. The appeal must be sent within two months of the NIPO's decision, and may take six to twelve months for the KFIR to make a final decision (see section 49, second para, and section 50, first para).

The outcome shall be recorded in the Trademark Register (not to be confused with the Norwegian Official Trademarks Gazette) and a notice thereof published (see section 29 of the Trademarks Act).

4. Initiating a Lawsuit

4.1 Actions to Pursue Infringement

The owner of a registered or unregistered trade mark may initiate legal proceedings if another party has infringed, aided and abetted thereto, or given grounds to fear that they will infringe the owner's rights pursuant to the Trademarks Act. Prior to the proceedings, the owner of a trade mark will typically send a cease-and-desist letter to the alleged infringer, and may initiate legal proceedings if the alleged infringer disregards the warning letter. Legal proceedings will typically be initiated by filing a request for a preliminary injunction, followed by a writ of summons initiating the main case. In the writ of summons, the trade-mark owner may request that the court establishes a prohibition against the aforementioned acts, including recalling/removing the goods from commercial channels, destroying or handing over the goods to the trade-mark owner, and/or claiming compensation and damages for the (potential) infringing act.

4.2 Initiating Infringement Proceedings

Infringement proceedings are initiated before a district court in the first instance, but the Norwegian legal system distinguishes between registered and unregistered trademarks in terms of in which district court the proceedings shall be brought.

The Oslo District Court is the mandatory legal venue in the first instance for registered trade marks, while unregistered trade marks follow the rules of ordinary venue. An action concerning the latter may therefore be filed with the district court of the ordinary venue of the defendant, or with the district court where the business enterprise's head office is located according to the Register of Business Enterprises (see section 62 of the Trademarks Act and section 4-4, first and third para of the Dispute Act).

4.3 Declaratory Judgment Proceedings

A party with a legal interest may initiate legal proceedings concerning, inter alia, a declaratory judgement. This requirement will be met as soon as an infringement is alleged. The same action may also be taken as a counter claim in an already existing infringement case.

4.4 Jurisdiction of Courts

If the decision from the NIPO has been brought before the KFIR pursuant to an appeal, and the KFIR has handed down a decision, the decision may be appealed to the Oslo District Court (see section 52 of the Trademarks Act). The Oslo District Court is also the mandatory legal venue of first instance for any actions concerning invalidity, deletion or infringement of a registered trade mark, as well as for cases concerning applicants and trade-mark owners who are not domiciled in Norway (see section 62).

All cases decided by the Oslo District Court shall have mandatory legal venue at the Borgarting Court of Appeal in Oslo.

The rules of ordinary venue apply for trade-mark cases that are not subject to section 62. The Norwegian Supreme Court shall have the final say in any and all cases, subject to the case being admitted by the Supreme Court's Appeals Committee. The Committee considers if the appeal concerns issues whose significance extends beyond the scope of the current case, or if it is important for other reasons that the case is determined by the Supreme Court (see section 30-4, first para of the Dispute Act).

Contributed by Kvale Advokatfirma DA ***Authors:*** Marie Vaale-Hallberg, Lars Trygve Jenssen, Kaia Bugge Fougner, Tarje Neergaard

4.5 Prerequisites to Filing a Lawsuit

It is required to send a notice including information about the claim and the basis for the claim, among other details (see sections 5-2, first para and 1-3 of the Dispute Act). However, the consequence of not sending such a notice is limited to considerations concerning costs, which may be reduced or not awarded if a notice has not been sent.

It is common practice to send a cease-and-desist letter, which is typically made out so that it fulfils the requirements of section 5-2.

4.6 Representation for Parties

The parties in trade-mark litigation are not obliged to have a lawyer, although the court may order that the party be represented by counsel if said party is unable to present the case in a comprehensible manner (see sections 3-1 and 3-2 of the Dispute Act).

4.7 Interim or Preliminary Injunctions

The trade-mark owner and/or licensee, depending on the licence agreement, may seek a preliminary injunction by filing a motion to the alleged infringer's ordinary venue. As trade-mark matters usually follow the Trademark Act's special provisions for legal venue, which establish the Oslo District Court as the mandatory legal venue, the ordinary rules of legal venue represent an exception from the provisions normally applied in trade-mark matters. If the defendant files a counterclaim prior to the preliminary injunction proceedings (eg, by claiming that the trade mark is invalid), the request for a preliminary injunction will normally constitute part of the main case proceeded before the Oslo District Court (for the special provisions for legal venue, see pt. 4.4.)

In order to obtain a preliminary injunction, the owner/licensee must first substantiate a claim by proving, on a balance of probabilities, that the plaintiff will prevail with the claim in a regular main case. Secondly, the plaintiff must substantiate the grounds for an injunction either by demonstrating that the defendant's conduct has made it necessary to secure the claim provisionally because the action or execution of the claim stands at risk of being considerably impeded, or by substantiating the need for a temporary arrangement in order to avert considerable future loss or inconvenience. The first option is considered to be the most practical in infringement cases.

When filing a motion for a preliminary injunction, the plaintiff may request that the court makes an ex parte decision, wherein the plaintiff must explain the reasons the case should be decided immediately. If the court finds these grounds present, it will give a decision ex parte and with due haste. If the court decides to grant the preliminary injunction ex parte, the defendant may demand a subsequent oral hearing to attempt to reverse the decision. Before the oral hearing, the Court will arrange for written pleadings to be exchanged between the parties.

If an ex parte decision has not been requested, or if the court does not decide to grant such request, the court will arrange for written pleadings to be exchanged between the parties and summon them to an oral hearing, normally within two to three weeks. After the oral hearing, the court will grant or deny the request in due course (see chapters 32 and 34 of the Dispute Act).

The decision may be appealed to a court of appeal, subject to the ordinary rules of legal venue. As a main rule, the court of appeal will undertake written case handling only, unless an oral hearing is required to ensure sound and fair legal proceedings (see section 29-15 of the Dispute Act). In trade-mark matters, as in most others, the main rule of written proceedings is normally applied in the appeal court.

4.8 Protection for Potential Defendant

In addition to disputing and or making counterclaims concerning both the likelihood of the plaintiff's stated claim and the stated reason for an injunction, a defendant may – as a final defence – claim that an injunction is disproportionate. The defendant may also demand that the plaintiff provides security as a prerequisite for an injunction.

Administrative reviews cannot be initiated if a counterclaim concerning invalidity and non-infringement has been brought but not yet finally decided. If the counterclaim is brought after the NIPO has initiated the administrative review, the NIPO shall await further procedure on the matter until the legal proceedings have been finally decided.

If the defendant has filed an application for an administrative review, they may not, however, bring a counterclaim to the court, nor may a defendant who has previously brought a counterclaim to court file an application for an administrative review if the application concerns the same matter. The defendant must therefore choose which of the processes is most suitable to safeguard their interests (see section 41 of the Trademarks Act).

4.9 Obtaining Information and Evidence

There are legal rules and mechanisms in the Norwegian legal system concerning disclosure and discovery.

If a party gives notice of a claim or contests a notified claim, the party shall provide information about important documents and evidence which they cannot expect the opposite party to be familiar with. The parties also have a duty of truth and disclosure, as well as a duty to testify and give evidence during the procedure before the court.

The duty to give evidence before proceedings have been initiated and during the proceedings applies irrespective of which of the parties the evidence favours (see the Dispute Act sections 5-3, first para, 21-4 and 21-5).

Any one person, including third parties, who has factual information of relevance to the trade-mark matter shall attend as a witness at a court hearing following a summons (see section 24-1).

Section 28 A-1, first para, is particularly relevant to trade-mark matters: when there is reasonable cause to believe that infringement has been made and the owner of the trade mark has petitioned the court, the court may instruct the alleged infringer to inform of the source of origin and the supply network for the goods and services to which the infringement relates. Such information may also be required from a party who has aided and abetted, been in possession of an infringing good or used/performed an infringing service as part of a business activity, who has been pointed out by anyone of the aforementioned parties, or who has made preparations to conduct an infringing activity.

4.10 Initial Pleading Standards

An action concerning trade-mark proceedings is started by submitting a writ of summons to the court, including the claim that is being made, the outcome the trade-mark owner is requesting by way of judgment, the factual and legal grounds upon which the claim is based, and the evidence that will be presented. Once filed, the court will set a date for the defendant to reply, and will thereafter set deadlines for further pleadings, until a final date for a final pleading is set, which is normally three weeks before the oral hearing.

4.11 Representative or Collective Actions

The Norwegian legal system does allow for both representative and collective actions, although they are uncommon in relation to trade marks. In order to bring a collective action, several parties must have claims or obligations whose factual or legal basis is identical or substantially similar and can be heard by a court with the same composition and substantially pursuant to the same procedural rules. In addition, the class procedure must be the most appropriate way of dealing with the claims and enable the nomination of a class representative. It is difficult to imagine a situation where this is done.

Another potential approach is the joinder of claims and actions, or the consolidation of cases, which enables two or more parties to act as claimants in one single action or to join the hearing of the separate cases insofar as certain requirements are met (see sections 15-2, second para, and 15-6 of the Dispute Act).

4.12 Restrictions on Trade-Mark Owners

There are no rules in Norwegian trade-mark law concerning restrictions on the trade-mark owner asserting their rights against others.

5. Infringement

5.1 Action for Infringement

An infringement action can be filed by any party with a legal interest, which essentially excludes any party who is not the owner of or a licensee to the trade mark (or a representative of either). As the right of action is regulated by the freedom of contract between the contracting parties, the owner may preclude the licensee's possibility of bringing legal proceedings concerning trade-mark infringement (see section 63 first para of the Trademark Act).

For legal actions against infringements of an unregistered trade mark, the owner or licensee must rely on proving that the trade mark has been established through use when bringing an action to court. If and when it is finally registered, a pending trade mark will have priority from the priority date, and all claims for infringement and damages will be effective from such date.

5.2 Signs and Infringement

In order to succeed on a claim for trade-mark infringement, the plaintiff must demonstrate that it owns a valid mark and that the defendant has used the mark or a similar mark in commerce in a manner that is likely to confuse consumers as to the origin or sponsorship of the goods or services offered in connection with the mark. The main issues in considering the likelihood of confusion are the similarities of the marks (strength of trade-mark elements key) and the proximity or similarities of the goods and services in question.

5.3 Use of a Sign by Defendant

An infringement requires use as a mark.

5.4 Defences Against Infringement

The primary defences are lack of danger of confusion, ie, lack of trade-mark similarity and goods and services similarity.

The alleged infringer may also make an invalidity objection, claiming that the trade mark is not valid due to lack of priority or distinctiveness, or that it has been subject to non-use or has been used by the owner in bad faith. Parody, satire, etc, are also possible, if such factors are present.

5.5 Role of Experts and/or Surveys

Expert witnesses may be appointed by a party or by the court (see section 25-2 of the Dispute Act). In the Norwegian legal system, the courts shall determine the case based on a free evaluation of evidence, so the weight of the expert opinion will depend on credibility, etc, as proven before the court, but it can be important.

Surveys are increasingly used to document claims in trade-mark matters, and will either substantiate that the mark has acquired distinctiveness through use or that the mark is well known. Although surveys shall be taken into consideration by the courts, there is some scepticism regarding the importance attached to them. The weight of the survey will, among other things, depend on how the questions of the survey are formulated.

5.6 Administrative or Criminal Offence

Serious trade-mark infringements, primarily counterfeiting, can constitute a criminal offence subject to imprisonment. If an infringer is to be sentenced to imprisonment, the proceedings must be public, ie, pursued by the prosecution authority. If the prosecution authority withdraws the case or decides not to pursue, the proceedings may be subject to private prosecution. As far as is known, the Norwegian courts' authority to penalise with imprisonment has not been used.

5.7 Custom Seizures

The Norwegian legal system provides for customs seizure of counterfeits and parallel imports. Relevant provisions are found under the Norwegian Act on Customs Duties and Movement of Goods (Customs Act), where it is stated that the customs authorities may – notwithstanding the duty of confidentiality – notify the trade-mark owner in cases of reasoned suspicion that imported or exported goods that are subject to control by the customs authorities will constitute a violation of a trade-mark right. The customs authorities are allowed to detain the goods for up to ten business days from the date the notice was given (see section 15-1). The above-mentioned rule does not apply to private import and/or export.

Furthermore, provided that the general requirements to request a temporary injunction under the Dispute Act are fulfilled, the court may order a temporary injunction against the recipient and decide that the customs authorities shall detain the goods as long as the import or export of the goods constitutes an infringement of the trade mark. The court may also make such an order if the proprietor of the goods is unknown. According to the Customs Act, the courts shall notify the customs authorities of any preliminary order.

6. Revocation/Cancellation

6.1 Remedies and Reasons

There are numerous grounds to revoke/cancel the registration of a trade mark in Norway, eg if the general conditions of registration are not met or if the trade mark conflicts with public interests or, where no consent has been given, with the rights of others. The trade mark may also be revoked/cancelled if it has become contrary to public order or is liable to cause offence, if it has become the general designation due to the owner's passivity, if it has become liable to deceive in respect of the kind, quality or geographical origin, if it has not been in actual use for five years after the registration, or if the use of the trade mark has been discontinued for five years.

Exemptions may, however, apply (see sections 35, 36 and 37).

In addition, if a registration of a trade mark, a renewal or an alteration of a registration has taken place by obvious mistake, the NIPO may cancel the registration in part or in full on its own initiative (see section 45, first para).

6.2 Trade Mark Office and Civil Courts

A revocation/cancellation action can be brought before the NIPO with a request for an administrative review under sections 35, 36 and 37. Such request may be made by anyone with a legal interest when the opposition time limit has expired and any opposition cases have been settled with a final decision (see sections 39 and 40).

A revocation/cancellation action can also be brought before the court, although only a party with a legal interest – ie, a trade-mark owner or licensee (or representative) – may bring such action. Should the owner or the licensee choose to bring a legal action, a notification shall be given to the NIPO and by registered post to each licensee with an address entered into the Trademark Register (see sections 63 and 64).

6.3 Statutory Limitation or Time Period

There is no statutory limitation or time period within which to file revocation/cancellation actions.

6.4 Initiation of Revocation/Cancellation Proceeding

Anyone with a legal interest can bring a revocation/cancellation action before the NIPO (see section 39). The request must be filed in writing and include the name and address of the requisitioner, the relevant trade-mark registration, the grounds on which the request is based, and necessary documentation supporting the request.

6.5 Partial Revocation/Cancellation

A trade-mark registration can be revoked/cancelled in part. If the basis for invalidity or deletion only applies to some of the goods or services for which the trade mark is registered, the registration shall be invalidated or deleted with effect only for these goods or services. This will typically be the case if the owner is able to prove use in only some of the registered categories (see section 38).

6.6 Possibilities of Amendment

The owner of a trade mark may request that the NIPO make alterations to a registered trade mark, normally on the condition that the pursuer retracts the revocation/cancellation proceedings. However, alterations may only be made if they are insignificant and do not affect the overall impression of the trade mark (see section 34).

Depending on the proceedings, the trade mark will either remain in its original form or be subject to revocation in part or in full.

6.7 Revocation/Cancellation and Infringement

An infringement action is often met with an invalidity and cancellation/revocation claim, in which case the matters are heard and decided by the same court.

7. Trial & Settlement

7.1 Special Procedural Provisions

The Oslo District Court is the mandatory legal venue for any trade mark cases related to actions concerning a review of a decision made by the KFIR, actions concerning invalidity or deletion of a trade-mark registration pursuant to sections 35, 36 and 37, and civil actions concerning infringements of a registered trademark. Legal actions concerning unregistered trade marks are subject to the ordinary rules of legal venue contained in the Dispute Act.

Cases concerning a request for a preliminary injunction follow the ordinary rules of venue. An action may therefore be filed with the district court of the ordinary venue of the defendant, or with the district court where the business enterprise's head office is located, according to the Register of Business Enterprises (see the Norwegian Dispute Act section 4-4, first and third para). As a request for a preliminary injunction is often followed by a non-infringement counterclaim, thus combining the cases and making the Oslo District Court the mandatory venue, it is primarily the Oslo District Court that deals with cases concerning requests for preliminary injunctions.

7.2 Determination of Cases

Trade-mark cases brought before the Oslo District Court are determined by a legal judge who specialises in trade-mark proceedings. If requested by one of the parties or if the court deems it necessary, the court shall sit with two expert lay judges, who may be appointed by the court upon its own initiative or upon the request of the parties. Expert lay judge with legal expertise, however, may only be appointed if nominated by both parties (see section 9-12, first to third para).

7.3 Possibilities of Settlement

The parties can choose to settle at any time until the judgment has been given. It is quite common to settle during court-sponsored mediation prior to the oral hearing in the court of first instance. If prudent, the judge will also remind and encourage the parties to discuss potential settlements during the main hearing.

7.4 Other Court Proceedings

Proceedings may be stayed by both the NIPO and the courts. If a legal action concerning invalidity or deletion of a registration of a trade mark is brought to court before a final decision has been made in a matter concerning an administrative review, the NIPO shall await further procedure. The procedure shall be postponed until the legal proceedings have been decided with legally binding effect. Please be advised that this only applies if the request for an administrative review was made by a party other than the trade-mark owner. The party who has requested an administrative review cannot, however, bring an action concerning invalidity or deletion to court while the case is currently subject to an administrative review by the NIPO. If the party has previously brought legal actions concerning invalidity or deletion to court, such a request cannot be made (see section 41).

In addition, the court may stay the proceedings in a case upon the request of a party if the outcome is fully or partly dependent on a legal issue that will be bindingly resolved in another case (see the Dispute Act section 16-18, first para).

8. Remedies

8.1 Existing Remedies

Compensation and damages for direct and indirect infringement of a registered or unregistered trade mark shall be determined on the basis of one of the following options, whichever is most favourable for the trade-mark owner:

- compensation corresponding to a reasonable licence fee for the use, as well as damages for any loss resulting from the infringement that would not have arisen in connection with licensing;
- damages for any loss resulting from the infringement; or
- compensation corresponding to the gain obtained by the infringer through the infringement (see section 58, first para).

In the event of wilful or gross negligent infringement, the infringer shall instead pay compensation corresponding to double a reasonable licence, if demanded by the rights-holder. In the event of infringement committed in good faith, the compensation shall correspond to a reasonable licence fee (see section 58, second and fourth para). Please be advised that the liability mentioned here may be reduced pursuant to the Act on Compensatory Damages if there are significant reasons to suggest such a reduction.

In addition, should a party be successful in an action against the infringer, said party is entitled to full compensation for their legal costs from the opposite party. Similar to the principle established in the Act on Compensatory Damages, the opposite party may be exempted from liability for legal costs in full or in part if the court finds significant reasons to do so (see the Dispute Act section 20-2, first and third para).

8.2 Rights and Remedies

Should the defendant prevail, he or she will be entitled to full compensation for legal costs from the opposite party, although the plaintiff's liability for legal costs may be exempted in whole or in part if the court finds significant reasons to do so (see section 20-2, first and third para). As the Court awards compensation for legal costs based on rough calculations, the awarded costs may not be enough to cover the actual legal costs.

In addition, in accordance with the alleged infringer's claim, the court will hand down a declaratory judgment stating that the prevailing defendant may continue the prior alleged infringing activity.

8.3 Different Types of Remedies

The remedies for trade marks are the same, regardless of the type and classification of the trade mark.

9. Appeal

9.1 Special Provisions

There are no special provisions concerning the appellate procedure for trade-mark proceedings.

9.2 Factual or Legal Review

The appeal will give rise to a new trial in which the case is heard again in full. New arguments and new evidence are allowed.

9.3 Length of Appeal from Trial Court

An appeal from a trial court decision will normally take one to two years to be decided.

10. Other Trade Mark Issues

10.1 Recognition of Dilution

The legal standard in Norway is that a trade-mark registration cannot be opposed or subject to legal proceedings concerning degeneration if the trade mark has not yet become fully degenerated. It is, however, possible to oppose a trade-mark registration or to prevent use of a trade mark in a lawsuit if the trade mark has become fully degenerated, ie that the trade mark has become the general designation in the relevant market for goods or services of the type for which it is registered (see section 36 litra b of the Trademarks Act).

10.2 Protection of Famous Marks

The Norwegian Trademarks Act does protect "famous marks", referred to in the Trademarks Act as "well-known" marks. According to section 4, an identical or similar trade mark that – through use – "takes unfair advantage of, or is detrimental to, the distinctive character or repute (goodwill) of the well-known trade mark", cannot be registered without the consent of the owner of the well-known mark, provided that the trade mark is also well known in Norway.

In addition, the Trademarks Act, as opposed to the Paris Convention Article 6bis, provides protection against the use of a trade mark "for similar or any other goods or services". Article 6 bis of the Paris Convention, on the other hand, only provides protection for "identical or similar goods".

Moreover, while Article 6 bis of the Paris Convention requires that the trade mark is "liable to cause confusion", section 4, second para of the Trademarks Act only refers to the "unfair advantage" obtained by the use of the trade mark, inter alia if the use of the trade mark constitutes a risk of it being associated (but not confused) with the well-known mark. The concept of "free riding" has therefore been satisfactorily addressed in the Norwegian legislation.

10.3 Special Rules Regarding Geographic Indicators

A trade mark cannot be registered if it:

- exclusively, or with only insignificant changes or additions, consists of signs or indications that indicate the geographical origin of the goods or services; or
- is liable to deceive in respect of the geographical origin of the goods or services (see sections 14, second and third para and 15 first para, litra b).

It is not permissible to register a trade mark that consists of or contains anything that is liable to be understood as a geographical indication of origin for wine and spirits, unless the geographical origin of the goods is in accordance with the indication (see section 15).

10.4 Special Rules Relating to Surnames

The trade-mark protection enjoyed by the owner does not include the right to prohibit a third party from using its own name in the course of trade, insofar as this does not in itself represent a breach of good business practice (see section 5, second para).

11. Costs

11.1 Costs Before Filing a Lawsuit
The costs that typically arise before filing a lawsuit are lawyer fees related to the time spent when considering the matter, writing cease-and-desist letters, etc.

11.2 Costs Regarding an Infringement Action
Costs for bringing an infringement action to conclusion in the first instance will depend on the complexity of the case – ie, the length of the case, the need to bring in expert opinions, etc. Typically, a case can be heard in one to three court days and would accrue costs of approximately NOK300,000 to NOK1 million, ex VAT.

11.3 Costs of Litigation
The party who is successful in an action is entitled to full compensation for his or her legal costs from the opposite party. This includes, as a legal starting point, court fees paid, the other party's costs for representatives and expert judges, presentation of evidence which is not deemed unnecessary or disproportionate, and the expenses of the party for travelling to the court hearing. In cases where the outcome of the case was uncertain or where the successful party has rejected a reasonable offer of settlement, the court may exempt the opposite party from liability for legal costs, in whole or in full, if it finds significant reasons to do so, such as cost efficiency (see sections 10-5, first para and 20-2, first and third para).

Kvale Advokatfirma DA
Haakon VIIs Gate 10
0161 Oslo
P.O. Box 1752 Vika
0122 Oslo

Tel: +47 22 47 97 00
Fax: +47 21 05 85 85
Email: post@kvale.no
Web: www.kvale.no

KVALE

12. Alternative Dispute Resolution

12.1 Common Way of Settlement
The parties are encouraged to attempt to reach an amicable settlement out of court, and shall therefore investigate whether there is a possibility to settle the dispute before an action is brought. The parties may make use of out-of-court mechanisms such as arbitration and judicial mediation. As the Norwegian Dispute Act aims to resolve disputes outside court, court-sponsored mediation is provided prior to the main hearing in the first instance. Judicial mediation is therefore the main rule, unless the parties refuse or have agreed otherwise. Other forms of ADR are uncommon, and arbitration is rarely used. Conciliation before a conciliation board is exempted for cases concerning trade marks.

13. Trade Marks and Other Intellectual Property

13.1 Protection by Copyright
It is possible for a trade-mark owner to accumulate the protection enjoyed by the principles related to the protection of trade marks with principles related to the protection provided by a copyright, insofar as the intellectual work fulfils the requirements set out in the Copyright Act. There are, however, nuances to this matter, as underscored by joined cases 16/00148, 16/00149, 16/00150, 16/00151, 16/00153 and 16/00154.

In the aforementioned case, the KFIR addressed whether it is possible to protect an expired copyright with a trade-mark right. The KFIR found, in short, that the municipal's systematic attempt to register all the creations in the Vigeland museum and park as trade marks would represent a breach of public order and the considerations that substantiate the need for limitations in the protection of a copyright. The trade marks could therefore not be registered. The arguments presented by the KFIR suggest that the Board would have come to the same conclusion regardless – ie, that it is not possible to protect either an expired or existent copyright with a trade-mark right.

Whether cumulative or subsequent protection via trademark registration is possible must therefore be considered and decided on a case-by-case basis.

SERBIA

Contributed by BDK Advokati

The 'Law & Practice' sections provide easily accessible information on navigating the legal system when conducting business in the jurisdiction. Leading lawyers explain local law and practice at key transactional stages and for crucial aspects of doing business.

Contributed by BDK Advokati ***Authors:*** Bogdan Ivanišević, Marko Popović

Law and Practice

Contributed by BDK Advokati

CONTENTS

Contributed by BDK Advokati ***Authors:*** Bogdan Ivanišević, Marko Popović

BDK Advokati is a full-service law firm with offices in Belgrade (Serbia), Podgorica (Montenegro) and Banja Luka (Bosnia and Herzegovina). It has significant experience and expertise in trade-mark protection and prosecution. Its wider intellectual practice group handles a range of associated issues such as: drafting and negotiating IP-related agreements (trade-mark licensing and assignments, know-how licensing, patent licensing and assignments, distribution agreements, sponsorship agreements, franchising agreements); protection of copyright, industrial design, and patents; plant-variety protection; IP litigation; cyber space issues; and advertising. BDK Advokati is a member of the South East Europe Legal Group, an organisation assembling leading independent law firms from 12 jurisdictions in South East Europe, which allows it to assemble regional teams quickly for cross-border transactions involving jurisdictions outside its direct coverage.

Authors

Bogdan Ivanišević is a partner at the firm and leads the firm's intellectual property practice. He also heads BDK Advokati's media and entertainment and life sciences sectors and co-leads the data protection and privacy team. He has contributed to leading intellectual property law blogs and magazines. World Trademark Review (WTR) included Bogdan among the leading trade-mark practitioners in Serbia in 2017. Bogdan previously spent 12 years working as a human-rights researcher and lawyer for Human Rights Watch and the International Centre for Transitional Justice.

Marko Popović is an associate at BDK Advokati, working in BDK's intellectual property and data protection practices. He has a special interest and expertise in trade mark and copyright law, domain names, data protection aspects of cloud computing and the internet of things (IoT). The interplay between law, technology and art is something that inspires and fuels his work.

1. Types of Trade Marks & Registration

1.1 Types of Trade Marks

The Trade Mark Act (2009) expressly refers to registered marks, service marks, certification marks, collective marks and famous marks. The Company Act employs the concept of company name. Furthermore, a provision in the Trade Act (2010) arguably serves as a statutory basis for the protection of unregistered marks, trade dress and trade names. The Act identifies as a mode of unfair competition the sale of goods with a mark, information or shape which reasonably creates confusion among consumers as to the origin, quality and other features of the goods. From publicly available information it cannot be concluded to what extent, if at all, participants in commerce rely on the Trade Act's unfair competition clause to protect their unregistered marks, trade dress and trade names.

1.2 Trade-Mark Rights

For trade mark rights to be obtained, the holder needs to register a mark. Mere use does not suffice. However, use of an unregistered trade mark may give rise to claims on unfair competition grounds

1.3 Standards for Registering

There are no different standards for registering different types of trade marks. For example, both a word mark and product configuration may acquire distinctiveness and meet conditions for registration if a broad section of the relevant public recognises it as a distinctive sign.

1.4 Trade-Mark Register

The Intellectual Property Office (Zavod za intelektualnu svojinu) (IP Office) maintains a Registry of Applications and a Trade Mark Registry. Both registries are open to the general public, online and offline.

1.5 Types of Registers

There are no different trade-mark registers, such as principal and supplementary.

1.6 Searching for Prior Trade Marks

Searching for prior trade marks, before applying to register a mark, is a common – albeit not generally accepted – practice.

1.7 Registration Requirements
For a mark to be registered it is necessary that the mark can be represented graphically.

1.8 Registering a Trade Mark
Natural persons and legal entities, both Serbian or foreign, may register a trade mark in Serbia.

1.9 Registering Signs
According to the Trade Mark Act, different types of signs can be registered as a trade mark. Examples include signs consisting of words, slogans, letters, numerals, images, colour combinations, three-dimensional shapes and sounds (if represented by musical notation). The IP Office does not grant protection to signs consisting of scent or taste. The IP Office holds that these signs may not be represented graphically and reproduced in the Trade Mark Registry.

1.10 Other Rights to Signs
Company names registered in the Company Registry enjoy limited protection pursuant to the provisions of the Company Act. Trade names do not explicitly enjoy protection under any legislative act, but the unfair competition clause in the Trade Act arguably enables such protection. One may register a domain name with the Serbian National Internet Domain Registry, but there is no specific right to a domain name. The Committee for the Resolution of Disputes Relating to the Registration of National Internet Domains, a body acting under the auspices of the Serbian Chamber of Commerce, resolves disputes relating to registered national domains (.RS and .СРБ), when such domains allegedly infringe protected trade marks.

1.11 Registration Procedure
The registration procedure begins by filing a trade-mark application. The IP Office first checks if the application satisfies formal requirements and then moves to the stage of substantive examination. Serbia does not use opposition proceedings, so the IP Office conducts examinations on relative grounds for refusal of registration, in addition to the absolute grounds. If the application meets the requirements for registration, the IP Office requests that an applicant pay a fee for the initial ten-year period as well as the costs of publication of the trade mark in the IP Office's gazette. After an applicant furnishes proof of payment, the IP Office enters the trade mark in the Trade Mark Registry and issues a registration certificate to the trade mark-owner.

The Serbian legal system allows multi-class applications.

1.12 Use in Commerce
It is not necessary to use a mark in commerce in order to obtain trade-mark registration. After registration, a trade mark-owner must begin using the trade mark before the expiry of a five-year period, otherwise any interested party may obtain revocation of the registration from the IP Office.

A trade mark-owner can renew the registration for an unlimited number of successive ten-year periods, upon the payment of renewal fees.

1.13 Registration of Series Marks
A trade-mark application may only contain one mark applied for. The Trade Mark Act does not know of the registration of series marks.

1.14 Length of Registration Process
The average duration of trade-mark registration proceedings before the Serbian IP Office is between six and nine months. If an applicant is a foreign natural person or legal entity, with no residency or registered office in Serbia, they must be represented by a Serbian lawyer or by a person registered with the IP Office as a trade-mark representative.

The official fee for a single word mark in up to three classes is approximately EUR400. From that amount, EUR130 must be paid for the trade-mark application, an additional EUR255 for obtaining the trade-mark registration and the first ten years of protection, and EUR15 for issuance of the registration certificate.

The attorney fees for registration of a single word mark vary from EUR250 to EUR450. The figure does not include the non-mandatory search of relevant online databases.

1.15 Grounds for Refusal
The IP Office will refuse a trade-mark registration if the mark cannot be represented graphically. Another obstacle to registration exists if the mark is incapable of distinguishing the goods or services from those of others, or if the mark is contrary to public policy or to accepted principles of morality. Furthermore, a mark cannot enjoy protection if it consists exclusively of the three-dimensional shape which results from the nature of the goods themselves; the shape of goods which is necessary to obtain a technical result; or the shape which gives substantial value to the goods. Marks consisting exclusively of signs or indications which may serve, in trade, to designate the kind, quality, quantity, intended purpose, value, geographical origin, or the time of production of the goods or of rendering of the service, or other characteristics of the goods or service may not be registered. Also, signs or indications which have become customary in the current language, or in the bona fide established practices of the trade, may not be registered as trade marks. A trade mark cannot be registered if it is of such a nature as to deceive the public, for instance as to the nature, quality or geographical origin of the goods or services. If a mark contains official marks or hallmarks of quality control or warranty, or imitations thereof, it cannot be registered, unless the written

consent of the competent authority has been given. A mark which represents or imitates a national or religious symbol may not be registered. A final group of marks not eligible for registration on absolute grounds is marks containing a national coat of arms or other public arms; a flag or an emblem; the name, or the abbreviated name of a country or of an international organisation; and the imitations thereof, except with the authorisation of the competent authority of the country or the organisation.

1.16 Process for Overcoming Objections

If the IP Office finds that an applied-for mark is devoid of distinctive character, is descriptive or has become customary in the current language or in the bona fide established practices of the trade, an applicant may claim that the mark has become capable of distinguishing goods and services in trade through its genuine use (ie, that the mark has acquired distinctiveness).

1.17 Consideration of Prior Rights

The IP Office examines not only the absolute grounds for refusal of a trade mark but relative grounds too. It also examines ex officio the existence of certain prior rights. A mark which is identical to an earlier trade mark (or applied-for mark) for identical goods and services cannot enjoy trade mark protection. Also, a mark will be refused protection if it is identical to the earlier trade mark (or applied-for mark) for similar goods and services; or if it is similar to an earlier trade mark (or applied-for mark) for identical or similar goods and services and, due to that identity or similarity, a likelihood of confusion, including the likelihood of association with the earlier trade mark (or applied-for mark), exists on the part of the relevant members of the public.

Furthermore, an applied-for mark cannot be protected if it is identical or similar to a mark for identical or similar goods and services, and the latter mark is well known in Serbia within the meaning of Article 6bis of the Paris Convention for the Protection of Industrial Property. Famous trade marks are protected regardless of the goods or services if the use of the later mark would result in taking unfair advantage from the reputation of the earlier famous trade mark, or be detrimental to its distinctive character or reputation.

Finally, an applied-for mark cannot be registered if by its appearance or content it infringes copyright or industrial property rights other than the trade mark. If the mark contains a name or personal portrayal of a person, it can be registered only with the consent of that person.

1.18 Third-Party Rights

Opposition proceedings are not available to trade mark-owners in Serbia. An interested party may make observations in writing to the IP Office as to the absolute and relative grounds for refusal to register a trade mark. The interested party does not need any sort of standing or commercial interest.

1.19 Revoke, Change, Amend or Correct an Application

An applicant may at any time during the process of registration withdraw the application or restrict the list of goods or services contained in the application. Designating the enumerated goods or services in a more specific manner, without adding new classes of goods or services, is also permissible.

The applicant may also introduce non-substantive modification of the representation of the mark applied for. Such a modification may not change the distinctive character of the mark. Determination of substantiveness requires a facts-specific inquiry, as even the change of an indistinctive element can amount to a change of distinctive character of the mark as a whole.

If the applied-for mark contains a non-distinctive element, and if inclusion of that element in the trade mark might give rise to doubts as to the scope of protection of the mark, the IP Office may request an applicant's written statement disclaiming any exclusive right to such an element.

1.20 Assigning an Application or Granting a Licence

An applicant may assign or grant a licence in relation to the trade-mark application.

1.21 Remedies Against the Trade Mark Office

If the IP Office refuses to register a trade mark, an applicant may lodge an appeal with the Administrative Commission of the Government of the Republic of Serbia, within 15 days from the receipt of the decision by the IP Office. If the Administrative Commission rules against the applicant, the latter may initiate judicial proceedings before the Administrative Court within 30 days from the receipt of the second-instance decision.

1.22 Use of a Trade Mark

An applicant does not have to use its mark in commerce before the registration is used.

The owner of the trade mark must use the registered trade mark in connection with the goods or services in respect of which it is registered. Upon application by an interested party, the IP Office revokes the trade mark if the owner, or a person authorised by them, has not put the trade mark to genuine use within a period of five years following registration, or for any uninterrupted period of five years from the date of its last use, unless there are proper reasons for non-use. Such proper reasons, according to the Trade Mark Act, include a decision by a government authority; an import ban; or any other prohibition affecting goods and/or services protected by the trade mark.

Only genuine, commercial use qualifies as the use for the purpose of maintaining trade mark rights. The quantity of goods or services for which the mark is used must indicate serious, rather than fictitious, economic activity. Mere advertising of a trade mark without the possibility of buying advertised goods or services does not amount to genuine use.

1.23 Dividing a Trade Mark

An applicant may divide a trade-mark application into two or more separate applications. In the request submitted to the IP Office, the applicant must indicate the goods and services which should remain in the original application and the goods and services to be included in the divisional application. The divisional application preserves the filing date and any priority date of the original application.

1.24 Length of Term of Protection

The term of protection for a trade mark is ten years from the date of filing an application. Trade-mark registration can be renewed for an unlimited number of successive ten-year periods. In order to renew trade-mark protection the owner has to pay an office fee.

The trade mark owner may renew the trade mark after the term of protection has lapsed, within the six-month grace period following the expiry of the term. The owner must, in that case, pay an additional 50% amount of the renewal fee.

If the trade-mark owner does not pay the office fee, and if a licence, pledge or other right has been entered in the Trade Mark Registry in favour of a third party, the IP Office notifies that third party so that it may maintain the registration by paying the office fee.

1.25 Requirements for an Exhaustion

In 2013, Parliament changed the Trade Mark Act in such a way that the principle of international exhaustion of trade-mark rights gave way to national exhaustion. Under the amended Act, a trade mark-owner cannot prohibit the use of the trade mark in relation to the goods which have been put on the market in Serbia by the trade mark-owner or with their consent. The owner of the goods may further place those goods on the market without infringing the trade mark.

Exceptionally, the trade mark-holder may lawfully oppose further sale of the trade-marked goods with deteriorated quality due to the impairment of the condition of the goods after they have been put on the market. Also, exhaustion does not apply where the trade mark-owner has other "legitimate reasons" to oppose further commercialisation of the goods. The law does not shed further light on what such "other conditions" might include.

1.26 Participation in the Madrid System

Serbia is a party to the Madrid Agreement and the Madrid Protocol. There are no requirements specific to Serbia for international trade-mark registrations.

1.27 Consequences for Providing Incorrect Information

There are no specific statutory rules and no case law concerning the provision of incorrect information in connection with a trade-mark application or other filing.

1.28 Updating or Refreshing a Design Mark

A mark may be modified during the application stage, within limits. An applicant may not modify the distinctive element of the mark. Modification of a non-distinctive element or elements of the mark may lead to impermissible changes of the distinctive character of the mark as a whole.

1.29 Denotation

A trade mark-owner is under no obligation to use symbols such as ® or TM to indicate trade-mark registration or use. Third parties using an identical or confusingly similar mark may not invoke the absence of such a sign as a defence against trade-mark infringement. At the same time, the use of such symbols has the benefit of raising awareness to consumers and competitors that the sign enjoys trade-mark protection.

2. Assignment and Licensing

2.1 Assignment Requirements or Restrictions

Assignment of a trade mark or an applied-for mark can be based on an assignment agreement, a change of the legal status of a trade mark-owner (if a legal entity), or on a court or administrative decision. An assignment agreement has to be in writing. For an assignment to be enforceable between the parties, no approval from the IP Office is necessary. However, a record of the assignment of the trade mark in the Trade Mark Registry is necessary for the assignment to have effect against third parties.

2.2 Procedure for Assigning a Trade Mark

After concluding a trade-mark assignment agreement in writing, both the trade mark-holder (the assignor) and the assignee are authorised (but not obliged) to request recordation of the assignment with the IP Office. If the IP Office receives such a request and does not identify any obstacles to an assignment, the IP Office issues a decision on recordation of the assignment.

2.3 Registering or Recording the Assignment

As long as the assignment of a trade mark is not recorded, an assignee may not bring proceedings for infringement of the trade mark against a third party. If the trade mark-owner does not pay the office fee, and if the assignment is not recorded, the assignee may not maintain the registration by paying the office fee.

2.4 Trade Marks and Security

A trade mark can be given as a security and be subject to rights in rem. A trade mark-holder may create a pledge on the trade mark in order to secure the rights of their creditor. Recordation of the pledge in the Trade Mark Registry has constitutive effect. Also, a trade mark can be assigned by way of security and be levied in execution.

2.5 Licensing Requirements or Restrictions

The licensing of a trade mark or an applied-for mark requires the conclusion of a written licence agreement. Approval from the IP Office is not necessary for the licence to be valid. However, recordation of the trade-mark licence in the Trade Mark Registry is necessary for the licence to be effective against third parties. The Obligations Act (1978) explicitly provides for exclusive and non-exclusive licences. However, the licensor and the licensee are free to set out the respective rights and obligations in a way that effectively turns the arrangement into a sole licence.

2.6 Procedure for Licensing a Trade Mark

After concluding a trade mark-licensing agreement in writing, both the trade mark-owner (the licensor) and the licensee are authorised, but not obliged, to request recordation of the licence with the IP Office. If there are no obstacles to the licensing, such as the licensor's contractual obligation vis-à-vis a third party not to license the trade mark, the IP Office will issue a decision on recordation of the licence.

2.7 Registering or Recording the Licence

If a licence is not recorded, a licensee may not make use of the Trade Mark Act provision authorising a trade-mark licensee to launch court proceedings against a third-party infringer. Also, in the absence of recordation, an exclusive licensee may not oppose a licence subsequently granted by the licensor to an unwitting third party. If a trade mark-owner does not pay the office fee, and if the licence is not recorded, the licensee may not maintain the registration by paying the office fee.

2.8 Reasons to Deny Granting a Perpetual Licence

A trade mark-owner can grant a perpetual licence. The perpetuity is preconditioned on the payment of a renewal fee after each ten-year term of protection.

3. Opposition Procedure

3.1 Legal Grounds and Timeframes

There is no opposition procedure under the framework set forth by the Trade Mark Act. The IP Office examines ex officio both the absolute and the relative grounds for refusal of trade-mark protection.

An interested party may make observations in writing to the IP Office as to the absolute and relative grounds for refusal to register a trade mark.

4. Initiating a Lawsuit

4.1 Actions to Pursue Infringement

The owner of a registered trade mark and a trade-mark applicant may file a lawsuit against the alleged infringing party, within three years of learning about the infringement and the infringer, but not after the expiry of a five-year period after the first occurrence of infringement. The plaintiff may request that the courts declare that the defendant was engaged in trade-mark infringement and to order the cessation of infringing activities. In addition, the lawsuit may include the requests for seizure, definitive removal, or destruction or alteration of the infringing goods; destruction or alteration of the tools and equipment used to manufacture the infringing goods; compensation of damages and reimbursement of costs; and publication of the judgment at the expense of the defendant. Finally, the plaintiff may request by means of the lawsuit that the defendant furnish information about third parties involved in the infringement.

The holder of an unregistered trade mark can launch court proceedings based on the unfair competition provision in the Trade Act. The provision applies if a competitor sells goods with a mark, information or shape which reasonably creates confusion among consumers as to the origin, quality and other features of the goods. The statute of limitations is six months after learning about the infringement and the infringer, but in no event longer than three years after the unlawful activity has ended. The plaintiff may request a declaration of unfair competition; an injunctive relief; rectification of the consequences of the unfair competition; compensation of damages; and publication of the judgment at the expense of the defendant.

Trade-mark infringement may be prosecuted as a criminal offence if the defendant, acting with the intent to deceive, used the mark or included elements of the mark in its own trade name, designation of geographical origin, trade mark, or other sign. Criminal prosecution may also encompass those who acquire, manufacture, process, place into commerce, lease or store the counterfeited goods with the intent to sell such goods in substantial quantities or value.

4.2 Initiating Infringement Proceedings
Jurisdiction of a particular type of court in a trade-mark case depends on the character of the parties to proceedings. The Organisation of Courts Act (2008) provides that commercial courts decide in trade-mark cases if both parties are commercial entities. If one or both parties are natural persons, the jurisdiction belongs to regular courts.

4.3 Effect of Decisions on Infringement Actions
Decisions of the trade-mark office are not binding on courts. Therefore, if the trade-mark office determines that a sign meets the conditions for registration, the courts are free to decide in infringement proceedings that the senior mark lacks distinctiveness and the junior mark does not infringe.

4.4 Declaratory Judgment Proceedings
Under the Civil Proceedings Act (2011), a party may start declaratory judgment proceedings if they have a relevant legal interest. Whether an alleged trade-mark infringer has such an interest is a factual matter for the courts to determine.

4.5 Jurisdiction of Courts
If a commercial court has the jurisdiction to hear a trade-mark case, the jurisdiction to try the case in the first instance belongs to the commercial courts in Belgrade. The Appellate Commercial Court, located in Belgrade, decides on appeals against a first-instance judgment.

If, exceptionally, a court of general jurisdiction decides a trade-mark case, the High Court in Belgrade hears the case in the first instance. Any appeals are then heard by the Appellate Commercial Court in Belgrade.

The Supreme Court of Cassation may hear a trade-mark case if the party that lost on appeal proves that conditions are in place for filing an extraordinary legal remedy (revision, application for review of the final and binding judgment, or application for reopening of proceedings).

4.6 Prerequisites to Filing a Lawsuit
There are no prerequisites to filing a lawsuit, such as issuing a formal demand letter, warning letters, engaging in mediation, or any other requirement.

4.7 Representation for Parties
A party in a trade-mark litigation matter does not need to be represented by a lawyer. Exceptionally, in third-instance proceedings, pursuant to an extraordinary legal remedy (revision, application for review of the final and binding judgment, or application for reopening of the proceedings), a lawyer must represent the party.

4.8 Interim or Preliminary Injunctions
Both preliminary and interim injunctions are available to a moving party. An injunction in a trade-mark case is easier to obtain than in other types of cases. Under the Trade Mark Act, it suffices for the moving party to show that infringement is likely to have occurred or would be likely to occur. In other types of disputes, the identity in kind between injunctive relief and the final relief sought is an obstacle to obtaining an injunction; however, this restriction does not apply in a trade-mark case. Also, the party seeking the injunction in a trade-mark case does not have to demonstrate the risk that, in the absence of an injunction, the other party is likely to frustrate or substantially hamper recovery of damages.

4.9 Protection for Potential Defendant
A defendant in a trade-mark case can protect itself by filing an answer to the complaint and filing protective briefs. If a trade mark-owner requests that the courts issue an injunction against the defendant, the defendant may require a bond to be posted by the trade mark-owner. The defendant may not subsequently start declaratory relief in another court asking for declaration of non-infringement, as it would involve the same cause of action between the same parties (litis pendentia).

4.10 Obtaining Information and Evidence
At the trial stage, if a party in trade-mark litigation relies on documentary evidence in the possession of the opposing party, the courts will call on the latter party to produce the document. The opposing party may lawfully refuse to produce the evidence if making the information available would be in breach of the obligation to maintain confidentiality of the relationship between a party and his or her legal representative; in breach of the priest-penitent privilege; or in breach of the duty to protect professional secrets. Likewise, the party may deny the request if the information would expose the party or a close person to heavy embarrassment, substantial economic damage or criminal prosecution. However, even in these cases the opposing party must produce the evidence if the party previously relied on the evidence, or if the document is "common to" that party and the moving party (for example a contract between the two parties, or an administrative decision referring to both parties), or the party is obliged to produce the document under a special law (such as the law on free access to information of general importance).

The courts may order a third party to produce a specific document if the document is common to that party and the party requesting the document's production, or if the requested party is obliged to produce the document under a special law.

4.11 Initial Pleading Standards

There are no special provisions concerning the initial pleading standards for lawsuits in trade mark proceedings that would differ from non-intellectual property proceedings. The complaint must specify the type or types of relief sought (declaration of infringement, permanent injunction, compensation of damages or other). The complaint must include all facts on which the claim is based and refer to the specific evidence corroborating the factual allegations. The complaint must also identify the value of the case. Finally, the complaint must contain all formal elements required for any kind of written submission: designation of the courts, the parties and their legal representatives.

The parties may supplement the initial pleadings with additional factual allegations only if it was not possible, for justifiable reasons, to advance such arguments before the conclusion of preliminary hearings.

4.12 Representative or Collective Actions

Serbian law does not permit class actions or other types of representative or collective actions in trade-mark proceedings.

4.13 Restrictions on Trade Mark-Owners

Under the general principles of civil law, also applicable in trade-mark law, abuse of rights is prohibited. For example, it would be arguably unlawful for trade mark-owner A to use registered trade mark A1 solely as a tool for threatening trade mark-owner B with initiation of cancellation proceedings based on the prior registration of A1, in the situation in which trade mark-owner A does not in fact use A1 in commerce and uses the threat of cancellation in order to extort other benefits from trade mark-owner B, unrelated to the A1.

5. Infringement

5.1 Action for Infringement

The only necessary party to an action for infringement is the infringer. Apart from a trade mark-owner, a trade-mark licensee is also authorised to file an action for infringement unless the licence agreement provides otherwise. An applicant for trade-mark registration is also authorised to lodge an action for infringement.

5.2 Signs and Infringement

The key factors which a court considers in determining whether the use of a sign constitutes trade-mark infringement is the degree of similarity between the trade mark and the sign, and between the goods or services concerned. The courts are more likely to find the likelihood of confusion if the similarity is more pronounced. The scope of protection the courts confer on a trade mark is also related to the degree of distinctiveness of the mark: the more distinctive the mark, the more probable is the finding of the likelihood of confusion.

Famous marks (marks with reputation) enjoy protection against an identical or similar sign even if the sign is used in relation to goods or services other than the goods and services for which the famous mark is protected, provided that the use of the sign causes detriment to the mark's distinctive character or repute, or takes unfair advantage of the mark's distinctive character or repute.

5.3 Use of a Sign by Defendant

The purely descriptive use of a trade mark does not amount to a trade-mark infringement. Conversely, for a court to establish a trade-mark infringement, the defendant must have used the sign to identify their goods or services, in connection with the sale, offering for sale, distribution or advertising of those goods or services.

5.4 Defences Against Infringement

An alleged infringer may rely on several defences against the allegation of infringement. If the allegedly infringing sign is a prior trade mark, this fact would negate an infringement. Also, the alleged infringer may object that the plaintiff has abandoned the trade mark by not using it for five years from the date of registration or for any uninterrupted period of five years from the date of its last use.

Furthermore, the Trade Mark Act provides for a number of limitations which the alleged infringer may use as a defence. Thus, the trade mark-owner cannot prevent a third party from placing in the line of commerce their goods or services under a sign identical or similar to the trade mark, if that sign represents the third party's company name or a designation acquired in good faith before the priority date of the trade mark. Also, the trade mark-holder cannot prohibit a third party from using, in the course of trade and in accordance with honest business practices, their own name or address, or indications concerning the kind, quality, quantity, intended purpose, value, geographical origin, the time of production or other characteristics of the goods and/or services. Finally, the trade mark-holder cannot prevent a third party from using the trade mark when it is necessary to indicate the intended purpose of a product or services, in particular as accessories or spare parts.

5.5 Role of Experts and/or Surveys

The courts do not look favourably on the use of expert opinions in infringement proceedings because the likelihood of confusion and other issues central to an infringement case require legal or factual determinations, which the courts are qualified to make by stepping into the shoes of an average consumer of the product or service. The use of surveys is permitted, but occurs extremely rarely due to the high costs involved.

5.6 Administrative or Criminal Offence

The Trade Mark Act prescribes that a legal entity which has infringed a trade mark or the right arising from the trademark application constitutes a commercial offence, punishable by a monetary fine.

The Criminal Code provides for the criminal offence of the non-authorised use of another's business name or of other indications of goods or services. The crime requires intent on the part of the defendant to deceive buyers or users. The penalty is a monetary fine or up to three years' imprisonment.

5.7 Custom Seizures

The Serbian legal system provides for customs seizure of counterfeits. A trade mark-owner may submit a request for the implementation of protective measures against counterfeit goods. The request may refer to a single shipment or shipments in general. The Customs Authority may grant the request for an initial period of one year. When the Customs Authority suspects that the goods held at customs might infringe intellectual property rights, the Authority suspends the release of the goods and notifies the trade mark-owner. The owner may inspect the goods and take photos and samples. The trade mark-owner may request destruction of the goods at their own expense or commence infringement proceedings before the competent court. If the trade mark-owner requests destruction of the goods, the Customs Authority will interpret any failure on the part of the customs declarant to respond as the declarant's consent. If the declarant opposes the destruction, the trade mark-owner may file a lawsuit seeking a court declaration that the trade mark has been infringed. In this case, the declarant bears the expense of the storage, maintenance and destruction of the goods.

As a result of the principle of national exhaustion, introduced in Serbia in 2013, a trade mark-owner may oppose the import of goods carrying the protected mark, if the owner first placed the goods, or consented that the goods be placed, in a foreign market. However, there are still no regulations in place detailing the procedures for customs' seizure of parallel imports, equivalent to the elaborated and frequently employed rules governing the seizure of counterfeits.

6. Revocation/Cancellation

6.1 Remedies and Reasons

A trade-mark registration may be revoked and removed from the Trade Mark Registry if the trade mark-owner (or a person authorised by them) has not used the trade mark for five years from the date of its registration or for any uninterrupted period of five years from the date of its last use.

Another ground for revocation exists if the trade mark has become a common name for the product or service for which it is registered. Also, the trade mark may be revoked if it deceives the public as to the nature, quality, geographical origin or other characteristics of the goods or services. Finally, if the trade mark becomes contrary to public policy or to accepted principles or morality, the IP Office may revoke it.

The trade mark is to be declared invalid if, at the time of its registration, the requirements for registration have not been met (absolute and relative grounds for invalidity).

6.2 Trade Mark Office and Civil Courts

A revocation application and the application for declaration of invalidity may be brought before the IP Office.

6.3 Statutory Limitation or Time Period

The Trade Mark Act poses limitations to bringing an action for declaration of invalidity, in consequence of acquiescence. If the holder of the prior right knew, during the five-year period preceding the filing of the application for declaration of invalidity, that the owner of the registered trade mark had used the mark, and during that time they did not object, they cease to be entitled to apply for a declaration that the trade mark is invalid, unless registration of the trade mark was applied for in bad faith.

6.4 Initiation of Revocation/Cancellation Proceeding

Any interested party may initiate revocation proceedings before the IP Office. However, only the holder of the prior right may file an application for invalidity based on the existence of an earlier identical or similar trade mark, well-known mark, famous mark, or on the infringement of copyright or industrial property rights.

The public prosecutor or any interested party may initiate proceedings for the declaration of invalidity before the IP Office.

6.5 Partial Revocation/Cancellation

Where grounds for revocation or declaration of invalidity exist in respect of only some of the goods or services, a trade mark is to be revoked or declared invalid only in part.

6.6 Possibilities of Amendment

During revocation proceedings or proceedings for the declaration of invalidity, a trade mark-owner may restrict the list of goods or services for which their trade mark is protected.

6.7 Revocation/Cancellation and Infringement

A commercial court or court of general jurisdiction hears a trade-mark infringement case, and the IP Office decides in revocation proceedings or proceedings for declaration of invalidity. The courts must stay proceedings pending a final decision by the IP Office.

7. Trial & Settlement

7.1 Special Procedural Provisions
Under Serbian law, there are no special procedural provisions for trade-mark proceedings.

7.2 Determination of Cases
A case is determined by legal judges. The parties have no influence on the allocation of a case to specific judges.

7.3 Possibilities of Settlement
The courts must advise parties on the possibility under civil procedure law to resolve a dispute amicably and to opt for mediation at any stage of proceedings. If the parties consensually propose mediation, the courts must stay proceedings and refer the parties to commence a separate mediation proceeding to which a distinct law applies.

The parties may also settle a case at any stage of proceedings. A case ending in court settlement is considered adjudicated.

7.4 Other Court Proceedings
If a trade mark-owner sues two unrelated infringers in separate proceedings, such proceedings run independently and neither court has to stay any proceedings pending the resolution of the other. See also **6.7 Revocation/Cancellation and Infringement**.

8. Remedies

8.1 Existing Remedies
The remedies available to a trade mark-owner include declaration of infringement; cessation of infringing activities; seizure, definitive removal or destruction or alteration of the infringing goods and the means for manufacturing such goods; compensation of damages and reimbursement of costs; publication of the judgment at the expense of the defendant; and provision of information on the other who took part in the infringement. In the case of wilful infringement or infringement caused by gross negligence, the trade mark-owner may claim damages in the amount of three times that of the licence fee the trade mark-owner would reasonably obtain. A judge has discretion in ordering the remedies.

8.2 Rights and Remedies
If a defendant prevails in a trial, they may obtain reimbursement of attorney fees, reimbursement of fees paid in relation to the filing of the submissions, compensation of the damage (if any) suffered as a consequence of preliminary or interim injunctions, and expenses incurred for the purpose of hiring an expert witness or a translator.

8.3 Different Types of Remedies
Under Serbian law, there are no different types of remedies for different types of trade marks.

9. Appeal

9.1 Special Provisions
There are no special provisions concerning the appellate procedure for trade-mark proceedings.

9.2 Factual or Legal Review
In appellate proceedings, if an appeal is based on the allegedly incomplete or erroneous findings of facts on the part of a trial court, the appellate court reviews the facts to the extent necessary to determine whether the appeal is well-founded.

If, after a retrial, the case against reaches the appellate court and the court again agrees with the appellant that the findings of facts are incomplete or erroneous, the appellate court itself must hold the hearings in order to establish the facts.

If the appeal is based on procedural issued or the erroneous application of substantive law, rather than on incomplete or erroneous findings of facts, the court may not review the facts of the case.

9.3 Length of Appeal from Trial Court
An appeal from a trial court decision may take anywhere between four and nine months to be decided.

10. Other Trade Mark Issues

10.1 Recognition of Dilution
The proprietor of a trade mark with a reputation may oppose registration of a trade mark which is identical with, or similar to, an earlier trade mark in relation to goods or services which are not similar to those for which the earlier trade mark is registered, where use of that sign without due cause would be detrimental to the distinctive character or the repute of the earlier trade mark, or would take unfair advantage of the mark's reputation. Likewise, the proprietor of a trade mark with a reputation is entitled to prevent all third parties from using in the course of trade a sign which is identical with, or similar to, the trade mark in relation to goods or services which are not similar to those for which the trade mark is registered, where use of that sign without due cause is detrimental to the distinctive character or the repute of the trade mark, or takes unfair advantage of the mark's reputation.

10.2 Protection of Famous Marks

The Trade Mark Act protects a trade mark with a reputation even if the mark is not used in Serbia. However, such a mark has to be registered in the country in order for the proprietor to be able to prevent registration or use of a dilutive sign.

In contrast, a "well known" mark within the meaning of Article 6bis of the Paris Convention does not have to be either registered or used in Serbia in order to enjoy protection against identical or similar marks for identical or similar goods or services.

10.3 Special Rules Regarding Geographic Indicators

The acquisition and legal protection of designations of origin and geographical indications is the subject matter of a separate piece of legislation, Indications of Geographical Origin Act, from 2000.

10.4 Special Rules Relating to Surnames

A trade mark-holder cannot prohibit a third party from using in the course of trade and in accordance with honest business practices his or her own surname as a mark.

BDK Advokati
Majke Jevrosime 23
11000 Belgrade
Serbia

Tel: +381 11 3284 212
Fax: +381 11 3284 213
Email: office@bdkadvokati.com
Web: www.bdkadvokati.com

11. Costs

11.1 Costs Before Filing a Lawsuit

A trade mark may pay between EUR300 and EUR800 for legal services for devising a cease-and-desist letter and sending it to a purported infringer.

11.2 Costs Regarding an Infringement Action

The costs for bringing an infringement to conclusion in the first instance, including attorney fees, in a case of standard complexity and duration range from EUR800 to EUR2,000.

11.3 Costs of Litigation

The losing party is required to reimburse the prevailing party for the costs of litigation, including court fees and attorney fees.

12. Alternative Dispute Resolution

12.1 Common Way of Settlement

Alternative dispute resolution is not a common way of settling a trade-mark case in Serbia. By far the largest number of trade-mark cases are resolved by courts.

13. Trade Marks and Other Intellectual Property

13.1 Protection by Copyright

Trade marks can also be protected by copyright or industrial design.

ST LUCIA

LAW AND PRACTICE: p.279

Contributed by Floissac, Fleming & Associates

The 'Law & Practice' sections provide easily accessible information on navigating the legal system when conducting business in the jurisdiction. Leading lawyers explain local law and practice at key transactional stages and for crucial aspects of doing business.

Contributed by Floissac, Fleming & Associates **Authors:** Brenda Floissac Fleming, André McKenzie

Law and Practice

Contributed by Floissac, Fleming & Associates

CONTENTS

Floissac Fleming & Associates is one of Saint Lucia's oldest and most reputable law firms. It specialises in banking, commercial and corporate law but is strong across the spectrum of legal work. Floissac Fleming & Associates' intellectual property practice covers trade marks, patents and designs, its services including, but not limited to, registration/filing, maintenance, renewal, enforcement, prosecution, due diligence services, searches and litigation. The firm has a well-balanced representation of domestic and international clients and represents a wide cross-section of industries. Alternative dispute resolution, real estate, employment and labour are other areas of expertise for the firm.

Authors

Brenda Floissac Fleming is the senior partner of Floissac Fleming & Associates, and enjoys over 30 years in private practice. Not only is she is the head of the firm's trade-mark practice group, but her practice also comprises, among other matters, banking and property; she has a wealth of experience in all areas of civil practice from basic and rudimentary debt actions to large commercial and corporate matters, including mergers and acquisitions. Brenda is the Honorary Consul for Chile and a member of the International Trade Mark Association (INTA).

André McKenzie is an associate in Floissac Fleming & Associates' intellectual property and litigation departments. His practice covers the full spectrum of trade-mark matters in Saint Lucia including, but not limited to, applications for registration, renewal, assignment and authorised user agreements. André's previous legal work experience includes internships with the Eastern Caribbean Supreme Court in Saint Lucia, the Supreme Court of Jamaica, the Attorney General's Chambers in Jamaica and the Jamaica Civil Aviation Authority.

1. Types of Trade Marks & Registration

1.1 Types of Trade Marks

In addition to the general trade mark for goods or services or both goods and services, Saint Lucia also contemplates the registration of collective marks, certification marks and defensive marks. No clear distinction is made in respect of service marks as they are considered trade marks associated with services and are registered in the same manner as trade marks for goods.

The rights in such trade marks are based on statutory law and are governed by the Trade Marks Act and Trade Marks Regulations of Saint Lucia, Cap. 13.30 of the Revised Edition of the Laws of Saint Lucia (hereafter referred together as the Act).

1.2 Trade-Mark Rights

While a trade mark must be registered in order to be protected, unregistered trade-mark rights may be afforded protection under common law.

1.3 Standards for Registering

Registration requirements are standard as outlined in **1.6 Registration Requirements**, save and except for the following:

- an application for the registration of a collective trade mark must be made by the association to which the mark belongs;
- in relation to certification marks, in addition to the standard requirements for the registration of a standard trade mark, an applicant must also submit a copy of the rules governing the use of the certification mark and the rules must include provisions regarding: the applicant's approved certifiers who may be approved for the purpose of certifying goods or services or both; the cases in which goods or services are to be certified; the conditions under which an approved user is allowed to use the certification mark; the use of the certification mark by the owner, if he or she intends to use it, and any approved user; and the settlement of disputes arising from a refusal to certify goods or services or to allow the use of the certification mark; and
- an applicant who is wanting to register a defensive mark must also show that it is likely that the use of the mark in relation to the goods or services in respect of which its registration as a defensive mark is sought will be taken to indicate that there is a connection between those goods or services and the registered owner.

1.4 Trade-Mark Register

In Saint Lucia, the Registry of Companies and Intellectual Property ("ROCIP") is statutorily charged with the responsibility for administering the registration of trade marks and keeping the Register of Trade Marks, which is publicly available.

1.5 Searching for Prior Trade Marks
Searches at the ROCIP are more commonly conducted to ascertain the status of existing/previous trade marks. That notwithstanding, searches are also conducted prior to registration to ascertain whether there are any similar trade marks already registered and whether there is likely to be an opposition to the registration of the trade mark.

1.6 Registration Requirements
To obtain registration of a trade mark, a formal application must be made to the ROCIP. The application must include:

- the full name and address of the applicant;
- an Authorisation of Agent authorising an agent to act on the applicant's behalf;
- the full name and address of the agent;
- an indication as to the type of trade mark protection sought, ie trade mark, collective trade mark, certification trade mark or defensive trade mark;
- whether the applicant is using or intends to use the trade mark, has authorised or intends to authorise another person to use the trade mark, or intends to assign the trade mark to a body corporate;
- a representation of the trade mark;
- whether the mark is a word mark;
- a description of the mark where the mark is not a word mark;
- the number of marks in the series where the application is for a series mark;
- whether the application claims priority and if so, the details of the priority claimed along with a certified copy of the application of which priority is claimed;
- specifications of the goods and services for which registration of the trade mark is sought based on the Nice classification and multi-class applications are allowed;
- if colour is claimed, an indication of the colours claimed;
- an indication of whether any limitations or disclaimers are claimed; and
- if the trade mark or any part thereof or any documents intended to be used in relation to the registration of the mark is not in English, a certified translation of the non-English documents or characters.

1.7 Registering a Trade Mark
A trade mark may be registered by a person inclusive of a body corporate or unincorporated body.

1.8 Registering Signs
The following signs may be registered as a trade mark in Saint Lucia: letters, words, names, signatures, numerals, devices, brands, headings, labels, tickets, aspects of packaging, shapes, colours, and any combination thereof.

1.9 Registration Procedure
An application must be accompanied by an Authorisation of Agent giving the agent the authority to act on the applicant's behalf. The applicant must provide a representation of the trade mark and where the mark is in a language other than English or contains characters not in English, a certified translation of the mark or non-English characters must accompany the application. Once the application is made, the ROCIP will examine the application and issue an examination report upon completion. If the examination report indicates that the trade mark is acceptable, the Registrar will publish a notice of application for registration of the trade mark in the Gazette and persons have three months from the date of publication in the Gazette to file an opposition to its registration. If no opposition is filed, the Certificate of Registration is issued approximately six weeks after the expiration of the opposition period.

The registration of a trade mark normally takes between six and eight months from application to the issuance of the Certificate of Registration.

1.10 Use in Commerce
There is no requirement to show use or use in commerce or intention to use in commerce in order to apply for registration. What is required is that an applicant must state whether he or she is the owner of the mark and is using or intends to use the trade mark.

1.11 Registration of Series Marks
A person may make a single application for the registration of two or more trade marks in respect of similar goods or services within a single class if the trade marks resemble each other in material particulars and differ only in respect of one or more of the following matters:

- statements or representations as to the goods or services in relation to which the trade marks are used or are intended to be used;
- statements or representations as to number, price, quality or names of places;
- the colour of any part of the trade mark; or
- any matter that is not inherently adapted to distinguish the goods or services and does not substantially affect the identity of the trade marks.

1.12 Grounds for Refusal
An application for the registration of a trade mark may be rejected on the following grounds:

- the trade mark contains or consists of a sign that is prescribed not to be used as a trade mark;
- the trade mark cannot be represented geographically;

- the trade mark is not capable of distinguishing an applicant's goods or services from the goods or services of other persons;
- the trade mark is scandalous or its use is contrary to law;
- the trade mark is likely to deceive or cause confusion; and
- the trade mark is substantially identical with or deceptively similar to a trade mark registered in respect of similar goods or closely related services or a trade mark whose registration in respect of similar goods or closely related services, is being sought by another person and the priority date for the registration of the applicant's trade mark is not earlier than the priority date for the registration of the other trade mark in respect of the similar goods or closely related services.

1.13 Process for Overcoming Objections
If an application for registration is rejected on the basis of a clerical error or obvious mistake or related to the specification of goods and services, an applicant may make an application to amend or correct his or her application to satisfy the Registrar and the requirements of the Trade Marks Act. An applicant may also appeal to the High Court against any decision of the Registrar that leads to the subsequent rejection of an application.

1.14 Consideration of Prior Rights
In conducting the examination of an application, the ROCIP will assess whether the application infringes any prior rights of a registered trade mark-owner. The ROCIP will assess whether the trade mark is identical to or resembles another trade mark so that it is likely to create confusion.

1.15 Revoke, Change, Amend or Correct an Application
A written request may be made to amend an application for registration of a trade mark before its registration, however, the permissible amendments are dependent on the stage of the registration process.

If the notice of application for registration has not been published in the Gazette and the request for amendment is made within 14 days of the date of the application for registration of a trade mark, an amendment may be made to correct a clerical error or an obvious mistake.

If the notice of application for registration has been published an amendment may be made to:

- the representation of the trade mark if the amendment does not substantially affect the identity of the trade mark as at the time when the notice of the application was published;
- correct a mistake of fact or an error in the classification of any goods or services specified in the application;
- change the type of registration sought in the application; or
- any particulars specified in the application other than the type of registration sought, unless the amendment would have the effect of extending the rights that, apart from the amendment, the applicant would have under the registration if it were granted.

1.16 Dividing a Trade Mark
A person who has made an application for the registration of a trade mark in respect of certain goods or services or both may make another application:

- for the registration of only part of the trade mark in respect of any or all those goods or services or both;
- for the registration of the trade mark in respect of only some of the goods or services or both in respect of which registration is sought under the initial application; or
- if the initial application has been amended to exclude some of the goods and services or both in respect of which registration was sought in the first place, or the registration of the trade mark in respect of any or all of the goods or services or both that have been so excluded.

A divisional application may only be made if the initial application for the registration of the trade mark is pending.

1.17 Length of Term of Protection
A registered trade mark is protected for a period of ten years from the filing date of the application for its registration.

An application for renewal of the registration of a trade mark may be made at any time within the ten-year period. Where the registration of a trade mark lapses, the owner of the trade mark may still make an application for renewal within 12 months after its registration expires, failing which the Registrar will remove the trade mark from the register upon the expiry of 12 months after its registration lapses.

1.18 Participation in the Madrid System
Saint Lucia does not take part in the Madrid System.

1.19 Denotation
Markings are not mandatory in Saint Lucia and the Trade Marks Act does not prescribe words or symbols to be used to indicate trade-mark use or signify registration.

2. Assignment and Licensing

2.1 Assignment Requirements or Restrictions
An application may be made to assign a registered trade mark or a trade mark whose registration is being sought. The application must be accompanied by written evidence of the assignment signed by both the assignor and assignee. A trade mark may be assigned with or without the goodwill of the business concerned in the relevant goods or services

or both and there is no requirement for there to be consideration for the assignment. An assignment may be partial in that it may apply to some of the goods and services of the trade mark but not partial in relation to the use of the trade mark in a particular area.

2.2 Procedure for Assigning a Trade Mark
An application for assignment is filed at the ROCIP together with the original or a certified copy of written evidence of the assignment and the Authorisation of Agent. The ROCIP will review the application and if acceptable, it will make the amendments to the Register and publish notice of the recording of the assignment and the registration of the beneficiary as the owner of the trade mark in the Gazette.

2.3 Registering or Recording the Assignment
The assignment of a trade mark must be registered at the ROCIP as the assignee will only have rights against third parties once registered. If the assignment is not recorded, the assignee will not be able to enforce his or her rights against third parties in relation to the trade mark.

2.4 Trade Marks and Security
A registered trade mark is personal property and a right in respect of a registered trade mark is enforceable in the same way as rights in respect of any other personal property.

2.5 Licensing Requirements or Restrictions
Legislation in Saint Lucia does not expressly provide for the licensing of trade marks, however, licences would be considered as an interest in or a right, or both, in respect of a trade mark. Interests or rights in a trade mark may be voluntarily recorded at the ROCIP. Therefore, a licence may be recorded at the ROCIP by making a joint application by the licensor and licensee.

If a person has applied for the registration of a trade mark and another person has an interest or right in respect of the trade mark (ie a licence), they may apply together to the Registrar for a record to be kept of the other person's claim.

2.6 Procedure for Licensing a Trade Mark
A joint application is made to the ROCIP by the parties to a licensing agreement. This is usually accompanied by a document setting out the terms of the licence and an Authorisation of Agent. The Registrar will then record the particulars of the licence in the Register.

2.7 Registering or Recording the Licence
Since the recordal of a licence is a voluntary procedure there is no requirement for registration. However, unless and until a licence is recorded, a licensee cannot realise the benefits afforded to him or her under the Act. For example, issuing a notice of objection to the importation of goods that infringe the trade mark to the Comptroller of Customs where the licensor fails to do so.

3. Opposition Procedure

3.1 Legal Grounds and Timeframes
The registration of a trade mark may be opposed on the following grounds:

- the applicant is not the owner of the trade mark;
- the applicant does not intend to use or authorise the use of the trade mark or to assign the trade mark to a body corporate;
- the opponent claims earlier use of a similar or identical trade mark;
- the trade mark is substantially identical or deceptively similar to a trade mark that has acquired a reputation in Saint Lucia and because of the said reputation of the other trade mark the use of the first mentioned trade mark would be likely to deceive or cause confusion;
- the trade mark consists of a false geographical indication;
- the application was amended contrary to the Trade Marks Act;
- the application contains certain signs prescribed by the Act not to be used as a trade mark or a sign so nearly resembling it as to be likely to be mistaken for it;
- the trade mark does not distinguish the applicant's goods or services;
- the trade mark is scandalous or its use is contrary to law; or
- the trade mark is likely to deceive or cause confusion.

3.2 Filing an Opposition
A third party may file a notice of opposition to the registration of a trade mark within three months of the date of publication of its acceptance in the Gazette, unless an extension is granted by the Registrar.

While representation is not mandatory, it is highly recommended that an opponent seeks legal representation. The official fee for filing a notice of opposition and supporting evidence is USD260 and an additional USD35 for the filing of the Authorisation of Agent. Professional fees vary and depend on, among other things, the issues and complexity of a case and the experience or seniority of counsel.

3.3 Opposition Procedure
A third party who wishes to oppose the registration of a trade mark (the opponent), must file a notice of opposition within three months of the date of publication of its acceptance in the Gazette, unless an extension is granted by the Registrar.

If the opponent intends to rely on evidence in support of the opposition, the opponent must serve a copy of the supporting evidence on an applicant within three months from the day on which the notice of opposition is filed. Within two days after the opponent serves a copy of the supporting evidence on the applicant, the opponent must file with the Registrar the original evidence and a statement setting out the date, place and manner of service of the copy of the evidence on the applicant. If the opponent does not intend to rely on evidence in support of the opposition, the opponent must, within three months from the day on which the notice of opposition is filed, serve on the applicant a copy of a notice stating that the opponent does not intend to rely on evidence in support of the opposition. The opponent must file with the Registrar, the original notice and a statement setting out the date, place and manner of service of the copy of the notice on the applicant as soon as practicable after serving the applicant. If the opponent does not file evidence in support or the notice or apply for an extension to do so, the opponent shall be deemed to have abandoned his or her opposition.

If the applicant intends to rely on evidence in answer to the opposition, the applicant must serve a copy of the evidence in answer on the opponent within three months from the day on which the opponent serves him or her with the evidence in support or notice. The applicant must file with the Registrar, the original evidence and a statement setting out the date, place and manner of service of the copy of the evidence on the opponent within two days of service. If the applicant does not intend to rely on evidence in answer to the opposition, the applicant must serve on the opponent, within the period for service of a copy of the evidence in answer, a copy of a notice stating that the applicant does not intend to rely on evidence in answer to the opposition. Within two days after the applicant serves a copy of the notice on the opponent, the applicant must file with the Registrar the original notice and a statement setting out the date, place and manner of service of the copy of the notice on the opponent. If the applicant does not file evidence in answer or the notice or apply for an extension of time to do so, he or she shall be deemed to have abandoned their application.

If an opponent intends to rely on evidence in reply to the opposition, the opponent must serve a copy of the evidence in reply on the applicant within three months after the service on the opponent of a copy of the evidence in answer. Within two days after the opponent serves a copy of the evidence in reply on the applicant, the opponent must file with the Registrar the original evidence and a statement setting out the date, place and manner of service of the copy of the evidence on the applicant. If an opponent does not intend to rely on evidence in reply to the evidence in answer to the opposition, the opponent must serve on the applicant, within three months after the service on the opponent of a copy of the evidence in answer, a copy of a notice stating that the opponent does not intend to rely on evidence in reply to the evidence in answer to the opposition. Within two days after the opponent serves a copy of the notice on the applicant, the opponent must file with the Registrar the original notice and a statement setting out the date, place and manner of service of the copy of the notice on the applicant. If the opponent does not file evidence in reply to the evidence in answer or the notice or apply for extension of time to do so, the evidence shall be deemed closed and opposition proceedings follow the normal course.

Upon completion of the evidence, the applicant or opponent may ask the Registrar to hear the parties to the opposition proceedings or the Registrar may, on his or her own initiative, give an opportunity to the parties to be heard. The Registrar must give notice to the parties of a date when he or she will hear arguments in the opposition proceedings, which must be a date at least 14 days after the date of the notice unless the parties consent to a shorter notice. Within seven days from the receipt of the notice any party who intends to appear must so notify the Registrar. The Registrar will then hear the proceedings and issue a ruling at the end of the proceedings.

3.4 Legal Remedies

An applicant can appeal decisions made by the Registrar to the High Court. Where the High Court hears an appeal from the decision of the Registrar an appeal does not go to the Court of Appeal except with that court's leave.

The appeal will follow the normal course of civil litigation matters in the High Court or Court of Appeal and may take approximately one to two years.

4. Initiating a Lawsuit

4.1 Actions to Pursue Infringement

An action for an infringement of registered or unregistered trade marks may be brought in the High Court. There are no specialised courts or tribunals for trade-mark matters in Saint Lucia.

In respect of registered marks, the Act additionally provides that the Comptroller of Customs may effect seizure and deal with goods that are imported into Saint Lucia if the importation infringes or appears to infringe a registered trade mark. The registered owner of a trade mark may give to the Comptroller a notice in the prescribed form objecting to the importation after the date of notice of goods that infringe the trade mark.

4.2 Declaratory Judgment Proceedings

If a person threatens to bring an action against another person on the grounds that the threatened person has infringed a registered trade mark or a trade mark alleged by the person to be registered, any person aggrieved by the threat may bring an action in the High Court against the person making the threat.

The alleged infringer may obtain from the court:

- a declaration that the defendant has no grounds for making the threat;
- an injunction restraining the defendant from continuing to make the threat; or
- recover any damages that he or she has sustained because of the defendant's conduct.

4.3 Jurisdiction of Courts
Trade-mark infringement proceedings are heard in the High Court at first instance. With leave of the Court of Appeal an appeal goes to the Court of Appeal against a judgment of the High Court. Prosecution for criminal offences committed under the Act is commenced in a District Court and an appeal goes to the High Court.

4.4 Prerequisites to Filing a Lawsuit
There are no prerequisites to filing a claim. However, pre-action cease-and-desist letters are typically issued to alleged infringers as a matter of practice.

4.5 Representation for Parties
There is no mandatory requirement that the parties to trade-mark litigation matters must be represented by a lawyer. However, as trade-mark litigation matters are treated as any other civil proceedings in the High Court, it is highly recommended that parties obtain legal representation.

4.6 Interim or Preliminary Injunctions
An injunction may be granted by the High Court subject to any conditions it deems fit. In deciding whether to grant an injunction the High Court will consider the standard requirements for the granting of injunctions in civil cases.

4.7 Protection for Potential Defendant
Prior to the commencement of legal proceedings, an alleged infringer may apply to the courts for the remedies outlined in **4.2 Declaratory Judgment Proceedings**. Where legal proceedings have commenced, a defendant may file a defence and any counterclaim, if applicable, to the claim brought against him or her.

4.8 Obtaining Information and Evidence
Disclosure of documents is always pursuant to an order of the courts. The judge typically orders standard disclosure at the case-management stage of court proceedings. A party may also make an application to the court for specific disclosure.

4.9 Initial Pleading Standards
There are no special provisions for pleadings in trade-mark proceedings as opposed to non-intellectual property civil proceedings. The claimant is required to set out clearly all the relevant facts which give rise to the claim and to prove his or her case on a balance of probabilities.

Pleadings may be supplemented by filing an amended Statement of Claim prior to case management or otherwise with leave of the courts.

4.10 Representative or Collective Actions
There are no specific rules for representative or class actions in trade mark proceedings. The rules of court in civil proceedings provide that, on the application of an appropriate person, the courts may appoint a body having a sufficient interest in the proceedings or one or more persons, to represent all or most or some of the persons with the same or similar interest.

5. Infringement

5.1 Action for Infringement
A registered owner of a trade mark has the exclusive rights to obtain relief if the trade mark has been infringed. If a trade mark is registered in the name of two or more persons as joint owners of the trade mark, the rights granted to those persons are to be exercised by them as if they were the rights of a single person.

Subject to the terms of the governing licence agreement, an authorised user of a registered trade mark may also bring an action for infringement of the trade mark.

5.2 Signs and Infringement
Where an alleged infringer has used a sign as a trade mark, the factors taken into consideration when assessing whether the trade mark has been infringed include:

- the degree of similarity between the trade mark and the sign used by the person;
- the degree of similarity between the goods and services associated with the registered trade mark and the sign;
- whether the trade mark is well-known in Saint Lucia; and
- the likelihood of confusion between the goods or services of the registered trade mark and the sign.

5.3 Defences Against Infringement
The defences to a claim of infringement of a registered trade mark include:

- the defendant used a sign in good faith to indicate the kind, quality, quantity, intended purpose, value, geographical origin, or some other characteristic of goods or services,

or the time of production of goods or of the rendering of services;
- the defendant used the trade mark in good faith to indicate the intended purpose of goods or services;
- the defendant used the trade mark for the purposes of comparative advertising;
- the defendant exercised a right to use the trade mark given to him or her under the Trade Marks Act;
- the court is of the opinion that the defendant would obtain registration of the trade mark in his or her name if he or she were to apply for it;
- the defendant has applied to use or has used the trade mark in relation to, the goods by, or with the consent of, the registered owner of the trade mark;
- the defendant can show that he or she or his or her predecessor in title has continuously used the trade mark in the course of trade in relation to those goods or services from a time before the registration of the trade mark or when the registered owner first used the trade mark; or
- an action against groundless threats.

5.4 Administrative or Criminal Offence

Trade mark infringements are enforced either through civil proceedings as outlined in **4.1 Actions to Pursue Infringement** or criminal proceedings. Under the Act, criminal offences are prosecuted by the Director of Public Prosecutions and would, in the first instance, be heard in the District Court. These decisions may be appealed to the High Court.

5.5 Custom Seizures

The Act makes provisions for the Comptroller of Customs to effect seizure and deal with goods that are imported into Saint Lucia if the importation infringes or appears to infringe a trade mark registered in Saint Lucia. The registered owner of the trade mark may give to the Comptroller a notice in the form prescribed objecting to the importation after the date of notice of goods that infringe the trade mark.

6. Revocation/Cancellation

6.1 Remedies and Reasons

The acceptance of an application for registration of a trade mark may be revoked if, before a trade mark is registered, the Registrar is satisfied that the application was accepted because of an error or omission in the course of examination or that, in the special circumstances of the case, the trade mark should not be registered, or should be registered subject to conditions or limitations, or to additional or different conditions or limitations. If the Registrar revokes the acceptance of an application the application is taken never to have been accepted. The Registrar's decision may be appealed to the High Court.

Where a third party seeks the cancellation of a registered trade mark, an application must be made to the High Court. An application made to the High Court in challenge of a registered trade mark can be made on the following grounds:

- any of the grounds on which the registration of the trade mark could have been opposed before the Registrar;
- an amendment of the application for the registration of the trade mark was obtained as a result of fraud, false suggestion or misrepresentation;
- because of the circumstances applying at the time when the application is made to the High Court the use of the trade mark is likely to deceive or cause confusion for a reason other than that the trade mark is likely to deceive or cause confusion or the trade mark is substantially identical with, or deceptively similar to, a trade mark registered in respect of similar goods or closely related services, or the trade mark is identical or deceptively similar to a trade mark that has acquired a reputation in Saint Lucia and because of said reputation of the other trade mark the use of the first mentioned trade mark would be likely to deceive or cause confusion;
- if the following circumstances apply:
  - (a) the Registrar accepted the application for the registration of the trade mark because he or she was satisfied, having regard to the extent to which the trade mark was inherently adapted to distinguish the goods or services of the applicant for registration from the goods and services of any other person and the intended use of the trade mark, that the trade mark would distinguish those goods or services as being those of the applicant;
  - (b) the application for rectification is made at least ten years after the filing date; or
  - (c) in the intervening period, the trade mark has not been used to an extent sufficient for it to distinguish, in fact, the goods or services of the registered owner from the goods or services of any other person;
- the application is in respect of an entry in the Register and the entry was made, or has been previously amended, as a result of fraud, false suggestion or misrepresentation;
- a condition or limitation entered in the Register in relation to the trade mark has been contravened;
- if the trade mark consists of, or contains, a sign that after the date of registration becomes generally accepted within the relevant trade as the sign that describes or is the name of an article, substance or service; and
- if the trade mark consists of, or contains, a sign that describes or is the name of an article or substance that was formerly exploited under a patent or a service that was formerly provided as a patented process and it is at least two years since the patent has expired or ceased, and the sign is the only commonly known way to describe or identify the article, substance or service.

6.2 Initiation of Revocation/Cancellation Proceeding

The revocation of a trade mark is at the instance of the Registrar acting of his or her own volition. An application for the cancellation of a trade mark by the owner is made to the ROCIP. However, a third-party application for the cancellation of a trade mark is made to the High Court.

7. Trial & Settlement

7.1 Special Procedural Provisions

There are no special procedural provisions for trade-mark proceedings before the courts as they are conducted as any normal civil proceeding and are governed by the rules of the court. Special procedural provisions apply to opposition proceedings which are highlighted in **3.3 Opposition Procedure**.

7.2 Determination of Cases

The case is determined by legal judges and the parties do not have any influence as to who the judge will be.

7.3 Possibilities of Settlement

In the course of legal proceedings the parties may, by consent, have the opportunity to have the matter settled by formal court-connected mediation. Aside therefrom, the parties are at liberty to settle the dispute at any time of their own volition.

8. Remedies

8.1 Existing Remedies

The remedies available to a successful trade-mark owner in an action for infringement include, among others, an injunction which may be granted subject to any condition the courts deem fit, damages or an account of profits at the option of the claimant and payment of legal costs.

8.2 Rights and Remedies

A successful defendant may obtain among others, a declaration of non-infringement from the courts, an injunction restraining the registered owner from making groundless threats and payment of legal costs.

9. Appeal

9.1 Special Provisions

There are no special provisions concerning the appellate procedure for trade-mark proceedings. The appellate procedure for trade-mark proceedings is provided by the relevant rules of the courts.

9.2 Factual or Legal Review

Only in very limited circumstances will a court exercising an appellate jurisdiction interfere with findings of fact. Accordingly, appeals are predominantly limited to a review of points of law.

10. Other Trade Mark Issues

10.1 Protection of Famous Marks

If a famous trade mark is not used or registered in Saint Lucia, the owner may, nonetheless, be able to pursue an infringement action under the common law tort of passing-off. The owner will need to prove that the famous trade mark is known to the Saint Lucia public and that there was an intention to deceive or confuse and that he or she has suffered damage as a result of the said deception or confusion.

11. Costs

11.1 Costs Before Filing a Lawsuit

Costs are typically determined by an agreement between a party and its chosen legal representative.

11.2 Costs Regarding an Infringement Action

The cost of litigation is assessed pursuant to the Eastern Caribbean Supreme Court Civil Procedure Rules 2000. Part 65 of the Rules, as amended, deals with the ways in which costs are to be quantified and specifies a scale of fixed and prescribed costs and outlines percentages to be allowed at various stages of any claim from filing to trial.

11.3 Costs of Litigation

Generally, the losing party is required to pay the successful party's costs of litigation.

12. Alternative Dispute Resolution

12.1 Common Way of Settlement

Mediation and arbitration (to a lesser extent) are both available to aggrieved parties to attempt resolution of their disputes by assisted negotiations outside of the more formal setting of the courts.

Arbitration becomes operational in the event of a dispute if, by agreement, the parties have decided previously to pursue this medium.

The courts in Saint Lucia favour settlement of disputes by mediation and there is a court-connected mediation programme in place to assist in this regard. Mediation is usually recommended in the first instance by the courts. A matter may, however, be referred to mediation only with the consent of the parties. In Saint Lucia an agreement reached by mediation may be duly filed in the High Court, which is made by an order (by consent) of the courts, thereby binding the parties.

Floissac Fleming & Associates
Cnr. Brazil & Mongiraud Streets
P.O. Box 722, Castries
Saint Lucia

FLOISSAC FLEMING & Associates

Tel: (758) 452-2887
Fax: (758) 453-1496
Email: info@floissaclawyers.com
Web: www.floissaclawyers.com

TAIWAN

LAW AND PRACTICE: p.291

Contributed by Deep & Far Attorneys-at-Law

The 'Law & Practice' sections provide easily accessible information on navigating the legal system when conducting business in the jurisdiction. Leading lawyers explain local law and practice at key transactional stages and for crucial aspects of doing business.

Law and Practice

Contributed by Deep & Far Attorneys-at-Law

CONTENTS

Deep & Far Attorneys-at-Law was founded in 1992 and is one of the largest law firms in this country. Deep & Far focuses on all aspects of intellectual property rights (IPRs) including patents, trade marks, copyrights, trade secrets, unfair competition, and/or licensing, counselling, litigation and/or transaction thereof. The firm's three-strong trade-marks team deal with all aspects of the trade marks process, including: consultation, search, registration, renewal, amendment, opposition, invalidation, cancellation, seizure, licensing, investigation, and dispute settlement (including mediation and litigation).

Author

Lu-Fa Tsai is a partner at Deep & Far. His key areas of expertise are general law, intellectual property – including trade marks – international investment and fair trade. Aside from his trade-mark practice, he is experienced in criminal, corporate and civil cases of all kinds. Lu-Fa Tsai is the author of Trademark Use, Taiwan in SMD International Country Index (2014), and is a member of Taipei Bar Association, Taiwan, R.O.C.

1. Types of Trade Marks & Registration

1.1 Types of Trade Marks

Taiwan has had service marks and goods marks in the past, but they are now all called trade marks. There are also certification marks, collective marks, and collective trade marks. There is no stipulation or clear definition in the laws regarding what makes a mark famous, nor is there a specific law directed to trade dress, although this is briefly provided in the Goods Labelling Act and the Fair Trade Act. Rights in such trade marks are basically provided in the statutory law, but are often better delineated by various court decisions.

1.2 Trade-Mark Rights

A trade-mark registration must be obtained in order to gain exclusive rights to the trade mark. Nevertheless, exclusive rights to a well-known trade mark may be acquired merely by using the trade mark. A registered well-known trade mark is positively protected by the trade-mark law, but an unregistered well-known mark is better protected by the fair trade law. Specifically, although an unregistered well-known trade mark can stop or cancel an identical trade-mark registration, it may enforce its trade-mark rights only after being registered.

1.3 Standards for Registering

Normally, a trade mark consisting of or containing a generic or descriptive term or design cannot be registered or must provide a disclaimer, unless it has obtained a secondary meaning, which is also known as acquired distinctiveness. This applies to trade dress or 3D trademarks where the Intellectual Property Office asks the applicant to show its secondary meaning or acquired distinctiveness before it may be registered. There might be a slight deviation for a certification, collective mark or collective trade mark because the geographical name (name for a place of origin) serves only to certify the place of origin of the goods or services.

1.4 Trade-Mark Register

There is a trade-mark register, which is publicly available (see http://tmsearch.tipo.gov.tw/RAVS/wfm10000.html).

1.5 Types of Registers

There are no different types of registers.

1.6 Searching for Prior Trade Marks

It is normal practice for big companies or international giants to search for prior trade marks before applying to register a trade mark, partly because the filing fees are low; small and medium companies would like the IPO to cover both the search and registration functions. Search resources include:

- Trademark Search System (for both earlier-filed trade marks and registered trade marks)
  - (a) Original Chinese version: http://tmsearch.tipo.gov.tw/TIPO_DR/index.jsp
  - (b) New Chinese version: https://twtmsearch.tipo.gov.tw/OS0/OS0101.jsp
  - (c) New English version: https://twtmsearch.tipo.gov.tw/OS0/OS0101.jsp?l6=en_US&isReadBulletinzh_TW=true
- Directory and Case Compilation of Well-known Trade marks
  - (a) Directory and case compilation of well-known trade

marks for the last five years: https://www.tipo.gov.tw/lp.asp?CtNode=7746&CtUnit=3810&BaseDSD=7&mp=1
(b) Directory and case analysis of well-known trade marks: https://www.tipo.gov.tw/lp.asp?ctNode=7066&CtUnit=3506&BaseDSD=7&mp=1

1.7 Registration Requirements
The requirements to register a trade mark are as follows:

- Formality Requirements: the submission of an application to the Trademark Office needs a petition and trade-mark specimens (see Article 19(1), Trademark Act).
- Substantive Requirements: registration can be refused (see Articles 29(1), 29(3), 30(1), 30(4), Trademark Act) on the following absolute and relative grounds:

  (a) the trade mark has no distinctiveness (Article 29(1));
  (b) a part of the trade mark has no distinctiveness, but the applicant does not make a disclaimer to that purpose (Article 29(3));
  (c) the trade mark is identical or similar to another person's registered trade mark, and the designated goods or services of the trade mark are identical or similar to those of the registered trade mark, so that there is a likelihood of confusion for relevant consumers (Article 30(1)(10));
  (d) a part of the trade mark is identical or similar to another person's registered trade mark, and the designated goods or services of the trade mark are identical or similar to those of the registered trade mark, but the applicant does not make a disclaimer to that purpose (Article 30(4)).

1.8 Registering a Trade Mark
Trade marks may be registered by domestic and foreign natural persons, legal persons (eg, companies, limited partnerships, corporations with legal status, foundations with legal status, associations with legal status, societies with legal status), groups (eg, businesses such as partnerships and sole proprietorships, factories, private schools, private hospitals) or government authorities/agencies (eg, the ministry of economic affairs, public schools, public hospitals). Any domestic and foreign legal persons, groups or government authorities/agencies that are competent to certify another person's goods or services can register a certification mark (see Article 81(1), Trademark Act). Any domestic and foreign associations, societies or any other groups that qualify as a legal person (corporations with legal status) may register a collective mark (see Article 85, Trademark Act).

1.9 Registering Signs
The following types of signs can be registered and/or protected as a trade mark (see Art. 18(1), Trademark Act): words, devices, symbols, colours, three-dimensional shapes, motions, holograms, continuous patterns, odours, positions, and any combination of the above.

1.10 Other Rights to Signs
The Taiwan legal system recognises other rights to sign or source-identifiers besides trade marks, such as:

- rights to company names, contained within Article 18(1) of the Company Act (for general company names) and Article 22(1) of the Fair Trade Act (for well-known company names);
- rights to trade names (business names), contained within Article 28(1) of the Business Registration Act (for general trade name) and Article 22(1) of the Fair Trade Act (for well-known trade names);
- rights to trade dresses (eg, containers, packages or appearances of goods), contained within Article 22(1) of the Fair Trade Act (for well-known trade dresses) and Articles 4(1) & 6(1) of the Goods Labelling Act; and
- rights to other source-identifiers (signs, symbols), contained within Article 22(1) of the Fair Trade Act (for well-known source-identifiers).

1.11 Registration Procedure
After filing an application, there is a procedural examination as to the formality requirements, followed by a substantive examination. After the mark has been found allowable, the procedure involves payment of the registration fee, publication of the registration and issuance of the registration certificate. The Taiwan legal system allows multi-class applications.

1.12 Use in Commerce
The system does not require demonstration of use of the filed trade mark in commerce, as of the date of filing the application. If the trade mark-owner has not used the trade mark for three years since its registration (the date of publication of its registration), the Trademark Office can cancel the registration of the trade mark ex officio or upon request (see Article 63(1)(2), Trademark Act).

The registration of a trade mark is effective for ten years from the date of publication of registration. The registration of a trade mark may be renewed for a further ten years after the renewal (see Article 33, Trademark Act). The request for renewal of a registration shall be made within the six months before the expiry of the period of registration; it may also be made within six months after the expiry of the period of registration, but this accrues double the renewal fee (see Article 34(1), Trademark Act). The renewal fee for trade marks (in the narrow sense) or collective trade marks is TWD4,000 per class of goods or services; the renewal fee for certification marks, collective marks or collective trade marks is also TWD4,000.

1.13 Registration of Series Marks
The registration of series trade marks is not permitted.

1.14 Length of Registration Process

The procedural and substantive examinations for an application for trade-mark registration take about eight months. Representation is not necessary for those applicants that are Taiwan (ROC) nationals and have a residence or business office in Taiwan (ROC), but those that have no residence or business office in Taiwan (ROC) (eg, overseas Taiwanese (Chinese)) do need representation. Applicants from Mainland China (PRC), Hong Kong or Macao that have a residence or business office in Taiwan (ROC) do not need representation, but applicants that have no residence or business office in Taiwan (ROC) do. Representation is necessary for applicants from foreign countries, regardless of whether or not there is a residence or business office in Taiwan (ROC).

Fees for obtaining a trade-mark registration are collected separately at the application and registration stages. At the application stage, the official fees (application fee) for under 20 items of the designated goods in Classes 1 to 34 are TWD3,000 per class, with TWD200 per additional item; fees for Classes 35 to 45 are fixed at TWD3,000 per class, except as designated those involved in connection with "retail" where the basic item number is 5, with excessive fees beyond that being TWD500 per item, Attorney fees are TWD10,000 for the first class and TWD6,000 for the second class, with TWD20 per each excess item. In the registration stage, the official fees (registration fees) are TWD2,500 per class, while the attorney fees are TWD6,000 for the first class and TWD3,600 for the second class.

1.15 Grounds for Refusal

Absolute grounds for refusal of a trade-mark registration include:

- lack of distinctiveness (eg, generic or descriptive designs) (see Article 29(1), Trademark Act);
- that the mark is barely required for exercising the function of goods or services (see Article 30(1)(1), Trademark Act);
- that the mark is identical or similar to the national flag, the national emblem, the national seal, a military flag, a military insignia, an official seal, or a medal of the Republic of China, or the national flag of a foreign country, or the national emblem, national seal or national insignia of a foreign country communicated by any member of the WTO under Article 6ter(3)(b) of the Paris Convention (see Article 30(1)(2), Trademark Act);
- that the mark is identical to the portrait or name of Dr Sun Yat-Sen or the head of state (see Article 30(1)(3), Trademark Act);
- that the mark is identical or similar to the mark of a government agency of the Republic of China or an official exhibition held thereby, or the medal or certificate awarded thereby (see Article 30(1)(4), Trademark Act);
- that the mark is identical or similar to the emblem, the flag, another insignia, the abbreviation or the name of an international intergovernmental organisation or a well-known domestic or foreign public interest institution, and is likely to cause mistakes or misconception among the public (see Article 30(1)(5), Trademark Act);
- that the mark is identical or similar to a domestic or foreign national sign or hallmark for quality control or warranty, and designated to be used on identical or similar goods or services (see Article 30(1)(6), Trademark Act);
- that the mark violates public order or good morals (see Article 30(1)(7), Trademark Act);
- that the mark is likely to cause the public to mistake or misconceive the nature, quality or place of origin of the goods or services (see Article 30(1)(8), Trademark Act); and
- that the mark is identical or similar to a geographical indication for wine or distilled spirits of the Republic of China or a foreign country, and designated to be used on goods identical or similar to wine or distilled spirits, where the foreign country and the Republic of China enter into an agreement or jointly accede to an international treaty, or reciprocally recognise the protection of geographical indication for wine or distilled spirits (see Article 30(1)(9), Trademark Act).

1.16 Process for Overcoming Objections

Any person may file an opposition to the registration of a trade mark that has a lack of distinctiveness (inherent distinctiveness) with the Trademark Office, within three months of the publication of registration (see Article 48(1), Trademark Act). By the same token, if an already registered trade mark has a lack of distinctiveness (inherent distinctiveness), an interested party may file an invalidation with the Trademark Office and, likewise, a trade-mark examiner getting known thereto may submit a proposal for an invalidation of the registration to the Trademark Office (see Article 57(1), Trademark Act). The trade mark-owner may, however, exhaust its efforts to demonstrate that the registered trade mark has distinctiveness in the opposition or invalidation process. The general basis for such demonstration is to show the obtainment of a secondary meaning (acquired distinctiveness), through which the mark may then be registered (see Article 29(2), Trademark Act).

1.17 Consideration of Prior Rights

Although the Trademark Office may take the initiative to consider the existence of prior rights in its examination of an application for registration, it does not normally do so if the relevant materials are not provided. Prior rights of others include registered trade marks, earlier filed trade marks, well-known trade marks and earlier used trade marks (see Articles 30(1)(10), 30(1)(11) and 30(1)(12)), while prior rights of the applicant are the well-known status (see Article 30(1)(11)).

1.18 Third-Party Rights
Third parties have the right to participate during the registration procedure, but it is not common practice to intervene before an application is allowed for registration. Third parties may file an opposition, invalidation or cancellation after registration of a trade mark if they find that such registration violates any of their interests. Anyone may file an opposition (see Article 48(1)) or a cancellation (see Article 63(1)), but only an interested party may file an invalidation (see Article 57(1)).

1.19 Revoke, Change, Amend or Correct an Application
No amendments shall be made to the design of a trade mark after filing the application, unless such amendment does not substantially change the trade mark (see Article 23). Similarly, no amendments shall be made to the designated goods or services of a trade mark after filing the application, unless such amendment is a restriction of the designated goods or services (see Article 23).

Changes to the name or address of the applicant, the trade-mark agent, or any other particulars of an application may be made upon request (see Article 24), while errors in the name or address of the applicant, errors of wording or copying and other obvious errors in the particulars of an application may be corrected upon request or ex officio (see Article 25(1)). In addition, an applicant may request to divide an application into two or more applications by allocating the designated goods or services included in the original application among the divisional applications (see Article 26), either for purposes of earlier partial registration or for strategic considerations. Finally, an applicant may request to withdraw an application itself.

1.20 Assigning an Application or Granting a Licence
An applicant may assign a trade-mark application to another person (see Article 27). Conceptually, only a registered trade mark has the right to be licensed for protection by the fair trade law, unless it is a well-known trade mark. The owner of a filed trade mark, however, is not prohibited from licensing the anticipatory trade-mark rights, if appropriate.

1.21 Remedies Against the Trade Mark Office
The remedies against the Trademark Office decision proceed sequentially as follows:

- administrative appeal before the Ministry of Economic Affairs (within 30 days of the refusal by the Trademark Office);
- administrative litigation before the Intellectual Property Court (within two months of the refusal by the Ministry of Economic Affairs); and
- administrative litigation appeal before the Supreme Administrative Court (within 20 days of the refusal by Intellectual Property Court).

1.22 Use of a Trade Mark
The Taiwan legal system does not require an applicant to use its trade mark in commerce before the registration is issued. Nevertheless, a prior use may safeguard the potential interests for a later registration if the former applicant or registrant has a contractual or other relationship with the prior user where any kind of reliable evidence – eg a contract or invoice – may establish a genuine use (Article 30(1)(12)).

1.23 Dividing a Trade Mark
It is possible to divide a trade-mark application. The requirements include a petition, a petition time before receipt of a final action for an application or a post-grant dispute from the Trademark Office, and a co-action by joint trade-mark owners or applicants (see Articles 26, 28(5), 31(3), 38(3), 46(4)). The second requirement is somewhat unnecessary or improper, because Articles 26 and 37 respectively provide that such petition may be made at any time before and after registration.

1.24 Length of Term of Protection
The term of trade-mark protection is ten years (see Article 33(1)). The trade-mark owner may renew the trade-mark registration before the term expires (see Article 34(1)), if the request is made within the six months before the expiry of the period of registration. The request for renewal of registration may also be made within six months after the expiry of the period of registration, but the renewal fee is doubled in this case (see Article 34(1)).

1.25 Requirements for an Exhaustion
Where goods have been put on the domestic or foreign market under a registered trade mark (domestic registered trade mark) by the trade-mark owner or with his or her consent, the trade-mark owner is not entitled to claim further trade-mark rights (rights to the domestic registered trade mark) for such goods, unless such claim is to prevent the condition of the goods from being changed or impaired after they have been put on the market, or if there is another reasonable ground (see Article 36(2)).

1.26 Participation in the Madrid System
Taiwan (ROC) does not participate in the Madrid system, for political reasons.

1.27 Consequences for Providing Incorrect Information
The consequences for providing incorrect information in the relevant proceedings (for example, if a trade-mark applicant forges the consent of the owner of a registered trade mark

or earlier filed trade mark to the trade-mark application) are as follows:

- Consequences under Trademark Law – the forged consent has not legally existed ab initio and thus is not effective. Therefore, the filed trade mark cannot be registered if it is likely to cause confusion among the relevant consumers (see Article 30(1)(10), Trademark Act).
- Consequences under Civil Law – the forged consent has not legally existed ab initio and thus is not effective. The earlier trade-mark applicant or registrant may claim damages, if any (Article 184(1), Civil Law).
- Consequences under Administrative Law – if the trade-mark application had been approved but the trade-mark registration was revoked through opposition or invalidated through invalidation filed by the prior trade-mark applicant or registrant, the applicant cannot claim protection of reliance, because its reliance deserves no protection (see Articles 117, 119, Administrative Procedure Act).
- Consequences under Criminal Law – if the applicant forges a private document and it is sufficient to cause damages to the public or another person, he or she may be sentenced to imprisonment for no more than five years (see Article 210, Criminal Code).

1.28 Updating or Refreshing a Design Mark

No amendments shall be made to the design of a trade mark after it has been filed or registered, so under no circumstances can a design mark be updated or refreshed (see Articles 23, 38(1)). However, a non-substantive revision to the trade-mark design is permissible before registration (Articles 23, 31(3)).

1.29 Denotation

There is no specific symbol that trade-mark owners should use to denote that a mark is registered, but the registrant may use a desired symbol or the international popular symbol (eg, ®) to denote the registration (Article 35(3)). Likewise, although there is no express provision about the TM symbol, it can be deduced from Articles 30(1)(12) and 35(3) that registrants may assert common-law rights in the mark by such symbol for declaration of potential trade-mark rights.

2. Assignment and Licensing

2.1 Assignment Requirements or Restrictions

There are no special requirements or restrictions applicable to assigning a trade-mark application or registration. However, the assignment of a trade-mark registration may not be claimed against any third party, unless it is registered at the Trademark Office (see Article 42).

2.2 Procedure for Assigning a Trade Mark

In order to assign a trade-mark application or registered trade mark, the original owner usually concludes an assignment agreement with the assignee, who then files an application for recordal of the trade-mark assignment with the Trademark Office. The required documents include an application form, a power of attorney and the original assignment agreement or a simplified one tailored to the recording purpose. The official fee for registration of a trade mark assignment is TWD2,000 per case.

2.3 Registering or Recording the Assignment

The assignment of a trade-mark registration (registered trade mark) needs to be recorded at the Trademark Office in order to win a locus standi against any third party. Although the assignment is effective even without official recordal, the new owner may only claim rights against the assignor assignee (see Article 42). Typical risks during the gap between the assignment taking place and its official recordal are as follows:

- the assignor assigns the trade mark to another person again. The first assignee may not use the first assignment to claim against the second assignee if the first assignment was not recorded or registered;
- the assignor licenses the trade mark to another person. The assignee may not use the assignment to claim against the licensee if the assignment was not registered; and
- the assignor creates a pledge of the trade mark for another person. The assignee may not use the assignment to claim against the pledgee if the assignment was not registered.

2.4 Trade Marks and Security

A trade mark – including the trade mark itself, the trade-mark registration and rights to the trade mark – can be given as a security or assigned by way of security (Article 44(2)). A trade mark can be the subject of a pledge (pledge of rights) (see Articles 44, 45, 46(1), 92, 93(1)(5), Trademark Act, and Article 900, Civil Code). A trade mark can be levied in execution (Articles 28(1), 46(1)).

2.5 Licensing Requirements or Restrictions

No special requirements or restrictions are applicable to licensing a trade mark to a licensee who has no locus standi to claim against any third party, unless it is registered at the Trademark Office (see Article 39(2)); any kind of licence is permissible. Nevertheless, the usual three types of licences are exclusive licence, non-exclusive licence and sole licence, which is different from exclusive licence in that it allows use by the licence, which an exclusive licence does not.

2.6 Procedure for Licensing a Trade Mark

In order to license a trade mark (registered trade mark), the trade-mark owner usually concludes a trade-mark licence agreement with an interested party, and the licensor or licensee then files an application for registration or recordal of the trade-mark licence with the Trademark Office. The required documents include an application form, a power of attorney and the trade-mark licence agreement. The official fee for registration of a trade-mark licence is TWD2,000 per case.

2.7 Registering or Recording the Licence

The licence of a trade mark (registered trade mark) needs to be registered or recorded at the Trademark Office in order to get a locus standi to claim against any third party. Without recordal, the licence is effective only between the licensor and the licensee (see Article 39(2)). Risks existing during the gap between the licence being entered into and its registration are typically as follows:

- the licensor assigns the trade mark to another person. The licensee does not have a locus standi to claim the licence against the assignee if the licence was not registered (see Article 39(3));
- the exclusive licensor licenses the trade mark to another person exclusively again. The first exclusive licensee does not have a locus standi to claim the first exclusive licence against the second licensee if the first exclusive licence was not registered;
- the exclusive licensor licenses the trade mark to another person non-exclusively. The exclusive licensee does not have a locus standi to claim the exclusive licence against the non-exclusive licensee if the exclusive licence was not registered;
- the non-exclusive licensor licenses the trade mark to another person exclusively. The non-exclusive licensee does not have a locus standi to claim the non-exclusive licence against the exclusive licensee if the non-exclusive licence was not registered (see Article 39(4)); and
- the licensor creates a pledge of the trade mark for another person. The licensee does not have a locus standi to claim the licence against the pledgee if the licence was not registered.

2.8 Reasons to Deny Granting a Perpetual Licence

There is no reason a trade-mark owner cannot grant a perpetual licence.

3. Opposition Procedure

3.1 Legal Grounds and Timeframes

The legal grounds for filing an opposition to a trade-mark registration include (see Article 48(1)):

- lack of distinctiveness (eg, generic or descriptive designs) (see Article 29(1));
- that the mark is merely necessary for exercising the function of goods or services (see Article 30(1)(1));
- that the mark is identical or similar to the national flag, the national emblem, the national seal, a military flag, a military insignia, an official seal, or a medal of the Republic of China, or the national flag of a foreign country, or the national emblem, national seal or national insignia of a foreign country communicated by any member of the WTO under Article 6ter(3)(b) of the Paris Convention (see Article 30(1)(2));
- that the mark is identical to the portrait or name of Dr Sun Yat-Sen or the head of state (see Article 30(1)(3));
- that the mark is identical or similar to the mark of a government agency of the Republic of China or an official exhibition held thereby, or the medal or certificate awarded thereby (see Article 30(1)(4));
- that the mark is identical or similar to the emblem, the flag, another insignia, the abbreviation or the name of an international intergovernmental organisation or a well-known domestic or foreign public interest institution, and is likely to cause mistakes or misconception among the public (see Article 30(1)(5));
- that the mark is identical or similar to a domestic or foreign national sign or hallmark for quality control or warranty, and is designated to be used on identical or similar goods or services (see Article 30(1)(6));
- that the mark violates public order or good morals (see Article 30(1)(7));
- that the mark is likely to cause the public to mistake or misconceive the nature, quality or place of origin of the goods or services (see Article 30(1)(8));
- that the mark is identical or similar to a geographical indication for wine or distilled spirits of the Republic of China or a foreign country, and designated to be used on goods identical or similar to wine or distilled spirits, where the foreign country and the Republic of China enter into an agreement or jointly accede to an international treaty, or reciprocally recognise the protection of geographical indications for wine or distilled spirits (see Article 30(1)(9));
- that the mark is identical or similar to another person's registered trade mark or earlier filed trade mark, and is designated to be used on goods or services identical or similar to those on which the registered trade mark or earlier filed trade mark is designated to be used, and is likely to cause confusion or mistake among the relevant consumers (see Article 30(1)(10));
- that the mark is identical or similar to another person's well-known trade mark or mark, where it is likely to cause confusion or mistake to the relevant public, or is likely to dilute the distinctiveness or reputation of the well-known trade mark or mark (see Article 30(1)(11));
- that the mark is identical or similar to another person's earlier used trade mark and designated to be used on goods or services identical or similar to those on which the earlier used trade mark is used, where the applicant is aware of the existence of the earlier used trade mark due to contractual, geographical, business or any other relationship with the

owner of the earlier used trade mark and files the application with the intent to imitate the earlier used trade mark (see Article 30(1)(12));
- that the mark contains another person's portrait or well-known name, stage name, pseudonym or alternative name (see Article 30(1)(13));
- that the mark contains the name of a well-known legal person, business or any other group, where it is likely to cause confusion or mistake among the relevant public (see Article 30(1)(14));
- that the mark is an infringement of another person's copyrights, patent rights or any other rights, where a final and binding judgment of the court has been rendered (see Article 30(1)(15)); and
- that using a trade mark identical or similar to the original registered device arbitrarily altered or affixed thereto a note to become identical or similar to a registered trade mark of other (see Article 65(3)).

An opposition to a trade-mark registration shall be filed within three months of the date of publication of registration (see Article 48(1)). The period of examination for an opposition against a trade-mark registration is about five months.

3.2 Filing an Opposition

Any person may file an opposition (see Article 48(1)). Representation is not necessary for opponents or opposers who have a residence or business office in Taiwan (ROC), but opponents or opposers that do not have such residence or business place in Taiwan (ROC) do need representation.

Fees for filing an opposition include an official fee of TWD4,000 per class and an attorney fee of about TWD25,000 for an average case.

3.3 Opposition Procedure

The opposition procedure normally runs as follows: filing of an opposition (by the opponent), procedural examination (by the Trademark office), submission of a response (by the trade-mark owner), substantive examination, submission of a supplementary statement (by the opponent), submission of a supplementary response (by the trade-mark owner), and the making of a decision.

3.4 Legal Remedies

Legal remedies against the decision of the Trademark Office regarding an opposition are sequentially as follows:

- administrative appeal before the Ministry of Economic Affairs (within 30 days of the decision of the Trademark Office). The period of examination is theoretically three months, subject to a discretional extension of another three months;
- administrative litigation before the Intellectual Property Court (within two months of the decision of the Ministry of Economic Affairs). The period for trial is theoretically six months; and
- administrative litigation appeal before the Supreme Administrative Court (within 20 days of the decision of the Intellectual Property Court). The period of trial is about one year.

4. Initiating a Lawsuit

4.1 Actions to Pursue Infringement

For the owner of a registered trade mark, the following actions are available to pursue infringement:

- to demand a person who infringes trade-mark rights to stop such infringement (see Article 69(1));
- to demand a person who is likely to infringe trade-mark rights to prevent such infringement (see Article 69(1);
- to demand a person who infringes trade-mark rights to destroy the infringing articles and the materials or implements used in infringing the trade-mark rights (see Article 69(2));
- to demand a person who infringes trade-mark rights intentionally or negligently to pay damages (see Article 69(3)); and
- to request Customs to seize articles that are suspected of infringing trade-mark rights (see Article 72(1)).

For the owner of an unregistered well-known trade mark, the following actions are available to pursue infringement:

- to demand a person who infringes trademark rights to stop such infringement (see Article 29, Fair Trade Act);
- to demand a person who is likely to infringe trade-mark rights to prevent such infringement (see Article 29, Fair Trade Act);
- to demand a person who infringes trade-mark rights to pay damages (see Article 30, Fair Trade Act); and
- to demand a person who infringes trade-mark rights intentionally to pay punitive damages, which may not exceed three times the amount of damages that are proven (see Article 31, Fair Trade Act).

The owner of an unregistered general trade mark has no trade-mark rights under the trade-mark law or the fair trade law, so no actions are available to pursue the use of its trade mark by another person.

4.2 Initiating Infringement Proceedings

A trade-mark owner normally initiates infringement proceedings before the Intellectual Property Court (see Article 3(1), Intellectual Property Court Organization Act), as such court is intended to be equipped with judges with competent IP knowledge. According to the statutes, a trade-mark owner may also initiate infringement proceedings before a competent court as other kinds of infringements. A special common court (ie, a district court) can also try the case if the trade-mark owner (plaintiff) and the alleged infringer (defendant) designate a common court to exercise jurisdiction by a written agreement (see Article 24, Code of Civil Procedure).

4.3 Effect of Decisions on Infringement Actions

Decisions of the Trademark Office are not binding on the courts trying an infringement action (see Article 16(1), Intellectual Property Case Adjudication Act). For example, when the trade-mark owner (plaintiff) initiates a trade-mark infringement action before the Intellectual Property Court and the alleged infringer (defendant) files an opposition or invalidation against the registration of the plaintiff's trade mark, the Trademark Office's decision to revoke or invalidate the trade-mark registration based on the similarity of trade marks and similarity of goods or services before the Intellectual Property Court renders a judgment on the infringement action is not binding on the Intellectual Property Court. The Intellectual Property Court may still find that the plaintiff's trade mark is not similar to another person's registered trade mark, or that the designated goods or services of the plaintiff's trade mark are not similar to those of another person's registered trade mark, so that the registration of the plaintiff's trade mark shall not be revoked or invalidated.

4.4 Declaratory Judgment Proceedings

The alleged infringer may start declaratory judgment proceedings – ie, an action for a declaratory judgment confirming the nonexistence of claims regarding trade-mark infringement – under the following circumstances:

- if the trade-mark owner has demanded that the alleged infringer stop infringement, prevent infringement or pay damages, etc (eg, through a warning letter) (see Articles 69(1)-69(3), 72(1), Trademark Act, and Article 247(1), Code of Civil Procedure); and
- if the alleged infringer initiates declaratory judgment proceedings before the trade-mark owner initiates a trade-mark infringement action (action demanding performance) or declaratory judgment proceedings (action for a declaratory judgment confirming the existence of claims regarding trade-mark infringement) (see Article 253, Code of Civil Procedure).

4.5 Jurisdiction of Courts

The following courts have jurisdiction to hear trade-mark matters.

For civil litigation:

- First instance: Intellectual Property Court (see Article 3(1), Intellectual Property Court Organization Act) or regular or consensual district court (see Article 24, Code of Civil Procedure).
- Second instance: Intellectual Property Court (see Article 3(1), Intellectual Property Court Organization Act) or regular higher court of the regular or consensual district court.
- Third instance: Supreme Court (see Article 20, Intellectual Property Case Adjudication Act).

For criminal litigation:

- First instance: District Court (see Article 23, Intellectual Property Case Adjudication Act).
- Second instance: Intellectual Property Court (see Articles 25(1), 25(2), Intellectual Property Case Adjudication Act) or collegiate bench of the District Court (see Article 455bis(1), Code of Criminal Procedure).
- Third instance: Supreme Court (see Article 26, Intellectual Property Case Adjudication Act).

For administrative litigation:

- First instance: Intellectual Property Court (see Article 3(3), Intellectual Property Court Organization Act).
- Second instance: Supreme Administrative Court (see Article 32, Intellectual Property Case Adjudication Act).

4.6 Prerequisites to Filing a Lawsuit

Disputes arising from property rights (including trade-mark rights) where the amount or value of the disputed subject is less than TWD500,000 shall be subject to mediation by court before an action is initiated (see Article 403(1)(11), Code of Civil Procedure). Formal demand letters or warning letters are popular, but are not formally required.

4.7 Representation for Parties

For civil litigation, in the first and instances, the parties do not need to be represented by a litigation agent (see Article 68, Code of Civil Procedure). In the third instance, the appellant needs to be represented by a litigation agent unless the appellant is a lawyer or a relative thereof, or its working staff is a lawyer (see Article 466bis(1), Code of Civil Procedure).

For criminal litigation, in the first and second instances, the accused does not, in principle, need to be represented by an advocate (see Articles 27(1), 29, 31(1), Code of Criminal Procedure). In the third instance, the accused does not need to be represented by an advocate in principle (see Articles 27(1), 31(1), 389(2), Code of Criminal Procedure), but the advocate must be a lawyer (see Article 389(2), Code of Criminal Procedure).

For administrative litigation, the parties do not need to be represented by an agent in the first instance (see Articles 49(1), 49(2), Code of Administrative Litigation), in the second or last instance, the parties do need to be represented by an agent in principle, who needs to be a lawyer (see Articles 241bis(1), 241bis(2), Code of Administrative Litigation).

4.8 Interim or Preliminary Injunctions

Interim or preliminary injunctions are available, and include provisional attachments, provisional injunctions and injunctions maintaining a temporary status quo.

The requirements of interim or preliminary injunctions are as follows:

• For provisional attachments:

A creditor may apply for a provisional attachment with regard to a monetary claim or a claim changeable into a monetary claim for the purpose of securing satisfaction of a compulsory execution (see Article 522(1), Code of Civil Procedure). No provisional attachment shall be granted unless it is impossible or extremely difficult to satisfy the claim by a compulsory execution in the future (Article 523(1), Code of Civil Procedure).

• For provisional injunctions:

A creditor may apply for a provisional injunction with regard to non-monetary claims for the purpose of securing satisfaction of a compulsory execution (see Article 532(1), Code of Civil Procedure). No provisional injunction shall be granted unless it is impossible or extremely difficult to satisfy the claim by a compulsory execution in the future due to a change in the status quo of the claimed subject (see Article 532(2), Code of Civil Procedure).

• For injunctions maintaining a temporary status quo:

Wherever necessary for the purpose of preventing material harm, imminent danger or other similar circumstances, an application may be made for an injunction maintaining a temporary status quo with regard to the disputed legal relationship (see Article 538(1), Code of Civil Procedure). A ruling for an injunction maintaining a temporary status quomay only be issued where the disputed legal relationship may be ascertained in an action on the merits (see Article 538(2), Code of Civil Procedure).

4.9 Protection for Potential Defendant

A potential defendant may institute declaratory judgment proceedings – ie, an action for a declaratory judgment confirming the non-existence of claims regarding trade-mark infringement – in order to protect itself. The trade-mark owner may petition to submit a bond for a provisional attachment or injunction, normally in the amount of one third of its claim, while the defendant may petition to lift off the provisional attachment or injunction by submitting a counter bond, normally in the full amount of the claim.

4.10 Obtaining Information and Evidence

In the Taiwan legal system, a party to a trade-mark matter can obtain relevant information and evidence from the other party or a third party by way of perpetuation of evidence. Specifically, whenever it is likely that evidence may be destroyed or that its use in court may become difficult, or with the consent of the opposite party, the party may move the court for perpetuation of such evidence; where necessary, the party who has legal interests in ascertaining the status quo of a matter or object may move for expert testimony, inspection or perpetuation of documentary evidence (see Article 368(1), Code of Civil Procedure, and Article 1, Intellectual Property Case Adjudication Act). Where no action on the merits has been initiated, a motion for perpetuation of evidence shall be made before the court where the action is to be brought; where the action has been initiated, such a motion shall be made before the court where the action is pending (Article 18(1), Intellectual Property Case Adjudication Act).

4.11 Initial Pleading Standards

To initiate an action, a complaint submitted to the court must state specific details, including:

- the parties and their statutory agents;
- the subject matter and its cause and facts; and
- the claim subject to decision (see Article 244(1), Code of Civil Procedure; Article 1, Intellectual Property Case Adjudication Act).

The complaint shall be plausible (see Articles 249(3), 449bis, 502(2), Code of Civil Procedure). There are no special provisions for trade-mark litigation proceedings that differ from those for non-intellectual property litigation proceedings. It is possible to supplement pleadings with additional arguments. Whenever the presiding judge considers that the preparation for oral argument has not been completed, he or she may order the parties to submit a supplementary pleading or response of full details within a specified period of time, and may also order them to state or declare in detail the evidence used for a specific matter (see Article 268, Code of Civil Procedure; Article 1, Intellectual Property Case Adjudication Act).

4.12 Representative or Collective Actions

The Taiwan legal system generally permits representative (collective) actions (such as class actions), including in trade-mark proceedings. Multiple parties that have common interests may appoint one or more persons from themselves to sue or to be sued in the interests of appointing and appointed parties (see Article 41(1), Code of Civil Procedure; Article 1, Intellectual Property Case Adjudication Act).

4.13 Restrictions on Trade Mark-Owners

Restrictions on the trade-mark owner asserting its rights against others can only be found in respect of substantive laws in the following instances:

- limitation of trade-mark rights under the trade-mark law (see Article 36, Trademark Act);
- prohibition of deceptive or obviously unfair conduct under the fair trade law (competition law) (see Article 25, Fair Trade Act); and
- prohibition of abuse of rights under the civil law (see Article 148, Civil Code).

5. Infringement

5.1 Action for Infringement

The necessary parties to an action for infringement are as follows:

- when there are no trade-mark licences: trade-mark owner and alleged infringer;
- when there is one or more non-exclusive licences: trade-mark owner, non-exclusive licensee(s) and alleged infringer;
- when there is one exclusive licence: exclusive licensee and alleged infringer;
- when there is one or more prior non-exclusive licences (by the trade-mark owner) and one later exclusive licence (by the trade-mark owner): non-exclusive licensee(s), exclusive licensee and alleged infringer; and
- when there is one prior exclusive licence (by the trade-mark owner) and one or more later non-exclusive licences (by the exclusive licensee): exclusive licensee, non-exclusive licensee(s) and alleged infringer.

The circumstances in which a third party who is not the trade mark-owner can file an action for infringement are as follows:

- when there are no trade-mark licences: it is not possible for a non-licensee to file an action for infringement under any circumstances;
- when there is one or more non-exclusive licences: a non-exclusive licensee must file an action for infringement jointly with the trade-mark owner (and the other non-exclusive licensees);
- when there is one exclusive licence: it is possible for the exclusive licensee to file an action for infringement independently;
- when there is one or more prior non-exclusive licence (by the trade-mark owner) and one later exclusive licence (by the trade-mark owner): a non-exclusive licensee must file an action for infringement jointly with the exclusive licensee (and the other non-exclusive licensees), and it is possible for the exclusive licensee to have a joint action with the non-exclusive licensee(s); and
- when there is one prior exclusive licence (by the trade-mark owner) and one or more later non-exclusive licence (by the exclusive licensee): it is possible for the exclusive licensee and a non-exclusive licensee to file an action for infringement jointly, while it is required for the non-exclusive licensee(s) to have a joint action with the exclusive licensee.

Within the scope of the licence, a licensee (exclusive or non-exclusive) may file an action for infringement in its own name when its trade-mark rights (exclusive rights) are infringed (see Article 39(4), Trademark Act). It is not possible for a trade-mark owner to take any action to stop infringement before its trade mark is registered, unless the trade mark is a well-known trade mark.

5.2 Signs and Infringement

The main factors to be considered in determining whether the use of a sign constitutes trade-mark infringement (ie, where it is likely to cause confusion or mistakes among the relevant consumers) are as follows:

- degree of distinctiveness of the registered trade mark and the used sign;
- degree of similarity between the registered trade mark and the used sign;
- degree of similarity between the designated goods or services of the registered trade mark and the goods or services on which the sign is used;
- degree of business diversification of the owner of the registered trade mark;
- actual cases of confusion or mistake;
- degree of familiarity of the relevant consumers with the registered trade mark and the used sign; and
- whether the use of the sign is in good faith.

5.3 Use of a Sign by Defendant

While it is not necessary for the plaintiff to establish that the defendant has used the sign as a trade mark, it is possible for the defendant to establish that it has not used the sign as a trade mark (eg, purely descriptive use). The burden of proof rests on the defendant (see Articles 36(1)(1), 36(1)(2)).

5.4 Defences Against Infringement

The main defences against trade-mark infringement are as follows:

- limitation of trade-mark rights (eg, use of own name, descriptive use, functional use, prior use in good faith or exhaustion of trade-mark rights) (see Article 36, Trademark Act);
- grounds for opposition (see Article 48(1), Trademark Act);
- grounds for invalidation (see Article 57(1), Trademark Act);

- grounds for cancellation (eg, non-use) (see Article 63(1), Trademark Act);
- forfeiture of trade-mark rights (eg, expiry of registration period or abandonment of trade-mark registration) (see Articles 33, 45, Trademark Act)
- prohibition of deceptive or obviously unfair conducts (see Article 25, Fair Trade Act); and
- prohibition of abuse of rights (see Article 148, Civil Code).

5.5 Role of Experts and/or Surveys

Expert testimony and/or surveys are permissible as evidence in actions, including trade-mark actions. In making a judgment, and taking into consideration the entire import of the oral argument and the result of evidence investigation, the court shall determine the facts by discretional evaluation (see Articles 222(1), Code of Civil Procedure). Expert testimony and surveys as evidence shall be investigated in the proceedings and taken into consideration by the court when making a judgment, but are not binding on the court.

5.6 Administrative or Criminal Offence

Trade-mark infringement is a criminal offence in Taiwan (see Articles 95 to 97, Trademark Act). It may arguably constitute an administrative offence before the Fair Trade Commission (FTC), so that the trade-mark owner may petition FTC to require the offender to affix a distinguishing indication in order to avoid the likelihood of confusion regarding the origin of goods or services (see Article 22(4), Fair Trade Act). A criminal procedure for a trade-mark infringement offence is typically as follows:

- the trade-mark owner files a complaint with a judicial police officer;
- the judicial police officer sends the result of his or her investigation to a public prosecutor;
- the public prosecutor initiates a public prosecution with a district court;
- the district court hands down a judgment of guilty;
- the accused (alleged infringer) appeals to the Intellectual Property Court;
- the Intellectual Property Court refuses the appeal of the accused;
- the accused appeals to the Supreme Court; and
- the Supreme Court refuses the appeal of the accused.

5.7 Custom Seizures

The Taiwan legal system provides for customs seizure of counterfeits but not parallel imports, because the import or export of counterfeits is illegal anyway under Taiwanese trade-mark law, but parallel import is legal due to the international exhaustion of trade-mark rights under Taiwanese trade-mark law (see Article 36(2), Trademark Act). The customs seizure procedure for counterfeits is typically as follows:

- Customs finds that the imported or exported articles are likely to be counterfeits (infringing articles);
- Customs gives a notice to the trade-mark owner or its representative or agent in Taiwan, requesting that it travels to customs for identification. Customs gives a notice to the importer or exporter at the same time, and requests the provision of relevant evidence of non-infringement;
- the trade-mark owner identifies the articles as counterfeits and provides relevant evidence of infringement;
- the importer or exporter provides relevant evidence of non-infringement;
- the trade-mark owner files an application for seizure of the articles with Customs;
- Customs seizes the articles; and
- the trade-mark owner brings a trade-mark infringement action before the Intellectual Property Court and gives notice to Customs.

6. Revocation/Cancellation

6.1 Remedies and Reasons

Remedies available for cancellation (revocation) of a trade mark include the following:

- administrative appeal before the Ministry of Economic Affairs (MOEA, within 30 days of receiving the decision of the Trademark Office);
- administrative litigation before the Intellectual Property Court (IPC, within two months of receiving the decision of the Ministry of Economic Affairs) if dissatisfied with the appeal decision of MOEA; and
- administrative litigation appeal before the Supreme Administrative Court (within 20 days of receiving the decision of the Intellectual Property Court) if dissatisfied with the decision of IPC.

Reasons for the cancellation (revocation) of a trade mark include the following:

- the trade mark is altered into a different form or supplemented with additional signs by the owner so that it is identical or similar to another person's registered trade mark, and the goods or services on which the trade mark is used are identical or similar to those on which another person's trade mark is designated to be used, so that it is likely to cause confusion or mistake to the relevant consumers (see Artickle 63(1)(1), Trademark Act);
- the trade mark is altered into a different form or supplemented with additional signs by a licensee so that the trade mark is identical or similar to another person's registered trade mark, and the goods or services on which the trade mark is used are identical or similar to those on which another person's trade mark is designated to be used, so that it is likely to cause confusion or mistake to the relevant

consumers, while the owner knows or should have known the conduct of the licensee, but shows no objection thereto (see Article 63(2), Trademark Act);

- the trade-mark owner has not used the trade mark for three years since its registration or has ceased to use the trade mark for three years after its registration without reasonable grounds for non-use, unless the trade mark has been used by a licensee (see Article 63(1)(2), Trademark Act);
- no appropriate distinguishing indication is added pursuant to Article 43 of the Trademark Act, unless the indication has been added before a decision of cancellation is rendered by the Trademark Office and thus there is no likelihood of confusion or mistake (see Article 63(1)(3), Trademark Act);
- the trade mark has become a generic mark, name or shape for the designated goods or services (see Article 63(1)(4), Trademark Act); and the actual use of the trade mark is likely to cause the public to mistake or misconceive the nature, quality or place of origin of the goods or services (see Article 63(1)(5), Trademark Act).

6.2 Trade Mark Office and Civil Courts

Cancellation (revocation) actions shall be brought before the Trademark Office (see Art. 63(1), Trademark Act). They cannot be brought before IP courts or civil courts.

6.3 Statutory Limitation or Time Period

The trade-mark registration shall not be cancelled (revoked) on the grounds prescribed in Article 63(1)(2) of the Trademark Act if the trade-mark owner has commenced or resumed the use of the trade mark before the cancellation is filed, unless such use was commenced or resumed within the three months before the cancellation is filed because the trade-mark owner became aware that the cancellation would be filed (see Article 63(3), Trademark Act). There is no statutory time period for filing cancellation actions.

6.4 Initiation of Revocation/Cancellation Proceeding

Any person may file a cancellation (revocation), and the Trademark Office may also initiate cancellation proceedings ex officio (Article 63(1), Trademark Act). There are no particular admissibility (standing) requirements (eg, legal or commercial interest) for initiating cancellation proceedings in Taiwan.

6.5 Partial Revocation/Cancellation

A partial cancellation (revocation) is possible (Article 63(4), Trademark Act). Specifically, where grounds for cancellation exist only in respect of some of the designated goods or services of the registered trade mark, the registration may be cancelled in respect of those goods or services (Article 63(4), Trademark Act).

6.6 Possibilities of Amendment

Amendments are possible in cancellation (revocation) proceedings, in the following circumstances:

- For the trade-mark device, no amendments shall be made to the design or device of a trade mark after the trade mark has been registered (see Article 38(1), Trademark Act). Therefore, amendments to the design or device of the trade mark are also not possible in cancellation proceedings.
- For goods or services, no amendments shall be made to the designated goods or services of a trade mark after the trade mark has been registered, unless such amendment is a restriction of the designated goods or services (see Article 38(1), Trademark Act). Therefore, amendments to goods or services are possible in cancellation proceedings, if such amendment is a restriction of the designated goods or services where the restriction of the designated goods or services shall be requested before a decision for the cancellation proceedings is rendered (see Article 38(2), Trademark Act).

The owner of a registered trade mark may request the Trademark Office to divide the registration into two or more registrations by distributing the designated goods or services included in the original registration among divisional registrations (see Article 37, Trademark Act). The division of the registration, however, shall be requested before a decision for the cancellation proceedings is rendered (see Article 38(2), Trademark Act).

6.7 Revocation/Cancellation and Infringement

Trade-mark cancellation (revocation) actions and trade-mark infringement actions are not heard together, with the former being heard by the Trademark Office, and the latter by the court (the IP Court, in principle). Nevertheless, the alleged infringer (the defendant in an infringement action) may defend that the trade-mark registration of the trade-mark owner (the plaintiff in an infringement action) shall be cancelled, and file a cancellation against the trade-mark registration with the Trademark Office at the same time. The court, however, shall determine on the alleged infringer's defence by itself. Specifically, it does not need to suspend the action, and the decision of the Trademark Office is also not binding on it (see Article 16(1), Intellectual Property Case Adjudication Act).

The court may render a judgment in the infringement action either before or after the Trademark Office renders a decision in the cancellation action. It does not need to suspend the action and wait for the decision of the Trademark Office, and also may deliver its own viewpoints or reasons.

Since the court opinions in a judgment in the infringement action are important reference or guidance of the Trademark Office while a decision in the cancellation action of the

Trademark Office might merely be possibly taken into consideration by the court, if the judgment and Office decision have overlapping issues related to grounds for cancellation, the Office decision always comes out after the judgment.

7. Trial & Settlement

7.1 Special Procedural Provisions

There are special procedural provisions for trade-mark proceedings, as follows:

- For civil litigation: Articles 6 to 22 of the Intellectual Property Case Adjudication Act expressly exclude the application of some articles in the Code of Civil Procedure, but clearly provide the confidentiality protective order.
- For criminal litigation: Articles 23 to 30 of the Intellectual Property Case Adjudication Act mainly provide for the venue of a case.
- For administrative litigation: Articles 31bis to 34 of the Intellectual Property Case Adjudication Act provide venue and how to deal with new evidence on the same cancellation or revocation ground.

7.2 Determination of Cases

The case is determined by legal judges. The parties have no influence on who the judge is, but may petition for recusal of a specific judge.

7.3 Possibilities of Settlement

The defendant may always settle the case before the case is decided. The defendants can present themselves at any time through their own strategic considerations, and shall present when the court tries or considers it necessary for settlement (see Article 378, Code of Civil Procedure). The court may seek settlement at any time irrespective of which phase the proceedings have reached, with either a commissioned judge or an assigned judge being authorised to do so (see Article 377(1), Code of Civil Procedure). Where both parties are close to agreeing on terms for a settlement, they may move the court, the commissioned judge or the assigned judge to make a settlement proposal within the scope specified by the parties (see Article 377bis(1), Code of Civil Procedure).

7.4 Other Court Proceedings

Other court proceedings (eg, administrative litigation proceedings for opposition, invalidation or cancellation before the IP Court or not) have no influence on the current court proceedings (eg, infringement proceedings before the IP Court). The court trying the infringement case may determine by itself whether a trade-mark registration shall be revoked, invalidated or cancelled, and need not suspend the infringement action and wait for the judgment of the court trying the opposition, invalidation or cancellation case (see Article 16(1), Intellectual Property Case Adjudication Act). Nevertheless, if both proceedings are pending before the IP Court, it tends to deliver harmonised reasoning.

8. Remedies

8.1 Existing Remedies

The existing remedies for a trade-mark owner are as follows:

- For the owner of a registered trade mark:
  - (a) cessation of infringement: to demand a person who infringes on its trade-mark rights to stop such infringement (see Article 69(1), Trademark Act);
  - (b) prevention of infringement: to demand a person who is likely to infringe on its trade-mark rights to prevent such infringement (see Article 69(1), Trademark Act);
  - (c) destruction of infringing articles: to demand a person who infringes on its trade-mark rights to destroy the infringing articles and the materials or implements used in infringing on the trade-mark rights (see Article 69(2), Trademark Act);
  - (d) damages: to demand a person who infringes on its trade-mark rights intentionally or negligently to pay damages (including an account of profits, not including punitive damages and recovery of attorneys' fees) (see Articles 69(3), 71, Trademark Act);
  - (e) Customs seizure: to request Customs to seize articles that are suspected of infringing on its trade-mark rights (see Article 72(1), Trademark Act);
  - (f) payment order: to apply for issuance of a payment order with a district court (see Articles 508(1), 510, Code of Civil Procedure, and Article 21, Intellectual Property Case Adjudication Act);
  - (g) preliminary injunction: to apply for a preliminary injunction with the IP Court (eg, freeze on bank accounts) (see Articles 522(1), 532(1), 538(1), Code of Civil Procedure, and Article 22, Intellectual Property Case Adjudication Act).
- For the owner of an unregistered well-known trade mark:
  - (a) cessation of infringement: to demand a person who infringes on its trade-mark rights to stop such infringement (see Article 29, Fair Trade Act);
  - (b) prevention of infringement: to demand a person who is likely to infringe on its trade-mark rights to prevent such infringement (see Article 29, Fair Trade Act)
  - (c) damages: to demand a person who infringes on its trade-mark rights to pay damages (including an account of profits, not including punitive damages and recovery of attorneys' fees) (see Article 30, 31(2), Fair Trade Act);
  - (d) punitive damages: to demand a person who infringes on its trade-mark rights intentionally to pay punitive damages of up to three times the proven amount

of damages (see Article 31(1), Fair Trade Act);

(e) publication of the judgment: to demand a person who infringes on its trade-mark rights to publish the content of the judgment in a newspaper at the infringer's expenses (see Article 33, Fair Trade Act);

(f) payment order: to apply for issuance of a payment order with a district court (see Articles 508(1), 510, Code of Civil Procedure);

(g) preliminary injunction: to apply for a preliminary injunction with a district court (eg, freeze on bank accounts) (see Articles 522(1), 524, 532(1), 533, 538(1), 538quinquies, Code of Civil Procedure).

8.2 Rights and Remedies

Normally, a prevailing defendant does not have any rights or remedies, such as being reimbursed for attorneys' fees. The court decision will make non-infringement clear in the decision, but is not likely to order declaration of non-infringement in any other medium.

8.3 Different Types of Remedies

There are no different types of remedies for different types of trade marks in Taiwan so far as the nature of remedies is concerned.

9. Appeal

9.1 Special Provisions

Special provisions concerning the appellate procedure for trade-mark proceedings involve mainly the jurisdiction. The courts with jurisdiction to hear an appeal in trade-mark proceedings are as follows:

- For Civil Litigation:
  (a) Second instance (first appeal): Intellectual Property Court (see Article 3(1), Intellectual Property Court Organization Act, and Article 19, Intellectual Property Case Adjudication Act);
  (b) Third instance (second appeal): Supreme Court (see Article 20, Intellectual Property Case Adjudication Act);
- For Criminal Litigation:
  (a) Second instance (first appeal): Intellectual Property Court (see Article 3(2), Intellectual Property Court Organization Act, and Article 25(1), Intellectual Property Case Adjudication Act) or collegiate bench of the District Court (see Article 455bis(1), Code of Criminal Procedure, and Article 1, Intellectual Property Case Adjudication Act);
  (b) Third instance (second appeal): Supreme Court (see Article 26, Intellectual Property Case Adjudication Act).
- For Administrative Litigation:
  (a) Second instance (appeal): Supreme Administrative Court (see Article 32, Intellectual Property Case Adjudication Act).

9.2 Factual or Legal Review

For civil cases, there are both factual and legal reviews in the second instance (first appeal), and it is a kind of successive instance. Specifically, the parties may present additional means of attack or defence, including additional arguments or defences, additional facts or additional evidence. The appellate court, however, does not review evidence that was presented and investigated in the first instance; nor does it review arguments, defences or facts that were presented and investigated in the first instance, if no additional evidence is presented in the second instance (see Article 447(1), Code of Civil Procedure, and Article 1, Intellectual Property Case Adjudication Act). In the third instance (second appeal), there is only legal review.

There are also both factual and legal reviews in the second instance (first appeal) in criminal cases, and it is a kind of repetitive instance. Specifically, the parties may present additional means of attack or defence, including additional arguments or defences, additional facts or additional evidence. The appellate court also reviews arguments or defences, facts or evidence that were presented and investigated in the first instance (see Article 364, Code of Criminal Procedure, and Article 1, Intellectual Property Case Adjudication Act). In the third instance (second appeal), there is only legal review.

For administrative litigation, there is only legal review in the second instance (appeal).

9.3 Length of Appeal from Trial Court

The first appeal (second instance) normally takes between six months and one year, and the second appeal (third instance) normally takes about one year.

10. Other Trade Mark Issues

10.1 Recognition of Dilution

Taiwan recognises dilution as a grounds to oppose or invalidate a trade-mark registration, or to stop or prevent use of a trade mark in a lawsuit (see Articles 30(1)(11), 48(1), 57(1), 70(1), Trademark Act). The protection from dilution, however, is only applied for well-known registered trade marks.

10.2 Protection of Famous Marks

Taiwan protects trade marks that are famous outside the nation but are not yet in use or registered within Taiwan. Nevertheless, such marks are positively protected by the fair trade law only (see Article 22(1), Fair Trade Act). In the trade-mark law, there is only passive protection to stop others from registering the same or similar marks (see Article 30(1)(11), Trademark Act).

10.3 Special Rules Regarding Geographic Indicators

There are special rules in Taiwan with regard to geographical indications, the protection of which is an absolute ground for refusal of trade-mark registration. That is, a trade mark shall not be registered if it is identical or similar to a geographical indication for wine or distilled spirits of the Republic of China or a foreign country, and designated to be used on goods identical or similar to wine or distilled spirits, where the foreign country and the Republic of China enter into an agreement or jointly accede to an international treaty, or reciprocally recognise the protection of geographical indication for wine or distilled spirits (see Article 30(1)(9), Trademark Act).

10.4 Special Rules Relating to Surnames

The following special rules related to the ability to use one's own name (including surname) exist in Taiwan:

- the owner of a registered trade mark is not entitled to prohibit a third party from indicating his or her own name in accordance with honest and credible practices of commercial transactions and not using it as a trade mark (Art. 36(1)(1), Trademark Act);
- the owner of an unregistered well-known trade mark is not entitled to prohibit a third party from using his or her own name in good faith, or from selling, transporting, exporting or importing goods or services bearing such name (Articles 22(1), 22(3)(1), Fair Trade Act).

11. Costs

11.1 Costs Before Filing a Lawsuit

No costs are statutorily required before filing a lawsuit. Nevertheless, the cost of warning letters typically arises before filing a lawsuit in order to ascertain whether an amicable resolution is possible.

Deep & Far Attorneys-at-Law
13th Fl., No. 27, Sec. 3,
Chung San N. Rd.
Taipei 104,
Taiwan, R.O.C.

Tel: 886-2-2585-6688
Fax: 886-2-25989900/25978989
Email: email@deepnfar.com.tw
Web:www.deepnfar.com.tw

11.2 Costs Regarding an Infringement Action

The typical costs for bringing an infringement action to conclusion in the first instance are as follows:

- the court fees for the first instance of civil litigation (eg, trade-mark infringement action) can be calculated by using a calculating programme (see http://www.judicial.gov.tw/assist/count.html).
- because there are no discovery proceedings, attorney fees are relatively small compared to the major industrial countries: for an average case, the attorney fees can be kept under USD30,000. Since the politicians always keep the country going in wrong directions so as to have an oversaturated domestic legal market, quite a few cases are handled for each instance under TWD80,000.

11.3 Costs of Litigation

The losing party is responsible for paying court fees (see Article 78, Code of Civil Procedure). The parties are responsible for paying their own attorney fees; specifically, the losing party is not required to reimburse the prevailing party for attorney fees.

12. Alternative Dispute Resolution

12.1 Common Way of Settlement

Alternative dispute resolution is compulsory for some disputes (Article 403, Code of Civil Proceedings), but it is neither a common nor compulsory element of settling a trademark case in Taiwan, although parties or the court may make an effort.

13. Trade Marks and Other Intellectual Property

13.1 Protection by Copyright

A trade mark can also be protected by copyright (eg, in the case of logo) or patent (eg, design patent). A trade mark is conceptually a special trade dress.

UK

LAW AND PRACTICE: p.311

Contributed by J A Kemp

The 'Law & Practice' sections provide easily accessible information on navigating the legal system when conducting business in the jurisdiction. Leading lawyers explain local law and practice at key transactional stages and for crucial aspects of doing business.

Law and Practice

Contributed by J A Kemp

CONTENTS

J A Kemp advises on trade-mark selection and strategy and files, defends and opposes trade-mark applications in the United Kingdom, Europe and the rest of the world. The firm obtains global protection for trade marks through international applications before the World Intellectual Property Organisation and by instructing filing and prosecution programmes worldwide. The firm works for a variety of clients, from start-ups, spin-outs and small and medium-sized enterprises to some of the largest corporate clients and most prestigious academic institutions in the world. J A Kemp also has a global network of attorney firms which instruct the firm on behalf of their clients.

Author

James Fish is head of J A Kemp's Trade Marks Group. His experience includes extensive handling of multi-jurisdictional clearance searching; advising on filing strategy; trade-mark prosecution of unusual marks; conducting trade-mark- related litigation; and handling anti-dilution campaigns. James works with a variety of clients worldwide in a number of sectors, in particular pharmaceuticals, electronics, medical devices and the wine industry. He also leads the firm's Paris-based trade-marks operation.

1. Types of Trade Marks & Registration

1.1 Types of Trade Marks
The United Kingdom provides for a number of different types of trade marks. The statutory system of registration makes a distinction between (i) an ordinary trade-mark that may include amongst other signs a word, logo, colour or shape covering goods and/or services; (ii) collective trade marks; and (iii) certification marks. As the UK is a common law jurisdiction that separately gives rise to a right of action to the holder of an unregistered trade-mark under the common law of passing off, the law in relation to trade marks is a combination of statute and case law.

1.2 Trade-Mark Rights
Trade-mark rights arise by virtue of use and/or registration in the United Kingdom.

1.3 Standards for Registering
Whilst the standard of official examination does not differ between different types of ordinary trade-mark, the capacity for certain signs to function as trade marks does. The consumer may need to be educated first that a colour or a shape, by way of an example, is being used as a trade-mark.

1.4 Trade-Mark Register
There is a public Register of Trade Marks in the United Kingdom, available at https://www.gov.uk/search-for-trademark.

1.5 Types of Registers
There is only one type of register.

1.6 Searching for Prior Trade Marks
It is usual to search for prior trade-mark applications and registrations before adopting a trade-mark for use and registration. In addition to searching the public trade-mark registers covering the UK, additional due diligence may include a search of the internet, Companies House and domain name registers.

1.7 Registration Requirements
The UK Trade Marks Act 1994 requires that an application to register includes the name and address of the applicant, a statement of goods and/or services to be claimed, and a representation of the trade-mark. The applicant must possess a bona fide intention to use the trade-mark in relation to the goods and/or services claimed.

1.8 Registering a Trade Mark
Anyone can register a trade-mark: individuals (subject to capacity), partnerships, companies and trusts.

1.9 Registering Signs
Any sign capable of graphical representation can be registered and/or protected as a trade-mark — such as words, images, sounds, numbers, shapes and colours — and that, in practice, at this time limits the possibility of obtaining protection for smell marks and holograms. An important but subtle amendment will be introduced to the Trade Marks Act with respect to the common definition of a trade-mark in the EU, where the graphical representation requirement will be

replaced with the words "being represented on the Register of… trade marks ('the Register'), in a manner which enables the competent authorities and the public to determine the clear and precise subject-matter of the protection afforded to its proprietor". This change is intended to make it easier to register non-traditional trade marks but where there remains the overriding requirement that the sign claimed must be clear and precise.

1.10 Other Rights to Signs
The UK legal system recognises other rights to signs or source-identifiers besides trade marks, but only at common law under the law of passing off and providing that the earlier use gives rise to a protectable trading goodwill.

1.11 Registration Procedure
The UK system provides for registration of multi-class applications covering goods and/or services. The UK abides by the Nice Classification (11th Edition). The application is filed and examined as to its formalities, where queries may arise in relation to the legal status of the applicant, the specification terms being claimed and whether the graphical representation is legible. The application is then substantively examined on absolute grounds, ie, whether the trade-mark applied for is capable of functioning as a trade-mark, is not devoid of any distinctive character, is not descriptive, misleading or generic. Specific provisions deal with shape marks. The application is also examined as to earlier applications and registrations that the examiner considers may present a conflict. Such applications and registrations are raised for information purposes only.

The applicant must decide whether or not to proceed with the application to publication and if they do, the examiner is obliged to contact the holders of UK applications and registrations, and UK designations under the International Registration systems raised in the report. Once the application has been approved, it is published for opposition purposes. The two-month opposition term is extendable by one month. In the absence of opposition, the application proceeds to grant within 14 days following the expiry of the publication term. From start to finish, grant of registration can be achieved within four months assuming that no official and/or third-party objection arises.

1.12 Use in Commerce
All that the law demands is that the applicant possesses a bona fide intention to use the trade-mark in relation to the goods or services claimed. The official fees associated with filing are GBP170 for the first class claimed and GBP50 for each additional class. A resulting registration should be renewed ten years following the filing date of the application. The official cost of renewal is GBP200 for the first class and GBP50 for each additional class.

1.13 Registration of Series Marks
Series marks are registrable. Up to six marks can be claimed within a series.

1.14 Length of Registration Process
A registration can mature within a period of four months. An applicant does not require professional representation to initiate the procedure. An applicant does require an address for service in the EU/European Economic Area (EEA) in order to receive official correspondence. The official cost of one trade-mark in one class is GBP170 when filed online. Attorney standard charge fees for filing vary across the UK profession but would typically amount to GBP300 for the first class.

1.15 Grounds for Refusal
The examiner can raise objection under the following:

- Section 3(1)(a): the mark does not function as a trade-mark;
- Section 3(1)(b): the mark is devoid of any distinctive character;
- Section 3(1)(c): the mark is descriptive;
- Section 3(1)(d): the mark is generic or misleading;
- Section 3(2): objections dealing specifically with shapes where they consist of the goods themselves, claim technical features or where the shapes add substantial value to the goods being claimed;
- Section 3(3): contrary to public policy or to accepted principles of morality;
- Section 3(4): contrary to any enactment or rule of law;
- Section 3(5): the trade-mark consists of a specially protected emblem; and
- Section 3(6): the mark has been applied for in bad faith.

1.16 Process for Overcoming Objections
Much would depend on the basis for objection. For example, a failure to provide applicant name, trade-mark or specification is fatal to the application in so far as it does not comply with the requirements of Section 32(3) of the Act. The first course of response is to argue against an objection, which can take the form of written observations. If the objection is maintained, a hearing can be sought before a senior registry official. Evidence of secondary meaning (if available) would generally be left in reserve given the cost of collating and adducing such evidence.

1.17 Consideration of Prior Rights
The UK office conducts a search of its own register amongst earlier applications and registrations covering the UK, including UK national, EU and international registrations designating the UK and EU. If appropriate, the examiner will raise the earlier application/registration for "information purposes" only. It is then up to the applicant to decide whether or not in the face of this information they wish to

proceed to publication for opposition purposes. If the applicant elects to proceed, the UK Intellectual Property Office (IPO) is only obliged to notify the holders of UK applications and registrations, and UK designations under the international registration system. The mere existence and presentation of an earlier application/registration creates no adverse presumption and does not preclude continuance of the application. In fact, unless the applicant withdraws their application prior to a two-month deadline created by the examination report, the application will proceed to publication without the need for the applicant to request this. This avoids the need for the holders of international registrations designating the UK to appoint local counsel.

1.18 Third-Party Rights

Given the change in the way that the IPO raises earlier rights for information purposes, the only mechanisms open to a third party to challenge an application on the basis of an earlier right would be to enter formal opposition. An application is published for an extendable period of two months (extendable by one month). A third party can assert their earlier rights by way of formal opposition during this period.

1.19 Revoke, Change, Amend or Correct an Application

Section 39 of the UK Trade Marks Act 1994 provides for withdrawal of an application or restriction of the goods or services covered by an application. In other respects, the application may be amended by correcting the name or address of the applicant, errors of wording or copying, or obvious mistakes and only where the correction does not substantially affect the identity of the trade-mark or extend the goods or services claimed.

1.20 Assigning an Application or Granting a Licence

It is possible to assign an application for a trade-mark or grant a licence in relation to it during the application process. However, neither transaction can be recorded until the application matures to grant of registration.

1.21 Remedies Against the Trade Mark Office

A reasoned statement of refusal of an application can be requested from the examiner. This then creates a deadline of 28 days by which the refusal may be appealed either to the appointed person, from which no further right of appeal lies, or to the Chancery Division of the High Court of England and Wales.

1.22 Use of a Trade Mark

The UK legal system does not have a requirement that an applicant use its mark in commerce before the transaction is issued. The law requires that a trade-mark be placed into genuine use during the five-year term post grant of registration and any subsequent five-year period. What is meant by genuine in these circumstances? The law requires more than mere token use. It requires the creation and preservation of a market share under the trade-mark by reference to the goods/services claimed.

1.23 Dividing a Trade Mark

Using a Form TM12 it is possible to divide an application into two or more separate applications (called divisional applications) to allow those classes that are acceptable to go forward for publication and for the objections to the remaining classes to be dealt with separately.

1.24 Length of Term of Protection

A trade-mark is registered for a period of ten years from the date of registration (the renewal date — calculated ten years from the filing date of the granted application) and may be renewed for further periods of ten years. It is possible to renew late up to six months following the renewal date, upon payment of an additional late fee. It is possible to restore a registration up to 12 months from the renewal date where an intention to renew can be shown. A witness statement and late renewal and restoration fees will be required in these circumstances.

1.25 Requirements for an Exhaustion

A registered trade-mark is not infringed by the use of the trade-mark in relation to goods that have been put on the market in the EEA under that trade-mark by the proprietor or with his or her consent. Note that this general presumption does not apply where there exist legitimate reasons for the proprietor to oppose further dealings in the goods and in particular where the condition of the goods have been changed or impaired after they have been put on the market.

1.26 Participation in the Madrid System

The UK is a member of the Madrid Protocol. There are no particular requirements for registration that differ from other Protocol countries.

1.27 Consequences for Providing Incorrect Information

Providing incorrect or incomplete information in relation to a trade-mark application may be fatal to the application. Certain information can be corrected and certain cannot (see **1.19 Revoke, Change, Amend or Correct an Application**). A decision of the registrar may be challenged before the appointed person or the High Court of England and Wales.

1.28 Updating or Refreshing a Design Mark

A registered trade-mark shall not be altered in the register. The registrar may, at the request of the proprietor, allow the alteration of a registered trade-mark where the mark includes the proprietor's name or address and the alteration is limited to alteration of that name or address and does not substantially affect the identity of the mark.

1.29 Denotation

The ® symbol is reserved for use in relation to registered trade marks only. The TM symbol may be used to denote a pending application or unregistered trade-mark at common law or a registered trade-mark.

2. Assignment and Licensing

2.1 Assignment Requirements or Restrictions

A registered trade-mark is personal property and is transmissible by assignment, testamentary disposition or operation of law. It is transmissible in connection with the goodwill of a business or independently. A registered trade-mark may be assigned in full or in part, or in relation to the use of the trade-mark in a particular manner or a particular locality. An assignment is not effective unless it is in writing signed by, or on behalf of, the assignor.

2.2 Procedure for Assigning a Trade Mark

An assignment must be made in writing and executed by, or on behalf of, the assignor. The assignment can be recorded before the IPO on a Form TM16 (official fee GBP50) signed by the assignor and the assignee or their legal representatives. It takes around four to six weeks to record the assignment.

2.3 Registering or Recording the Assignment

It is highly advisable that an assignment be recorded without delay before the trade-mark office. In the absence of recordal, the transaction is ineffective as against a person acquiring a conflicting interest in or under the registered trade-mark in ignorance of it and a person claiming to be a licensee by virtue of the transaction does not have the protection of the general provisions under the Trade Marks Act 1994 extending to licensees. Furthermore, following a period of six months from the date of assignment, the assignee is not entitled to claim damages for infringement in respect of any infringement of the registered trade-mark occurring after the date of the assignment and before the assignment is registered.

2.4 Trade Marks and Security

A trade-mark can be given as a security, be subject to rights in rem, be assigned by way of security and be levied in execution.

2.5 Licensing Requirements or Restrictions

A licence to use a registered trade-mark may be general or limited, ie, it may apply to all goods or services, or part thereof. The licence may also restrict the use of the trade-mark in a particular manner or a particular locality. A licence is not effective unless it is in writing signed by, or on behalf of, the grantor. A licence may be exclusive, meaning that the licensee has the same rights against a successor in title who is bound by the licence as he or she has against the person granting the licence; non-exclusive; and sub-licensed.

2.6 Procedure for Licensing a Trade Mark

A licence must be in writing in order to be effective and must be executed by, or on behalf of, the grantor. A licence should be recorded before the IPO using Form TM50 (official fee GBP50). It takes around four to six weeks to record the licence.

2.7 Registering or Recording the Licence

In the absence of recordal, the transaction is ineffective as against a person acquiring a conflicting interest in or under the registered trade-mark in ignorance of it and a person claiming to be a licensee by virtue of the transaction does not have the protection of the general provisions under the Trade Marks Act 1994 extending to licensees, which includes specific provisions dealing with exclusive licensees. These include the ability of the non-exclusive licensee to call upon the trade-mark proprietor to take infringement proceedings and, where they fail to do so within a two-month period, to bring proceedings in their own name as if they were the proprietor, providing they join the proprietor as claimant. The court can take into account the damage suffered by the licensee and give directions as to how any proceeds for any pecuniary remedy be shared with a licensee.

2.8 Reasons to Deny Granting a Perpetual Licence

In theory, it is possible to grant a perpetual licence. However, the court will approach the question of whether something is truly perpetual by way of construction, ie, does it mean "operating without limit of time" or "never-ending". There may still be termination provisions relevant to both interpretations.

3. Opposition Procedure

3.1 Legal Grounds and Timeframes

A trade-mark application can be opposed during the extendable publication term of two months, which may be extended by an earlier rights-holder by filing a Form TM7A (Notice of Threatened Opposition) that has the effect of (i) extending the opposition term by one month and (ii) formally placing the applicant on notice of possible opposition, thereby allowing the applicant to claim their costs on the statutory scale when filing formal opposition and on the assumption they are successful. An opposition can be grounded on absolute grounds (see **1.15 Grounds for Refusal**).

An opposition can also be filed by the owner of an earlier identical trade-mark application or registration covering identical goods or services (S.5(1)), an identical/similar mark covering similar/identical goods or services and where there exists a likelihood of confusion on the part of the relevant consumer (S.5(2)(a)) or where there is a similar mark covering similar goods or services and where there exists a likelihood of confusion on the part of the relevant consumer (S5(2)(b)) or where the trade-mark is identical/similar and where the later application covers different goods or services and where the earlier mark has a reputation in the UK (or in the case of an earlier EU TM, a reputation in the EU) and the later trade-mark without due cause would take unfair advantage of, or be detrimental to, the distinctive character or the repute of the earlier trade-mark (S5(3)). Further, it is possible to base opposition on an earlier unregistered trade-mark under S5(4)(a) where the applicant is afforded with a right of action under the common law of passing off. S5(4)(b) further provides for a right of action grounded upon the ownership of an earlier right such as copyright, design right or registered design.

Specific provisions of the UK Act deal with the ability of the owners of well-known marks (S56) (not registered in UK but the subject of registration in a Paris Convention country) to raise opposition and under S60 for the proprietor of a trade-mark in a Paris Convention country to complain of the acts of an agent or representative.

3.2 Filing an Opposition

Only the proprietor of an earlier application/registration or an earlier right may file opposition based upon an earlier application/registration/right unless they are specifically provided with specific authority from the right-holder. There must be locus standi (standing requirements). Anyone can object based on absolute grounds. There is no requirement for legal representation in order to oppose. A party must have an address for service in the UK/EEA for correspondence purposes.

The official cost of entering opposition varies depending on the ground/grounds used. In the simplest case, the official fee is GBP100 for a fast-track opposition based on S5(1) or S5(2) grounds and where the earlier registration is not vulnerable to proof of use challenge being more than five years old from the date of grant of registration. The fee rises to GBP200 where the grounds for opposition are not limited to S5(1) or S5(2). Attorney fees will vary enormously for opposition depending on the complexity of the ground of opposition, evidence preparation, whether proof of use is requested, whether the proceedings are based on the papers or whether a hearing is granted at which counsel is present, whether cross-examination is required and so forth. Fees may range from the low thousands of pounds for a straightforward matter up to many tens of thousands of pounds for a complex matter.

3.3 Opposition Procedure

The opposition procedure can briefly be described as follows.

- File Form TM7 (Notice of Opposition) and Statement of Grounds.
- Opposition examined as to its formalities and, if accepted, communicated to the applicant.
- Applicant is set a two-month term to file a Form TM8 and counter-statement. This two-month deadline also serves as the cooling-off period designed to facilitate settlement.
- The cooling-off term must be extended before expiry of deadline. If so, it will automatically be extended by nine months (Form TM9C) and a further nine months (Form TM9T) on the request of both parties. No further extension is possible. Suspension of the proceedings may be available as an alternative. The cooling-off term can be terminated by either party at any stage (Form TM9T), resulting in a two-month term for filing the Form TM8 and counter-statement.
- If no cooling-off extension is filed, the Form TM8 and counterstatement (defence) must be filed. If not, the registrar may treat the application as abandoned.
- The Form TM8 and counterstatement is filed. The applicant may place the opponent to proof of use of an earlier registration that is more than five years old from the date of grant immediately preceding the publication term.
- The evidence rounds are set.
- A period of two months is provided for the opponent to substantiate the opposition and to respond to the defence raised.
- A period of two months is provided for the applicant to adduce evidence in defence.
- A period of one month is provided for the opponent to serve evidence in reply.
- The parties are invited to submit written observations in lieu of a hearing or request a hearing, including any request for cross-examination of any witness.
- Either a decision results on the papers or the parties submit skeleton arguments (with mutual exchange) and thereafter attend a hearing — usually for half a day — that may occur in person or via videolink. A decision is usually reserved and follows some weeks after the hearing.

3.4 Legal Remedies

A decision may be appealed within a period of 28 days from the adverse decision to either the appointed person (from which no further right of appeal lies) or the Chancery Division of the High Court of England and Wales. A further right of appeal is possible with the leave of the court to the Court of Appeal where the judge has made an error of principle in applying the law to the facts and again with leave to the Supreme. In rare circumstances, a decision of the registrar can be set aside by way of an administrative judicial review where the procedure and decision-making is flawed.

4. Initiating a Lawsuit

4.1 Actions to Pursue Infringement
The available actions may typically include: (i) where the mark is registered, a claim for trade-mark infringement and (ii) where the mark is unregistered but has been used in trade, a claim for passing off.

4.2 Initiating Infringement Proceedings
Generally speaking, claims must be brought in the High Court (Chancery Division) or in the Intellectual Property Enterprise Court (IPEC), which is a specialist court with jurisdiction to hear claims not exceeding GBP500,000 in value, or in certain county courts.

4.3 Effect of Decisions on Infringement Actions
Generally speaking, an office decision will not bind the court or determine the outcome of an infringement case. In some (limited) circumstances an issue of fact or law determined by the office could be given binding effect between the parties and in some cases an attempt to relitigate in the court issues whichhave the subject of extensive evidence and argument in office proceedings, might be regarded as an abuse of process.

4.4 Declaratory Judgment Proceedings
A claim for a declaration of non-infringement can be brought where a question or threat of infringement has arisen.

4.5 Jurisdiction of Courts
At first instance, the courts will generally be one or other of those specified in **4.2 Initiating Infringement Proceedings**. Appeals lie (with permission) to the Court of Appeal and, thence, with permission and only where the appeal raises a point of law of general public importance, to the Supreme Court of the United Kingdom. (In some circumstances, questions of EU law or interpretation of EU legislation may be referred by the English court to the Court of Justice of the European Union.)

4.6 Prerequisites to Filing a Lawsuit
Unless a failure to do so can be justified (for example, in cases of real urgency), if a lawsuit is filed without first raising and seeking to resolve the matter in correspondence, there could be adverse costs consequences for the claimant.

4.7 Representation for Parties
In the case of individuals, parties in trade-mark litigation matters do not need to be represented by a lawyer. Companies are usually represented by a lawyer or other permitted legal representative, but can instead be represented by an employee, with the permission of the court.

4.8 Interim or Preliminary Injunctions
Preliminary or interim injunctions may be granted where the claimant shows there is a serious question to be tried and where the "balance of convenience" favours the grant of the injunction (usually pending trial or further order). The claimant must undertake to the court to compensate the defendant for any losses it suffers if it turns out that the injunction should not have been granted (eg, because the claimant loses at trial).

4.9 Protection for Potential Defendant
Depending upon the facts, the defendant may have grounds for commencing proceedings for a declaration of non-infringement, or a declaration that the claimant's trade-mark is invalid. In some cases — for example, where a customer had been threatened with infringement proceedings in respect of its sales — it may be possible for the trade mark-owner to bring an "unjustified threats" action seeking an injunction to restrain a repetition of the threat and damages.

4.10 Obtaining Information and Evidence
Disclosure of relevant documents or categories of documents may be ordered by the court, where justified.

4.11 Initial Pleading Standards
Pleadings (statements of case) must set out concisely all facts and (especially in the IPEC) arguments relied on so that the issues in the case are known before trial. The facts alleged must be verified by a statement of truth. Arguments may be developed at trial in the written skeleton argument and oral submissions but if an aspect of a case has not been pleaded, permission of the court may be required to introduce that aspect at trial. Permission might be refused, especially if further evidence might have been adduced by the opposing party, had the new aspect been pleaded before.

4.12 Representative or Collective Actions
Collective actions are in principle possible but in practice extremely rare in trade-mark cases. Occasionally multiple claimants join together to bring a case where, for example, a cybersquatter has engaged in a pattern of similar behaviour towards them all.

4.13 Restrictions on Trade Mark-Owners
Threats (express or implied) of trade-mark proceedings can in some circumstances lead to claims for injunctions restraining repetition of the threat and damages. This is more likely to be the case where, rather than the person who applied the offending mark or imported the goods, his customer is threatened. If the threat of, or bringing, a trade-mark infringement action amounted to an abuse of a dominant position or was otherwise contrary to competition law, that could in principle provide a defence, or lead to a counterclaim for damages. Such defences/claims are not commonly raised in a typical trade-mark case.

5. Infringement

5.1 Action for Infringement
Actions for trade-mark infringement may be brought by the (i) proprietor or (ii) (if the licence so provides) an exclusive licensee. Further, unless the licence provides otherwise, a licensee (exclusive or non-exclusive) may call upon the proprietor to bring infringement proceedings and, if he or she fails to do so, may bring such proceedings in the licensee's own name. Infringement proceedings cannot be commenced before the mark is registered.

5.2 Signs and Infringement
Infringement may arise in three circumstances:

- Use of an identical mark for goods or services identical to those for which the mark is registered will generally amount to infringement without the need to establish confusion.
- Where the mark and/or the goods/services are not identical, but similar, there will be infringement if there is a likelihood of confusion. In assessing likelihood of confusion, all relevant factors will be weighed, including the doctrine of imperfect recollection; the overall impression of the marks, including their dominant and distinctive components; whether a lesser degree of similarity between the goods/services is offset by a greater degree of similarity between the marks, or vice versa; and the degree of distinctiveness of the registered mark (either inherent distinctiveness or distinctiveness acquired through use). If there is a risk that the public might believe that the goods or services come from the same or economically linked undertakings, there is a likelihood of confusion.
- In the case of a mark with a reputation, use of an identical or similar mark in relation to goods or services similar or dissimilar to those for which the mark is registered will amount to infringement where the use, without due cause, takes unfair advantage of, or is detrimental to, the distinctive character or repute of the registered mark.

5.3 Use of a Sign by Defendant
There will be no infringement if the use relied on does not affect or is not liable to affect the functions of the trade-mark, in particular its essential function of guaranteeing to consumers the origin of the goods or services. Accordingly, in the relevant legislation, certain uses for purely descriptive purposes are expressly excluded from the scope of the exclusive right. It is not an infringement to use "indications concerning the kind, quality, quantity, intended purpose, value, geographical origin, the time of production of goods or of rendering of services, or other characteristics of goods or services", or to use a registered mark "where it is necessary to indicate the intended purpose of a product or service (in particular, as accessories or spare parts)", provided in each case that "the use is in accordance with honest practices in industrial or commercial matters". Generally speaking, it is for the defendant to raise and prove a defence of non-trade-mark use, not for the claimant to prove that the use complained of amounts to trade-mark use.

5.4 Defences Against Infringement
In addition to the above, available defences may include the following.

- Use of own name or address (pending compliance by the UK with an EU Directive; in the case of a UK national mark this defence can be available for both companies and individuals, but in the case of a European Union Trade Mark (EUTM) is available to individuals only).
- Use of another registered mark for the goods or services for which it is registered (provided the registration relied upon by way of defence is valid).
- Use in a particular locality of an earlier right that applies only in that locality.
- Exhaustion of rights (no infringement in the case of genuine goods put on the market in the EEA by the proprietor or with his or her consent).
- Acquiescence in the use of a later registered mark for a period of five successive years. (Whether acquiescence or estoppel could provide a defence in any other circumstance is presently uncertain.)
- Where the registration of a mark is subject to a disclaimer or limitation, the rights conferred are restricted accordingly. So, for example, if a mark is registered subject to a particular colour limitation, the registration is not infringed by an otherwise confusingly similar mark in different colours.
- Invalidity/revocation: where available, a declaration of invalidity or revocation for five years' non-use may also, in practice, afford defences.

5.5 Role of Experts and/or Surveys
Except where survey evidence is permitted, expert evidence is unusual in trade-mark cases. An exception might be where the goods or services are unusual and the court needs the services of an expert in the particular field to understand the market or relevant technical issues. Where survey evidence is permitted, a survey expert commonly gives evidence concerning the manner in which the survey was conducted and any statistical conclusions that might be drawn. However, the courts are sceptical about survey evidence and will only give permission for it to be adduced where satisfied that it will be of real value. This is more likely to be possible where the evidence is designed to test distinctiveness, rather than confusion.

5.6 Administrative or Criminal Offence
Trade-mark infringement can amount to a criminal offence. Although the relevant statutory provisions are aimed primarily at counterfeiting, they are drafted so broadly that many other activities that amount to civil infringement may be criminal offences too. Although local weights and meas-

ures authorities are given responsibility for enforcement, any person (including the trade-mark proprietor) can bring a (private) criminal prosecution. Having said that, it would be rare for a prosecution to be brought in connection with an ordinary commercial dispute where no counterfeiting issue arises.

5.7 Custom Seizures
Counterfeit goods may be seized at the border by UK Customs under EU Regulation No 608/2013. A trade mark -owner who wants Customs action at the border needs to complete an Application for Action, providing relevant details of his rights and (to the extent known) the shipment. Where goods are seized by Customs they may be destroyed if the owner of the goods consents or fails to object to their destruction. Where the owner objects, the goods may be released unless the trade mark owner commences infringement proceedings within ten working days (three in the case of perishables). Customs' powers of seizure under Regulation 608/2013 do not extend to parallel imports but, under the Trade Marks Act 1994, a trade mark-owner may give notice that parallel imports from outside the EEA (or within that area but not entered for free circulation) will infringe and should therefore be treated as prohibited. Such goods may be seized under UK customs law.

6. Revocation/Cancellation

6.1 Remedies and Reasons
Section 46 of the UK Trade Marks Act 1994 provides that a trade-mark registration may be revoked for reasons of:

- five years' non-use from the date of grant of registration;
- any subsequent five-year term;
- that owing to acts or inactivity on the part of the owner, the mark has become generic; or
- as a result of the use made of it, the mark is liable to mislead as to the nature, quality or geographical origin of the goods/services claimed.

6.2 Trade Mark Office and Civil Courts
Under S46(4) of the Act, an action for revocation can be brought before the UK Intellectual Property Office. It can additionally be raised by way of counterclaim to an action for infringement in the IPEC or High Court.

6.3 Statutory Limitation or Time Period
A revocation action under S.46 may be brought at any stage once the registration is more than five years old from the date of grant. An application for invalidation under S.47 can be brought at any stage unless acquiescence under S.48 can be shown. To this end, where the proprietor of an earlier trade-mark or other earlier right has acquiesced for a continuous period of five years in the use of a registered trade-mark in the United Kingdom, being aware of that use, they shall cease to be entitled to apply for a declaration of invalidity and to oppose use. Where acquiescence applies, it is counterclaimed by way of defence.

6.4 Initiation of Revocation/Cancellation Proceeding
In the United Kingdom there are no locus standi in relation to an application for revocation (there being good public policy reasons to allow this) nor in relation to the filing of an application for a declaration of invalidity on absolute grounds (see **1.15 Grounds for Refusal**). There are locus standi requirements in relation to the filing of an application for a declaration of invalidity based upon relative grounds for refusal under Section 5 or Section 56.

6.5 Partial Revocation/Cancellation
Partial revocation and partial invalidation are possible. The scope of the application will specify the extent, ie, should the registration be revoked/cancelled in full or in part. Where the claimant requests revocation/invalidation of the registration in its entirety, it is open to the tribunal/court to revoke/cancel in part. Partial revocation may be ordered where a registration has only been used in part. Similarly, invalidation may be ordered in part where the earlier mark/right only creates a conflict in part and where the remainder of the specification is valid as filed.

6.6 Possibilities of Amendment
It is open to the registered proprietor to surrender partially specification terms that have not been used or that give rise to invalidity.

6.7 Revocation/Cancellation and Infringement
Actions for revocation and invalidation may be joined and heard in parallel.

7. Trial & Settlement

7.1 Special Procedural Provisions
The Civil Procedure Rules of England and Wales apply to all civil cases including trade-mark infringement proceedings in the UK and Part 63 of the CPR contains specific provisions dealing with IP including registered trade marks. The IPEC, which is a specialist list of the Chancery Division, operates its own rules of procedure. See the following IPEC Guide: https://assets.publishing.service.gov.uk/government/uploads/system/uploads/attachment_data/file/543307/intellectual-property-_enterprise-court-guide.pdf.

There is a general principle in the UK that parties should see if matters can be settled before any proceedings are issued. There are no specific guidelines for trade-mark disputes but a general pre-action conduct guideline is available at http://

www.justice.gov.uk/guidance/courts-and-tribunals/courts/procedure-rules/civil/contents/practice_directions/pd_pre-action_conduct.htm.

7.2 Determination of Cases
Trade-mark infringement cases are decided by a judge. In the IPEC, the judge will likely have experience of IP matters. The presiding judge HHJ Richard Hacon was a barrister specialising in IP prior to his appointment. Given the increased caseload before the IPEC it is also common to see deputy High Court judges sitting, such as Daniel Alexander, QC, David Stone and Melissa Clarke, all of whom have experience in IP matters. In the Chancery Division of the High Court the position is quite different. It is not guaranteed that the judge hearing the case will have any experience of trade-mark matters at all as the Court hears matters ranging from disputes relating to business, property or land, disputes over trusts, competition (anti-trust) claims under either European or UK competition law, commercial disputes (domestic and international), disputes over the validity of a will ("probate disputes") and hear claims relating to partnerships (eg, dissolution), cancelling, setting aside or correcting ("rectifying") errors in deeds and other legal instruments, breaches of trust or contract and professional negligence. The parties have no influence over who the judge will be.

7.3 Possibilities of Settlement
A defendant may invite settlement at any stage either upon receipt of the letter before claim (which is the precursor to formal proceedings) or at any stage up to or post a decision. The court expects the parties to attempt to reach a settlement in order to avoid incurring unnecessary costs and may suspend proceedings in order to allow the parties to negotiate or mediate a settlement. Indeed, a failure to settle may have an adverse impact on costs awarded to the successful or losing party. Settlement correspondence is generally made "without prejudice", rendering it confidential between the parties and not available for submission before the court unless it is made "save as to costs", where it may be inspected to show unreasonable conduct post decision or where a Part 36 Offer is made to show that a monetary sum and undertakings were made earlier in the proceedings and that were better than those ultimately awarded at trial.

7.4 Other Court Proceedings
The principle of "lis alibi pendens" or "action pending elsewhere" can have an effect on UK court proceedings. This typically applies in the case of an application for invalidation of an EU trade-mark registration that may present itself as the basis for a claim in the UK courts. The so-called EUIPO torpedo may provide for a stay of proceedings in the UK until it is determined by the EUIPO and any subsequent appeal route, which can last many years. However, the torpedo must have been fired before the claim form is filed. Otherwise, all relevant issues are usually dealt with in the one action in the UK by way of counterclaim.

8. Remedies

8.1 Existing Remedies
In civil cases, the claimant for infringement can seek a permanent injunction, damages (either on a reasonable royalty basis or else an account of profits), their reasonable costs (limited to GBP50,000 in the IPEC in relation to the issue of liability and where this figure does not include court fees, any wasted costs ordered and any recoverable VAT) (costs are unlimited in the High Court), delivery up and/or destruction of infringing goods. Payment into court may be ordered where the defendant is outside the jurisdiction of the Court. A freezing order can be obtained in relation to the defendant's bank accounts/assets in the jurisdiction in certain circumstances. A search-and-seize order may also be ordered. The judge has discretion in ordering remedies.

8.2 Rights and Remedies
A prevailing defendant has the rights/remedies of a declaration of non-infringement and their reasonable costs.

8.3 Different Types of Remedies
There are no different types of remedies for different types of trade marks.

9. Appeal

9.1 Special Provisions
In general, there are no special provisions concerning the appelate procedure for trade-mark proceedings. If a party wishes to appeal, permission is required. Permission may be sought from the judge making the order or from the court to which the appeal is addressed. Depending on the nature of the order being appealed, the destination of an appeal from the multi-track in the IPEC is the Court of Appeal or the High Court (Chancery Division). Final orders are appealed to the Court of Appeal, whereas interim orders are appealed to the High Court (Chancery Division). Appeals from the High Court (Chancery Division) lie to the Court of Appeal.

9.2 Factual or Legal Review
Appeals are limited to a legal rather than factual review, ie, the judge must have erred in law. In practice, however, points of law and their application are driven by the facts so it is inevitable that an appeal will look to the facts. In extremely limited circumstances it may be possible to file fresh evidence on appeal and raise a new point of law but there is an extremely heavy burden to discharge.

9.3 Length of Appeal from Trial Court
It is usual to seek permission to appeal from the trial judge, which is invariably refused. An application to appeal directly to the Higher Court must be made within 21 days and the appeal grounds served on the other party, who has 14 days in which to enter reasons why permission should not be granted. If permission is granted, an appeal in a non-urgent civil case will be heard by the Court of Appeal within a period of 12-18 months. An appeal up to the Supreme Court where permission is granted will take a similar period of time.

10. Other Trade Mark Issues

10.1 Recognition of Dilution
Dilution or 'blurring' of the distinctive character or repute subsisting in an earlier trade-mark is recognised in both Section 5(3) (dealing with opposition) and 10(3) (which deals with infringement) of the UK Trade Marks Act 1994. The sections make provision for opposition and infringement where the later trade-mark applied for or sign used in the course of trade is identical or similar to the earlier trade-mark and claims is used in relation to goods or services that are not similar to the goods or services for which the earlier trade-mark is registered and where the trade-mark has a reputation in the UK and where use registration of the later mark/sign would without due cause take unfair advantage of, or be detrimental to, the distinctive character or repute of the trade-mark.

10.2 Protection of Famous Marks
The United Kingdom is a member country of the Paris Convention and Article 6bis (protection of well-known trade marks) is implemented under S.56 of the Act.

10.3 Special Rules Regarding Geographic Indicators
Geographical indications comprise protected geographical indications, protected designations or origin and traditional speciality guarantees. Pages 112-118 of the UK Trade Marks Registry Work Manual provide an excellent summary regarding the registrability of geographical indications, for example, "Rioja" for wine. See: https://assets.publishing.service.gov.uk/government/uploads/system/uploads/attachment_data/file/690003/Trade-Marks-Manual.pdf.

10.4 Special Rules Relating to Surnames
See Pages 177-178 of the UK Trade Marks Registry Work Manual, shown below:

"In the CJEU's judgment in Case C-404/02, Nichols plc v Registrar of Trade Marks, the Court confirmed that assessing the distinctive character of a surname must be carried out according to the specific circumstances of the case, and that (like all other types of marks) the presence or absence of distinctive character depends upon the perception of relevant consumers, having regard to the essential function of a trade-mark identified in Article 2 of the Directive.

"Consequently, the nature of the relevant trade and the use of surnames as an indicator of trade origin within that trade must be taken into account. If the relevant public's expectation was that there would be numerous undertakings trading in the relevant sector under the name in question, with the result that the public would have no expectation that the relevant goods or services under that name would originate from any particular undertaking, then it would be legitimate to conclude that the name is devoid of any distinctive character and subject to an objection under section 3(1)(b). Internet research will usually be required to ascertain whether it is common in the relevant trade to use surnames as trading practice. However, in some instances it will not be necessary to carry out that research. For example, it is well known that the surname 'Smith' is common, and from that it is reasonable to assume there will be large number of doctors named Smith practising in the UK. Therefore, it is unlikely that consumers or end users of medical services will regard that name, by itself, as distinguishing the medical services of one undertaking from those of other such undertakings. Other sectors in which it is common to trade under a surname is that of solicitors.

Surnames With Other Meanings
"Where a word which is a surname has another meaning, that meaning may be open to an objection, for example, the trade-mark BROWN would face an objection under sections 3(1)(b) and (c) if applied for in relation to 'sauces' because it is a word which may serve, in trade, to designate a kind of product, namely brown sauce. Similarly, the same word would not be acceptable as a trade-mark for 'paints' because it designates a characteristic of those goods (colour).

Surnames With Initials and Full Personal Names
"Full names and/or surnames with initials have a greater capacity to distinguish the goods or services of one undertaking than a surname alone, and are therefore likely to be acceptable."

11. Costs

11.1 Costs Before Filing a Lawsuit
It would be usual to conduct due diligence around the later sign in order to determine whether any rights are owned and, if not, how long the sign has been in use and what for. This may necessitate trade-mark register searches, domain name searches, company searches and a commercial investigation. A credit check of the defendant may also indicate their ability to defend but with the rise of after-the-event insurance, this is always difficult to predict. Investigative

work and searches prior to issuing the claim letter will cost in excess of GBP1,000. The cost of drafting a claim letter including the undertakings sought in reply will be around GBP1,250-1,500.

11.2 Costs Regarding an Infringement Action

The costs for bringing an action to trial can vary enormously under English procedure depending on whether the action is filed in the IPEC or High Court, the basis for the claim and availability of any counter-claims, and the advocate(s) appointed. On the one hand the IPEC, which was set up in order to provide a cheaper alternative to litigating IP matters in UK, operates different court fees, evidence is limited, the availability of discovery and expert witnesses is limited and the number of days set down for trial is much shorter, leading to lower overall costs. A straightforward action for infringement based on similarity of marks and identical goods/services may cost up to GBP100,000. Costs exposure is limited to GBP50,000 (excluding court fees, wasted costs and any recoverable VAT) but also means that you would likely only expect to recover half of any total outlay. With all options being open in the High Court, costs can vary enormously and costs would likely exceed GBP150,000-200,000 for a basic action. However, actions can run into many hundreds of thousands of pounds and upwards into the millions depending on the complexity of the matter, the evidence, whether a survey or surveys are deemed necessary and admissible, and so on.

11.3 Costs of Litigation

The general rule under English law is that the winner takes all. What this means in practice is that they can generally be expected to recover around 75% of their reasonably incurred costs, including court fees, professional fees and expenses. Court costs are capped in the IPEC at GBP50,000 (excluding court fees, wasted costs and any recoverable VAT). Court costs are unlimited in the High Court. When giving judgment in the claimant's or defendants favour there will be an indication that the losing party will be liable to pay costs if not agreed then by assessment.

J A Kemp
14 South Square
Gray's Inn
London
WC1R 5JJ

Tel: +44 203 077 8600
Fax: +44 20 7430 1000
Email: jfish@jakemp.com
Web: www.jakemp.com

J A • KEMP
PATENT ATTORNEYS • TRADE MARK ATTORNEYS

12. Alternative Dispute Resolution

12.1 Common Way of Settlement

ADR in the form of mediation is available to parties in the UK. The court will generally expect an attempt to resolve matters amicably before recourse to court action and a failure to negotiate a settlement may have a bearing on costs. However, mediation is not compulsory. It is not common to mediate but mediation is growing in popularity and efforts to educate IP right-holders as to its benefits continues.

Arbitration may be provided for in the context of a contractual dispute.

13. Trade Marks and Other Intellectual Property

13.1 Protection by Copyright

A trade-mark representation may give rise to other forms of protectable IP right, such as copyright, ie, it may embody an artistic work such as a logo, or registered or unregistered (design right) design.

USA

The 'Law & Practice' sections provide easily accessible information on navigating the legal system when conducting business in the jurisdiction. Leading lawyers explain local law and practice at key transactional stages and for crucial aspects of doing business.

The 'Trends & Developments' sections give an overview of current trends and developments in local legal markets. Leading lawyers analyse particular trends or provide a broader discussion of key developments in the jurisdiction.

Law and Practice

Contributed by Kirkland & Ellis LLP

CONTENTS

Contributed by Kirkland & Ellis LLP **Authors:** Claudia Ray, Bonnie L. Jarrett, Jordan Romanoff

Contributed by Kirkland & Ellis LLP ***Authors:*** Claudia Ray, Bonnie L. Jarrett, Jordan Romanoff

Kirkland & Ellis LLP's copyright, trade mark, internet & advertising (CTIA) practice group is comprised of a core group of 40 attorneys in the New York, Chicago, Los Angeles, Palo Alto, and Washington, D.C. offices; the group draws upon the resources of Kirkland's 230-person intellectual property practice with additional offices in Houston, London, and San Francisco. The firm's CTIA group has handled some of the highest-profile matters in the copyright, trade mark, internet and advertising law areas, with notable results; its experience spans a wide range of industries, including technology, consumer products, entertainment and media, fashion, and financial services. Key practice areas include: copyright, trade mark and internet-related litigation; trade dress (product packaging and design); unfair competition; false advertising; defamation; rights of privacy and publicity; domain name disputes; the DMCA; NAD disputes; and trade secrets. The authors would like to thank Miranda Means and Chrissy Milanese for their additional contributions to this chapter.

Authors

Claudia Ray is a partner at Kirkland & Ellis and a member of the firm's IP department. She represents clients in such industries as technology, financial services, consumer products, apparel, and entertainment in connection with adversarial proceedings relating to copyright and trade-mark infringement and theft of trade secrets, among other issues. She also advises on corporate transactions, licensing matters, and overall IP strategy. Claudia is a member of several professional legal bodies, including the International Trademark Association's US Amicus Subcommittee, previously chaired the New York City Bar Association's Trademarks and Unfair Competition committee, and frequently lectures and publishes on trade marks and other IP-related issues.

Bonnie L. Jarrett is a partner at Kirkland & Ellis and a member of the firm's IP department. Her practice focuses on intellectual property litigation, including trade marks, copyrights, false advertising, and trade secrets. She represents clients across a wide range of industries, including entertainment and media, technology, pharmaceuticals, and consumer products. Bonnie also represents clients in trade-mark proceedings before the US Patent and Trademark Office and the Trademark Trial and Appeal Board, and counsels clients regarding the acquisition, retention, and enforcement of intellectual property rights worldwide. She is a member of a number of legal professional bodies, including the trade-mark litigation committee of the ABA's intellectual property law section and has published widely on the subject of copyright and trade marks.

Jordan Romanoff is an intellectual property litigation associate in the New York office of Kirkland & Ellis and a member of the firm's IP department. His practice focuses on litigation and counselling in the fields of copyright, trade mark, right of publicity, art, internet, and advertising law. He represents and advises clients across a wide range of industries, including entertainment and media, fashion, technology, and consumer products. Jordan is a member of the International Trademark Association's copyright committee.

1. Types of Trade Marks & Registration

1.1 Types of Trade Marks

The federal trade-mark statute, the Lanham Act, recognises that a trade mark may be "any word, name, symbol, or device, or any combination thereof" that is used "to identify and distinguish... goods... and to indicate the source of the goods." See 15 U.S.C. § 1127. Put more simply, anything that can serve as a unique source-identifier, including a word, a design, a colour or a sound, can function as a trade mark. US law protects various types of trade marks, including service marks, design marks, certification marks, collective marks, and trade dress. See id. §§ 1052-54. Protectable rights in a trade mark are based on the use of a mark, and may be enforced under both statutory law and common law. Although it also is possible to obtain a registration for a mark from an individual state, because federal registrations confer nationwide priority, the following discussion focuses primarily on the federal system. State systems are broadly consistent with the federal system.

1.2 Trade-Mark Rights

A registration is not necessary to have a valid trade mark. Federal registration of trade marks is governed by the Lanham Act, 15 U.S.C. §§ 1051 et seq. Unregistered marks are protectable under Section 43(a) of the Lanham Act. States also have laws governing the registration of trade marks and the protection of unregistered marks under common law.

1.3 Standards for Registering
In general, to be protectable a mark must either be inherently distinctive or it must be shown to have acquired secondary meaning, but there are exceptions. For example, although product-design trade dress must have acquired secondary meaning to be registrable and protectable, secondary meaning is not required for product-packaging trade dress.

1.4 Trade-Mark Register
The US Patent & Trademark Office ("USPTO") maintains a Principal Register and a Supplemental Register that are publicly accessible through its website, located at <www.uspto.gov>.

1.5 Types of Registers
Marks are eligible for inclusion on the Principal Register if they are either inherently distinctive or have become distinctive through continued use in commerce (ie, have acquired secondary meaning).

Marks that are "capable of distinguishing applicant's goods or services and not registrable on the Principal Register," but are not otherwise barred from registration, may be registered on the Supplemental Register. Such marks are generally descriptive terms that have not acquired secondary meaning. They are not entitled to any presumptions of validity, ownership or the exclusive right to use the mark, cannot be cited to prevent the importation of counterfeit products, and do not become incontestable. If a mark on the Supplemental Register acquires secondary meaning, the owner may file a new application to register it on the Principal Register. States also maintain their own registers.

1.6 Searching for Prior Trade Marks
Mark owners often conduct a search before applying to register a mark with the USPTO to determine whether there are any marks in use and/or registered that might conflict with their mark. Federal trade-mark records can be searched online using the Trademark Electronic Search System, available at www.uspto.gov or at the Public Search Facility in Alexandria, Virginia. Private firms also can be used to conduct trade-mark searches. Applicants also may wish to consider searching state trade-mark registries, company names, news articles, industry-specific resources, and the internet before using and/or applying to register a trade mark.

1.7 Registration Requirements
To obtain a federal registration, a mark-owner must complete and file an application with the USPTO, pay the required fee (the USPTO publishes a schedule of fees; currently the application fee ranges from USD225 to USD400 per mark, per class of goods and services), and provide a verified statement together with specimens of the mark as it is used in commerce. The applicant must provide information about its "domicile and citizenship, the date of [its] first use of the mark, the date of [its] first use of the mark in commerce, the goods in connection with which the mark is used, and a drawing of the mark." TMEP § 801.02. The specimen included in the application must show the manner in which the trade mark is used in interstate commerce, ie, how it appears on product packaging, on a tag, or in advertising.

Once the USPTO approves the mark and specimen, if no one opposes the mark it will proceed to registration and a registration certificate will be issued to the trade mark-owner.

1.8 Registering a Trade Mark
Natural persons, firms, corporations, unions, associations, and other organisations all may register trade marks.

1.9 Registering Signs
In addition to words and designs, colours, sounds and scents can be registered as marks.

1.10 Other Rights to Signs
Trade names and domain names may be protected under both federal and state law. A trade name (the corporate name under which a company does business) may be registered through the Secretary of State or the county clerk's office, depending on the state. In many states, the registration of a trade name does not grant the registrant exclusive rights to use the name as a mark. The registrant may, however, gain such rights through use of the name as a mark. Domain names are protected by the Anti-Cybersquatting Consumer Protection Act, which prohibits the use or registration of a domain name that is confusingly similar to a senior user's trade mark.

1.11 Registration Procedure
An application to register a trade mark may be filed online with the USPTO at www.uspto.gov, or by sending a paper application to the USPTO. Multi-class applications are permitted. If the application meets the minimum filing requirements described above, the USPTO assigns the application a serial number and a trade-mark examiner reviews the application to determine whether the trade mark is registrable. If the examiner determines that it is registrable, the USPTO will publish the mark in the Official Gazette, which provides public notice of the application and an opportunity for third parties to oppose its registration.

If the examiner determines that there is some barrier to registration (eg, likelihood of confusion or defective goods and services' description), the examiner will issue a non-final office action. An applicant will then have six months to respond. If it does not respond, the application will be deemed abandoned. If the applicant responds and the USPTO is satisfied with the response, the mark will be published. If the USPTO is not satisfied with the office action response, it will issue a final office action. The applicant may then either submit a final response or file an appeal to the Trademark Trial and Appeal Board ("TTAB"), which will decide whether the mark may be registered despite the examiner's refusal.

If the mark is published and the registration is not successfully opposed, a registration certificate is issued to the trade mark-holder. The issuance of the registration after the expiry of the opposition period typically takes approximately three months.

The states each maintain similar procedures with respect to the registration of marks, the details of which vary from state to state.

1.12 Use in Commerce

Subject to certain exceptions, including for applications based on foreign registrations, the US requires that a mark be used in commerce before a federal registration will issue. Use need not be shown as of the date of filing an application, as the US allows trade-mark owners to file applications on an intent-to-use ("ITU") basis with a priority date based on the date the application is filed.

The ITU application process generally is similar to that for a use-based application, except that the registration does not issue immediately after the expiry of the opposition period if no opposition is filed (or if an opposition is filed but ultimately is unsuccessful). Instead, a notice of allowance is issued within two months of publication of the ITU application, indicating that the registration will issue once a statement of use is filed. The applicant then has six months from the issuance of the notice of allowance in which either to file a statement of use or file a request for a further six-month extension. The statement of use must be filed with the required fee (currently USD125 per class), a specimen showing use, and a verified statement alleging ownership, use in commerce, and the date of first use. If the applicant does nothing, the application will be deemed abandoned. After the statement of use is filed, if all of the required elements are met the USPTO will approve it and register the mark. If the statement of use is defective, for example because the filing fee was not paid or there is a defect in the specimen, then the examiner will issue an office action, to which the applicant will have to respond, as described above with respect to use-based applications.

After a mark has been registered, to maintain the registration the owner must file, within the sixth year following the issuance of the registration, a declaration of continuing use, which is commonly referred to as a "Section 8" affidavit, attesting that the mark is still in use. The mark-owner must then file a further renewal after the end of the ninth year, but before the tenth year, following registration and every ten years thereafter. The applicant also may file a "Section 15" affidavit, attesting that the mark has been in continuous use in commerce for five years following registration and there is no adverse decision or pending proceeding involving rights in the mark. The registration will then become "incontestable" and the available grounds for challenging the registration will be limited to genericness and fraud on the USPTO during the application process. The fees for the Section 8 and 15 affidavits are set forth in a schedule issued by the USPTO, and currently are USD125 per class and USD200 per class respectively.

1.13 Registration of Series Marks

The USPTO does not allow applicants to include series marks within the same application. Instead, each mark must be set forth in a separate application, for which a separate filing fee is paid. If a prospective mark is similar to an applicant's existing mark, the applicant may indicate that common ownership in the application.

1.14 Length of Registration Process

Prosecuting an application takes approximately seven to 13 months, depending on whether the examiner has issued an office action or an opposition has been filed. Although an applicant does not need an attorney to file an application, the USPTO recommends consulting a trade-mark attorney to help conduct a more comprehensive search and deal with any issues that arise during the review process. Official filing fees for a trade-mark application are set by the USPTO, as noted above. Attorneys' fees for trade-mark searches and legal services relating to trade-mark applications vary widely.

1.15 Grounds for Refusal

The Lanham Act provides that the USPTO may refuse to register a trade mark that is (a) is "immoral, deceptive, or scandalous... ; or... disparag[ing] or falsely suggest[s] a connection with persons, living or dead, institutions, beliefs, or national symbols... "; (b) an incorrect geographical indication for wines and spirits; (c) "a name, portrait, or signature identifying a particular living individual except by his written consent, or the name, signature, or portrait of a deceased President of the United States during the life of his widow, if any, except by the written consent of the widow"; (d) confusingly similar to an existing mark; (e) "merely descriptive or deceptively misdescriptive"; (f) "primarily geographically descriptive"; (g) "primarily geographically deceptively misdescriptive"; (h) primarily merely a surname; or (i) functional. See 15 U.S.C. § 1052. The US Supreme Court recently held that the ban on registration of "scandalous, immoral, or disparaging marks" violates the First Amendment, however, so that basis no longer applies. See Matal v Tam, 137 S. Ct. 1744 (2017).

1.16 Process for Overcoming Objections

If an examiner issues an office action objecting to the registration of a mark, an applicant has six months in which to submit a response addressing the objections.

1.17 Consideration of Prior Rights

The USPTO considers prior rights when reviewing an application by searching its database for any registrations for the same or similar marks. If the examiner concludes that a registered mark is likely to cause confusion, the USPTO may reject the application. If the applicant can show that they had used the mark before the earlier registration, the USPTO may grant a concurrent registration, which allows a prior user to continue to use the mark for the user's existing goods or services within the geographic area in which the user operates and the "zone of natural expansion" in which the user is likely to operate in the future.

1.18 Third-Party Rights

Third parties may participate in the registration process in several ways. For example, a third party may file a "letter of protest" with the USPTO before the mark's publication for opposition in the Official Gazette. Such a letter may provide the examiner with information regarding the mark's registrability, including whether it is likely to cause to confusion with another mark or whether the mark is generic or descriptive. Letters of protest are filed with the USPTO, but they are not part of the official record, nor are they sent to the applicant.

Once a mark is published in the Official Gazette, third parties may oppose it during the 30-day window following publication. An opposing party may request an extension of the opposition period within 30 days of publication in the Official Gazette or within an extension period set by the TTAB.

1.19 Revoke, Change, Amend or Correct an Application

A trade-mark applicant may revoke, change, amend, or correct an application during the registration process in certain limited ways. The applicant may amend the class of goods or services for which it seeks registration or alter the description of those goods, but any such amendment cannot broaden the goods or services for which registration is sought. Between the filing of an ITU application and its approval by the examiner for publication, the applicant can amend the application to allege use. After a notice of allowance is issued, the applicant may only amend the application to delete certain goods/services or provide a change of attorney address. Allegations of use may be added after that time by filing a statement of use.

1.20 Assigning an Application or Granting a Licence

A trade-mark application may be assigned if it is based on use. Any such assignment must be accompanied by an assignment of the goodwill associated with the mark. Generally speaking, an ITU application may not be assigned until after a statement of use is filed in order to prevent "trafficking" in marks. There is an exception, however, for situations where the entire business associated with the mark is also sold.

1.21 Remedies Against the Trade Mark Office

If the USPTO issues an office action and the applicant is not able to overcome the examiner's objection(s), the USPTO may refuse to register the mark. If registration is refused, the applicant may appeal to the TTAB. If the TTAB affirms the refusal, the applicant may appeal to the US Court of Appeals for the Federal Circuit.

1.22 Use of a Trade Mark

An applicant may demonstrate use in commerce by filing a specimen of use with the USPTO. Appropriate specimens include goods or product-packaging bearing the mark, labels, tags, packaging material, and advertising materials.

1.23 Dividing a Trade Mark

An applicant may divide a trade-mark application into two separate applications "upon payment of a fee for each new application created and submission by the applicant of a request" to divide. The request must be made between the date of filing and the date on which the trade mark is approved for publication, or during an "opposition, concurrent use, or interference proceeding, upon motion granted by the" TTAB.

1.24 Length of Term of Protection

Trade-mark rights are potentially perpetual if the owner continues to use the mark and, for registered marks, complies with the USPTO's renewal requirements. If the mark-owner does not file a declaration of use and renewal affidavit, and pay the required fee, the registration will be cancelled. A cancelled registration may not be renewed.

1.25 Requirements for an Exhaustion

There is no concept of trade-mark exhaustion in the US. Once a trade mark is registered, as long as the renewal requirements are met and the mark is not abandoned, trade-mark rights may last in perpetuity. Certain rights do end upon sale of a good bearing a mark, however. For example, trade-mark law does not prohibit a bona fide purchaser from reselling a good bearing a trade mark, provided that the good is not altered and the reseller does not suggest that the sale is authorised.

1.26 Participation in the Madrid System

The US participates in the Madrid system. The holder of an international trade-mark registration may request an extension of its protection to cover the US if it submits a declaration attesting to a bona fide intent to begin using the mark in commerce in the US.

1.27 Consequences for Providing Incorrect Information

Fraud on the USPTO occurs where the trade-mark owner knowingly makes a false, material representation with the intent to deceive the trade-mark office. Claims of fraud may arise in proceedings before the TTAB or a court. If either the TTAB or a court finds that a mark-owner has committed fraud on the USPTO in connection with its mark, the registration for that mark will be cancelled.

1.28 Updating or Refreshing a Design Mark

The drawing of a mark may not be changed if the result is that "the character of the mark is materially altered," see 37 C.F.R. § 2.272,ie, whether the mark shown in the new drawing creates "essentially [the] same commercial impression" as the old mark. See TMEP 807.14.

1.29 Denotation

Owners of trade marks on either the Principal Register or the Supplemental Register may use the "®" symbol. The "TM" symbol may be used for an unregistered, or common-law, mark.

2. Assignment and Licensing

2.1 Assignment Requirements or Restrictions

A mark-owner may assign the mark to another provided it is transferred with the good will of the business for which it is used. Good will refers to the reputation of a mark and consumer expectations associated with the use of that mark on particular goods and services. A transfer of good will requires that the assignee continue the assignor's business, or that its goods or services be sufficiently similar to those of the assignor that consumers will not be misled by the transfer. Assigning a trade mark without its accompanying good will is an assignment "in gross" and can lead to abandonment of the mark.

If a mark has never been used in connection with the sale of goods or services (ie, used as a trade mark), no goodwill is associated with it and it therefore cannot be assigned. A trade mark that has been abandoned due to non-use also cannot be assigned.

An assignment of a federally registered trade mark or application must be in writing. Approval from the USPTO is not required for an assignment to be valid. The assignment of a common-law trade mark does not have to be in writing, and the validity of an oral assignment may be proven through the clear and uncontradicted oral testimony of a witness with actual knowledge of the oral agreement.

2.2 Procedure for Assigning a Trade Mark

To be valid, an assignment of a federally registered trade mark or application must be executed in writing and supported by valid consideration, such as a money payment. An assignment should specify in writing the assignor, assignee, mark being assigned, and accompanying good will. See 37 C.F.R. § 3.31. As discussed above, common-law trade-mark rights can be assigned without a writing.

2.3 Registering or Recording the Assignment

An assignment may, but need not, be registered or recorded at the USPTO to be valid. Recordation is advisable because (i) an assignee may only obtain a federal certificate of registration in its name if the assignment has been recorded, (ii) a recorded assignment is prima facie valid in form, and (iii) an assignment is void against a subsequent bona fide purchaser of the same mark unless the assignment was recorded with the USPTO within three months of that assignment or before the subsequent purchase.

To record an assignment with the USPTO, the assignor must pay a fee, submit a legible cover sheet in English, and provide either (i) a copy of the original assignment document, (ii) a copy of an excerpt from that document evidencing the assignment of title, or (iii) a signed statement by both the assignor and assignee explaining how the conveyance affects title in the mark. The necessary materials can be submitted to the USPTO by mail or through its website.

2.4 Trade Marks and Security

Trade marks can be given as security for a debt, often as a conditional assignment, ie, an agreement that the assignment will occur at some point in the future if a triggering event such as default occurs. Because they operate as assignments, security interests must include the mark's good will in order to be valid.

Because trade marks are considered "general intangibles" under the Uniform Commercial Code (UCC), a creditor should file a UCC financing statement in the appropriate state office in order to protect a security interest in a trade mark. For federally registered marks, some practitioners also record security interests with the USPTO, although it is not clear whether doing so is legally required.

Trade-mark actions generally require in personam jurisdiction. US law does recognise in rem rights where another party's use of a certain domain name allegedly infringes a trade-mark owner's mark and in personam jurisdiction is absent because the alleged infringer either is based in a foreign country or cannot be located. - See 15 U.S.C. 1125(d)(1)–(2). - In such instances, the owner can assert: (1) infringement of a registered trade mark; (2) infringement of an unregistered trade mark; (3) dilution of a famous mark; and/or (4) cyberpiracy of a trade mark. See id., §§ 1114(1); 1125(a), (c), (d).

2.5 Licensing Requirements or Restrictions
An owner may license a mark to another for use, but the owner must continue to exercise control over the nature and quality of the goods the licensee offers under the mark. Failing to exercise control can result in partial or total abandonment of the licensor's rights in the mark.

A licence without quality control, known as a "naked licence," will erode a mark's capacity to serve as an accurate source-identifier and can lead to the abandonment of the mark. The operative question is whether the control exercised by the licensor is sufficient under the circumstances to satisfy the public's expectation of quality assurance arising from the presence of the trade mark on the licensee's goods or services. Sufficient quality control might include contractual provisions regarding permissible ingredients or parts supplied or approved by the licensor, specifications governing how the mark may appear on packaging, the types of goods on which a mark may be used, and/or how the mark may be used in advertising.

Trademarks may be licensed to a single licensee or to multiple licensees simultaneously on a non-exclusive basis.

There is no requirement that a trade-mark licence be in writing; an oral licence can be valid. A licence need not be recorded with the USPTO, and the name of the licensor does not have to appear on the licensed uses of the mark. Parties to a trade-mark licence should specify the duration of the licence in their licence agreement, as the law of some states provides that a licence without a specified duration is terminable at the will of either party upon reasonable notice.

2.6 Procedure for Licensing a Trade Mark
There is no particular procedure required to create a valid trademark licence. It can be helpful, however, to specify the licensor, the licensee, the licensed mark, the goods and/or services with which the mark may be used, how the mark must be depicted, the territory in which the mark may be used, whether the licensee may sub-license the mark, the royalties to be paid, the duration of the licence, and a quality-control provision. A licence also may include audit rights for the licensor, acknowledgments that the licensor is the owner of the trade mark and that the licensee's use of the mark will inure to the benefit of the licensor, and an agreement by the licensee to co-operate in protecting the mark and obtaining and maintaining trade-mark registrations.

2.7 Registering or Recording the Licence
A trade-mark licence does not need to be registered or recorded with the USPTO or any other governmental department in order to be valid. Licences of federally registered marks and applications may be recorded with the USPTO, which gives the advantage of putting the public on notice of the licensed rights.

2.8 Reasons to Deny Granting a Perpetual Licence
Although legally a trade-mark owner may grant a perpetual trade-mark licence, doing so can be risky because some states' contract laws allow courts to interpret perpetual licences as terminable at the will of either party.

3. Opposition Procedure

3.1 Legal Grounds and Timeframes
Once a party establishes proper standing, its opposition may be based on any of the statutory grounds discussed above that render a mark unregistrable. The opposer also may argue that the applicant: (i) applied for an invalid "phantom mark," meaning it incorporated multiple marks into its single application; (ii) misused the federal trade-mark registration symbol ("®") before obtaining a registration with intent to deceive or mislead; (iii) was not the mark's true owner as of the filing date; and/or (iv) did not make bona fide use of the mark in commerce before filing a use-based application or did not have a bona fide intent to use a mark before filing an ITU application. The opposer may assert that the mark's registration is barred by claim or issue preclusion.

3.2 Filing an Opposition
Any person or entity who is likely to be damaged by registration of the applicant's mark may file an opposition, provided it states valid legal grounds for the opposition. Both natural and juristic persons (ie, corporations, associations, firms, unions, and other organisations) may initiate oppositions. The opposer need not be represented by an attorney, although a juristic person must designate a representative who is (i) an officer or partner of the entity and (ii) authorised to represent the entity. The filing fee for an opposition is USD400 per class of goods and services for electronically filed oppositions, and USD500 per class for paper filings. The average attorneys' fees, if the opposer has representation, vary depending on the number of classes for which the mark will be opposed and the complexity of the grounds for opposition.

3.3 Opposition Procedure
An opposition is commenced by filing a notice of opposition with the USPTO. The notice may be filed online or in paper format. The notice must provide a short statement as to why the opposer believes it would be damaged by the registration and the grounds for the opposition, supported by relevant

facts. Once the notice is filed, the TTAB will notify the applicant of the opposition by email. The applicant must then file an answer, presenting any denials or defences, and also may file a counterclaim requesting cancellation of any registration pleaded in the notice. If the applicant does not file an answer, the case will proceed to default.

The opposer may withdraw the notice without prejudice at any time before an answer is filed. Once the answer is filed, the opposition may not be withdrawn without prejudice unless the applicant consents in writing.

After the applicant submits its answer, the parties engage in fact and expert discovery, including making initial disclosures, producing documents, completing written interrogatories and requests for admission, and taking depositions of witnesses. At the end of the testimonial period, the parties submit briefs to the TTAB. The opposer's brief is due 60 days after the conclusion of the rebuttal testimony period and the applicant's brief is due 30 days later. The opposer also may file an optional reply brief within 15 days of the applicant's filing. The TTAB will hear oral argument on the matter only if requested by the parties. The TTAB will then weigh the evidence and arguments presented, and the opposer will prevail if it proves its case by a preponderance of the evidence. The only remedy available in an opposition proceeding is refusal to register the mark. The TTAB cannot enjoin use of a mark or award damages.

3.4 Legal Remedies

A party may move for reconsideration of the TTAB's decision in an opposition proceeding within one month from the decision. An applicant may appeal a final refusal of registration to the TTAB within six months of the date of issuance of the final action. A party also may appeal a TTAB decision to the Court of Appeals for the Federal Circuit, or seek review in a civil action in federal district court. The district court will conduct a de novo review, and the parties may introduce new evidence and raise additional claims such as infringement. The Federal Circuit's review is limited to the TTAB record. The timeline for appeals in federal court varies depending on many factors. An appeal to the Federal Circuit generally takes between nine months and one year from the time it is docketed until the time of a final decision on the merits.

4. Initiating a Lawsuit

4.1 Actions to Pursue Infringement

An owner of a registered mark may file a lawsuit under either 15 U.S.C. § 1114 (Section 32 of the Lanham Act) or 15 U.S.C. § 1125(a) (Section 43 of the Lanham Act). Section 32 of the Lanham Act creates a cause of action against any person who creates or uses in commerce any reproduction or counterfeit of the registered mark in connection with the sale, distribution or advertising of goods and services where such use is likely to cause confusion. Section 43 allows the owner of a registered or unregistered trade mark "who believes that he or she is or is likely to be damaged by" a third party's (i) use in commerce of "any word, term, name, symbol, or device, or any combination thereof" in connection with goods or services, or (ii) false designation of the origin of the goods or services to bring suit against that third party. In addition to these federal claims, most states have statutory and/or common law causes of action prohibiting trade-mark infringement and unfair competition.

4.2 Initiating Infringement Proceedings

A trade-mark owner may sue for infringement in federal or state court. Assuming the allegedly infringing mark is being used in interstate commerce, trade-mark owners typically prefer to proceed in federal court under the Lanham Act. Related state-law claims may be asserted in the federal action. If the mark is not used in interstate commerce, a plaintiff may be limited to seeking relief in state court. In some circumstances, litigants may prefer to proceed in state court for strategic reasons, such as lower costs.

Another option is to bring a claim of trade-mark infringement in the US International Trade Commission ("ITC") if the trade mark is being used on goods that are imported into the United States. The ITC has the authority to exclude infringing products from entering the United States.

4.3 Effect of Decisions on Infringement Actions

In 2015, the Supreme Court held that federal courts should give preclusive effect to TTAB decisions on the issue of likelihood of confusion if the ordinary elements of issue preclusion are met. See B&B Hardware v Hargis Industries, 135 S. Ct. 1293 (2015). Issue preclusion prevents a party from relitigating an issue if (i) the same issue was raised in a previous proceeding; (ii) the issue was actually litigated and decided in the previous proceeding; (iii) the parties had a full and fair opportunity to litigate the issue; and (iv) the resolution of the issue was necessary for a valid and final judgment on the merits. Because TTAB decisions often do not consider "marketplace usage," many TTAB decisions do not meet the standard for issue preclusion in federal cases.

4.4 Declaratory Judgment Proceedings

An alleged infringer who satisfies the case or controversy and standing requirements for federal district court by alleging a concrete, actual or imminently threatened injury that is redressable by the court may initiate a declaratory judgment proceeding. The receipt of a cease-and-desist letter by the alleged infringer, though not required for a declaratory judgment action, is often enough to meet the imminently threatened injury requirement.

4.5 Jurisdiction of Courts
A district court decision may be appealed as of right to the circuit court of appeals in the circuit in which the case was initially decided. The circuit court's decision may then be appealed to the United States Supreme Court, which has discretionary but not mandatory review power over circuit court decisions.

The state court system in the US is comprised of trial courts, intermediate courts of appeals, and the highest court of appeals, often, but not always, called the state supreme court. The intermediate court of appeals' decision may be appealed to the highest court of the state, which has discretion to hear the case.

4.6 Prerequisites to Filing a Lawsuit
There are no procedural prerequisites or requirements for filing a trade-mark infringement lawsuit, although a lawsuit often is preceded by a cease-and-desist letter or a period of prior communications between the parties.

4.7 Representation for Parties
As in an opposition, an individual may choose to appear in a lawsuit without an attorney (ie, pro se), although US laws generally require that a corporation be represented by an attorney.

4.8 Interim or Preliminary Injunctions
Temporary restraining orders ("TROs") and preliminary injunctions are available in trade-mark lawsuits to provide relief from irreparable harm pending a full trial on the merits, just as they are available in other cases.

A TRO may be granted without notice to the adverse party, although the party seeking such relief in federal court typically must certify in writing any efforts made to give notice to the adverse party or explain why such notice should not be required. The movant also must provide an affidavit or a verified complaint setting forth specific facts showing that it will suffer immediate and irreparable injury before the opposing party can be heard. TROs typically expire within 14 days unless the court extends the order for good cause.

A court may issue a preliminary injunction only on notice to the adverse party and where the party seeking relief demonstrates that (a) it is likely to succeed on the merits and suffer irreparable harm in the absence of preliminary relief, (b) the balance of equities tips in its favour and (c) a preliminary injunction is in the public interest.

A court has discretion to order that a party seeking either a TRO or preliminary injunction post a bond or provide other security against damages to the enjoined party if the injunctive relief was improvidently granted.

4.9 Protection for Potential Defendant
To protect itself, as discussed above, a potential defendant in a trade-mark action may pre-emptively initiate a court proceeding seeking a declaratory judgment that it is not infringing or has not infringed the plaintiff's trade mark. Once sued, the defendant may bring counterclaims, including asserting that it, and not the plaintiff, is in fact the true trade-mark owner or has prior rights. Alternatively, it may assert defences to negate the plaintiff's claim of infringement by, for example, challenging the validity of the claimed trade mark or pleading a defence such as waiver. A defendant also may request that the court require a bond or other security before issuing a TRO or preliminary injunction.

4.10 Obtaining Information and Evidence
In federal court, once litigation has commenced the parties can obtain discovery from each other pursuant to the Federal Rules of Civil Procedure. Each state also has its own rules governing discovery. Discovery typically includes (a) responding to interrogatories, (b) producing documents and other evidence related to the case, (c) requests for admission and (d) pre-trial depositions under oath. The parties also may obtain discovery from third parties through a subpoena. Pre-litigation discovery is limited, but it is possible to take a pre-litigation deposition to perpetuate testimony.

4.11 Initial Pleading Standards
The initial pleading in a federal case must contain "a short and plain statement" of the claim, including sufficient facts to support a finding that the claim is plausible. A party may amend an initial pleading once as a matter of course within 21 days of serving a complaint or, in some cases, within 21 days after service of a responsive pleading from the other party. Otherwise, a party may only amend its pleading with the court's leave or with the opposing party's written consent.

4.12 Representative or Collective Actions
It is possible to assert trade-mark claims in a representative or collective action, commonly called a class-action lawsuit. A class action in federal court will only be certified if the class of potential plaintiffs is so numerous that joinder of all potential plaintiffs in the litigation is "impracticable." As a practical matter, it would be unusual for there to be a group of people large enough to satisfy this requirement who also collectively hold the rights to a trade mark.

4.13 Restrictions on Trade Mark-Owners
A trade-mark owner may be subject to a defence or counterclaim of trade-mark misuse if the defendant can show that the rights-holder has used the trade mark illegally, for example as a means to violate antitrust laws or to perpetuate a fraud.

The availability of sanctions in federal court may also serve as a deterrent to a trade mark-owner's aggressive assertion of rights in federal court if the trade mark-owner does not have a good-faith basis for its claim. A plaintiff bringing a claim for an improper or frivolous purpose may be sanctioned by the court; sanctions may include, among other things, an unfavourable ruling against the plaintiff or monetary fines.

Procedural restrictions such as the running of the statute of limitations on a claim may also pose barriers. The Lanham Act does not contain a specific statute of limitations, so the law of the state in which the action is brought typically governs the applicable limitations period.

5. Infringement

5.1 Action for Infringement

Under the Lanham Act, both the owner of a mark (whether registered or unregistered) and its "successors and assigns" may sue a purported infringer. See 15 U.S.C. §§ 1114, 1127.

Whether a licensee has standing to sue a potential infringer under Section 32 of the Lanham Act depends on the terms of the relevant licence. If they are such that the licence essentially functions like an assignment, for example by excluding the licensor from using the mark, then the licensee will have standing to sue for infringement of that mark.

A non-owner can sue for infringement under Section 43(a), which allows claims "by any person who believes that he or she is or is likely to be damaged" by a violation of that section. Exclusive licensees have standing to sue under that section.

5.2 Signs and Infringement

To succeed on a claim for trade-mark infringement, a plaintiff must demonstrate that (a) it owns a valid mark, (b) it has priority in that mark, and (c) the defendant has used the same or a similar mark in commerce in a manner likely to confuse consumers as to the origin, affiliation, or sponsorship of the goods or services offered in connection with the mark. See 15 U.S.C. §§ 1114, 1125.

In evaluating whether a likelihood of confusion exists, courts consider many factors. They vary from circuit to circuit, but generally include the (i) strength of plaintiff's trade mark; (ii) similarity of the marks; (iii) proximity of the products and whether they compete; (iv) likelihood of expansion; (v) evidence of actual consumer confusion; (vi) defendant's intent; and (vii) the degree of care likely to be exercised by consumers. A plaintiff must prove that there is a "probability of confusion" by ordinary prudent purchasers, not a mere possibility of confusion.

5.3 Use of a Sign by Defendant

A plaintiff need not establish that a defendant has used the mark as a source identifier, only that there is a likelihood of confusion based on the defendant's use of the mark issue "in commerce." A defendant may plead descriptive use as a defence to infringement, ie, use to describe, rather than identify the source of, the defendant's products.

5.4 Defences Against Infringement

In addition to arguing that there is no likelihood of confusion, a defendant also may challenge the validity of the plaintiff's mark by arguing that the mark: (a) was fraudulently obtained; (b) has been abandoned; (c) was used by the defendant with the plaintiff's permission; (d) does not have priority over the defendant's use; (e) is being misused in violation of antitrust laws; and/or (f) is functional. In addition, a defendant may argue that its use is a use other than as a mark, ie, of the allegedly infringing party's name, or of a term or device which is used to describe its goods and services. A defendant also may argue that equitable principles, such as laches, estoppel, and acquiescence, bar the claim. Depending on the circuit, a defendant may also assert unclean hands, First Amendment protections, parody, and nominative fair use (ie, using the mark to refer accurately to the plaintiff's mark, as in comparative advertising).

It is important to bear in mind that if a plaintiff's mark has become incontestable, the defendant may not challenge the mark's validity, although the other defences mentioned above still would be available.

5.5 Role of Experts and/or Surveys

Expert testimony often is important in trade-mark infringement cases. Experts may be used for a variety of purposes, including to show a likelihood of confusion, secondary meaning, fame, or genericness. For example, parties often will offer a survey conducted by an expert as proxy evidence of actual confusion. Courts generally view survey evidence favourably. Surveys used to establish likelihood of confusion, or secondary meaning, in a litigation are subject to different standards and must be designed differently from surveys or focus groups that companies use in the ordinary course of business to gain insight into their consumers.

5.6 Administrative or Criminal Offence

Under the Trademark Counterfeiting Act of 1984, the federal government may bring criminal charges against those who "intentionally" traffic or attempt to traffic in goods or services using a counterfeit mark (ie, merchandise bearing a mark that is "identical with, or substantially indistinguishable" from a registered mark). An individual defendant may be fined up to USD2,000,000 and imprisoned for not more than ten years, or both, with the penalties increasing to fines up to USD5,000,000 and imprisonment of not more than 20 years if there is a subsequent offence. If an entity is convicted of trade-mark counterfeiting, it may be fined up to USD5,000,000 for a first offence and up to USD15,000,000 for a subsequent offence. Prosecutors often bring claims after warehouse raids or other sting operations.

5.7 Custom Seizures

The US Customs and Border Protection ("CBP") agency has the authority to seize and destroy merchandise that infringes federally registered trade marks and/or is the subject of an exclusion order by the ITC. See 19 U.S.C. § 1526. To assist with and benefit from CBP's enforcement efforts, trade-mark owners should register their marks online with the CBP at <iprr.cbp.gov>. The CBP's database of registrations is accessible at all ports of entry. A trade-mark owner also may provide additional information or trainings to assist seizures.

If counterfeit merchandise is seized, CBP will report back to the trade-mark owner with (a) the date of importation; (b) the port of entry; (c) the description of the merchandise from the notice of seizure; (d) the quantity as set forth in the notice of seizure; (e) the country of origin of the merchandise; (f) the name and address of the manufacturer; (g) the name and address of the exporter; and (h) the name and address of the importer.

Parallel imports (otherwise known as grey-market goods) consist of foreign-made goods that bear either a genuine trade mark or a trade name that is identical or indistinguishable from a US trade mark, and which are imported into the US without authorisation from either the US owner or exclusive licensee. With limited exceptions, the CBP will deny parallel imports entry into the US and detain the merchandise for 30 days. After the expiry of the 30-day period, if the importer has not demonstrated that it falls under an exception the CBP will seize the merchandise and institute forfeiture proceedings. The CBP will allow entry where the goods originate from a foreign trade-mark owner that has common ownership with the US owner. The CBP also will allow in merchandise that is materially different from that offered by the US owner if the "merchandise or its packaging bears a conspicuous and legible label designed to remain on the product until the first point of sale to a retail consumer in the US stating that: 'This product is not a product authorised by the United States trade-mark owner for importation and is physically and materially different from the authorised product.'" 19 C.F.R. § 133.23.

6. Revocation/Cancellation

6.1 Remedies and Reasons

If a mark is not yet incontestable, the grounds for cancellation include that the mark: (a) is likely to cause confusion with a prior mark; (b) is likely to cause dilution by blurring or tarnishment; (c) is descriptive without secondary meaning; (d) has not been used in commerce; (e) includes an allegedly descriptive term in a composite without a disclaimer; or (f) misuses the federal registration symbol. If a mark is incontestable, the possible grounds for cancellation are limited to those that may be asserted at any time.

One can petition for cancellation of a mark at any time on the ground that the mark: (a) is or has become generic; (b) is functional; (c) was fraudulently registered; (d) has been abandoned; (e) is used to misrepresent the source of goods or services; (f) misuses a certification mark; or (g) is a previously registered mark that was not republished under the 1946 Lanham Act.

As with oppositions, the following statutory bars to registration may also be raised at any time as a basis for cancellation: (a) the mark consists of immoral, deceptive or scandalous matter; (b) the mark consists of matter that will suggest a false connection with persons, institutions, beliefs, or national symbols; (c) the mark uses a geographical indication on wines or spirits and identifies a place other than the origin of the goods; (d) the mark uses the flag, coat of arms, or other insignia of a state or country; (e) the mark consists of the name, portrait, or signature of a living person without consent; or (f) the mark contravenes the strict provisions for using collective and certification marks. Again, however, the ban on the registration of "scandalous, immoral, or disparaging marks" recently was found unconstitutional and no longer applies.

6.2 Trade Mark Office and Civil Courts

Both the TTAB and the federal courts have the power to cancel a trade-mark registration.

6.3 Statutory Limitation or Time Period

A registration on the Principal Register can be cancelled at any time. A party also may petition to cancel a registration on the Supplemental Register or a mark that was registered under the 1881 or 1905 trade-mark laws and not republished under the Lanham Act at any time.

6.4 Initiation of Revocation/Cancellation Proceeding

As with an opposition, any party or entity "who believes that he is or will be damaged" by a mark's registration may initiate a cancellation proceeding with the TTAB. A petitioner must have a "real interest" in the cancellation proceedings and a "reasonable" basis for believing that it will be damaged.

6.5 Partial Revocation/Cancellation

The USPTO may order cancellation of a mark "in whole or in part," "modify" a registration by "limiting the goods or services specified," and "otherwise restrict or rectify the register." 15 U.S.C. § 1068.

Partial cancellation may be invoked in a number of circumstances. For example, certain goods or services may be deleted from a registration because the registrant has abandoned the mark with respect to some but not all of the goods included in the registration. Partial cancellation also is used where a multi-class trade-mark registration has become generic with respect to one class of the goods for which it was registered, but not the others. Partial cancellation is not available to restrict a registration geographically, as such a remedy is only available in a concurrent-use proceeding.

A petitioner seeking partial cancellation generally need only plead "a short and plain statement of the claim showing that the pleader is entitled to relief." Where the petitioner seeks to restrict the goods or services listed in another's registration to avoid a finding of likelihood of confusion, it must plead and prove that (a) restricting the goods or services in the registration will avoid a likelihood of confusion, and (b) the registrant is not using its mark on the goods or services sought to be stricken.

6.6 Possibilities of Amendment

A registration subject to a cancellation proceeding may not be amended in substance or disclaimed in part unless (1) the opposing party consents to the amendment and the TTAB approves, or (2) the TTAB grants the registrant's motion to amend.

6.7 Revocation/Cancellation and Infringement

A cancellation proceeding may not include an infringement claim because the TTAB does not have jurisdiction to hear infringement actions. If a dispute arises in federal court, the court may hear claims for both cancellation and infringement. Where the same parties have actions pending both in federal court and before the TTAB, the TTAB will usually suspend its proceeding until the district court litigation is resolved.

7. Trial & Settlement

7.1 Special Procedural Provisions

There are no special procedural provisions for trade-mark proceedings in the United States.

7.2 Determination of Cases

There are no specialised trade-mark judges in the US court system. In any trade-mark case, questions of law will be determined by a judge, whereas questions of fact typically will be determined by a jury (unless the parties have agreed to a "bench trial" where the judge will serve as fact-finder). A party may move the court for summary judgment as a matter of law prior to trial. If the judge concludes that there is "no genuine dispute as to any material fact," the judge can grant summary judgment in favour of the moving party and thus decide the case without any jury involvement or a trial.

Actual damages may include (a) the defendant's profits, (b) any damages sustained by the plaintiff, and (c) the costs of the action, and may be heard by either a judge or a jury. If a plaintiff seeks treble damages for the defendant's intentional use of a counterfeit mark the judge may award the plaintiff three times its actual damages, together with reasonable attorneys' fees. If the owner of a registered mark elects to seek statutory rather than actual damages, its damages' claim will be determined at the court's discretion.

7.3 Possibilities of Settlement

The parties may settle their dispute at any time. Depending on the jurisdiction and the judge's individual practices, a court may require the parties to engage in one or more settlement conferences or other alternative dispute resolution ("ADR") procedures prior to trial. The parties may choose to engage in mediation, a non-binding ADR process whereby the parties and their attorneys meet with a neutral third party who is trained to facilitate settlement discussions. A mediator typically helps the parties reach their own voluntary settlement by assessing the strengths of the parties' positions and identifying potential areas of agreement or disagreement.

7.4 Other Court Proceedings

In the ordinary course, there cannot be parallel infringement actions proceeding in tandem in the US. Because the US system is comprised of separate state and federal courts as well as numerous regulatory and administrative bodies, the potential for adjudicatory overlap does exist, but courts and governing agencies are encouraged to, and often do, work together to ensure that matters involving the same subject-matter do not run simultaneously.

In general, once an issue has been resolved by a final judgment, that judgment will be given preclusive effect in other courts under the doctrine of issue preclusion, such that a party to the initial action cannot re-litigate the same issue or cause of action in a different court in the hope of achieving a different result.

Where a party has brought a claim in the ITC simultaneously with TTAB and district court proceedings, the TTAB and district court proceedings typically will be stayed until ITC reaches a final judgment (which generally will happen faster in the ITC than in a TTAB or district court proceeding).

8. Remedies

8.1 Existing Remedies

In a federal infringement action, once liability is established a trade-mark owner may seek a permanent injunction preventing the defendant from using the infringing mark and/or monetary damages.

The owner of an unregistered mark is limited to seeking its actual damages, including (a) defendant's profits, (b) any damages sustained by the plaintiff, and (c) the costs of the action. The plaintiff must prove only the defendant's sales, after which the burden shifts to the defendant to establish "all elements of cost or deduction claimed." 15 U.S.C. §1117(a).

The owner of a registered mark may elect to recover either actual or statutory damages. If the defendant intentionally used a counterfeit mark, the plaintiff may recover three times its actual damages, together with a reasonable attorney's fee, unless the court finds extenuating circumstances. If the plaintiff elects to seek statutory damages, the court may award an amount between USD1,000 andUSD200,000 per infringed mark per type of good or service sold or offered for sale. If the defendant wilfully infringed the plaintiff's mark, the court has discretion to increase this award up to a maximum of USD2,000,000 per infringed mark per type of good or service. See 15 U.S.C. §1117(b), (c).

In general, under US law each party is responsible for paying its own attorney fees and costs in a litigation. The Lanham Act allows courts to award reasonable attorney fees to the prevailing party in "exceptional" cases. Attorneys' fees generally are not awarded unless the plaintiff is able to show intentional, deliberate or wilful infringement. The US Supreme Court recently held, in a patent case, that exceptional cases generally involve either an unusual discrepancy in the merits of the positions taken by the respective parties or a situation where the losing party litigated the case in an unreasonable manner. See Octane Fitness, LLC v. Icon Health & Fitness, In., 34 S. Ct. 1749 (2014). Several circuits have imported that standard into trade-mark law. See SunEarth, Inc v Sun Earth Solar Power Co, 839 F.3d 1179, 1181 (9th Cir. 2016); Georgia-Pacific Cons. Prods. LP v von Drehle Corp., 781 F.3d 710, 721 (4th Cir. 2015); Fair Wind Sailing, Inc v Dempster, 764 F.3d 303, 315 (3d Cir. 2014).

For cases involving intentional and knowing use of a counterfeit mark, a plaintiff can recover reasonable attorneys' fees.

8.2 Rights and Remedies

If a defendant is the prevailing party in a federal case, it may recover an award of its attorneys' fees if it is able to show that the case is "exceptional," as discussed above.

A defendant also may move for sanctions under Rule 11 of the Federal Rules of Civil Procedure if the plaintiff brought a frivolous or improper claim in bad faith. If the defendant prevails, it may be awarded part or all of the reasonable attorneys' fees arising directly as a result of the Rule 11 violation.

Alternatively, if a defendant prevails on a counterclaim alleging that the plaintiff infringed the defendant's mark, the defendant may seek an injunction or monetary damages. See Fed. R. Civ. P. 65; 15 U.S.C. §1117.

8.3 Different Types of Remedies

The injunctive relief available for registered or unregistered trade marks is the same but the monetary remedies available differ. Owners of unregistered trade marks are limited to actual damages, whereas owners of registered marks also may obtain treble damages and statutory damages.

9. Appeal

9.1 Special Provisions

There are no special provisions concerning the appellate review of trade-mark proceedings. Grants or denials of preliminary injunctions may be appealed immediately, without the need to wait for a final judgment.

9.2 Factual or Legal Review

Appellate review encompasses the factual findings of the trial court, which are reviewed for clear error, as well as legal conclusions, which are reviewed de novo. Different circuits have different positions as to whether likelihood of confusion, which is the central test for trade-mark infringement, is a question of fact (to be reviewed for clear error), a question of law (to be reviewed de novo, without regard for the decision below), or a mixed question of fact and law (where the standard of review varies depending on a number of factors).

9.3 Length of Appeal from Trial Court

It is not unusual for the federal appellate process to take anything from several months to several years. The process involves substantive briefing by both parties to the appeal, which can take several months. Circuit court appeals often involve oral argument before an appellate judge or panel of appellate judges. Circuit courts have discretion in scheduling the oral argument date for an appeal. Once the briefing and oral argument have been completed, the court has discretion in issuing a decision.

10. Other Trade Mark Issues

10.1 Recognition of Dilution

The US recognises dilution as a basis for opposing a trade-mark registration or enjoining another party's use of a mark under the appropriate circumstances. A plaintiff seeking relief on a dilution theory must show that (1) its mark is famous and distinctive, (2) the defendant began using its mark in commerce after the plaintiff's mark became famous and distinctive, and (3) the defendant's mark is likely to dilute the plaintiff's mark by either "tarnishment" or "blurring." With respect to the first element, "a mark is famous if it is widely recognised by the general consuming public of the US as a designation of source of the goods or services of the mark's owner."

The US recognises dilution by blurring and dilution by tarnishment. Dilution by blurring occurs when a mark previously associated with the mark-owner's goods or services is used on other goods or services, thus weakening the mark's ability to evoke the prior user's goods in the minds of consumers. Dilution by tarnishment refers to an association that arises from another's use of a similar mark on goods or services in a manner that harms the reputation of the famous mark.

10.2 Protection of Famous Marks

Under the "well-known marks" rule, trade marks that have not been used or registered in the US but are so famous elsewhere that their reputations are known domestically may be given priority. Although the TTAB traditionally has recognised the well-known marks doctrine in its proceedings, federal courts that have addressed the doctrine's availability have come to inconsistent conclusions. See Grupo Gigante SA De CV v Dallo & Co, 391 F.3d 1088 (9th Cir. 2004) (applying the doctrine); ITC Ltd v Punchgini, Inc, 482 F.3d 135 (2d Cir. 2007) (explicitly rejecting the doctrine).

10.3 Special Rules Regarding Geographic Indicators

In the US, geographically descriptive terms — or those that designate geographical locations and that consumers tend to regard as descriptive of the geographic location of the goods or services — are not considered inherently distinctive and can only be protected if they acquire secondary meaning. It is not possible to have trade-mark rights in the US in a term that is primarily geographically deceptively misdescriptive of the goods and services on which it is used.

The mere inclusion of a geographical term within a mark does not render the entire mark geographically descriptive. Instead, the composite mark is evaluated in light of its total commercial impression. Similarly, a party may use the name of a geographic location arbitrarily as a trade mark, meaning in a manner that consumers are unlikely to understand in its geographical sense when placed on the party's goods or services.

Even where a party has obtained trade-mark rights in a geographical term, any junior user who is in fact located in the place described will have a limited right to tell consumers of its location, provided such a statement of geographic origin is made in a purely descriptive, non-trade-mark sense.

10.4 Special Rules Relating to Surnames

A person may protect his or her own surname as a trade mark if it has secondary meaning. There is no absolute right to use one's own name as a mark when someone else has established rights in the name first and the junior user's mark is likely to cause consumer confusion. Courts often are reluctant to issue injunctions banning all use of the junior user's personal surname as a mark, seeking to balance the parties' competing interests by crafting an injunction that limits or modifies the junior user's name to prevent confusion yet still allows the junior user to retain some form of his or her own surname. For example, a court may require the junior user to add prefixes or suffixes, include a disclaimer on the mark, change the mark's stylisation, or use the surname in a non-trade-mark manner on the mark to communicate participation in the business. See Gucci v Gucci Shops, Inc, 688 F. Supp. 916 (S.D.N.Y. 1988); Pizitz, In. v Pizitz Mercantile C of Tuscaloosa, Inc, 467 F. Supp. 1089 (N.D. Ala. 1979).

11. Costs

11.1 Costs Before Filing a Lawsuit

Pre-filing costs will depend on the nature and complexity of the suit. A mark-owner will often send a demand letter to the alleged infringer before filing suit, explaining its claim to the mark and asking the other party to cease its use. There is no set cost for such a letter. After the alleged infringer receives the cease-and-desist letter, the parties typically engage in discussions in attempt to resolve the matter. The negotiation costs will depend on the amount of time spent and the resources the attorney must expend on the negotiation. A party receiving a demand letter often will have an attorney research the matter and conduct a preliminary investigation to determine whether it should litigate or settle the matter out of court.

A mark-owner may choose to hire an expert to conduct a trade-mark survey before filing suit. A survey will generally cost between USD30,000 and USD50,000 in the simplest cases but can cost far more depending on the complexity of the issues, survey design, universe polled, and experience of the expert retained.

11.2 Costs Regarding an Infringement Action

Suing in federal court involves several components of cost, including drafting a complaint to be filed with the court and paying the court's administrative filing fee of USD400 (for federal court).

Litigation costs will vary, depending on factors such as the value of the marks at issue, whether counsel is retained, the number and complexity of claims brought, the types of evidence needed (such as surveys or expert accounts), and the jurisdiction. See AM. INTELLECTUAL PROPERTY LAW ASS'N, REPORT OF THE ECONOMIC SURVEY (2015). The average cost of trade-mark litigation is generally estimated to be between USD150,000 and USD1 million, though these numbers tend to rise when the marks at issue are more valuable. See id.

12. Alternative Dispute Resolution

12.1 Common Way of Settlement

As discussed above, the parties to a trade-mark case may use ADR to resolve their dispute. Many courts facilitate ADR at the beginning of the litigation process. In some jurisdictions, some attempt at ADR is mandatory before parties can proceed to trial.

ADR sometimes can offer advantages over traditional litigation. For example, parties sometimes can resolve their disputes more quickly through ADR than they would in court, which can save costs. The parties are largely in control of the ADR schedule and therefore have more flexibility to tailor the process to their unique needs. Many types of ADR are confidential, which can be appealing for parties who do not want the details of their dispute made public through court records.

The most common forms of ADR used in trade-mark cases are mediation and arbitration. As discussed above, mediation is non-binding. In arbitration, a neutral third party known as an "arbitrator" typically will issue a written decision resolving the case on the merits. Parties may agree to arbitrate after a conflict arises, although often the parties will have agreed in a prior contract (such as a licensing agreement) to resolve future disputes through arbitration. In an arbitration proceeding, the parties present evidence and arguments supporting their positions to the arbitrator.

Kirkland & Ellis LLP
601 Lexington Avenue
New York, NY 10022
United States

Tel: +1 212-446-4800
Fax: +1 212-446-4900
Email: info@kirkland.com
Web: www.kirkland.com

KIRKLAND & ELLIS

The applicable procedural and evidentiary rules are usually determined by the parties' arbitration agreement. Arbitration generally is less rigid than litigation but more formal than mediation. Depending on the type of arbitration, the arbitrator's decision can either be binding or non-binding. In non-binding arbitration, the parties are usually bound by the decision unless one of them rejects it and requests a trial. In binding arbitration, the parties agree that the arbitrator's decision will be the final resolution of the case, and the parties will generally not have the opportunity to appeal.

13. Trade Marks and Other Intellectual Property

13.1 Protection by Copyright

In the US, patent, trade mark, and copyright are separate and independent forms of legal protection for intellectual property assets. Plaintiffs can, and frequently do, assert infringement under more than one of these regimes based on the same conduct.

A party can have overlapping rights in a single product or design. For example, one can secure a design patent or a copyright for a product's design, which at the same time that design provides trade-mark protection through acquired secondary meaning in the product's design. This can be significant given the varying durations of protection and remedies available under trade-mark, copyright, and patent law. Although copyright has a limited duration, a trade mark can be enforced perpetually if the mark remains in use. Therefore, trade-mark rights in a logo or design can be enforced even after expiry of the copyright.

Courts may be wary of claims under one intellectual property regime that over-extend into other areas. Although parties may plead several IP theories in the same case, courts will not allow a party whose claim fails under one IP regime to reassert the claim under a different regime where the court does not feel it truly fits. See, for example, Dastar Corp v Twentieth Century Fox Film Corp, 539 U.S. 23 (2003).

Contributed by Cowan DeBaets Abrahams & Sheppard LLP ***Authors:*** Eleanor M. Lackman, Joshua B. Sessler, Scott J. Sholder, Nancy Wolff

Trends and Developments

Contributed by Cowan DeBaets Abrahams & Sheppard LLP

Cowan DeBaets Abrahams & Sheppard LLP is a boutique firm located in New York, NY, and Beverly Hills, CA. Cowan DeBaets Abrahams & Sheppard has approximately 35 attorneys who specialise in media, entertainment, and non-patent IP law (copyrights, trade marks, publicity rights, unfair competition, etc); clients include leading names in the motion pictures, digital media, fashion, sports, e-commerce, music, social media, travel and leisure, consumer goods, and technology industries. The firm's trade-mark practice encompasses clearance and counselling, prosecution domestically and through its foreign networks internationally, licensing, brand enforcement, domain proceedings, and litigation in federal courts and before the USPTO Trademark Trial and Appeal Board.

Authors

Eleanor M. Lackman is a partner at the firm and co-chair of its litigation and trade-mark practice groups. She specialises in copyright law, trade-mark law, and litigation. She is currently a member of the International Trademark Association's (INTA) Amicus committee, and of the Media Law Resource Center's copyright and trade mark committee; she is a former member (two terms) of INTA's internet committee, and of the New York City Bar Association's trade-mark and unfair competition committee. Eleanor has published a number of articles on trade-mark issues and speaks frequently on the topic.

Joshua B. Sessler is a partner at Cowan DeBaets Abrahams & Sheppard and co-practice leader of its corporate department. His key areas of expertise are trade marks, corporations/mergers & acquisitions, information technology and licensing. Joshua has almost 20 years of experience advising entrepreneurs, investors, content-owners and companies in the full range of corporate, intellectual property and internet technology legal matters. He represents a broad range of creative individuals and companies who are using new media and technology to create innovative business paradigms.

Scott J. Sholder is a partner at CDAS. His key practice areas are copyright and trade-mark litigation; media defence litigation (defamation, false light, etc); entertainment and media commercial litigation/ADR; right of publicity and privacy litigation; domain-name disputes. He is co-chair of the Media Law Resource Center's media copyright and trade-mark committee, and a member of the New York City Bar Association's entertainment law committee. He has published extensively on trade-mark matters, and has presented in-house Continuing Legal Education (CLE) lectures regarding trade-mark basics and risk management in online image/content use and licensing.

Nancy Wolff is a partner at the firm and co-chair of its litigation department, which includes trade marks. Her primary practice areas are copyright, trade mark and digital media, particularly as it relates to licensing digital media. Nancy advises her clients on the registration and protection of intellectual property in the area of copyright and trade mark, also advising when releases are necessary under various publicity laws and on how to promote the clients' products and services without running foul of complex and evolving advertising and privacy rules. She is a member of the American Bar Association's IP section and has contributed to the association's magazine, Landslide; she is also a member of the Media Law Resource Center's copyright and trade-mark section.

USA TRENDS AND DEVELOPMENTS

Contributed by Cowan DeBaets Abrahams & Sheppard LLP ***Authors:*** Eleanor M. Lackman, Joshua B. Sessler, Scott J. Sholder, Nancy Wolff

Trends and Developments in Trademark Use and Risk in the Media and Entertainment Industries

Brands are part of everyday life, and their depiction in media and entertainment (including music, motion pictures, television and video games) is no exception. This essay provides an overview of the legal context framing the use of trade marks in expressive works under US law, as well as some recent developments in this area.

What Potential Claims do Plaintiffs Assert When They See Their Names or Brands Used in Expressive Works?

Common claims include the following:

- trade-mark infringement or unfair competition resulting from the argument that the public is confused, or that the party using the brand is doing so in order to ride on a brand's cachet;
- false advertising pertaining to an express or implied message about the brand within the entertainment product;
- false endorsement arising from the suggestion that the brand-owner endorses the creator or contents of the song, film or game; and
- dilution, in cases where the use of the trade mark blurs the brand's distinctiveness or tarnishes the brand's reputation.

How Does US Law Apply in the Context of Media and Entertainment?

United States law has a strong tradition of upholding free speech and free expression, as encompassed in the First Amendment of the US Constitution. This includes the right to use a brand as part of a title of an expressive work or within an expressive work. The leading case is *Rogers v Grimaldi*, 875 F.2d 994 (2d Cir. 1989), which set out the standard for when the trade-mark laws will not apply to use of a trade mark in expressive works. *Rogers* held that the trade-mark laws are not applicable if the use of the trade mark is "artistically relevant" to the work, and not "explicitly misleading" as to the source or content of the work. Although *Rogers* applies within a certain region, covering New York City, the appellate courts covering the entertainment capitals in California have also adopted the *Rogers* test in *Mattel, Inc. v. MCA Records, Inc.*, 296 F.3d 894 (9th Cir. 2002).

Of all intellectual property doctrines, the law is most permissive of the use of trade marks, but a court will not always find that use of a trade mark is permissible. Practitioners should also bear in mind that use with respect to an expressive work may not be advisable if such use is intended to spill into ancillary rights such as the merchandising of products related to the expressive work.

Examples of How Courts Have Applied the Rogers Test

The following examples help to illustrate the breadth of the *Rogers* test, as well as its boundaries.

Motion Pictures and Television

Two cases involving titles of works help to show the *Rogers* test in practice. A court found that the use of the name "Dairy Queens" – the name of a well-known fast-food chain – as the title of a "mockumentary" about beauty contests in rural Minnesota was infringing. The judge opined that the use was gratuitous and bore no artistic relevance to the film.

In contrast, an appellate court held that the use of the term "Empire" for a television show about a record company did not infringe a record company's rights in the same term. The court also pointed out that "Empire" was used in its common sense – as a reference to the show's setting in "the Empire State" of New York and to the empire that the fictional business in the show was depicted to be. Notably, the court appeared to extend its findings to cover for-sale promotional activities, which runs counter to other rulings that have found movie merchandise to involve a different test than the test for the motion pictures themselves.

Incidental use of brands in motion pictures has generally been accepted. For example, a court rejected a claim brought by Caterpillar over the use of Caterpillar-branded bulldozers in a scene where the "bad guys" bulldoze the jungle in "George of the Jungle". A court also rejected a claim that the makers of the "Slip 'N' Slide" toy would be injured by the lead character's misuse of the product in the film. In that case, the court observed that studios have a general practice of not asking permission to use name-brand products in films.

Music

The *Mattel* case mentioned above involved the title of a song, "Barbie Girl", which poked fun at the shallow materialism identified with Mattel's brand of dolls, rather than simply using the brand in order to get attention. This is what the court concluded may have happened in a case involving the OutKast song "Rosa Parks", which was not about the famous civil-rights leader Rosa Parks at all, and which could have been used just to enhance the song's potential sale to the public.

Video Games

The US Supreme Court ruled in 2011 that video games are fully protected by the First Amendment, and courts have treated them in the same way as motion pictures, books, music and other expressive works. Courts have rejected the use in *Grand Theft Auto* of a strip club named "Pig Pen" that made fun of a real "Playpen" strip club, and the use of "Delta Force" in a *Call of Duty* military game. However, a court refused to give an early win to Electronic Arts over a military game that made extensive use of depictions of several of Bell Helicopter's well-known military aircraft. The case settled, but the ruling suggests that using a trade mark in a pervasive way that might suggest co-sponsorship or co-production could end up failing the second element of the *Rogers* test.

Contributed by Cowan DeBaets Abrahams & Sheppard LLP ***Authors:*** Eleanor M. Lackman, Joshua B. Sessler, Scott J. Sholder, Nancy Wolff

An appeals court recently affirmed the dismissal of trademark claims brought by a Formula One race sponsor over Sony's *Gran Turismo* video game. Sony used the brand on a virtual replica of the same bridge on which the brand-owner's trade mark appears in the real race. The court found that the realism of the races bore "at least some" artistic relevance to the games, and the test is only whether the relevance is more than zero. The court also did not find that the use did not explicitly mislead the consumer, regardless of whether or not consumer confusion actually existed.

Copyright and Publicity Law are Different

Generally, the policies involving the use of trade marks do not come into play in the same way when the right alleged to be violated is a copyright or publicity right. In those cases, fair use (which considers First Amendment principles, but under a different test) or "de minimis" (minor or incidental) use tend to come in as defences that are asserted when a violation is shown. The fact that so many different types of issues can arise in the typical expressive work suggests that, when other parties' content or material is used in media or entertainment, producers should consult with an attorney who is experienced in vetting for risk involving copyright, trade mark, trade dress and publicity rights.

Trends and Developments to Come

With few exceptions, courts have almost uniformly given creators of expressive works a wide berth in making use of trade marks and trade dress in books, films, video games, music and other expressive media. Even creative works that are sometimes deemed to be promotional – such as music videos used to advertise songs – tend to fall under the same level of protection as traditional expressive works, and the "Empire" decision seems to confirm that broad scope. However, as sponsored content and other types of creative or long-form promotions become standard in the digital age, courts may view the test through a narrower lens: they may find that the speech in the work is more "commercial" than "expressive," as Hyundai learned when it lost its motion to dismiss a claim by Louis Vuitton over the use of its "toile" monogram in a longer-form Super Bowl commercial. The next battles in this area may centre on what constitutes an expressive work and how much brand usage is too much in an age when the public increasingly expects short-form and long-form content to be wrapped up in some sort of sponsorship or promotion.

Regardless of where the law goes concerning new forms of content, remedies against exploitation of that content are narrowing. Due to changes in the law, those who use brands in conjunction with expressive works have recently seen more protection against injunctions that may restrict such use. Courts in the United States are increasingly adopting a higher standard for obtaining injunctions: in many courts, a brand-owner must prove more than confusion, which was all that was previously required to obtain an injunction (except in rare exceptions). Now, the brand-owner must establish not only confusion but that they are irreparably harmed by the use, and that the public interest will not be harmed if an injunction issues. While actual confusion can certainly persuade a court that the use should not be permitted, the combination of the *Rogers* test – which tolerates some level of confusion – and the growing requirement that a plaintiff must establish several factors together may give content creators more confidence that their use of others' trade marks and brands is something that cannot be easily stopped and may be limited to, at worst, the payment of some money damages.

Cowan, DeBaets, Abrahams & Sheppard LLP
41 Madison Avenue, 38th Floor
New York
NY 10010

CDAS
Cowan DeBaets Abrahams & Sheppard

Tel: 212 974 7474
Fax: 212 974 8474
Email: elackman@cdas.com
Web: www.cdas.com

Index

Introduction

BRAZIL

INDEX

CANADA

Law and Practice p.33

Contributed by Blaney McMurtry LLP

CHILE

Law and Practice p.55

Contributed by Cooper & Cía

INDEX

CHINA

COSTA RICA

Law and Practice p.87

Contributed by Castro & Pal Abogados

INDEX

ETHIOPIA

Law and Practice p.99

Contributed by Tamrat Assefa Liban Law Offices

FRANCE

Law and Practice p.115

Contributed by Jacobacci Coralis Harle

INDEX

GERMANY

ISRAEL

MACAU

MALAYSIA

NORWAY

SERBIA

ST LUCIA

TAIWAN

UK

Contributed by J A Kemp

USA